W9-BYG-786

Marketing Management, Second Edition by Michael R. Czinkota and Masaaki Kotabe

Vice President/Publisher: Dave Shaut
Acquisitions Editor: Pamela Person
Developmental Editor: Bryant Editorial Development, Jamie Gleich Bryant
Executive Marketing Director: Steve Scoble
Media Technology Editor: Kevin von Gillern
Media Production Editor: Robin Browning
Production Editor: Amy S. Gabriel
Manufacturing Coordinator: Sandee Milewski
Photo Research: Feldman & Associates, Inc.
Photo Manager: Cary Benbow
Internal Design: Jennifer Lynne Lambert
Cover Design: Jennifer Lynne Lambert
Cover Photo: © Bruce Rogovin/Tony Stone Images
Production House: Lachina Publishing Services, Inc.
Compositor: Lachina Publishing Services, Inc.
Printer: RR Donnelley & Sons Company
          Roanoake Manufacturing Division

COPYRIGHT ©2001 by South-Western College Publishing, a division of Thomson Learning. The Thomson Learning logo is a registered trademark used herein under license.

All Rights Reserved. No part of this work covered by the copyright hereon may be reproduced or used in any form or by any means—graphic, electronic, or mechanical, including photocopying, recording, taping, or information storage and retrieval systems—without the written permission of the publisher.

Printed in the United States of America
1 2 3 4 5 03 02 01 00

For more information contact South-Western College Publishing, 5101 Madison Road, Cincinnati, Ohio, 45227 or find us on the Internet at http://www.swcollege.com

For permission to use material from this text or product, contact us by
- **telephone: 1-800-730-2214**
- **fax: 1-800-730-2215**
- **web: http://www.thomsonrights.com**

Library of Congress Cataloging-in-Publication Data

Czinkota, Michael R.
    Marketing management / Michael R. Czinkota, Masaaki Kotabe.—2nd ed.
        p. cm.
    Includes indexes.
    ISBN 0-324-02203-4 (hardcover)
    1. Marketing—Management. 2. Marketing—Management—Case studies. I. Kotabe, Masaaki. II. Title.

HF5415.13 .C95 2000
658.8—dc21   00-026225

This book is printed on acid-free paper.

Marketing Management

Second Edition

Michael R. Czinkota
Georgetown University

Masaaki Kotabe
Temple University

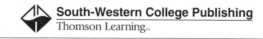
South-Western College Publishing
Thomson Learning

Australia • Canada • Denmark • Japan • Mexico • New Zealand • Philippines
Puerto Rico • Singapore • South Africa • Spain • United Kingdom • United States

To Ilona and Maggie! MRC

To Kay, MK

Brief Contents

Contents

Chapter 1

AN OVERVIEW OF MARKETING

Chapter 2

MARKETING PLANNING

Chapter 3

UNDERSTANDING THE ENVIRONMENT AND THE COMPETITION

Chapter 6

ESTIMATING THE MARKET DEMAND

Chapter 7

MARKET SEGMENTATION, POSITIONING, AND BRANDING

Chapter 8

PRODUCT AND SERVICE DECISIONS

Chapter 9

NEW PRODUCTS

Chapter 10

PRICING DECISIONS

Chapter 11

DISTRIBUTION AND SUPPLY CHAIN MANAGEMENT

Chapter 12

DESIGNING EFFECTIVE PROMOTION AND ADVERTISING STRATEGIES

Chapter 13

DIRECT MARKETING, SALES PROMOTION, AND PUBLIC RELATIONS

Chapter 14

SELLING AND SALES MANAGEMENT

Chapter 15

THE FUTURE OF MARKETING

Preface

Thank you for giving up your time to read what we have to say about marketing. You are our customers, the targets of our marketing effort; it is you we aim to delight!

We believe that exciting new changes are coming to the marketing field and that we can help teach present and future marketers to do their work better. By improving your understanding of marketing, we hope to help you increase your efficiency and effectiveness and leave a mark for the better on society. Our approach to marketing sets us apart from the competition, which, we believe, will allow us to capture market share. Here are the features that make this book special.

OUR APPLIED APPROACH

Marketing used to be a very practical field. It was generally accepted that business transactions could be carried out more effectively, that there were many needs that had been left unsatisfied, and that the field of marketing could contribute to improving the quality of life of individuals. Over time, however, the approach to marketing in universities began to suffer from "lab coat" syndrome. Complexity became fashionable; esoteric approaches were in demand. Many researchers and authors began to talk more about models than about people, to substitute tools for insights, and to examine printouts instead of consumers. It seemed that obscurity, not enlightenment, had become the ultimate goal.

Yet, in our minds, marketing is still a very practical discipline. People still have practical needs, firms still face practical problems, and solutions still have to work in real life. Most marketers cannot and should not hide in labs. Marketing is a social science based on theories and concepts, but it also requires that most marketers visit with people, observe them, talk to them, and understand their activities. In essence, marketing is a "dialogue" between marketers and their customers.

Our book reflects this applied approach. Together with important concepts and theories, we provide you with the experience that we have obtained through our work with numerous companies—both large and small, domestic and international—for many years. You will recognize this applied orientation when we talk about advertising, trading, selling, and segmentation. You will sense it when we present you with "Manager's Corners" features and cases that show you how marketers work. You will enjoy it when we provide you with down-to-earth "Marketing in Action" examples that you can explore and analyze. Most important, you will understand it when you get to your professional activities and discover the direct relevance of what you have learned.

OUR GLOBAL PERSPECTIVE

Markets have become global. Mark Twain once wrote, "There is a road ahead of you: If you stand still, you will get run over." No longer is competition limited to your home market. If you stand still in your domestic market, you will likely be trampled by competitors from abroad. Economies have become intertwined, firms have become linked to each other across national boundaries, and markets are open to most anyone. Never before have the risks from unexpected market entrants been so large—and never before have the opportunities for global success been so bountiful. But opportunities must be recognized and seized; risks must be understood and evaluated. This book assists you in that task by removing national blinders and exposing you to the interplay of global business forces. As you go through the text, you will benefit from our combined in-depth expertise in North and South America, Asia, and Western, Central, and Eastern Europe. You will understand how marketing can adapt to new environments and demands and see marketing for what it really is: a discipline that knows no regional or political borders when it comes to improving the way societies function. You will learn about the limited rewards that are given to those who come in second, and you will appreciate the need to be world class in your performance.

OUR INCORPORATION OF TECHNOLOGY

Societies, and the people within them, change. Never before has the change been so rapid, resulting in the downfall of so many old icons and the emergence of new paradigms. Consider technology: The separation of the location of production and consumption in the services area offers us new ways of living and working. Banks are no longer confined to their large buildings on Main Street; insurance companies no longer need their downtown palaces; teachers are no longer limited to the classroom; and analysts no longer have to stay in their offices. Rather, we can all spread our wings and reach out to individuals and businesses or, better yet, have them come into our homes. This spatial freedom profoundly recasts the activities of marketers. We encounter new ways of communicating with our customers, presenting them with our offerings, and reaching them with our services. We can structure our offers to be more precise and more distinct. We can use electronic data interchange and techniques such as just-in-time delivery to make the marketing offering less expensive and more satisfying. However, unless marketers make use of these new possibilities, they run the danger of falling behind, using the equivalent of bronze tools in the Iron Age. We recognize these changes and have given much thought to their implications for marketers. You will discover in every chapter our identification of change drivers and our analysis of change. As a result, we believe you will be empowered to deploy your judgment in preparation to work with change and its challenges.

OUR SOCIAL AWARENESS

Today's society demands more of marketers than was expected in the past. Issues such as diversity, ethics, responsibility, concern about the natural environment, and privacy are becoming integral parts of the marketing discipline. Marketing managers are increasingly challenged not only to adapt to existing rules but to lead the way. To be at the forefront of social transformation, marketers must encompass a new breadth of perspective and embrace a much greater variety of social activities than ever before. The marketing function can no longer confine itself to one organization and the marketing activities within it. Instead, it needs to encompass a broad range of stakeholders, suppliers, and customers. We help you gain such a perspective by presenting you with the primary elements of social change, developing the implications of such change on the marketing discipline, and offering ways to synthesize them into marketing strategy. For example, we develop a postmortem perspective of the product cycle that considers producer responsibilities after the product has been withdrawn from the market. We also fully incorporate the marketing of services into our discussions and include aspects of nonprofit marketing. In addition, you will discover that we have fully integrated societal concerns into all of our materials.

OUR RESEARCH ORIENTATION

Notwithstanding our practical emphasis, we fully recognize that marketing theory has an important role to play. It provides us with the conceptual tools that allow us to abstract, analyze, understand, and predict phenomena. Theory offers broad perspectives and assists in the formulation of decision rules. It permits us to recognize the underlying fundamentals, to discover commonalities, and to appreciate differences. The use of theory allows us to avoid repetition of past mistakes, provides us with context, and enables us to understand quality. Theory, when relevant to the field, is quite practical in that it allows us to improve the practice of marketing. Therefore, we have delved deeply into the existing marketing theories and have incorporated them into our presentation. We have also made an effort to point out leading-edge work and use it to highlight future developments in the marketing field. Because of our own extensive international work, we have not been confined to the research literature of any one country but can present you with leading-edge information from the United States, Europe, and Asia. At the same time, we have made an effort to present theory with a critical eye, highlighting the benefits as well as the limits of its application.

OUR POLICY ORIENTATION

Marketing does not function only in business environments. Rather, it needs to interact closely with governments and legal frameworks that are expressions of societal expectations and demands. The public policy dimensions of marketing need to be incorporated into marketing planning if the firm is to be successful in the long run. But marketing must also be an active player in the formulation of such policy. Marketing's closeness to the customer allows it to make a unique contribution to the emergence of new policies when they are concerned with the well-being of individuals and the betterment of society. Our policy background and ongoing work with government agencies enables us to bring a realistic perspective of this public/private interaction into our discussion of marketing strategies.

OUR USER FRIENDLINESS

Learning is, unfortunately, often seen as the mental equivalent of medicine: Unless it is painful and tastes bad, many people do not believe that it works. While we cannot argue on behalf of the medical profession, we do know that such a conclusion is incorrect as far as marketing is concerned. Marketing is an exciting, energizing, and enthusiastic discipline. One's exposure to marketing should not deteriorate into an onerous chore. We have therefore worked hard at making our book intelligible, interesting, and a good read. We want you to see this work as a page turner; we intend to stimulate your curiosity and your desire to find out what happens next. We have provided you with our best writing combined with superior design and layout to make this book easy—and perhaps even fun—to read.

OUR TARGET ORIENTATION

As you will discover in the book, good marketing requires good customer identification. Trying to be everything to everyone may cause one to miss all the targets. This book has been written for MBA students and advanced undergraduates who wish to go into business. It will provide you with the information, perspectives, and tools necessary to get the job done in the marketing field. We intend to assist you in practicing marketing by building on the existing skills and knowledge you already possess. Our aim is to enable you to make better decisions.

OUR INSTRUCTOR SUPPORT

A textbook is about teaching, and we have made a major effort to present the instructor and the student with the best possible pedagogical value. Some of the specific teaching features are as follows:

- The "Manager's Corner" features bring specific examples from the marketing world into the classroom. These features are intended to help students understand and absorb the presented materials. The instructor can highlight them to exemplify theory or use them as minicases for class discussion.

- The "Marketing in Action" sections ask students to apply concepts and theory to actual business situations.

- "Questions for Review" allow the student to rapidly reassess the chapter content and determine the degree of understanding gained.

- "Questions for Discussion" invite the instructor and the students to expand the depth of the topics addressed and to explore further implications and practical applications.

- Ten full-length cases present students with real business situations. They encourage in-depth discussion of the material covered in the chapters and allow students to apply the knowledge they have gained.

- The *Instructor Manual with Test Bank* (ISBN 0-324-02204-2) is designed to provide major assistance to the professor. The manual includes the following materials.

  Teaching plans: Alternative teaching plans and syllabi are presented to accommodate the instructor's preferred course structure and varying time constraints. Time plans are developed for the course to be taught in a semester format, on a quarter basis, or as an executive seminar.

  Discussion guidelines: For each chapter, specific teaching objectives and guidelines are developed to help stimulate classroom discussion.

  Answers to Questions for Review and Questions for Discussion

  Notes for Manager's Corners and Cases

  Testing material consists of in-depth essay questions, short essay questions, and multiple-choice questions. Through *ExamView™ Testing Software*, the test bank portion of the *Instructor Manual* is also computerized and available to adopters in PC format (ISBN 0-324-02208-5).

- PowerPoint Slides (ISBN 0-324-00205-0) are available to support every chapter. Should instructors choose to make the presentation available to their students, they can easily generate a set of Power Notes from the files.

- Color *Transparency Acetates* (ISBN 0-324-02206-9) are provided for figures and tables presented in the text. A brief teaching note accompanies each transparency to help instructors organize their in-class presentations of the material.

- A comprehensive *Video Package* (ISBN 0-324-02207-7) features segments for nearly every chapter. Each segment presents the situation of a well-known company in view of the topic at hand. Profiled companies include Burton Snowboards, Burke Marketing Research, the Toronto Bluejays, Red Roof Inn, and many others. Segment summaries and lengths are provided in the *Instructor Manual.*

Most important, we personally stand behind our product. Should you have any questions or comments on this book, you can contact us, talk to us, and receive feedback from us.

Professor Michael R. Czinkota
(202) 687-4204
e-mail: czinkotm@msb.edu

Professor Masaaki Kotabe
(215) 204-7704
e-mail: mkotabe@sbm.temple.edu

ACKNOWLEDGMENTS

We thank the many colleagues, students, and executives who have permitted us to work with them and allowed us to learn with and through them. We also thank the following reviewers for the constructive and imaginative comments and criticisms, which were instrumental in increasing the quality of the manuscript.

For their help with the first edition:

Casey Donoho
Northern Arizona University
Richard C. Leventhal
Metropolitan State College
Faye S. McIntyre
Rockhurst College
Bruce I. Newman
DePaul University
Richard D. Nordstrom
California State University–Fresno
Elaine M. Notarantonio
Bryant College
Alphonso O. Ogbuehi
Christopher Newport University

Thomas L. Powers
University of Alabama at Birmingham
Robert G. Roe
University of Wyoming
Peter B. Shaffer
Western Illinois University
Carolyn Simmons
Lehigh University
Mark T. Spriggs
University of Oregon
Ken Williamson
James Madison University

For their help with the second edition:

Thomas L. Baker
University of North Carolina at Wilmington
Carol L. Bruneau
University of Montana
Debra K. Cartwright
Truman State University
Newell Chiesl
Indiana State University
James Finch
University of Wisconsin–La Crosse
Stephen J. Gould
Baruch College, The City University of New York

Wesley H. Jones
University of Indianapolis
Pankaj Kumar
Cornell University
Satya Menon
University of Chicago
Al Rosenbloom
Benedictine University
John Tsalikis
Florida International University
Shaoming Zou
University of Missouri, Columbia

And to those reviewers who helped us understand the particular needs of distance-learning students:

John DeNigris
University of Phoenix
Gary Eckert
Nova Southeastern University

Craig Eslinger
University of Phoenix
Phyllis K. Goodman
College of Dupage

John E. Hawes
MIM; American Graduate School of
International Management
Yvonne Phelps
University of Phoenix
Marilyn Pike
University of Phoenix
Donald L. Reinhart
University of Phoenix

Debbie Schrager
University of Phoenix
Philip C. Spivey
University of Phoenix
Allen K. Sutton
University of Phoenix

Thanks also go to the Dryden Press for the kind permission to use selected materials from the *International Marketing* text of Michael R. Czinkota and Ilkka Ronkainen. Thanks also to Victoria Crittenden (Boston University), who made important contributions to the content of this book. We must also acknowledge the work of Susan Peterson (Scottsdale Community College), who revised the Instructor Manual, Test Bank, and PowerPoint presentation. A very special word of thanks goes to Jamie Gleich Bryant of Bryant Editorial Development and to our team at South-Western College Publishing, in particular David Shaut and Steve Scoble, for their enthusiasm and support. At Georgetown University, Marc De Buretel De Chassey, Ahn Nguyen, and Kristen M. Mehlum were of great help in producing the manuscript. At the University of Texas at Austin, Aldor Lanctot of Dell Computer and Steve Giamporcaro helped us with ever-changing technology issues in marketing, and Preet Aulakh of Michigan State University and Arvind Sahay of London Business School, both former Ph.D. students of the second coauthor at Texas, provided intellectual insight. Fundação Getúlio Vargas (FGV), São Paulo, Brazil, has been an intellectual home to the second coauthor during the summer. Particularly, Maria Cecilia Coutinho de Arruda and Wilton de Oliveira Bussab of FGV deserve our special word of appreciation for our maintaining and honing a truly global perspective during the course of writing this textbook. At Temple University, Harsh Mishra is credited for his insight into many of the recent examples throughout the book. James Wills and Laurel King at the University of Hawaii at Manoa offered the second coauthor a homey environment for his intensive work toward completion of this edition. Finally, Junzo Ishii of Kobe University, Japan, should be acknowledged for his insights into the myths of many marketing concepts that helped us better formulate our marketing textbook.

We are deeply grateful to you, the professors, the students, and the professionals using this book. Your interest demonstrates the need for more knowledge about marketing. As our customers, you are telling us that our product adds value to your lives. As a result, you add value to ours. We enjoy maintaining our "dialogue" with our customers. Thank you!

Michael R. Czinkota is on the faculty of marketing and international business of the Graduate School and the Robert Emmett McDonough School of Business at Georgetown University. He also serves as Chairman of FIBER, the Foundation for International Business Education and Research, in Washington, D.C. He has held professorial appointments at universities in Asia, Australia, Europe, and the Americas.

Dr. Czinkota served in the U.S. government as Deputy Assistant Secretary of Commerce. He was responsible for macro trade analysis, departmental support of international trade negotiations and retaliatory actions, and policy coordination for international finance, investment, and monetary affairs. He also served as head of the U.S. Delegation to the OECD Industry Committee in Paris and as senior trade advisor for Export Controls.

Dr. Czinkota's background includes eight years of private sector business experience as a partner in an export-import firm and in an advertising agency and seventeen years of research and teaching in the academic world. He has been the recipient of research grants from various organizations, including the National Science Foundation, the National Commission of Jobs and Small Business, and the Organization of American States. He was listed as one of the three most published contributors to international business research in *Journal of International Business Studies* and has written several books, including *International Marketing, The Global Marketing Imperative,* and *Trends in International Business.*

Dr. Czinkota serves on the Global Advisory Board of the American Marketing Association and on the Board of Governors of the Academy of Marketing Science. He is on the editorial boards of *Journal of Business Research, Journal of the Academy of Marketing Science, International Marketing Review,* and *Asian Journal of Marketing.* He was named a Distinguished Fellow of the Academy of Marketing Science. For his work in international business and trade policy, he has been awarded honorary degrees from the Universidad Pontificia Madre y Maestra in the Dominican Republic and the Universidad del Pacifico in Lima, Peru.

Dr. Czinkota advises a wide range of individuals and institutions in the United States and abroad. He serves on several corporate boards and has worked with corporations such as AT&T, IBM, GE, Nestlé, and US WEST. He also has assisted various governmental organizations in the structuring of effective trade promotion policies.

Dr. Czinkota was born and raised in Germany and educated in Austria, Scotland, Spain, and the United States. He studied law and business administration at the University of Erlangen–Nürnberg and was awarded a two-year Fulbright Scholarship. He holds an MBA in international business and a Ph.D. in logistics from The Ohio State University.

Masaaki "Mike" Kotabe holds the Washburn Chair of International Business and Marketing, and is Director of Research at the Institute of Global Management Studies at the Fox School of Business and Management at Temple University. Before joining Temple University in 1998, he was Ambassador Edward Clark Centennial Endowed Fellow and Professor of marketing and international business at the University of Texas at Austin. Dr. Kotabe also served as the Vice President of the Academy of International Business in the 1997 to 1998 period. He received his Ph.D. in marketing and international business at Michigan State University. Dr. Kotabe teaches international marketing, global sourcing strategy (R&D, manufacturing, and marketing interfaces), and Japanese business practices at the undergraduate and MBA levels and theories of international business at the Ph.D. level. He has lectured at various business schools around the world, including Austria, Germany, Finland, Brazil, Colombia, Mexico, Japan, Korea, Indonesia, and Turkey. For his research, he has worked closely with leading companies, such as AT&T, NEC, Philips, Sony, and Ito-Yokado (parent of 7-Eleven stores). Dr. Kotabe currently serves as advisor to the United Nations' and World Trade Organization's Executive Forum on National Export Strategies.

Dr. Kotabe has written many scholarly publications. His research work has appeared in such journals as *Journal of Marketing, Journal of International Business Studies,* and *Strategic Management Journal.* His books include *Global Sourcing Strategy: R&D, Manufacturing, Marketing Interfaces* (1992), *Japanese Distribution System* (with Michael R. Czinkota, 1993), *Anticompetitive Practices in Japan* (with Kent W. Wheiler, 1996), *MERCOSUR and Beyond* (1997), *Trends in International Business: Critical Perspectives* (with Michael R. Czinkota, 1998), *Japanese Distribution Strategy* (with Michael R. Czinkota, 2000), and *Global Marketing Management* (with Kristiaan Helsen, 2001).

He is the associate editor of *Journal of International Business Studies* and the co-editor of *Journal of International Management.* He serves on the editorial boards of *Journal of Marketing, Journal of International Marketing, Journal of World Business, Journal of Business Research, Latin American Economic Abstracts,* and *Thunderbird International Business Review.* He also serves as an advisor to the *National Competitiveness Report* of the Institute of Industrial Policy Studies (IPS).

In the 1997 issue of *Journal of Teaching in International Business,* Dr. Kotabe was ranked the most prolific international marketing researcher in the world in the last ten years. He has been recently elected a Fellow of the Academy of International Business for his lifetime contribution to international business research and education. He is also an elected member of the New York Academy of Sciences.

chapter **1**

An Overview of Marketing

You are about to begin an exciting, important, and necessary undertaking: the exploration of marketing. Marketing is exciting because it combines the science and the art of business with many other disciplines, such as economics, psychology, anthropology, cultural studies, geography, history, jurisprudence, statistics, and demographics. This combination will stimulate your intellectual curiosity and enable you to absorb and understand the phenomenon of market-based exchange. The study of marketing has been compared to mountain climbing: challenging, arduous, and exhilarating.

Marketing is important and necessary because it takes place all around us every day, has a major effect on our lives, and is crucial to the survival and success of firms and individuals. Successful marketing provides the promise of an improved quality of life, a better society, and, as suggested in Manager's Corner 1.1, even a more peaceful world. After your study of marketing you will see what happens, understand how it happens, and, at some time in your future, perhaps even make it happen. This is much better than standing by and wondering what happened.

Manager's Corner 1.1

Does marketing create peace?

One of the biggest surprises of the postwar era has been that historic enemies, such as Japan and the United States, or France and Germany, have not had the remotest threat of war since 1945. Why should they? Anything Japan has that we want we can buy, and on very easy credit terms, so why fight for it? Similarly, why should the Japanese fight the United States and lose all those profitable markets? France and Germany, linked intimately through marketing and the European Union, are now each other's largest trading partners. Closed countries build huge armies and waste money on guns and troops; open countries spend their money on new machines and tools to crank out Barbie dolls and consumer electronics. Their bright young people figure out how to run the machines, not how to fire the latest missile. For some reason, they not only get rich fast but also lose interest in military adventures. Japan, that peculiar superpower without superguns, confounds everyone simply because no one has ever seen a major world power that got that way by selling you to death, not shooting you to death. In short, if you do a great deal of trade with someone, why fight? The logical answer—you don't—is perhaps the best news mankind has had in millennia.

Source: Richard N. Farmer, "Would You Want Your Granddaughter to Marry a Taiwanese Marketing Man?" *Journal of Marketing* 51 (October 1987): 114–115.

WHAT IS MARKETING?

The essence of marketing is a state of mind. In making marketing decisions, the manager adopts the viewpoint of the customer. Decisions therefore are driven by what the customer needs and wants. Much of what the marketing manager does is concerned with making decisions that revolve around how the goods or services of the organization can be made to match the customer's needs and wants.

> the key to
> **success of marketing**
> is adopting the customer's viewpoint

But the key to success of marketing is adopting the customer's viewpoint.

Marketing theory is part of the social science domain. As such, a key focus of its analysis is human behavior, which is mutable, unpredictable, and reactive.[1] Marketing is also heavily context dependent. More so than most other fields of inquiry, the nature and scope of marketing can be substantially affected when one of its contextual elements, such as the economy, societal norms, demographic characteristics, or new technologies, changes.[2] Therefore, marketing is far from an exact science and allows plenty of room for different interpretations. But several fundamental dimensions form the underpinnings of all marketing thinking.

Peter Drucker stated that "every business can be defined as serving either customers or markets or end users."[3] The marketing dimension has recognized this service dimension most explicitly. The key elements of all marketing are outward-looking and firmly centered on the customer. This orientation requires marketers to look at their organization, activities, and processes through their customers' eyes. Communication with customers, measurement of their satisfaction levels, and designing programs to improve customer satisfaction allow marketing the greatest influence within the firm.[4]

We will see that this customer focus can be applied to almost all types of organizations, even those in the nonprofit sector that have traditionally viewed themselves as exempt from normal commercial processes. The needs and wants of the customer or client should almost always be paramount: The difficulty for many organizations is deciding who their customers are and what their needs and wants are.

The reason for this **customer focus** is the fundamental marketing tenet of competition. Firms must compete for resources in the marketplace, which offers a host of alternative ways for the customer to spend funds. Only if a firm competes successfully—that is, if it can convince customers to spend money on its products rather than on others—will the firm be able to survive. The dimension of competition makes the customers reign supreme, because the customer's decisions will determine the winners of the competition.

A practical metaphor for **marketing** is a **dialogue**. The marketer must communicate specific exchange advantages, even though communication often takes place by such indirect means as advertising or coalition building. More importantly, though, the marketer must spend a great deal of effort and time listening to the customer through marketing research. The marketer who listens to customers and understands their viewpoints is the most effective manager. If you have any

---

1. George M. Zinkhan and Ruby Hirschheim, "Truth in Marketing Theory and Research: An Alternative Perspective," *Journal of Marketing* 56 (April 1992): 80–88.
2. Jagdish N. Sheth and Rajendra S. Sisodia, "Revisiting Marketing's Lawlike Generalizations," *Journal of the Academy of Marketing Science* 27, no. 1 (1999): 71–87.
3. P. F. Drucker, *Managing for Results* (New York: Harper & Row, 1964), 51.
4. Christian Homburg, John P. Workman, and Harley Krohmer, "Marketing's Influence Within the Firm," *Journal of Marketing* 63 (April 1999): 1–17.

doubt as to what might be good marketing, simply think of it in the context of this dialogue: Would it work face-to-face with the customer? Another key marketing dimension is the adaptation of a long-term perspective. Individuals and firms are potential customers long before they become actual customers. Working with them in order to make them party to a transaction—through analysis and communication—is an important aspect of marketing. It is of equal, if not greater, importance to continue to work with customers after they have engaged in a transaction. In many instances, it is at this point when the customer is the most valuable to the marketer. In essence, the sale merely consummates the courtship, at which point the marriage begins. How good the marriage is depends on how well the seller manages the relationship. The quality of the marriage determines whether there will be continued or expanded business, or troubles and divorce.[5] **Repeat purchases** from current customers are easier to achieve than finding new customers. Current customers have a lifetime value based on their ongoing expenditures, which by far overshadow any of their specific transactions. For example, a customer may spend only $55 at any given visit to a supermarket. However, if the customer is likely to live in the area for 10 years and comes in twice a week to shop, the lifetime value of that customer to the supermarket will exceed $57,000. With this long-term perspective in mind, marketers treat the customer differently from those who see only the individual sale. Of course, the same perspective also applies to the marketer's relations with suppliers. If one considers the cost of building a relationship with suppliers, including aspects such as trust, reliability, and consistency, such a relationship takes on an important value and makes it worthwhile to invest in developing linkages such as direct order entry methods or online information exchanges.

Recognizing innovation and adapting to change are other key features of marketing. Doing so improves the performance of the marketing function in two ways. First, servicing the customer is likely to be more efficient, because it takes advantage of improvements in product quality advances, production process changes, and communication enhancements. Second, improvements are likely to come about more quickly due to the desire to stay ahead of the competition. For example, marketers are key drivers in implementing new aspects of electronic commerce in the business field. All this results in better service and more choice for the customer. Each of these dimensions is a key component of marketing. Their implementation in marketing practice will be addressed throughout this book.

DEFINITIONS OF MARKETING

The American Marketing Association defines marketing as "the process of planning and executing the conception, pricing, promotion, and distribution of ideas, goods, and services to create exchanges that satisfy individual and organizational goals."[6]

www.ama.org

It is useful to focus on some of this definition's components in order to fully understand its meaning. Viewing marketing as a *process* highlights the idea that the activity goes beyond a single transaction. Rather, the aim is to develop ties and relationships that require the maintenance of systemic perspectives. Use of the terms *planning* and *executing* emphasizes that marketing as a discipline consists of

> marketing . . . goes beyond a single transaction. Rather, the aim is to develop ties and relationships

5. Theodore Levitt, "After the Sale Is Over," *Harvard Business Review* 61 (September 1983): 87–93.
6. Peter D. Bennett, ed., *Dictionary of Marketing Terms*, 2d ed. (Chicago: American Marketing Association, 1995), 166.

the theoretical approach as well as the practical implementation that makes concepts come alive. *Conception, pricing, promotion,* and *distribution* then explain the variety of marketing components that can be used in this planning and execution. The application of marketing not just to *goods* but also to *services* and *ideas* makes the field broad and useful for producers of soap as well as for think tanks and government services. The term *exchanges* clarifies that something is given and something is received by the participants in the marketing process. It might not necessarily be money that is exchanged for goods; it might just as well be performance of a service (coaching Little League) in exchange for obtaining a good feeling and a sense of fulfillment. The word *create* gives marketing an anticipatory dimension and emphasizes the forward-looking approach necessary to identify future needs and wants. *Satisfaction* is a crucial component of marketing. It means that all the participants in the exchange feel better after the marketing transaction has taken place. As we will see later in the discussion on pricing, even though individuals seek to exchange equal value, after a successful transaction they will perceive themselves as being better off than before, and on the way to increased affluence. *Individuals* and *organizations* are the participants in the marketing process. The fact that marketing is responsive to their *goals* indicates that the discipline and its orientation are dynamic and subject to ongoing change.

As you can see, this definition is full of meaning, packs a lot of punch, and lets marketing make a major contribution to the welfare of individuals. Nevertheless, based on our view of marketing, we will expand this definition on several dimensions. The fact that marketing "creates" exchanges highlights the fact that the exercise of marketing can cause new activities to happen. However, the term *creation* overemphasizes transactions as one-time events. Therefore, we prefer the addition of the term *maintain,* to reflect the long-term relationship nature of marketing activities. We also believe that, as the scope of marketing is broadened, the dimension of *societal goals* needs to be added to individuals and organizations, properly reflecting the overarching reach and responsibility of marketing as a societal change agent that responds to and develops social concerns about the environment, technology, and ethics. It is also very important to recognize that, as a discipline, marketing will make progress principally by acknowledging the connections among the different players in the marketing process. Strengthening the interaction with the consumer has to be accompanied by closer association with producers, suppliers, and channel members. The firm, its suppliers, and its customers form one common system whose approaches need to be optimized. Marketers need to understand the systemic context of their actions by understanding how their approaches affect the entire system and all of its members. All of this will be accomplished primarily by making increased use of technology to link the different partners. Equally important is the need to broaden our marketing understanding beyond national borders to include the world. Today, sourcing and supply linkages exist around the globe, competition emerges from all corners of the earth, and market opportunities evolve worldwide. As a result, many crucial dimensions of marketing need to be reevaluated and adapted. It is therefore imperative to include the *global dimension* to the definition of marketing. Based on these considerations, our expanded definition of marketing is "the process of planning and executing the conception, pricing, promotion, and distribution of ideas, goods, and services to create and maintain exchanges that satisfy individual, organizational, and societal goals in the systemic context of a global environment."

A BRIEF HISTORY OF MARKETING THOUGHT

To appreciate the structure of marketing theory, it is useful to understand how this theory has evolved.

Marketing has existed for millennia, ever since people first started to barter accumulated **surpluses**. For most of that time, though, marketing was seen as a peripheral activity, because, in subsistence economies, such surpluses represented a relatively small part of the total. Most marketing activities were confined to disposing of surplus agricultural products. After the Industrial Revolution made such surpluses more commonplace, the "marketing" of these became the province of the "salesman," with his specialized skills.

Writings about activities that are now part of marketing can be found as early as the nineteenth century. For example, a book titled *The History of Advertising* was published in England in 1875. However, little of this material contributed to the formation of marketing thought. Jones and Monieson suggest that the first academic discussions of marketing can be traced back to the turn of the twentieth century.[7] At that time, marketers began to set themselves apart from economists by conducting studies that were more empirical, practical, and descriptive of the marketplace. They analyzed issues from the standpoint of the firm rather than that of public administration. As early as 1902 courses were developed in the area of distribution, which, for the first time, recognized that intermediaries can add value to the production process rather than just add cost.[8] In large part, these distribution issues were most relevant in the agricultural sector, which is why the early marketing pioneers emerged in universities close to agricultural producers, such as the University of Michigan, the University of Pennsylvania, and Ohio State University. Over the following years, marketers boldly postulated, and later proved, that demand could be increased and shaped by factors other than the mere existence of supply. They also moved the concept of price away from mere cost considerations and sought new explanations of price formations in the market.

During and after the 1930s, scholars began to integrate the various components of marketing, formulating the first marketing theories and developing the body of marketing thought. Researchers began to evaluate consumers and their behavior in the context of business decisions, leaving their mother disciplines such as psychology behind and calling themselves *consumer behaviorists*. Simultaneously, in the wider sphere of practical business management, the newly fashionable advertising agencies began to redefine the discipline in a way that came close to the modern concept of marketing. In the late 1950s and early 1960s, U.S. society benefited from a great surge in demand for goods, a major expansion of production capacities, and an increase in competition, far exceeding the economic welfare levels of other nations. As a result, the United States became the cradle of marketing thinking. This era encouraged the development of marketing in its modern form, based on a customer focus that made extensive use of market research to investigate customers' needs and wants, and it emerged on the scale that we now witness. The discipline further matured in the 1970s as the ideas that had developed from practical experience were codified and substantiated with quantitative research. Marketing became routinized as an increasingly important function of business. The leading edge of marketing moved on, at least in part, to the service industries—particularly to retailing and financial services and to nonprofit institutions and activities—which were experiencing massive changes. In the 1980s, however, marketing began to lose much of its previous self-confidence. Evolving ideas focused attention on more of an environmental perspective. Warren Keegan summarized the changes as follows:

> By 1990 it was clear that the "new" concept of marketing was outdated and that the times demanded a strategic concept. The strategic concept of marketing, a major evolution in the history of marketing thought, shifted the

7. B. D. G. Jones and D. D. Monieson, "Early Development of the Philosophy of Marketing Thought," *Journal of Marketing* 54 (1990): 102–113.

8. Robert Bartels, *The History of Marketing Thought*, 2d ed. (Columbus, Ohio: Grid, 1976), 12.

> ## Knowing everything there is to know about the customer is not enough.

focus from the customer or product to the firm's external environment. Knowing everything there is to know about the customer is not enough. To succeed, marketers must know the customer in a context which includes the competition, government policy and regulation, and the broader economic, social and political macro forces that shape the evolution of markets.[9]

Today, there is once again increasing use of marketing techniques and increasing confidence in the outcome, but this is now a usage that recognizes the inherent limitations of traditional marketing. Continuous subtle changes in the context and application of marketing are leading to a paradigm shift in the new millennium. Two main dimensions account for that change.

First, to remain a viable discipline, marketing must become more responsive to new societal demands and realities that require the incorporation of a global perspective, social responsibility, ethics, and human interaction with the environment. In an era in which old ideological delineations such as central planning have decayed and new ones are emerging, marketing must broaden its reach to become a key change agent to improve our quality of life, thereby contributing to the betterment of society.[10] For example, as one looks at the current transformation of the emerging market economies of Central Europe, one can see the many new challenges confronting marketing: How does the marketing concept fit into these societies? How can marketing contribute to economic development? How can and should one get the price mechanism to work? What role should advertising play?

In the area of social responsibility and ethics, marketing managers are increasingly challenged not only to adapt to existing rules but to lead the way. Simply using the standard of existing law is no longer sufficient for a discipline that intends to be at the forefront of social transformation. When it comes to issues such as monitoring environmental pollution, maintaining safe working condition, copying technology or trademarks, and paying bribes, the problem becomes even more complex for the international marketer who is facing a multicultural environment with differing and often inconsistent legal systems.[11] In addition, the passage of time results in new expectations and awareness by customers, who often evaluate past actions by current standards. Therefore, the marketer must not only be sensitive to current societal expectations and the effects that the firm's actions in one country may have on customers in another country, but also proactively assert leadership in implementing standards of the highest level. Even though such a position may have negative repercussions on short-term profits, the firm is likely to benefit in the long run through consumer goodwill and the avoidance of later recriminations. In addition, the firm may well be able to boost its competitive position through its efforts to create an improved quality of life through marketing.

The second key force of change in marketing is a result of both new technology and the need to view both suppliers and customers as part of the **marketing system**. If marketers remain focused only on their own firm or organization, they are likely to be overtaken by strategists and management experts who are preach-

---

9. W. K. Keegan, *Global Marketing Management*, 5th ed. (Upper Saddle River, N.J.: Prentice Hall, 1995), 5.
10. Reiner Springer and Michael R. Czinkota, "Marketing's Contribution to the Transformation of Central and Eastern Europe," *Thunderbird International Business Review* 41, no. 1 (1999): 29–48.
11. Robert W. Armstrong and Jill Sweeney, "Industry Type, Culture, Mode of Entry, and Perceptions of International Marketing Ethics Problems: A Cross-Cultural Comparison," *Journal of Business Ethics* 13, no. 10 (1994): 775–785.

ing a new gospel. In an era of just-in-time (JIT) production, early supplier involvement (ESI) in product planning, and direct order entry in purchasing, confinement of one's perspective to a single organization and a short-term transaction becomes limiting and soon even noncompetitive. Marketing has been transformed by the arrival of the information revolution, which is restructuring the performance of marketing tasks. Never before has it been so easy for customers and suppliers worldwide to establish direct contact with each other. Never before has it been possible to know so much about each other. Today, firms can use huge panels of people who register via the Internet to gather, track, cross-reference, manipulate, analyze, and disseminate information.[12] As a result, firms can offer much more precision in their marketing activities. Predictions of an Internet-based economy of more than $1.4 trillion by 2003 presage a major effect on the marketer's interaction with customers, particularly in the industrial or business-to-business field.[13] Making use of technological innovation in marketing has direct effects on the efficiency and effectiveness of all business activities. Integration of these capabilities into a firm's marketing strategy opens entirely new horizons. Products can be produced more quickly, obtained less expensively from sources around the world, distributed at lower cost, and customized to the individual client's needs. Most importantly, forms can differentiate their market transactions based on the content of the transaction, the context in which it occurs, and the infrastructure that makes the transaction possible.[14] Technology opens up a **market space** rather than a marketplace by allowing the firm to keep the content while changing the context and the infrastructure completely, such as when a newspaper is distributed globally online rather than house-to-house on paper. All this presents firms with unprecedented new opportunities to serve and satisfy their customers. The discipline of marketing is therefore poised on the hinges of business practice, either swing-

> Marketing has been **transformed by** the information revolution

ing the door wide open to encompass a new breadth of perspective and to embrace a much larger portion of business activities, or closing the door to its further development and growth. Yet, if history is a guide, marketing will be able to adapt to these new needs, since adjustment to change is at the heart of the discipline. As one of the early pioneers of marketing stated, "No systems of marketing remain static; all are in stages of adaptation to continuing change, both in the external environment and with the marketing organization itself. In a general theory of marketing, provision would be made for accounting for and anticipating change in the processes, systems and behavior patterns."[15]

THE STRUCTURE OF MARKETING THEORY

So far, we have defined marketing in general terms and offered some categorizations. However, one of the first things you should come to appreciate about a genuine, practical marketing approach to problems is that it abhors pigeonholing any situation into neat categories. Rather, it prefers to look at the customers' specific

12. Seymour Sudman and Edward Blair, "Sampling in the Twenty-First Century," *Journal of the Academy of Marketing Science* 27, no. 2 (1999): 269–277.
13. Maricris G. Briones, "On Ramp: How Three Companies Took Different Roads to Doing Business on the Information Highway," *Marketing News* (April 26, 1999): 1, 13.
14. John J. Sviokla and Jeffrey F. Rayport, "Mapping the Marketspace: Information Technology and the New Marketing Environment," *Harvard Business School Bulletin* 71 (June 1995): 49–51.
15. Robert Bartels, "The General Theory of Marketing," *Journal of Marketing* 32 (January 1968): 29–33.

needs and wants. This apparent contradiction can, however, be resolved. Frameworks are often a valuable aid to organizing ideas. Simple diagrams and categories are useful in helping you understand the complexity of linkages and are also effective memory aids. This book uses such diagrams, but you should recognize that they are simplifications intended to illuminate ideas rather than to define them. A danger arises only when the categories are allowed to replace the ideas. An analogy is useful here: When you tell your family doctor your symptoms, he or she will usually follow a framework as an aid to diagnosis. If you have a temperature, a headache, a cough, drowsiness, and aching in the limbs, you might have the flu. If the doctor checks further, however, and finds that you also have a slow pulse and a rash on the upper abdomen, you might have typhoid fever. One moral from this analogy is that the doctor, who has spent years learning how to use categories, applies expert judgment to all the factors observed. The use of frameworks as a guide to marketing diagnosis can be just as valuable, but the whole picture must never be forgotten.

With this warning in mind, we now examine the dimensions that have the widest application across the breadth of marketing activities.

GOODS VERSUS SERVICES

Marketing applies to tangible goods, such as a refrigerator that is manufactured in a factory by the supplier, as well as to intangible services, such as a haircut. Some goods, such as personal computers, have a great deal of "service" attached to them; the total package is sometimes described as the extended product. On the other hand, some services, such as a haircut, depend on physical products; the hair-care treatments used are very important and are clearly physical. There are differences in the way in which organizations might market a good and a service. A good is often promoted on the basis of its physical features, whereas promotion of a service is associated more with the quality of the organization providing it. In general, however, we will see that the basics of marketing are shared by both goods and services. Marketing in Action 1.1 discusses how Walgreens is battling the blurring of the goods/services distinction for prescription refills.

PRODUCT CATEGORIES

Even within this overall categorization, marketers often presume that there are significant differences between the various product types. In the general category of consumer goods, for example, there are both nondurable and durable consumer goods. Nondurable consumer goods, the archetypal marketed goods, are heavily advertised to build awareness, trial, and preference. Groceries are an example. Consumer durables, sometimes further subdivided into white goods (refrigerators, for example) and brown goods (such as furniture and electronic devices), are the "capital" goods of the consumer sector. These may require more personal selling and support.

CONSUMER VERSUS INDUSTRIAL MARKETS

There are significant differences in approach to consumer and industrial markets. Individual consumers who buy a product for themselves or their families typically spend less, but each individual may be the sole decision maker. Their suppliers, the mass consumer goods manufacturers, have to deal with such consumers by indirect means. This traditionally requires that suppliers find out about consumer needs through market research and communicate with them via advertisements in the mass media. Industrial marketing, however, often requires

Marketing in Action 1.1

Walgreens battles the virtual pharmacy

Walgreens (www.walgreens.com) began in 1901 in Chicago, Illinois (USA), when Charles R. Walgreen, Sr. purchased a neighborhood drugstore for $6,000. Since that time, the company has opened almost 3,000 stores. Walgreens pioneered the drive-through pharmacy windows and has become known in the industry for its freestanding buildings. However, drive-through windows and freestanding buildings are now making way for online pharmacies.

Pharmacy companies such as CVS (www.cvs.com) and Rite Aid (www.riteaid.com) have bought their way into the Web-based pharmacy arena through acquisitions of Soma.com and Drugstore.com, but Walgreens is sticking to its policy of growing from within rather than through acquisitions. As a major provider of prescriptions online, the company plans to take advantage of what it is currently doing—allowing customers to order refills via the company's Web site. By 1999, the company was filling 1,400 online refill requests daily.

To battle the virtual pharmacies, Walgreens is expanding its current online refill program to a full prescription service through the Internet. In addition to ordering prescriptions online (new prescriptions will still have to be called in by the doctor's office or mailed/faxed), customers will be able to request mail delivery or store pickup as well as access patient information online. Such patient information will include a prescription history, potential drug and food interactions, and a complete drug description. Patient-specific information will be secured by each customer once they have obtained a Walgreens password.

Can Walgreens turn its online pharmacy into a competitive advantage? Is the online service itself any different from what the virtual pharmacies have to offer? How will the company build on its century of drugstore retailing to market its Web-based service?

Sources: www.walgreens.com; James Frederick, "Walgreens Gears for Opening of its Own Internet Pharmacy," *Drug Store News*, July 19, 1999, CP1.

face-to-face interaction, which is justifiable when the value of the individual sale is higher. The interaction is with someone who merely represents the buying organization and perhaps is not the only decision maker. It is the nature and extended length of these negotiations, coupled with the technical demands on the marketing professionals involved, that frequently offer the most telling difference from consumer goods marketing. On the other hand, technology may make it possible to erase some of these differences, particularly if the communication between customers and their supplier becomes more direct and the marketing effort more precise.

PROFIT VERSUS NONPROFIT

One of the divisions often debated is that between profit-making organizations and nonprofit-making sectors such as universities or charities. The former are easy to deal with. They are, at least in theory, driven by the primary motive of making a profit, and good marketing is an excellent way of increasing the bottom-line profit figures. On the other hand, employees of the nonprofit sectors frequently have difficulty in seeing how marketing, which is too often associated with hard-selling advertisements for consumer goods, applies to their own organization. Exactly how it may be of use will become more obvious as we progress, but at this stage it should be understood that all organizations necessarily have links with the outside world. For example, MADD (Mothers Against Drunk Driving), an organization that strives to encourage motorists not to drink and drive, needs to use market research to discover the motivations of those who do and the most effective means of influencing them not to. MADD then uses the mass media to convey its messages. The smallest charity has to decide who its clients are and

www.madd.org

what their needs are, before communicating with them. As Manager's Corner 1.2 shows, even religious institutions can make use of marketing approaches.

INTERMEDIARIES VERSUS END USERS

Many of the marketing processes use intermediaries, such as retailers and wholesalers, to provide the product to the end user or customer. These intermediaries themselves represent a significant proportion of the service sector, and they make very different demands on the suppliers of products. They are seeking profit, as well as a match with their own marketing needs, which may be very distinct from the desires of end users. Technology may dramatically affect the marketing perspective and actions of both intermediaries and end users.

DOMESTIC VERSUS INTERNATIONAL

When a firm shifts from the domestic market to the international market, many new factors enter into its marketing horizon, including exchange rates, tariffs, and conflicting government policies. In addition, new modes of transportation might

---

Manager's Corner 1.2

Nuns in the midwest use marketing to attract new recruits

Marketing is becoming more and more important to anyone wishing to get a message across to the public. For public institutions and private organizations alike, for profit or not-for-profit enterprises, marketing is a useful tool. The following examples show how religious institutions use marketing techniques.

The sisters of St. Benedict Monastery in Ferdinand, Indiana, are using marketing to increase the number of sisters recruited to their religious order. In 1990 the order faced a serious risk of extinction, common in many orders in the United States. In St. Benedict, there were 275 nuns at the monastery, 60 percent of them were over 70, and only one new person was recruited per year. The sisters decided to seek professional marketing help to increase the number of recruits. It was important to see how the profession of a nun was viewed by the public. Using questionnaires, telephone interviews, and focus groups, they discovered that 98 percent of the respondents thought of nuns in robes, closeted in the convent, although most nuns do not wear habits and often work outside the monastery as lawyers, educators, and nurses.

The order placed ads in newspapers, explaining the modern role of nuns. As soon as someone responded, that person was put on a mailing list for information and invitations to visit the monastery and interact with the resident nuns. Marketing the profession of a nun seems successful, since the order has been recruiting three members a year for the last six years. The nuns from St. Benedict now teach religious orders all around the world how marketing can help them too. At these meetings they discuss, not the Bible, but "Selling on the Fast Track" and "Guerrilla Marketing Attack."

Many churches in America, like the Church of Jesus Christ of Latter Day Saints, the Southern Baptist Church, or the United Methodist Church, use television ad campaigns to enhance their image and their appeal to people of other denominations or non-believers. Each denomination has to define who their "customers" are. The Southern Baptist Church tailors its ads to different demographic groups: Generation X, baby boomers, urban poor, and working professionals. Other churches are turning to marketing consultants to learn that new members can be won by giving them spirituality in the context of ample parking and child care.

Sources: Daniel Akst, "When Business Gets Religion," *New York Times,* October 4, 1998, 5; Meera Louis, "Modern Marketing Helps Sell Life as a Nun," *Wall Street Journal,* May 11, 1999, B1, B14; Lisa Miller, "Religious Advertising Converts, Moving Toward a Tougher Sell," *Wall Street Journal,* February 24, 1998, B2.

Exhibit 1.1

Shifting from a domestic to an international market is a complex transition requiring special attention to all business functions, not the least of which is evaluation of new consumer preferences. Campbell's soups are sold internationally, but strategy in Europe—where soups are most often sold in powdered rather than condensed form—will need to be different than strategy in the United States, where consumption of condensed soups is higher than of powdered soup varieties.

be needed, the inventory pipelines lengthen, and payment flows slow down. A new set of customers has to be listened to, and their attitudes, behavior, culture, and socioeconomic position have to be understood. Although marketing internationally deals with the same marketing dimensions, it requires a new perspective of both the environment and the customer. The marketer must either search for "marketing universals"—such as segment—and product-specific consumer behaviors that are invariant across cultures or countries[16] (see Exhibit 1.1) or find ways of adapting to different settings.

SMALL FIRMS VERSUS LARGE FIRMS

Small firms are just as susceptible to marketing solutions as large ones. The difference is that they usually do not have the resources or expertise to exploit marketing in its most sophisticated forms and are unlikely to make much of an impact on their environment. Some claim that small firms have a distinctive marketing style. For example, there is generally little or no adherence to formal structures and frameworks; the marketing style relies heavily on intuitive ideas and decisions and, probably most importantly, on common sense.[17] Common sense is a very valuable commodity in marketing, and the proprietors of small businesses are usually much closer to their customers than the marketing vice presidents of many multinational firms.

---

16. Niraj Dawar and Philip Parker, "Marketing Universals: Consumers' Use of Brand Name, Price, Physical Appearance, and Retailer Reputation as Signals of Product Quality," *Journal of Marketing* 58 (1994): 81–95.

17. D. Carson and S. Cromie, "Marketing Planning in Small Enterprises: A Model and Some Empirical Evidence," *Journal of Marketing Management* 5, no. 1 (1989).

Industry Sector Specificity

Other dimensions are particularly important to specific industry sectors. For example, whether the sector is largely controlled by government regulation, as is the ethical pharmaceuticals industry, or whether an industry is subject to subsidized competition from abroad can be crucial for the development of a successful marketing strategy. Fortunately, most of these different categories of organization have more marketing theory and practice in common than not. Indeed, most of the marketing activities described in this book are widely applicable. Even pricing, which at the surface has little relevance for noncommercial organizations, turns out to offer them many lessons.

MARKETING AND INTERNAL RESOURCES

Marketing theory emphasizes the necessity of viewing the needs of the customer/consumer/client as the prime focus of all marketing activity. In practice there may be even greater justification for such a focus, because most organizations are preoccupied with internal problems, and it takes a great deal of effort to shift their attention to the outside. On the other hand, what gets lost in this single-minded concentration on the customer is the relationship of the marketing function with the organization's resources. Much as the organization cannot exist in isolation from its market, neither can marketing exist in isolation from the rest of the organization or its suppliers and intermediaries, although that is often what marketing departments attempt. After all, marketing's primary role is to serve the organization, even if its first task is then to remind the organization that it is there to serve the customer. Marketing has to work with available resources, no matter what the market demands. Some of the most spectacular failures have arisen from very strong marketing visions that drove their adherents to commit their organizations beyond any reasonable expenditure of resources. For example, the British air carrier Laker Airways, which introduced discounted fares across the Atlantic, was immensely popular with its customers but lost its investor's funds when it went bankrupt. Apple Computers almost lost sight of the need to live within organizational constraints and had some close brushes with demise.

www.apple.com

Paradoxically, therefore, the starting point for the marketer is the organization itself. To get ready for a marketing orientation, the organization needs to address the following dimensions:

1. **Develop an understanding of what resources the organization has at its disposal.** This requires a considerable degree of sophistication, for the important resources are not those shown on the balance sheet. Above all, it demands an understanding of what the product package is, including all the service, physical, and image elements within and outside of the organization. IBM managed the transition from punched-card tabulators to mainframe computers because even its name embodied the concept that its market was (International) Business Machines. It had the necessary skills along with the culture—unlike Exxon, which tried to jump from oil to information technology and failed.

www.ibm.com

www.exxon.com

2. **Develop a suitable filter for marketing data.** This is one of the most difficult stages because it requires the marketer to focus attention, when looking at the outside world, on just those aspects that are relevant to the organization's future. It poses problems of **marketing myopia**, wherein the marketer simply does not see changes emerging because they are outside his or her frame of reference. On the other hand, a tight focus is necessary if the marketer is to handle masses of data and to avoid data overload. More importantly, a tight focus means that input can be transformed so that it is useful to the organization.

3. **Use this filter to find out about the customer.** This is the conventional starting point for marketing theory. The difference here is that the marketer conducts this examination in the context of the lessons about the organization's resources that were learned in the first two steps; thus the search for information is an informed one.

4. **Review the processes to date.** This step, which requires an extraordinary degree of professional detachment, is the hallmark of great marketers. The marketer must repeat the earlier steps, this time taking into account the lessons learned. This may mean that the filter developed in step 2 has to be modified in light of what has since been discovered in step 3. This iteration needs to be continually conducted. It required Ray Kroc to understand that the marketing formula developed by a small hamburger restaurant in the backwoods could be turned into a worldwide McDonald's chain, and Michael Dell to see that the direct marketing and just-in-time production concepts could be applied successfully to the personal computer industry.

www.mcdonalds.com
www.dell.com

5. **Manipulate resources to achieve the resulting marketing objectives.** Traditional marketing theory frequently assumes that only the resources specifically made available to the marketing department should be taken into account. In reality, all the resources from both within and outside of the organization must be brought into play. Capturing resources that are traditionally the prerogative of other departments or outside firms can be very difficult and often hazardous to one's career, but it can pay massive dividends when a systems approach is implemented.

THE COMPLEXITY OF MARKETING

Some marketers have an inclination to assume very simple theoretical relationships between firms and customers. Although doing so may make comprehension easier, it does not prepare you for real-life marketing. By its very nature, marketing has to deal with complex dimensions, particularly when addressing the following five main features:

MULTIPLE DECISION MAKERS

In many buying situations there is more than one person involved in the buying decision. This is especially true of those customers in industrial marketing, but it can just as easily apply to those in consumer goods marketing. Even the purchase of a food staple may need the tacit agreement of the whole family; conflicts are likely to arise if a parent buys cereal, no matter how inexpensive or nutritious, that the children do not like.

MULTIPLE FACTORS

The purchase decision is often dependent on many other decisions. Thus, the decision of whether to buy cereal may depend on whether any milk is available. It may depend upon what budget is available, or on what higher priority items have already laid claim to that budget.

INTERACTION

The buyer does not make the purchase decision in isolation from the supplier. Perceptive marketers employ partnership techniques, in which both suppliers and purchasers are actively involved in the decision-making processes. For example, Japanese multinationals work so closely with their suppliers that it is often difficult to know where the boundary between firms is.

TIME FRAME

It is overly simplistic to assume that a purchase decision stands by itself, without any influence from previous experience. Even the purchaser of the box of cereal has a rich history of exposure to advertising, as well as personal experience with product usage. Yet, watch television almost any night and you will see some brand being promoted on a totally different platform from that of a few months ago—the marketers having made the (usually incorrect) assumption that there is no historical effect. Cadillac found, much to its dismay, the existence of such a historical effect when it tried to promote its Catera brand to young buyers and found that most purchasers were still traditional middle-aged customers.

www.cadillac.com

GLOBAL FACTORS

Global influences on the consumer and the marketers cannot be ignored. For example, a drought in Brazil will have an impact on coffee production and consumption around the world. Exchange rate changes and government tariffs affect the cost and availability of products. Introduction of the euro in the European Union has affected the degree of price transparency across borders and has reduced the pricing flexibility of wholesalers and retailers. Innovations and new market entrants from abroad, or production shifts of domestic firms, can change the type of competition, product composition, and product selection. Demand surges abroad might result in price increases and product scarcity. To ignore the influence of global factors may place the very survival of the firm at risk.

THE MARKETING MIX

Once customer needs or wants are determined, the marketer has to satisfy them. The first aspect of this implementation is the product itself, which is the ultimate basis for the customer to determine whether his or her needs are being met. The marketer must, therefore, match the product as closely as possible to those needs. This may be accomplished by offering a tailor-made, existing product, by radically changing the product, by modifying its features or its packaging, or even by describing the product in a different way. The second aspect is the delivery system: The producer must get the product within reach of the customer in a timely manner. Third, the customer must be made aware of the availability and benefits of the product. The marketer needs to communicate with the customer and persuade the customer to purchase the product, perhaps by using an advertisement. Fourth, the product must be priced right so that the customer can afford it and is willing to choose it from among competing offers.

These separate aspects may be categorized in a number of ways. One customary framework is McCarthy's four Ps: Product, Price, Place, and Promotion.[18] "Product" refers to the product-related elements and includes both goods and services. Perhaps influenced by economics, "price" is split off as an element worthy of separate consideration, although this may overemphasize its importance. The other two Ps are parts of the delivery system: "Place" refers to delivering the product, and "promotion" to delivering the message. Figure 1.1 shows the four components of the marketing mix and their many dimensions.

> McCarthy's
> four Ps:
> Product, Price, Place, and Promotion

---

18. E. J. McCarthy, *Basic Marketing: A Managerial Approach,* 8th ed. (Burr Ridge, Ill.: Irwin, 1984), 46.

Figure 1.1

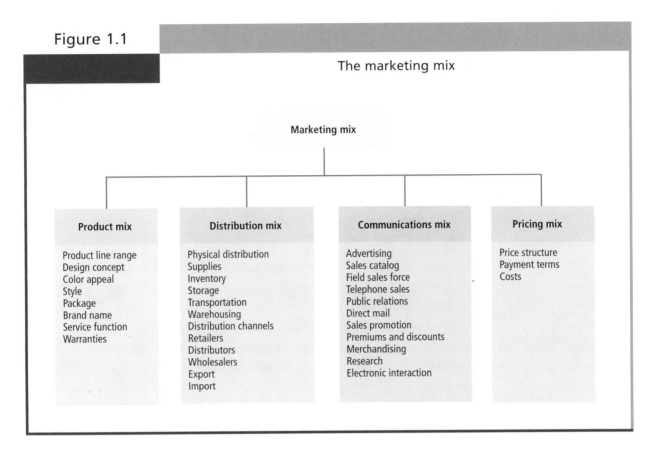

The marketing mix

Product mix	Distribution mix	Communications mix	Pricing mix
Product line range	Physical distribution	Advertising	Price structure
Design concept	Supplies	Sales catalog	Payment terms
Color appeal	Inventory	Field sales force	Costs
Style	Storage	Telephone sales	
Package	Transportation	Public relations	
Brand name	Warehousing	Direct mail	
Service function	Distribution channels	Sales promotion	
Warranties	Retailers	Premiums and discounts	
	Distributors	Merchandising	
	Wholesalers	Research	
	Export	Electronic interaction	
	Import		

The four Ps offer just one, albeit frequently used, approach to marketing. Some pundits propose just two factors: the "Offering" (product and price) and the "Methods and Tools" (including distribution and promotion). Still others argue for the need to subdivide these categories further, differentiating, for example, between sales and advertising as forms of promotion. Perhaps the most significant criticism of the four Ps approach is that it emphasizes the inside-out view (looking from the company outward) instead of the outside-in approach.[19] Nevertheless, the four Ps offer a memorable, useful guide to the major categories of marketing activity, as well as a framework within which they can be used.

SELLING VERSUS MARKETING

Selling has long suffered from a tarnished image. Dubious selling practices occasionally result in a sale if the customer is particularly gullible. However, good marketing, which encompasses a far wider range of skills, will lead the customer to buy again from the same company. Seldom can an organization survive in the long run based on single purchases made by first-time customers. Repeat business and the lifetime purchases of customers generate the most profit. Much of the selling effort of the well-organized marketing function is directed toward keeping the number of delighted customers high and the number of dissatisfied customers to a minimum. In such organizations, feedback from the market will alert the

> **Repeat business and the lifetime purchases of customers generate the most profit.**

19. G. Morgan, *Riding the Waves of Change* (San Francisco: Jossey-Bass, 1988), 37.

company to the main reasons that customers do not buy again. Such feedback will lead, if necessary, to an improvement or modification of the product. Effective selling is not about half-truths or overrated claims—these practices are almost always counterproductive in the longer term.

Many of the criticisms of selling are valid, because there are many poor salespeople and almost as many poor sales managers. It is also true that good sales managers and sales personnel have long recognized and supported the basic tenets of sound marketing. On the other hand, you should be aware that the term *marketing* is often adopted by those who are in reality engaged exclusively in pure selling activities. For example, for a number of years the term *marketing executive* has applied to salespeople in general. As early as 1964, Peter Drucker observed, "Not everything that goes by that name deserves it. But a gravedigger remains a gravedigger even when called a 'mortician'—only the cost of the burial goes up. Many a sales manager has been renamed 'marketing vice president'—and all that happened was that costs and salaries went up."[20]

Seven common elements distinguish marketing-oriented companies:

1. The use of market share, rather than volume, as the primary measure of marketing success.

2. The understanding and use of market segmentation principles.

3. The process for monitoring customer needs, usage, and trends, as well as competitive activity—that is, market research.

4. A set of specific marketing goals and targets.

5. A structure or process for coordinating all nonmarketing functions toward the achievement of marketing goals.

6. A corporate style and culture in which marketing integrates process participants both within and outside of the firm.

7. A market-based business concept that provides unique value to the customer.[21]

The key difference is that selling is an inward-looking function in which you persuade the customer to take what you have. In selling, product development is detached from the marketplace: Only when the product is ready does the search for customers start. Marketing, on the other hand, is an outward-looking function in which you try to match the real requirements of the customer. The company looks for market opportunities and creates product solutions in response. These two approaches are contrasted in Figure 1.2. In practice, a mix of both approaches is often used. It is a very poor salesperson who does not instinctively, rather than as a matter of theory, use sound marketing principles when questioning a customer to find out what he or she wants. Equally, it is a fortunate marketer who can produce a new product to match exactly the discovered gap in the market; most new products emerge from nonmarketing processes and are only then opportunistically matched to markets. The most successful approaches seem to be the ones in which the sales function collaborates closely with marketing in order to reach and delight customers. Manager's Corner 1.3 provides examples of how the tensions between sales and marketing can be overcome.

> Marketing . . . is an outward-looking function in which you try to match the real requirements of the customer.

---

20. Drucker, *Managing for Results*, 38.
21. M. Bower and R. A. Garda, "The Role of Marketing Management," in *Handbook of Modern Marketing*, 2d ed., ed. V. P. Buell (New York: McGraw-Hill, 1986), 1–6.

Figure 1.2

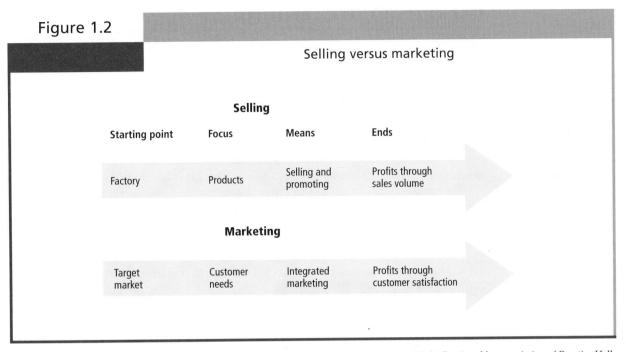

Selling versus marketing

Selling

Starting point	Focus	Means	Ends
Factory	Products	Selling and promoting	Profits through sales volume

Marketing

Target market	Customer needs	Integrated marketing	Profits through customer satisfaction

Source: Philip Kotler, *Marketing Management,* 9th ed. (Upper Saddle River, N.J.: Prentice Hall, 1997), 20. Reprinted by permission of Prentice Hall, Inc., Upper Saddle River, N.J.

Manager's Corner 1.3

Overcoming tension between sales and marketing

When there is too much tension or too little communication between sales and marketing divisions, business is bound to suffer. Formal communications are useful because they are verifiable and offer a record of events. In situations where two departments have different styles, a formal procedure for communication can help reduce conflict. Yet, achieving good communication is often quite elusive. The sales team often sees marketing as disconnected from the real world. The marketing people in turn think that salespeople do not really understand the intricacies of dealing with consumers. The tension between sales and marketing is bred by physical and philosophical separation and by differing objectives. Sales staff concentrates on quarterly revenue; marketing aims for more long-term results. In an overcrowded marketplace where customers are deluged with different signals, you can't hope to differentiate yourself without a consistent, unified message.

Xerox (www.docuworld.com) launched a program, called DocuWorld, to capture new customers for digital printing equipment. This complex marketing initiative could only take place with the joint efforts of the sales and marketing teams. DocuWorld demands the involvement of local salespeople, who are responsible for audience acquisition. Marketing produces databases and distributes leads. As a result of the cooperation, a measurable increase in revenues was seen following the launch of the program.

Coca-Cola's national accounts program has long been noted as a leader in integrating sales, marketing, and any other group that might touch the customer. Coke (www.coke .com) devotes to each national account a team that includes employees from sales, marketing, finance, operations, and support. They converge on a market, research the people, culture, and sociology, and then debrief each other. Through this process they understand their objectives better and are able to outdistance the competition.

Sources: Regina Fazio Maruca, "Getting Marketing's Voice Heard," *Harvard Business Review* (January/February 1998): 10–11; Sarah Lorge, "Marketers Are from Mars, Salespeople Are from Venus," *Sales and Marketing Management* (April 1999): 26–33.

MARKETING AND CORPORATE STRATEGY

In establishing the context for marketing, we must first understand how it fits into the organization's overall corporate strategy. The study of corporate strategy is often treated as a separate academic discipline, although it is closely related to the processes of marketing planning. Marketing's input into the corporate strategy processes comprises both external and internal elements. A number of external influences affect an organization, such as the prevailing social and economic climate and, more directly, the accompanying legislation. A closer look at the meaning of *market orientation* will help us to understand the connection between marketing and strategy. Market orientation is the organizationwide generation of market intelligence pertaining to current and future customer needs, dissemination of the intelligence across departments, and organizationwide responsiveness to it.[22] Put even more succinctly, market orientation is composed of customer orientation, competitor orientation, and interfunctional coordination.[23]

Just as General Charles de Gaulle remarked that war is too important to be left to the generals, a market orientation is clearly too important to be left to the marketers. Rather, the entire organization needs to be informed about customers and competitors and has to be responsive to that information. What is needed is companywide coordinated response and action. Now we can see why marketing planning processes often seem indistinguishable from those of corporate strategy itself. In both cases, the needs of the customer have to be understood, the internal constraints and capabilities have to be assessed, and the external environment has to be analyzed.

> the entire organization needs to be **informed about customers and competitors** and has to be responsive to that information

THE DIFFERENCE BETWEEN PRODUCTS AND BENEFITS

The contrast between a market orientation and a product orientation has been a source of controversy since the 1950s. In order to provide some context for later chapters, you must fully understand the product perspective, because it is the demand for the product that the marketer is trying to optimize. Behind the statement "Customers don't buy products; they seek to acquire benefits" lies a basic principle of successful marketing: When people purchase products, they are motivated first not by the physical attributes of the product but by the benefits that those attributes offer. An indication of what tangible and intangible qualities make up a product can be found by looking closely at the difference between what customers appear to buy and what they actually want (see Exhibit 1.2). When customers buy a 2-mm drill, what they really want is a 2-mm hole. The drill vendor

> "Customers don't buy products; **they seek** to acquire benefits"

22. Ajay K. Kohli and Bernard J. Jaworski, "Market Orientation: The Construct, Research Propositions, and Managerial Implications," *Journal of Marketing* 54 (April 1990): 1–18.

23. John C. Narver and Stanley F. Slater, "The Effect of a Market Orientation on Business Profitability," *Journal of Marketing* 54 (October 1990): 20–35.

Exhibit 1.2

This advertisement for Program flea control medication for dogs is a perfect example of the product versus benefit orientation. Novartis, the maker of Program, is marketing the benefit of a flea-free pet and of having a flea-free pet that can still be a part of the family. The tag line, "Prevent sticky flea treatments from keeping you apart," conveys the double benefit of Program medication. Novartis has found a way to deliver the benefits its customers—perhaps both animal and human—are seeking.

is in grave danger of losing business if a better means of making holes is invented. Ignoring such alternatives has led to the demise of many businesses. For example, the personal computer with word-processing software has largely replaced the typewriter, and compact discs have replaced phonograph records, in both cases because they offer better ways of delivering the benefits the customer is seeking. Not recognizing this difference between products and benefits has been described as marketing myopia.[24] Marketing in Action 1.2 discusses the distinction between products and benefits in the ethical context of marketing Tantra.

The solution to this problem of perception is for the supplier to look at the product through the eyes of the customer—and even then there are pitfalls. Many sales trainers, for example, emphasize selling the benefits and not the product's physical features. Unfortunately, too many sales representatives then feel free to decide for themselves what the benefits are, based on what they see rather than the thoughts and attitudes of the customer.

MARKETING AND SERVICE CULTURES

Some service-sector organizations have been at the forefront of marketing. In general, however, much of this sector's management has been antipathetic toward marketing for a number of reasons, all of which are mainly self-imposed limitations and do not relate to any genuine problems inherent in marketing itself. Some of these so-called reasons are as follows:

---

24. Theodore Levitt, "Marketing Myopia," *Harvard Business Review* 38 (July 1960): 45–56.

Lack of tangibility. The intangible nature of services makes them less immediately responsive to marketing techniques. For example, it is more difficult for customers to try out a service than a manufactured good. The difference, however, only means that marketing approaches have to be more personal, more direct, and more customer interactive.

Lack of mass marketing. Many service suppliers, such as accountants, have only small offices that are very individualized in their contact with customers. As the emergence of large chains such as H & R Block have shown, however, there is ample opportunity to introduce national communication and a central marketing structure for such services.

Lack of direct competition. Some organizations, such as banks, have traditionally not seen themselves as having customers. At times they have behaved almost as if they themselves were the customers. Such organizations used to be in the fortunate position where the supply of their offering was swamped by considerably more demand than could be met, and their role was to ration this scarce supply. Now, however, the situation has changed in many countries, and service providers need to face the test of competition every day.

Professional status. Other groups of service providers have long been organized into professions, such as lawyers, physicians, or dentists. Their professional organizations, due to their monopoly power, often effectively removed direct competition—and with it marketing. Many professions used to have rules that specifically barred their members from almost every form of marketing activity. As these prohibitions have been weakened or removed, however, marketing thinking has been quick to emerge.

Marketing in Action 1.2

The art and science of marketing as applied to Tantra

Is Tantra (www.tantramagazine.com) really a 4,000-year-old religious doctrine or is it an entrepreneur's dream—a dream of selling sex combined with New Age psychology? *Tantra— The Magazine Online* addressed the question, "What is Tantra?" Tantra is described as being both an art and a science. The scientific component is based on increasing awareness to expand consciousness. As an art, Tantra is described as the beauty, flow, and grace of the physical form. The online description of Tantra explains that most Westerners believe it to be a sacred style of sexuality that utilizes improved communication, breath, and energy. Some colleges and universities include Tantra theory in their religious studies programs.

Where do the art and science of marketing mingle with the art and science of Tantra? Is Tantra implementing a marketing program?

Tantra uses niche marketing by focusing upon the adult "feel-good" industry. The product is religion (a service), with tangible brand extensions (e.g., E-sensuals catalog, online magazine, weekend seminars, balms, and books). The company's pricing resembles a penetration pricing strategy. Distribution is direct to the consumer, with e-commerce playing a major role in the firm's integrated marketing communications program. Strategically, increasing market share appears to be a major organizational objective.

Are entrepreneurs using religion as a disguise for selling sex? Is there anything wrong with the use of marketing to match the buyers of sexuality with the sellers of sexuality? Have the marketers behind Tantra's marketing program crossed the line ethically, or are they just practicing great marketing?

Sources: www.tantramagazine.com; D. Kirk Davidson, "The Marketing of Tantra: Over the Line?" *Marketing News*, February 15, 1999, 7.

MARKETING AND NONPROFIT ORGANIZATIONS

Nonprofit organizations have the greatest difficulty in coming to terms with marketing, probably because much of marketing theory is described in terms of improving profit performance. Using profit as the main gauge of marketing effectiveness allows for a practical and measurable approach in commercial organizations but can pose major problems for organizations that cannot assess their performance in such terms. One resulting problem, therefore, is that some nonprofit organizations simply do not recognize the requirement to meet their customers' needs.

What can replace profit in the nonprofit context? The measure most frequently suggested appears to be "match." Nonprofit organizations should seek the best match between the use of their resources and the needs of their customers or clients. In this context, marketing is a means of most productively matching the resources available to provide what the users need and want—exactly as in any commercial operation. One apparent complication in the case of nonprofit organizations is that there are several types of customers: The clients for the service, those who decide who the clients will be, and the donors of the funds to provide that service. Each of these groups has a different set of needs and has to be marketed to separately. As a result, there may be multiple objectives, and activities may be subject to public scrutiny. In this way the nonprofit is no different from the for-profit organization, which has to deal with shareholders, management, employees, suppliers, and customers, all of whom may have different goals and requirements.

SUMMARY

Marketing is a particularly practical business discipline. There may be many definitions of marketing, but all of them consider the customer to be the focus of decision making, and all of them describe the dialogue between the producer and the customer—increasingly as it takes place in a global context. Marketing efforts vary, depending on the different circumstances within which they are practiced. However, it is important to see marketing's role in an overarching context, reaching beyond the organization to encompass the entire client and supplier system in an outward-looking way that matches corporate capabilities with the requirements of customers and permits them to acquire desired benefits most efficiently.

The various elements of marketing that are employed in marketing campaigns are known as the marketing mix and are often described in terms of the four Ps: product, price, place, and promotion. This mix can be applied not just to the goods sector but also to services and the nonprofit arena. The implementation of the marketing mix, however, is complex due to multiple decision makers, the interaction of multiple decision factors on the part of buyers, and global demand and supply linkages.

In light of the need to exercise growing responsiveness to changing societal demands and expectations in areas such as the environment and ethics and the expanding ability of marketers to use technology in order to understand customers and respond to them, a new marketing paradigm is emerging where marketers are poised to become the strategic leaders of the corporate supply system.

QUESTIONS FOR REVIEW

1. How and why has the definition of marketing by the American Marketing Association been expanded here? Comment on the complexity of marketing and some of the factors that are important.

2. The starting point for a marketer is the organization itself; how is that paradoxical? In order to get ready for a marketing orientation, the organization needs to address what dimensions? Are marketing and corporate strategy striving for the same goals? How must these work together to obtain a clear objective?

3. What were the inherent limitations of traditional marketing thought? How were they addressed in the evolution of the modern marketing concept? What crucial new perspectives did marketers have as compared to economists? How has technology influenced this change in thought?

4. What are the elements of the marketing mix? Into what four categories are they traditionally grouped? Can these categories be further subdivided? What are their limitations?

5. Explain marketing orientation. What are the seven common elements that exist in marketing-oriented companies? What is the key difference between selling and marketing approaches?

6. "Customers don't buy products; they seek to acquire benefits." What is the reasoning behind this statement and what are its pitfalls? What are tangible and intangible qualities of products? Name some.

7. Does the applicability of marketing differ for service companies? What are the four reasons why some service sector managers have shunned marketing? Evaluate which of these are viable reasons.

8. Does marketing exist solely to increase profit? If this is the case, then marketing in nonprofit organizations can be said to be useless. Discuss.

QUESTIONS FOR DISCUSSION

1. In 1997, Mercedes-Benz unveiled its sporty CLK coupe to the world in Verona, Italy, and since then, it has become a much-sought-after luxury sports car. Only 9,000 of the 43,000 cars Mercedes intended to produce that year were slated for U.S. markets, so long waiting lists and Internet brokering became common features of a CLK purchase. Stories abound still of people offering to pay higher than list prices for the privilege of owning Mercedes' newest and hottest coupe. When demand so outstrips supply, is there a need to consider the use of marketing? Why or why not?

2. In recent years, the book publishing industry has experienced numerous mergers and acquisitions. In addition, technological advances such as the Internet have caused major changes in the distribution of intellectual content. Identify some of the traditional marketplace activities of the book publishing industry and evaluate their chance for future success. How will these activities change in the context of the emerging market space? Is it possible to attribute the increase in merger activity to the developing market space of book publishing? Why or why not?

3. The Red Cross provides numerous services around the world, including disaster relief, nursing, youth involvement, and biomedical services. One important activity is the collection of donated blood, with the Red Cross receiving over six million volunteer blood donations a year. In the United States alone, someone needs a blood donation approximately every two seconds. The high demand for blood, coupled with concerns about the safety of giving and of receiving blood and the hectic lives of potential donors, can make soliciting donations a challenge. How can you apply the marketing concept to this activity?

4. Marketing ethics has sometimes been called an oxymoron. An example of this can be found in recent corporate sponsorship of Girl Scout badges, such as the Fashion Adventurer program offered by the retailer Limited Too. Combining fashion and sewing education with in-

store visits and coupons redeemable after completion of the program, such initiatives are considered by some to be little more than artful sales pitches cloaked in a sash full of contemporary patches. What is your assessment of corporate sponsorship of Girl Scout badges? Can you, by using the marketing concept, develop a rationale for ethics to be fully incorporated into marketing thinking?

5. How does international marketing differ from domestic marketing? Consider again the examples of Mercedes-Benz from question 1 and the Red Cross from question 3. Mercedes' rollout of its new CLK in Verona and the Red Cross' international relief efforts can both be related to international marketing activities. What are the primary marketing dimensions that need special attention in the international marketing context? How do these dimensions apply to the situations of Mercedes-Benz and of the Red Cross and how do they differ from each other?

FURTHER READINGS

Czinkota, Michael R., and Ilkka A. Ronkainen. *International Marketing.* 6th ed. Fort Worth, Tex.: Dryden Press, 2000.

Donaldson, Thomas, and Patricia Werhane, eds. *Ethical Issues in Business: A Philosophical Approach.* 6th ed. Upper Saddle River, N.J.: Prentice Hall, 1999.

Friedman, Thomas L. *The Lexus and the Olive Tree: Understanding Globalization.* New York: Farrar, Straus and Giroux, 1999.

Kurtz, David L., and Kenneth E. Clow. *Services Marketing.* New York: John Wiley & Sons, 1998.

Levitt, Theodore. *The Marketing Imagination.* New York: Free Press, 1986.

Lovelock, Christopher H. *Principles of Services Marketing and Management.* Upper Saddle River, N.J.: Prentice Hall, 1999.

Sargeant, Adrian. *Marketing Management for Non-Profit Organizations.* Oxford: Oxford University Press, 1999.

Schlegelmilch, Bodo. *Marketing Ethics: An International Perspective.* London: International Thomson Business Press, 1998.

chapter **2**

Marketing Planning

In practice, corporate strategy and marketing are closely related, and much of corporate strategy is derived from marketing. The development of the organization's mission and objectives largely determines its marketing strategy. Therefore, this chapter first examines corporate strategy, then moves to strategic marketing, and finally discusses marketing planning, which is, in theory, the central function of marketing (see Manager's Corner 2.1).

Manager's Corner 2.1

What is in the marketing plan?

Firms may think that they have a marketing plan when, in fact, they do not. They have a business plan, instead. A marketing plan is defined as "a broad set of guidelines as to how the firm is going to accomplish its strategic goals, a living document that guides the company throughout the year, a blueprint for future activity. It is a coordinated, integrated outline of everything that will be done by a firm in each of the marketing functions such as research, planning, advertising, public relations, sales promotion, direct marketing, sales management, product development, pricing and delivery channel management—to support the firm's strategic plan and business plan." In other words, a marketing plan states what will be done, who will do it, when they will do it, why it will be done, how it will be done, and how much it will cost in terms of budget, staff, technology, and facilities. It may even state where it will be done. The plan is not written in a vacuum! That is why a marketing plan should reflect and support the objectives and goals of the company's strategic and business plans.

Key elements that should be included in a marketing plan follow.

Situational analysis. It examines the internal environment, the external environment, the current marketing mix, and the continuing relevancy of current market targets. It should also include a geographic study of the competition, an analysis of what is going on in the market, as well as a study of the advertising revenues. For example, this element of the plan should note whether the financial institution is in a merger mode or consolidation mode.

Marketing objectives. These objectives are based on the conclusions drawn from the situational analysis. They can be broad-based and timeless statements. They may never be accomplished, yet they are indications of the general direction in which a firm wishes to progress. Marketing objectives are always based on the company's strengths, weaknesses, opportunities, or threats; they are always written to reflect a direction that will address one or more of the firm's strategic or business objectives. Each marketing objective must have subordinate goals that can be accomplished and demonstrate progress toward the objective. Goals are specific and time sensitive in nature.

Strategy and tactics. A third major element of a marketing plan involves both strategy and tactics. Although these words are often used interchangeably, they do not mean the same thing. Each goal must have one or more strategies to accomplish the goal. Each tactic must include four elements—a specific action (what is to be done), an accountability (who is to do it), a deadline (when it should be completed), and a budget (how much this action step will cost to complete).

Monitoring and evaluation.

1. *Tracking:* What will be tracked and why? By whom will it be tracked, and how often? How will it be tracked?

2. *Reporting:* What will be reported, and why? By whom (and to whom) will it be reported and how often? How will it be reported?

3. *Evaluation:* What will be evaluated, and why? By whom will it be evaluated, and how often? How will it be evaluated?

4. *Corrective Action:* What corrective action may be needed if a goal is not met, and why? Who will take that corrective action? Are new procedures needed to evaluate the success of that corrective action?

Source: Vicki Gerson, "Arming Yourself with a Marketing Plan," *Bank Marketing,* September 1998.

MARKETING PLAN

The need for planning is almost universally accepted by managers, even though it is not so widely put into practice. Some of the benefits of planning include the following:

- **Consistency.** The individual marketing action plans will be consistent with the overall corporate plan and with the other departmental or functional plans. They should also be consistent with those of previous years, minimizing the risk of management "firefighting"—that is, incoherent, case-by-case action plans.

- **Responsibility.** Those who have responsibility for implementing the individual parts of the marketing plan will know what their responsibilities are and can have their performance monitored against these plans.

- **Communication.** Those implementing the plans will also know what the overall objectives are, the assumptions that lie behind them, and the context for each of the detailed activities.

- **Commitment.** Assuming that the plans are agreed upon by those involved in their implementation, as well as by those who will provide the resources, the plans should stimulate a group commitment to their implementation.

Plans must be specific to the organization and to its current situation. There is not one system of planning but many systems, not one style but many styles, and a planning process must be tailor-made for a particular firm in a specific set of circumstances.[1]

PLANNING PROCESS

In most organizations strategic planning is an annual process, typically covering just the year ahead. Occasionally, a few organizations may look at a practical plan that stretches three or more years ahead.

To be most effective, the plan must be formalized, usually in written form, as an identifiable *marketing plan.* This process typically follows a number of distinct steps, as shown in Figure 2.1. The process moves from the general to the specific, from the overall objectives of the organization down to the individual action plan for a part of one marketing program. Although at first glance this looks complex, it is, in fact, a very functional flowchart of the whole planning process and nicely illustrates the relationships between the various components. It is also an iterative process, so that the draft output of each stage is checked to see what impact it has on the earlier stages—and is amended accordingly.

1. E. R. Alexander, "Planning and Implementation: Coordinative Planning in Practice," *International Planning Studies* 3 (October 1998): 303–320.

Figure 2.1

Marketing planning in a corporate framework

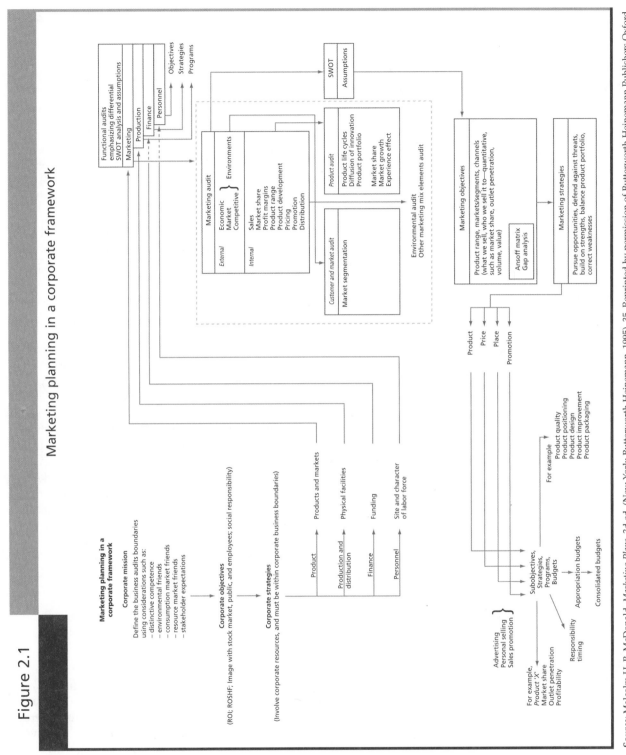

Source: Malcolm H. B. McDonald, *Marketing Plans*, 3d ed. (New York: Butterworth Heinemann, 1995), 35. Reprinted by permission of Butterworth Heinemann Publishers Oxford, a division of Reed Educational & Professional Publishing Ltd.

There are three main approaches, in terms of involvement of the organization as a whole. They are:

Top-down planning. Here top management sets both the goals and the plans for lower-level management. While decision making may be quick at the top level, implementation of the plans may not be as quick because it takes time for various units (divisions, groups, and departments) to learn about the plans and to reorganize their tasks accordingly to accomplish the new goals.[2]

Bottom-up planning. In this approach, the various units of the organization create their own goals and plans, which are then approved (or not) by higher management. This can lead to more creative approaches, but it can also pose problems for coordination. More pragmatically, strategy all too frequently emerges from a *consolidation of tactics.*[3]

Goals-down-plans-up planning. This is the most common approach, at least among the organizations that invest in such sophisticated planning processes. Top management sets the goals, but the various units create their own plans to meet these goals. These plans are then typically approved as part of the annual planning and budgetary process.[4]

CORPORATE PLAN

The starting point for the marketing plan, and the context within which it is set, is the **corporate plan**. In most marketing-oriented organizations the contents of the corporate plan will closely match those of the marketing plan itself, but it will also include the plans for the disposition of the other internal resources of the organization. Thus, the corporate plan is likely to contain three main components: (1) where the organization is now, (2) where the organization intends to go in the future, and (3) how the organization will organize its resources to get there.

The first category is intimately involved with the customers. In marketing terms, although there are many other factors to take into account, the most important definition of where the company *is* revolves around where it is in the market (and hence where it is with its consumers). The same is largely true of the second stage as well; because, no matter how much its managers may wish otherwise, where the company can realistically expect to go is totally in the hands of its customers. It is only at the third stage that the four Ps of the marketing mix come into play as vehicles for moving the company to reach its objectives (see Chapter 1 for a definition of the four Ps).

CORPORATE OBJECTIVES

The overall objectives of commercial organizations are conventionally supposed to be financial, such as maximizing revenue, maximizing profit, maximizing return on investment, or minimizing cost. However, other aims are also possible. Many companies choose long-term growth (which may be quite different from revenue maximization in the short term). Almost all have an implicit, and very powerful, aim of survival, which John K. Galbraith spelled out so forcefully in his book *The Affluent Society.*[5]

2. William Ouchi, *Theory Z: How American Business Can Meet the Japanese Challenge* (Boston: Addison Wesley, 1981).

3. Myung-Su Chae and John S. Hill, "The Hazards of Strategic Planning for Global Markets," *Long Range Planning* 29 (December 1996): 880–891.

4. H. Igor Ansoff and Edward J. McDonnell, *Implanting Strategic Management,* 2d ed. (Upper Saddle River, N.J.: Prentice Hall, 1990).

5. John K. Galbraith, *The Affluent Society* (London: Hamish Hamilton, 1958).

One of the best-known alternatives to profit maximization, that of "satisficing," comes from Herbert Simon,[6] who pointed out that managers can neither know nor contend with all the factors influencing a decision. Because you cannot know the optimum solution with perfect precision, you should choose a solution that "satisfices," or reaches your corporate objectives satisfactorily. Of course, the terms *best, better, satisfactory,* and *good enough* are to be understood in terms of marketing managers' customer-based objectives, such as customer satisfaction and perceived product quality, as well as marketing objectives, such as market share and sales growth rate. If we accept the traditional assumption that the objectives of the corporate plan are financially based, then it follows that these objectives are meant to be measured in numerical and, in particular, financial terms.

In the most general terms, though, the objectives behind a strategy address two questions: *Where* do we want to be? and *When* do we expect to be there? For example, First National Supermarkets' annual report states its objective in terms of direction and scope: "Solidify our market leadership position in the greater Cleveland area, expand elsewhere in Ohio, and become a dominant retail supermarket chain in southern New England and eastern New York." In line with

> the objectives behind a strategy address two questions: *Where* do we want to be? and *When* do we expect to be there?

our earlier discussion of the overall aims of the marketing planning process, these objectives should provide for a sense of purpose, help achieve consistency, and provide a basis for control.

Furthermore, to fulfill these functions, objectives should have a number of characteristics. They should be measurable, be acceptable and agreeable, be consistent, and be realistic. It is unlikely that First National Supermarkets executives and shareholders can visualize the company's specific strategy plans to accomplish those objectives as stated above. However, its objectives would be considered realistic if it were stated that "First National Supermarkets strives to capture 10 percent of the grocery market and achieve a 5 percent return on sales after tax within four years of implementation of a new strategy."

OBJECTIVES FOR NONPROFIT ORGANIZATIONS

In the case of nonprofit organizations, the objectives may be even less clear. Five main reasons can be suggested for the differences from commercial organizations.[7]

1. **Ambiguous goals.** More actors and groups of actors are involved.
2. **Lack of agreement in means-end relationships.** Even where there is consensus on the goal there may be disagreement on how to get there.
3. **Environmental turbulence.** Nonprofit organizations seem to be exposed more to turbulence than commercial ones.
4. **Unmeasurable outputs.** By definition, nonprofit organizations do not have the classically convenient simplicity of bottom-line profit.
5. **Unknown effects of management intervention.** The lack of precision caused by factors 1 through 4 is problem enough, but the "culture" seems to add further barriers to managing these organizations.

---

6. Herbert A. Simon, "Relational Decision Making in Business Organizations," *American Economic Review* 69 (September 1979).
7. Keith J. Blois, "Managing for Non-Profit Organizations," in *The Marketing Book,* 3d ed., ed. M. J. Baker (Boston: Butterworth Heinemann, 1994).

www.redcross.org

For example, the mission of the American Red Cross in greater New York is to improve the quality of human life; to enhance self-reliance and concern for others; and to help people avoid, prepare for, and cope with emergencies. It does this through services that are governed and directed by volunteers and are consistent with its congressional charter and the principles of the International Red Cross.[8] Although these objectives are not concise, they nonetheless provide a sense of purpose and a basis for control.

Even so, Kotler and Andreasen[9] suggest some possible objectives for such organizations:

Surplus maximization—equivalent to profit maximization

Revenue maximization—just as for profit-making organizations

Usage maximization—maximizing the numbers of users and their usage

Usage targeting—matching the capacity available

Full cost recovery—breaking even

Partial cost recovery—minimizing the subsidy

Budget maximization—maximizing what is offered

Producer satisfaction maximization—satisfying the wants of staff

It is important that you recognize the complexity that lies behind corporate objectives and are not seduced by those who would argue that simplicity is the order of the day. Although the problems may have to be artificially simplified to make them easier to handle, this should not blind you to their true nature. It should also alert you to the fact that, with so many variables that periodically may be in a state of flux, each new situation will be unique. Despite the fact that rules of thumb will help, the solutions must be built anew for each problem.

> It is important that you **recognize the complexity** that lies behind corporate objectives

CORPORATE MISSION

Behind the corporate objectives, which offer the main context for the marketing plan, lies the **corporate mission**, which in turn provides the context for these corporate objectives. This corporate mission can be considered a definition of what the organization is and of what it does: "Our business is . . ."

www.ibm.com

This definition should not be too narrow or it will constrict the development of the organization. A too rigorous concentration on a narrow view, such as "We are in the business of making meat-scales," IBM's focus during the early 1900s, might limit subsequent development into other areas. On the other hand, it should not be too wide or it will become meaningless: "We want to make a profit" is not too helpful a tool in developing specific plans.

www.intel.com

The definition should cover three dimensions: *customer groups* to be served, *customer needs* to be served, and *technologies* to be utilized.[10] Thus, the definition of Intel's corporate mission in the 1980s and 1990s has been to provide computer users around the world (customer group) with the state-of-the-art, fastest, and most energy-efficient computing experience (customer need) by continual improvement and development of microprocessor technology (technology). However, the corpo-

---

8. www.arc-gny.org/index.html, accessed May 1, 1999.

9. Philip Kotler and Alan R. Andreasen, *Strategic Marketing for Nonprofit Organizations,* 5th ed. (Upper Saddle River, N.J.: Prentice Hall, 1996).

10. Derek F. Abell, *Managing with Dual Strategies: Mastering the Present Preempting the Future* (New York: Free Press, 1993).

rate mission may need to be changed accordingly when market environments change. How Miller Brewing Company has met these kinds of changes is the topic of Marketing in Action 2.1.

For example, Intel is currently going through such a change caused by the revolutionary expansion of the Internet use that it has helped create. People will only buy the newest processor if it makes their software run faster. But the software that matters most these days is the Internet, and hot new Intel microprocessors do not necessarily improve that experience much. A recent study shows that for beginning and intermediate PC users, processor speed came in fifth on a list of purchasing criteria. A few years ago, consumers wished Microsoft PowerPoint would create graphics faster. Now what matters is the speed of the Internet access you have to your home or office. It is bandwidth that matters. This worsens another Intel problem, the overall slowdown in the PC market, because users have less reason to upgrade their machines. Intel needs to seriously rethink its corporate existence.[11]

www.microsoft.com

CORPORATE VISION. Perhaps the most important factor in successful marketing is the **corporate vision**. Surprisingly, it is largely neglected by marketing textbooks, although not by the popular exponents of corporate strategy—it was perhaps the main theme of the book by Peters and Waterman,[12] in the form of their "superordinate goals." Indeed, nothing drives progress like a strong vision.[13]

nothing drives
progress
like a strong vision

Marketing in Action 2.1

Miller Brewing Company may need some innovation in its marketing planning

"Heritage. Quality. Innovation." The rich heritage of Miller Brewing Company (www.millerbeer.com), founded a century and a half ago, has helped make it the second largest brewer in the United States and the third largest in the world. The mission statement, "Quality, uncompromising and unchanging," clearly states the company's commitment to quality. In regard to innovation, Miller Brewing was the first with low-calorie beer, packaged draft beer, and domestic ice beer and was the first national brewer to develop a curbside recycling program. However, it looks like it might take an innovative marketing program to get this Milwaukee, Wisconsin (USA)-based company out of the doldrums.

As a distant number two in the beer market behind Anheuser-Busch Cos. (www.anheuser-busch.com), Miller's total 1998 sales and income both dropped by approximately 2 percent. This decline came even after two years of discounting in an attempt to regain market share. Although Miller Brewing is only 4 percent of Philip Morris' (www.philipmorris.com) operating income, the parent company is clearly demanding growth from the beer maker.

In an attempt to satisfy both corporate goals and distributor demands, while battling Anheuser-Busch, late 1998 saw Miller introducing beer packaged in 20-ounce recyclable plastic bottles. Other planning included keeping prices down, more in-store promotions, and buying smaller brands to broaden the company's portfolio. However, one distributor had expressed concern that Miller was still missing the boat. This distributor sees the beer industry as an image-driven business, with Miller's advertising being ineffective in this area.

What can Miller Brewing Company do in its market planning that will lead to satisfaction among its distributors and within the home office of Philip Morris?

Sources: www.millerbrewing.com; Richard A. Melcher, "It's Still Not Miller Time," *Business Week,* November 16, 1998, 52.

---

11. David Kirpatrick, "Intel's Got a Bigger Problem than the FTC," *Fortune,* July 6, 1998, 30–32.
12. T. J. Peters and R. H. Waterman, *In Search of Excellence* (New York: Harper & Row, 1982).
13. Theodore Levitt, *The Marketing Imagination* (New York: Free Press, 1986).

Superordinate goals. Superordinate goals are a cultlike devotion to accomplishing difficult tasks as if they were a corporate driving principle. For example, when battered by the Japanese competitors in the global competition for dynamic RAM chips in the 1980s, Motorola's executives felt humbled and began to get the "quality message." Its chief executive, George Fisher, said, "The issue was survival; the challenge was quality; the solution would come from the people of Motorola. We didn't have a detailed map, but with unity of purpose, we set out to completely change the way we serve our customers." Sometime in 1986, "total customer satisfaction" was articulated as the superordinate goal for everyone in the corporation.[14] And so began Motorola's renewed journey—which, in the beginning, was very much a process of stumbling and fumbling—to find the way to total customer satisfaction.[15]

If the organization in general, and its chief executive in particular, has a strong vision of where its future lies, then there is a good chance that the organization will achieve a strong position in its markets (and attain that future). The organization's strategies will be consistent and will be supported by its staff at all levels. In this context, all of IBM's marketing activities are underpinned by its philosophy of customer service, a vision originally promoted by the charismatic Watson dynasty. Similarly, at Matsushita, a maker of Panasonic, Quasar, and Technics product lines, it means never cheating a customer by knowingly producing or selling defective merchandise.[16]

In some cases, there is a sense of mission, which is a feeling that the group has banded together to create something new and exciting. This is common in new organizations[17] and is probably common at a company like America Online, Inc. (AOL). AOL's strategy to shift from online/Internet service provider to pop culture brand assumed a new prominence. Stressing the twin values of communications and convenience, AOL is artfully positioned as a rival to industries ranging from television to retail. AOL increasingly has become an acronym designed to rival MTV, NBC, and QVC. AOL's innovative leadership by its president and chief operating officer, Bob Pittman, suggests that AOL may ultimately be a bigger brand than MTV.[18]

The problem for marketers is that this vision is often unrelated to the markets. IBM and Matsushita are fortunate, because their creeds are of general applicability and of almost religious fervor. Many other organizations have a much narrower scope of vision and may only be successful while they approximate to market needs. The vision will move from being a major advantage to being an overwhelming disadvantage if the market shifts. As Peter Drucker[19] says, "Every *right* product sooner or later becomes a *wrong* product."

> "Every *right* product sooner or later becomes a *wrong* product."

The message for the marketer is that the marketing strategies, to be most effective, must be converted into a powerful long-term vision. Peter Drucker,[20] once again, says:

14. Bob McIvor, "Building the Factories of Tomorrow," *Financial Management* 22 (spring 1993): 24–25.

15. Ajay K. Kohli, Bernard J. Jaworski, and Ajith Kumar, "MARKOR: A Measure of Market Orientation," *Journal of Marketing Research* 30 (November 1993): 467–477; Subhash Sharma, Ronald W. Niedrich, and Greg Dobbins, "A Framework for Monitoring Customer Satisfaction," *Industrial Marketing Management* 28 (May 1999): 231–243.

16. Richard T. Pascale and Anthony G. Athos, *The Art of Japanese Management* (New York: Simon & Schuster, 1981).

17. Henry Mintzberg, Bruce Ahlstrand, and Joseph Lampel, *Strategy Safari: A Guided Tour Through the Wilds of Strategic Management* (New York: Simon & Schuster, 1998).

18. "The IQ Q&A: Bob Pittman," *Adweek,* September 21, 1998, IQ22–IQ31.

19. Peter F. Drucker, *Managing in Turbulent Times* (New York: Harper & Row, 1980).

20. Drucker, *Managing in Turbulent Times.*

www.motorola.com

www.panasonic.co.jp

www.aol.com

www.mtv.com
www.nbc.com
www.qvc.com

In many markets one prospers only at the extremes: either as one of the few market leaders who set the standard, or as a specialist. . . . What is not tenable is a strategy in between.

MARKETING MYOPIA.   In a very influential article, Theodore Levitt[21] stated:

The viewpoint that an industry is a customer-satisfying process, not a goods-producing process, is vital for all businessmen to understand. An industry begins with the customer and his needs, not with a patent, a raw material, or a selling skill. Given the customer's needs the industry develops backwards, first concerning itself with the physical *delivery* of customer satisfactions. Then it moves back further to *creating* the things by which these satisfactions are in part achieved. How these materials are created is a matter of indifference to the customer, hence the particular form of manufacturing, processing, or what-have-you cannot be considered as a vital aspect of the marketing.

> ". . . that an industry is a customer-satisfying process, **not a goods-producing process,** is vital for all businessmen to understand."

Levitt's reason for this emphasis—which was supported by considerable anecdotal evidence in the rest of the article—was that most organizations defined their corporate missions too narrowly, typically on the basis of the technological processes that they employed. For example, it would be myopic for Paramount Pictures to consider itself in the moviemaking business rather than the "audio and visual entertainment" business. For a similar reason, Saatchi & Saatchi's chief executive, Kevin Roberts, has redefined his firm's identity: "We're not an ad agency, we're an idea factory."[22]

www.paramount.com

www.saatchi.com

Levitt's view, which was enthusiastically seized upon by the more adventurous organizations, was that the link with the consumer, the "customer franchise," was the most important element. Adopting a customer perspective has helped many organizations to better appreciate how they could develop a corporate mission. Honda, once a motorcycle manufacturer, came to define itself as a "personal transportation" company and diversified into automobiles with its Civic and Accord models.

www.honda.com

However, some organizations have also taken the process too broadly. Holiday Inns, for example, decided that it was not in the "hotel business" but in the "travel industry" and acquired a number of businesses, including a bus company. However, it soon learned that its management skills were not in those areas and divested itself of them, retrenching to the business it knew best.[23] Obviously, finding an optimum level breadth of scope is crucial for successful business.

www.holidayinn.com

Indeed, it is worth noting that such merger and acquisition activities must be considered as viable alternatives to traditional marketing developments. A useful list of the available alternatives is presented in Table 2.1. The world's automobile industry is an excellent case in point in recent years. Daimler-Benz and Chrysler merged into DaimlerChrysler to create a horizontal integration in the hope that the former could gain a market position in the midlevel passenger car and minivan segments as well as in economies of scale. Ford's purchase of the automobile unit of Volvo has a similar objective in mind. BMW is determined to stay concentrated on what it does best with a strong focus on the

www.daimlerchrysler.com

www.ford.com
www.volvocars.com
www.bmw.com

21. Theodore Levitt, "Marketing Myopia," *Harvard Business Review* (July/August 1960): 45–56.
22. Bernice Kanner, "The Badman Cometh," *Chief Executive* (December 1998): 26–30.
23. David J. Teece, Richard Rumelt, Giovanni Dosi, and Sidney Winter, "Understanding Corporate Coherence: Theory and Evidence," *Journal of Economic Behavior & Organization* 23 (January 1994): 1–30.

Table 2.1

Strategic alternatives

Strategic alternative	Focus	External or internal	Purpose or function
Status quo	Stability	Internal	Continue in present products/markets temporarily or permanently, depending on product life cycle
Concentration	Single product line	Internal	Do one thing well
Horizontal integration	Ownership or control of competitors	External	Gain market power and economies of scale
Vertical integration	Transformation of cost center to profit center	External	Improve economies of scale; reduce dependence on suppliers or distributors
Diversification	Broadening of product line	External or internal	Reduce competitive pressures; gain greater profitability; spread risk
Joint ventures	Complementary benefits	External	Spread risk; bring about synergy
Retrenchment	Reduction of activity or operations	Internal	Temporarily respond to adversity by permanent phaseout
Divestiture	Removal of entity that does not fit	Internal	Realign products/markets or organization
Liquidation	Removal of entity that does not fit	Internal	Same divestiture alternative but situation is usually more severe
Innovation	Seizing of leadership position	Internal	Take initiative; gain position early in product life cycle
Restructuring	Cost reduction, growth potential	External	Concentrate on products and divisions with high potential

Source: A. J. Rowe, R. O. Mason, K. E. Dickel, and N. H. Snyder, *Strategic Management: A Methodological Approach,* 4th ed. (Reading, Mass.: Addison Wesley, 1989). Reprinted by permission of Alan J. Rowe.

upper segment of status-conscious, high-performance car lovers. General Motors, on the other hand, is restructuring to identify its niches in an ever-congested automobile market.[24]

MARKETING AUDIT

As the first formal step in the marketing planning process, the marketing audit should only involve bringing together the source material which has already been collected throughout the year as part of the normal work of the marketing department.

> A marketing audit is a *comprehensive, systematic, independent* and *periodic* examination of a company's—or business unit's—marketing environment, objectives, strategies, and activities with a view to determining problem areas and opportunities and recommending a plan of action to improve the company's marketing performance.[25]

Although some organizations have successfully employed external consultants to conduct marketing audits, they are generally best undertaken by management who "owns" the marketing process. This is partly because they are the

24. G. Pascal Zachary, "Big Business: Let's Play Oligopoly!—Why Giants Like Having Other Giants Around," *Wall Street Journal,* March 8, 1999, G1.; Alex Taylor, III, "U.S. Carmakers: Masters of Delusion? Asleep at the Wheel," *Fortune,* March 15, 1999, 34–35.

25. Philip Kotler, W. T. Gregor, and W. H. Rodgers III, "The Marketing Audit Comes of Age," *Sloan Management Review* (winter 1977): 25–43.

best people to understand the subtleties of the information revealed (assuming that they have set aside their preconceptions and prejudices). Even more important, though, the audit is the best possible learning process for these managers because it introduces them to the factors that are most important to their management of marketing. Finally, and most important of all, it ensures that those who will have to implement the results of the planning process understand, and are committed to, the assumptions that lie behind it.

In this context some factors related to the customer that should be included in the material collected for the audit may be:

- *Who are the customers?*

    What are their key characteristics?

    What differentiates them from other members of the population?

- *What are their needs and wants?*

    What do they expect the "product" to do?

    What are their special requirements and perceptions?

- *What do they think of the organization and its products or services?*

    What are their attitudes?

    What are their buying intentions?

A "traditional"—albeit product-based—format for auditing materials includes:

1. Financial data from management accounting, costing, and finance sections
2. Product data from production, research, and development
3. Sales and distribution data from sales, packaging, and distribution sections
4. Advertising, sales promotion, and merchandising data information from these departments
5. Market data and miscellany from market research, who would in most cases act as a source for this information

It is apparent that a marketing audit can be a complex process, but the aim is simple: *It is only to identify those existing (external and internal) factors that will have a significant impact on the future plans of the company.*

It is clear that the basic input material for the marketing audit should be comprehensive. As suggested earlier, the best approach is to continuously accumulate this material as it becomes available. This method avoids the otherwise heavy workload involved in collecting it as part of the regular, typically annual, planning process itself—when time is usually at a premium. Even so, the first task of this annual process should be to check that the material held in the current data file actually *is* comprehensive and accurate and can form a sound basis for the marketing audit itself.

the basic input material for the marketing audit should be comprehensive

The structure of the data file should be designed to match the specific needs of the organization, but one simple format may be applicable in many cases. This format splits the material into three groups:

1. **Review of the marketing environment.** A study of the organization's markets; customers; competitors; and the overall economic, political, cultural, and technical environment; covering developing trends, as well as the current situation.

2. **Review of the detailed marketing activity.** A study of the company's marketing mix; in terms of the four Ps—product, price, promotion, and place.

3. **Review of the marketing system.** A study of the marketing organization, marketing research systems, and the current marketing objectives and strategies.

The last item is too frequently ignored. The marketing system itself needs to be regularly questioned, because the validity of the whole marketing plan relies on the accuracy of the input from this system, and "garbage in, garbage out" applies with a vengeance.

> the validity of the whole marketing plan
> **relies on the accuracy**
> of the input from [the marketing] system

Two important bureaucratic audits should also be added: a marketing productivity audit, to see where marketing costs could be reduced, and a marketing function audit, to identify weaknesses.

ANALYSIS

What is important and will need to be taken into account in the marketing plan that will eventually emerge from the overall auditing process will be different for each product or service in each situation. One of the most important skills to be learned in marketing is being able to concentrate only on what is important.

www.compaq.com

www.dell.com
www.ibm.com

In the case of Compaq, it was an awareness of a gap between products that customers wanted and products that were available on the market. In the case of Dell, it was an appreciation of competitive pricing structures. In the case of IBM, it was an understanding of overall environmental factors. Each of these companies, with broadly similar products and operating in the same market, probably asked very different questions in their respective marketing audits.

In addition, all the analytical techniques that are described in this book can be applied and should be applied where relevant. It is important to say not just what happened but also why. The marketing planning process encompasses all of the marketing skills. However, a number of these may be particularly relevant at this stage, including the following:

- **Positioning.** As already stated, the starting point for the marketing plan must be the customer. The techniques of positioning and segmentation therefore usually offer the best starting point for what has to be achieved by the whole planning process.

- **Portfolio planning.** In addition, the coordinated planning of the individual products and services can contribute towards the balanced portfolio. A product portfolio analysis provides a very useful pictorial device that summarizes this information (see Figure 2.2). On this diagram, the *segments* the organization is operating in are plotted, with the market attractiveness (value to the organization) of each plotted on the vertical axis and the strength of the organization in that segment along the horizontal axis. In this example the size of the solid circles shows the relative amount of the organization's total turnover that they represent. The dotted circles, on the other hand, show where the organization wants to be (including the volume) in three years' time.

- **80/20 Rule.** To achieve the maximum impact, the marketing plan must be clear, concise, and simple. It needs to concentrate on the 20 percent of the products or services, and on the 20 percent of the customers, that will account for 80 percent of the volume and 80 percent of the profit.

Figure 2.2

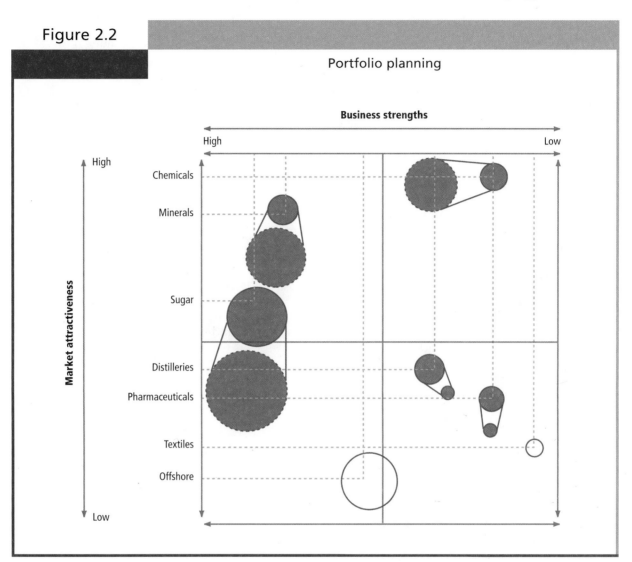

Portfolio planning

Source: Malcolm H. B. McDonald, *Marketing Plans*, 3d ed. (New York: Butterworth Heinemann, 1995), 43. Reprinted by permission of Butterworth Heinemann Publishers Oxford, a division of Reed Educational & Professional Publishing Ltd.

- **Four Ps.** As we have seen, the four Ps can sometimes divert attention from the customer, but the framework they offer can be very useful in building action plans.

SWOT ANALYSIS

One particularly useful technique in the analysis of the material contained in the marketing audit is that of a SWOT (Strengths, Weaknesses, Opportunities, Threats) analysis. It groups some of the key pieces of information into two main categories (internal factors and external factors) and then sorts by their dual positive and negative aspects (Strengths and Opportunities, as the positive aspects, with Weaknesses and Threats representing the negative aspects):

- **Internal factors.** Strengths and weaknesses internal to the organization, its strategies, and its position in relation to its competitors.
- **External factors.** Opportunities and threats presented by the external environment and the competition.

The internal factors that may be viewed as strengths or weaknesses depending upon their impact on the organization's positions (they may represent a strength for one organization but a weakness, in relative terms, for another), may include all of the four Ps, as well as personnel, finance, and so on. The external factors, which again may be threats to one organization whereas they offer opportunities to another, may include such matters as technological change, legislation, and sociocultural changes, as well as changes in the marketplace or competitive position. One such framework for a SWOT analysis is illustrated in Figure 2.3.

You should note, however, that SWOT is just one aid to categorization. It is not the only technique. It has its own weaknesses in that it tends to persuade companies to compile lists rather than to think about what is really important to their business. It also presents the resulting lists uncritically without clear prioritization, so that, for example, weak opportunities may appear to balance strong threats.

> **SWOT is just one aid to categorization. It is not the only technique.**

The aim of any SWOT analysis should be to isolate the key *issues* that will be important to the future of the organization and that subsequent marketing planning will address.

Figure 2.3

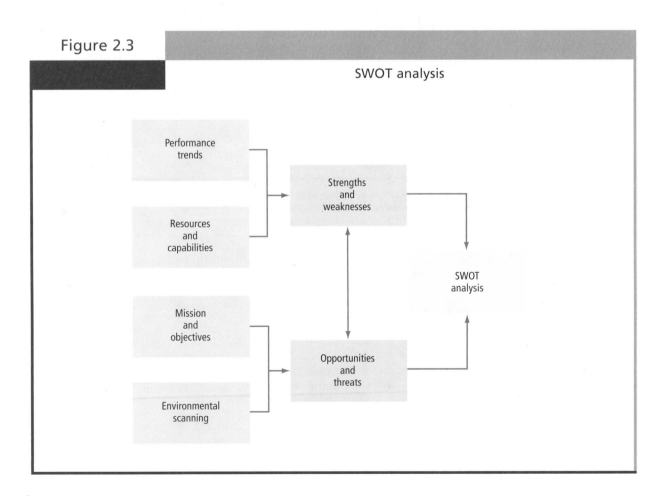

SWOT analysis

ASSUMPTIONS

It is essential to spell out assumptions in a marketing audit. However, most companies do not even realize that they make such assumptions. Canon, for example, depends on Sunset Direct, a database marketing company, to find customers for its computer printers and scanners.[26] The customer database is assumed to be accurate, and such an assumption is often the key to understanding Canon's marketing plan. You should, however, make as few assumptions in the audit as possible and very carefully explain those you do make.

www.canon.com
www.sunsetdirect.com

As an extension to this process, when you estimate the results expected from your strategies, you should also explore a range of alternative assumptions in the same way that it was suggested earlier that there might be a range of forecasts, each meeting different needs. For example, if you have assumed that the market will grow by x percent, you might estimate sales from your chosen strategy at $\$y$. However, you should also estimate sales at lower and higher rates of growth in the market ("At rate of growth of $x - 2$ percent, sales will be $\$y - 3$. At a growth rate of $x + 2$ percent . . .").

The most useful component of this exercise may well be a sensitivity analysis. Sensitivity analysis is designed to measure how a small change in one factor (for example, prices) will affect the other factor (for example, sales). This determines which factors have the most influence over the outcomes—and hence which factors should be managed most carefully.

MARKETING OBJECTIVES

With the results of the audit available, the active part of the marketing planning process begins. This stage in marketing planning is indeed the crux of the whole marketing process. The marketing objectives state just where the company intends to be at some specific time in the future.

Marketing objectives are essentially about the match between products and markets—what products or services will be in what position in what markets—so they must be based on realistic customer behavior in those markets. Objectives for pricing, distribution, advertising, and so on are at a lower level and should not be confused with marketing objectives, although they are part of the marketing strategy needed to achieve marketing objectives.

> marketing planning
> **is indeed the crux**
> of the whole marketing process

To be most effective, objectives should be *measurable*. This measurement may be in terms of sales volume, money value, market share, or percentage penetration of distribution outlets. As it is measured, it can, within limits, be unequivocally monitored and corrective action taken as necessary. Usually marketing objectives must be based, above all, on the organization's financial objectives; financial measurements are converted into the related marketing measurements. An example of a measurable marketing objective might be "to enter the market with product Y and capture 10 percent of the market by value within one year." An example of a nonmeasurable marketing objective was stated by Kevin Roberts, the chief executive officer of Saatchi & Saatchi Worldwide. He stated, "My goal is to have Saatchi revered as the hottest ideas shop on the planet—hotter than

www.saatchi.com

---

26. "Sunset Shines in Database Marketing," *Austin American-Statesman*, October 9, 1995, D1, D5.

Exhibit 2.1

Marketing myopia can change the paths of even successful companies for the worse. Recognizing the business of the business is critical for survival and for prosperity. The statement by Saatchi & Saatchi's chief executive, Kevin Roberts, that "We're not an ad agency, we're an idea factory" is broadcast in many ways via the company's Web site. The company mission is clearly communicated, as is the primacy of idea generation in the company's daily activities.

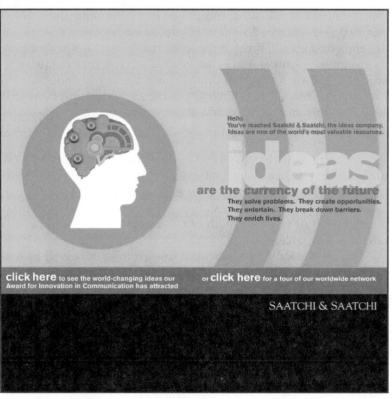

disney.go.com
www.mit.edu
www.microsoft.com

Disney, hotter than MIT or Microsoft."[27] Exhibit 2.1 shows the conviction behind his statement. Mr. Roberts's statement was not intended as a marketing objective, for as you can see, it clearly would not meet the criterion of being measurable.

MARKETING STRATEGIES

As James Quinn points out, "Goals [or objectives] state *what* is to be achieved and *when* results are to be accomplished, but they do not state *how* the results are to be achieved."[28] That is where marketing strategies enter the picture. A marketing strategy is essentially a pattern or plan that integrates an organization's major goals, policies, and action sequences into a cohesive whole.[29] As explained in Chapter 1, marketing strategies are generally concerned with the four Ps:

> "Goals state *what* is to be achieved and *when* results are to be accomplished, but they do not state *how* the results are to be achieved."

- Product strategies

    Developing new products, repositioning or relaunching existing ones, and scrapping old ones

    Adding new features and benefits

---

27. Bernice Kanner, "The Badman Cometh," *Chief Executive* (December 1998): 26–30.

28. James B. Quinn, *Strategies for Change: Logical Incrementalism* (Burr Ridge, Ill.: Richard D. Irwin, 1980).

29. Quinn, *Strategies for Change: Logical Incrementalism.*

Balancing product portfolios

Changing the design or packaging

- Pricing strategies

  Setting the price to skim or to penetrate

  Pricing for different market segments

  Deciding how to meet competitive pricing

- Promotional strategies

  Specifying the advertising platform and media

  Deciding the public relations brief

  Organizing the sales force to cover new products and services or markets

- Placement strategies

  Choosing the channels

  Deciding levels of customer service

In principle, these strategies describe how the firm's marketing objectives will be achieved. The four Ps are a useful framework for deciding how the company's resources will be manipulated to achieve the objectives. It should be noted, however, that the four Ps are not the only framework, and may divert attention from the real issues. The focus of marketing strategies must be the objectives to be achieved—not the process of planning itself. Only if it fits the needs of these objectives should you choose to use the framework of the four Ps.

> ## The focus of marketing strategies must be **the objectives to be achieved—** not the process of planning itself.

The strategy statement can take the form of a purely verbal description of the strategic options that have been chosen. Alternatively, and perhaps more positively, it might include a structured list of the major options chosen.

One often-overlooked aspect of strategy is timing. Choosing the best time for each element of the strategy is often critical. Sometimes, taking the right action at the wrong time can be almost as bad as taking the wrong action at the right time. Timing is, therefore, an essential part of any plan and should normally appear as a schedule of planned activities. Lotus Development Corp. was a victim of bad timing when it recently announced to its biggest customers that it would soon ship a new version of its popular Notes program, which would be priced 50 percent less than its current product. Naturally, the customers stopped ordering in anticipation of the better and cheaper upcoming version. As a result of the announcement's bad timing, revenue from Notes fell 40 percent from the previous quarter.[30]

www.lotus.com

> Sometimes, taking the right action at the wrong time
>
> ## can be almost as bad as
>
> taking the wrong action at the right time.

After completing this crucial stage of the planning process, you will need to recheck the feasibility of your objectives and strategies in terms of the market share, sales, costs, and profits that these demand in practice. As in the rest of the marketing discipline, you will need to employ judgment, experience, market research, or anything else that helps you to view your conclusions from all possible angles.

---

30. Kathy Rebello, "Can Jim Manzi Get Out of This Lotus Position?" *Business Week*, May 8, 1995, 36–37.

The following is a list of criteria for evaluating individual strategies:[31]

1. Does it contribute to the proposed strategic structure or to a proposed primary strategy?
2. Is it likely to show a return on investment that exceeds the company's cut-off rate?
3. Is its risk profile acceptable?
4. Does it make use of or reinforce strategic strengths?
5. Does it rely on weaknesses or do anything to reduce them?
6. Does it exploit major opportunities?
7. Does it avoid, reduce, or mitigate the major threats? If not, are there adequate contingency plans?
8. Does it accord with company morals?
9. Is it consistent with other primary or secondary strategies?
10. Are the managers fully confident that this strategy can be carried out in the real practical world?

Strategy deals with the unknowable, not the uncertain. It involves forces of such great number, strength, and combinatory powers that you cannot predict events in a probabilistic sense. Pragmatically speaking, you should never forget to proceed flexibly and experimentally from broad concepts toward specific commitments, making the latter concrete as late as possible in order to narrow the bands of uncertainty and to benefit from the best available information.[32] **Yield management** is one such technique used by an increasing number of companies to maximize revenues under uncertainties of customer purchase by discounting, overbooking, and limiting early sales for capacity-contained services[33] (see Manager's Corner 2.2).

Manager's Corner 2.2

Yield management

Yield management is now commonly used in the allocation of airline seats, hotel rooms, railroad cars, rental cars, advertising space, elective surgeries, satellite transmission, and printing press runs. It is the defining feature of the demand management, order-booking, and capacity planning processes of a variety of firms. Yield management provides two benefits to the firm's financial performance.

First, it manages capacity to avoid unused capacity *and* stock-outs. Second, it protects profit margins by decreasing the attractiveness of across-the-board price discounting by competitors. The proliferation of information technology has enabled the use of yield management to increase significantly. Companies that do not incorporate yield management into their planning process may find themselves at a considerable competitive disadvantage. For example, American Airlines (www.aa.com) estimates that it saves $470 million per year through the use of yield management.

Firms with relatively high levels of the following characteristics are most likely to benefit from using yield management:

1. Fixed capacity
   Adding capacity may be infeasible or prohibitively expensive
   Example: adding a room to a hotel
2. Perishable inventory
   How long unsold merchandise can be stored for future sale
   Example: an unused yet available rental car

31. John Argenti, *Systematic Corporate Planning* (Walton-on-Thames, England: Thomas Nelson, 1974).
32. Quinn, *Strategies for Change: Logical Incrementalism.*
33. Ramarao Desiraju and Steven M. Shugan, "Strategic Service Pricing and Yield Management," *Journal of Marketing* 63 (January 1999): 44–56.

3. Demand uncertainty

With random demand, both unused capacity and stock-outs (lost sales) are more likely

4. Fixed costs

Costs of providing goods or services are not affected by demand

Example: fuel costs are high for an airline flight regardless of whether the plane is occupied

These characteristics make a firm more willing to use yield management. The next question is the feasibility of the implementation. Three factors in the external environment make the use of yield management more feasible: (1) segmentable markets, (2) ease of preventing arbitrage, and (3) advance reservation requirements.

Segmenting. Two key components to make yield management work are segmenting markets and setting strategic price differentials. In the airline industry, the corporate market is less price sensitive than the travel market. Airlines have instituted discounts for "staying over the weekend" precisely to prevent corporate clients from getting the lower prices targeted for noncorporate passengers. Measuring demand and price sensitivity for each segment is a necessity for setting differential pricing and allocating capacity to each segment.

Preventing Arbitrage. Obviously, this is to prevent low-margin customers from subsequently selling to high-margin customers. Referring again to the airline industry, tickets are typically booked in the passenger's name and can only be used by that passenger.

Advanced Reservation. The availability of historical demand information on a per-segment basis greatly assists in the process of profit maximization through price and capacity setting.

The ease of yield management implementation is also increased if a firm has the following internal competencies: (1) a historical sales database, (2) sales forecast accuracy, and (3) market information system (MIS) sophistication. The first deals with measuring sales performance and could include estimations of price sensitivity or low and peak demand periods. The second is a separate but related capability. The third, MIS sophistication, is especially important to the kind of dynamic reallocation employed in yield management. Capacity is allocated for each segment in advance. However, given advanced and last minute bookings, the segment capacity must be constantly reallocated to adjust for current bookings or orders. People Express airlines lacked the MIS infrastructure to handle last-minute bookings for its business travelers, and thus lost this high-margin segment to competitors such as Piedmont.

Because of the perishability of service inventory, yield management has been largely a service industry phenomenon, including lodging, transportation, rental firms, hospitals, and satellite transmission (see Exhibit 2.2). However, the advance of information technology is facilitating the use of yield management, so this discipline is being introduced into new industries.

This highly complex, multiperiod pricing system is both popular and profitable among many airlines. However, there has also been a movement to simplified pricing. Attempts at simplification of pricing are finding more success in other industries. For example, railroads and other freight and transportation services are trying to simplify their pricing schedules. Companies such as AT&T (www.att.com), American Hawaii Cruises (www.cruisehawaii.com), Premier Hospital Alliance, Yellow Freight System (www.yellowfreight.com), Novell (www.novell.com), CIX, Infonet (www.infonet.com), and Dow Jones News/Retrieval (www.dowjones.com) have recently moved to more simplified pricing.

Sources: Frederick H. Harris and Peter Peacock, "Hold My Place, Please," *Marketing Management* 4 (fall 1995): 34; Ramarao Desiraju and Steven M. Shugan, "Strategic Service Pricing and Yield Management," *Journal of Marketing* 63 (January 1999): 44–56.

DETAILED PLANS AND PROGRAMS

You will need to develop your overall marketing strategies into detailed plans and programs. Although these detailed plans may cover each of the four Ps, the focus will vary, depending on your organization's specific strategies. A product-oriented company will focus its plans for the four Ps around each of its products. A market- or geographically-oriented company will concentrate on each market or geographical area. Each will base its plans on the detailed needs of its customers and on the strategies chosen to satisfy these needs.

Exhibit 2.2

Although yield management strategy is being implemented across multiple industries, from foodservice to transportation to computer software to news retrieval services, it is still the hallmark of the travel industry. Hoping to fill hotel rooms and vacant seats on planes, many companies have created programs with deep discounts for last-minute bookings and weekend travel. Holiday Inn is one such company. Offering different weekend specials each week, the goal is to encourage the kind of spontaneous travel that will maximize company revenues.

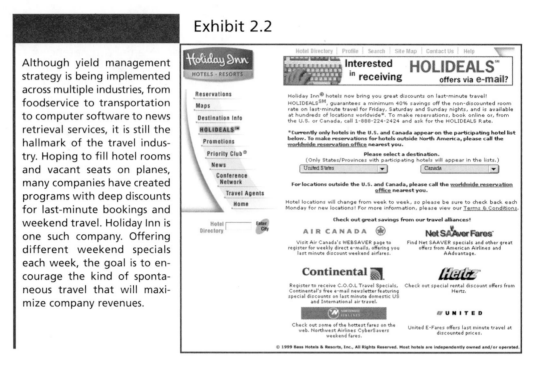

Again, the most important element is the detailed plans, which spell out exactly what programs and individual activities will take place over the period of the plan (usually over the next year). Without these specified—and preferably quantified—activities the plan cannot be monitored, even in terms of success in meeting its objectives. It is these programs and activities that will then constitute the "marketing" of the organization over the period. As a result, these detailed marketing programs are the most important, practical outcome of the whole planning process. These plans should therefore be:

- *Clear*—they should be an unambiguous statement of *exactly* what is to be done.
- *Quantified*—the predicted outcome of each activity should be, as far as possible, quantified, so that its performance can be monitored.
- *Focused*—the temptation to proliferate activities beyond the numbers that can be realistically controlled should be avoided. The 80/20 rule applies in this context, too. Bonoma and Crittenden,[34] reporting the results of their research into marketing implementation, noted, "The number of marketing programs in a firm, compared to relevant competitors, will be inversely related to the quality of marketing practices observed."
- *Realistic*—they should be achievable.
- *Agreed upon*—those who are to implement them should be committed to them and agree that they are achievable.

The resulting plans should become a working document that will guide the campaigns taking place throughout the organization over the period of the plan.

---

34. Thomas V. Bonoma and V. L. Crittenden, "Managing Marketing Implementation," *Sloan Management Review* (winter 1988).

If the marketing plan is to work, every exception to it (throughout the year) must be questioned, and the lessons learned must be incorporated in the next year's plan.

It is at this stage that all the various elements of the plan—objectives, strategies, and detailed plans—are finally brought together.

REASONS FOR INADEQUATE PLANNING

The marketing plan, no matter how detailed and well planned it is, may not work as expected for various reasons. One study shows that there are 10 main factors that lead to problems in the marketing planning process.

The main messages deriving from this study are:

Commitment. The management involved, and particularly top management (and above all the chief executive), must be committed to the planning process and to the implementation of the plans it produces. They must be involved in the process and understand that it is highly relevant—indeed essential—to their own management activities, not just a once-a-year ritual that they must endure.

Time. Implementation of the planning process takes longer than people expect or wish. It should not be expected to produce fully operational plans for perhaps three years, which is very much longer than the few weeks normally allowed. In part, this time is needed for all the individuals to develop their communication processes (and understand each other's terminology), as well as to understand that there is more to planning than numbers and unconnected details.

Understanding. The managers must also recognize what the various planning processes are, including operational planning, as opposed to strategic planning; how the marketing plan integrates into the corporate plan; and what the role of the planner is.

MARKETING PLAN STRUCTURE

The marketing plan itself should, of course, be formalized as a written document, although in practice too few companies take this seriously. The shape that this document takes will depend on the exact requirements of the business, but it might contain the following sections:[35]

1. Mission statement
2. Summary of performance (to date, including reasons for good or bad performance)
3. Summary of financial projections (for three years)
4. Market overview
5. SWOT analyses of major projects/markets
6. Portfolio summary (a summary of SWOTs)
7. Assumptions
8. Setting objectives
9. Financial projections for three years (in detail)

---

35. Malcolm H. B. McDonald and Warren Keegan, *Marketing Plans That Work: Targeting Growth and Profitability* (Boston: Butterworth Heinemann, 1997).

CONTINGENCY PLAN

Few marketing plans are ever implemented exactly as intended: The marketing environment is a particularly uncertain one, so it is essential to include full backup plans to cover for the eventuality that some of the assumptions are proved incorrect. One can imagine the difference in IBM's fortunes had it fully considered the possibility that mainframes might someday be replaced by personal computers. Given a different set of assumptions, IBM might have remained the dominant computer manufacturer in the world. The following questions should be answered for each assumption.[36]

- What is the basis of assumption?
- What event would have to happen to make this strategy unattractive?
- What is the risk of such an event occurring (% or high/low)?
- What is the impact if the event occurs?
- What is the trigger point for action?
- What actual contingency action is proposed?

BUDGETS AS MANAGERIAL TOOLS

The classic quantification of a marketing plan appears in the form of budgets. Because these are so rigorously quantified, they are particularly important. They should represent an unequivocal projection of actions and expected results, and they should be capable of accurate monitoring. Indeed, performance against budget is the main (regular) management review process.

The purpose of a marketing budget is to pull all the revenues and costs involved in marketing together into one comprehensive document. It is a managerial tool that balances what is needed to be spent against what can be afforded and helps make choices about priorities. It is then used in monitoring the performance in practice. The marketing budget is usually the most powerful tool with which you think through the relationship between desired results and available means. Its starting point should be the marketing strategies and plans that have already been formulated in the marketing plan itself. In practice, the two will run in parallel and will interact. At the very least, the rigorous, highly quantified budgets may cause a reconsideration of some of the more optimistic elements of the plans.

> The marketing budget is usually the most powerful tool by which you think through the relationship between desired results and available means.

Many budgets are based on history, and they are the equivalent of time-series forecasting. It is assumed that next year's budgets should follow some trend that is discernible over recent history. Other alternatives are based on a simple "percentage of sales" or on "what competitors are doing." However, there are many other approaches, including the following.

AFFORDABILITY. This may be the most common approach to budgeting. Someone, typically the managing director on behalf of the board, decides on a "reasonable" promotional budget—what can be afforded. This figure is most often based on historical spending. This approach assumes that promotion is a cost; sometimes it is seen as an avoidable cost.

---

36. McDonald and Keegan, *Marketing Plans.*

PERCENTAGE OF REVENUE. This is a variation of "affordable," but at least it forges a link with sales volume, in that the budget will be set at a certain percentage of revenue, and thus follows trends in sales. However, it does imply that promotion is a result of sales, rather than the reverse.

COMPETITIVE PARITY. In this case, the organization relates its budgets to what the competitors are doing. For example, it matches their budgets, beats them, or spends a proportion of what the brand leader is spending. On the other hand, it assumes that the competitors know best, in which case the service or product can expect to be nothing more than a follower.

ZERO-BASED BUDGETING. This approach takes the objectives as set out in the marketing plan, together with the resulting planned activities, and then costs them out.

Both the affordability and percentage of revenue methods are considered by many managers to be realistic in that they reflect the reality of the business strategies as those managers see it. On the other hand, neither makes any allowance for change. They do not allow for development to meet emerging market opportunities and, at the other end of the scale, they continue to pour money into a dying product or service (known as a "dog").

MEASUREMENT OF PROGRESS

The final stage is to establish targets (or standards) against which progress can be monitored. Accordingly, it is important to put both quantities and timescales into the marketing objectives (for example, to capture 20 percent by value of the market within two years) and into the corresponding strategies.

Changes in the environment mean that often the forecasts and the related plans may need to be changed. Continuous monitoring of performance against predetermined targets represents a most important aspect of this. Perhaps even more important is the enforced discipline of a regular formal review. As with forecasts, the best (most realistic) planning cycle will revolve around a quarterly review in many cases. Best of all, at least in terms of the quantifiable aspects of the plans if not the wealth of backing detail, is probably a quarterly rolling review—planning one full year ahead each new quarter. Of course, this does absorb more planning resource; but it also ensures that the plans embody the latest information, and—with attention focused on them so regularly—forces both the plans and their implementation to be realistic.

PERFORMANCE ANALYSIS

The following elements of marketing performance are most important to track.

SALES ANALYSIS. Most organizations track their sales results, or, in nonprofit organizations for example, the number of clients. The more sophisticated track them in terms of *sales variance*—the deviation from the target figures—that allows a more immediate picture of deviations to become evident. *Micro-analysis*, which is a nicely pseudoscientific term for the normal management process of investigating detailed problems, then investigates the individual elements (individual products, sales territories, or customers) that are failing to meet targets.

MARKET SHARE ANALYSIS. Relatively few organizations, however, track their market share, and in some circumstances, this may well be a much more important measure. In an expanding market, sales may still be increasing, while

Marketing in Action 2.2

A marketing plan to change misperceptions about Roswell Park Cancer Institute

Roswell Park Cancer Institute (rpci.med.buffalo.edu) is a premier cancer research, treatment, and education center. Located in Buffalo, New York, it was the first such institute opened in the United States and is now the third largest. With a $241.5-million rebuilding project underway, the Institute opened a new hospital in 1998.

Roswell Park's market share is estimated to be less than 20 percent of the potential market, although it has a staff of 2,700 devoted to patient care and research. Interestingly, many Western New Yorkers do not even know what happens at the Institute. Both Kaleida Health System (www.chob.edu/main/home.html), the largest single provider of cancer treatment in the area, and Catholic Health System's Sisters Hospital, strong in breast cancer surgery, are major competitors for the local business.

Recognizing that the Institute needed more cancer cases, focus groups (consisting of both former patients and those who chose not to use Roswell) were used to gather information about the market's perception of the facility. Results suggested that the Institute was perceived to be a research-oriented facility that cancer patients would go to for experimental therapy—a "last resort" facility—and that the Institute was too expensive.

Executives at Roswell are considering an approximately $500,000 one-year media campaign to address such misperceptions. The only significant hospital advertising that has occurred in the Buffalo area has been by Erie County Medical Center (www.ecmc.edu). Instead, local medical facilities have focused attention on doctors. Unfortunately, Roswell has never formed a good referral network with local community physicians.

Is consumer advertising the best way to increase Roswell's market share? Are there other elements of the marketing plan that Roswell might be overlooking in its focus on a media campaign?

Sources: http://rpci.med.buffalo.edu; Henry L. Davis, "Roswell Park Targets Area Residents in Advertising Blitz," *Buffalo News*, June 4, 1999, 1B.

---

share is actually decreasing—boding ill for future sales when the market eventually starts to drop. Where such market share is tracked, there may be a number of aspects that will be followed, including:

- Overall market share
- Segment share—in the specific, targeted segment
- Relative share—in relation to the market leaders

Marketing in Action 2.2 shows how market share can be a driver—for good or for bad—of marketing activities.

EXPENSE ANALYSIS.   The key ratio to watch in this area is usually the marketing expense to sales ratio, although this may be broken down into other elements (advertising to sales, sales administration to sales, and so on).

FINANCIAL ANALYSIS.   The bottom line of marketing activities should, at least in theory, be the net profit. For nonprofit organizations, the comparable emphasis may be on remaining within budgeted costs. There are a number of separate performance figures and key ratios that need to be tracked, such as:

- Gross contribution
- Gross profit
- Net contribution
- Net profit

- Return on investment
- Profit on sales

There can be considerable benefit in comparing these figures with those achieved by other organizations (especially those in the same industry), using, for example, the figures that can be obtained from 10-K reports. The most sophisticated use of this approach, however, is typically done by those who use PIMS (Profit Impact of Management Strategies). Initiated by the General Electric Company and then developed by Harvard Business School, PIMS is now run by the Strategic Planning Institute and covers nearly 4,000 Strategic Business Units (SBUs) across North America and Europe.[37]

www.ge.com
www.hbs.edu
www.thespinet.org

The above performance analyses concentrate on the quantitative measures that are directly related to short-term performance. However, there are a number of indirect measures tracking customer attitudes that can also indicate the organization's performance in terms of its long-term marketing strengths and may accordingly be even more important indicators. Some useful measures are the following:

- Market research—including customer panels (which are used to track changes over time)
- Lost business—the orders that were lost because, for example, the stock was not available or the product did not meet the customer's exact requirements
- Customer complaints—how many customers complain about the products, services, or the organization itself and what they complain about

RELATIONSHIP ANALYSIS. Relationship marketing has become important for a company's long-term success, since it costs five times more to get a new customer than to keep a current one.[38] Clearly, companies that value commitment and trust relationships with their customers will outcompete those that believe in a "hand over the money, and we will deliver" school of thought. Although it is not easy to measure the "quality" of relationship marketing, both inputs and outputs need to be examined.[39] Input factors that have direct bearing on relationship marketing that a company can manage are:

- Understanding customer expectations
- Building service partnerships with customers
- Empowering employees
- Total quality management

Based on these inputs, various relationship-based outputs can be measured by:

- Customer satisfaction
- Customer loyalty
- Customers' perception of product and service quality
- Profitability

---

37. Robert D. Buzzell and Bradley T. Gale, *The PIMS Principles* (New York: The Free Press, 1987); Jinuk Chowdhury and Ajay Menon, "Multidimensional Components of Quality and Strategic Business Unit Performance: A PIMS Test," *Journal of Managerial Issues* 7 (winter 1995): 449–465.
38. Joshua Levine, "Relationship Marketing," *Forbes*, December 20, 1993, 232–233.
39. Thomas L. Baker, Penny M. Simpson, and Judy A. Siguaw, "The Impact of Suppliers' Perceptions of Reseller Market Orientation on Key Relationship Constructs," *Journal of the Academy of Marketing Science* 27 (winter 1999): 50–57.

Summary

In general, the use of marketing plans conveys a number of advantages: consistency, responsibility, communication, and commitment.

The *corporate plan* should contain three main components:

- Where the organization is now
- Where the organization intends to go in the future
- How it will organize its resources to get there

Corporate objectives, which are usually more complex than just financial targets, should reflect the *corporate mission* (including customer groups, customer needs, and technologies), which may reflect a strong corporate vision.

The starting point of the marketing planning process is the marketing audit, the output of which may be one or more facts books, covering a wide range of questions about internal (product-related) and external (environmental, as well as market) factors and the marketing system itself, as well as the following basic questions:

- Who are the customers?
- What are their needs and wants?
- What do they think of the organization and its products or services?

A SWOT analysis may be used to collate the most important information about the organization's strengths and weaknesses and the opportunities and threats of the environment in which it operates. Whatever the form of analysis, the inherent *assumptions* must be spelled out.

This will lead to the production of *marketing objectives* and subsequently to *marketing strategies* (typically covering all elements of the four Ps).

A suggested structure for the marketing plan document itself might be:

1. Mission statement
2. Summary of performance (to date, including reasons for good or bad performance)
3. Summary of financial projections (for three years)
4. Market overview
5. SWOT analyses of major projects or markets
6. Portfolio summary (a summary of SWOTs)
7. Assumptions
8. Setting objectives
9. Financial projections for three years (in detail)

All of these detailed plans should be, as far as possible, number based and deadlined, briefly described, and practical. These programs must be controlled, particularly by the use of budgets, for which the overall figures may be derived by affordable, percentage of revenue, competitive parity, or zero-based budgeting.

Finally, the actual performance of the marketing strategy needs to be examined. The most important elements of marketing performance are sales analysis, market share analysis, expense analysis, financial analysis, and relationship analysis. Although much of the relationship analysis may not be quantifiable, it has become an increasingly important determinant of a company's long-term success.

QUESTIONS FOR REVIEW

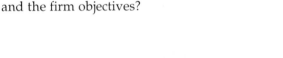

1. What advantages accrue to the use of the plans in general? What would be contained in the corporate plan?

2. How may corporate objectives be derived from the corporate mission? What elements may they contain? Where does corporate vision fit in?

3. What may be contained in the marketing audit?

4. How may a SWOT analysis be carried out? How are assumptions dealt with?

5. What are the differences between marketing objectives and marketing strategies? What should marketing strategies cover?

6. What might the structure of a marketing plan look like? What rules might be applied to its content?

7. What is the relationship between the mission statement and the SWOT analysis? What is the relationship between the mission statement and the firm objectives?

QUESTIONS FOR DISCUSSION

1. Evaluate the following marketing plan:

   A consortium of 2,200 independent grocers under the IGA Inc. umbrella has stepped up its marketing and advertising efforts to compete for shoppers. The collective resources of IGA, or Independent Grocers Alliance, enables the owner of a single supermarket in Iowa to market as effectively as a 15-store chain in Connecticut. The benefit has become more important in recent years, as rapid industry consolidation has created huge regional chains such as Wal-Mart and Kroger with enormous purchasing power and hefty marketing budgets. As a result, IGA has nearly doubled its annual marketing and advertising budget in the last five years to about $100 million.[40]

2. Soft Sheen Products Inc., which sells products like Care Free Curl, Optimum Care, Sportin' Waves, and Baby Love, is bringing out Alternatives, a line of relaxer and styling products aimed at black women, primarily ages 18 to 25. The marketing plans for the new brand—developed and produced after a year of research—are infused with elements meant to appeal to that younger consumer. They range from packaging the product in bold, vibrant colors to a television commercial centered on a hot trend, poetry recitals at urban clubs.[41]

   Find other such examples that are emblematic of the changes marketers and media are making to capitalize on a rising number of female consumers in their teens and early 20s.

---

40. Dana Canedy, "A Consortium of Independent Grocers Is Stepping Up Efforts to Compete with Supermarket Chains," *New York Times*, January 15, 1998, 10.

41. Stuart Elliott, "Soft Sheen Aims at Women Who Really Like to Style Their Hair," *New York Times*, December 16, 1997, 9.

3. Known for maintaining a fierce tempo of producing one film a month, on average, including commercial successes like *The Exorcist* and *Superman*, while being a senior Warner Brothers executive, John Calley turned the troubled Sony Pictures Entertainment around after taking over as its president. Sony's two studios, Columbia Pictures and Tristar Pictures, brought in several hundreds of millions of dollars at the box office at a record pace for the film industry. Calley oversaw last-minute changes in the marketing plans and expanded the promotional budget, moves widely credited for turning potentially popular films into blockbusters.

   Substantiate Calley's marketing plan with his specific project successes. It may require a bit of research on Sony Pictures as well as on the film production industry.

4. ServiceMaster Industries Inc. corporate objectives reads: "To honor God in all we do, to help people develop, to pursue excellence, and to grow profitably"—precisely in that order. For the last 10 years profits have been growing at an annual compound rate of 31 percent, and stockholders' equity has increased 17 percent.

   ServiceMaster got its start 32 years ago cleaning furniture and mothproofing car-pets in homes and offices. Among the more famous places its specialists spruce up: Buckingham Palace, the Houses of Parliament, and the White House. But the company's biggest business is cleaning hospitals. About 95 percent of ServiceMaster's hospital contracts are renewed, but so far the company has cornered business from only 11 percent of the nation's 7,100 hospitals.

   Make a five-year marketing plan for ServiceMaster that is compatible with its corporate objective as well as the nature of its market.

5. Superdrug changed its vision statement from "to be the No. 1 retailer of toiletries in the UK, in terms of consumer perception, market share, and profitability" to "to be the customer's favorite, up-to-the-minute health and beauty shop, loved for its value, choice, friendliness, and fun" to give employees and suppliers a clear understanding of what the firm is trying to do in the business. Evaluate this change in terms of its ability to be a "touchable" statement, which appeals to individual employees and helps move Superdrug towards its mission.

6. Gap Inc. will continue to build its brands this year by rolling out 300 to 350 stores in the United States and abroad, opening a store a day, and an aggressive $225 million marketing plan. Gap's first-quarter comp-store sales are expected to increase 10 percent. While the Gap division will add 80 to 90 units, Banana Republic will open 35 to 40 new stores and GapKids will open 45 to 50 stores.

   Evaluate the justification and competitiveness of such marketing plans in the light of prevailing industry characteristics.

7. The number of berths and the lushness of the new ships expected in the North American cruise market is increasing. The number of berths is increasing at 7.5 percent a year whereas the attractiveness of ship features (such as show lounges, miniature golf courses, and wine-and-caviar bars) also improves. Seventy percent of the new tonnage in the next four years is being built by the three industry leaders. Meanwhile, passenger growth in this industry has slowed to 2.2 percent a year. What assumptions are the three major cruise lines making about the future of this industry?

FURTHER READINGS

Ansoff, H. Igor, and Edward J. McDonnell. *Implanting Strategic Management*, 2d ed. Upper Saddle River, N.J.: Prentice Hall, 1990.

Beck, David. "The Rise and Fall of Great Companies." *Journal of Business Study* 12 (July-August 1991): 62–64.

Duffy, Michael F. "ZBB, PBB, and their Effectiveness within the Planning-Marketing Process." *Strategic Management Review* 10 (March-April 1989): 163–173.

McNamee, Patrick B. *Strategic Market Planning: A Blueprint for Success.* New York: John Wiley & Sons, 1998.

Rowe, Alan J., Richard O. Mason, Karl E. Dickel, and Neil H. Snyder. *Strategic Management: A Methodological Approach*, 3d ed. Reading, Mass.: Addison Wesley, 1989.

Zinkhan, George M., and Arun Pereira. "An Overview of Marketing Strategy and Planning." *International Journal of Research in Marketing* 11 (June 1994): 185–218.

chapter **3**

Understanding the En
and the Competition

Understanding the Environment and the Competition

No organization is completely self-contained; each is embedded in an environment composed of federations, associations, government agencies, customers, suppliers, and competitors. Societal expectations, customs, and laws define and control the nature and limits of an organizations's relationships within this environment. Most organizations' bottom-line profits are dependent more on the vagaries of external environmental events than on how well their internal operations are managed.[1] Moreover, this **external environment** is not only changing, it is changing fast. Consider historian Arthur Schlesinger Jr.'s observation that "a boy who saw the Wright brothers fly for a few seconds at Kitty Hawk in 1903 could have watched Apollo II land on the moon in 1969. The first electronic computer was built in 1946; today the world rushes from the mechanical into the electronic age. The double helix was first unveiled in 1953; today biotechnology threatens to remake mankind."[2] As a result of this quickening pace, the impact of environmental change has become more unpredictable. Figure 3.1 illustrates how this turbulence has increased and how a greater speed of change and a decreased visibility of the future lead to a lower familiarity with events.

Most organizations devote immense efforts to optimizing the internal factors that are within their control. However, firms also need to be aware of their external environment and its current and potential effects. Any changes in the business environment, whether at home or abroad, may have serious repercussions on the marketing activities of the firm. Managers must therefore spend an increasing amount of their time on matters external to the firm and try to understand their effects on the company. In doing so, they must first develop a firm grasp of those environmental dimensions that are likely to influence corporate activities the most. This step involves a close scrutiny of societal, cultural, demographic, technological, economic, political, and legal factors. Next, the manager needs to analyze the changes in the environment in terms of their impact on the firm, including a clear identification of the desires and needs of the different publics that the company serves. In addition, the marketer should develop an in-depth understanding of the position, motivation, and capabilities of competing organizations, as well as these organizations' responses to the actions of other firms. All this knowledge is then used to develop competitive strategies that allow the firm to strengthen its position in the market. Manager's Corner 3.1 outlines some of the effects that one change in technology—the Internet— has on corporate marketing practice. Many more practical details of this effect can be explored in the case study on Amazon.com, which is presented at the end of this book.

---

1. S. Lieberson and J. F. O'Connor, "Leadership and Organizational Performance: A Study of Large Corporations," *American Sociological Review* 37 (April 1972): 117–130.
2. Arthur M. Schlesinger Jr., *The Cycles of American History* (Boston: Houghton Mifflin, 1986), xi.

Figure 3.1

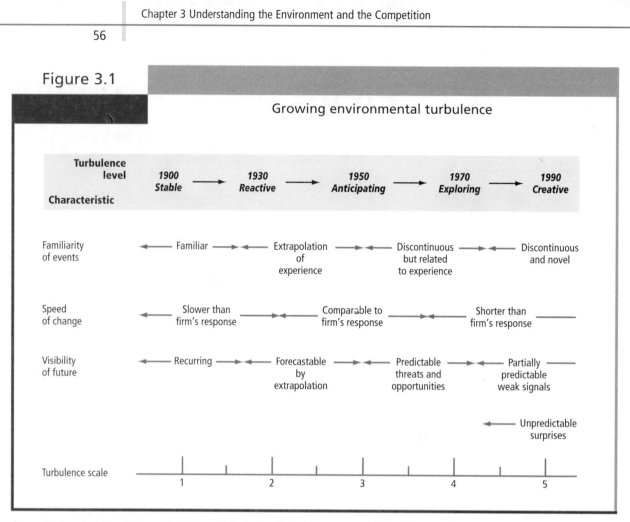

Source: H. Igor Ansoff and Edward J. McDonnell, *Implanting Strategic Management,* 2d ed. (Upper Saddle River, N.J.: Prentice Hall, 1990), 13. Reprinted by permission of Prentice Hall, Inc., Upper Saddle River, N.J.

Manager's Corner 3.1

The impact of the Internet

The information revolution promises to reverse many of the social trends that characterized the 20th century. Clearly, this has important implications for marketers. More splintered media are changing the rules for niche manufacturers and mass marketers alike. An example of this is the Internet.

The Internet empowers consumers. Already 16 percent of car buyers shop online before showing up at a dealership, arming themselves with information on dealer costs. The Internet represents the ultimate triumph of consumerism. Though the Internet still represents a minute fraction of total purchases, its growth is mind-boggling. A study by Jupiter Communications (www.jup.com) reported that 10 million people in the United States had bought something over the Internet in 1997 and that 17 million were expected to do so in 1999. In 1996 only 4 percent of Americans used the Internet every day. In 1999 the figure grew to 25 percent. There is no other channel where revenues are growing at anywhere near this rate.

Here are three ways in which the Internet is changing the market and how companies are rushing to take advantage of them. First, in the off-line world, the cost of directly comparing products or services was often high. Online, mediocrity will have no place to hide. CompareNet (www.compare.com) is typical of the new breed of neutral brokers, where consumers can compare products feature for feature and dollar for dollar. Skeptical customers can read unbiased product reviews and participate in online discussion groups. In this environment, it is hard to make a second-rate product a success. Second, before the Internet, goods and services were often planned and built far in advance of customer needs, and there was little customers could do to configure those products to their own requirements. Dell Computers (www.dell.com) allows customers to configure PCs and servers to their liking. With Dell, customers can specify their choice of sound card, video card, video monitor, speakers, and memory capacity from a pulldown menu on Dell's Web site. Dell Computers will even tell a customer if choosing a particular part would delay shipment or cause a compatibility problem with some other part.

It is no wonder that Dell is selling $6 million of products a day over its Web site and believes that 50 percent of its sales will be Web-based by the end of 2000. Third, no longer will geography tie down a company's aspirations or the scope of its market. Amazon.com spans the globe, selling 20 percent of its books to foreign destinations. A physical bookstore serves an area of a few square miles, and you cannot peruse its inventory without getting into your car. But whether you're in Albania or Zambia, Amazon.com is just a click away.

Sources: Gary Hamel and Jeff Sampler, "The E-Corporation: More Than Just Web-based, It's Building a New Industrial Order," *Fortune,* December 7, 1998, 80–92; David Soberman, "Into the Upside-down Age," *Financial Times,* November 9, 1998.

THEORETICAL FRAMEWORKS

Figure 3.2 likens the environment surrounding the firm to the layers of an onion. This model distinguishes between three different types of environments: the internal environment, which focuses on activities contained totally within the organization; the marketing environment, which is composed of those suppliers and competitors that have the most immediate impact on the marketing efforts of the organization; and the general external environment, which contains additional major factors affecting the performance of the organization. These external factors are often referred to as the STEP (Sociocultural, Technological, Economic, and Political/Legal) factors. We will look at each of these factors separately but also examine their interaction. In each case we will not only consider the issues involved but also search for the main drivers of change.

Figure 3.2

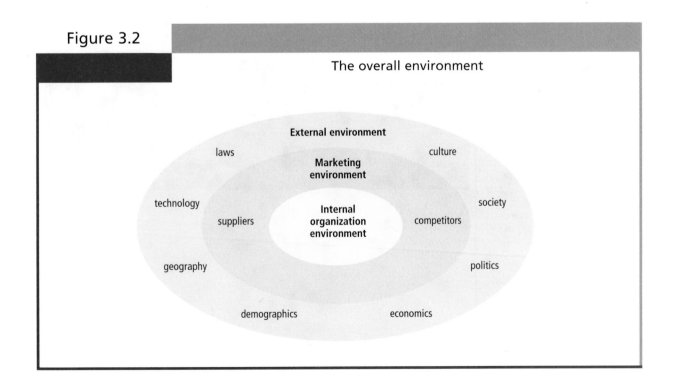

THE SOCIOCULTURAL ENVIRONMENT

Cultural traditions are not easily overturned, but over the years they can change quite significantly. In the latter half of the last century, for example, the role of women in society—and in particular their role at work—has changed dramatically. This change is obviously of considerable significance to those marketers supplying services to women: No longer can they assume that the average woman is a traditional housewife. The women's magazine industry, for example, was changed beyond all recognition due to these shifts.

Over the past decades, there have been major changes in several other areas of the sociocultural environment. For example, most industrialized nations have experienced a shift from a goods-producing to a service-based economy, and occupations have changed with the rise of professional and technical expertise. This shift is evoked in Exhibit 3.1. Innovations in communications and computer technology have further accelerated the pace of change by collapsing what is known as the **information float**; the amount of time information spends traveling through communication channels has been reduced from a few days for a letter to only a matter of seconds for electronic mail. As a result, responses are now expected almost instantaneously, leaving less time for contemplation and evaluation.

New information technologies are also giving birth to new activities, processes, and products. For example, Robert Reich, Secretary of Labor in the former Clinton Administration, noticed the creation of a new class of workers, the **symbolic analysts**, who are employed by firms that concentrate not on production but on analysis. Reich stated that in the "new world-economy, symbolic analysts hold a dominant position."[3] With this shift in focus, process innovation now has to be applied to learning in the same way it is applied to all other economic activities. Terms like *learning efficiency, effectiveness, retention,* and *relevance* are likely to emerge as key performance criteria. The use of new learning technologies, self-paced instruction, the tailoring of content to specific individual learning needs and the development of just-in-time learning approaches are likely to become commonplace in the business education industry.[4] Overall, these changes affect

Exhibit 3.1

Drastic changes in the socio-cultural environment have been felt across the globe in this century. Gender roles, industrialization levels, technological advances, and countless other innovations, evolutions, and paradigm shifts have resulted in a rate of change unequalled by any other historical moment. This ad for ABB evokes some of these changes.

3. Robert Reich, *The Work of Nations* (New York: Knopf, 1991), 244.
4. Peter Dickson and Michael R. Czinkota, "How the U.S. Can Be Number One Again: Resurrecting the Industrial Policy Debate," *Columbia Journal of World Business* 31 (fall 1996).

how people live, where they live, how they learn and work, and how they expect to satisfy their needs. Understanding these shifts is crucial for the formulation of winning market strategies.

Another important sociocultural change may be the move from a materialist to a postmaterialist society in industrialized nations. Inglehart and Appel postulate that "the most basic values that motivate the publics of Western societies have been changing gradually but steadily during recent decades." Newer generations appear to replace materialist values and economic and physical security with "Post-Materialist values that place greater emphasis on such goals as self-expression and belonging."[5]

Such a reprioritization of values may already be taking place around the globe. In some societies, the goals of financial progress and further improvements in the quantitative standard of living may well give way to new priorities. Such reorientations would result in major reversals of currently held business values. For instance, the abandonment of a consumption orientation would require a substantial readjustment of the activities of marketers. Consider, for example, Western Europe's growing concern about the **physical environment**. No longer are all corporate actions acceptable simply because they are profitable and legal. Customers demand that firms consider the environmental impact of their products and that they take measures to reduce harmful effects. If firms are not responsive to such expectations, they face declining customer interest in their products or, worse, active consumer boycotts of their goods. Some of the adjustments marketers have had to make in response to this reorientation include the production of more environmentally responsible products, less wasteful packaging, and the use of recyclable materials.

Among the most predictable changes are those resulting from **demography**. The western baby boom of the 1950s and 1960s and the subsequent dramatic decline in birth rates have produced very different cohorts of population, with accompanying changes in earnings and consumption. Any marketer is well advised to develop or acquire up-to-date demographic analyses. As an indication of some of the global trends that should be watched, Table 3.1 shows the rapidly increasing population domination by the less-developed world. Demographic shifts result in increasingly youthful populations in Asia and increasing aging populations in almost all western countries. Figure 3.3 shows the population variations of age groups in the United States. Differences in the size of age groups have major implications for consumption patterns as well as for social expenditures such as education, health care, and pensions. For example, the growth in demand for housing is likely to decrease, which will have repercussions for the furniture industry.

THE TECHNOLOGICAL ENVIRONMENT

The impact of changing technology is another major factor in the external environment. The rapid growth of fax machines, cellular telephones, and modems demonstrates the evolution of unrestricted communication flows. Data communications are exploding, propelled by the Internet and the rapid convergence of data and video with traditional voice traffic. Data have already overtaken voice on American telephone networks. At current growth rates, data traffic in 2004 will be 25 times heavier than voice traffic.[6] Concurrently the availability of information to be communicated is increasing dramatically. Since all this information includes details about lifestyles, opportunities, and aspirations, the implications of this technology revolution for marketers are major. For example, a growing

---

5. R. Inglehart and D. Appel, "The Rise of Postmaterialist Values and Changing Religious Orientations, Gender Rules and Sexual Norms," *International Journal of Public Opinion Research* 1, no. 1 (1989).
6. "And Then Came the Europeans," *Economist*, March 13, 1999, 73–74.

Table 3.1

World population by region and development category: 1950 to 2025 (predicted)

Region	1950	1960	1970	1980	1990	2000	2010	2025
WORLD	2,556	3,039	3,707	4,454	5,278	6,082	6,846	7,921
Less-Developed Countries	1,749	2,129	2,703	3,372	4,136	4,901	5,639	6,708
More-Developed Countries	807	911	1,004	1,081	1,142	1,181	1,207	1,213
AFRICA	228	283	360	468	621	798	995	1,323
Sub-Saharan Africa	184	227	289	378	502	652	820	1,108
North Africa	44	56	71	90	119	146	175	216
NEAR EAST	44	57	75	101	135	175	223	307
ASIA	1,368	1,628	2,038	2,498	2,987	3,451	3,863	4,398
LATIN AMERICA AND THE CARIBBEAN	166	218	286	362	443	523	596	695
EUROPE AND THE NEW INDEPENDENT STATES	572	639	703	750	787	799	802	786
Western Europe	304	326	352	367	375	386	385	366
Eastern Europe	88	100	108	117	122	122	124	121
New Independent States	180	214	242	266	289	290	293	298
NORTH AMERICA	166	199	227	252	278	306	332	374
OCEANIA	12	16	19	23	27	30	34	39

Sources: Direct access to this table and the International Data Base is available through the Internet at www.census.gov/ipc/www; *World Population Profile: 1998,* U.S. Bureau of the Census, U. S. Government Printing Office, Washington, D.C., 1999: A3.

Figure 3.3

Population variations in U.S. age groups

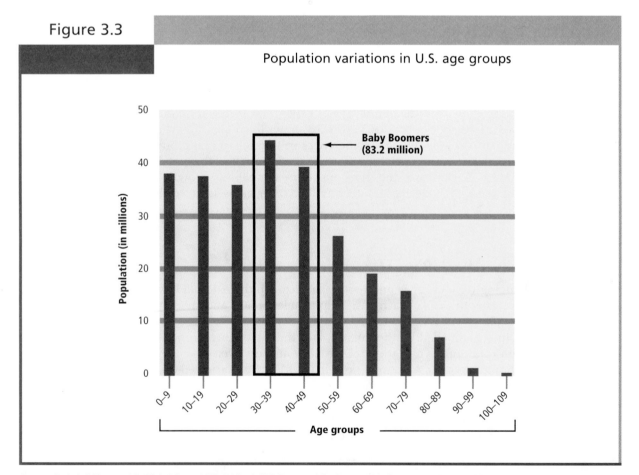

Source: *Statistical Abstract of the United States: 1998,* 118th ed., U.S. Bureau of the Census, U.S. Government Printing Office, Washington, D.C., 1998: 15–16.

global awareness of products is likely to ease international product introductions. At the same time, such greater ease will also encourage the emergence of greater global competition for market share both at home and abroad.

THE IMPACT OF INFORMATION TECHNOLOGY ON MARKETERS.   The use of electronic data interchange (EDI), merchandise scanning, and increased data sharing is restructuring the ways firms do business. Technology affects the entire marketing strategy framework and covers the relationships with suppliers and manufacturers, the internal organization of the firm, and the firm's interaction with its customers. Even though the technology has been available for some time, we are entering a new era in terms of its application. As Bill Gates, Chairman and CEO of Microsoft Corporation, stated, "The tools and connectivity of the **digital age** now give us a way to easily obtain, share, and act on information in new and remarkable ways. For the first time, all kinds of information—numbers, text, sound, video—can be put into a digital form that any computer can store, process, and forward. Standard hardware combined with a standard software platform has created economies of scale that make powerful computing solutions available inexpensively to companies of all sizes. And the 'personal' in personal computer means that individual knowledge workers have a powerful tool for analyzing and using the information delivered by these solutions."[7] Because much of marketing is a dialogue, and information technology both enhances and restructures the existing forms of communication, marketers will be affected by information innovations more than ever before.

www.microsoft.com

> marketers will be affected by information innovations more than ever before.

UPSTREAM RELATIONSHIPS.   The key to technology application rests with the building of information exchange relationships that convey vital knowledge accurately and rapidly and enable the recipients of the knowledge to respond by adapting their activities to the market realities. The vast majority of supermarkets and drugstores in the United States already uses electronic data entry and shares data with vendors in order to develop new models of production.[8] For example, The Limited retail chain set up **electronic data interchange** (EDI) links with its clothes makers in Hong Kong. Computer-aided design and air freight have combined to reduce the lag between order and delivery to three weeks instead of the nine months once standard for department stores. The system also allows The Limited to adjust the sizes, colors, and patterns of its collections in response to actual sales, rather than relying purely on its buyers' intuition.[9] Similarly, Wal-Mart and Procter & Gamble have developed an EDI linkage that allows P&G to receive information on store sales directly from Wal-Mart's scanner system. Thus P&G can plan production and delivery to precisely match customer shopping habits.[10] Some firms have gone even further in their upstream relationships by fully integrating some marketing aspects with their vendors. For example, Ahold Zaandam in the Netherlands has made one of its vendors, Heineken, fully responsible for maintaining supplies at its warehouses and for determining when and how to make its deliveries. As a result, the firm holds as little as four hours' demand worth of inventory at the warehouse.[11]

www.wal-mart.com
www.pg.com

www.heineken.com

7. Bill Gates, *Business @ The Speed of Thought* (New York: Warner Books, 1999), xv.

8. "The Impact of Information Technologies," *Chain Store Age Executive* 69, no. 5 (1993): 14.

9. "Stores of Value," *Economist,* March 4, 1995, R5.

10. Eric K. Clemons and Michael C. Row, "Information, Power, and Control of the Distribution Channel: Wisdom from Wharton," *Chief Executive* 85 (May 1993): 64.

11. James Fallon, "U.K. Is Seen Ahead in ECR, Technology: Efficient Consumer Response," *Supermarket News,* October 17, 1994, 11.

The use of information technology has also had distinct implications for the power relationships between manufacturers and their channel members. Increasingly, the point of purchase represents a crucial node of information. This is where critical information is accumulated regarding consumer behavior and promotional response. The available information lets retailers know what they are selling in each of their stores, how much money they are making on each sale, and who their customers are. Retailers no longer need to be saddled with stock that does not sell or run out of items that customers want to buy.[12] Consequently, retailers have amassed so much power over manufacturers and other supply chain members that they can dictate the structure of the relationships and are able to force their vendors to either implement and adapt to information systems or lose the account. In light of the global sourcing policies of corporations, participation of vendors in information systems will become increasingly important for manufacturers around the world. Firms in countries that are not able to provide an adequate information infrastructure will be severely handicapped in their ability to compete internationally.

> the point of purchase **represents a crucial node** of information

INTERNAL EFFECTS OF INFORMATION TECHNOLOGY. The information revolution also has major effects on the internal operations of firms. Leading-edge users of technology are able to develop cost advantages that permit them to assume leadership positions in their industry. For example, Tesco, the second largest food retailer in the United Kingdom, has used information technology to control its ordering and stocking levels, with the following results:

www.tesco.co.uk

- Major reduction of total stocks at its distribution centers
- Lead times of one to two days on fresh foods
- Out-of-stock conditions reduced by 30 percent
- Reduction of storage space from 40 percent to 20 percent of total store floor space
- Productivity benefits of more than $31.7 million[13]

Such improvements are at the core of developing a position of strategic advantage and are therefore crucial to the marketer. These types of improvements enabled Wal-Mart to surge ahead of its competitors Kmart and Sears to become the leading retailer in the United States.

www.wal-mart.com
www.kmart.com
www.sears.com

Information also has an effect on the structure of firms and their hierarchies. For example, with better information flow, smaller organizations may be able to achieve economies of scale more quickly. In larger organizations, information availability can transform corporate structure by encouraging horizontal communications—for example, via electronic mail—and reducing the need for the traditional hierarchical organizational structure. New ways of handling information can also be decisive in determining the location of the firm's activities. For example, the ability to conduct banking via automatic teller machines has enabled financial institutions to greatly expand their reach of customers. With the increasing use of banking by telephone, this expansion will also diminish the importance and value of old-fashioned bank buildings.

INFORMATION TECHNOLOGY AND THE CUSTOMER. Technology also permits marketers to work with customers in more efficient ways. By linking pur-

---

12. "Change at the Check-out," *Economist*, March 4, 1995, R3.
13. Fallon, "U.K. Is Seen Ahead in ECR, Technology."

chases with specific customers, marketers can develop promotional programs based on specific purchase behavior. At the checkout point, for example, coupons can be automatically issued based on the scanned purchases. A customer who purchases Coke may receive a coupon to try Pepsi next time; a customer who buys Pampers may get a coupon for baby food. Similarly, by using frequent shopper cards, customers can be identified and promotions can be targeted. For example, a family with a child can receive information on and coupons for diapers, baby formula, or breakfast cereal depending on the age of the child.[14] Alternatively, given the proper pieces of information, mail-order companies can compose individual catalogs based on specific customer profiles.[15] Information will also offer major new opportunities for customers. For example, television shopping decreases the need to visit stores, and online product information makes price comparisons easier and reduces the ability of marketers to differentiate prices based on location. Simply put, information provides greater transparency of the market and therefore enhances the customer's ability to make better decisions.

www.coke.com
www.pepsiworld.com
www.pampers.com

> Information provides greater **transparency of the market and enhances** the customer's ability to make better decisions.

OTHER TECHNOLOGY FACTORS. Information is not the only technology driver, of course. The development of superconductive materials and composite materials has made progress possible in fields such as transportation and electric power, pushing the frontiers of human activity into yet unexplored areas such as outer space and the depths of the oceans. Concerns about the environment are leading to new perspectives on products, production processes, and consumption and are likely to lead to new technologies that will provide substitute products and enhanced environmental "friendliness." The development of biotechnology is already leading to revolutionary progress not only in agriculture, medicine, and chemistry, but also in manufacturing systems.[16] For example, California-based Calgene (part of the Monsanto Company) has planted fields of cotton that are already colored red, blue, black, and tan by the use of color-producing bacteria rather than toxic dyes. IBG of Baton Rouge, Louisiana, has cultivated a fat-eating strain of bacteria to produce McFree, which is sold to the McDonald's Corporation to clean french-fry fat from restaurant drains. Proteins are beginning to be used to "stone wash" blue jeans and chinos.[17]

www.monsanto.com

www.mcdonalds.com

All these changes in technology are likely to introduce major discontinuities into the marketer's life. Although no one can foresee all changes, the marketer must at least be open-minded enough to be ready for them. In addition, it is important to avoid four common errors that can lead to the downfall of the firm:

- The belief that an evolutionary approach to technology will be enough
- The assumption that there will be ample early warning about a coming discontinuity
- The expectation that customer contact and input is sufficient preparation for change (customers may well be wrong in predicting what they want, particularly when new technology is concerned)
- The conviction that one's firm can always react fast enough to change[18]

14. Clemons and Row, "Information, Power, and Control of the Distribution Channel."
15. Laura Mazur, "Evolution in the Workplace," *Marketing*, September 15, 1994, vi.
16. Shinji Fukukawa, *The Future of U.S.-Japan Relationship and Its Contribution to New Globalism* (Tokyo: Ministry of International Trade and Industry, 1989), 10–11.
17. Kathleen Day, "Biotech's Other Benefits," *Washington Post*, August 27, 1995, H1.
18. Richard N. Foster, *Innovation: The Attacker's Advantage* (New York: Summit Books, 1986), 35.

THE ECONOMIC ENVIRONMENT

Although the market is clearly at the heart of marketing, it is also central to economic theory and to the basic philosophy of capitalism. The way in which each of these two disciplines approaches the concept of the market is, however, quite different.

Modern microeconomics theory has no problem describing the activities of the perfect firm. This ideal organization is involved in perfect competition, with price as the one factor to be manipulated in the many economic equations used to describe that firm. All decisions are made rationally, based on profit, and all the relationships are exactly known and can be plotted with definitive graphs.

Yet microeconomists find considerable difficulty dealing with imperfect competition, since no generally accepted model for representing this state has yet emerged. Worse still, particularly in a climate of uncertainty, microeconomics recognizes, but cannot easily handle those relationships that do not fit neatly into exact equations. As the economist John Kenneth Galbraith has observed, management decision making is often anything but rational. It is frequently not designed to achieve the simple monetary outcomes that are the staple of economics; instead it reflects more complex motivations.[19] With an increase in conflicting priorities within and between societies, this complexity appears to be on the rise.

Marketing, conversely, thrives on precisely these elements, which constitute the real business world. Thus the aim of every brand manager is to make competition ever more imperfect, aiming for the ideal brand that holds a monopoly over its customers, who will stridently demand their favorite brand of cola or beer and reject any alternatives. In this environment the intangible, and often seemingly irrational, needs and wants of the consumer predominate. The tools of marketing are frequently the creative approaches used to formulate the most attractive good or service and to develop the most effective promotions. Having to compete on price alone, as many microeconomists wish, is usually seen as defeat by such marketers.

The marketer is also affected by shifting economic factors, primarily **globalization**, regional economic integration, and exchange rates. World markets today are more intertwined than ever before. In the past two decades, world trade has expanded from $200 billion a year to more than $6.3 trillion.[20] As a result, a global reorientation of production strategies has taken place. For example, only a few

> competition does not emanate only from established domestic competitors, but can appear overnight from foreign shores.

decades ago, it would have been thought impossible to produce parts for a car in more than one country, assemble the car in yet another nation, and sell it in still other countries. But such global investment strategies, coupled with production and distribution sharing, are occurring with increasing frequency. In the late 1990s, the total number of transnational corporations—firms that own or control production or service facilities outside the country in which they are based—exceeded 53,000, with 450,000 affiliates around the world. The global sales for foreign affiliates of multinationals are estimated at $9.5 trillion, more than 50 percent greater than the volume of world trade.[21] The 600 largest multinationals are estimated to generate between one-fifth and one-fourth of the value added in the global production of goods and services.[22] In addition, the ownership of **multinational corporations** is changing dramatically. In the 1970s, half of all

19. John Kenneth Galbraith, *The New Industrial State* (Boston: Houghton Mifflin, 1967), 83.
20. World Trade Organization, "International Trade," www.wto.org, accessed January 1999.
21. United Nations, *World Investment Report, 1998: Trends and Determinants* (New York: United Nations, 1998), xvii.
22. "Perspectives: The Heart of the New World Economy," *Financial Times*, October 1, 1997, 12.

multinational corporations were based in the United States or Britain. At the end of the century, there are 2,728 companies around the globe with a capitalization of $1 billion or more. Of these, 1,634 are headquartered outside of the United States.[23] Marketers must therefore broaden their horizons when looking at market opportunities and threats. A firm's customer base is no longer restricted to one home country, but can be found around the world; likewise, competition does not emanate only from established domestic competitors, but can appear overnight from foreign shores.

Regional **economic integration** is another major phenomenon affecting the marketer. Increasingly, countries engage in economic cooperation to use their respective resources more efficiently and to provide larger markets for member-country producers. Integration efforts have facilitated marketing activities across borders but, on occasion, inhibited them between trading blocs. The emergence of regional economic agreements such as the European Union; the North American Free Trade Agreement (NAFTA) between the United States, Mexico, and Canada; Mercosur in South America; and ASEAN in Asia are profoundly changing the landscape for the marketer. Often these changes mean that one has to do business within a given bloc, mainly through direct investment, in order to remain competitive. At the same time, global integration has also successfully reduced red tape, documentation hassles, and transportation difficulties. Harmonization of rules and standards have made the achievement of economies of scale easier. By reducing the barriers between markets, such integration has also increased the levels of efficiency and competition—a boon for customers and for marketers on the cutting edge but a bane of traditionalists who long to keep doing things the old-fashioned way.

www.nafta.org
www.mercosur.org

The economic environment has also been greatly affected by the powerful effects of exchange rates. Traditionally, exchange rates were mainly the consequence of trade flows between nations and were relatively stable in the short and medium term. But because of liberalized **currency flows** around the world, **exchange rates** today have taken on a power of their own and have begun to determine the level of trade between nations. International capital flows in 1998 of more than $1.5 trillion per day[24] greatly exceeded the reserves of any central bank and made exchange rates much more volatile. For example, in December of 1994, within a mere week the value of the Mexican peso dropped by more than half. Such rapid changes in currency value have a major effect on the marketer, particularly when doing business internationally. Long-term strategic plans can be ruined if major shifts in exchange rates occur. Viable trade relations or investment projects may have to be shifted or even abandoned because of exchange rate effects. For example, the entire business strategy of Airbus Industry was placed at risk because of the decline in the value of the dollar. The consortium quoted the sales price of its airplanes in dollars but had to pay for production inputs in deutsche mark, francs, and pesetas. When the underlying assumption of an exchange rate of 2 mark to the dollar met the market reality of a value of less than 1.40 mark per dollar in the early 1990s, it became impossible to produce and sell the planes at a profit.

www.airbus.com

THE POLITICAL AND LEGAL ENVIRONMENT

Politics and laws play a critical role in marketing. Even the best-laid plans can go awry as a result of unexpected political or legal influences, and the failure to anticipate these factors can be the undoing of an otherwise successful venture. Governments affect firms through their legislation and regulations, which might

---

23. Leila Heckman and Holly Sze, Solomon Smith Barney Research, May 1999.
24. Bank for International Settlements, *Central Bank Survey of Foreign Exchange and Derivatives Market Activity, 1998* (Basle: BIS, 1999).

specify anything from the ingredients that firms may put into their products to the buildings in which their employees may work. Interest groups can place pressure on firms and alter corporate activities by shaping selective dimensions of the way the public sees the firm, for example its environmental responsibility or its position towards child labor. In addition, other stakeholders can demand the acceptance of their views by the firm's management.

LAWS AND REGULATIONS.   Many laws and regulations may not be designed specifically to address marketing issues, yet they can have a major impact on a firm's opportunities. Minimum wage legislation, for example, affects the international competitiveness of any firm using production processes that are highly labor intensive. Similarly, the cost of adhering to safety regulations may significantly affect the pricing policies of firms. **Intellectual property rights** legislation and the extent of its enforcement may either allow a firm to recoup its investment into innovation or deprive it of its rightful returns, thereby determining the firm's ability to invest in further research and development to create new products. In addition, firms are often affected by administrative regulations that are developed by agencies in order to implement broader laws, particularly in the international arena. For example, the case "Water from Iceland," presented at the end of this book, shows how federal and local regulations can affect the import of water into the United States.

> ## Most aspects of
> ## marketing transactions are covered
> ## by one or another form of legislation

Most aspects of marketing transactions are covered by one or another form of legislation, and at least by contract law. The marketing manager must be aware of the legal aspects that directly affect the firm. These effects vary from industry to industry and from country to country. The chemical industry, for instance, is driven by legislation on safety, whereas financial services providers may operate under the jurisdiction of the Interstate Banking Act. Legal issues must be handled expertly, because only some of the vast array of laws affect individual industries or organizations in specific countries, and many of them change quite rapidly. The recent worldwide move to deregulation, for example, has had major implications for organizations in areas as diverse as financial services and airline operation. Both of these industries have seen many new entrants, while a significant number of their traditional members have gone out of business.

Because political viewpoints can be modified or even reversed, and new laws can supersede old ones, existing legal and regulatory restraints need not always be accepted. To achieve change, however, there must be some impetus for it, such as the clamors of a constituency. Otherwise, systemic inertia is likely to allow the status quo to prevail. In dealing with onerous laws, the marketer has various options. One is to simply ignore prevailing rules and expect to get away with it. This is a high-risk strategy because of the possibility of objection and even prosecution. A second, traditional option is to accept all existing rules. The drawback to this option is, of course, the cost and opportunity loss due to restrictive rules. A third option involves the development of **coalitions** or **constituencies** with like interests that can motivate legislators and politicians to consider and ultimately implement change. This option can be pursued in various ways. The marketer can explain the employment and economic effects of certain laws and regulations and demonstrate the benefits of change. The picture can then be enlarged by including indirect linkages; for example, suppliers, customers, and distributors can be asked to participate in demonstrating the benefit of change to political decision makers. Developing such coalitions is not an easy task, and companies often seek assistance in effectively influencing the government decision-making process. Such help is particularly beneficial when narrow economic objectives or single-issue campaigns are needed. Typical providers of this assistance are **lobbyists**, well-connected individuals and firms that can provide access to policymakers and legislators.

Foreign countries and companies have been particularly effective in their lobbying efforts in the United States. For example, the U.S. Department of Justice reports that over 2,000 lobbyists representing foreign principals have registered with the department.[25] As an example, Brazil alone has held on average nearly a dozen contracts per year with U.S. firms covering trade issues. Brazilian citrus exporters and computer manufacturers have hired U.S. legal public relations firms to provide them with information on relevant U.S. legislative activity. Likewise, the Banco do Brasil lobbied for the restructuring of Brazilian debt and favorable banking regulations. A crucial factor in successful lobbying, however, is the involvement of citizens and companies. Manager's Corner 3.2 explains how one country has gained such participation, and Exhibit 3.2 shows the successful results of Compaq's lobbying efforts in China.

www.usdoj.gov

Manager's Corner 3.2

Backbone of the new China lobby: U.S. firms

Every year, the U.S. government reviews whether China's Most Favored Nation (MFN) status should be extended. Since this status conveys the benefit of low tariffs on Chinese exports, one would expect the Chinese government to be the principal lobbyist in Washington. However, as the MFN debate showed, it was U.S. corporations that played the leading role. Because China is the fastest-growing major market for U.S. exports, some U.S. companies anticipate potentially tremendous business opportunities. They made sure to argue their case for keeping low tariffs for Chinese exports, which Beijing has demanded as a condition for buying American products.

Corporations involved in lobbying usually focus their efforts on the issue of U.S. jobs. According to one U.S. official involved, "We're dealing directly with CEOs, who are dealing with opportunities they can grasp. You're not talking about a theoretical China market—you're talking about jobs next year." CEOs from such giants as Boeing and Motorola met with President Clinton on China's importance to their industries. Other *Fortune* 500 executives visited the Departments of Commerce and State, bringing with them estimates that exports to China create 157,000 U.S. jobs. Retail footwear lobbyists distributed results of a study showing that cheap imported shoes from China save U.S. consumers $16 billion a year; they then proceeded to flood the White House with letters from thousands of shoe store managers pleading for MFN's extension.

Because relations between the two countries were normalized in 1979, China has not had a strong lobbying presence in Washington. According to U.S. analysts, the real power of the China lobby comes from a strategy dating from imperial times: "Use barbarians to control barbarians." Beijing will open the trade door just enough to show the profitability of the Chinese market. It is then up to the profit seekers to wield whatever political influence is needed to keep the door open. Beijing certainly knows how to set business forces in motion. During the 1993 MFN debate, Chinese trade delegations in the United States went on a well-publicized, cross-country shopping spree. "China has been very effective in using its market opening to get maximum leverage over the American business community, motivating it to work their own government on MFN and other trade issues," says a former assistant to President Bush. Threats of cancellation of orders or a loss of future deals if MFN is not renewed are provided regularly by China, making it clear that it is in an enlightened American company's best interest to press the government to approve MFN without conditions.

Source: Michael Weisskopf, "Backbone of the New China Lobby: U.S. Firms," *Washington Post*, June 14, 1993, A1.

25. www.usdoj.gov.

Exhibit 3.2

One way of enhancing lobbying efforts in foreign countries is to sponsor, underwrite, or contribute to social programs. Compaq has done just that. Pictured here is Eckhard Pfeiffer, CEO and president of Compaq Computer Corporation, with Zhang Ruisi, age 12, at the opening of a Compaq Internet classroom in a Beijing youth center. Compaq also launched Beijing's first online bookstore as part of a jointly developed project by Compaq China and China Information Highway Corporation (CIHC).

Although representation of the firm's interests to government decision makers and legislators is entirely appropriate, the marketer must also consider that major questions can be raised if such representation becomes very strong. In such instances, short-term gains may be far outweighed by long-term negative repercussions if the marketer is perceived as exerting too much political influence.

INTEREST GROUPS. Political action is not confined just to governments and legislatures; it can result from other groups as well. Pressure groups campaign often to change legislation but also work to change the public's awareness and buying habits. For example, in the mid 1990s, after negotiating governmental permission, Shell Oil company planned to dump a massive oil-storage buoy in the Atlantic Ocean. A massive publicity effort by Greenpeace, however, led millions of consumers to boycott Shell's gasoline stations. Shell therefore had to abandon its plans.[26]

www.shell.com
www.greenpeace.org

Firms themselves may also join pressure groups to force the government to protect their entrenched positions, and they are often successful. It might be thought that only the larger organizations are the direct targets of pressure groups or have the resources to be involved in pressure groups themselves, but it is just as important that the smaller organizations understand that the number of interest groups and nongovernmental organizations (NGOs) is rising around the world. Some groups focus on issues, others on organizations or constituents. For example, the Sierra Club and Greenpeace concentrate on the environment, Transparency International scrutinizes corporate behavior, while the AFL-CIO focuses on worker rights around the world. Exhibit 3.3 shows Greenpeace demonstrators in Brazil protesting against climbing fossil fuel usage and the effects of global warming. Common to all groups are their broad reach and use of very sophisticated information and communication tools to affect the political and economic process. Defending an organization against pressure groups requires skill and tact. Most important, it requires a sound understanding of their viewpoint and, to be most effective, a sympathetic approach. It is rarely possible to defeat such groups head-on without incurring heavy costs; it may be much more realistic to focus them on solutions that are attractive to them and preferable to the organization.

www.sierraclub.org
www.transparency.de
www.aflcio.org

26. "Oil Platforms: Hollow Shell," *Economist*, June 24, 1995, 76.

Exhibit 3.3

Interest groups are an influential force in the external marketing environment. Often able to garner support very quickly, special interest groups can have a dramatic impact on a company's marketing efforts. The environmental group Greenpeace is known for relentlessly pursuing companies perceived as violating environmental laws and ignoring environmental concerns. Here, members stage a demonstration in front of Royal Dutch Shell Oil company headquarters in Buenos Aires.

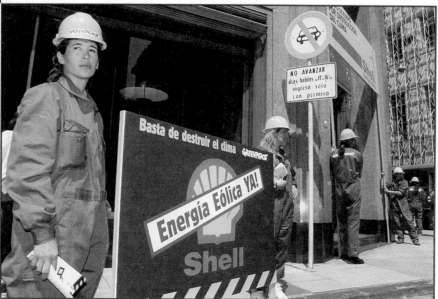

MULTIPLE STAKEHOLDERS. A number of different groups can also claim an interest or stake in the organization. The public of an organization is defined as "any group which has an actual or potential interest or impact on an organization's ability to achieve its objectives."[27]

Some believe that only the owners are legitimately entitled to an interest in what the organization does. But today the belief that "the fundamental goal of all business is to maximize shareholder value" may be either commonplace or controversial, depending on one's location. For example, in the United States, management is expected to achieve maximum shareholder value. If this is not the case, activist shareholders may exert pressure or even launch a hostile takeover bid. In many other countries, however, legislation and societal expectations have brought about greater consideration of different stakeholder positions. Maximizing shareholder value is often seen as short-sighted, inefficient, simplistic, and even antisocial.[28] Such a perspective, of course, brings trade-offs that shift resources from one group to another. For example, in Japan the social desirability and acceptance of small retail stores run by pensioners have resulted in a very complex distribution system that in turn results in relatively high consumer prices.[29] In Germany, employees have the right to share in the decision making of firms and elect half of the representatives of the company's supervisory board directly. **Worker's councils** composed of nonexecutive employees have the power to share decisions in personnel and social matters.[30]

Clearly, the actions of marketers are affected by the degree to which different stakeholders must be considered. However, such consideration should be taken into account even when not mandated by law or expected by society. Good marketing requires an understanding of and responsiveness to the local environment. Nevertheless, an increasingly global marketplace for financial resources will encourage investment flows to those areas, countries, and firms where the returns

---

27. R. F. Lusch and V. N. Lusch, *Principles of Marketing* (Boston: Kent, 1987).
28. Thomas E. Copeland, "Why Value Value?" *The McKinsey Quarterly* 4 (September 1994): 97.
29. Michael R. Czinkota and Jon Woronoff, *Unlocking Japan's Markets*, 2d ed. (Rutland, Vt.: Charles E. Tuttle, 1993), 25 ff.
30. Copeland, "Why Value Value?"

are greatest. The marketer must therefore strike a balance by focusing on the shareholders—the providers of capital—while conducting good marketing with the divergent publics.

Overall, as this environmental analysis has shown, we are living in a time of very rapid and significant change. Economically advanced nations seem to be approaching a historic turning point. The 200-year-old industrial era is winding down, but the postindustrial era has not yet come into focus. Coinciding with the coming of the postindustrial era is a shift in paradigm. How we think of the world largely shapes how we behave in it. There are ample signs in all the major institutions that new paradigms are being developed.[31] The increasing scale of the discontinuous changes means that marketers must be ever more sensitive to these potential, dramatic shifts in the environment. They must also develop the ability, based on adequate resources and prior planning, to cope with such changes.

> There are ample signs in all the major institutions that new paradigms are being developed.

ENVIRONMENTAL ANALYSIS

To cope with all the changes in its external environment, the firm must first discover what opportunities and threats this environment holds for the organization. This process requires an environmental analysis. Three main mechanisms that serve to conduct such an analysis are environmental scanning, Delphi studies, and scenario building.

ENVIRONMENTAL SCANNING

To identify changes in the business environment, corporations need to track new developments and obtain continual updates. Some organizations have formed environmental scanning groups to carry out this task. They receive ongoing information on political, social, and economic affairs; on changes of attitudes held by public institutions and private citizens; and on possible upcoming alterations in markets. Environmental scanning models can stretch the minds of managers to incorporate new dimensions, assist in the development of broad strategies and long-term policies, and help in formulating action plans and operating programs.

Obviously, the precision required for environmental scanning varies with its purpose. Whether the information is to be used for mind stretching or for budgeting, for example, must be taken into account when constructing the framework and variables that will enter the scanning process. The more immediate and precise the exercise is to be in its application within the corporation, the greater the need for detailed information. At the same time, such heightened precision may lessen the utility of environmental scanning for the strategic corporate purpose, which is more long-term in its orientation.

Environmental scanning can be performed in various ways. One method consists of obtaining factual input regarding many variables. For example, the International Data Base (IDB) of the U.S. Census Bureau collects, evaluates, and compares a wide variety of demographic, social, and economic characteristics of countries all over the world. Estimates are developed particularly on economic variables such as labor force statistics, GNP, and income statistics, but also on health and nutrition variables. Similar factual information can be obtained from organizations such as the World Bank or the United Nations.

www.census.gov/ipc
/www/idbnew.html
www.worldbank.org
/data/
www.un.org/Depts/unsd
/social/main.htm

---

31. L. J. Rosenberg, "Revisioning Marketing: Management for the New Paradigm Era," in *Changing the Course of Marketing: Alternative Paradigms for Widening Marketing Theory*, Supplement 2 (Greenwich, Conn.: JAI Press, 1985).

Frequently, corporations believe that such factual data alone are insufficient for their information needs. Particularly for forecasting future developments, other methods are used to capture underlying dimensions of social change. One significant method is **content analysis.** This technique investigates the content of communication in a society and entails literally counting the number of times preselected words, themes, symbols, or pictures appear in a given medium. It can be used productively in marketing to monitor the social, economic, cultural, and technological environment in which the organization is operating. The use of content analysis is facilitated by tools such as optical scanners and software packages that can accommodate texts in Chinese, Japanese, Hebrew, Korean, and Arabic.[32] By attempting to identify trendsetting events, corporations can pinpoint upcoming changes in their line of business as well as new opportunities. Marketing in Action 3.1 is an example of successful environmental scanning.

By monitoring the use of the names of corporate products in online chat groups, a firm can determine how interested and aware the public is about a product, how much such a product is part of the lives of individuals, how and where these individuals live, and what complaints users are sharing with each other. Such information can then be useful not only in developing product improvements but also in developing entire new product families and marketing strategies. For example, a growing mention of fruit-enhanced cereal by inner-city parents may lead to the rethinking of the advertising theme and focus by a cereal producer.

Environmental scanning is conducted by a variety of groups within and outside of the corporation. Frequently, small corporate staffs are created at headquarters to coordinate the information flow, but subsidiary staff can be used to provide occasional intelligence reports. Groups of volunteers are also formed to gather and analyze information and feed individual analyses back to corporate

---

Marketing in Action 3.1

Mannesmann and the global economy—from tubes to telecom

A German-based company, Mannesmann (www.mannesmann.com) operates in four core business sectors: engineering, automotive, telecommunications, and tubes. The company has a workforce of 116,000 employees (over one third of whom are based outside of Germany) and had annual sales of DM 37.3 billion in 1998. Founded over 100 years ago, the company was the first to produce steel tubes by rolling a solid ingot.

In 1994 the company identified telecommunications as the growth market of the future. Since the company began to seriously transform itself from a manufacturer to a service provider, it has attained the number two position in both the German and Italian telecommunications marketplaces. As a result, the company's share price rose 116 percent in 1998.

Mannesmann's feat was accomplished in a German economy plagued with high unemployment and declining growth. However, Germany's economic decline may be masking several strong points within the German business market: (1) the stock market has doubled, (2) use of venture capital has tripled, (3) ROE is at record highs, (4) corporate profits are at a decade high, and (5) the number of mergers and acquisitions has risen dramatically.

As Mannesmann keeps pace with changes in both the German and worldwide markets and as German businesses reinvent themselves, company executives need to continually evaluate its business sectors. With the tubes business contributing only 12 percent of group sales (compared to 36 percent for engineering, 28 percent for automotive, and 24 percent for telecommunications), where does it fit in Mannesmann's competitive strategy? Should the company maintain its status as a conglomerate in the rapidly changing German business environment?

Sources: www.mannesmann.com; Cait Murphy, "Will the Future Belong to Germany?" *Fortune*, August 2, 1999, 129–136.

---

32. David R. Wheeler, "Content Analysis: An Analytical Technique for International Marketing Research," *International Marketing Review* 5 (winter 1988): 34–40.

headquarters, where they serve as input into the "big picture." Increasingly, large corporations also offer services in environmental scanning to outsiders. In this way, profits can be made from an in-house activity that has to be conducted anyway.

Typically, environmental scanning is designed primarily to aid the strategic planning process rather than the tactical activities of the corporation. A survey of corporate environmental scanning activities found that CEOs who experience greater environmental uncertainty tend to do more scanning. They are most interested in keeping themselves informed about their customers, regulations, and the competition.[33] Although environmental scanning is perceived by many corporations as quite valuable for the corporate planning process, there are dissenting voices. For example, it has been noted by researchers that "in those constructs and frameworks where the environment has been given primary consideration, there has been a tendency for the approach to become so global that studies tend to become shallow and diffuse, or impractical if pursued in sufficient depth."[34] Obviously, this trade-off between the breadth and the depth of information presents a major challenge. However, the ever-increasing capabilities of data processing may at least reduce the scope of the problem. Possibly the simplest and best advice is for all employees to cultivate a deep, ongoing curiosity about the external world, coupled with an ability to recognize which signals, from the mass of data that arrive every day, are relevant and important to the future of the organization.

Delphi Studies

To enrich the information obtained from factual data, corporations also resort to the use of creative and highly qualitative data-gathering methods, such as **Delphi studies**. These studies are particularly useful because they are "a means for aggregating the judgments of a number of experts who cannot come together physically."[35] This type of research approach clearly aims at qualitative rather than quantitative measures by collecting the information of a group of experts. It seeks to obtain answers from the few who know instead of the average responses of many with only limited knowledge.

Typically Delphi studies are carried out with groups of about 30 well-chosen participants who possess particular in-depth expertise in an area of concern, such as future developments in the marketing environment. These participants are asked, via mail, fax, or e-mail, to identify the major issues in an area—say, the effect of concerns about the physical environment on packaging. They are also requested to rank their statements according to importance and to explain the rationale behind the order. Next, the aggregated information is returned to all participants, who are encouraged to clearly state their agreements or disagreements with the various rank orders and comments. Statements can be challenged, and in another round, participants can respond to the challenges. After several rounds of challenge and response, a reasonably coherent consensus is developed.

The Delphi technique is particularly valuable because it is able to bridge large distances and therefore makes individuals quite accessible at a reasonable cost. It does not suffer from lack of interaction among the participants, which is the drawback of ordinary mail investigations. One problem with the technique is that it requires several iterations, so much time may elapse before the infor-

---

33. Ethel Auster and Chun Wei Choo, "CEOs, Information, and Decision Making: Scanning the Environment for Strategic Advantage," *Library Trends* 43, no. 2 (1994): 38.

34. Lothar G. Winter and Charles R. Prohaska, "Methodological Problems in the Comparative Analysis on International Marketing System," *Journal of the Academy of Marketing Science* 11 (fall 1983): 421.

35. Andre Delbecq, Andrew H. Van de Ven, and David H. Gustafson, *Group Techniques for Program Planning* (Glenview, Ill.: Scott, Foresman, 1975), 83.

mation is obtained. Moreover, substantial effort must be expended in selecting the appropriate participants and in motivating them to participate in this exercise with enthusiasm and continuity. When obtained on a regular basis, Delphi information can provide crucial augmentation to the factual data available to the marketer.

SCENARIO BUILDING

For information enrichment purposes, some companies use scenario analysis. The principal method here is to have a group of participants from across the organization identify the forces of change and look at different configurations of key variables in the market.[36] For example, economic growth rates, import penetration, population growth, and political stability can be varied. By projecting such variations for medium- to long-term periods, companies can envision completely new environmental conditions. These conditions are then analyzed for their potential domestic and international impact on corporate strategy.

Of major importance in scenario building is the identification of crucial trend variables and the degree of their variation. Frequently, experts are consulted to gain information about potential variations and the viability of certain scenarios. A wide variety of scenarios must be built to expose corporate executives to multiple potential occurrences. Ideally, even far-fetched variables deserve some consideration, if only to build worst-case scenarios. For example, oil companies need to work with scenarios that factor in dramatic shifts in the supply situation, precipitated by, for example, regional conflict in the Middle East, and that consider major alterations in the demand picture due to, say, technological developments or government policies.

Scenario builders also need to recognize the **nonlinear nature** of factors. To simply extrapolate from currently existing situations is insufficient. Frequently, extraneous factors may enter the picture with a significant impact. Finally, the possibility of joint occurrences must be recognized, because changes may not come about in an isolated fashion but may be spread over wide regions. An example of a joint occurrence is the possibility of "wholesale" obsolescence of current technology. Quantum leaps in computer development and new generations of computers may render obsolete the technological investment of a corporation. For example, the rapid development of digital photography may place great pressures on the viability of traditional photo labs.

For scenarios to be useful, management must analyze and respond to them by formulating contingency plans. Such planning will broaden horizons and may prepare management for unexpected situations. Familiarization can in turn result in shorter response times to actual occurrences by honing response capability. The difficulty, of course, is to devise scenarios that are unusual enough to trigger new thinking yet sufficiently realistic to be taken seriously by management.[37]

> scenarios [must be] unusual enough **to trigger new thinking yet sufficiently realistic** to be taken seriously by management

An organization's environmental analysis should also mesh closely with the corporate strategy. For example, organizations using a differentiation strategy can scan for opportunities, whereas organizations with a cost leadership strategy can scan for threats.[38] Overall, environmental analysis can aid the ongoing decision

---

36. David Mercer, "Simpler Scenarios," *Management Decision* (June 1995).
37. David Rutenberg, "Playful Plans," Queen's University, working paper, 1991.
38. Daniel F. Jennings and James R. Lumpkin, "Insights Between Environmental Scanning Activities and Porter's General Strategies: An Empirical Analysis," *Journal of Management* 18 (December 1992): 791.

process and become a vital corporate tool in carrying out the strategic planning task. Only by observing and absorbing global trends and changes can the firm maintain and improve its competitive position.

COMPETITION

Competition is a major factor in most markets. The marketer must therefore understand the relative performance of his or her offering when compared to the competition. Only with an in-depth understanding of the competition is it possible to formulate competitive strategies that permit the firm to prevail in the fierce battle for resources.

THE INDUSTRY

The first level of the competitive environment is the industry within which the organization operates. **Industry** is defined as a group of organizations that offer products that are near substitutes for each other; in economic terms, these products have a high cross-elasticity of demand. The character of a given industry largely determines the competitive activities taking place within it and the profits of most of the participants. Some of the factors that contribute to this overall character are the size of the market, its age, and its structure.

The larger the market, the more attractive it is to new entrants; but the larger the market, the more likely it is to become segmented as well. Segmenting allows niche marketing, thus reducing direct competition. The age of a market and its rate of change also have an impact on the players within it. The older markets are often more competitive, as growth slows down and the competitors look for growth at the expense of each other.

The number of organizations competing and the concentration of the industry are also important. It might seem that a greater number of organizations in a market increases competition. This is generally true if the brands are of roughly the same size. But the level of competition is also affected by the degree of concentration of the overall industry in the hands of major players. A monopoly or oligopoly will significantly reduce competitive forces. The most stable and profitable markets (apart from a pure monopoly) usually have one or two dominant brands and a few smaller brands. On the other hand, if the comparable number of brands—say four or five—are all of the same size, then the market may be viciously competitive.

COMPETITIVE STRUCTURE

Economies of scale are often the main feature of a market. The theory is that the greater the economies of scale, the greater the benefits accruing to those with large shares of the market. As a result, the competition to achieve larger shares is intense. **Economies of scale** can come about because larger plants are more efficient to run, and their cost per unit of output may be relatively less. There may be overhead costs that cannot be avoided—even by the smaller organizations—but can be spread over larger volumes by the bigger players. Economies of scale may also be the result of learning effects; with increasing cumulative production the manufacturer learns more and finds more efficient methods of production. All of these effects tend to increase competition, by offering incentives to buy market share in order to become the lowest-cost producer. By the same token, economies of scale also produce significant barriers against new entrants to the market. The higher the initial investment, the more difficult it is to justify the investment for a new entry. But such economies of scale do not always last forever, particularly in view of the new computer-based manufacturing technologies and the increasing trend in many markets to offer a wider choice to consumers through niche marketing.

In many instances, the existing firms in large markets have managed to persuade government (paradoxically, often as a response to complaints about cartels) to enact legislation to govern the competitive behavior of the main players. Such government intervention can erect nearly impenetrable entry barriers. This situation is perhaps most obvious in the medical profession, but it also applies to the suppliers of the defense industry. On an international level, firms are often able to convince governments to erect formidable barriers to the entry of foreign competitors. Such actions are justified with the **infant industry argument**—"our industry is too young to compete and needs to grow first"—or with the invocation of some higher good, such as the protection of bank depositors or telephone customers from fly-by-night foreign operators. Such barriers often serve only to provide ample income to the protected industries and to deprive customers of choice and lower prices. Even though international negotiations and economic integration have begun to reduce the scope of this type of barrier, many marketers are still handicapped in their activities through such impediments.

It is also important to understand the competitive history of firms. The previous reactions of competitors to a large extent determine what the new competitive moves will be, particularly in terms of reactions to new entrants. If existing brands have shown that they will react strongly by defending their position with aggressive promotion and pricing, then new entrants may be deterred. Instability may be created, however, if the organizations in the market differ in their structures, goals, and cultures and cannot easily read the intentions of their competitors. Michael Porter suggests that there are good and bad competitors. Good competitors play by the rules that the industry has tacitly recognized; they typically limit price competition, help to expand the industry, and do not aim to destroy other competitors. Bad competitors, on the other hand, usually do the opposite: They break the rules, buy market share (often by starting a price war), and upset the equilibrium. To optimize their results, good competitors should, within the very strict legal guidelines, aim to constrain the bad.[39] However, competitive history may pale in significance in the face of shifts outside of the market. For example, the oil market was very stable until the 1973 Arab-Israeli war, which resulted in major market discontinuities.

Distribution channels can also have a major effect on the structure of competition. For example, if distribution channels can be denied to competitors, then competition can be limited. Forward integration, or the development of arrangements that tie distributors to their suppliers through measures such as financing or trade credit, can be very effective at limiting distribution access. Oil companies have succeeded in limiting the distribution of their gasoline to tied outlets. The development of close relationships with distribution outlets can have a similar effect. For example, many retailers will stock only a few leading brands of consumer goods, thus effectively limiting competition. If firms have been able, through collaboration, technical advice, or other support activities, to build close ties with their distributors, any new competitor must break these bonds and create new ones to use the existing distribution channel. The only other option is to set up an alternative distribution system, which may be prohibitively expensive.[40] Distribution can also be a barrier to international market entry. For example, international trade negotiations between the United States and Japan have long focused on the existence of captive distribution channels, which greatly inhibited

39. Michael Porter, *Competitive Strategy* (New York: Free Press, 1980), 20–36.
40. Thomas S. Gruca and D. Sudharshan, "A Framework for Entry Deterrence Strategy: The Competitive Environment, Choices, and Consequences," *Journal of Marketing* 59 (July 1995): 44–56.

the market entry of foreign goods into Japan.[41] It is perhaps significant that Japanese corporations have invested heavily in distribution and sales and marketing infrastructure to aid their overseas penetration.

The capacity configuration in a market is also an important factor. If firms in an industry have insufficient capacity to fulfill demand, the incentive is high for new market entrants. However, such entrants need to consider the time it takes to bring new or additional capacity online, the likelihood of such capacity being developed by existing suppliers, and the possibility of changes in demand. Firms also often have overcapacity of supply. In such instances, particularly when economies of scale play a role, competitors are likely to focus on sales levels and market share, almost regardless of price. This tends to lead to low, commodity-based prices.

Michael Porter has developed a framework that adds five other influences on competition:

1. Industry competitors that determine the rivalry among existing firms

2. Potential entrants that may change the rules of competition but can be deterred through entry barriers

www.opec.org

3. Suppliers whose bargaining power can change the structure of industries, as OPEC did in the 1970s

4. The bargaining power of the buyers—for example, the retailer's control of the destiny of many consumer goods suppliers

5. The threat of substitute products or services that can restructure the entire industry, not just the existing competitive structure (as the World Wide Web is doing to the publishing industry)[42]

Substitutes are a particularly important element of competition, because they normally appear from unexpected sources. Perhaps the most famous example is that of the U.S. motorcycle industry, which was almost destroyed not by domestic competition but by the Japanese, to whose growing experience the U.S. manufacturers had remained blind. In the case of service organizations, the choices offered by substitutes may sometimes represent the main competition. Figure 3.4 illustrates the chain of competitive decisions facing the audience that eventually arrives in a theater.[43] Unless the decision makers in the theater recognize their competition and offer performances that the public prefers to alternative forms of entertainment, the longevity of the theater may be endangered.

COMPETITIVE RESPONSE

An important aspect of any competitive assessment is the determination of how competitors will respond to future changes:

- **Nonresponse (or slow response).** This competitor will not respond directly to any changes in the environment, or at least will not do so in the short term. It may be a dominant brand leader that can afford to ignore most competitive threats, or it may be a competitor in a particularly weak position.

www.pg.com

- **Fast response.** A few organizations, such as Procter & Gamble, have a policy of immediate and substantial response. Such a strategy is usually the most effective and the most profitable, because the sooner the threat is removed, the sooner high profits can again be generated.

41. Czinkota and Woronoff, *Unlocking Japan's Markets*, 2d ed., 75 ff.

42. Porter, *Competitive Strategy*, 36.

43. Philip Kotler and A. R. Andreasen, *Strategic Marketing for Nonprofit Organizations*, 5th ed. (Upper Saddle River, N.J.: Prentice Hall, 1996), 176.

Figure 3.4

Types of competitors facing a theater

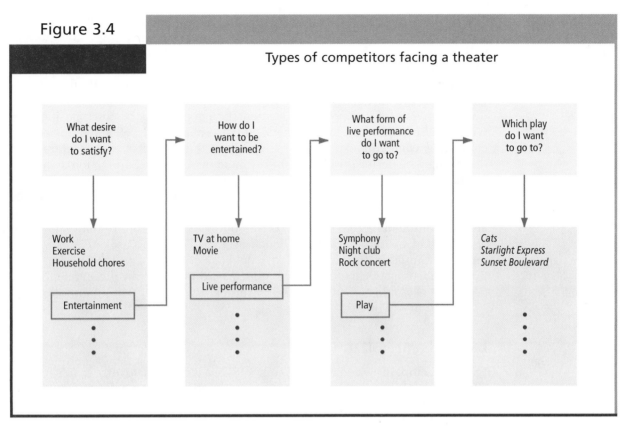

Source: Philip Kotler and A. R. Andreasen, *Strategic Marketing for Non-Profit Organizations,* 5th ed. (Upper Saddle River, N.J.: Prentice Hall, 1996), 176. Reprinted by permission of Prentice Hall, Inc., Upper Saddle River, N.J.

- **Focused response.** Some competitors will respond only to certain types of challenges (typically challenges to price), either refusing to accept or simply not recognizing other forms of challenge, particularly those in the form of new product developments.

The type of response varies depending on the change that has occurred and the specific situation of a competitor at that time. It has been found, for example, that more firms will react to a new product introduction than to a new firm entering the market.[44] Similarly, aggressive reactions are more likely in industries that have high patent protection than in those with low patent protection, perhaps because competitors in patent-rich industries are more sensitive to each other's moves and less willing to allow momentum to shift to a competitor.[45] Response analysis must therefore investigate the degree to which firms are likely to respond to a particular change rather than to change in general.

COMPETITIVE STRATEGIES

Michael Porter, a leading exponent of competitive strategy, states that there are just three potentially successful generic strategic approaches to outperforming other firms in an industry: overall cost leadership, differentiation, and focus.[46]

44. Douglas Bowman and Hubert Gatignon, "Determinants of Competitor Response Time to a New Product Introduction," *Journal of Marketing Research* 32 (February 1995): 42–53.
45. Thomas S. Robertson, Jehoshua Eliashberg, and Talia Rymon, "New Product Announcement Signals and Incumbent Reactions," *Journal of Marketing* 59 (July 1995): 1–15.
46. Porter, *Competitive Strategy,* 7.

The first alternative, overall cost leadership, has come to prominence in recent years, as organizations have invested vast sums to achieve economies of scale. Markets have been expanded to entire continents to support massive new plants, as in the European car industry. Porter's second and third alternatives, however, rely on factors other than price to contain competition. Product differentiation, particularly branding, removes the product from some of the most direct elements of competition. Segmentation focus and product positioning, which will be discussed in Chapter 7, are also particularly effective devices for containing competitive pressure. They allow the marketer to concentrate on defending the offering within a small segment of the market and to make inroads on the most vulnerable competitive goods or services.

www.kraft.com

www.honda.com

www.gm.com

However, firms do not need to concentrate on just one strategy. For example, the Maxwell House division of Kraft General Foods has established a cost leadership position in regular ground coffee but carved out a differentiated position with several of its other coffees, such as Rich French Roast and Colombian Supreme. Similarly, the Honda Civic hatchback occupies a cost leadership position in subcompact cars, but the Honda Accord occupies a differentiated position.[47] An example of General Motors' competitive strategy in Japan follows in Marketing in Action 3.2.

LEADERS AND FOLLOWERS

Firms can employ a wide range of competitive actions. However, a firm's market position largely determines the range of such actions. One useful differentiation can be made between leaders, whose products typically have a market share of 50 percent or more, and followers, who have minor shares and marginal positions.

Leaders stand to gain significantly from market expansion. Therefore, the two main strategies of a market leader are market expansion and defense of market share. To expand the total market, the firm can search for new users by, for

---

Marketing in Action 3.2

Has General Motors gone too Japanese with its Saturn?

In general, American imports have not fared well in the Japanese car market. Nonetheless, in 1997 General Motors introduced Saturn (www.saturn.com) cars in Japan. In order to position it as an everyday car for the average Japanese customer, GM's Japanese Saturn has right-hand drive, folding side mirrors for the narrow streets, its own Japanese dealerships with friendly Japanese employees, and ads featuring Japanese salespeople. The car is also competitively priced with Japanese models. The only apparently non-Japanese aspect of the car is the selling approach. The company's "no-haggle" sales approach has met with positive feedback. But despite GM's efforts to place Saturn cars in the mainstream Japanese car market, the overall marketing efforts have resulted in disappointing sales.

Not all imports implement a strategy like that of Saturn. In fact, Japanese buyers of imported cars tend to select imports because of their distinctive, non-Japanese look and design. American imports that have been successful in Japan include the Cadillac Seville and the Jeep Cherokee—two cars that are quintessentially American, with larger bodies and more powerful engines than Japanese models. And the majority of imported car sales can be attributed to distinctive European models.

Based on the information given, evaluate Saturn's competitive strategy in Japan. How should Saturn modify its competitive strategy in order to increase sales? Should Saturn simply pull itself out of the Japanese car market? Why or why not?

Sources: www.gm.com; Lisa Shuchman, "How Does GM's Saturn Sell Cars in Japan?" *Wall Street Journal*, August 25, 1998, B1+.

---

47. Praveen R. Nayyar, "On the Measurement of Competitive Strategy: Evidence from a Large Multiproduct U.S. Firm," *Academy of Management Journal* 36 (December 1993): 16–54.

www.mci.com

instance, attracting nonusers to the brand. Alternatively, it can develop new uses by finding other things for the product to do. Finally, the firm can seek to encourage more usage by persuading existing users to buy more. For example, MCI, the telephone firm, used all three strategies. To find new users, the firm expanded into Europe from the United States. It encouraged card calls and collect calls while on travel and also offered special rates on weekends to increase the willingness of subscribers to make telephone calls.

In defending market share, the firm also has several alternatives: **position defense** by making the brand position impregnable, **preemptive defense** by launching an attack on a competitor before it can be established (this defense also discourages other potential competitors), and **counteroffensive defense**, which attacks the competitor's home territory so that it has to divert its efforts into protecting its existing products.[48] For example, some U.S. firms have entered the Japanese market mainly to force Japanese firms that had entered the U.S. market to reconcentrate their efforts back in their home market. Of these three strategies, position defense is the most risky, because, as the long history of fortifications has shown, supposed impregnability often results in being blindsided by innovative competitors.

In terms of competitive activity, companies with major brand leaders will typically concentrate their efforts on advertising. With their large sales, they can easily generate large advertising budgets. A 10 percent advertising budget on a $20 million brand produces $2 million of advertising, which will probably dominate advertising in the sector. A comparable 10 percent cut in price would probably go unnoticed. The advertising messages may well stress the brand or particular attributes of the offerings, which are likely to be positioned close to the customer's ideal.

On the flip side of the coin, the strategy for followers is fiercely competitive, aiming to grab the largest possible piece of the existing pie. The main competitive device is likely to be price competition, because the small volume of business means that followers often cannot generate significant advertising budgets. A 30 percent price cut may be seen by the consumer as significant, whereas a similar 30 percent advertising budget, even on a $1 million brand, would generate only $200,000, barely enough for one small campaign. A more profitable approach, however, is to avoid the main competitors altogether by using niche marketing, which concentrates on small segments that are not addressed by the major brands. Most successful are those followers that are able to hone in on two types of customers—those that are "switchable" at relatively low acquisition costs and the "high profit customers" that generate the most return.[49]

Several alternative strategies are available to the firm that wishes to improve its position. Using military analogies, researchers have identified five key attack options, shown in Figure 3.5.[50] In a **frontal attack**, the challenger takes on the market leader in its own territory and attacks the opponent's strengths rather than its weaknesses. Considerable resources are needed for this strategy. The outcome depends on who has the greater firepower and endurance, but can be very profitable if successful. In a **flank attack**, the challenger zeros in on a segment (or geographical region) where the market leader is most vulnerable. An alternative is to target market needs not covered by the leaders, a strategy used very effectively by Japanese corporations. The **encirclement strategy** involves launching a grand offensive against the enemy on several fronts where the aggressor has, or is able to muster, enough force to break the opponent's will to

48. Philip Kotler, *Marketing Management*, 9th ed. (Upper Saddle River, N.J.: Prentice Hall, 1997), 377–381.
49. Adrian J. Slywotsky and Benson P. Shapiro, "Leveraging to Beat the Odds: The New Marketing Mind Set," *Harvard Business Review* 79 (September/October 1993): 76.
50. P. Kotler and R. Singh, "Marketing Warfare in the 1980s," *Journal of Business Strategy* 2 (winter 1981): 30–41.

Figure 3.5

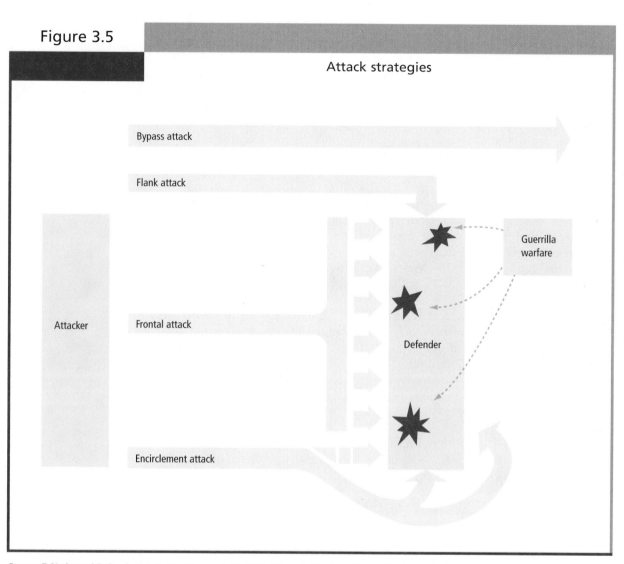

Source: P. Kotler and R. Singh, "Marketing Warfare in the 1980s," *Journal of Business Strategy* 2 (winter 1981): 30–41. © Faulkner & Gray, Inc. Republished with Permission.

resist. **Bypass attacks** are most prevalent in high-tech markets, where a challenger puts its efforts into bypassing existing technology and winning the battle for the next generation of technology to be brought to the market. Such a move needs significant funding, but it can put the winner in an almost impregnable position. In **guerrilla warfare** the attacker makes intermittent forays, typically on ground of its own choosing, so that the cost to the attacker is minimized and that to the opponent maximized. The sole aim is to weaken and demoralize the market leader, eventually leading to concessions.

On a final note, the Boston Consulting Group makes the following observations, based on its experience of market warfare:

- If there are many competitors, a shakeout is nearly inevitable.
- All but the two largest share competitors will be either losers (and eventually eliminated) or marginal cash traps.
- Anything less than 30 percent of the relevant market or at least half the share of the leader is a high-risk position.

- The quicker any investment is cashed out, or a market position second only to the leader gained, the lower the risk and the higher the probable return on investment.[51]

As difficult as it may be to maintain a leadership position, it is even harder to be a follower; hence the great attraction of segmentation, which splits the market into smaller, though still viable, pieces, and allows the firm to be the market leader in the segment of its own choosing.

SUMMARY

An understanding of the environment is important for the marketer. Social, technological, economic, and political factors can have a major impact on the firm's opportunities and threats. Key social and cultural elements to consider are the redefinition of occupations, a societal trend toward postmaterialism, and major demographic shifts. In the area of technology, the outlook for marketers is likely to be thoroughly changed by transformations in information processing and the subsequent shifts in business practices as well as the emergence of new materials, new biotechnological products, and growing environmental concern. In the economic area, increasing globalization, regional integration, and exchange rate effects represent major influences on marketing practice. The political environment is characterized by legislative and regulatory actions that influence the firm but that can also be influenced by the firm. However, the political arena is also increasingly defined by the activities of special-interest groups whose actions can have a major effect on firms. Furthermore, the marketer is likely to be required, either by regulation or by good marketing sense, to take into account various stakeholders beyond the shareholders if the firm and its products are to remain acceptable to society at large.

In order to deal with the environment, the firm must first analyze and understand it. Such analysis can be accomplished by environmental scanning, Delphi research, and scenario building. To understand the competition, however, more specific issues such as market structure, products and production processes, and industrial changes taking place must be evaluated.

After understanding these dimensions, a successful strategic position can be achieved through economies of scale, political clout, and captive distribution systems. Victory in the halls of government in particular is increasingly sought by firms that are unable to win the competitive battle in the field of commerce. Building and maintaining a successful position also requires an understanding of the likely competitive response from adversaries and the different strategies that can be employed by leaders and followers. Overall, it should be remembered that as difficult as it may be to maintain a leadership position, it is even harder to be a profitable follower.

QUESTIONS FOR REVIEW

1. What are the four main dimensions of the external environment? How do they relate to the marketing environment?

2. What might be the main technological drivers over the near to medium term? What social changes is the information revolution leading to?

51. B. D. Henderson, "The Rule of Three and Four," *Perspectives* (Boston: Boston Consulting Group, 1985).

3. List some major recent changes in lifestyles and demographics.

4. How and why is the role of pressure groups changing?

5. How can one conduct environmental analyses?

6. How do economies of scale and the concentration of business affect competition in an industry?

7. What are some of the main entry barriers into an industry?

8. What are the key competitive strategies for market leaders and followers?

QUESTIONS FOR DISCUSSION

1. Due to the success of such Internet concerns as Autobytel.com and CarPoint.com, coupled with like pressure from Ford and Chrysler, General Motors has been forced to respond in kind with a more customer-oriented Web site that provides expanded pricing information. Ready for rollout in 1999, such initiatives were unheard of only five years previous.[52] What are some of the marketing effects of increased price transparency?

2. In April of 1999, the Federal Trade Commission began to implement the Children's Online Privacy Act passed by the U.S. Congress in the fall of 1998. The new FTC rules require parental consent of children entering chat rooms, posting information on online bulletin boards, or providing personal data on a Web site targeted at children. Parents can convey consent by fax, e-mail, phone, or submission of credit card information. Despite seemingly broad parental support, Web operators fear that the burden of parental responsibility in this area may shift to their industry.[53] Why should governments regulate businesses? Won't the marketplace take care of any problems itself? Consider this and other examples, such as OSHA standards, radiated beef, cigarette advertising, and minimum wage.

3. As it attempts to overhaul its stumbling economic system, China needs many of its M.B.A. graduates to fill positions in its industrial and service sectors. Unfortunately, those jobs may not be as attractive as ones with companies dealing in less concrete products. In fact, many M.B.A. students quit jobs in these sectors to go

to school and then gravitate toward careers in consulting, investment banking, and information technology upon graduation. This trend leaves many important managerial positions in the industrial sector open for long periods of time. Manufacturers have tended to respond by offering higher salaries, training, and experience abroad and by grooming current employees to take important managerial positions.[54] If society shifts to symbolic analysts, what about all those who can't or won't participate? Will all the predicted benefits of efficiency really materialize if unemployment is a major side effect?

4. Despite a close relationship that has Procter & Gamble and Wal-Mart sharing sales information and inventory responsibilities, the largest U.S. retailer will go head-to-head with its largest supplier when it rolls out its own brand of laundry detergent under the Sam's Choice label. The new detergent is aimed directly at Tide, the leading brand in the U.S. and one of Procter & Gamble's flagship products, with like colored packaging and powder and liquid varieties. Sam's Choice would be priced at 25 to 43 percent lower, posing a serious threat to Tide's 38.6 percent U.S. market share.[55] Will the growing strength of retailers due to the technology revolution result in the ultimate integration and absorption of all manufacturing by retailers?

5. Merck–Medco Managed Care, a division of Merck & Co., uses the Internet and tailored software programs to communicate with doctors and patients about medications and other

---

52. Gregory White, "General Motors to Take Nationwide Test Drive on Web," *Wall Street Journal*, September 28, 1998, B4.

53. John Simons, "New FTC Rules Aim to Protect Kid Web Privacy," *Wall Street Journal*, April 21, 1999, B1, B4.

54. Kenneth Howe, "China's Nascent Managers, Seeking Fame and Fortune, Shun Factories," *Wall Street Journal Interactive*, July 27, 1999.

55. Emily Nelson, "Wal-Mart Launches Laundry Soap, Competing with Procter & Gamble," *Wall Street Journal*, August 6, 1999, B1.

products relative to patient health. By entering the patient's name in the computer, along with the diagnosis and potential prescription remedies, the doctor can gain a wealth of information on the patient's medical status and history as well as perform numerous transactions relative to the office visit and general medical care of the patient. The software archives the list of medications the patient is currently taking, identifies possible contraindications for drugs the doctor is thinking of prescribing, and recommends alternative drugs, should the one the doctor intends to prescribe not be the best suited according to the diagnosis entered. Merck also uses technology to communicate directly with the patient, using the Internet to send personalized messages and allowing the patient to process prescription refills. Soon, Merck will have the capability to send electronic reminders for refills to participating patients.[56]

How is the increased personal information flow likely to affect individual interaction with fellow humans and society in general? With increasing concerns about privacy, will the social discipline of marketing become a vehicle for antisocial change?

6. In order to gain ground in the competitive market of printers and cartridges, Lexmark drastically reduced the price on its 1100 Color Jetprinter to $89 in 1999. The company was able to sustain such a steep reduction by subcontracting the assembly of its printers to companies in South Korea and China, where labor is cheaper than in the United States.[57] With wages in developing countries only one-tenth of those in industrialized nations, how can industrialized countries hope to compete in the long run?

7. The Center for Science in the Public Interest is well known for its contribution to increased nutrition labeling and to lobbying for closer monitoring of food safety. One of its larger on-going campaigns regards Olestra, the fat substitute found in popular fat-free snack foods. CSPI dedicates an entire page on its Web site to Olestra-related articles, press releases, research and findings, and chat rooms. Visitors are invited to post accounts of their bad experiences with Olestra and are given the hope of having an impact on future food regulations. Has the power of interest groups gone too far or does it represent the birth of a new form of democracy?

8. Capitalization levels of many Web-based companies has skyrocketed in recent years, and many of these newer ventures are enjoying much deeper pockets than their traditional rivals: Amazon.com has a greater level of capitalization than Barnes & Noble, Charles Schwab than Merrill Lynch, eToys than Toys "R" Us. Market values are a point of competition and comparison, yet many company mission statements—including those of the companies cited—place the consumers and their needs first among customers. Why shouldn't shareholders be the top priority of every firm and its managers? What are the consequences of devaluing the importance of the source of capital?

FURTHER READINGS

Choo, Chun Wei. *Information Management for the Intelligent Organization: The Art of Scanning the Environment*, 2d ed. Medford, N.J.: Information Today, 1998.

Gates, Bill. *Business @ The Speed of Thought*. New York: Warner Books, 1999.

Hufbauer, Gary Clyde, and Kimberly Ann Elliott. *Measuring the Costs of Protection in the United States*. Washington, D.C.: Institute for International Economics, 1994.

Naisbitt, John. *Unraveling the Global Paradox*. Washington, D.C.: Food Marketing Institute, 1998.

Negroponte, Nicholas. *Being Digital*. New York: Vintage Books, 1996.

Porter, Michael. *The Competitive Advantage of Nations*. New York: Free Press, 1990.

56. Elyse Tanouye, "Web Links Give Drug Reps Foot in Doctors' Door," *Wall Street Journal*, March 18, 1999, B18.
57. Alec Klein, "As Cheap Printers Score, H-P Plays Catch-Up," *Wall Street Journal*, April 21, 1999, B1, B4.

chapter

4

Understanding the Buyer

Two keys to successful marketing are understanding and responding to the wishes and needs of the buyer. This **customer-consumer orientation** is what sets marketing apart from all other business disciplines. Since each individual good or service evokes a specific, and possibly unique, response from its set of buyers, each buying situation is unique. Those employing face-to-face selling or one-on-one internet marketing can exploit this uniqueness, whereas those in mass markets need to deal in terms of groups and averages. But all suppliers need to determine their customers' specific needs and wants. The focus of this chapter is, therefore, on the buyer, both as consumer and as customer. We will first concentrate on the consumer, or end user, analyze how buying decisions are made, and explore the factors that influence these decisions. We will then look at customers, or organizational buyers in industrial markets, and highlight their purchase decision processes.

A MODEL OF CONSUMER BEHAVIOR

The question "How do consumers make their decisions?" is more difficult to answer than one might expect. Consumers do not approach each **buying decision** with conveniently blank minds and then rationally consider all the options. Their decision making is an extended, complex, and often confused process. Typically, the consumer's behavior is the result of the influence of a variety of factors and the interaction between them. Figure 4.1 presents a total model of consumer behavior, which shows the different dimensions and factors and their connections to each other. Starting with **need recognition**, which is triggered either internally or by outside stimuli, the consumer proceeds to search for fulfillment of that need. Influenced by past experiences and by environmental influences, the consumer begins to evaluate different alternatives. This evaluation is affected by individual aspects such as resources, knowledge, and lifestyle and leads eventually to a purchase decision. After this decision comes the consumption or use process, which, through a **post-purchase evaluation**, results in consumer satisfaction or dissatisfaction. This result in turn is fed back into the search process as a component used for future evaluations. Although this model does not allow us to fully understand each particular purchase, it serves as a framework to explain the kinds of information required to understand different consumer decision processes and provides essential insights for marketing strategy.[1] In the following pages we will explore the most relevant individual components of this model in more detail.

---

1. James F. Engel, Roger D. Blackwell, and Paul W. Miniard, *Consumer Behavior*, 8th ed. (Orlando: Harcourt Brace and Company, 1995), 47.

Figure 4.1

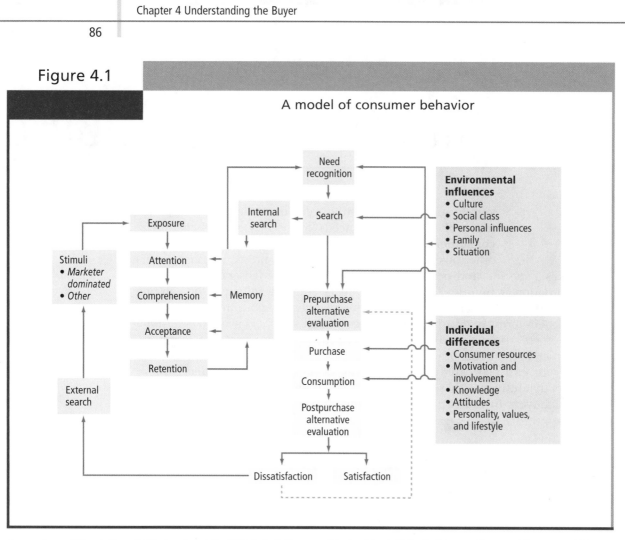

A model of consumer behavior

Source: James F. Engel, Roger D. Blackwell, and Paul W. Miniard, *Consumer Behavior,* 8th ed. (Orlando: Harcourt Brace and Company, 1995), 153. Copyright © 1995 by Harcourt, Inc. Reproduced by permission of the publisher.

THE CONSUMER DECISION-MAKING PROCESS

To appreciate some of the complexities in the way consumers make their purchase decisions, let us examine the apparently simple case of buying a can of tuna. A purchaser in a supermarket may have many factors in mind when faced by the large number of competing brands. The purchaser probably has tried several brands and decided that some are acceptable and others are not. There may have been a bad experience with a particular brand, or one brand may have been found to be especially good. Or, perhaps the purchaser is simply bored with the taste of the "usual" brand. **Experience** is a much undervalued factor, particularly by those who believe that creative marketing is all it takes to move a product. The consumer usually takes practical experience into account before any other factors. If the product is not liked, no amount of advertising will succeed. Experience will, of course, change over the years. Consumers learn from their consumption decisions and adjust their expectations and behavior. As a result, a certain approach that once worked does not necessarily keep on working.

Apart from the physical experience of the product, the prospective purchaser will also demand that it conform to his or her **values** and **attitudes**. Some consumers seek out cans of tuna packed in water because these match their need to be weight conscious. Others may decide to discontinue the consumption of tuna due to the dangers that tuna fishing nets pose to dolphins. The marketing communication that they have been exposed to in the past such as advertising has to some extent shaped the consumer's views—at least, that is the fervent hope of marketers. But it should be recognized that the most influential promotion may come by way of recommendation from a friend, from an opinion leader (i.e., someone who is looked up to or whose opinion is valued), or from a family member. Faced with choices, the purchaser compares the value, or benefit, derived from the various brands. In this evaluation, consumers balance the benefits of the purchase against the cost or price. Some consumer groups or segments are more sensitive toward price, whereas others may be more benefit oriented.[2] For example, some consumers may always buy the cheapest brand, or try a new brand because it's on sale that week. Unless willing to make a visit to another supermarket, the purchaser is also limited in the choice to be made by the brands available. It is often said that **consumers** have the ultimate **sovereignty**, because their purchasing decisions decide who will survive in the market. However, the decisions made by intermediaries such as retailers often dictate or limit the selections of merchandise from which consumers can choose. The willingness to experiment with new products may therefore reflect more the willingness on the part of retailers than of consumers. Marketing in Action 4.1 discusses one company's response to consumer reluctance to purchase new products. If it's not on the shelf, it won't be sold very often holds true in the consumer goods sector. Once the purchase has been made, the buyer will evaluate the purchase—and promptly apply the results of this evaluation to future purchasing decisions.

Marketing in Action 4.1

Acer America Corp. attempts to understand the novice computer buyer

The third-largest PC manufacturer in the world, the Acer Group maintains its worldwide headquarters in Taiwan. Acer America Corporation (www.acer.com), based in San Jose, California (USA), is a wholly owned subsidiary of the Acer Group. The company offers a wide range of personal computers, including laptops, notebooks, servers, desktops, and mini/micro towers. Products are distributed through a variety of consumer and industrial channels.

Acer America Corporation is facing stiff competition in the U.S. home computer market. Company giants such as Hewlett-Packard (www.hp.com) and Compaq (www.compaq.com) are making aggressive moves into this market. Although this is a relatively common story for midsized personal computer manufacturers in today's rapidly changing technological marketplace, Acer is battling these major companies by gaining a better understanding of the computer buyer.

A series of focus groups indicated that approximately two-thirds of home computer buyers are first-time owners. This finding prompted additional research on the first-time buyer and focused on the "negatives" in the purchase of a home computer. A major negative from the first-time buying experience was the complexity of setting up a home computer for the first time.

The research on consumer buying behavior has prompted Acer America Corporation to target its home computer sales to first-time buyers. It has decided to offer the company's Aspire model to the novice buyer. What does such a shift in company strategy mean to Aspire's marketing program? Will this strategy distinguish Acer from the competition? Is this a risky strategy, as first-time buyers will probably be hit hardest by an economic slowdown?

Sources: www.acer.com; Jim Carlton, "Acer Is Targeting the First-Time Buyers in PC Launch," *Wall Street Journal*, October 14, 1998, B11.

---

2. Dhruv Grewal, Kent B. Monroe, and R. Krishnan, "The Effects of Price-Comparison Advertising on Buyer's Perceptions of Acquisition Value, Transaction Value, and Behavioral Intentions," *Journal of Marketing* 62 (April 1998): 46–59.

PROBLEM OR NEED RECOGNITION

The **buying process** starts with the stimulus of a consumer's **recognition** of a **need**. That recognition may be internally generated or externally imposed by environmental factors or by a supplier's promotional stimulus. As a general rule, the marketer cannot do much about the internal processes, except to recognize them. On the other hand, the marketer can do a great deal in terms of external environmental influences, from recognizing them to steering them in the direction most favorable to the supplier's intentions.

INFORMATION SEARCH

For most goods and services the consumer obtains information passively, by subconsciously absorbing messages from the media and from friends and acquaintances. For particularly important decisions the information search is active. Instead of just absorbing information, the consumer is looking for it. Matters are discussed with friends and experts, and knowledge is sought from sources such as consumer magazines or a Web search. The marketer enters the picture during this information search stage by making certain that suitable information, for example in the form of carefully planned advertising, is available to the consumer. The consumer then decides how much attention to devote to the communication, based on the degree of interest toward the message and the environment in which the exposure occurs. The next step is comprehension of the message, which may not be the same comprehension the marketer expects. When noise clutters the communication process, the consumer may misinterpret a message. If the message conflicts with the beliefs of the consumer, the message may even be distorted to conform with expectations. Acceptance of the message follows, together with retention, which ensures that the message will be remembered for future use. At any time, the communication can be screened out, and, in fact, most information communicated by marketers is ignored or dismissed. That is why so much money is spent on sending messages and devising ways to make them stick with the consumer.

EVALUATION OF ALTERNATIVES

www.coke.com

Most products have numerous competing brands on the market, ranging from internationally distributed brands, such as Coca-Cola, to those that can be obtained only in a few local shops. The process of choosing between alternative brands can be represented as a series of filtering stages, some of which are under the consumer's control and some under the supplier's.

The first consideration is whether the consumer is even aware of a particular product or brand. **Awareness** is mostly under the control of the supplier and reflects the intensity and the success of the communication strategy. A second issue is whether the consumer has access to the product. Availability is mainly under the control of the producers and the distribution chains. How far the consumer is prepared to venture in search of a difficult-to-obtain product depends on the characteristics of the product and the specificity of the consumer's desire. A can of beans has to be on the shelf of the supermarket visited by the consumer just when needed. On the other hand, some consumers will wait several months and travel hundreds of miles to see a star-studded musical performance. The information revolution makes it increasingly easier for suppliers to cope with the availability factor. Ongoing analysis of consumer behavior enables more precise pinpointing of where and when consumers will be looking for a product. Close linkages between producers and distributors through, for example, electronic data interchange and direct order entry methods, permit rapid information flow about sales levels and order replenishment, thereby reducing or even avoiding out-of-stock situations on the retail level.

Except in pure commodity markets, not all brands are identical. Some are clearly more suitable, at least in the consumer's eyes, and some are definitely unsuitable. Typically, the consumer chooses products based on the benefits they offer. First, the consumer decides which benefits are sought and which **attributes** of the product are necessary to obtain these benefits. At the same time, an image of each brand is built in terms of these attributes. Consumers then match attributes of competing brands, somehow keeping track of the importance of the attributes and the varying degrees of match or mismatch. These attributes are not, however, just the physical features beloved by suppliers but rather include a wide range of attitudinal factors. Some claim that consumers buy into a **consumption system**, from which they expect product and service satisfaction, which changes over time.[3] For example, initially, the customer of a Lexus automobile may be equally thrilled by the automobile as well as the service by new dealerships. Later on, the automobile itself may turn out to be more important, whereas after some years, the service again comes to the forefront.

www.lexus.com

The marketer must understand that the process of evaluating and comparing benefits and attributes varies among consumers. For example, some consumers may use a **lexicographic decision strategy**, in which they compare only the most important attribute of similar products. The product that performs best on this one attribute is then selected. If two or more brands are perceived as equally good they are then compared on the second most important attribute. The comparisons continue until the tie is broken. Alternatively, consumers may use a **conjunctive decision rule**, in which minimum standards are set for all attributes, and only those products that meet all the standards are chosen. Consumers may also rate the importance of attributes and allow a high rating on one to compensate for a low rating on another. In light of these and other decision-making strategies, varying multiple-attribute models of consumer decision making have been developed to assist the marketer in responding better to consumers. Suppliers often use segmentation (discussed later) as a means of targeting the brand to a specific group within the market. Segmentation tries to match brand attributes to a group of consumers with similar needs. This ensures a better fit, but in the process the attributes become less suitable to buyers in other segments of the market.

PURCHASE DECISION

At this stage the consumer's choice takes place. A selection is made from the brands that remain after the previous filtering stages. To the consumer the choice is rational; the brand chosen best meets the perceived needs. Yet lack of information or lack of market transparency may lead to decisions that, to the marketer at least, seem irrational. However, given the increasing availability of comparative information and the growing capability of organizing such information, this entire decision process may well undergo substantial change. For example, if a consumer can browse on the Internet to check the availability and the price of a product, retailers may be less inclined to offer the product at sharply different prices. Similarly, the consumer may find it easier to compare features of different products and thus make a more informed decision, in which case the main differentiating feature of retailers may become their ability to assist the consumer in understanding and fulfilling needs. If that is so, we may

---

3. Vikas Mittal, Pankaj Kumar, and Michael Tsiros, "Attribute-Level Performance, Satisfaction, and Behavioral Intentions over Time: A Consumption-System Approach," *Journal of Marketing* 63 (April 1999): 88–101.

well see a return of the expert function of retailers, which goes far beyond today's prevalent function as product locator, product guardian, or cash register operator.

POSTPURCHASE BEHAVIOR

After a purchase has been made the product is consumed or used. During and after this process, **cognitive dissonance** may have an interesting effect on consumer behavior. According to cognitive dissonance theory, if there were conflicting elements in the original decision to buy (the negative aspects of the product purchased versus the positive elements of the alternatives not purchased), there will be postpurchase tension in the consumer's mind. Buyers tend to read promotional material even more avidly after the purchase than before, in order to justify their decisions and to displace the dissonant elements by concentrating on those aspects of the promotion that stress the good points of the product purchased.[4] Thus marketers need to recognize the role of their promotion in general, and of their advertising in particular, in the postpurchase period. Whether the buyer's expectations have been met and whether the consumer is satisfied are the crucial issues. Clearly the experiences after the purchase process become part of the future evaluation of buyers in similar decision processes. This ongoing feedback loop after the purchase is what motivates suppliers to check on the satisfaction of consumers and to try to rectify any problems that may lead to dissatisfaction. That is why marketers should keep in touch with consumers after the sale and build a relationship that goes beyond the sales transaction.

> marketers should keep in touch with consumers **after the sale and build a relationship** that goes beyond the transaction

WHAT FACTORS SPECIFICALLY INFLUENCE CONSUMERS?

In making a final decision, and indeed throughout the whole decision-making process, consumers are influenced by a wide range of factors, not just those relating to the obvious features of the product. Figure 4.2 shows some of the factors most discussed by marketing theorists. Some of these factors exert a direct, measurable influence on buying decisions, whereas others are less tangible and may only suggest patterns of buying behavior. In many cases intangible factors, such as the perception of the product or the relationship between supplier and consumer, may be important. A good understanding of the different factors that influence consumer behavior is crucial to marketers and is therefore the subject of much market research. Comprehension of these factors is instrumental in segmenting and positioning products and in motivating consumers to buy.

ECONOMIC FACTORS

To many theorists, economic factors constitute the main influence on purchasers. One primary consideration is the economic well-being of the consumers. Put simply, if consumers have more money, they are likely to spend more. One of the methods of categorizing consumers, therefore, is by income group. Income alone, however, provides insufficient information because the behavior of different income groups is modified by the overall economic climate. If an economic boom

---

4. Leon A. Festinger, *A Theory of Cognitive Dissonance* (Evanston: Row, Peterson, 1957), 135.

Figure 4.2

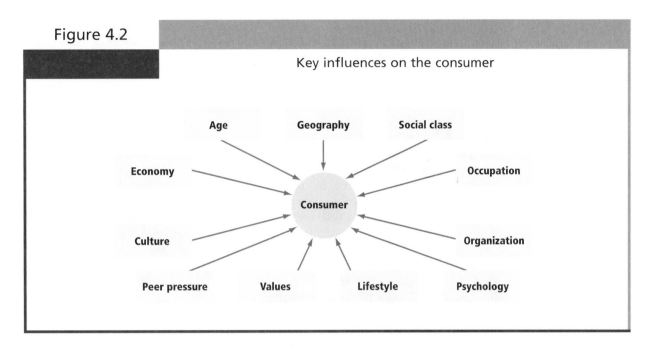

Key influences on the consumer

is under way, the consumer is likely to spend more money and will sometimes borrow in order to spend even more than he or she earns. The industrialist will also spend more, investing in new capacity to take advantage of the favorable economic climate.

AGE AND LIFE CYCLE

The activities of individuals and families vary over time. Age and family status are likely to influence the needs of consumers and the time and resources available to fulfill these needs. Traditionally, for example, young singles are interested mostly in entertainment, and childless professional couples demand many luxury goods. Couples with children tend to be less able to spend money on non-essentials, while older couples without children at home may again be able to afford luxuries.

Many of these traditional **life cycle** implications remain valid. For example, couples who marry and have children early tend to display behavioral patterns consistent with the above description. However, new groupings are emerging, based on nontraditional or delayed life cycles. For example, many couples today may postpone marriage and parenthood in order to pursue dual careers.[5] A life cycle grouping developed by Gilly and Enis takes new societal developments into account and focuses only on current household composition.[6] The model explicitly incorporates such nontraditional paths as delayed marriage and parenthood, childlessness, and remarriage, and includes middle-aged or older singles, never-married or widowed single parents, cohabiting couples, and mature families. Research has shown this categorization to outperform other models in its ability to differentiate groups.[7] Of course, because different societies have varying family

---

5. Charles M. Schaninger and William D. Danko, "A Conceptual and Empirical Comparison of Alternative Household Life Cycle Models," *Journal of Consumer Research* 19, no. 4 (1993): 583.

6. Mary C. Gilly and Ben M. Enis, "Recycling the Family Life Cycle: A Proposal for Redefinition," in *Advances in Consumer Research*, vol. 9, ed. A. Mitchell (Ann Arbor, Mich.: Association for Consumer Research, 1982), 271–276.

7. Schaninger and Danko, "A Conceptual and Empirical Comparison," 582.

patterns, the marketer is well advised to ensure that the assumptions used regarding such patterns are based on facts from the specific society that will be exposed to the marketing effort.

Much work has also been conducted on individual age subcategories. In many countries, for example, a longer life span has resulted in a larger proportion of mature consumers. The implications of age effects such as increased ear length, expanded nose breadth, and diminishing height may be profound for marketers catering to older groups, such as garment manufacturers and designers of eyeglasses and hats.[8] Manager's Corner 4.1 provides some examples of how marketers position themselves to appeal to customers at different age levels.

By better understanding the connection between age and life cycle and by analyzing the simultaneous occurrence of consumer needs, the marketer can improve the servicing of these needs and increase sales. For example, management at a large warehouse club noticed a correlation between the sales of disposable diapers and beer. When investigating the matter, they found that young fathers coming to the store after work to buy diapers would also pick up a six-pack of beer on the same trip. The store decided to move a beer display next to the diapers, and sales jumped by 10 percent.[9]

Manager's Corner 4.1

Marketers seek to "graduate" buyers

How do companies keep customers as they grow older and their lifestyles change? Clothing manufacturers have long recognized the importance of aiming for an array of demographics and lifestyles. A growing number of retailers "graduate" customers, not by pushing them to the next level within their stores, but by creating different store environments and clothing geared toward specific demographic groups. Gap (www.gap.com) is the leader in this concept, starting with BabyGap for babies, then kids at its GapKids stores, then teenagers at its low-priced Old Navy outlets. Later on, customers are moved to the mid-priced Gap stores and then to the Banana Republic boutiques, which offer more expensive fabrics and career suits. Likewise, if times get tough, the chain hopes customers might trade down to Old Navy again, which protects the company during penny-pinching times.

Retailers say one reason they're looking to graduate customers is that busy shoppers want to be targeted and don't have time to browse. Other chains have been following Gap's example. Abercrombie & Fitch (www.abercrombie.com), a staple for college students, recently introduced Abercrombie stores for young teens and adolescents who want to mimic their older siblings. Talbots Inc. (www.talbots.com) has been opening Talbots Kids stores. Wet Seal Inc. (www.wetseal.com), owner of the Contempo stores known for "club" clothes, is rapidly expanding their age category, opening Wet Seal stores for teens, Limbo Lounges for young adults, and Arden B boutiques for women ranging 20–40.

However, the plan to shift to a new age group of customers does not always work. Take the car industry and the case of Cadillac (www.cadillac.com), for example. The Cadillac Catera is a sporty sedan aimed at bringing in affluent buyers 35–50 years old. Instead, half of the Catera's owners are at least age 65. Cadillac's problem, in actuarial terms, is this: Older people "have fewer cars left in them." Younger buyers can grow with the franchise and support future business. But younger buyers are gobbling up other brands of entry-level luxury cars such as the Mercedes-Benz C280 (www.mercedes.com), the BMW 328i (www.bmw.com), or the Lexus ES300 (www.lexus.com).

Sources: Warren Brown, "The Caddy They Ducked," *Washington Post*, September 11, 1997, E1–E2; Stephanie Stoughton, "The Customer's New Clothes," *Washington Post*, March 20, 1999, E1–E2.

---

8. Charles D. Schewe and Geoffrey E. Meredith, "Digging Deep to Delight the Mature Adult Consumer," *Marketing Management* 3, no. 3 (1994): 21–35.

9. Schaninger and Danko, "A Conceptual and Empirical Comparison," 585.

GEOGRAPHY

For some goods or services, geographical variations may be quite important. In the United States, for example, distinctly different taste preferences for food exist when comparing the North and the South or the East Coast and the West Coast, ranging from what to eat for breakfast to what to drink with dinner. These **geographic differences** are even greater around the world. For example, in the United Kingdom, northerners prefer white pickled onions, whereas southerners prefer brown ones. Few people drink orange juice for breakfast in France, but many do so during the day as a refreshment. In Japan, soup is consumed mainly for breakfast.

To better understand existing consumer differences based on geography, marketers go to great lengths to research and analyze behavioral patterns. In the United States, Claritas has developed a **segmentation** database named PRIZM that classifies every U.S. **zip code** into one of 40 categories ranging from "Blue Blood Estates" to "Public Assistance." Each of these categories is defined by detailed demographic, lifestyle, and consumption information and often includes data on specific brands. For example, the "Shotguns and Pickups" cluster is partly defined by high usage of chain saws, snuff, canning jars, frozen potato products, and whipped toppings. Its members are very unlikely to use car rental services, belong to country clubs, read *Gourmet* magazine, or drink Irish whiskey. In contrast, members of the "Furs and Station Wagons" cluster are much more likely than the average U.S. consumer to have a second mortgage, buy wine by the case, read *Architectural Digest,* drive BMW 5-series cars, and eat natural cold cereal and pumpernickel bread. They are unlikely to chew tobacco, hunt, drive a Chevette, use nondairy creamers, eat canned stews, or watch "Wheel of Fortune."[10]

The availability of such geographic information can help the marketer target mailings, advertisements, or personal sales pitches that will be most effective and efficient. **Geographic clustering** can also be done by region. For example, it has been suggested that Europe can be subdivided into nine superregions and a financial district that offer a better framework for analyzing and anticipating trends in the continent than the current national borders of Europe. The regions suggested are as follows:

- *Latin Crescent:* most of Spain, southern Portugal, southern France, and most of Italy
- *Baltic League:* Sweden, Finland, the Baltic republics, Russia down to St. Petersburg, the coastal regions of Poland and Germany, the eastern half of Denmark, and a corner of Norway
- *Atlantic Coast:* Great Britain, Ireland, and virtually the entire western coast of Europe, running from northern Portugal through Oslo and along the Norwegian Swedish border
- *Mitteleuropa:* Germany, most of Belgium, the Netherlands, Luxembourg, northern and central France, the northwestern corner of Switzerland, the Czech Republic, and western Poland
- *Capital District:* the triangle formed by Brussels, Paris, and Strasbourg, including Luxembourg City
- *Financial District:* London
- *Alpine Arc:* Alpine regions of France, most of Switzerland, western Austria, parts of Italy down to Milan, and Germany up to Munich

www.claritas.com

www.gourmet.com

www.archdigest.com
www.bmw.com
www.chevrolet.com

10. Basil G. Englis and Michael Solomon, "To Be and Not to Be: Lifestyle Imagery, Reference Groups, and the Clustering of America," *Journal of Advertising* 24, no. 1 (1995): 13.

www.ecb.int

- *Danube Basin:* from Bavaria east of Munich through eastern Austria, including Slovakia, all of Hungary and Romania, the former Soviet republic of Moldova, the northern half of Bulgaria, the new republics of Slovenia and Croatia, and the Adriatic coast of northern Italy as far west as Milan
- *Balkan Peninsula:* Serbia, Bosnia, Montenegro, Macedonia, Albania, Greece, southern Bulgaria, and the European part of Turkey
- *Slavic Federation:* Ukraine, Belarus, Russia west of the Ural Mountains, and parts of Poland east of Warsaw[11]

Not all observers agree with these groupings. For example, some claim that the city of Frankfurt, with the seat of the European Central Bank (ECB), will either join with or fiercely compete against London to form a broader financial district. Similarly, the war in Serbia has been a setback to the emergence of a Slavic Federation. Nonetheless, if, as the researcher claims, these divisions indeed reflect cohesive groupings of people and economies, the marketer can use the superregions to develop products, devise marketing campaigns, and make location decisions.

SOCIAL CLASS

One traditional differentiation used by marketers has been that of social class. Depending on the society under consideration, the role and importance of social class may very significantly. In some countries, social class is a position inherited,

> rather than a trickle-down effect from classes above,
> **the new opinion leadership**
> comes from persons within the same social class

assigned by birth or by tradition. In others, the level of social standing is closely linked with an individual's occupation or the income level attained. It used to be assumed that the upper classes were the first to try new products, which then trickled down to the lower classes. Historically, there may have been some justification for this. The refrigerator, the washing machine, the car, and the telephone were all adopted first by the higher social classes. Recently, however, as affluence has become more widespread, the process has become much less clear. It is now argued that rather than a trickle-down effect from classes above, the new opinion leadership comes from persons within the same social class.

Nevertheless, the occupation of the individual, or the head of the household, can significantly affect his or her way of life. A manager in a high-tech industry may have a different set of values from those of a worker on a production line in a declining industry or from those of a university professor. When comparing data sets on **occupation** across countries, the marketer is well advised to exercise caution in ensuring that the categories used are indeed comparable. For example, a blue-collar occupation in one nation may well be a white-collar occupation in another. Even occupational titles may vary in their meaning: An "engineer" in one nation may have a different education, social position, and income than in another, because the term can either designate a degree or a supervisory role in the production process.

CULTURE

Culture is another important factor affecting consumer behavior, and one most noticeable in terms of nations. The culture of the United Kingdom, with its per-

---

11. Delamaide Darrell, *The New Superregions of Europe* (New York: Dutton, 1994), 20.

sisting class consciousness, differs in many ways from that of the United States. The way of life under the Mediterranean sun is quite different from Nordic life in the cold. Even within the overall culture of a nation there are smaller subcultural groupings with their own distinctive values. These are perhaps most obvious in ethnic or religious groupings, which attract their own specialist suppliers.

The **Asian American community** in the United States may serve as an example. Only recently have marketers begun to understand that a special focus on this community may be worthwhile. However, lumping everybody into one basket may be a mistake, according to one researcher. Vietnamese Americans, for example, desire a great deal of information about products to help them make a decision. They are "label readers," expecting an advertiser to persuade them by explaining how a product will benefit them. Korean Americans tend to be extremely brand-loyal and are interested in quality and well-established brand names. Many speak exclusively Korean at home and are best reached by Korean TV and other Korean language media. Recent Chinese American immigrants from Hong Kong and Taiwan read and watch Chinese media, even though they speak and understand English. Indian Americans, particularly recent immigrants, miss service the most. They are used to cheap labor and are drawn to products that promise to make life easier and more convenient.[12]

The marketer must take such differences into account when targeting consumer groups. Moreover, great care must be taken when communication appeals are being adapted to a subculture. A simple translation may not only be insufficient, it may be downright dangerous. For example, when a U.S. chicken supplier's slogan, "It takes a tough man to make a tender chicken," was translated to advertise to Hispanics, it was understood by the offended target group to say, "It takes a sexually excited man to make a chick sensual." Even if the language part is working, the projected environmental setting must also be synchronized with the targeted subculture. For example, a promotion will not be successful if it characterizes the average Hispanic in the United States as playing golf at a country club with $400 clubs or fly-fishing in the high mountain countryside of Colorado while drinking beer. One promotion fizzled when a radio station offered two tickets to Disneyland to Hispanics as a prize. Two tickets were considered far too few for the family-oriented Hispanic.[13] Manager's Corner 4.2 shows how firms have successfully improved their focus on the Hispanic market in the United States.

disney.go.com
/Disneyland/

Manager's Corner 4.2

Focusing on a consumer culture: Hispanics in the United States

Businesses are increasingly paying attention to a growing consumer population in the United States—the Hispanics. This market is $300 billion strong, and in the next fifteen years it is expected to grow to an aggregate purchasing power worth $965 billion. There are 35 million Hispanics in the United States today, and this number should grow to more than 80 million by 2040, when one out of every four Americans will be of Hispanic descent. The burgeoning Latino middle-class market is of special interest to marketers.

Studies show that during the 1980s the number of middle-class Latinos in Southern California grew 3.5 times more than the number of poor Latinos.

The publishing industry is one that has been trying hard to conquer Latino readers. Several magazines have been launched that are specifically targeted to the Hispanic audience. Among them are *Latina, Sí, People En Español, Moderna*, and *Latina Style*. Until then few magazines showed Hispanic models or talked about Hispanic preoccupations. Few

12. John Steere, "How Asian-Americans Make Purchase Decisions," *Marketing News* 3, no. 13 (1995): 9.
13. Linda Devine, "Reaching the Hispanic Market: It All Adds Up," *San Diego Business Journal* 15, no. 43 (1994): 7A.

beauty tips specifically for Hispanic women were given, even though market research shows that they buy more lipstick, perfume, and shampoo than non-Hispanics. These magazines are tailored to appeal to an upwardly mobile Hispanic with solid education, a steady job, and a pocketful of cash. Readers of any cultural background want to look at magazines and see themselves mirrored within its glossy pages. A housekeeper from Rockville, Maryland, says, "The people are real Hispanics. It's so nice to see them in a first class magazine." Market research points to the fact that Latino parents in the United States want shows to expose their children to Spanish. So television decided to follow the press's footsteps by beginning to air sports and children's programs in Spanish. And Hispanic Internet sites such as latinolink.com and the newly launched quepasa.com are gaining momentum in the Latin community.

The trend toward a marketing strategy for Latinos is by no means restricted to the media industry. Car manufacturers, such as Honda (www.honda.com), began to advertise to Hispanic consumers, who spend $11 billion annually on cars. Honda ranked as the fifth largest car manufacturer in 1989 in the Hispanic market. Less than half a decade after it began its new marketing approach, it became number one.

Sources: Marie Arana-Ward, "Magazines, Latinos Find Themselves on the Same Page," *Washington Post,* December 5, 1996, A1, A23–A24; Lisa De Moraes, "Tuning to Latino Viewers," *Washington Post,* October 21, 1998, D2.

PEER PRESSURE

Within cultures and subcultures, there is a powerful force at work requiring members to conform to the overall values of their group. There are membership groups in which the individual is formally a member (for example, of a political party or trade union). Individuals may also have **reference groups** (social cliques, such as yuppies) to which they would like to belong. They may also recognize groups with which they would not wish to associate. Typical group behavior results in pressure on an individual to conform. Such peer pressure can sometimes be used to great effect by marketers. If they can sway the few opinion leaders in the reference group, they may capture a large portion of the group. Figure 4.3 gives one example of how these groups interrelate.

Perhaps the most influential peer group is the **family**. Since family structure can vary widely between countries, cultures, and subcultures, an analysis of the

> Perhaps the most **influential peer group** is the family.

target consumer's family structure can be crucial. For example, in **nuclear families**, the number of immediate family members and their importance to the individual is limited, whereas in extended families, there are numerous important family members available to exercise an influence on the individual's decision making. Consequently, the influence of peers and referents other than family members is relatively less powerful in **extended families**, so the use of a nonfamily peer in a promotion may not be successful.[14]

Family relations are dynamic as the interplay between generations changes. For example, it has been found in the United States that members of **Generation X** (usually referring to people born in the 1970s) tend to continue to live at home through their late 20s. As a result, many "Xers" have become designated decision makers for their parents or other relatives, particularly in areas where young adults have expertise, such as electronic equipment, computers, or automobiles.[15] Marketers ignore this influence at their own peril when designing communication strategies for their target groups.

14. Terry L. Childers and Akshay R. Rao, "The Influence of Familial and Peer-Based Reference Groups on Consumer Decisions," *Journal of Consumer Research* 19 (September 1992): 198–211.
15. Karen Ritchie, "Marketing to Generation X," *American Demographics* 17 (April 1995): 36.

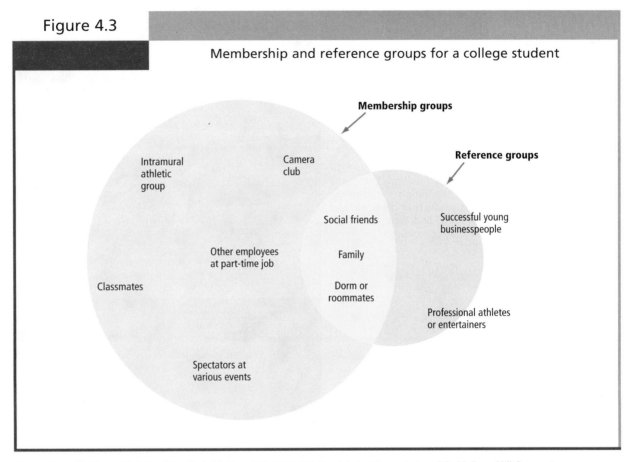

Figure 4.3

Membership and reference groups for a college student

Source: James H. Myers, *Marketing* (New York: McGraw-Hill, 1986), 223. Reprinted with permission of the McGraw-Hill Companies.

LIFESTYLE AND VALUES

Although many firms still use class and age (see Exhibit 4.1) as the main discriminators, increasing affluence has resulted in spending patterns that now vary considerably, even within the same age and class groups; they now reflect individual lifestyles. Marketers wish to appeal to such lifestyles and therefore increasingly develop **lifestyle classification** methods that link different dimensions of consumers, such as activities, interests, and opinions, with their spending or product use patterns. For example, in order to better understand the behavior of consumers who use high technology information and communication methods, the market research company Odyssey conducted 4,000 consumer interviews and 28 focus groups in 14 cities. The result was the development of six technology consumer lifestyle segments: New Enthusiasts, Hopefuls, Faithfuls, Oldtimers, Independents, and Surfers.[16] Perhaps best known is the Values and Lifestyles (VALS™) system developed by SRI International. Unlike many other segmentation systems, VALS divides consumers into groups based on psychological characteristics (such as status-seeking and excitement-seeking) and several key demographics found to be predictive of consumer behavior. VALS yields insights into why people act as they do and the ways enduring internal psychological traits are expressed in external buying patterns and lifestyles. VALS classifies U.S. adults into eight cosumer groups based on their answers to 35 attitudinal and four demographic

www.future.sri.com/vals

16. Rebecca Piirto Heath, "Qu'est-ce que c'est?" *American Demographics Marketing Tools* (November/December 1995): 74.

Exhibit 4.1

Traditionally considered a brand for mature consumers, Oldsmobile is trying to attract younger buyers. With its *Wizard of Oz* graphic and the inset of the children in the back seat, this ad highlights a new on-board entertainment system to target consumers with growing families. The crossover marketing with Blockbuster further defines the lifestyle and age of the intended consumer.

questions. The VALS classification battery is integrated into several large national syndicated consumer surveys. It is also integrated into clients' custom questionnaires so that their respondents can be VALS-typed. The major tendencies of the four VALS groups with greater resources (for example, education, income, self-confidence, health, and eagerness to buy) are:

- *Actualizers:* successful, sophisticated, active, "take-charge" people. Purchases often reflect cultivated tastes for relatively upscale, niche-oriented products.
- *Fulfilleds:* mature, satisfied, comfortable, reflective. Favor durability, functionality, and value in products.
- *Achievers:* successful, career- and work-oriented. Favor established, prestige products that demonstrate success to their peers.
- *Experiencers:* young, vital, enthusiastic, impulsive, and rebellious. Spend a comparatively high proportion of their income on clothing, fast food, music, movies, and video.

The major tendencies of the four VALS groups with fewer resources are:

- *Believers:* conservative, conventional, and traditional. Favor familiar products and established brands.
- *Strivers:* uncertain, insecure, approval-seeking, resource-constrained. Favor stylish products that emulate the purchases of those with greater material wealth.
- *Makers:* practical, self-sufficient, traditional, family-oriented. Favor only products with a practical or functional purpose such as tools, utility vehicles, and fishing equipment.

- *Strugglers:* edlerly, resigned, passive, concerned, resource-constrained. Cautious consumers who are loyal to favorite brands.[17]

Figure 4.4 summarizes the structure of the VALS system. Getting the lifestyles of consumers right can make a big difference to the satisfaction of consumers and the profitability of marketing undertakings. For example, Marriott Corporation has developed several time-share locations, where clients buy the right to occupy a property for one week during a specified season. To be successful, Marriott must market the same vacation place to different prospects. A location in Vail, Colorado, can be sold to some during the winter season for skiing but also to others for a summer season of hiking, fishing, and horseback riding. By being able to match the marketing approach, the season, and the type

www.marriott.com

Figure 4.4

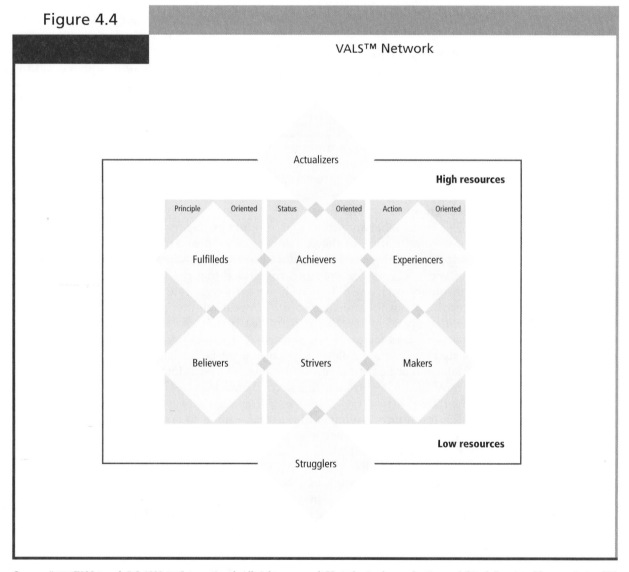

Source: "VALS™ Network," © 1999 SRI International. All rights reserved. Unauthorized reproduction prohibited. Reprinted by permission SRI Consulting.

17. "VALS 2 Psychographic Segmentation System" (Menlo Park, Calif.: SRI International, 1994): 4.

of home to the right individual, the company can save large amounts of promotion expenditures and achieve high rates of closings.[18]

Lifestyles can also be used by nonprofit organizations. One Wisconsin blood donation center reportedly turned a deficit of 7,000 donors into a surplus of 7,000 by concentrating its attention on people who were affluent, busy, and had close-knit families. Clearly, lifestyles depend on the environment in which the consumer lives, so socioeconomic variables can play an important role.

DIFFUSION OF INNOVATION

One aspect of consumer behavior that is closely related to lifestyles and has attracted considerable interest relates to the way new products or new ideas are adapted. Gatignon and Robertson suggest that the so-called diffusion process can be characterized in terms of three dimensions: the rate of **diffusion**, the pattern of diffusion, and the potential penetration level.[19] The rate of diffusion reflects the speed at which sales occur over time. The pattern of diffusion refers to how a new idea or product spreads to different groups. The potential penetration level is a separate dimension indicating the size of the potential market, that is, the maximum cumulative sales (or adoption) over time. Marketing actions are important in influencing the speed of diffusion as well as the process of diffusion by segment. Indeed, in most cases marketing actions are designed to achieve faster penetration, to block competition, and to establish a market franchise.

> marketing actions are designed to achieve faster penetration, to block competition, and to establish a market franchise

This is just what ambitious new product managers look for in their launches. But one complication of the consumer decision-making process is the fact that the adoption of new products is not necessarily uniform throughout the population. Everett Rogers, for example, concluded that there are five separate groups of consumers, each one of which shows a different rate of new product adoption. Proceeding from the quickest to the slowest adopters, they are innovators (2.5 percent), early adopters (13.5 percent), early majority (34 percent), later majority (34 percent), and laggards (16 percent).[20] A careful look at these categories will indicate that they are following a normal (or bell) distribution curve. The early and later majorities are captured by one standard deviation, the early adopters and most of the laggards by the second standard deviation, and the innovators by the third.

The **innovators** are adventurous and willing to take risks, whereas the early adopters are the main opinion leaders in their community. This classification suggests that the marketer should take a particular interest in these two leading groups when contemplating a product launch. But innovations may have consequences or costs for the consumption system in which they are placed. For instance, the adoption of an innovation might require other changes in the consumption system or the adoption of ancillary services, which raise the total cost of innovating.[21] Manager's Corner 4.3 shows how innovations in technology can precipitate new derivative

---

18. Cathy Asato, "Marriott's Time-Share Club Chooses DB Software that Performs Like a Marketer, not a Scientist," *DM News*, December 11, 1995, 17.

19. H. Gatignon and T. S. Robertson, "A Propositional Inventory for New Diffusion Research," *Journal of Consumer Research* 11 (March 1988): 26.

20. E. M. Rogers, *Diffusion of Innovations* (New York: Free Press, 1962), 247.

21. Gatignon and Robertson, "A Propositional Inventory."

Manager's Corner 4.3

Paradoxes of technology and marketing challenges

Technology promises to make us more efficient, entertain us, and put us in touch with one another. At the same time, we also accuse technology of disruptively wasting our time as well as isolating us from other people. A technological advance is likely to bring about multiple changes, and the key to making a success of new technology is to understand how the buyer feels about it.

Take the example of two new products that have been hailed as the next generation VCRs—TiVo (www.tivo.com) and Replay (www.replay.com). These devices, called "personal video recorders," work with television programming as well as cable and satellite and capture programming on computer-style hard drives instead of videotapes. They let users create "virtual channels" reflecting personal tastes. Like VCRs, Replay and TiVo are boxes that attach to the TV and are used to record shows. But TiVo and Replay are more like computers than cassette recorders. Using elaborate on-screen menus of television list-

ings, a telephone line connection, and a remote control, a consumer can click on a favorite show to record it. TiVo and Replay also bring VCR-type capabilities to live television, in the sense that viewers can rewind, pause, and create their own instant replay of live events. With this new technology consumers will create customized viewing channels by typing in their interests, such as history or the name of an actor, and have all programs around this topic recorded. A person will control what is viewed and see only what is of interest.

Personal video recorders are likely to have a significant impact on advertisers. Replay's remote control has a "Quick Skip" button that makes a show jump ahead 30 seconds—the standard length of an American commercial. If people do start skipping commercials, broadcast networks will need to find other sources of income or use other forms of promotion that cannot be skipped, such as product placement or banners directly in programs.

Sources: David Champion, "Marketing: Technology's Garden of Paradox," *Harvard Business Review* (July/August 1998); Bruce Haring, "Personalized TV No Longer Remote," *USA Today*, March 3, 1999, D5; "Taking the Ads out of Television," *Economist*, May 8, 1999, 64.

challenges for marketers. One crucial aspect of the adoption process is the changing importance of external influence (mass media) relative to internal influence (word of mouth) over time, as illustrated in Figure 4.5.[22]

It should also be noted that research finds the rates of innovation and diffusion vary not only between customers but also between countries. A comparison within the European Union determined that innovativeness tends to decrease with higher ethnocentrism. Consumers in more individualistic countries tended to be more innovative. Innovativeness was found to be lower in national cultures that emphasize uncertainty avoidance.[23] In an analogy to the diffusion proposition that consumers who innovate go beyond their social system boundaries, cosmopolitanism has also been shown to be positively related to the population's propensity to innovate.[24] Marketers with innovative products that require the enthusiasm of early adopters should therefore pay close attention to the propensity to innovate in the countries that they are considering for entry.

22. Vijay Mahajan, E. Muller, and F. M. Bass, "New Product Diffusion Models in Marketing: A Review and Directions for Research," *Journal of Marketing* 54 (January 1990): 27.

23. Jan-Benedict E. M. Steenkamp, Trenkel ter Hofstede, and Michel Wedel, "A Cross-National Investigation into the Individual and National Cultural Antecedents of Consumer Innovativeness," *Jorunal of Marketing* 63 (April 1999): 55–69.

24. Hubert Gatignon, Jehoshua Eliashberg, and Thomas S. Robertson, "Modeling Multinational Diffusion Patterns: An Efficient Methodology," *Marketing Science* 8, no. 3 (summer 1989): 231–247.

Figure 4.5

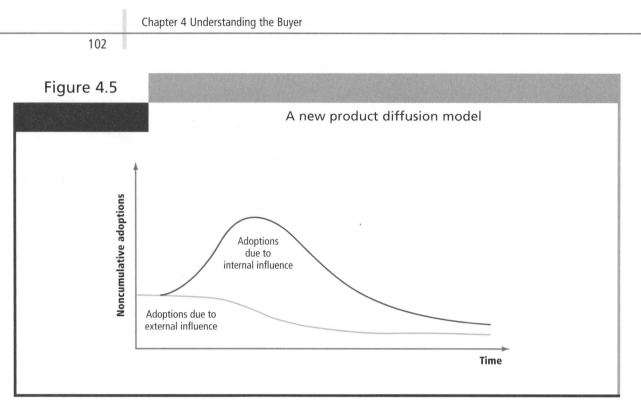

A new product diffusion model

Noncumulative adoptions

Adoptions due to internal influence

Adoptions due to external influence

Time

Source: Vijay Mahajan, E. Muller, and F. M. Bass, "New Product Diffusion Models in Marketing: A Review and Directions for Research," *Journal of Marketing*, 54 (1990), No. 1: 4. Reprinted by permission of the American Marketing Association.

PSYCHOLOGICAL FACTORS

A number of psychological factors also influence buyer behavior, ranging from the teachings of Freud to Herzberg's discussion of **dissatisfiers** (characteristics that prevent a product's purchase by a given customer) and **satisfiers** (characteristics that will positively persuade the customer to choose that brand).[25] In the context of marketing, perhaps the most widely quoted psychological approach is that of Abraham Maslow.[26] He developed a **hierarchy of needs**, shaped like a pyramid, which ranges from the most essential immediate physical needs such as hunger, thirst, and shelter to the most luxurious nonessentials. It was Maslow's contention that the individual addresses the most urgent needs first, starting with the physiological. But as each need is satisfied, and the lower-level physical needs are satiated, attention switches to the next higher level, resulting ultimately in the level of self-actualization or fulfillment. It has been argued that marketers in industrialized nations should increasingly focus their attention on the two highest levels for the citizens of their countries. However, it appears that even in relatively rich countries, the elementary needs of many remain unfulfilled. An interesting phenomenon—the **foreign concern**—emerges as an additional post-Maslowian level. Many who themselves have achieved high levels of needs fulfillment begin to focus on individuals in other countries. Seeing that they are comparatively worse off, these poorer individuals and countries are encouraged to seek and offer self-actualization, without addressing their own often unfulfilled basic needs such as nourishment and housing. Such approaches can lead to disagreement and even conflict, particularly in the international trade and policy areas, without necessarily improving the quality of life.

25. F. Herzberg, *Work and Nature of Man* (New York: William Collins, 1966).
26. Abraham Maslow, *Motivation and Personality* (New York: Harper & Row, 1954).

COORDINATING CONSUMER DIMENSIONS

To most effectively use the dimensions discussed so far, the marketer must design the right approach for each type of consumer and ensure that the approach reaches the consumer. Therefore, the marketer must coordinate all activities, whether in service, pricing, or communications; otherwise, the consumer receives confusing and sometimes even conflicting messages. Information technology can be very useful in assigning consumers to their appropriate groups and then ensuring that the marketing effort extended toward them fits appropriately.

> the marketer must coordinate
> **all activities, whether in service,**
> pricing, or communications

ORGANIZATIONAL PURCHASING

So far our discussion has focused mainly on consumer products. However, different categorizations are often applied to **industrial products**, which are sold to businesses and institutional or government buyers to be incorporated into their own products, resold, or used within their organizations. These tend to be purchased in larger quantities and are often of higher value than consumer products. Industrial products are also much more amenable to marketing with the use of new technology, because the business partners tend to be well informed about the market and typically have the use of market-specific, state-of-the-art technology (see Exhibit 4.2). Therefore, new approaches to doing business can gain rapid acceptance. For example, when measured in sales volume, industrial marketing has made much more use of Internet technology than consumer marketing. Consequently, organizational purchasing has dimensions that are distinct from consumer behavior. Industrial buying processes are often grouped at the most basic level by broad product type:

> organizational purchasing has
> **dimensions that are distinct**
> from consumer behavior.

- **Basic raw materials**, such as steel for a car manufacturer. These are usually sold on a contractual basis with tight specifications. Sales are often achieved by competitive pricing, credit terms, and delivery reliability.
- **Components**, such as radiators. These differ from basic materials because of their wider variation. Product quality and reliability become extremely important.
- **Capital goods**, such as lathes. These are normally dominated by high technical capability.
- **Supplies**, such as detergents for floor cleaning. These are consumable items, usually of low unit value, and often sold through distributors.

Marketers of industrial goods must pay particular attention to what makes industrial market activities different from consumer goods markets. Examples are **reciprocity,** in which firms engage in interrelated business transactions; relationship marketing, in which long-term interaction rather than short-term transactions govern the relationship between firms; and **reverse marketing** structures, in which firms need to collaborate in order to accommodate the flow of products from the end user back to the manufacturer, for reasons such as safety

Exhibit 4.2

Although industrial buying typically centers around manufactured products, it also includes services that are generally considered consumer-oriented. Resorts are an example of this, with many sites often competing for a company's annual sales meeting or other large event. Marriott Hotel's Web site even has a meeting planning page to help locate the optional Marriott facility for corporate events (www.marriott.com/search/meetingsearch.asp).

or environmental responsibility. We will address these dimensions specifically throughout the book in the context of marketing strategy development. At this stage, the most important differences to keep in mind are demand structures and decision processes.

DEMAND PATTERNS

The demand for industrial goods or services often depends on some other product or process; this is known as **derived demand**. The industrial marketer selling steel, for example, also needs to be concerned about the demand for the ultimate consumer product, such as the automobile. In recent years this has led to a more partnership-style relationship between some industrial sellers and their customers. This concept of customer partnership is explored in more detail later in this text.

Joint demand occurs when the demands for two or more products are interdependent, normally because they are used together. The demand for razor blades depends on the number of razors in use, which is why razors have sometimes been sold as loss leaders in order to increase demand for the associated blades.

DECISION MAKERS AND INFLUENCERS

In industrial marketing, organizational factors tend to dominate the decision process. There is much theory about the interaction between the various decision makers and **influencers** (those who can only influence but not decide). Decisions are frequently made by groups rather than individuals, and the official buyer often does not have authority to make the decision.

A more complex view of industrial buying decisions suggests three levels of decision making:

1. *Economic buying influence* exerted by the decision maker who can authorize the necessary funds for the purchase

2. *User buying influences* exerted by the people in the buying company who will use the product and will specify what they want to purchase

3. *Technical buying influence* exerted by the experts (including, typically, the buying department) who can veto the purchase on technical grounds[27]

An even finer differentiation identifies six roles within the buying center:

1. *Users* who will actually use the product or service

2. *Influencers*, particularly technical personnel

3. *Deciders*, or the actual decision makers

4. *Approvers* who formally authorize the decision

5. *Buyers*, or the department with formal purchasing authority

6. *Gatekeepers* who have the power to stop sellers from reaching other members of the buying center[28]

One important aspect of organizational purchasing is its interactive nature, which the International Marketing and Purchasing Group, a pan-European group of researchers, has investigated in some detail. Both the buyer and the seller contribute to the purchasing process, so the discussions and meetings—which may extend over a considerable period—are designed to achieve a negotiated outcome that is satisfactory to both sides. Both sides must win for the successful emergence of a customer partnership and the maintenance of a relationship.

ETHICS AND INDUSTRIAL BUYING

Although ethics is important both for consumer as well as industrial markets, differences in ethical perspectives can loom particularly large in the industrial buying process. For example, in some markets, the relationship itself, not the performance, is the overriding determinant of who gets the contract. Sometimes such relationships are developed through the paying of **bribes** in order to influence the decision. In some markets the practice may be so widespread that firms that do not pay bribes will never win a contract. Such situations are particularly onerous for firms that are prohibited by their governments from participating in such business practices. For example, the U.S. government, by enacting the **Foreign Corrupt Practices Act**, made it a crime for U.S. executives of publicly traded firms to bribe a foreign official in order to obtain business, even if they are competing with other foreign executives who offer bribes. More recently, the Organization for Economic Cooperation and Development (OECD) has agreed to antibribery rules on a much broader level that makes it more difficult for anyone to bribe and thus levels the international playing field.

> differences in ethical perspectives can
> ## loom particularly large
> in the industrial buying process.

www.oecd.org

The problem is one of ethics versus practical needs and, to some extent, of the amounts involved. For example, it may be hard to draw the line between providing a generous tip and paying a bribe in order to speed up a business transaction. Many business executives believe that the United States should not apply its moral principles to other societies and cultures in which bribery and corruption are endemic. To compete internationally, executives argue, they must be free to use the most common methods of competition in the host country. On the other hand, it is difficult to apply different standards to executives and firms based on whether they do business abroad or domestically. Furthermore, bribes may open the way to shoddy performance and loose moral standards

---

27. R. B. Miller and S. E. Heiman, *Strategic Selling* (New York: Kogan Page, 1989), 81.

28. F. E. Webster and Y. Wind, *Organizational Buying Behavior* (Upper Saddle River, N.J.: Prentice Hall, 1972), 79.

among executives and employees and may result in the spread of general unethical business practices. Unrestricted bribery could cause firms to concentrate on the best way to bribe rather than on the best way to produce and market their products. Even though the extreme case of business by bribery is easy to dismiss, real business situations are usually much less clear-cut and often present the protagonists with difficult decisions. Manager's Corner 4.4 describes one such dilemma.

USAGE AND LOYALTY

For both business and consumer marketers, usage status, usage rate, and loyalty are the most important outcomes of all purchasing processes. **Usage status** refers to the experience of the customer with the product or brand. Customers can be grouped into a number of categories, such as nonusers, former users, potential users, first-time users, or regular users. **Usage rate** is the frequency with which customers use (and purchase) a product. Often the Pareto 80/20 Rule applies here; that is, 20 percent of users account for 80 percent of usage. **Loyalty** determines whether the customer is committed to the brand. Four typical patterns of loyalty behavior have been proposed:

- *Hard-core loyals* who buy the brand all the time
- *Split loyals* who are loyal to two or three brands
- *Shifting loyals* who move from one brand to another
- *Switchers* who have no loyalty; they may be deal prone (looking for bargains) or vanity prone (looking for something different)[29]

Manager's Corner 4.4

Ethics in a shrinking world

As organizations expand their relationships with other cultures, employees abroad are faced with some interesting dilemmas. One central question is whether ethics policies grounded in unique American values are exportable or whether the attempt to apply these policies in foreign countries basically amounts to cultural imperialism.

An actual case study will help make our point. An American company executive in Tokyo has just selected a Japanese company to distribute his product in the Far East. The day before the executive leaves, the Japanese CEO presents him with a set of golf clubs and a leather bag that sells for at least $2,000 in the United States and probably $4,000 in Japan. This act is in keeping with a Japanese custom of giving gifts. The American executive feigns ignorance of the custom, allowing himself to avoid giving a gift in return, but the decision remains as to what he should do

with the golf clubs. Refusing the gift would cause the Japanese CEO to lose face in front of his employees and probably sour the relationship—not a wise idea. The only option seems to be to accept the gift and then present the clubs to the home company. One unfortunate consequence of this situation, however, is that each time the Japanese CEO visits the United States, the executive who made the deal has to pretend to be either sick or out of town on the day set aside to play golf.

In the rush to create ethics policies, all players should be aware that their way of doing things isn't the only way and that customs of other cultures have value and validity. If rules of behavior are going to be written in the global economy, they must be framed in the context of world citizenry so that employees have the ability to adapt to local customs yet comply with the values that define their corporate character.

Source: David Fagiano, "Ethics in a Shrinking World," *Business Credit* 96 (February 1994): 48.

---

29. Philip Kotler, *Marketing Management*, 9th ed. (Upper Saddle River, N.J.: Prentice Hall, 1997), 262–263.

In industrial markets, organizations regard the **heavy users** as major accounts to be handled by senior sales personnel, whereas the **light users** will be handled by the general sales force or by a dealer. In consumer markets such differentiations, although quite sensible, are more difficult to find. However, some service providers, such as hotels, rental car agencies, or airlines, have developed registration or loyalty programs that not only encourage customers to come back but also allow the provider to quickly identify (and respond to) heavy users.

For the marketer, the achievement of repeat purchases is crucial. It is very rare that a single purchase by each customer is sufficient for the attainment of long-term profitability. The marketer therefore looks at the series of transactions that such repeat purchasing implies. The consumer's growing experience over a number of such transactions is often the determining factor in future purchases. All the succeeding transactions are interdependent, and the overall decision-making process may

> ## For the marketer, the achievement of repeat purchases is crucial.

thus be as complex as that in any industrial buying process. Challenges generating sustained, repeat business are addressed in Marketing in Action 4.2.

In the case of **capital goods** (such as washing machines for households or machine tools for companies) or rarely purchased goods (such as silverware, which the typical household buys only twice in a lifetime), it may be possible to achieve repeat buying only over very extended periods. However, the experience of one purchase, such as a washing machine, may be extended to a similar

Marketing in Action 4.2

Levi's attempts to keep the Bob Dylan generation, while enticing the electronica generation

Envision yourself as an executive at Levi Strauss & Co. (www.levistrauss.com) sitting in the San Francisco, California (USA), headquarters watching videos of teenagers talking about Levi's. One after another, the teenagers of the Echo Boom generation refer to Levi's as "uncool," "more suitable for their parents or older siblings," not "with it," and a "has-been." What would you do?

Levi Strauss & Co., founded in 1853, was rated the 15th most-admired U.S. corporation and the number one most-admired apparel firm in *Fortune* magazine's 1996 annual survey. Apparently the voters were not kids of the Baby Boomers. The indifference of these Echo Boom kids to Levi's products led to a dramatic drop in Levi's blue-jean market share (30.9 percent in 1990 to 18.7 percent in 1997). Such market-share erosion resulted in the closing of 11 U.S. manufacturing facilities and the layoff of one-third of the North American workforce.

Levi's marketing response to this teenage indifference has affected every component of its marketing program. New initiatives include:

- Withdrawal of the company's newest line of blue jeans, Special Reserve (appealed to the 25-plus crowd)
- Focus on the Silver Tab brand (median buying age of 18)
- Evaluation of the 67-year relationship with ad agency of Foote, Cone & Belding
- Sponsorship of concerts for bands playing electronica (echo boom) music
- Placement of Levi's products on characters in *Friends* and *Beverly Hills 90210*
- Opening of flagship stores instead of planned mall stores
- Jazzier, colorful packaging for an exciting, youthful look

What do you think about Levi's revamped strategy? Will the new strategy entice teenagers to wear Levi's for the rest of their lives?

Sources: www.levistrauss.com; Linda Himelstein, "Levi's Is Hiking Up Its Pants," *Business Week*, December 1, 1997, 70+.

purchase, such as a clothes dryer. Without such prior experience, though, the typical consumer will seek reassurance from other sources, such as reports in consumer magazines, resort to the reputation of the vendor, or else be influenced by word-of-mouth experiences of friends and acquaintances. However, marketers can try to make such acquisitions easier by offering warranties or by providing ample return privileges. For example, some automobile manufacturers have begun to offer one-month return privileges for their cars, in effect providing the customer with a no-risk trial period.

THE CUSTOMER FRANCHISE AND BRAND EQUITY

One of the best ways for any firm to maintain its focus on the buyer is to regard its relationship with its buyers as a prime asset of the business—one that has been built up by a series of marketing investments over the years. This asset is often referred to as the **customer franchise**. As with any other asset, this investment can be expected to bring returns over subsequent years as long as it is protected and nurtured.

At one extreme, the customer franchise may be derived from the individual relationships developed by the sales professionals. At the other extreme, it is the cumulative image held by the consumer, resulting from long exposure through a number of interactions with the firm. In some markets the customer franchise may be so strong as to be exclusive, in effect giving the supplier a monopoly with those customers. For example, banks used to be reasonably confident that once they recruited a consumer as a teenager, he or she would generally remain loyal to them forever. Today this is no longer the case. Consumers regularly switch brands for variety but may retain a positive image of the original brand. Thus the customer franchise may still have a value (upon which the advertiser can build) even if the current purchasing decision goes against the firm. A later decision may once again swing in its favor. The customer franchise is, therefore, a tangible asset in terms of its potential effect on sales, even if it is intangible in every other respect.

The customer franchise is based on an accumulation of experiences over time. Unfortunately too many marketers fail to recognize the importance—and long-term nature—of this investment. They treat each new campaign as if it could exist in isolation, no matter how well or how badly it meshes with previous messages that have been delivered to the consumer. The evidence shows that consumers do not view the advertising and promotion in this way; instead they incorporate it into their existing image—to good or bad effect—depending on how well the new campaign complements the old. All these efforts affect the brand value of a product or the brand equity of a firm, which can be quite major. When looking at the high prices paid for firms acquired through mergers or for stocks offered in an Initial Public Offering (IPO), the buyer almost always makes such payments in recognition of the value of **brand equity**. Just as the number of signed-up customers for a cable television company conveys a particular consumer franchise value, so does the number of "hits" on a Web site indicate the attractiveness of the site to Internet users.

SUMMARY

Focus on the buyer is the key dimension of marketing and is what sets the discipline apart from all other business fields. The marketer must therefore understand how buyers come to the decision to purchase a product. This decision-making process is a complex one, both for consumers who are end users and for industrial buyers. For consumers, the process includes the effects of experience, lifestyle, promotion, and price. More general factors influencing consumers may be culture, geography, social class, occupation, psychological factors, and peer pressure. Marketers have conducted much research to understand the consumer decision process better and, as a result, have developed the tools of lifestyle analysis and segmentation to be able to serve consumers more efficiently and more profitably.

On the industrial side, organizational purchasing is subject to a different set of influences, both because it is usually based on derived demand and because the decision is often split between decision makers and influencers. Other factors that affect buyers' product acceptance are the diffusion of innovation, usage, and loyalty and the existence of a customer franchise.

QUESTIONS FOR REVIEW

1. What specific factors, at the time of purchase, may affect the buying decision?

2. What general factors may affect consumer buying behavior? How does social class compare with age as a predictor of behavior? How may residential neighborhoods be used? Are there dangers in following categorizations too closely?

3. What are the two main models of lifestyle? How do these compare with the various psychological approaches?

4. What is diffusion of innovation? How does the customer franchise relate to customer usage and loyalty?

QUESTIONS FOR DISCUSSION

1. Review Manager's Corner 4.1 on graduating consumers. Has the Gap family of stores been successful in its attempts among people you know? Would the concept of graduating consumers work better in some industries over others? Why or why not? Examine some of your (possible) future lifestyle changes and analyze how they are likely to affect your product choices in clothing and other areas.

2. In 1998, Josten's Inc. sold $193.4 million in school and athletic rings to high school and college students. Marketing memories is a large part of their marketing pitch, but class jewelry can be considered a once-in-a-lifetime purchase. If a product is not inherently conducive to repeat purchase, what incentive does the marketer have to provide good service? In addition to the Josten's example, consider

Batesville Casket Company, a leading manufacturer of caskets in the United States.

3. As more people are pressed for time, shopping has taken on a new look focusing on convenience and speed. In this respect, several Internet retailers pose serious threats to their more traditional counterparts. One such company is eToy. The company attempts to reduce the amount of steps needed to buy a toy and provide hassle- and kid-free shopping for busy parents.[30] Given that some groups have less time to devote to shopping, can one expect their purchase behavior to change from an optimizing to a satisfying strategy? Analyze the role of the Internet retailer in this dynamic.

4. Luxury-car makers have discovered a new marketing tool in the invitation-only party for prospective customers. Makers like Lexus and BMW have sponsored such lavish parties with gourmet food, racing-type test drives, and free tickets to exclusive events. "A Taste of Lexus" will cost Toyota $10 million to host 25,000 prospects, or $400 per person. This is much higher than the $35 to $45 per person spent to reach potential customers through traditional advertising. The invitations to these galas, however, are only extended to people who have the "right" zip code or who drive the "right" cars.[31] Is it ethical for marketers to target mainly large consumer groups with lots of disposable income? What about the small groups with less money?

5. In 1998, Daewoo began pitching its cars to college students through a unique campus-based sales force comprised of "student advisors." Considering the relatively low purchasing power of the typical college students and their openness to new types of sales approaches, Daewoo invested $20 million in training college advisors how to sell its low-end models on their campuses. The results of this innovative one-to-one marketing effort have met with success in this niche market despite the company's generally weak presence in the overall U.S. car market.[32] Should we be pleased or worried about the fact that marketers are increasingly able to fine-tune their approach to individual consumers?

6. During the 1970s, soda rivals Coke and Pepsi were targeting their U.S. marketing efforts at youth, while large coffee roasters were using more mature spokespeople. In the 1990s major coffee roasters like Maxwell House and Folger's find that they have missed an entire generation of would-be coffee drinkers with their marketing message. Now they are faced with trying to convince long-time soda drinkers not only that coffee isn't just a breakfast drink, but that their supermarket varieties can stand up against popular gourmet varieties like Starbucks.[33] If it were possible to identify "switchers," should the marketer treat them differently from "loyal users"? If so, what should some of these differences be? Identify ways the major coffee roasters could market to each of these groups.

30. George Anders and Ann Grimes, "eToys Shares Nearly Quadruple in IPO As Market Value Outstrips Toys 'R' Us," *Wall Street Journal*, May 21, 1999, A3, A6.

31. Frederic M. Biddle, "Luxury-Car Makers Try the Party Scene," *Wall Street Journal*, August 4, 1999, B8.

32. Andrea Puchalsky, "Daewoo May Revamp College-Based Bid to Sell Cars in Wake of Suit by Students," *Wall Street Journal*, March 23, 1999, B11G.

33. Nikhil Deogun, "Joe Wakes Up, Smells the Soda: Coffee Roasters Beaten by Pop Try to Be Hip," *Wall Street Journal*, June 8, 1999, B1.

FURTHER READINGS

Assael, Henry. *Consumer Behavior and Marketing Action.* Cincinnati: South-Western, 1998.

Hutt, Michael D. *Business Marketing Management: A Strategic View of Industrial and Organizational Markets.* 6th ed. Fort Worth, Tex.: Dryden Press, 1998.

Peter, J. Paul, and Jerry C. Olson. *Consumer Behavior and Marketing Strategy.* 5th ed. Boston: Irwin/McGraw-Hill, 1999.

Rogers, Everett M. *Diffusion of Innovations.* 3d ed. New York: Free Press, 1983.

Sheth, Jagdish N., Bruce I. Newman, and Barbara L. Gross. *Consumption Values and Market Choices: Theory and Applications.* Cincinnati: South-Western, 1991.

Zollo, Peter. *Wise Up to Teens: Insight into Marketing and Advertising to Teenagers.* 2d ed. Ithaca, N.Y.: New Strategist Publications, 1999.

chapter **5**

Marketing Research and Information

The tool for listening to customers is marketing research. Before firms can offer new or improved products, they must understand what customers need, how they think, and what their questions are. Much of the marketing research process therefore aims to get close to the customer and to permit the organization to understand the customer's perspective and needs. Manager's Corner 5.1 shows how firms try out new ways to get to know their customers.

Marketing research also assists managers in **decision making**. Marketers are often faced with a lack of information and therefore with uncertainty; information can lead to better decisions under these conditions. **Uncertainty** is normally greater in those markets that are changing and greatest in those that are changing rapidly. Many markets have experienced major shifts in recent years because of

Manager's Corner 5.1

New ways to know your customer

Companies are increasingly relying on research to tell them where to put their marketing resources. Through research they are able to know who their customers are and what they are looking for. Here are three examples of how companies are using research methods to improve their profits.

Before a Miramax movie is released in theaters, a psychiatrist usually screens the previews based on the responses of moviegoers around the country. As people watch the previews and answer the psychiatrist's questions, their body language is analyzed. Based on these observations, the psychiatrist may recommend a change in previews to Disney's Miramax (www.miramax.com) unit so they are compelling to audiences. Because trailers aren't about being true to the movie but about generating ticket sales, they may be adapted to fit the expected audience for a particular film.

Companies are using people's homes, schools, offices, and after-work hangouts as a way of really getting to know their customers. For example, employees of E-Lab (www.elab .com), a market research company, are watching and filming people in their kitchens in order to see what utensils are used the most and how they are used. E-Lab uses professional recruiting firms to find subjects and typically pays them $100 to participate in the study. E-Lab also conducts beeper studies, which are a way to track customers' tastes without actually trailing them around. In a beeper study, participants are instructed to write down what they are doing when they are paged.

Interscope Records does research via its Web site, www.interscoperecords.com. When preparing to release a new album by the platinum R & B artists Blackstreet, the firm offered the "Blackstreet Focus Group" on its Web site. By going to this "group," fans could listen to five 30-second clips of unreleased songs from a new album due out in a few months by Blackstreet and then offer their opinions and commentary. Fans were even able to select the song they thought should be a single. Interscope Records was then able to produce a record that was directly targeted to Blackstreet's fans.

Sources: Don Jeffrey, "Who's Buying What Music, and Where Are They Buying It?" *Billboard,* March 13, 1999, 63, 89; Hillary Rosner, "Hocus Focus," *Village Voice,* December 15, 1998, 43; Melanie Wells, "New Ways to Get into Our Heads," *USA Today,* March 2, 1999, 01B.

global competition. Even industries thought to be stable or mature enough to be unaffected by change, such as car production or shipbuilding, have experienced dramatic changes in market structure and customer expectations.

Marketing research is also useful for analyzing organizational performance. Leading-edge firms constantly strive to improve their service delivery, their customer responsiveness, and their product assortments. To do so, they need information on their activities and performance. Marketing research therefore requires a constant flow of information, which typically covers markets, customers and consumers, competitive activities, the impact of environmental factors such as governments or sociocultural changes, and the organization's own marketing activities.

EVALUATING THE BENEFITS OF RESEARCH

Marketing research requires both time and money—two typically scarce commodities. To make a justifiable case for allocating resources to research, management must understand what the value of the research will be. It should clearly aid management in improving the decision-making process and thus should aim at managerial rather than statistical significance. At the same time, market research should be recognized as a tool and not a substitute for judgment. Enough of the "right" information is never obtained within the time constraints to dictate the action or course to follow. However, research will help avoid gross errors and compensate for inadequate experience or unreliable intuition.

> market research should be recognized as a tool and not a substitute for judgment

The value of research can be assessed from two perspectives. One approach analyzes the benefits the firm receives from research; the other identifies the downside risk that the firm incurs if it does not carry out research.

The context of the decision under consideration must be evaluated when determining the extent and expense of research. The value of a decision with the benefit of research should be greater than the value of the same decision without research by an amount exceeding the cost of the research. In addition, the firm needs to have adequate resources to act on the insights gained by the research. Otherwise, the findings will not contribute to the decision-making process, and the research would be a waste of resources.

Often, however, researchers neglect to assess this **cost-benefit** relationship, particularly when the individual risks and benefits are difficult to quantify (which frequently happens). If insufficient attention is paid to the outcome of research and its cost, the firm risks conducting either too much or insufficient research. Using a cost-benefit justification for research, however, may place the researcher at risk, because once the research is carried out, the actual benefits are measurable and can be compared with the anticipated ones. If the benefits do not materialize, the researcher may be charged with having inappropriately inflated the benefit expectations.

THE RISKS OF INADEQUATE RESEARCH

As an alternative to the benefit strategy, the researcher can construct "what if" scenarios that outline the risks the company may incur by operating without sufficient information. Such risks might include a loss of market penetration effectiveness or creation of ill will that precludes any further expansion. In the long run, this justification is easier for the researcher to use than the benefit formula, because he or she can point out that some of the worst-case scenarios have not materialized.

THE MARKETING INTELLIGENCE SYSTEM

As a result of the widening availability of computerized databases, the process of collecting and distributing marketing information has become systematized. The system that handles these processes in a controlled and coordinated fashion has come to be called the **Marketing Intelligence System** (MIS). Such a system collects and organizes data that are relevant to the marketer in terms of planning, implementation, and control. Manager's Corner 5.2 shows how some companies are using their intelligence system.

It is important to understand that the MIS system does not simply take in facts and pass them on. Rather, the system adds value by transforming data and facts into a finely honed tool that will help answer the marketer's specific questions.

Data are collections of facts; for example, the demographic figures of certain neighborhoods making up the area in which a superstore chain is considering opening another branch. **Information** consists of data that have been selected and ordered with some specific purpose in mind; for example, the overall profile of those neighborhoods. **Intelligence** is the interpretation of the analysis of information; for example, the resulting profile of the superstore's likely customers and its optimal location.

The power of facts increases as they go through the process from raw data to selected prime information to analyzed intelligence, but so does the potential bias applied to the data. At the first stage one can make errors of omission, as relevant data are left out. Later on, errors may consist of attributing meaning to the information that is not really there, but that one wants to be there. Much research information is like the psychologist's Rorschach inkblot test, in which the viewer might "see" anything that he or she can imagine.

Manager's Corner 5.2

The global spyglass

Both Corning (www.corning.com) and Digital Equipment Corporation (www.dec.com) are strong believers in global computer networks for the gathering and dissemination of competitive intelligence. Corning started its global system, the Business Information Exchange Network, with a pilot program in early 1989. One key feature is a news-search service that lets users inform the system of topics that interest them. The system then automatically clips articles and places them in the user's electronic mailbox.

Digital Equipment launched its Competitive Information System (CIS) in 1984. Initially, it was used mainly to collect and distribute data on domestic competitors, but after four years it became truly global. CIS contains product descriptions, announcements, internal and external competitive analyses, and a direct feed from an external news wire. "Our data set serves both strategic and tactical needs," explains Laura J. B. Hunt, Digital's manager of information access services. Digital's competitive analysts use data from CIS for strategic decision making and planning. Its sales representatives use other pieces of CIS data to formulate sales tactics. The system now has more than 10,000 registered employee users and generates more than 100,000 daily log-ins worldwide.

Source: Kate Bertrand, "The Global Spyglass," in *Annual Editions: International Business,* ed. F. Maidment (Guilford, Conn.: Dushkin/McGraw-Hill, 1992), 90–92.

SYSTEM STRUCTURE

Many data sources can be entered into an MIS, but they need to be oriented to the particular information needs of management. The value of marketing information results from having the right information available at the right time. Many elements of information available to the marketer are based on data held within the organization, particularly performance analyses and sales reports.

PERFORMANCE ANALYSES. In most organizations the data on performance, typically derived from order processing and invoicing, are available on computer databases, which should provide accurate sales data by product and by region. If the computer systems been designed to cope with the level of detail needed, performance figures should be available down to individual customers or clients. On the other hand, this poses the potential problem of information overload: There will be so much information, most of it redundant, that it will effectively be useless as a management tool. There are two possible solutions to this avalanche of data:

- **ABC analysis.** Typically the reports are sorted in terms of volume (or value) of sales, so the customers are ranked in order of their sales. The highest-volume or "A-level" customers are at the top of the list, and the many low-volume or "C-level" customers are at the bottom, because it matters less if they are not taken into account in decisions. As we have seen, the 80/20 Rule says that the top 20 percent of customers on such a list are likely to account for 80 percent of total sales, so this approach can be used to reduce the data that need to be examined by a factor of five.

- **Variance analysis.** In this approach, management sets performance criteria such as budgets or targets, against which each of the products or customers is subsequently monitored. Only performance that falls outside the expected range is highlighted, so only those items that constitute variances need to be reviewed. However, the variances are only as good as the criteria set. Setting criteria is a major task and is particularly problematic when parameters change over time.

SALES REPORTS. The performance data described above have the great advantage of being numerical; this makes abstraction and manipulation easy. Many of the data within an organization are available only as memos or reports, which provide verbal, rather than numerical, information. From the marketing viewpoint, sales reports are perhaps the most useful of these verbal reports. In some respects the reliance on words rather than figures may seem to make the manager's job easier, because many managers are more at ease with words than with numbers. But this is something of an illusion, and problems can occur in the analysis stage. Because **verbal data** are apparently so approachable, there is a tendency to accept them at face value, particularly if their message reinforces the reader's own prejudices. Even if a critical approach is retained, the data are often difficult to analyze; the writers of such reports tend to use the same words to mean different things, and the importance they attach to events often reflects their own enthusiasm. In addition, collating a number of such reports and distilling them into an overall impression becomes a matter of judgment rather than of a simple analysis and all too often results in "evidence" used to bolster the manager's own preconceived ideas. To a certain extent some of these problems may be corrected by a well-designed reporting system or by the use of electronic mail, which can be structured to help standardize the reporting format and even the language of replies.

All too often, access to key data is limited to a few people; a memo, especially from sales personnel in the field, rarely circulates to more than half a dozen people. The traditional system then requires the recipient (say, the regional sales manager) to recognize important data and incorporate them into his or her own reports to upper management. The management thus travels hierarchically through the organization, being filtered and distorted at each stage. More importantly, it

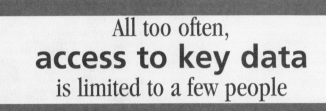

demands that a number of intermediaries recognize the significance of data. If just one of them chooses to ignore them, the data never make it to those in the chain above.

The increasing use of electronic mail should have a dramatic effect on the availability of such information, because it is almost as easy to send a memo to a hundred recipients as to one. Indeed, most e-mail systems have standard distribution lists. This has a number of important implications: The speed of distribution increases because the data become available immediately. The breadth of distribution also increases because the data are distributed to many more employees, providing them with a better perspective of what is happening throughout the organization. Employees are likely to be involved in a lateral transfer of information (between members of a department, and even across departmental boundaries) as well as—or even instead of—hierarchical communications through the normal management structure.

All these changes are a mixed blessing. The fact that memos may be distributed to ten times as many employees also means that each of them now receives many more memos than before. If one is not to sink under the torrent of data, new techniques of information transmission must be developed. For example, the originators of data will have to find ways to make the content more immediately understandable. The title of the memo will need to be meaningful in itself and may have to be associated with an equally meaningful keyword. A brief summary or abstract will, in any case, be needed for the reader who is skimming the mail to see which items are relevant and should be read in more detail. The verbal data themselves will need to be clearly structured. There will be every incentive to learn these new techniques, because those who send long unstructured memos will soon find that they are not read.

Another shortcoming of verbal material is its **retrieval**. If not "filed" in the wastepaper basket, memos and reports are often consigned to the vagaries of the manager's or department's often outdated filing systems. Electronic mail databases can be useful here. Better, though, are the specially developed computer applications for storing and retrieving vast quantities of verbal information. The most useful of these programs index every word in the documents so that an inquirer at a terminal can ask for only those documents that mention a given keyword or topic anywhere in their contents. This way, **repeat problems** can be systematically assessed. By organizing such verbal data on a customer-specific basis, firms can also achieve much greater levels of customer satisfaction. When a customer calls, the sales representative can immediately pull up any earlier correspondence with the customer. For example, Promus Hotels, which owns Hampton Inns, Embassy Suites, and Doubletree Inns, guarantees not to charge visitors for their current stay if they have any complaint. By tracking all complaints on a central database, Promus management can see where the complaints are coming from. Any hotel repeatedly experiencing the same complaint can be helped to fix the weak points. The system also allows identification of customers

www.promus.com

who might be tempted to take advantage of the generous guarantee. If a pattern develops, Promus sends a nice letter to the customer suggesting that if the hotel chain can't meet a high enough standard of quality to consider staying in a competitor's facility.[1]

Input can also come from informal reports, which are the staple diet of management. But if it is difficult to abstract useful data from written paperwork, it is not even considered worthwhile mentioning oral data—yet they probably represent the most important source of data available to a manager. For example, researchers have found that "Japanese-style market research relies heavily on two kinds of information: **soft data** obtained from visits to dealers and other channel members and **hard information** about shipments, inventory levels, and retail sales. Japanese managers believe that these data better reflect the behavior and intentions of flesh-and-blood consumers."[2] To make such informal interactions useful requires their condensation into written reports and their entry into the MIS system.

One additional issue to be considered here is that of **data longevity**. The long-term storage of information can be useful in developing a corporate memory, which may be increasingly important in an era where people leave firms more easily and quickly. In this context, the storage medium is important in order to avoid data deterioration. At the same time, many firms are wary of accumulating too many data and preserving them for too long, not so much because of the cost of storage space but because of a concern for changing societal standards. Corporate decisions that may have been sound twenty years ago may come under fierce attack when measured against the standards of today. A memo written long ago by a marketing manager may have major implications for a company exposed to a lawsuit. Therefore, many firms increasingly initiate **data reduction** programs, which eliminate information about old corporate decision processes and therefore reduce corporate exposure to the retroactive application of new standards.

SECONDARY DATA

Two types of external data are available to the marketer. These are secondary data and primary data, both available from outside the firm. The main source of external data is usually published data, often referred to as secondary data because they have been generated in response to someone else's questions. Finding secondary data is the key to sound research. Some useful sources of data are discussed below.

LIBRARIES

The widest-ranging source of published data is usually a library, possibly one within the organization itself, but more often a public library. Many published data are located in journals and specialized periodicals. Libraries often also have available special publications, yearbooks, and directories, many of them accessible either online or via CD-ROM. Such information can cover industry groups, abstracts, or company-specific data. The more specialized libraries run by trade associations or government agencies, such as the Federal Trade Commission, can also be good resources.

www.ftc.gov

DIRECTORIES AND NEWSLETTERS

The most important directories are available in your library, but again, the more specialized ones may be found only in the trade association libraries. Directories

1. Bill Gates, *Business @ The Speed of Thought* (New York: Warner Books, 1999), 187–189.
2. Johny K. Johansson and I. Nonaka, "Market Research in the Japanese Way," *Harvard Business Review* 65 (May/June 1987): 16–29.

primarily identify firms and provide very general background information, such as the name of the chief executive officer, the location, the address and telephone number, and some information on a firm's products. The quality of a directory depends, of course, on the quality of input and the frequency of updates. Many **newsletters** are devoted to specific marketing issues such as new product developments, industry or regulatory changes, or consumer demand patterns. Typically published by special interest groups or commercial providers, newsletters cater to narrow audiences but can supply important information to the manager interested in a specific area. The use of newsletters is particularly important if the firm intends to keep informed about events in a geographically dispersed area. National and international newsletters can provide insights into, say, the newest chemical regulation developments in the European Union, thus alerting the firm to international changes and new market conditions.

COMMERCIAL INFORMATION PROVIDERS

In addition to organizations that provide data in published form, others specialize in providing information in response to specific requests. For example, certain agencies, such as Dun and Bradstreet, provide credit ratings on particular organizations and shed insights on their corporate structure and business activities. A list of such information providers is provided in the appendix to this chapter.

TRADE ASSOCIATIONS

An excellent source of data, particularly informal data acquired during conversations at meetings, is trade associations. The membership fee is usually a very good value for the amount of information that can be gleaned from peers' experiences (see Exhibit 5.1). Some of these associations, such as the National Association of Wholesaler-Distributors or the National Association of Manufacturers, focus on

www.nawpubs.org
www.nam.org

Exhibit 5.1

Trade shows allow the gathering of a large amount of competitive information very quickly. Often many direct competitors exhibit at the same show, and conventioneers are able to comparison shop with little effort. This can be of critical importance in industries where new products are developed very quickly and very secretively. COMDEX, the world's largest computer trade show, routinely welcomes around 225,000 conventioneers to its Las Vegas show held annually in the fall.

www.ari.org

www.ama.org

types of firms across industries. Others, such as the Air Conditioning and Refrigeration Institute, are more specific, encompassing firms in a particular industry. Alternatively, some associations, such as the American Marketing Association, focus on certain activities of their members. In all instances, however, like-minded individuals have an opportunity to meet and exchange views. In addition, many associations publish summary industry data, which, although not informative about any specific competitor, can be very useful in terms of general **benchmarking** information, which allows firms to compare their performance and processes to the industry average.

ELECTRONIC INFORMATION SERVICES

Obtaining marketing information rapidly is often the key to success. When information is needed, managers cannot spend a lot of time, energy, or money finding, sifting through, and categorizing it. Consider the idea of laboring through every copy of a trade publication to find out the latest news about how environmental concerns are affecting marketing decisions. With the proliferation of new technologies, such information is now more readily available than ever before. Online databases and the Internet can link computer users worldwide. Databases provide information on products and markets or on companies and what they buy and sell. Market and trade statistics are available from the United Nations, the OECD, and the European Union.

www.un.org
www.oecd.org
europa.eu.int

Compact Disk/Read-Only Memory (CD-ROM) technology allows for massive amounts of information (the equivalent of 300 books of 1,000 pages each, or 1,500 floppy disks) to be stored on a single, 12-centimeter plastic disk. A CD-ROM service widely used in the United States is the National Trade Data Bank (NTDB), a monthly product issued by the U.S. Department of Commerce's Office of Business Analysis. The NTDB includes more than 170,000 documents such as full-text market research reports, import and export statistics, domestic and foreign economic data, all compiled from 26 government agencies.[3]

www.stat-usa.gov
/tradtest.nsf

Using data services for research means that professionals do not need to leave their offices, going from library to library to locate the facts they need. Many online services have late-breaking information available within minutes to the user. These techniques of research are cost effective as well. Stocking a company's library with all the books needed to have the same amount of data available as is online or with several CD-ROMs would be too expensive and space consuming. A listing of selected databases useful for marketing is presented in the appendix to this chapter.

Rapidly growing communication technology allows firms to gather information through **electronic bulletin boards** and discussion groups. For example, some firms use **search engines** or software programs to comb through thousands of newsgroups for mention of a particular product. If they find frequent references to the product, they can find out what customers are saying.[4] In a further

www.dec.com
www.sgi.com
www.sun.com

step, some firms, such as Digital Equipment Corporation, Silicon Graphics, and Sun Microsystems, systematically use the Internet to get closer to their customers by developing and interacting with discussion groups about their products. Not only do these activities shed light on customer thinking, but the interaction also saves large amounts of money by reducing customer service calls.[5] The marketer should use all these tools, but should also recognize some specific limitations of electronic information services. First, search engines are likely to uncover only a

3. "National Trade Data Bank," Government Documents Department, Lauinger Library, Georgetown University, 1999.

4. David A. Andelman, "Betting on the 'Net," *Sales and Marketing Management* (June 1995): 47–59.

5. Stephanie Losee, "How to Market on the Digital Frontier," *Fortune*, May 1, 1995, 88.

fraction of the information sought. Therefore, the user should not be misled into thinking that the information provided is comprehensive. Also, most Internet activities and search engines work in the English language. Although this fact makes life easier for native English speakers, it also does carry the risk that information in other languages is being ignored. Because the sources of innovation are quite global in nature, the marketer should also use other tools to ensure broad international coverage.[6]

EVALUATING SECONDARY DATA SOURCE AND QUALITY

Before too many resources are spent obtaining secondary data, evaluate the quality of the data source, the quality of the actual data, and the compatibility of the data with information requirements.

SOURCE QUALITY

In evaluating the quality of the data source, the researcher should determine who collected the data, the purpose of the original data collection, and how the data were collected. Ideally, the researcher would obtain the initial **research specifications** that were drawn up for the data collection. If these are not readily available, the organization that collected the data is occasionally willing to supply the specifications. By reviewing the specifications, the researcher can determine the purpose and the method of the original data collection and therefore evaluate the data quality and fit. Checking the quality of the source is important because there may be ulterior motives behind a specific form of data presentation. As an example, some countries may wish to demonstrate that their economy is improving in order to attract foreign investment. As a result, some descriptions of the domestic economy may be overstated.

DATA QUALITY

The relevance of data to the researcher's information requirements plays a major role in assessing the quality of the data. The first test is to determine whether the data provide responses to the firm's particular questions.

The **accuracy** and **reliability** of the data must be determined. For example, some international data are notoriously imprecise. As a result, the margin of error of some international statistics can be as high as 25 percent.[7] Exploring the accuracy of the data, as far as possible, can be carried out by investigating two dimensions. First, the researcher should determine the primary data source, because this allows an evaluation of source credibility. Further, the primary source usually provides the most detail about data-collection methods. The collection methods should be examined to determine whether proper research procedures were followed and whether definitions used are acceptable. **Data currency** can also be important, because secondary data are often outdated. In many nations, the most recent data available may be three to five years old. The effect of economic changes during these years on a firm's marketing operations may be quite significant. Obtaining misleading information may lead to inappropriate decisions, a result that runs contrary to the intent of marketing research. For example, changes in transportation infrastructure that are not available to the cursory researcher may lead to location decisions that turn out to be inefficient.

---

6. Michael R. Czinkota, "International Information Cross-Fertilization in Marketing: An Empirical Assessment," *European Journal of Marketing* 34 (2000).

7. K. Ramachandran, "Data Collection for Management Research in Developing Countries," in *The Management Research Handbook*, ed. N. C. Smith and P. Dainty (London: Routledge, 1991), 300–309.

Marketing in Action 5.1

Can Burger King believe its marketing research?

Research conducted by North Carolina (USA)-based Hardee's Food Systems, Inc. confirmed that Hardee's (www.hardees.com) was the favorite fast food of the surveyed consumers. So, how can it be that Burger King's (www.burgerking.com) marketing research study of 700 consumers reported the following rankings about the favorite hamburger of this set of surveyed consumers?

- 33 percent picked the Whopper
- 12 percent liked McDonald's Big Mac
- 9 percent chose Wendy's single hamburger
- 9 percent liked the Wendy's Big Bacon Classic
- 3 percent favored Burger King's Big King
- 2 percent selected Hardee's Frisco Burger
- 2 percent preferred Hardee's Monster Burger

Based on these research results, Burger King worked with its ad agencies to create general market ads, ads targeted to the Hispanic market, and ads targeted to the African-American market. The ads position the Whopper as the premier sandwich in the fast-food industry and claim that the Whopper is "America's Favorite Burger."

McDonald's (www.mcdonalds.com) does not see Burger King's ad and accompanying claim as threats. The response has been that consumers vote with their choices and that McDonald's serves 20 million customers a day in the United States. Therefore, why bother as long as consumers continue to "vote across the counter"? McDonald's might have a good point. Its 1998 market share was 42.3 percent on U.S. sales of $18.12 billion, whereas Burger King's was 20 percent on U.S. sales of $8.54 billion.

A spokesperson from Hardee's suggests that the validity of Burger King's results depends on the survey design, including the sample composition. How would you conduct marketing research if you worked at Burger King or any of its fast-food competitors?

Sources: www.burgerking.com; Gregg Cebrzynski, "Burger King Touts the Whopper as 'America's Favorite Burger,'" *Nation's Restaurant News*, April 5, 1999, 4.

Before data are acquired, both data sources and data quality must be carefully evaluated in terms of coverage, availability, accuracy, and timeliness.[8] This step is necessary not only to screen out data that may be expensive to obtain but also to minimize unnecessary cluttering of information. Even if data are free, working through them requires scarce corporate resources. The researcher therefore must ensure that the right data are obtained, using parsimony as the criterion. Otherwise, large data acquisitions are likely to lead to **information overload** within the firm, with the result that either the data are not used at all or their use becomes so time consuming that the research is inefficient. Marketing in Action 5.1 describes a situation where conflicting results may call into question the quality of the data collected.

> data sources and data quality
>
> **must be carefully evaluated in terms**
>
> of coverage, availability, accuracy, and timeliness

DATA COMPATIBILITY

The compatibility and **comparability of data** must also be considered. In marketing research, the researcher must often compare different sets of data from different sources. Great care must therefore be taken to ensure that identical, or at least similar, units of measurement, definitions, and categories are used. For example, the term *middle class* is likely to have very different implications for income and consumption patterns in different countries around the world.

---

8. G. Rice and Essam Mahmoud, "Forecasting and Data Bases in International Business," *Management International Review* 24, no. 3 (1984): 59–70.

PRIMARY MARKETING RESEARCH

Primary marketing data are collected from consumers or customers usually on a sample basis. The stereotypical market research interviewer, standing on the street corner accosting passersby or walking the streets, clipboard in hand, knocking on closed doors, probably collects only a very small part of the data available to any organization. However, these are particularly important data, because they often provide the only true listening part of the dialogue with the consumer.

SUPPLIERS OF PRIMARY MARKETING RESEARCH

Many organizations offer market research services, for only very large and sophisticated organizations will have the resources to handle all aspects of their own research. Table 5.1 lists the largest market research organizations in the United States. These suppliers can offer syndicated research and custom research to clients.

SYNDICATED RESEARCH.   These suppliers usually offer the easiest and quickest service and, typically, have ongoing or ad hoc research programs, the results of which they sell to a number of clients. Some of this can be standard research, such as the ACNielsen store audits that provide information on retail purchases by consumers. Shared cost is one advantage of such an approach, but the quality of the research is even more important. Some research can be ad hoc in that a supplier (often one specializing in the industrial field) sees a topic that it believes will be of interest to a number of companies; it then conducts the research and sells the results off the shelf. Some researchers with ongoing programs (especially those conducting opinion polls) will sell space or, more accurately, interviewer time on the back of their **omnibus surveys** (discussed below), so that one or two simple questions will be asked of a large sample at a relatively low cost.

www.acnielsen.com

Apart from the ease and speed of obtaining the research information, the great advantage of all these approaches is usually cost. Because the overall cost is shared among a number of customers, the cost to any one client is that much lower. This allows research that few individual organizations could afford to carry out themselves. In most cases it is also quick and easy to organize and therefore serves as a pilot for more complex studies.

The main types of **syndicated research** are retail audits, panel research, and omnibus surveys. **Retail audits** are one of the most sophisticated market research operations in terms of logistics. The concept, however, is simple. An auditor regularly visits each retail outlet on the panel, which has been recruited randomly. The auditor carries out a physical stock check on the products being surveyed. The change in stock from the previous visit (combined with the other stock movements, receipt of stock, and so on, which are obtained from the store's records) gives the consumer sales. Such retail audits are generally believed to offer the most accurate results of the volume of consumer sales and, in particular, of the value of such sales. These data are the main basis for brand-share calculations, for the all-important figures of price and distribution levels, and for the level of retailers' stocks, which is often very important where supply management in response to promotions is a feature.

Panel research is another way to measure consumer behavior. At its best, this may approach the accuracy of retail audits, with the added advantage that it offers consumer profiles. These panels adopt a variety of techniques and cover a range of subjects. The two main approaches are the **home audit** and the **diary method**. In the home audit the panel member is required to save packaging in a special receptacle. Once a week, an auditor checks the contents of the receptacle and the stocks of products in the house and asks the householder a short list of questions. This technique is particularly successful if respondents have a low attrition rate and provide long-term feedback. With the diary method the

Table 5.1

	Top 50 U.S. marketing research organizations					
'98 rank	Organization	Headquarters	Phone	Total research revenues[1] (millions)	Percent and revenues from outside U.S. ($ in millions)	
1	ACNielsen Corp.	Stamford, Conn.	(203) 961-3330	$1,425.4	72.6%	$1,035.0
2	IMS Health Inc.	Westport, Conn.	(203) 222-4200	1,084.0	62.0	672.5
3	Information Resources Inc.	Chicago	(312) 726-1221	511.3	22.4	114.3
4	Nielsen Media Research Inc.	New York	(212) 708-7500	401.9	2.6	10.4
5	NFO Worldwide Inc.	Greenwich, Conn.	(203) 629-8888	275.4	39.9	110.0
6	Westat Inc.	Rockville, Md.	(301) 251-1500	205.4		
7	The Arbitron Co.	New York	(212) 887-1300	194.5	3.9	7.6
8	Maritz Marketing Research Inc.	St. Louis	(314) 827-1610	169.1	25.0	42.3
9	The Kantar Group Ltd.	London	(44-171) 656-5599	150.6	19.3	29.1
10	The NPD Group Inc.	Port Washington, N.Y.	(516) 625-0700	138.5	16.0	22.2
11	Market Facts Inc.	Arlington Heights, Ill.	(847) 590-7000	136.5	14.9	20.3
12	Taylor Nelson Sofres Intersearch	Horsham, Pa.	(215) 442-9000	68.9	18.5	12.7
13	J.D. Power and Associates	Agoura Hills, Calif.	(818) 889-6330	64.8	10.5	6.8
14	United Information Group	New York	(212) 599-0444	59.0		
15	Audits & Surveys Worldwide Inc.	New York	(212) 627-9700	58.3[2]	33.3[2]	19.6[2]
16	Opinion Research Corp. International	Princeton, N.J.	(908) 281-5100	58.2	31.0	18.0
17	Burke Inc.	Cincinnati	(513) 241-5663	52.4	20.2	10.6
18	Roper Starch Worldwide Inc.	Harrison, N.Y.	(914) 698-0800	51.3	20.7	10.6
19	Macro International Inc.	Calverton, Md.	(301) 572-0200	48.7	39.0	19.0
20	Abt Associates Inc.	Cambridge, Mass.	(617) 492-7100	45.8	30.0	13.7
21	MORPACE International Inc.	Farmington, Mich.	(248) 737-5300	45.1	21.9	9.9
22	The M/A/R/C Group Inc.	Irving, Texas	(972) 506-3400	39.8		
23	Wirthlin Worldwide	McLean, Va.	(703) 556-0001	38.7	16.3	6.3
24	Total Research Corp.	Princeton, N.J.	(609) 520-9100	36.8	30.4	11.2
25	Diagnostic Research International Inc.	Los Angeles	(323) 254-4326	35.5	4.3	1.5
26	Lieberman Research Worldwide	Los Angeles	(310) 553-0550	34.8	12.1	4.2
27	C&R Research Services Inc.	Chicago	(312) 828-9200	34.5		
28	Elrick & Lavidge Marketing Research	Tucker, Ga.	(770) 938-3233	32.7	3.4	1.1
29	Market Strategies Inc.	Southfield, Mich.	(248) 350-3020	30.6	3.3	1.0

householder records the required information in a diary, which is collected by the interviewer (or, less successfully but more cheaply, returned by mail). Both methods have, over long periods, been shown to provide accurate share data. Most importantly, these panels can show trend data, repeat purchasing, and **brand-switching** information, which are almost impossible to obtain when using other methods.

Omnibus surveys are very similar to ad hoc surveys, except that space on the questionnaire is "sublet" to different researchers, providing, in effect, their own minisurvey. Omnibus surveys are often run on the back of ongoing research, such as political or opinion polls. The cost benefits can be significant, because field-work forms the major element of most market research costs. Such surveys may also provide a faster turnaround of results, particularly if the survey is conducted by telephone. However, the questionnaire needs to be short, its questions cannot be

Table 5.1

Top 50 U.S. marketing research organizations (*cont.*)

'98 rank	Organization	Headquarters	Phone	Total research revenues[1] (millions)	Percent and revenues from outside U.S. ($ in millions)	
30	Ipsos-ASI Inc.	Norwalk, Conn.	(203) 840-3400	30.5		
31	Custom Research Inc.	Minneapolis	(612) 542-0800	30.2	12.3	3.7
32	Walker Information	Indianapolis	(317) 843-3939	29.4	28.3	8.3
33	Harris Black International Ltd.	Rochester, N.Y.	(716) 272-9020	27.8	7.5	2.1
34	Yankelovich Partners Inc.	Norwalk, Conn.	(203) 846-0100	27.2		
35	IntelliQuest Inc.	Austin	(512) 329-0808	26.6	25.2	6.7
36	ICR-International Communications Research	Media, Pa.	(610) 565-9280	22.7		
37	Data Development Corp.	New York	(212) 633-1100	21.6	5.6	1.2
38	Market Decisions	Cincinnati	(513) 721-8100	19.1		
39	RDA Group Inc.	Bloomfield Hills, Mich.	(248) 332-5000	18.8	31.9	6.0
40	National Research Corp.	Lincoln, Neb.	(402) 475-2525	17.7		
41	Strategic Marketing Corp.	Bala Cynwyd, Pa.	(610) 667-1649	16.6	17.8	3.0
42	Lieberman Research Group	Great Neck, N.Y.	(516) 829-8880	16.1	2.5	.4
43	Directions Research Inc.	Cincinnati	(513) 651-2990	14.8		
44	Convergys MR&DCS	Cincinnati	(513) 841-1199	14.5	34.5	5.0
44	Questar Inc.	Eagan, Minn.	(651) 688-0089	14.5		
46	Greenfield Consulting Group Inc.	Westport, Conn.	(203) 221-0411	13.8	4.4	.6
47	The PreTesting Co. Inc.	Tenafly, N.J.	(201) 569-4800	13.5	5.5	.7
48	Marketing and Planning Systems Inc.	Waltham, Mass.	(781) 890-2228	13.2	15.2	2.0
48	Schulman, Ronca, & Bucuvalas Inc.	New York	(212) 779-7700	13.2		
50	Marketing Analysts Inc.	Charleston, S.C.	(843) 797-8900	13.0	6.0	.8
			Subtotal, Top 50	$5,943.3	37.9%	$2,250.5
	All other (133 CASRO member companies not included in Top 50)[3]			484.0		
			Total (183 organizations)	$6,427.3		

[1] Total revenues that include nonresearch activities for some companies are significantly higher. This information is given in the individual company profiles.

[2] Estimated.

[3] Total revenues of 133 survey research firms beyond those listed in Top 50 that provide financial information, on a confidential basis, to the Council of American Survey Research Organizations (CASRO).

Source: "Top 50 U.S. research organizations," The Honomichl, *Marketing News* (June 7, 1999): H4. Reprinted with permission of The American Marketing Association.

complex, and the context may be unpredictable because the questions asked by the other researchers cannot be controlled. Such surveys can also be used to locate individuals belonging to target groups so that they can be followed up by conventional ad hoc surveys.

As computer ownership rises within the general population, it will also be more likely for respondents to participate in electronic research. Large **cyber panels** will make it easier to receive input from highly targeted populations, thus providing better information at relatively lower cost. Given the rapid developments in technology, it may well be that electronic surveys and cyber panels become dominant forms of data collection.[9]

9. Seymour Sudman and Edward Blair, "Sampling in the Twenty-First Century," *Journal of the Academy of Marketing Science* 27, no. 2 (1999): 269–277.

CUSTOM RESEARCH.   Custom research is the staple diet of the market research industry. The research organization is commissioned by a client to undertake a specific research task, and it accepts responsibility for all aspects of the research. There is usually quite a distinct split between organizations that specialize in the consumer fields—the province of the large random surveys—and those in the industrial field, where research often revolves around extended interviews with individual organizations. There are also clear divisions between those involved in retail audits, those conducting questionnaire surveys on individual consumers, and those conducting group discussions or in-depth psychological interviews. In addition, many research firms concentrate mainly on the measurement of marketing performance—by investigating, for example, the effectiveness of advertisements. This latter form of research is growing quite rapidly, particularly because of the expansion of interactive media. For example, Nielsen Media Research founded a joint venture with Internet Profiles in order to provide firms with information about individuals using the Internet to visit a World Wide Web home page. With the help of a profile card filled out by browsers, firms can then structure follow-up activities.[10]

Within the market research community, firms often specialize in performing research subtasks. For example, an agency that has been commissioned by a client will typically plan and design the research itself but may appoint a subcontractor to provide the sample based on a specialist database, another organization to pretest the research, a further company to conduct the main series of interviews in the field, and yet another to analyze the results.

THE MARKETING RESEARCH PROCESS

Figure 5.1 presents an overview of the key steps necessary to plan and conduct primary marketing research and also serves as an outline for the subsequent discussion in this chapter. Although it may sometimes appear attractive to take a shortcut and skip some of the steps, it is unwise to do so because each step assesses the conditions particular to the research and therefore focuses the subsequent activities more tightly. By taking a shortcut one risks losing this focus and spending more rather than less effort.

DEFINING THE OBJECTIVES

This is the most important stage of all market research, and the one at which the research is most likely to be misdirected. Only the client can know the problem area that he or she wants the research to investigate. However, problem identification can be a great challenge. All too often, symptoms are mistaken for problems, and, as a result, research programs are developed that chase shadows instead of substance. An instance of such a mistake would be research conducted by Federal Express with the intention of avoiding loss of market share to UPS, when the real problem may be the increased use of fax machines. A marketing research expert can help to translate the client's ideas into a suitable framework. Without expertise it is all too easy to pursue the wrong issue or to introduce bias that will skew the results.

The objectives need to be clearly stated and unambiguous. On the other hand, they should not prejudge the issue. Market research will fail if it is merely asked to confirm the existing theories of the commissioning organization. This can be the result of **errors of commission** by slanting questions to produce the answers

www.nielsenmedia.com
www.ipro.com

www.fedex.com
www.ups.com

---

10. Kevin Goldman, "Nielsen, I/Pro Form Joint Venture to Measure the Internet's Activity," *Wall Street Journal*, September 6, 1995, B2.

Figure 5.1

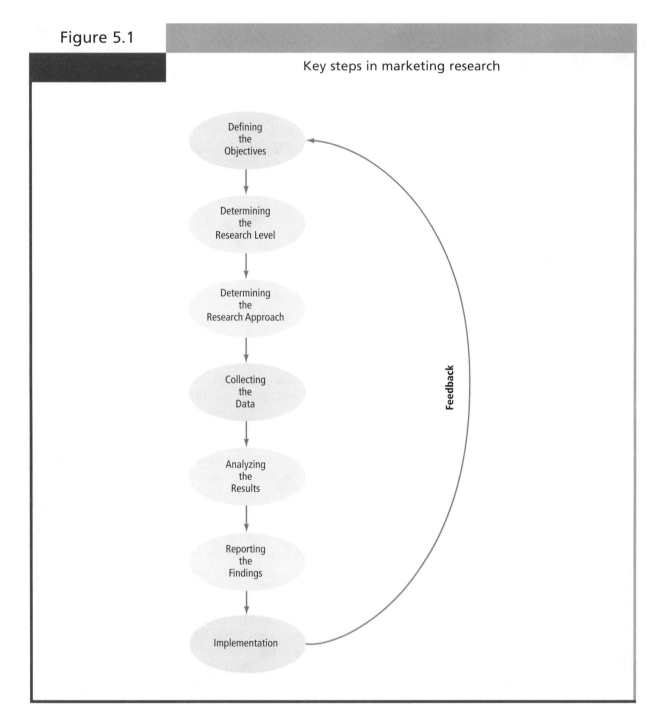

Key steps in marketing research

that the organization expects or wants. A good market research agency should detect such bias and remove it. **Errors of omission**—key questions never asked— are more difficult to deal with; this is a problem that few market research organizations are in a position to detect unless they are thoroughly familiar with the issues under study.

DETERMINING THE RESEARCH LEVEL

There are three possible research levels: **exploratory**, **descriptive**, or **causal**. The differentiation is necessary because each level requires varying commitments of time and funding. Furthermore, the answers supplied have varying utility to the

Figure 5.2

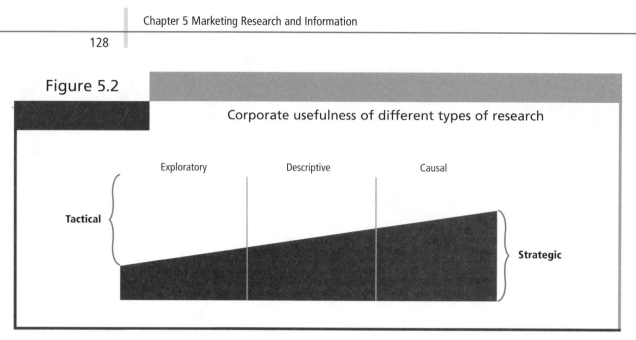

Corporate usefulness of different types of research

Exploratory   Descriptive   Causal

Tactical

Strategic

Source: Michael Czinkota and Ilkka A. Ronkainen, *International Marketing,* 4th ed. (Orlando: Harcourt Brace and Company, 1995). Copyright © 1995 by Harcourt, Inc. Reproduced by permission of the publisher.

corporation, ranging from mainly tactical at the exploratory level to strategic and long-term at the causal level. Figure 5.2 depicts the changes in corporate usefulness of the three types of research. Each objective has merit, depending on corporate needs, but the strategic insights are most useful for the long-run success of the firm.

EXPLORATORY RESEARCH. Exploratory research is most appropriate when the primary objective is to identify problems, to define problems more precisely, or to investigate the possibility of new, alternative courses of action. Exploratory research can also aid in formulating hypotheses regarding potential problems or opportunities that are present in the decision situation.[11] Frequently, exploratory research is only the first step in further research activity. To some extent, it can be compared to a fishing expedition or to a charting of the waters for the uninitiated.

> ## Defining and formulating the problem are often far more essential than its solution

Exploratory research can be very useful to gain initial insights into the new environment, its customers, and its suppliers. Exploratory research is often characterized by the need for great flexibility and versatility. Because the researcher is not knowledgeable about the phenomenon under investigation, there is a need to quickly adapt to newly emerging situations in order to make the research worthwhile. The emphasis is on **qualitative** rather than **quantitative data collection**, and on quick rather than slow answers. This, of course, means that exploratory research is less subject to the rigors of more precise research and is therefore less reliable. Exploratory research can be most useful in answering the basic question for the researcher, "What is the problem?" Defining and formulating the problem are often far more essential than its solution, which may be merely a matter of mathematics or experimental skill. If the basic research objective is to define a problem or to gain a feel for a situation or to provide an overview, exploratory research may be the most appropriate activity from the standpoint of both time and money.

11. Thomas C. Kinnear and James R. Taylor, *Marketing Research: An Applied Approach,* 3d ed. (New York: McGraw-Hill, 1987), 125.

DESCRIPTIVE RESEARCH. Descriptive research provides information about existing market phenomena. For example, market characteristics such as the socio-economic position of customers or their purchasing intent may be analyzed. Such research is often used to determine the **frequency** of marketing events, such as the frequency of customers visiting the store or of machines needing to be replaced, and investigates the degree to which marketing variables are associated with one another. Based on this determination, predictions can then be made regarding future occurrences in the market. The researcher typically uses descriptive work to look for similarities and differences between markets and consumer groups. Similarities can then be exploited through standardization, and differences can assist in the formulation of an adaptive business strategy.

Although several interviews may be sufficient for exploratory research, descriptive studies often require larger quantities of data because the requirements for an accurate portrayal of the population under study are much more stringent. To carry out descriptive work, the researcher needs a substantial amount of information about the phenomenon under study. Hypotheses are customarily pre-formulated and subsequently tested with the accumulated data. The research design needs to be carefully planned and structured. The intent of descriptive research is to maximize accuracy and to minimize systematic error. The researcher aims to increase reliability by keeping the measurement process as free from random error as possible. Descriptive research does not provide any information about causal interrelationships, but this does not necessarily detract from its value. Quite often, firms have little interest in the underlying causes for interaction and are satisfied if linkages can be described. As an example, a firm may benefit from knowing that in January, soft drink sales will drop by 30 percent from December's levels. Whether this development results from lower temperatures or from decreased humidity may be much less useful information.

> The intent of descriptive research **is to maximize accuracy** and to minimize systematic error.

CAUSAL RESEARCH. Causal research identifies precise cause-and-effect relationships present in the market. The level of precision is higher than that for other types of research because reasonably unambiguous conclusions regarding causality must be presented. Therefore, causal research is often the most demanding type in terms of time and financial resources. It intends to present answers for why things happen and to highlight details of the relationships among variables. To extract the causality from a variety of unrelated factors, investigators often need to resort to longitudinal and experimental measures. **Longitudinal measures**, which are measurements repeated over time, are required because after-the-fact measurement alone cannot fully explain the effect of causality. Similarly, **experimentation** is often necessary to introduce systematic variation of factors and then measure the effect of these variations. Take the example of soft drink sales. If one were to measure only the sales of a particular brand at one time, it would be difficult to detect usage patterns over time. **Repeat measurements** can assist in tentatively identifying the effects of temperature and time of year. However, in order to understand the relationship precisely, it is also important to control for factors such as competitive prices, promotion, and store shelf location. Therefore, experimentation is required in order to cleanly filter out other causal effects. Obviously, causal research is useful only if the research objective is to identify interrelationships and if this knowledge makes a sufficient contribution to the corporate decision process to justify the investment.

Descriptive studies constitute the vast majority of marketing research. Exploratory research is often seen as an insufficient basis for major corporate decisions, and causal research is seen as too time consuming, too expensive, and insufficiently beneficial to be justified. Corporations are mostly satisfied when management believes that a thorough understanding of a market situation has been obtained and that reasonable predictability is possible. Since corporate research is usually measured by its bottom-line effect, descriptive studies often appear to be most desirable.

DETERMINING THE RESEARCH APPROACH

Although there are many different types of research approaches, one principal differentiation is their type of data yield, which can be either qualitative or quantitative. The qualitative approach intends to gain informed insight and a better understanding of a phenomenon—without too many pretenses about generalizability. The quantitative approach is the numerical one, where researchers intend to manipulate numbers to extract information such as correlations. In the latter case, conditions of representativeness of data must be met (often through random sampling) together with minimum numbers of data points. Only if these conditions are fulfilled can statistical procedures be applied.

QUALITATIVE RESEARCH. Among the types of qualitative data-gathering techniques, observation, in-depth interviews, and focus groups are the most frequently used.

Observation involves watching participants as they undertake some activity, simply to see what happens. The pattern of customer flow in a supermarket is best determined by simply watching it (albeit using sophisticated video recording and computer analysis to make the data more meaningful). Observation can also help in understanding phenomena that would have been difficult to assess with other techniques. For example, Toyota sent a group of its engineers and designers to southern California to nonchalantly observe how drivers get into and operate their cars. They found that women with long fingernails have trouble opening the door and operating various knobs on the dashboard. Based on their observations, Toyota's researchers redesigned some of the automobile exterior and interior features.[12]

In-depth interviews can last an hour or more. One format is the nondirective approach, in which the interviewer allows the respondent to answer in any form to the semistructured interview. By keeping the answers totally open-ended, the freedom of expression often leads to a less-constrained view of true attitudes, but the responses must be analyzed by skilled personnel.

In *focus groups* a selected, relatively homogeneous group of 6–10 participants is encouraged to discuss the topics that the researchers are investigating. The moderator, who is often a trained psychologist, carefully leads the discussion, ensuring that all of the group members express their views. The interviewer's role is essentially a passive one, mainly to foster group interaction and to control any individual who is dominating the group. The goal of a focus group is for the participants to develop their own ideas in an unstructured fashion, interacting with and stimulating others. The whole session is usually captured on tape or video for later in-depth analysis. This often allows insights that are hidden by the preconceived questions posed in conventional surveys.

The concept of focus groups is based on the assumption that individuals are more willing to talk about a problem amid the security of others sharing the same problem.[13] Focus groups are a superb mechanism for generating

www.toyota.com

12. Michael R. Czinkota and Masaaki Kotabe, "Product Development the Japanese Way," in *Trends in International Business: Critical Perspectives,* ed. M. Czinkota and M. Kotabe (Oxford: Blackwell Publishers, 1998), 153–158.
13. D. N. Bellenger, K. L. Bernhardt, and J. L. Goldstucker, *Qualitative Research in Marketing* (Chicago: American Marketing Association, 1976), 7.

hypotheses when little is known and thus constitute a particularly productive approach to developing the first stage of larger research projects. Focus groups are often used as a cheaper and faster alternative for those organizations that cannot afford full-scale research. However, the researcher should beware of attributing too much generalizable significance to the results—in particular to any purported statistical outcome—because nonrandom samples do not allow for any statistical conclusions. In addition, the conclusions are dependent upon the researcher's interpretations. With the advances that have occurred in the communication field, focus groups can now be conducted electronically, thus saving time and money, as Manager's Corner 5.3 shows.

> Focus groups are a superb mechanism for generating hypotheses when little is known

QUANTITATIVE RESEARCH. Quantitative research provides a sufficient number of scientifically collected data points to permit the application of statistical techniques in the analysis. The importance of such techniques varies by individual manager and culture. In some countries, for example, primary emphasis is on understanding a phenomenon through creative—and sometimes daring—interpretation of limited data. In others, such as the United States, the accumulation of large quantities of data, their subsequent manipulation through sophisticated analytical procedures, and the discovery of statistically significant results

Manager's Corner 5.3

Online focus groups

Conducting focus groups over the Internet has its advantages and disadvantages. Marketing researchers say the groups are cheaper to conduct online, results can be tallied quickly, and developing technologies, like simultaneous language translation, make them more attractive. Reviewing Web sites is a natural subject for online focus groups and, not surprisingly, this is the service for which these groups are used most. A market researcher at Atlanta-based Turner Broadcasting Systems (www.turner.com) used virtual focus groups to find out if the reason one of TBS's Web sites wasn't getting as many hits as expected was because the graphics-heavy site took too long to download. The researcher in this case found using focus groups online an easy and quick way to get the information he wanted. Another advantage of online groups is their effectiveness in bringing together people from different parts of the country, especially those in higher income brackets who cannot spare the time to travel to the site of a traditional focus group. The most significant drawback is that unlike the traditional focus groups, body language and nuances of speech cannot be observed.

Another form of online research uses specially designed software instead of a moderator to conduct focus groups. To use the software, group members assemble in a room wired with networked computers. They then type their ideas about the object they are discussing onto their screens. All group ideas are printed on a large screen in the middle of the room. Research indicates that the process can be better controlled because each group member has an equal voice and it is difficult for any one person to dominate the discussion. When using the specially designed software, members tend to remain more focused on the task at hand, brainstorm more effectively, and make decisions faster. The hitch is that the computer lab atmosphere tends to be a negative experience for the members. So although more useful information can be obtained in the short term, the participants may be alienated. In the future this problem could be solved by having people use the software on electronic mail from their homes.

Sources: Thomas Kiely, "Wired Focus Groups," *Harvard Business Review* (January/February 1998): 12–16; Rachel Weissman, "Online or off Target," *American Demographics* (November 1998): 20–21.

are seen as important components of research. Regardless of the approach taken, the key is the **managerial significance** of data, which refers to the resulting knowledge that permits the manager to make better decisions. Typical quantitative research approaches are experimentation and surveys.

Experimental research exposes selected participants to different treatments. It may range from testing new products to viewing commercials and measuring responses to them. In theory this approach may be used to establish causal relationships. In practice it is more frequently used to select the best alternative from a range of products or advertising concepts or even more pragmatically to check that the one already chosen is acceptable.

The basis of much experimental research is a comparison between groups. In a before-and-after setting, which is the most customary approach, the subject is tested prior to and after exposure to a stimulus, typically a product or commercial. The performance of the product or commercial is judged by the change in the measurements taken of the subject, normally in terms of attitudes. An example for such an approach may be a taste test of different colas administered to consumers. In a split-run approach, the different stimuli are applied to separate but statistically equivalent groups and the results are compared. For example, cable TV systems permit the broadcasting of different direct response advertisements in the same test market city. This way, the effectiveness of the various advertisements can be measured.

The most widely used marketing research is survey, or questionnaire-based research. Typically, this may be designed to discover the participants' habits, attitudes, wants, and so on, simply by asking the respondent a number of questions. The **question structure** must be developed carefully and skillfully. First, the questions must be comprehensive, because a question not asked will not be answered. Second, they need to be in a language that the respondent understands, so that the answers will be clear and unambiguous. Many words used by researchers and their clients, even those from their everyday language, may be unfamiliar to the respondents they are testing, particularly if their respondents are less well educated. Even a word such as *incentive* is likely to be fully understood by only about half the population. The key is to keep questions clear by using simple words, by avoiding ambiguous words and questions, by omitting leading questions, and by asking questions in specific terms, thus avoiding generalizations and estimates.[14]

The researcher must also pay close attention to **question content**. Questions must reflect the ability and willingness of respondents to supply the answers. The knowledge and information available to respondents may vary substantially because of different educational levels, and that may affect their ability to answer questions. Further, societal demands and cultural restrictions may influence the willingness of respondents to answer certain questions. For example, in countries where the tax collection system is consistently eluded by taxpayers, questions regarding level of income may be deliberately answered inaccurately. For some respondents, the focus of a particular question may be sensitive, so one may want to address a topic indirectly. For example, rather than ask, "How old are you?" one could ask, "In what year were you born?"

To ensure that the questions asked are valid and meaningful, it is sound practice to **pretest** the questionnaire on a number of respondents so that potential problems can be debugged before the cost of a full survey is incurred. The communications elements of questionnaire design are too easily forgotten by researchers—and confusion is as much a problem in research work as bias. It is

---

14. Gilbert A. Churchill, Jr., *Marketing Research: Methodological Foundations,* 6th ed. (Fort Worth, Tex.: Dryden Press, 1995), 292.

worth remembering at all times that marketing is about a dialogue—a two-way communication. Clarity in the questionnaire and in the ideas behind it is rewarded by clarity in the results.

Questions can be unstructured or structured. **Unstructured questions** allow respondents to answer in their own words. Although the question is fixed, there is no preconceived set of expected answers.

> It is worth remembering at all times that marketing is about a dialogue

This means, however, that to be statistically useful, the resulting answers later have to be categorized into groups that make sense. This imposes extra costs and requires that the person coding the results understands what the cryptic comments from the respondent really mean. These open questions may take simple forms such as "Why did you buy Brand A?" With **structured questions**, the respondent is asked to choose from among several alternatives, or the interviewer is asked to listen to and then code the respondent's answer to an apparently open question against a number of preconceived answers. The advantage of structured questions is that the answers are easy to analyze and are unambiguous. The obvious disadvantage is that this precludes the respondent from giving an answer outside these limits, although often one choice is "Other," allowing for a free-form explanation.

In structured questionnaires, respondents are often asked questions such as "How frequently do you purchase Brand A?" or "How much did you pay?" This may require almost impossible feats of memory for many respondents unless the process being investigated is a very regular one. Mitigating this problem is the development of categories, which can be handled more easily. For example, the basic question can be expanded to cover a number of alternatives from which the respondent is asked to select one or more. Also useful are semantic differentials, in which the respondent is asked to choose a position on a scale between two bipolar words or numbers (for example, Excellent, Good, Adequate, Poor, Inadequate; or from 5, powerful, to 1, weak). As originally developed by Osgood, there were 20 specific rating scales.[15] One widely used form of scaling, developed by Likert, asks the respondent to rate opinion statements presented one at a time in terms of Strongly Agree, Agree, Neither Agree nor Disagree, Disagree, and Strongly Disagree.[16]

COLLECTING THE DATA

At this stage of the research an army of interviews descends upon the unsuspecting public. Among the possible methods of contacting respondents are mail, telephone, and personal interviewing.

MAIL.   Mail is the least expensive solution to data collection. Large overall samples can be used, allowing investigation of small market groups—especially in industrial markets—while still remaining within acceptable statistical levels. But in many respects a mail questionnaire is the least satisfactory solution because the questions have to be simple and the questionnaire short. The mail questionnaire must be particularly well designed in order to keep the respondent interested and motivated to reply. Still, the **response rates** are sometimes so low that the statistical validity of the results may be questioned, because it is arguable

15. E. C. Osgood, G. J. Succi, and P. H. Tannenbaum, *The Measurement of Meaning* (Urbana: University of Illinois Press, 1957), 129.
16. R. Likert, "A Technique for the Measurement of Attitudes," *Archives of Psychology* 140 (1932).

that the nonresponding majority might behave differently from those who have responded. This problem may be addressed in several ways. One can attempt to increase the response rate by prenotifying individuals that they will receive a survey, by offering participants some form of reward in return for the completed questionnaire, or by conducting follow-up mailings that ask nonrespondents again for their participation. One can also attempt to reduce the **nonresponse bias** of sampling by following up, typically by telephone, on a subsample of those not completing the questionnaire, to see if their views are different from those replying. If they are not different, the assumption is made that those responding are representative of the sample as a whole.

TELEPHONE. Using a telephone to contact respondents is a very fast survey technique; results can be available in a matter of hours. Therefore, this approach is often used for opinion polls where time is of the essence. It is also relatively inexpensive and thus affordable. **Telephone interviews** can last only a short time, and the types of questions are limited, particularly because the interviewer cannot check visually to see that the question is understood. However, the interviewer can follow up on questions, clarify issues, and adapt the entire questionnaire to the respondent's specific situation during the questioning.

PERSONAL INTERVIEWS. This is the traditional face-to-face approach to marketing research, and it is still the most versatile. The interviewer has much control of the interview and can observe the respondent's body language as well as his or her words. It is, however, the most expensive approach, and it is heavily dependent on the reliability and skill of the interviewer. This means that the quality of the supervision provided by the field research agency is critical. In order to avoid interviewers making up interviews, reputable agencies do exert the necessary control over their personnel, usually by having a field manager conduct followups of a subsample.

SAMPLES. With all quantitative techniques it is important to obtain a representative sample, although local conditions may make such a task difficult. In some regions, reliable mailing addresses may not be available—for example, in Venezuela, most houses are not numbered but are given names like "Casa Rosa" or "El Retiro." Mailing lists may not exist, and only limited records may be available about the number of occupants in a dwelling. Telephone ownership may be unevenly distributed among the population under study, or some subgroups may have more unlisted numbers than others. When privacy laws prohibit random dialing, important groups may not be represented in the research findings.

The basic principle of sampling is that one can obtain a representative picture of a whole population—the total group of people being investigated—by looking at only a small subset. This is a very cost-effective way of obtaining information. Samples are important in terms of understanding the accuracy that may be placed on the results. They also offer a good indication of the quality of the work being carried out. To guarantee accuracy, the respondents to any respectable market research should be chosen to offer a statistically valid sample, which permits valid statistical analyses. The typical ways in which a sample is chosen are the random approach and the quota approach.

Random samples are the classically correct method. A list of the total population to be sampled is used as the basis of selecting the sample, most rigorously by using tables of random numbers, but most simply by selecting every "*n*th" name. A reasonable degree of accuracy may be achieved with samples as small as a few hundred. Occasionally much larger overall samples are used in order to also observe smaller subsamples. An alternative and cheaper approach is **cluster sampling**, which may lose little accuracy if correctly employed. This consists of selecting the districts for interviewing on a random basis. Within these districts respondents can also be specified randomly or can be obtained quasirandomly, by "random walk" (that is, by querying every tenth house on a given street). In the case of a stratified sample the original population is categorized by some parameter—age, for example—and random samples are then drawn from each of these strata. This method ensures that there are adequate numbers in each of these subsamples to allow for valid statistical analyses.

The advantage of random samples is that they are statistically predictable. Apart from any questions on how comprehensive the original lists are, they are unlikely to be skewed or biased. Even then, results from poorly controlled research may be biased by poor sampling. This may be due to inadequate coverage, attributable to incomplete lists of the overall population. It is more likely due to a high proportion of nonrespondents. It has to be assumed that their responses would have been different from those who did respond, with the result that particular groups of respondents are overrepresented. Whatever the circumstances, the statistics, particularly those related to the degree of confidence that can be placed on the results, are easily applied.

Statistical theory assumes that the results will follow a **normal distribution**, with *normal* being used in a particular statistical sense to describe a symmetrical bell-shaped curve (see Figure 5.3). Under these circumstances, the statistical chance of deviation from the central part of the curve, the mean, is given by the standard error. Statistically, this means that 68 percent of any results would lie within one standard error of the mean, and 95 percent within two standard errors.

The formula for the standard error (SE) is

$$SE = \sqrt{\frac{p(100 - p)}{n}}$$

where p is the percentage of the population having the attribute being measured and n is the sample size. Thus if 10,000 households are included in the sample and we find that 10 percent of them record the behavior we are measuring, then we can calculate that

$$SE = \sqrt{\frac{10(100 - 10)}{10,000}} = 0.3\%$$

This would enable us to say that we were 68 percent confident that the result lies between 9.7 and 10.3 percent, and 95 percent confident that it was between 9.4 and 10.6 percent. If, on the other hand, the sample was just 400, the range within which we could be 95 percent confident would need to be much wider (between 7 and 13 percent—as the standard error would then be 1.5 percent). It is clear, therefore, why sample sizes often approach 1,000 respondents.

Quota samples aim to achieve an effect similar to stratified random samples by asking interviewers to recruit respondents to match an agreed quota of subsamples. This is supposed to guarantee that the overall sample is an approximately representative cross-section of the population as a whole. For example, the interviewer may be required to select certain numbers of respondents to match specified ages and social categories. This technique clearly may be subject to bias, because interviewers select only the more accessible respondents and exclude the more elusive elements of the population. In the strict theoretical sense, it is inappropriate to apply statistical tests to these data. However, quota sampling is significantly cheaper than using random samples, and so it is an approach frequently used for commercial research. Despite its apparent theoretical shortcomings, it often works well. As the quality of quota sampling depends directly upon the quality of the interviewer, it is the approach most likely to suffer from sacrificing quality to achieve cost savings. If poorly controlled, it may all too easily degenerate into "convenience sampling" or interviewing whoever is easiest—not a genuine form of sampling by any standard.[17]

---

17. J. Coulson, "Field Research: Sample Design, Questionnaire Design, Interviewing Methods," in *Handbook of Modern Marketing*, 2d ed., ed. V. P. Buell (New York: McGraw-Hill, 1986).

Figure 5.3

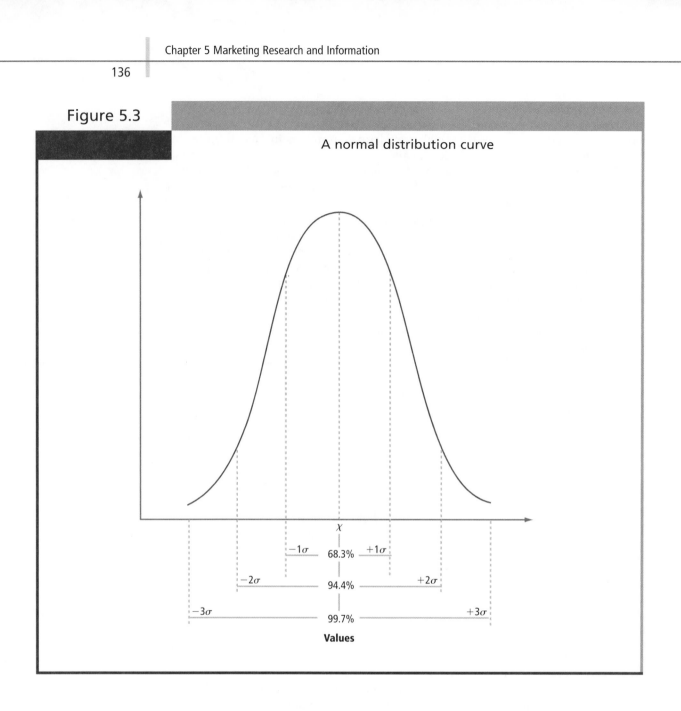

A normal distribution curve

The drawing of large samples is relatively easy in consumer market research, because there are usually large numbers of consumers available. The application of sampling is less easy in an industrial market setting. At one extreme, the industry itself may be so small that a survey will cover all the customers—therefore becoming a census. Because of this small population, there may be problems in individual willingness to respond, as even aggregate data may be too revealing of a specific firm's data. In larger industries, with a few industry leaders, there may also be the problem of information request overload. For example, the firms on the Fortune 500 list often receive hundreds of questionnaires a week and are therefore no longer able and willing to participate in survey research. Furthermore, it is increasingly difficult to ensure that a mail questionnaire, for example, actually reaches the intended recipient. Often such research instruments are either screened out by a gatekeeper or are responded to by individuals who are not well informed about the phenomenon under study. Unless a particular line of inquiry is of special importance to the industrial recipient of a questionnaire, response willingness tends to be low. Low response rates, in turn, prompt doubts

www.pathfinder.com
/fortune/fortune500/

about the validity of the results. However, technology again comes to the rescue—at least momentarily. E-mail permits surveys to be administered quickly, at a low cost, and to the precise respondent intended.

ANALYZING THE RESULTS

Collected data can be analyzed in a variety of ways. Increasingly, analysts use the massive computing power now available to cut through the superficial results. The mathematics of these various techniques is beyond the scope of this book; the practical skill needed is that of finding the best expert to implement them and knowing how much reliance to place on his or her judgment. The researcher should, of course, use the best tools available and appropriate for analysis. On the other hand, researchers should be cautioned against using overly sophisticated tools for unsophisticated data. Even the best of tools will not improve data quality. Therefore, the quality of data must be matched with the quality of analytical tools.

Some examples of the more popular analytical tools used by practitioners include multiple regression analysis, factor analysis, cluster analysis, and conjoint analysis. All of them can serve to identify common elements or connections within the data. By grouping data into related variables, these techniques reduce the scope of the data set and achieve stronger differentiations between groups, which in turn allows the marketer to focus better on each one of them.

REPORTING THE FINDINGS

The final research stage is to disseminate the results. This process may require more effort, and be more important, than the simple clerical task that it superficially seems to be. For one thing, one needs to identify those to whom the results are useful. Equally important, the language of the report may need to be "translated" for different audiences; very few managers may care about the detailed terminology of market research. This poses some problems. The process of simplification may result in the loss or alteration of some meaning. One favorite approach in presentation to top management is to augment the dry statistics that have already been considerably simplified with verbatim quotes from individual respondents. Instead of mysterious symbols and dull tables, there are direct quotations in which believable people give their views at length and in their own words. For many clients this is the texture of the world.[18] The particular danger here is that senior management unversed in market research skills will merely remember the most striking comments (particularly the ones that reinforce their existing prejudices) rather than the boring statistics.

Many managers find themselves on the receiving end of research reports yet are poorly trained in the skills needed to make sense of such reports. As a result, they tend to read the related conclusions uncritically, accepting or sometimes rejecting them at face value, usually based on what they think of the researcher presenting them or on whether these results confirm their own prejudices. In evaluating a report, a number of initial guidelines should be kept in mind:

- **Relevance.** Before you even look at the first page of the report, you should ask yourself whether the subject is relevant to your specific needs. Fortunately, the relevance can usually be deduced from a quick scan through the summary, coupled with an understanding of where the report has come from and why it was produced.

---

18. W. D. Wells, "Group Interviewing," in *Handbook of Marketing Research,* ed. M. J. Baker (New York: Butterworth Heinemann, 1987).

- **Reliability.** Perhaps the most important question, but the one least often asked, is how reliable the reported results are. What weight can be put on them and on the judgment of the researchers and experts who are recommending some form of action to be taken on the basis of the findings? Here one can examine the methodology, such as the questionnaire and sample design, because this is likely to give the best indication of the quality of the work, or consider the past performance and reputation of the researcher.

- **Accuracy.** After establishing that the material is both relevant and reliable, the next step is to determine its accuracy. All too often accuracy is a technicality that is buried deep in dense appendixes that never reach the general reader. Accuracy is not the same as reliability. As long as it is allowed for, low accuracy may be quite reliable and useful in decision making. The problem is to establish what accuracy can be tolerated. In marketing research the answer can normally be deduced from the sample size. If the sample size is greater than 500, the results are likely to be accurate to within 2 to 3 percent. If the sample is greater than 1,000, it may be accurate within 1 percent. Below 100, though, as many of the more dubious pieces of so-called quantitative research are, any statistical accuracy may be almost nonexistent. Nevertheless, some of the qualitative aspects of such research may still be quite meaningful.

- **Bias.** Most research reports contain bias, whether conscious or unconscious. It is very difficult for even the most professional researcher to remove all of his or her biases. You would be wise to assume that the material still contains some elements of distortion. This bias may not be without value: The best research starts with a strong thesis as to what is likely to be found. Although this will inevitably color the results, it also ensures that the research is focused and provides meaningful insights, as long as you recognize what the focus or bias is.

KNOWLEDGE IS THE BUSINESS

There is a danger that market research may become an end in itself, and that the marketer is drowned by the vast quantities of information that are unleashed. The marketer should never, therefore, lose sight of why research is conducted. Ford Motor Company learned this lesson in the 1950s, when it designed and launched the first car to be based on market research. Every feature of the Edsel was researched to make sure that it was the choice of the majority of consumers. The result was a disastrous failure for a number of reasons, not the least of which was uncritical use of the market research information. For instance, the majority that liked one feature was not necessarily the same majority that liked another. Thus it has been suggested that everyone was able to find at least one feature that they hated so much that they would not buy the car. Marketing in Action 5.2 may describe a similar example of this situation.

www.fordvehicles.com

> The marketer should never lose sight of why research is conducted.

Peter Drucker said, "Knowledge is the business fully as much as the customer is the business. Physical goods or services are only the vehicle for the exchange of customer purchasing power against business knowledge. . . . For business success, knowledge must first be meaningful to the customer in terms of satisfaction and value."[19] His words offer a useful focus for any market research, although he

---

19. P. F. Drucker, *Managing for Results* (New York: Butterworth Heinemann, 1964).

was talking of wider knowledge, particularly knowledge of what the organization does well and the great depth of specialist, technical expertise that usually lies behind it.

To be able to do something as well as others is not enough: It does not provide the leadership position without which a business is doomed. Only consistent excellence earns a profit, and the only genuine profit is that of the innovator. Economic results are the results of differentiation. The source of this specific differentiation, and with it of business survival and growth, is a specific, distinct knowledge possessed by a group of people in the business. To be most useful, market research also has to address what the organization itself does well, to explore those elements of the market and the customers in it.

One final thought on marketing research concerns major discontinuities in the overall environment, which can change all the factors to such an extent that the market research may be largely useless. One shortcoming of most marketing research is that it essentially measures the historical position, unearthing data on what has gone before, even though the future will be different. Consumer research will be largely valueless in periods of major transition, because consumers will (incorrectly) base their answers on their existing perspective without knowing what they would want or do if new, currently unknown alternatives were available. Some of the most successful new products have not emerged from incremental, researched changes, but have been genuine innovations. For

Marketing in Action 5.2

CIM reports that *Star Wars* merchandise should be targeted to adults

The Chartered Institute of Marketing (CIM) (www.cim.co.uk), located in the United Kingdom, is an international organization of marketing professionals. Research conducted by the institute may hold surprises for the manufacturers and distributors of *Star Wars* merchandise in the United Kingdom. Quantitative results from their research include:

- 31 percent of UK adults intend to see *Star Wars, Episode 1: The Phantom Menace*
- 20 percent of these adults will go to accompany their children

Additionally, the CIM reports that *Star Wars* (www.starwars.com) merchandise such as action toys, puppets, and video games appeal more to UK adults than to UK children. The basis of this attraction appears to be nostalgia. Examining initial reaction in the United States to the release of *Star Wars, Episode 1:*

The Phantom Menace, CIM reports that adult collectors were the buyers of *Star Wars* merchandise. Apparently, there was a lull in purchasing soon after the release of the film, perhaps indicating that *Star Wars* merchandise did not spark a critical flame in the younger generation.

Because film success is judged both by box-office sales and merchandise sales, what should be done? Holiday giving in December may bring a surge in demand, yet the movie will have been out for quite a while by then. With initial sales slow, will large toy manufacturers be prepared to stock store shelves with *Star Wars* merchandise? What should food producer Heinz (www.heinz.com) expect from its *Star Wars* pasta shapes in tomato sauce (including R2-D2, Darth Maul, Anakin Skywalker, Jar Jar Binks, and a Battle Droid)? Is the report out of the Chartered Institute of Marketing even of any relevance to Heinz?

Sources: www.cim.co.uk; Sheetal Mehta, "Adults Are the Best Star Wars Targets," *Supermarketing, Reed Business Information, Ltd.,* July 9, 1999, 13.

www.sony.com

example, the emergence of the Walkman was not the result of gradually growing customer desire, but rather the determination of Sony's CEO Akio Morita that this is the way things "ought" to be.

Innovations themselves are of major benefit to marketing. If we didn't keep finding new ideas, there would be limits to growth. It is the whole process of discovery that causes growth.[20] Even if such innovations devalue the importance of past research, obtaining the best possible information about the outside world is still the key to successful marketing. The more you understand about the environment in general, and customers in particular, the more effective your marketing is likely to be.

SUMMARY

This chapter explored the search for information about the customer and the market. This constitutes the listening part of the marketing dialogue. Marketing research is also needed to assist managers in the decision-making process and to analyze organizational performance. To be viable, however, the benefits derived from marketing research need to exceed the cost of conducting such research.

A systematic research approach will lead to the development of a marketing intelligence system (MIS) that contains information both internal and external to the firm. Important internal data sources are performance analyses and sales reports. The more data the intelligence system receives, the better it can serve the manager. It is therefore important to develop ways of entering nonnumerical reports, such as accounts from a sales conversation or information about customer interests. New technology can enable an MIS to alter communication and decision structures within a firm but also requires careful planning of information distribution and retention.

External information can be derived from either secondary or primary data. Secondary data, collected in response to someone else's questions, are obtained through desk research and are available quickly and at low cost. Main sources are libraries, directories, newsletters, commercial information providers, trade associations, and electronic information services. To ensure their usefulness, the researcher must determine the quality of the data source, the quality of the actual data, and the compatibility of the data with information requirements. Primary data are collected directly on behalf of a specific research project. Typical ways of obtaining such data are through syndicated research—such as retail audits, panel research, or omnibus surveys—and custom research.

The first step of primary marketing research is to clearly define the objectives in order to ensure the usefulness of the research. Next the research level needs to be decided. Exploratory research will help mainly in identifying problems, descriptive research provides information about existing market phenomena, and causal research sheds light on the relationships between market factors. The research approach then determines whether qualitative or quantitative data will be collected. Observation, in-depth interviews, and focus groups are primary techniques to yield qualitative data, which may be very insightful but are not fully generalizable and cannot be analyzed statistically. Quantitative data overcome these problems but require the systematic collection of large numbers of data. Experimentation and survey research are the primary research tools. Good survey research must concentrate on question design and structure in order to elicit useful responses. Data can then be collected by mail, by telephone, or in per-

20. Peter Robinson, "Paul Romer in the Shrine of Gods," *Forbes ASAP,* June 15, 1995, 72.

son after an appropriate sample frame is constructed. The data need to be analyzed with appropriate techniques in order to make the data set comprehensible, insightful, and useful for management. This usefulness is at the heart of the research report, which in essence is a communication process persuading recipients to use the information.

QUESTIONS FOR REVIEW

1. What is the difference between data, information, and intelligence?

2. What are the main internal sources of information? What analyses can be applied to the numerical data? What problems may be encountered with verbal reports?

3. What are the main sources of external data?

4. What are the differences among retail audits, panel research, and omnibus surveys?

5. What are the main stages of the marketing research process?

6. What is the difference between quantitative and qualitative research? What are the main tools of qualitative research?

7. What are the most important aspects of questionnaire design? What techniques may be used on questionnaires in order to categorize answers?

8. How may primary research data be collected? What are the advantages of each method? What are the differences between random and quota samples?

9. What should you look for when you use marketing research reports?

QUESTIONS FOR DISCUSSION

1. Gaylord Entertainment, owner and operator of Nashville's renowned Opryland hotel complex, will be adding two new Opryland hotels, one in Dallas and one in Orlando, by the year 2002. Some analysts are concerned that there will be consumer disappointment once guests and conventioneers realize that the new hotels will not follow the country music theme. But market research conducted among a much smaller group of Opryland's core customers—meeting planners—indicates that the Opryland name is not inextricably linked to country music, but to value and quality service. As a result, the Opryland Orlando will have a 4.5-acre Everglades swamp and a manufactured beach enclosed under its signature atriums.[21] From this example, it would appear that information gathered from a few knowledgeable people is more valuable than data collected from many uninformed persons. Why

is it, then, that so many marketing researchers prefer to collect quantitative rather than qualitative data?

2. Wal-Mart's success can be linked to its extensive data collection efforts. By recording information about every sales transaction, Wal-Mart has built a database that is the envy of many of its suppliers. This treasure trove of data is instrumental to managers making decisions about store layout because it provides instant information about sales, inventory, and profitability of each individual item the store carries.[22] What kind of information would you like to see as part of a sales report? Why? How can this information be formatted to be part of an MIS?

3. In his new book titled *The Control Revolution*, Andrew Shapiro discusses how the Internet and technology in general have shifted the

---

21. Karen Lundegard, "Heard in Florida: Some Investors Are Getting Anxious For the Next Big Break at Gaylord," *Wall Street Journal*, August 11, 1999.
22. Emily Nelson, "Why Wal-Mart Sings, 'Yes, We Have Bananas!'" *Wall Street Journal*, October 6, 1998, B1.

balance of power between consumers and organizations, corporations, and the media. With consumers now better able to take control of information and resources, one possible end is the elimination of traditional middlemen. Examples cited include day traders greatly reducing or even eliminating brokerage fees, musicians broadcasting their songs through the Internet rather than through a record label, and readers filtering information through search functions to obtain only exactly what they want. Clearly the Internet has expanded the scope of how marketing information is disseminated.[23] How can the wider dissemination of marketing information change the managerial structure of a firm? Can these changes also affect the firm's marketing appeal and performance? How?

4. Early in the 20th century, tobacco usage was considered chic and even salubrious (asthmatics were prescribed medicated cigarettes as remedies against attacks). The marketing efforts of industry leaders reflected the societal perception of the time. Late in the 20th century, however, the same companies were held accountable by U.S. courts for these aggressive marketing strategies according to latter-day standards. Is it appropriate to measure the actions that firms may have taken decades ago by the standards of today? Should firms adjust their information banks to reflect such a trend?

5. The impact the Internet has had on the dissemination of information is profound. Hoards of secondary databases are published on the Internet and are accessible to all. Savvy corporations have built or are building very detailed internal secondary databases to maintain information culled from various sources. But the Internet has also increased the ease of conducting primary research, mainly through Internet surveys. One such example is the increased surveying of teenage girls by market research firms such as SmartGirl and Girl Games, as well as by consumer goods manufacturers like Bonne Bell, *YM* magazine, Frito Lay, and Artcarved. What will the increasing availability and accessibility of secondary data mean to the importance of primary research?

Consider this example also as you consider the question posed in number 7 below: How does the technology of the Internet affect the quality and validity of primary data collected there? Will traditional primary research maintain a primacy over electronically conducted primary research? Will primary research in either form carry more weight that the widely available secondary data emerging today? Why or why not?

6. A recent innovation by Miracom Corp. may drastically increase the efficiency of collecting primary data. The Miratouch system is a computer kiosk with touch-screen functionality that can be installed at participating retailers. By rewarding customers who respond to the survey posted by the kiosk with giveaways, discounts, and other enticing offers, companies using the Miratouch system hope to collect firsthand demographic and purchasing behavior information before people leave their stores. Some traditional data-collection agencies, such as J. D. Power, are not as enthusiastic about the possibilities of the Miratouch system, citing the age-old "garbage in, garbage out" axiom. And they argue that the clipboard and pencil method can still do everything Miratouch is claiming to do better.[24] Evaluate how changes in technology can alter the data-collection process. How will such shifts affect the quality and validity of data?

7. The publisher of *Apple Daily*, a Hong Kong newspaper, has recently jumped headlong into e-commerce by opening a discount retailer that sells an extremely wide variety of products and takes orders via phone, fax, and Internet. In the congested urban center of Hong Kong, the promise of 24-hour delivery goes a long way to luring consumers into becoming adM@rt customers, particularly when conventional supermarkets are dingy, cramped, and without parking. Despite the success of adM@rt, most Asians still do not own computers, so the ultimate success of the electronic supermarket has yet to be decided.[25] How can marketing research help in identifying discontinuities between levels of societal acceptance and technological advances?

23. Carl S. Kaplan, "Writer Seeks Balance in Internet Power Shifts," *New York Times*, June 18, 1999, B10. Cybertimes, Technology section.

24. Greg Winter, "With Kiosks Connected to the Net, Marketing Research Goes Real-Time," *Wall Street Journal*, July 28, 1999.

25. Michael Flagg, "Hong Kong Publisher Irks a Few with Foray into Online Retailing," *Wall Street Journal*, August 6, 1999.

FURTHER READINGS

Churchill, Gilbert A., Jr. *Marketing Research: Methodological Foundations.* 7th ed. Fort Worth, Tex.: Dryden Press, 1999.

Directory of Online Databases. Santa Monica, Calif.: Cuadra Associates, published annually.

Douglas, Susan P., and C. Samuel Craig. *International Marketing Research: Concepts and Methods.* 2d ed. New York: John Wiley & Sons, 1999.

Kent, Raymond A. *Marketing Research, Measurement, Method and Application.* London: International Thomson Business, 1999.

Malhotra, Naresh K. *Marketing Research.* 3d ed. Upper Saddle River, N.J.: Prentice Hall, 1999.

McDaniel, Carl D., and Roger H. Gates. *Contemporary Marketing Research.* Cincinnati: South-Western College Publishing, 1999.

Appendix
Selected Information Sources for Marketing Issues

American Bankers Association
1120 Connecticut Avenue NW
Washington, DC 20036
www.aba.com

American Bar Association
750 N. Lake Shore Drive
Chicago, IL 60611
and
1800 M Street NW
Washington, DC 20036
www.abanet.org/intlaw/home
.html

American Management Association
440 First Street NW
Washington, DC 20001
www.amanet.org

American Marketing Association
311 S. Wacker Drive, Suite 5800
Chicago, IL 60606
www.ama.org

American Petroleum Institute
1220 L Street NW
Washington, DC 20005
www.api.org

Asia-Pacific Economic Cooperation Secretariat
438 Alexandra Road
#41-00, Alexandra Road
Singapore 119958
www.apecsec.org.sg

Asian Development Bank
2330 Roxas Boulevard
Pasay City, Philippines
www.asiandevbank.org

Association of South East Asian Nations (ASEAN)
Publication Office
c/o The ASEAN Secretariat
70A, Jalan Sisingamangaraja
Jakarta 11210
Indonesia
www.asean.or.id

Canadian Market Data
www.strategis.ie.gc.ca

Chamber of Commerce of the United States
1615 H Street NW
Washington, DC 20062
www.uschamber.org

Commission of the European Communities to the United States
2100 M Street NW
Suite 707
Washington, DC 20037
www.eurunion.org/

Conference Board
845 Third Avenue
New York, NY 10022
and
1755 Massachusetts Avenue NW
Suite 312
Washington, DC 20036
www.conference-board.org

Deutsche Bundesbank
Wilhelm-Epstein-Str. 14
P.O.B. 10 06 02
D-60006 Franfurt am Main
www.bundesbank.de

Electronic Industries Association
2001 Pennsylvania Avenue NW
Washington, DC 20004
www.eia.org

Export-Import Bank of the United States
811 Vermont Avenue NW
Washington, DC 20571
www.exim.gov

Federal Reserve Bank of New York
33 Liberty Street
New York, NY 10045
www.ny.frb.org

Federation of International Trade Associations
11800 Sunrise Valley Drive, #210
Reston, VA 20191-4345
www.fita.org

FIBER
Foundation for International Business Education and Research
11800 Sunrise Valley Drive
Reston, VA 20191
www.fiberus.org

Inter-American Development Bank
1300 New York Avenue NW
Washington, DC 20577
www.iadb.org

International Bank for Reconstruction and Development (World Bank)
1818 H Street NW
Washington, DC 20433
www.worldbank.org

International Monetary Fund
700 19th Street NW
Washington, DC 20431
www.imf.org

Source: © Michael R. Czinkota

International Telecommunication Union
Place des Nations
Ch-1211 Geneva 20
Switzerland
www.itu.int

Michigan State University Center for International Business Education and Research
www.ciber.bus.msu.edu/busres

Marketing Research Society
111 E. Wacker Drive
Suite 600
Chicago, IL 60601

National Association of Manufacturers
1331 Pennsylvania Avenue NW
Suite 1500
Washington, DC 20004
www.nam.org

National Federation of Independent Business
600 Maryland Avenue SW
Suite 700
Washington, DC 20024
www.nfib.org

Organization for Economic Cooperation and Development
2 rue Andre Pascal
75775 Paris Cedex Ko, France
and
2001 L Street NW
Suite 700
Washington, DC 20036
www.oecd.org

Organization of American States
17th and Constitution Avenue NW
Washington, DC 20006
www.oas.org

Society for International Development
1401 New York Avenue NW
Suite 1100
Washington, DC 20005
www.aed.org/sid

Transparency International
Otto-Suhr-Allee 97-99
D-10585 Berlin
Germany
www.transparency.de

World Trade Centers Association
1 World Trade Center
Suite 7701
New York, NY 10048
www.wtca.org

EUROPEAN UNION

Europa
The umbrella server for all institutions
europa.eu.int

I'M - EUROPE
Information on telematics, telecommunications, copyright, IMPACT program for the information market
www2.echo.lu

CORDIS
Information on EU research programs
www.cordis.lu

EUROPARL
Information on the European Parliament's activities
www.europarl.eu.int

Delegation of the European Commission to the US Press releases, EURECOM:
Economic and Financial News, EU-US relations, information on EU policies and Delegation programs
www.eurunion.org

Citizens Europe
Covers rights of citizens of EU member states
citizens.eu.int

EUDOR (European Union Document Repository)
Bibliographic database
www.eudor.com

European Agency for the Evaluation of Medicinal Products
Information on drug approval procedures and documents of the Committee for Proprietary Medicinal Products and the Committee for Veterinary Medicinal Products
www.eudra.org/emea.html

European Central Bank
www.ecb.int

European Environment Agency
Information on the mission, products and services, and the organizations and staff of the EEA
www.eea.dk

European Investment Bank
Press releases and information on borrowing and loan operations, staff, and publications
www.eib.org

European Training Foundation
Information on vocational education and training programs in Central and Eastern Europe and Central Asia
www.etf.it

Office for Harmonization in the Internal Market
Guidelines, application forms, and other information for registering an EU trademark
europa.eu.int/agencies/ohim/ohim.htm

Council of the European Union
Information and news from the Council with sections Covering Common Foreign and Security Policy (CFSP) and Justice and Home Affairs
Under Construction
ue.eu.int

Court of Justice
Overview, press releases, publications, and full-text Proceedings of the court;
europa.eu.int/cj/en/index.htm

Court of Auditors
Information notes, annual reports, and other publications
www.eca.eu.int

European Community Information Service
200 Rue de la Loi
1049 Brussels, Belgium
and
2100 M Street NW
7th Floor
Washington, DC 20037

European Bank for Reconstruction and Development
One Exchange Square
London EC2A 2EH
United Kingdom
www.ebrd.corn

European Union
200 Rue de la Loi
1049 Brussels, Belgium
and
2100 M Street NW
7th Floor
Washington, DC 20037
www.eurunion.org/

UNITED NATIONS

www.un.org

Conference of Trade and Development
Palais des Nations
1211 Geneva 10
Switzerland
www.unicc.unctad.org

Department of Economic and Social Affairs
1 United Nations Plaza
New York, NY 10017
www.un.org/ecosocdev/

Industrial Development Organization
1660 L Street NW
Washington, DC 20036
and
Post Office Box 300
Vienna International Center
A-1400 (Vienna, Austria)
www.unido.org

International Trade Centre
UNCTAD/WTO
54-56 Rue de Montbrillant
CH-1202 Geneva
Switzerland
www.intracen.org

UN Publications
Room 1194
1 United Nations Plaza
New York, NY 10017
www.un.org/pubs/

Statistical Yearbook
1 United Nations Plaza
New York, NY 10017
www.un.org/pubs/

Yearbook of International Trade Statistics
United Nations
United Nations Publishing Division
1 United Nations Plaza
Room DC2-0853
New York, NY 10017
www.un.org/pubs/

U.S. GOVERNMENT

Agency for International Development
Office of Business Relations
Washington, DC 20523
www.info.usaid.gov/

Customs Service
1301 Constitution Avenue NW
Washington, DC 20229
www.customs.ustreas.gov/

Department of Agriculture
12th Street and Jefferson Drive SW
Washington, DC 20250
www.usda.gov/

Department of Commerce
Herbert C. Hoover Building
14th Street and Constitution
Avenue NW
Washington, DC 20230
www.doc.gov/

Department of State
2201 C Street NW
Washington, DC 20520
www.state.gov/

Department of the Treasury
15th Street and Pennsylvania
Avenue NW
Washington, DC 20220
www.ustreas.gov/

Federal Trade Commission
6th Street and Pennsylvania
Avenue NW
Washington, DC 20580
www.ftc.gov/

International Trade Commission
500 E Street NW
Washington, DC 20436
www.usitc.gov/

Small Business Administration
409 Third Street SW
Washington, DC 20416
www.sbaonline.sba.gov/

STAT.USA
HCHB Room 4885
U.S. Department of Commerce
Washington, DC 20230
www.stat-usa.gov

U.S. Trade and Development Agency
1621 North Kent Street
Rosslyn, VA 22209
www.tda.gov/

Council of Economic Advisers
www.whitehouse.gov/gov/wh/eop/cea

Department of Defense
www.dtic.dla.mil

Department of Energy
www.osti.gov

Department of Interior
www.doi.gov

Department of Labor
www.dol.gov

Department of Transportation
www.dot.gov

Environmental Protection Agency
www.epa.gov

National Trade Data Bank
www.stat-usa.gov

National Economic Council
www.whitehouse.gov/gov/wh
/eop/nec

Office of the U.S. Trade Representatives
www.ustr.gov

Office of Management and Budget
www.whitehouse.gov/gov/wh
/eop/omb

Overseas Private Investment Corporation
www.opic.gov

U.S. Information Agency
www.usia.gov

INDEXES TO LITERATURE

Business Periodical Index
H. W. Wilson Co.
950 University Avenue
Bronx, NY 10452

New York Times Index
University Microfilms
International
300 N. Zeeb Road
Ann Arbor, MI 48106
www.nytimes.com

Public Affairs Information Service Bulletin
11 W. 40th Street
New York, NY 10018
www.pais.internet

Reader's Guide to Periodical Literature
H. W. Wilson Co.
950 University Avenue
Bronx, NY 10452
www.tulane.edu/~horn.rdg.html

Wall Street Journal Index
University Microfilms
International
300 N. Zeeb Road
Ann Arbor, MI 48106
www.wsj.com

DIRECTORIES

American Register of Exporters and Importers
38 Park Row
New York, NY 10038

Arabian Year Book
Dar Al-Seuassam Est. Box 42480
Shuwahk, Kuwait

Directories of American Firms Operating in Foreign Countries
World Trade Academy Press
Uniworld Business Publications Inc.
50 E. 42nd Street
New York, NY 10017

Directory of International Sources of Business Information
Pitman
128 Long Acre
London, WC2E 9AN, England

Directory of North American International Trade Associations
11800 Sunrise Valley Drive, #210
Reston, VA 20191-4345

Encyclopedia of Associations
Gale Research Co.
Book Tower
Detroit, MI 48226

Polk's World Bank Directory
R. C. Polk & Co.
2001 Elm Hill Pike
P.O. Box 1340
Nashville, TN 37202

Verified Directory of Manufacturer's Representatives
MacRae's Blue Book Inc.
817 Broadway
New York, NY 10003

World Guide to Trade Associations
K. G. Saur & Co.
175 Fifth Avenue
New York, NY 10010

ENCYCLOPEDIAS, HANDBOOKS, AND MISCELLANEOUS

A Basic Guide to Exporting
U.S. Government Printing Office
Superintendent of Documents
Washington, DC 20402

Doing business in . . . Series
Price Waterhouse
1251 Avenue of the Americas
New York, NY 10020

Economic Survey of Europe
The United Nations
United Nations Publishing Division
1 United Nations Plaza
Room DC2-0853
New York, NY 10017

Economic Survey of Latin America
The United Nations
United Nations Publishing Division
1 United Nations Plaza
Room DC2-0853
New York, NY 10017

Encyclopedia Americana, International Edition
Grolier Inc.
Danbury, CT 06816

Encyclopedia of Business Information Sources
Gale Research Co.
Book Tower
Detroit, MI 48226

Europa Year Book
Europa Publications Ltd.
18 Bedford Square
London WC1B 3JN, England

Export Administration Regulations
U.S. Government Printing Office
Superintendent of Documents
Washington, DC 20402

Exporters' Encyclopedia—World Marketing Guide
Dun's Marketing Services
49 Old Bloomfield Rd.
Mountain Lake, NJ 07046

**Export-Import Bank of the
United States Annual Report**
U.S. Government Printing Office
Superintendent of Documents
Washington, DC 20402

Exporting for the Small Business
U.S. Government Printing Office
Superintendent of Documents
Washington, DC 20402

Exporting to the United States
U.S. Government Printing Office
Superintendent of Documents
Washington, DC 20402

Export Shipping Manual
U.S. Government Printing Office
Superintendent of Documents
Washington, DC 20402

**Foreign Business Practices:
Materials on Practical Aspects of
Exporting, International
Licensing, and Investing**
U.S. Government Printing Office
Superintendent of Documents
Washington, DC 20402

A Guide to Financing Exports
U.S. Government Printing Office
Superintendent of Documents
Washington, DC 20402

**Handbook of Marketing
Research**
McGraw-Hill Book Co.
1221 Avenue of the Americas
New York, NY 10020

Periodic Reports, Newspapers, Magazines

Advertising Age
Crain Communications Inc.
740 N. Rush Street
Chicago, IL 60611
www.adage.com

Advertising World
Directories International Inc.
150 Fifth Avenue Suite 610
New York, NY 10011

Arab Report and Record
84 Chancery Lane
London WC2A 1DL, England

Barron's
University Microfilms
International
300 N. Zeeb Road
Ann Arbor, MI 48106
www.barrons.com

Business America
U.S. Department of Commerce
14th Street and Constitution
Avenue NW
Washington, DC 20230
www.doc.gov

Business International
Business International Corp.
One Dag Hammarskjold Plaza
New York, NY 10017

Business Week
McGraw-Hill Publications Co.
1221 Avenue of the Americas
New York, NY 10020
www.businessweek.com

Commodity Trade Statistics
United Nations Publications
1 United Nations Plaza
Room DC2-8053
New York, NY 10017

Conference Board Record
Conference Board Inc.
845 Third Avenue
New York, NY 10022

Customs Bulletin
U.S. Customs Service
1301 Constitution Avenue NW
Washington, DC 20229

Dun's Business Month
Goldhirsh Group
38 Commercial Wharf
Boston, MA 02109

The Economist
Economist Newspaper Ltd.
25 St. James Street
London SWIA 1HG, England
www.economist.com

Europe Magazine
2100 M Street NW
Suite 707
Washington, DC 20037

The Financial Times
Bracken House
10 Cannon Street
London EC4P 4BY, England
www.ft-se.co.uk

Forbes
Forbes, Inc.
60 Fifth Avenue
New York, NY 10011
www.forbes.com

Fortune
Time, Inc.
Time & Life Building
1271 Avenue of the Americas
New York, NY 10020
Pathfinder.com/fortune

Global Trade
North American Publishing Co.
401 N. Broad Street
Philadelphia, PA 19108

Industrial Marketing
Crain Communications, Inc.
740 N. Rush Street
Chicago, IL 60611

International Financial Statistics
International Monetary Fund
Publications Unit
700 19th Street NW
Washington, DC 20431
www.imf.com

Investor's Daily
Box 25970
Los Angeles, CA 90025

Journal of Commerce
100 Wall Street
New York, NY 10005
www.joc.com/

**Sales and Marketing
Management**
Bill Communications Inc.
633 Third Avenue
New York, NY 10017

Wall Street Journal
Dow Jones & Company
200 Liberty Street
New York, NY 10281
www.wsj.com

World Agriculture Situation
U.S. Department of Agriculture
Economics Management Staff
www.econ.ag.gov

Pergamon Press Inc.
Journals Division
Maxwell House
Fairview Park
Elmsford, NY 10523

**World Trade Center Association
(WTCA) Directory**
World Trade Centers Association
1 World Trade Center
New York, NY 10048

**International Encyclopedia of
the Social Sciences**
Macmillan and the Free Press
866 Third Avenue
New York, NY 10022

**Marketing and Communications
Media Dictionary**
Media Horizons Inc.
50 W. 25th Street
New York, NY 10010
www.horizons-media.com/

Market Share Reports
U.S. Government Printing Office
Superintendent of Documents
Washington, DC 20402
www.access.gpo.gov/

**Media Guide International
Business/Professional
Publications**
Directories International Inc.
150 Fifth Avenue
Suite 610
New York, NY 10011
www.clubi.ie/bdi/index.html

Overseas Business Reports
U.S. Government Printing Office
Superintendent of Documents
Washington, DC 20402
www.access.gpo.gov/

Trade Finance
U.S. Department of Commerce
International Trade
Administration
Washington, DC 20230
www.doc.gov/

**World Economic Conditions in
Relation to Agricultural Trade**
U.S. Government Printing Office
Superintendent of Documents
Washington, DC 20402
www.access.gpo.gov/

SELECTED TRADE DATABASES

News Agencies
Comline-Japan Newswire
Dow Jones News
Nikkei Shimbun News
Database Omninews
Lexis-Nexis
Reuters Monitor
UPI

**Trade Publication References
with Bibliographic Keywords**
Agris
Biocommerce Abstracts &
Directory
Findex
Frost (short) Sullivan Market
Research Reports
Marketing Surveys Index
McCarthy Press Cuttings Service
PTS F & S Indexes
Trade and Industry Index

**Trade Publication References
with Summaries**
ABI/Inform
Arab Information Bank
Asia-Pacific
BFAI

Biobusiness
CAB Abstracts
Chemical Business Newsbase
Chemical Industry Notes
Caffeeline
Delphes
InfoSouth Latin American
Information System
Management Contents
NTIS Bibliographic Data Base
Paperchem
PIRA Abstract
PSTA
PTS Marketing & Advertising
Reference Service
PTS PromtRapra Abstracts
Textline
Trade & Industry ASAP
World Textiles

Full Text of Trade Publications
Datamonitor Market Reports
Dow Jones News
Euromonitor Market Direction
Federal News Service
Financial Times Business Report
File
Financial Times Fulltext
Globefish
ICC Key Notes Market Research
Investext
McCarthy Press Cuttings Service
PTS Promt
Textline
Trade & Industry ASAP

Statistics
Agrostat (diskette only)
ARI Network/CNS
Arab Information Bank
Comext/Eurostat
Comtrade
FAKT-German Statistics
Globefish
IMF Data
OECD Data
Piers Imports
PTS Forecasts
PTS Time Series
Reuters Monitor

Trade Statistics
Tradstat World Trade Statistics
TRAINS (CD-ROM being
developed)
US I/E Maritime Bills of Lading
US Imports for Consumption
World Bank Statistics

Price Information
ARI Network/CNS
Chemical Business Newsbase
COLEACP
Commodity Options
Commodities 2000
Market News Service of ITC
Nikkei Shimbun News Database
Reuters Monitor
UPI
US Wholesale Prices

Company Registers
ABC Europe Production Europe
Biocommerce Abstracts &
Directory
CD-Export (CD-ROM only)
Company Intelligence
D&B Duns Market Identifiers
(U.S.A.)
D&B European Marketing File
D&B Eastern Europe

Dun's Electronic Business
Directory
Firmexport/Firmimport
Hoppenstedt Austria
Hoppenstedt Germany
Hoppenstedt Benelux
Huco-Hungarian Companies
ICC Directory of Companies
Kompass Asia/Pacific
Kompass Europe (EKOD)
Mexican Exporters/Importers
Piers Imports
Polu-Polish Companies
SDOE
Thomas Register
TRAINS (CD-ROM being
developed)
UK Importers
UK Importers (DECTA)
US Directory of Importers
US I/E Maritime Bills of Lading
World Trade Center Network

Trade Opportunities, Tenders
Business
Federal News Service
Huntech-Hungarian Technique
Scan-a-Bid
Tenders Electronic Daily
World Trade Center Network

Tariffs and Trade Regulations
Celex
ECLAS
Justis Eastern Europe (CD-ROM
only)
Scad
Spearhead
TRAINS (CD-ROM being
developed)
US Code of Federal Regulations
US Federal Register
US Harmonized Tariff Schedule

Standards
BSI Standardline
Noriane/Perinorm
NTIS Bibliographic Database
Standards Infodisk ILI (CD-ROM
only)

Shipping Information
Piers Imports
Tradstat World Trade Statistics
US I/E Maritime Bills of Lading

Others
Fairbase
Ibiscus

chapter

6

Estimating the Marke
ng the Market Dema   Estimating the Market Dema

Estimating the Market Demand

Estimating the Mar

A key marketing activity is planning, and the key precursor to planning is to forecast market demand conditions. With many business environments changing rapidly, it is no longer possible simply to repeat the actions that have worked in the past. It is now necessary to estimate and predict the best you can what will happen in the planning period in question.

For most organizations the future is clouded by a degree of uncertainty. The more uncertainty, the greater the risk to the organization. The primary task of market forecasting is to reduce uncertainty to the lowest possible level. The changes that are taking place in the organization's environment will result in both opportunities and threats. Another task of market forecasting, therefore, is to identify and quantify these changes.

> The primary task of market **forecasting is to reduce uncertainty** to the lowest possible level.

As we all have observed in the last several years, e-commerce has mushroomed above anyone's expectation. As shown in Manager's Corner 6.1, making a forecast of what business opportunities will emerge in the information technology field, particularly in e-commerce, has proved to be extremely difficult.

Manager's Corner 6.1

Forecasting marketing opportunities in the e-commerce market with certainty is its uncertainty

If you flip open almost any magazine in the information technology (IT) field, you will find a graph or a bar chart forecasting the growth of the e-commerce market. Most of the predictions will prove as hopelessly wrong in five years as they have in the past. Remember videotext? Back in 1983, a leading research firm confidently forecast that consumer sales of videotext would be $7 billion by 1987. The actual figure was less than 10 percent of the forecast.

Market forecasters arrive at extremely different predictions for the same thing. The National Sales Federation's (nrf.com) prediction for online consumer sales for the 1998 holiday season was $174 billion, whereas Jupiter Communications' (www.jup.com) estimate was a meager $2.3 billion. Forecasters cannot even agree on what has already happened. In 1997, Forrester Research (www.forrester.com) and International Data Corp. (www.idc.com) re-ported different numbers on the size of the 1996 e-commerce market—$9.5 billion and $5.4 billion, respectively.

These predictions and postdictions clearly show how difficult it is to define the domain and size of the e-commerce market. The real challenge to the marketer is how to plan when you cannot predict. To do so, don't ask what the future will be. Instead, ask how different the future needs to be from what it is today before it disrupts your business model and requires you to move aggressively. For example, what percentage of your industry's or company's customer base or operating market can you afford to lose before your business becomes unprofitable? In retailing, if a mall loses 10 percent of its customers permanently, it will have to close. A rule of thumb is that a permanent margin cut of about 15 percent would turn the standard business version into a liquidation sales candidate.

Of course, there are many areas in which IT has to place bets on specific technologies and vendors. But the forecasts have historically proven time and time again to be wrong. They suffer from the fallacy that the future is a linear extension of the present and the past. This is exemplified by Exhibit 6.1. Who could have anticipated the competitive companies of today, including Cisco (www.cisco.com), Qwest (www.quest.com), Lucent (www.lucent.com), Netscape (www.netscape.com), AOL (www.aol.com), Yahoo! (www.yahoo.com), Nokia (www.nokia.com), Ariba (www.ariba.com), and Exodus (www.exodus.com)?

Is it time for your company to jump into e-commerce? One piece of information to be used for your decision making: Online advertising revenues in 1998 reached $2.1 billion. The estimate for 1999 (at the time of writing this chapter in 1999) was an eye-popping $5.5 billion, or a 162 percent increase over 1998. By 2002, online ad revenues are expected to reach over $7 billion.

Sources: "Net Ads to Break $7 Billion in 2002," *The Industry Standard*, March 29, 1999, 44; Peter G. W. Keen, "Stop the Forecasts!" *ComputerWorld*, May 10, 1999, 48.

Exhibit 6.1

Matt Spangler and others are pictured here picking orders from the media cage at Amazon.com's Seattle distribution center. With combined sales for all units climbing as fast as new customers—up 171 percent from 1998 to 1999—the company has yet to turn a profit. In fact, in the second quarter of 1999 losses rose to 21 percent of net revenue, double the figure for the same period in 1998. It would seem that Amazon.com is experiencing the linear fallacy of forecasting—where the present is an extension of the past—but how long can negative profitability continue without compromising the reputation and the health of the business?

Forecasting's complexion and its complexity vary depending on whether it is short term or long term; on the importance of the resulting decision to firm survivability; and on whether it is a true forecast or, as is more often the case, a budget. The approach may also be macro or micro. This chapter explores the main techniques in some detail. These are divided into qualitative techniques (including scenarios), usually linked to the longer term, and quantitative (numerical) techniques, directed at the shorter term. Alternative approaches to reducing the risk of future developments are also discussed.

FORECASTS VERSUS BUDGETS

There often is confusion between **forecasts** and **budgets**, which are two closely related activities. As a result, the names of the two are sometimes interchanged. They are defined as follows:

- **Forecasting.** In its simplest sense, this predicting what will happen in the future, all other things being equal (usually in terms of statistics—especially in terms of the organization's own variables of interest).

- **Budgeting.** In its simplest sense, the budget (including the all-important *sales budget*, which is easily confused with a *sales forecast*) states what the organization believes is achievable—and intends to achieve. It is essentially a planned allocation of tasks and budgets to accomplish the goal set by the organization.

There are more complex definitions, but, even so, it is obvious from the preceding definitions that many of the so-called forecasts prepared by organizations are really budgets. The forecast is the basis for planning and has to be as accurate and unbiased as possible. The budget is directly linked to implementation and has to be practically achievable. The requirements of the two are, therefore, very different, and to confuse them weakens both processes.

The first part of this chapter will examine the various techniques in terms of their forecasting elements.

SHORT-TERM, MEDIUM-TERM, AND LONG-TERM FORECASTS

There may be different types of forecasts to meet different needs. One of the main differences is the time span that the forecast covers:

- Short term (tactical)—monthly and quarterly, for example, as input to the normal business planning and control processes

- Medium term—annually, as the main input to the budget planning processes

- Long term (strategic)—typically for five years, as the basis for the organization's strategies

SHORT TERM

Most organizations need to predict the events on a monthly or a quarterly basis for a number of reasons. Particularly, the recent development of the Internet permits short-term predictions with increased accuracy. These reasons include:

- **Production scheduling.** The classical use of short-term forecasting is that of scheduling production capacity. The input may come from the sales force, and its forecasts for the near future should represent a very confident measure of what will happen. On the other hand, the input may come from the marketing department, which may provide short-term forecasts based on recognized seasonal trends or short-term promotional activities. The Internet can be useful in accurate sales forecasting. With its headquarters in Europe, Heineken had traditionally been forced to work with a long lead time in receiving forecasts and getting product distributed throughout the United States. To process sales forecasts and orders efficiently, Heineken now uses an "extranet," a private network connecting Heineken to customers and suppliers using Internet technology based on the integrated value chain planning software developed by Logility, an Atlanta-based software developer.[1]

www.heineken.com

www.logility.com

---

1. "Heineken Redefines Collaborative Planning through the Internet," *Beverage Industry*, September 1998, 47.

www.netscape.com

- **Information transmission.** As can be seen from the previous example, one element of short-term forecasts has little to do with predicting unknown quantities; instead it is simply the formal process of transferring known information from one part of the organization to another. Thus, the order processing department produces forecasts, which are actually the totals for the orders already received and being processed for the production scheduling system. Heineken's system is known as HOPS (Heineken Operational Planning System) and allows for real-time forecasting and ordering interaction with distributors. Heineken can deliver customized forecasting data to distributors through individual Web pages. Distributors just need Netscape Navigator to access the Heineken program, eliminating the high cost of a direct line from the distributor to Heineken's offices.

- **Control.** Forecasts, especially short-term ones, are frequently used as a key element of control. Thus, what the sales force is predicting will happen in the near future gives advance warning of problems that will need to be rectified. It is likely, in practice, that most of these short-term forecasts will actually be sales budgets. Heineken's distributors have the option of approving or modifying the forecast online for better control of inventory needs. This approved or modified forecast is immediately forwarded to Logility's Replenishment Planning module, which calculates the distributor's inventory needs by comparing actual inventory to the newly forecasted levels. The replenishment plan is then transmitted to the distributor, who is still logged on to the Web site. Once the distributor approves the replenishment plan, the system creates an electronic purchase order, and the order cycle begins.

MEDIUM TERM

The classical image of forecasting revolves around those hectic few weeks in the year when the planning processes, usually driven by the budgets, demand the preparation of the annual forecasts—medium-term forecasts. Much of the quantitative section on forecasting later in this chapter will address this type of forecast.

LONG TERM

The long-term, or strategic, forecast (the subject of much of the qualitative forecasting described later in this chapter) is less common than short- or medium-term forecasting. As it typically covers a period of five years or longer, it is often seen as a luxury that only the larger organizations and those in more stable environments can afford. In reality, it is probably the most important forecast of all—certainly in terms of setting the direction for the overall marketing plan and increasing the chances of long-term survivability. Three types of decisions are associated with long-term forecasts:

- **Strategic direction.** The long-term forecast usually consolidates the long-term strategy. Having to quantify this strategy as a forecast, or a series of forecasts, helps to concentrate attention on practical and meaningful ideas.

- **Resource planning.** The long-term planning period should be chosen to cover the period over which the long-term investments, in plant or research, for example, will be completed.

- **Communication.** A long-term forecast tells everyone in the organization—workers and management—where the organization intends to go. As a result, it is also one of the key bases for the organizational culture, which is an essential, if still largely unrecognized, aspect of most organizations.

Long-term forecasts are the least likely to be confused with budgets and are perhaps less biased by the organization's view of its own activities. On the other hand, they are just as likely to be constrained by an organization's parochial view of the future. This market myopia may well preclude its forecasters from taking into account all of the factors involved.

DYNAMICS OF FORECASTING

It is often assumed that forecasts are immutable and static—the annual forecast will be renewed in 12 months' time, and not a moment earlier; the five-year plan will only be replaced in five years' time. It is somehow an admission of failure if such forecasts have to be changed.

In practice, forecasts should be amended as the environment changes. Thus, the best-managed organizations probably have a quarterly review of their annual forecast (and associated budgets) so that forecasts for the remaining quarters can be based on the latest information. The most sophisticated indulge in **rolling forecasts**, whereby at each quarter a full year ahead is forecast—in other words, a new fourth quarter is added to the plan. This takes much of the drama out of the annual planning cycle.

> In practice, forecasts **should be amended as the environment changes.**

More important, and less well recognized perhaps, is the fact that even five-year forecasts may need to change quite dramatically each time they are reviewed annually. Over the preceding year it is more than likely that the external environment, as well as the organization's internal environment, will have changed significantly—and in ways that were not predicted. The overall economy may have changed direction, competitors may have changed strategies, and consumers may have changed their tastes.

Then why bother to create five-year forecasts? The answer lies in the three reasons listed in the preceding section—strategic direction, resource planning, and communication. These decisions have to be made, with or without the forecasts, deliberately or by default. They still need to incorporate the best thinking, even if it is recognized that in a year's time new information may invalidate some of the decisions.

FORECASTS INTO BUDGETS

If forecasts have been kept separate from the budgets (and as we have already seen, this is often not the case), the first, and most important, decision is what budgets to set. Among these will be budgets that parallel the forecasts themselves. For example, a sales budget (or target) will parallel the sales forecast. As we have already explained, the budget represents what the organization has *decided* to do. These planned (budget) figures are a commitment within the overall plans and consider the planned actions to be taken in terms of the controllable (internal) factors.

HIGH AND LOW BUDGETS.　In many organizations a series of subtly different budgets are produced for different audiences in much the same way that in some countries there are two sets of accounts, one for the owner and one for the tax authorities. There always has to be an original forecast, which must be as accurate as possible. However, it should be recognized that there may be a number of

www.ibm.com

budget variants based on this, although, confusingly, they are often also referred to as forecasts. These variants are as follows:

- **Sales force targets.** It is often thought that salespeople need very challenging targets, so these are usually set very optimistically. On the other hand, IBM quite deliberately sets its sales force targets rather pessimistically because it wants 80 percent of its staff to be "successful" and beat their target.
- **Manufacturing forecast.** Most organizations do not want to be out of stock and will accept some spare capacity, so these are usually somewhat optimistic.
- **Profit forecast.** Every organization dreads not achieving its profit targets, so these are often deliberately pessimistic.

MACRO- AND MICROFORECASTS

Forecasts can also be categorized by the breadth of the factors that they encompass. Some companies have the resources—and the need—to undertake these forecasts of whole markets—indeed sometimes of whole national economies. These macroforecasts attempt to predict what large-scale forces at work will result in *macro* changes in the market environment. In the automobile industry, geopolitical situations in the Persian Gulf could affect the worldwide supply of petroleum, as we experienced in oil crises twice in the 1970s. The global warming trend may sway the government to introduce a more stringent automobile emission control, affecting the car prices.

This has led to the emergence of very sophisticated and complex econometric models. The most important input to these models may be the various *leading indicators*, including housing starts, prime lending rates, and wholesale prices. When pushed to these limits, however, this type of forecasting is both very elaborate and expensive; thus, it is seldom undertaken.

At the other end of the spectrum, microforecasting builds on the predictions of individual (or group) customer behavior. It typically accumulates overall forecasts for sales of particular products or services. In the case of the automobile industry, increased sales of trucks and minivans in the past decade encouraged automakers to raise their sales forecast for trucks and minivans in the near future. But, again, we need to be forewarned that immediate near-future sales forecasts are also affected by the longer-term trends and political mood. These forecasts are classically based on projections of observed historical trends. Before we examine such techniques we need to examine a problem behind historical projections (see Figure 6.1).

Figure 6.1a may be seen as a typical sales graph, covering two or three years (which is the historical period that many organizations look at when they produce forecasts), with the minor fluctuations smoothed out. It is possible that a four-year *trade cycle* lies behind this two- to three-year curve, as, indeed, there has been until very recently. The long-term sales chart may thus look like a rising wave, as presented in Figure 6.1b.

If this is the pattern, but the sales projections are made on the "traditional" basis of two-years' historical data, then the picture will emerge that is shown in Figure 6.1c. As the shape of the diagram suggests, this is known as the **fishbone effect**. It clearly can produce significant mismatches of organizational resource to opportunities—expecting a bumper crop when famine is about to set in or conserving just when a bumper crop is about to return. On the other hand, if the product life cycle is taken into account, the results of such forecasting may even be counterproductive when a downturn does not follow from a temporary hiccup in the economy but rather represents the onset of the decline phase for the product.

Having issued this caveat, however, estimates based on past sales are very widely used, and, in the absence of the more advanced forecasting tools, can justifiably be used as the main indicators in many situations. However, they must be

Figure 6.1

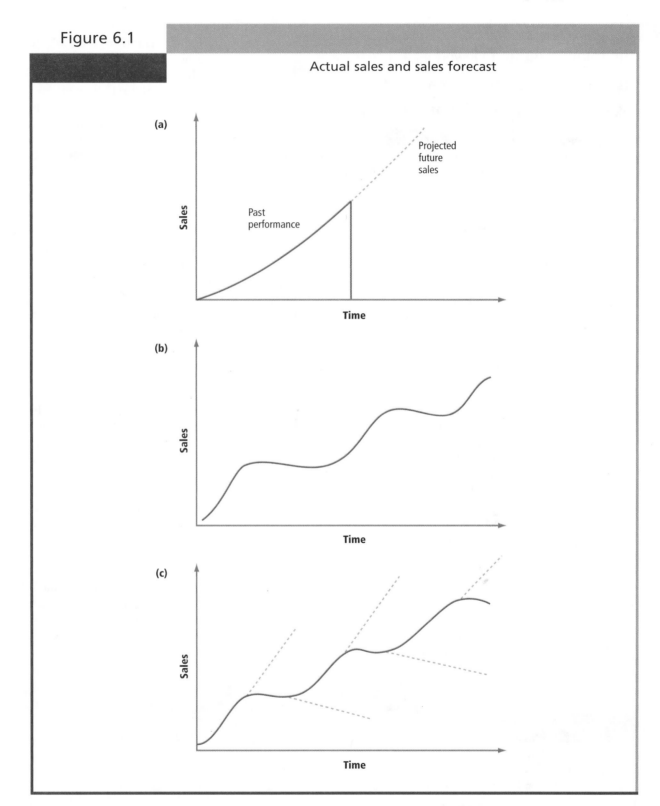

Actual sales and sales forecast

(a) Sales / Time — Past performance, Projected future sales

(b) Sales / Time

(c) Sales / Time

checked as far as possible against predictions derived from other sources—and always treated as predictions of an uncertain future.

Again, the automakers have begun to realize that the Internet can bring them closer to customers so that sales forecasting could be reduced to "order-to-delivery" cycle times with higher certainty. In the United States, about 30 percent of car purchases were made with some use of the Internet, from basic viewing of

> **The Internet, at first viewed as a threat, is now seen as helping make better on-site sales forecasts with near certainty.**

www.autobytel.com

cars to setting up deals via Web sites such as Autobytel. Information technology and the Internet allow networks of car dealers to collect and analyze customer data. The Internet, at first viewed as a threat by both automakers and dealers because it made customers dangerously knowledgeable about comparative price and product data, is now seen as a possible helpmate, as it helps them make better on-site sales forecasts with near certainty.[2]

DERIVED FORECASTS

All forecasts are based on a series of assumptions that the environmental factors will remain unchanged. In practice, though, specific forecasts can also be successfully derived from **global forecasts** made at aggregate levels. For example, if an automobile unit sales volume is predicted on the basis of the change in a country's GNP and prime lending rates over time, such a prediction is called a **derived forecast**. The more advanced forecasters, especially those whose organizations have large shares of their markets, may thus choose to split their forecasting process into a number of stages, as shown in Figure 6.2.

www.oecd.org

WORLD AND NATIONAL ECONOMIES. The OECD (Organization for Economic Cooperation and Development) usually provides the most widely respected *environmental forecasts* for the world economy. For each country, comparable figures are provided by government departments, although other expert institutions also provide their own (sometimes conflicting) versions. The ability of governments to actually collect the correct information is increasingly questioned. The U.S. government spends more than $3 billion per year collecting data that is characterized by some as "a stream of statistics that are nothing but myths and misinformation."[3] Given the U.S. government's relatively large expenditure on data, it is easy to suspect that data from less wealthy governments are even more unreliable.

Prior to the 1980s, these **national forecasts** were often predicated on the existence of *cycles* of economic activity—moving from boom to recession and back again over a four- or five-year period, although larger cycles of up to 60 years have been postulated (known as the Kondratieff Cycle, named after the Russian economist, Nicholai D. Kondratieff). These country-level forecasts are, however, often ignored by organization-level forecasters.

Figure 6.2

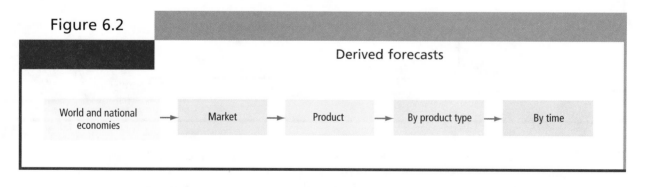

Derived forecasts

World and national economies → Market → Product → By product type → By time

2. "Business: Break Down," *Economist*, May 22, 1999, 70.
3. Michael J. Mandel, "The Real Truth About the Economy: Are Government Statistics So Much Pulp Fiction? Take a Look," *Business Week*, November 7, 1994, 110–118.

Marketing in Action 6.1

E&Y Kenneth Leventhal Real Estate Group predicts surge of new immigrants

The E&Y Kenneth Leventhal (EYKL) Real Estate Group is the provider of international real estate advisory services within the larger Ernst & Young (www.ey.com) global network. Ernst & Young, one of the world's leading accounting, tax, and consulting firms, has over 685 worldwide offices. The EYKL group provides professional services to real estate owners, developers, builders, lenders, and users.

In the late 1990s, EYKL completed "The 1999 National Lodging Forecast." Some very interesting immigration trends emerged from the study. Amazingly, if immigration trends continue as they did between 1991 and 1996, at a rate of approximately 1,000,000 annually, immigration by the year 2000 will be the highest of any decade in U.S. history. Many of today's immigrants come from Mexico and Asia. Approximately 68 percent of immigrants in 1996 resided in only six U.S. states (California, New York, Texas, Florida, New Jersey, and Illinois). By 2002, no single ethnic group will account for more than 50 percent of these states' populations. If trends continue, 30 million housing units will be needed nationally by the year 2050 just to accommodate new immigrants and their offspring.

What do the immigration forecasts mean in terms of real estate marketing? How will real estate firms need to think about target marketing? What about building design issues (e.g., many cultures believe strongly in the notion of extended families)? Will service providers in the real estate market need to be educated in cultural differences, as immigrants tend to cluster in ethnic communities? What do the trends mean in terms of recreation, retail, service, and entertainment issues?

Sources: www.ey.com/realestate; "Casa Sweet Casa," *Business Week,* January 11, 1999, 136.

MARKET.   The most important aggregate forecast, particularly for those organizations with high market shares, is that of the market (or *industry*). This forecast will, of course, be affected by external factors and will also take into account factors more specific to that market itself—whether it is relatively new, with large numbers of potential customers still to be recruited, or mature with little further growth potential.

> **The most important aggregate forecast,**
> **for those organizations with high market shares,**
> **is that of the market (or industry).**

Market forecasts tend to be based, as do individual product forecasts, on historical trends. However, they may also be based on modeling the numbers of different customers and the prediction of their changing usage patterns. This is particularly useful in new markets, although it is not necessarily an easy technique to implement. Who are the potential users? How much will they each use? These may be very difficult questions to answer for a really innovative new product or service. Marketing in Action 6.1 describes the impact of immigration forecasts on the market forecast.

PRODUCT.   Most forecasting takes place at the product (or company) level and is based on historical data. On the other hand, if the market forecasts have already been completed, the alternative approach is to derive the product forecast from that of the market by forecasting the changes in brand share. This is a rather different process, because it mainly focuses on competitive positions that may be underweighted in other forecasts.

Markov's brand-switching model, a popular marketing tool, is illustrative. In the Markov model the current probabilities of brand switching (measured from consumer intentions) by existing users of each brand are known. As these switches actually occur over time, this will lead to new levels of brand share (based on a cumulative historical buildup) that can, accordingly, be calculated. For example, in Table 6.1a, 50 percent of the users of Brand A will remain with it

Table 6.1

Markov's brand-switching model

a. Probability that consumers will switch brands

	A	B	C
	A	**B**	**C**
A	stay	change	change
	0.5	0.3	0.2
B	change	stay	change
	0.4	0.4	0.2
C	change	change	stay
	0.3	0.3	0.4

b. The application of probabilities to the existing brand shares to determine the postswitch market shares

				New brand share anticipated
A	0.5 of 20% = 10%	0.4 of 30% = 12%	0.3 of 50% = 15%	37%
B	0.4 of 30% = 12%	0.3 of 20% = 6%	0.3 of 50% = 15%	35%
C	0.4 of 50% = 20%	0.2 of 20% = 4%	0.2 of 30% = 6%	30%

annually, and it will gain (looking down the related vertical column) 40 percent from B and 30 percent from C. If, as shown, Brand A had an existing share of 20 percent (with B holding 30 percent and C 50 percent) this will result in a growth in share to 37 percent (Table 6.1b) in just one year.

Although apparently simple, this is actually an extremely sophisticated forecasting process, but it is of dubious practical value, because brand-switching intentions are rarely known with the degree of accuracy assumed by the model.

The wise forecaster will try to use both historical and derived forecasting methods and compare the results. In general, preparing the forecasts from many different bases results in greater confidence in the final outcome. However, the comparison will often pose difficult problems for the forecaster, as various forecasts are quite likely to generate differing projections. The process of explaining the differences (assuming that this is carried out with intellectual rigor, rather than just to reinforce existing prejudices) will often give the forecaster greater insight into the processes at work and will give a valuable indication of the likely accuracy of the final forecast.

> The wise forecaster will try to use **both historical and derived forecasting** methods and compare the results.

By type of product. From the product forecast it will often be necessary to forecast the sales of the individual types, or variants, of the product (or service). These are frequently calculated as a simple percentage split, but the wise forecaster will also investigate any trends that may be present, such as changes in consumer preference for different features in Swatch watches.

By time. The forecasts, or budgets, will also need to be expressed in terms of the budgetary periods (usually months), to take account of seasonality and special activities such as point-of-sales (POS) in-store promotions.

FORECASTING TECHNIQUES

In the business community, the term *forecasting* is typically associated with figures; the annual sales forecast is an example. In the social sciences, however, forecasts are frequently produced in a qualitative, verbal form. Both of these are valid, and both offer useful insights.

In general, the qualitative forecasts come into their own in the long term (in strategic and macroforecasting). In these cases the process may also sometimes be described as **technological forecasting** because this is the discipline in which many of the techniques were first developed. The short-term (tactical and micro) forecasts are usually more quantitative.

The following subsections will examine the qualitative techniques, which are mainly used to describe the longer term. Most sound policy making looks first at the longer term (for its strategy) before examining the shorter term in more detail (for its tactics). We shall extend this principle to forecasting, as it helps put the processes into context.

QUALITATIVE METHODS

Qualitative methods describe in words what will happen and the impact that it will bring about. In some cases, this may include significant amounts of statistics, but the context will differ from that of the more normal, numerical quantitative forecasts based on trends. Qualitative forecasts can be compiled from several sources.

INDIVIDUAL OR EXPERT OPINION. In practice, most forecasts are prepared by an individual. In a small company it may be the owner and in a larger organization it may be the marketing manager. In the largest of all it may be the brand manager or even the manager of the forecasting department. The individual forecast is inevitably a personal judgment, an opinion often based on experience and industry rules of thumb.

Sales force forecasts are normally viewed as quantitative, because they typically result from forecast sales figures, which may in turn be derived from customers' forecasts. They are then aggregated to give the total forecast. In reality, they fundamentally incorporate the **qualitative judgment** of each salesperson despite their apparent numerical accuracy. One problem with this technique is that it is often used in conjunction with commission systems, where the sales representative, in submitting his or her forecast, is very aware that this will be used as the basis for the following year's targets and hence his or her income. The process becomes not one of forecasting but one of negotiating targets. This is a poor basis for **unbiased forecasts**. A more advanced, and time-consuming, approach is to survey *all* customers to record their buying intentions for the coming year.

An important but rarely used input is the forecasts of the large customers themselves. For example, if you are selling steel to the car industry, you need to understand how that industry is forecasting its own future. The account planning process described later in this book is an ideal mechanism for this invaluable input.

EXPERT PANEL METHOD. This is the first of the formal ways of applying scientific method to individual opinion. It involves bringing together a panel of experts (business consultants, academic researchers, or corporate executives) to pool their individual forecasts. The individual forecasts may be based on various insights ranging from the respective experts' time-honed personal experiences in industry to econometric analyses. Then, having confirmed (or at least discussed) their individual cases, a corporate forecast "emerges" and is agreed upon.

As the quality of the forecast depends on the quality of the participants, the panel should consist of the best possible team of relevant experts—both from

> the [expert] panel should consist of
>
> **the best possible team of relevant experts—**
>
> both from within the organization and from outside it

within the organization and from outside it. As with the jury system, such a panel does seem to determine which really are the best forecasts, particularly when the members of the panel also must implement these forecasts. In general, however, the uncertainty associated with future events is underestimated by others who later review these forecasts. The participants in the forecasting usually recognize all too well the limitations of this method.

www.almanac.com

One type of expertise is provided by the experts who write various predictions in the *Old Farmer's Almanac*. Recently a number of these almanacs predicted huge snowfalls for the winter of 1995. As a result, prewinter sales of salt were up 42 percent from the previous year, snowmobile sales increased 46 percent, snowblower sales rose 120 percent, and employment at one snowplow maker had to be tripled to keep up with demand.[4] Ironically, however, the huge snowfalls failed to materialize!

www.rand.com

Another type of expert panel method is the Delphi technique, originally developed at the Rand Corporation. In this case the (anonymous) experts are quite deliberately *not* brought together, so as to avoid any bandwagon effect. Instead, a general questionnaire is circulated to the team, asking only for predictions of major changes. The collected replies, including, for example, predictions of technological changes, are then distributed to the team together with a questionnaire that asks more pointed questions, such as predicting dates for the introduction of new technology or forecasting its impact on the organization. Successive rounds of questioning become increasingly specific, until a sufficiently detailed picture is obtained.

www.bicc.co.nz
www.mdm.com

Dawn Jarisch, group company purchasing manager for BICC Cables, recently won a highly coveted *Modern Distribution Management* (formerly *Supply Management*) magazine's Idea of the Year award in the United Kingdom for developing a new technique incorporating elements of the Delphi method—a form of structured brainstorming based on collation and analysis of expert opinion. She worked in a small central team to devise and promote an alternative technique to produce price predictions for materials budgets. Its iterative approach canvassed and distilled internal opinion—supplemented where necessary by industry and macroeconomic forecasts—to produce minimum and maximum predictions and a reliable mean.[5]

A variation on the use of expert opinion is **role playing** or **simulation**, in which the experts involved attempt to deduce how they might react in the equivalent real-life situations. This is an expensive approach that is little used.

Still another technique is to ask experts about events similar to the issue under investigation in order to formulate an analogy. For instance, this analogy may come from history, from another field, or from another country. If the analogy matches the parameters involved it can offer a useful insight into the processes at work. For example, how China's socialistic regime might crumble in the future can be conjectured by experts who examine how the Soviet regime collapsed.

TECHNOLOGICAL FORECASTING.   This series of techniques is associated with plotting very long-term trends and, in particular, with changes in technology. The estimates are typically based on a plot of the previous changes over time (a **growth curve**), showing, for example, the increasing performance or decreasing cost. One classic example is shown in Figure 6.3. The brightness of the lamp,

4. Gary McWilliams, "The Farmer's Almanacs Start a Storm," *Business Week*, December 12, 1994.
5. "A What and Why Forecast," *Supply Management* (Idea of the Years Awards Supplement), March 26, 1998, 6.

Figure 6.3

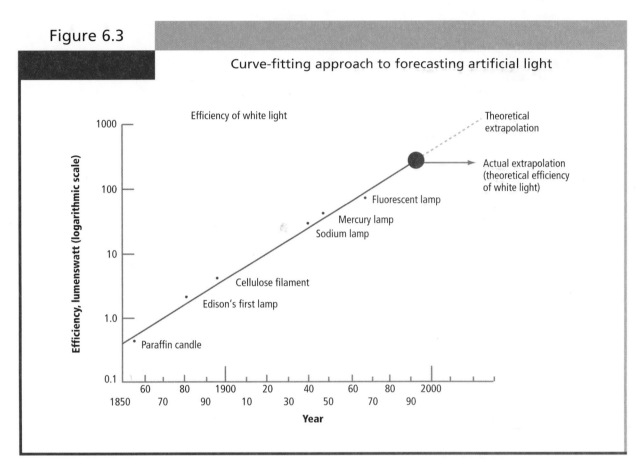

Curve-fitting approach to forecasting artificial light

Efficiency of white light

Theoretical extrapolation

Actual extrapolation (theoretical efficiency of white light)

Fluorescent lamp

Mercury lamp

Sodium lamp

Cellulose filament

Edison's first lamp

Paraffin candle

Efficiency, lumenswatt (logarithmic scale)

Year

Source: Spyros Makridakis and Steven C. Wheelwright, *Forecasting Methods for Management*, 5th ed. (New York: John Wiley & Sons, 1989), 321. © 1989 by John Wiley & Sons, Inc. Reprinted by permission of John Wiley & Sons, Inc.

measured by lumenswatt per energy unit, has increased at an exponential rate as a result of significant inventions over the years. Using this historical line, one can forecast the brightness of a yet-to-be-developed lamp in the future with a reasonable level of certainty.

Another related technological forecasting method is an **envelope curve** extrapolation. An envelope curve expects technology to develop by quantum leaps, with new techniques gradually being improved until they reach the ceiling of their performance, at which point they are then overtaken by the next development. The hypothetical graph in Figure 6.4 illustrates this approach in the context where it is usually deployed.

DECISION TREE.   One aid to qualitative forecasting is the use of tree structures. The main factors affecting the organization's environment, for example, are plotted, and the possible alternatives or decisions (hence the name **decision trees**) are shown at each stage, branching at each level like a tree. An example is the choices facing an inventor (Figure 6.5). At the end of this process, all of the various possible contributions, or at least all that the forecaster chooses to take into account, will have been documented, including some that might not otherwise have been considered. This is the main value of the technique, although an obvious problem is dealing with the sheer number of alternatives that becomes apparent.

One application of the decision tree approach is to apply probabilities to each of the decisions. Bayes's Theorem offers a simple formula for dealing with conditional probability. The resulting probabilities of all the possible outcomes can then be calculated. This process can be taken even further by calculating the composite **payoffs** (the product of the calculated value of the outcome multiplied by the probability) for each alternative. With computing power now easily available,

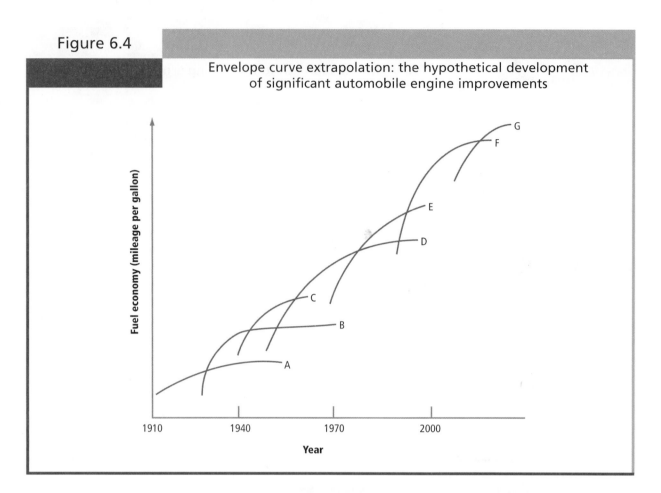

Figure 6.4

Envelope curve extrapolation: the hypothetical development of significant automobile engine improvements

Fuel economy (mileage per gallon)

A B C D E F G

1910 1940 1970 2000

Year

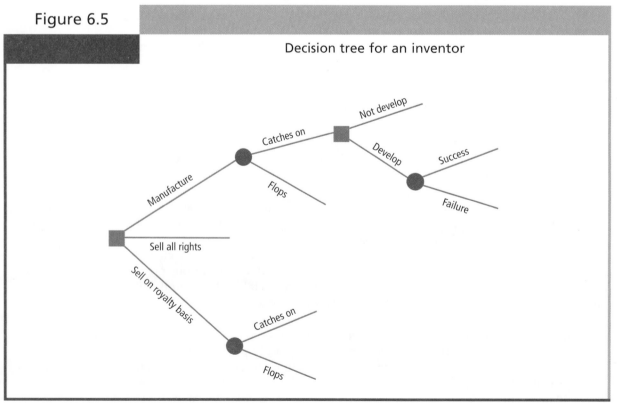

Figure 6.5

Decision tree for an inventor

Manufacture

Catches on

Flops

Not develop

Develop

Success

Failure

Sell all rights

Sell on royalty basis

Catches on

Flops

these quantified outputs can help give a good measure of the optimum outcomes, as long as, once more, it is recognized that all the input factors are opinions rather than hard facts. The wise forecaster also tries to understand how the various elements interact. The same payoff may be achieved by low risks on low-return activities or high risks on high returns—and most organizations would probably favor the former.

SCENARIO. This method combines the input from various forecasting techniques, especially the expert opinion and Delphi methods, to give an integrated view. Regrettably, it is rarely used because it requires some significant effort. The fleshing out of the bare-bones forecasts and their integration into a whole scenario means, on the one hand, that it is easier to detect incompatibilities between the various forecasts. On the other hand, it allows extrapolations of these individual forecasts to cover all the activities of the organization.

The identification of crucial trend variables and the degree of their variation is of major importance in scenario building. Frequently, key experts are used to gain information about potential variations and the viability of certain scenarios. Manager's Corner 6.2 provides an example of input from such experts.

A wide variety of scenarios must be built to expose corporate executives to multiple potential occurrences. Ideally, even far-fetched factors deserve some consideration to build scenarios ranging from the best to the worst. A scenario for Union Carbide Corporation, for example, could have included the possibility of a

www.unioncarbide.com

Manager's Corner 6.2

Advice from Kissinger Associates

Kissinger Associates is a New York-based consulting firm established in 1982 by former Secretary of State Henry Kissinger, former Undersecretary of State Lawrence S. Eagleburger, and former National Security Advisor Brent Scowcroft. For its corporate clients, the firm offers broadbrush pictures of political and economic conditions in particular countries or regions along with analyses of political and economic trends. Because none of the founders is particularly known for his business or economic expertise, an investment banker and an economist were brought on board.

Some have argued that the pointing out of political trends is an insufficient base from which to make a living. Kissinger himself stated that to provide only abstract information on the political condition in a foreign country is not fair to the client. The firm considers its primary strength to be its sensitivity to the international political situation and its continued closeness to information sources. Although Kissinger Associates offers no voluminous country reports, the principals believe that by correctly assessing, for example, the political outlook in Greece for the next five years, they can help a client decide whether

to make new investments there or preparations to leave in anticipation of a hostile socialist government. Similarly, the firm might help a U.S. Oil company with limited Middle East experience in its first attempts to negotiate and work with a government in that region. Although this type of work does not deeply involve Kissinger Associates in specific business decisions, it does require a good understanding of clients' businesses and goals.

One practical reason for using high-powered consulting input was explained by a former member of Kissinger Associates: "These days, in case an investment goes sour, it is useful for [management] to be able to say, 'We got this expert advice and acted on that basis.' They have to show due diligence in exercising their fiduciary duties."

Even though client identities and fees are well-guarded secrets, congressional confirmation hearings for former employees of Kissinger Associates revealed that clients such as Union Carbide, Coca-Cola (www.coke.com), Volvo (www.volvocars.com), Fiat (www.fiat.com), and Daewoo (www.daewoo.com) pay between $150,000 and $400,000 per year for the firm's services.

Source: Christopher Madison, "Kissinger Firm Hopes to Make Its Mark as Risk Advisors to Corporate Chiefs," *National Journal*, June 22, 1985, 1452–1456. Reprinted by permission of National Journal, Inc.

Exhibit 6.2

In scenario building some factors remain unpredictable. For this reason, extrapolating from currently existing conditions is insufficient, for unexpected events can have significant impact on the environment in which the scenario was created. The devastating effects of recent natural disasters and exceptional seasonal weather trends like El Niño and La Niña were felt by insurance companies. Although contingency plans could account for some of the damage, the repeated devastation was neither expected nor planned for.

disaster such as occurred in Bhopal, India. Similarly, oil companies need to work with scenarios that factor in dramatic shifts in the supply situation, such as those precipitated by regional conflict in the Middle East. They should consider major alterations in the demand picture, due to, say, technological developments or government policies.

Scenario builders also need to recognize the unpredictability of some factors. To simply extrapolate from currently existing situations is insufficient. Frequently, unexpected factors may enter the picture with significant impact. For example, despite some prediction about the climatic effects of El Niño and El Niña, insurance companies never expected the level of devastations wrought by hurricanes and tornadoes in the United States due to the cyclical warming and cooling of the tropical water in the Pacific (see Exhibit 6.2). Finally, given large technological advances, the possibility of "wholesale" obsolescence of current technology must also be considered. For example, quantum leaps in computer development and Internet technology may render obsolete the technological investment of a corporation or even a country.

For scenarios to be useful, management must analyze and respond to them

> The difficulty is to devise scenarios that are unusual enough
> **to trigger new thinking yet sufficiently realistic**
> to be taken seriously by management.

by formulating contingency plans. Such planning will broaden horizons and may prepare management for unexpected situations. Familiarization in turn can result in shorter response times to actual occurrences by honing response capability. The difficulty, of course, is to devise scenarios that are unusual enough to trigger new thinking yet sufficiently realistic to be taken seriously by management.

The development of a marketing decision support system is of major importance to many firms. It aids the ongoing decision process and becomes a vital corporate tool in carrying out the strategic planning task. Only by observing global trends and changes will the firm be able to maintain and increase its competitive position. Many of the data available are quantitative in nature, but attention must also be paid to qualitative dimensions. Quantitative analysis will continue to improve as the ability to collect, store, analyze, and retrieve data increases through the use of high-speed computers. Nevertheless, qualitative analysis will remain a major component of corporate research and strategic planning.

QUANTITATIVE METHODS

In general, most quantitative techniques revolve around time-series analysis of historical statistics. They treat the systems involved as a *black box*. As such, they can only be as reliable as those statistics at best, and hence are best applied to in-house statistics, such as sales figures, where the accuracy (and likely limitation) is better understood.

On the other hand, **explanatory models** try to set out how these systems work so that the effect of future changes can also be predicted. They are consequently more powerful, but significantly more difficult to build.

Sales trend forecasting is the scientific approach favored by most management, because it is seen to project forward the historical trends that they have already observed. Thus, if sales have increased by 15 percent for each of the previous three years, the assumption is that they will also increase by around 15 percent in the coming year. We have already seen, though, how the fishbone effect may sometimes invalidate these confident assumptions. Also, as the base broadens, growth rates will be more difficult to maintain.

The simplest and most common form of forecasting is handled manually or by using the now omnipresent electronic pocket calculator or personal computer. The processes are still simple mechanized analogues of the manual processes. These forecasts project the trends shown by recent historical sales figures. Again, this is best viewed as a variation of pure judgment.

Although these simple manual techniques have great strengths, they are limited by the subjectivity of their conclusions. The more sophisticated techniques (explained below) have almost as many assumptions built into them but, because these value judgments are not immediately obvious, they tend to be seen (incorrectly) as having inherently greater accuracy. Whether you use manual or more sophisticated techniques, you should be always aware of their limitations and assumptions before making any decision based on your forecast.

MATHEMATICAL TECHNIQUES.   There are a number of mathematical techniques (some of great complexity) that apparently provide a strong scientific basis. However, in essence, most of them allow for just four components in any such forecast:

- **Trend.** The ongoing growth (or decline) of the product or service is determined by fitting a straight or, occasionally, a curved line to the historical sales data (Figure 6.6).

- **Cyclical.** Any wavelike movement over the years reflects, for example, general business trends (Figure 6.7). The problem in this cyclical case is identifying which (if any) is the true cycle and not just an artifact. It is more difficult still to determine whether the cycle will be repeated again in the future. The decades-long Kondratieff Cycles, which are often discussed in economic

Figure 6.6

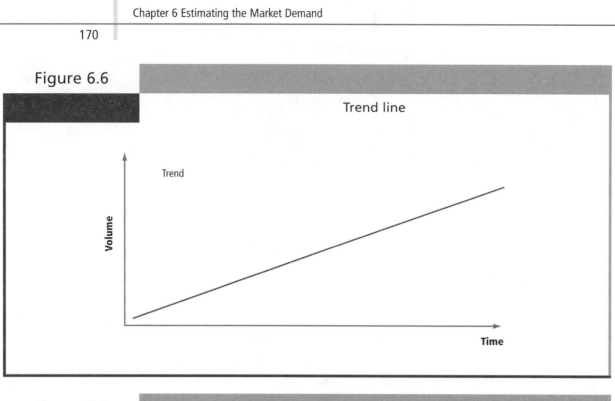

Trend line

Figure 6.7

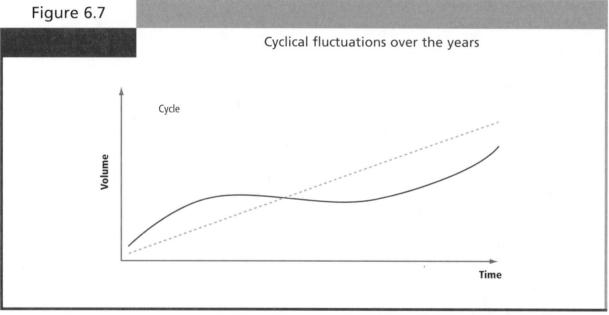

Cyclical fluctuations over the years

theory, are more difficult to observe (if they are present at all) and are consequently more controversial. However, Yoshihiro Kogane[6] offers one succinct analysis of these cycles over the past two centuries (Table 6.2).

- **Seasonal.** Many products or services are seasonal with some distinctive fluctuations, usually over a period of a year, that remain rather consistent over time, and this pattern is overlaid on the others (Figure 6.8).

- **Random events.** Most sales graphs show unpredictable effects, such as industry disputes, although some (such as planned promotional campaigns) may be predictable to a certain extent.

6. Yoshihiro Kogane, "Long Waves of Economic Growth: Past and Future," *Futures* (October 1988).

Table 6.2

Long waves and technological revolutions

Era	Actor(s)	Technological revolutions	Historical landmarks
1770s–1820s	UK	Factories (mines, farms) with machines driven by energy extracted from mineral fuels in place of "natural" energy of man, animal, wind, water	Industrial revolution U.S. independence French Revolution *Wealth of Nations* (1776)
1820s–1870s	Europe, USA	Railway network as transportation infrastructure integrating production units, markets, and residences of workers	American Civil War Formation of German empire Meiji Restoration *Das Kapital* (1867)
1870s–1920s	Europe, USA, Japan	Electric power network as energy infrastructure	Germany and the USA catch up with the UK First World War Russian Revolution
1920s–1970s	Europe, USA, Japan, NICs	Automated (with conveyor belts) factories in place of factories that are simply containers of machines	Second World War Japan catches up with Europe Independence of ex-colonies Oil crises
1970s–2020s?	Europe, USA, Japan, NICs, some LDCs	Information-communication network as information infrastructure integrating producers and users of information and services	Communications satellites Financial revolution

Source: Yoshihiro Kogane, "Long Waves of Economic Growth: Past and Future," *Futures* (October 1988): 532–548. © 1988. Reprinted with kind permission of Elsevier Science.

Figure 6.8

Seasonal fluctuations: consistent from year to year

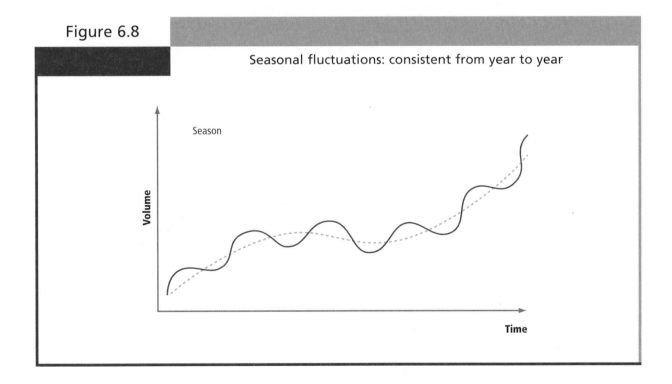

PERIOD ACTUALS AND PERCENTAGE CHANGES. The forecast may simply and, most frequently, continue the trends observed in previous periods. This may be achieved either by calculating the average percentage increase or by drawing the best-possible straight line through the historical figures when plotted on a graph. There are three related methods of this forecast, using period actuals and percentage changes.

- **Moving annual total.** This technique smoothes out short-term fluctuations (especially seasonality) by moving forward the accumulated total for the preceding 12 months. Thus, each new month's figures are added to the previous (MAT) total, and the comparable figures from a year ago are deducted. The forecast is once more obtained by extending the trend line; this time *smoothed* by the incorporation of the whole year's data.

- **Cumulative totals.** This measure is normally used in the context of control (measuring how cumulative sales are performing against target, for example) rather than as a forecasting tool.

- **Z charts.** As shown in Figure 6.9, all of these data (for one year) can be neatly combined on one graph, a Z chart. The bottom bar of the Z is made up of the monthly actuals, whereas the top bar is the moving annual total. The diagonal eventually joining them is the cumulative figure (equal to the first month actual at the left and the moving annual total at the end of the year at the right).

Figure 6.9

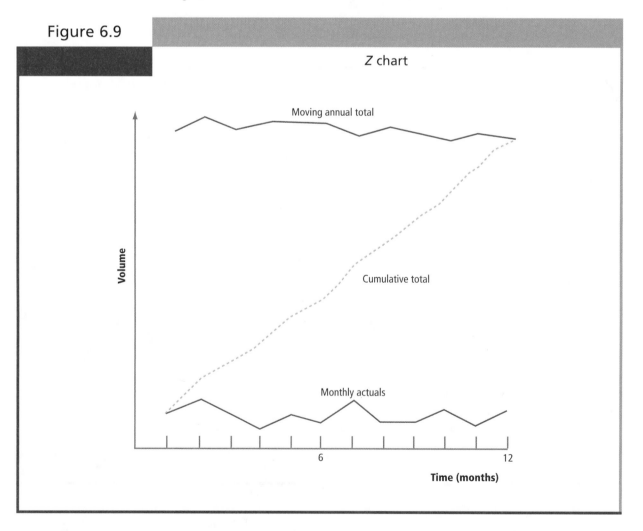

EXPONENTIAL SMOOTHING. This is a simple but useful mathematical technique that allows greater weight to be given to recent periods. For example, instead of the average trend over the whole of the last year being calculated, the sales data for each of the months is given a weighting, depending on how recent that month was.

In a manner somewhat akin to the moving annual total, it takes the previous figure, in this case the moving forecast, and adds on the latest *actual* sales figure. However, it does this in a *fixed* proportion that is chosen to reflect the weighting to be given to the latest period. The general formula is:

$$F_{t+1} = F_t + aE_t$$

where F_{t+1} is the new forecast, F_t is the previous one, and E_t is the deviation (or *error*) of the actual new performance recorded against the previous period forecast; a is the weighting to be given to the most recent events. In this simple form, exponential smoothing will not allow for seasonality, although more advanced (but less easily understood) versions can do this. These more advanced versions are discussed next.

ADVANCED TIME-SERIES ANALYSES AND MODELS. In general, to account for the variations due to seasonal trends as well as for those due to long-term trends, more sophisticated calculations, such as mathematical modeling, are needed. **Models** are merely more complex equations.

General time-series models can be built by arithmetically removing a steady overall trend (the straight line showing the long-term average increase) and by measuring deviations from it to give the underlying, average, seasonal pattern. Models can also be built by visual inspection (as the Z chart was).

Auto-Regressive Moving Average (ARMA) techniques are the most sophisticated of the simple time-series methods. They filter out the various effects of cycle and seasonality to detect the underlying growth. The most commonly reported method is **Box-Jenkins** (Figure 6.10). Although widely reported in the literature, these advanced techniques are relatively little used in practice.

MULTIPLE REGRESSION ANALYSIS. At the more advanced level, computers are extensively used to conduct **regression analyses** on the elements of the model. Regressional analysis determines the strengths of the relationship of one variable with other variables involved.

In simple regression, a linear, *straight line* relationship of the form

$$y = a + bx$$

is assumed, where a and b are the constants (to be found). Regression analysis is designed to explain or to predict a criterion variable (y), based on a predictor variable (x). This does not even require the use of a computer, but such simple relationships are rare.

Usually a number of predictor variables are involved for prediction, so that *multiple* regression analyses become necessary. Then computer programs are used to determine statistically from the historical data and the changes in the various variables what the likelihood is of each of the predictor variables having an impact on the criterion variable. The parameters of the model and the overall probabilities of each outcome can then be determined. For example, in order to predict annual automobile sales for first-time buyers in the United States, various factors can be considered in the regression model, as follows:

Annual automobile sales = a + b$_1$x (number of college graduates)
+ b$_2$x (interest rate) + b$_3$x (unemployment rate) + . . .

Figure 6.10

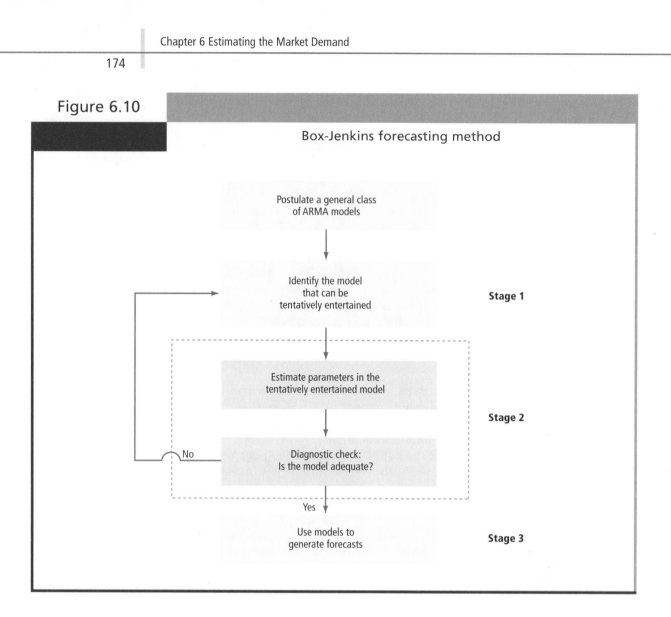

ECONOMETRIC MODELS.   Very large econometric models, which simulate the workings of national economies, can contain hundreds of factors spread across dozens of linked equations and can require large amounts of computing power. Unfortunately, as a result, they are barely understandable even to those running them. A relatively simple econometric model is illustrated in Figure 6.11. This econometric model shows how the various factors in boxes will affect, and be affected by, other factors. Arrows represent causal effects. However, these models are often seen as almost infallible largely due to their immense complexity. This is despite, or possibly because of, the general ignorance of many of those involved. Changes in government policy, for instance, are often run against the models of the national economy to see what *will* happen rather than what *might* happen.

www.compaq.com

Econometric-type models are also being used to help manage the new-product introduction strategy. As illustrated in Manager's Corner 6.3, Compaq employed a complex simulation software to plan the timing of the switch from 486-based to Pentium-based computers. The program was designed to model the latest trends in consumer demand, pricing, and dealer inventories. Based on the model, Compaq decided to wait several months after their competitors to introduced its own Pentium machines. The decision preserved the value of Compaq's 486 inventory and led to a 61 percent increase in fourth-quarter 1994 earnings, boosting profits by $50 million. However, as initially developed by Dell Computer, the "build-to-order" model of product development and sales fulfillment has started replacing the "build-to-forecast" model, and the traditional role of sales forecasting has begun waning into the 21st century.

www.dell.com

Figure 6.11

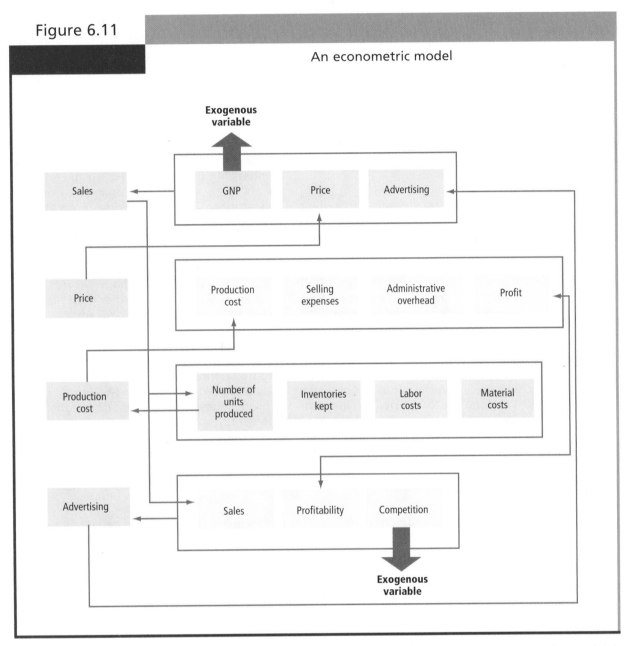

An econometric model

Source: Spyros Makridakis and Steven C. Wheelwright, *Forecasting Methods for Management,* 5th ed. (New York: John Wiley & Sons, 1989), 212. © 1989 by John Wiley & Sons, Inc. Reprinted by permission of John Wiley & Sons, Inc.

Manager's Corner 6.3

Forecasting methods are rapidly changing!

The personal computer business is characterized by the neck-breaking speed of new product development. As soon as a new technology emerges, it is immediately adopted in new products. You cannot miss the boat in this business. A PC model that comes out late, lacks the right features, or has the wrong price not only spells a foregone opportunity but also turns into piles of unusable components. IBM (www.ibm.com), for example, mis-

judged the market and suffered a 6 percent plunge in PC sales and a $1 billion loss in 1994. Compaq (www.compaq.com) also passed up $50 million in sales by underpredicting demand for PCs in the same year.

Can we ever forecast a future in an industry in which constant change is the only constant feature? In order to not repeat the same mistake, Compaq employed a complex simulation software it developed to plan the switch from 486-based to Pentium-based (www .pentium.com) computers. It took eight months of intense effort to develop the computer model. The program was designed to model, among other things, the latest trends in component price changes, fluctuating demand for a given feature or price, and the impact of rival models. By modeling supplier and competitor behavior, the program lets managers consider the risk of certain actions before taking them.

Based on the model results, Compaq elected to wait several months after their competitors to introduce their own Pentium machines—contrary to the PC industry norm. Competitors and pundits were loudly criticizing Compaq for its slow switch to PCs using Intel's Pentium chip. While rivals including Dell Computer (www.dell.com) and Gateway 2000 (www.gateway.com) immediately jumped into Pentiums, Compaq amassed a huge inventory of 486-based PCs, because the simulation model suggested that corporate buyers would not turn to Pentiums until early 1995. Indeed, the decision preserved the value of Compaq's 486 inventory and led to a 61 percent increase in fourth-quarter earnings. Not too long ago, PC vendors followed a simpler, more traditional marketing model: first forecast demand and then push finished goods into markets via multitiered channels with many players. Although that model continually suffered from inaccurate forecasts, business survival was possible just by churning out the hottest new technologies every 18 months or so. That was 1994.

Since then, Michael Dell has successfully introduced a new way for PC companies to compete—not by technology alone, but by emphasizing the needs of the customers with an ability to satisfy and serve them quickly and efficiently. Dell put pressure on the industry's traditional players with a simple concept: Sell personal computers directly on the Internet to customers with no complicated channels. By 1999, major PC companies are compressing the supply chain via such concepts as "build to order" rather than "build to forecast." Compaq's ability to accommodate those customers is at least as significant as their new products.

In a high-tech environment, the role of traditional forecasting methods is being gradually displaced by the "build-to-order" model of product development that does not require forecasting but instead constant monitoring of the market and quick response.

Sources: "At Compaq, a Desktop Crystal Ball: But Will Its Forecasting Software Really Make a Cutthroat Business Less Risky?" *Business Week*, March 20, 1995, 96–97; John Teresko, "The New PC Game," *Industry Week*, May 18, 1998, 50–53.

LEADING INDICATORS.   It may be possible to establish that certain factors are **leading indicators** in that they provide *advance* warning of future trends. For example, it may be that suppliers of pop CDs should study the birthrate statistics to see how their total teenage market may vary in future years.

In the United States, there are a range of useful published statistics that are widely used as indicators: *U.S. Durable Goods Orders*, movements of which may indicate the general economy some six months ahead; *Housing Starts*, perhaps 10 to 12 months ahead; and *Interest Rates on Three-Month Certificates of Deposit*, which is supposed to give an indication for 18 months ahead. One of the most useful—and most obvious in its workings—is the leading indicator offered by the Conference Board's *Consumer Confidence Index*. Other useful leading indicators include *Stock Prices, Corporate Bond Yield, Industrial Materials Prices, Business Failures, Money Supply, Unemployment Rate, Producer Price Index, Consumer Price Index,* and *Business Inventories*. Marketing in Action 6.2 discusses particular indicators used by DaimlerChrysler.

www.conference-board .org

In forecasting the market conditions of foreign countries, marketers can use a country's leading indicators similar to the ones available in the United States and also the country's trade balance and exchange rates as international leading indicators. A country's continued trade deficit usually indicates either that its government will tighten its fiscal and monetary policy, thereby reducing domestic consumption, or that its currency will depreciate, thereby making imported products more expensive. Either way, a country's trade deficit will portend its reduced purchasing power. To predict a foreign country's purchasing power, marketers may simply look at 180-day forward exchange rates in the Foreign Exchange Rate section of the *Wall Street Journal*. If forward exchange rates seem to be depreciating fast, then it generally indicates a pending reduction in purchasing power as explained above.

www.wsj.com

Marketing in Action 6.2

DaimlerChrysler's eight stoplight indicators of a downturn

With corporate headquarters in both Stuttgart, Germany, and Auburn Hills, Michigan (USA), DaimlerChrysler (www.daimlerchrysler.com) is a company with many internationally recognized brands. These brands include Mercedes-Benz, Chrysler, Plymouth, Jeep, Dodge, Freightliner, Airbus, Sterling, Eurocopter, and Ariane. With manufacturing facilities in 34 countries, a workforce of almost 450,000, and sales in over 200 countries, DaimlerChrysler sold 4.5 million passenger cars and commercial vehicles in 1998.

Like other automobile companies, Daimler-Chrysler invests considerable time, energy, and dollars in economic forecasting. Currently, the company can predict economic downturns 14 months into the future. Eight economic indicators are watched closely. These indicators, which are divided into two main categories, include:

Consumer's ability to buy:
1. Disposable household income
2. Household debt levels
3. Interest rate yield on government bonds
4. Inflation rate

Consumer's willingness to buy:
5. Consumer confidence
6. New unemployment claims

7. Changes in manufacturing workweek
8. Stock market

DaimlerChrysler's analysts closely watch each of these indicators and assign a red, yellow, or green status to upward or downward changes. A composite category indicator is then developed by determining the color that is in the majority in each of the two categories. For example, a red composite indicator means that a recession is six to nine months away, yellow implies that economic conditions could easily go either way, and a green composite indicator implies that no recession is predicted for the near future.

How could these stoplight indicators influence decisions in the company's various functional areas (e.g., marketing, production, personnel, and so on)? Where do you think DaimlerChrysler obtains the information on each of these eight indicators? Given the global scope of DaimlerChrysler's operations, would it be feasible to use a single set of globally amalgamated indicators, or should the company generate forecasts for each national market based on the indicators in that particular country? What other types of forecasts could be important to automobile manufacturers?

Sources: www.daimlerchrysler.com; "Where Is Consumer Demand Going?" *Profit, 1999 CB Media Limited* (June 1999), 17.

GAME THEORY. Defined as "the study of rational behavior in situations involving interdependence," game theory has recently received enhanced notoriety on two fronts. First, in 1994 three game theorists received the Nobel Prize in economics, and second, game theory was used extensively by the U.S. Federal Communications Commission to assist in auctioning off the wavelengths necessary to support pagers and pocket telephones.

www.fcc.gov

Before game theory, most economic models assumed that firms were basically acting in a vacuum. The actions of one firm were not assumed to impact the actions of other firms. That economic assumption is true as long as markets are *perfectly* competitive or where pure monopolies exist. Game theory allows for corporate action, competitor reaction, corporate action, and on and on. Unfortunately, game theory is difficult to use because of its complex mathematics. However, it is now being taught at many leading MBA programs, which means that it will be increasingly used in coming years.[7]

SPREADSHEETS

In the context of forecasting and planning, probably the most useful tool that personal computers provide is the now ubiquitous spreadsheet. Despite its apparent

7. Rajiv Lal and Ram Rao, "Supermarket Competition: The Case of Every Day Low Pricing," *Marketing Science* 16, no. 1 (1997): 60–80.

simplicity, even this tool is often misused by managers, who see it merely as a more sophisticated calculator. In the present context, however, it has a number of powerful contributions to make.

One important use of spreadsheets is the mechanization of routine budgets. The whole planning cycle is bedeviled by the grind of cranking out large numbers of routine figures. Many, if not most, of these are derived from other figures and ultimately lead back to a relatively few indirect variables entered into the model. Once these linkages are entered onto a spreadsheet, the planning cycle becomes much easier. However, there are dangers even in this seemingly straightforward approach, not least of which is that spreadsheets lock into the model all the existing assumptions about the relationships. There are two solutions to this dilemma:

- **Clear structure.** The spreadsheet should be designed in such a way that the linkages (and hence the assumptions) are obvious and are easy to change.

- **Process of challenge.** Some of the time saved by using the spreadsheet should be used routinely to challenge the assumptions to ensure that they are still valid.

Perhaps the most important use of spreadsheets is to question these assumptions. The ease with which calculations can be repeated with different assumptions means that the marketing manager can try out *all* of the different alternatives. This iterative process is called **sensitivity analysis**, and can then be used to fine-tune, or optimize, the key parameters. Although widely used spreadsheets, such as Microsoft Excel and Lotus 1-2-3, remain useful, spreadsheet add-ons, such as Palisade Corporation's @Risk, could provide more powerful analytical tools for decision making.

www.microsoft.com
www.lotus.com
www.palisade.com

MODELING. As indicated above, spreadsheets can be used to build crude models. For example, a model of the seasonal, trend, and cyclic components of sales figures (as well as the impact of promotions) can be created from eyeballing the graphs of historical sales and fine-tuning the resulting model parameters until the results obtained most closely fit the historical results. This process may be time consuming and lacking the elegance of the advanced techniques, but it may also produce results that are almost as good (and more easily understood).

ALTERNATIVES TO FORECASTING

There are a number of alternatives to forecasting that can also help reduce risk—including that due to poor forecasting—if not the need for some form of formal planning.[8]

- **Insurance.** Future movements in exchange rates, for instance, may be covered by *hedges* on the financial futures market.

- **Portfolios.** Risk can be spread by entering a number of different markets or introducing a number of different products that are unlikely to face the same economic downturns or competition.

- **Flexibility.** The Japanese in particular have developed means for coping rapidly with unexpected changes.

---

8. Robert Fildes, "Forecasting: The Issues," in *The Handbook of Forecasting*, 2d ed., ed. S. Makridakis and S. C. Wheelwright (New York: John Wiley & Sons, 1987).

FLEXIBILITY. Of the alternatives listed above, flexibility is emerging as the most important. This is most evident in the development, mainly by Japanese corporations, of flexible manufacturing and dramatically reduced development lead times for high-tech goods. But similarly accelerated time scales can be even more easily applied where technological development is less demanding and the promotional activities need to be changed rapidly.

This approach, although not superseding others, simply requires that once change has been detected (probably by some form of environmental analysis, as described in Chapter 3) the reaction time should be so fast that the response may be implemented before the change reaches a significant level. More importantly, the response time should be faster than that of competitors who might otherwise be able to take advantage of the change. However, such an approach requires a very sophisticated early detection method for environmental change.

FACTORS LIMITING FORECASTS

Spyros Makridakis[9] sums up the most likely errors and biases in forecasting in Tables 6.3 and 6.4. The most frequent mistake in practice is sometimes called the **hockey stick effect**. When actual results fail to live up to optimistic forecasts, the starting point of the new forecast is changed to allow for this, but the slope of the forecast line remains (still optimistically) unchanged. Nobody in the forecasting process asks why the forecast was missed—and nobody learns from experience.

Perhaps the greatest practical limitation on forecasting, however, is its incorrect use due to a lack of knowledge by managers. A survey by McHugh and Sparkes[10] came to the now classic conclusion that

> the greatest practical limitation on forecasting is its incorrect use due to a lack of knowledge by managers

> . . . despite the need and the fact that the results of past forecasting performance reveal a high level of inaccuracy it seems that not only do naive techniques dominate (representing 90% of techniques currently utilized) but also very few respondents are taking steps to improve the situation. . . . The main problem seemed to be that there was a total lack of specific techniques, particularly the Delphi method, cross-impact analysis and Box-Jenkins and in the case of causal model-building, regression and correlation analysis, the problem seems to be a lack of working experience of the particular techniques.

In fact, users prefer simple, intuitive, easy-to-use, easy-to-comprehend methods. It is these factors, rather than accuracy, that are ultimately desired, which determine when and how forecasting is used. The practical effect of all these limitations often results in a forecasting phenomenon, usually relating to long-range forecasting, known as the cliff. In essence, management uses forecasting for a period of time (albeit often without fully understanding why and how it should be carried out) until the point at which problems arise. All formal forecasting is then summarily stopped, as if dropped off a cliff.

---

9. Spyros Makridakis, "Metaforecasting: Ways of Improving Forecasting Accuracy and Usefulness," *International Journal of Forecasting* 4 (1988): 467–491.
10. A. K. McHugh and J. R. Sparkes, "The Forecasting Dilemma," *Management Accounting* (March 1983): 30–34.

Table 6.3

Forecasting errors and types of future uncertainty

Causes of forecasting errors		Types of future uncertainty			
		Expected		Unexpected	Inconceivable
		Normal	Unusual		
Random fluctuations		95% of the errors around the average pattern or relationship	The remaining 5% of errors; that is, large errors that would occur, on average, about one time out of 20	A not-too-serious car accident	
Changes in patterns/relationships	Temporary	Special events (such as a colder than average winter) and special actions (such as a promotional campaign, a new product introduced by a competitor)	An "average" recession not too different from previous ones A fire	A serious recession of the 1974–1975 type The energy crisis (for planning and strategies considered at the end of the 1970s)	The 1973–1979 energy crisis (for planning and strategies being considered in the 1960s)
	Permanent	Gradual changes in consumer attitudes and buying trends caused by technological innovation and concerns about health and quality of life	Big changes in attitudes and buying trends caused by new technologies or governmental intervention (such as the deregulation of the airline industry at the end of the 1970s)	A collapse of the international financial system The Industrial Revolution (for people living at the beginning of the 18th century)	A large meteorite hits and destroys life on Earth A major nuclear accident or war destroying life on Earth (to someone living before 1930)

Source: Spyros Makridakis, "Metaforecasting: Ways of Improving Forecasting Accuracy and Usefulness," *International Journal of Forecasting* 4, no. 3 (1988): 474. Reprinted with kind permission of Elsevier Science.

Table 6.4

Common biases in judgmental forecasting and proposed ways of reducing their negative impact

Type of bias	Description of bias	Ways of reducing the negative impact of bias
Optimism, wishful thinking	People's preferences for future outcomes affect their forecast of such outcomes	Have the forecasts made by a third, uninterested party Have more than one person make the forecasts independently
Inconsistency	Inability to apply the same decision criteria in similar situations	Formalize the decision-making process Create decision-making rules to be followed
Recency	The importance of the most recent events dominates those in the less recent past, which are downgraded or ignored	Realize that cycles exist and that not all ups or downs are permanent Consider the fundamental factors that affect the event of interest
Availability	Ease with which specific events can be recalled from memory	Present complete information Present information in a way that points out all sides of the situation to be considered
Anchoring	Predictions are unduly influenced by initial information, which is given more weight when forecasting	Start with objective forecasts Ask people to forecast in terms of changes from statistical forecasts and demand the reasons for doing so
Illusory correlations	Belief that patterns exist and/or two variables are causally related when this is not true	Verify statistical significance of patterns Model relationships, if possible, in terms of changes
Conservatism	Failure to change (or changing slowly) one's own mind in light of new information/evidence	Monitor systematic changes and build procedures to take action when systematic changes are identified
Selective perception	Tendency to see problems in terms of one's own background and experience	Ask people with different backgrounds and experience to prepare the forecasts independently
Regression effects	Persistent increases or decreases might be due to random reasons that, if true, would increase the chance of a change in trend	Explain that in the case of random errors the chances of a negative error increase when several positive ones have occurred

Source: Spyros Makridakis, "Metaforecasting: Ways of Improving Forecasting Accuracy and Usefulness," *International Journal of Forecasting* 4, no. 3 (1988): 476. Reprinted with kind permission of Elsevier Science.

SUMMARY

Forecasts predict what may happen, all other things being equal. Budgets go beyond this to incorporate the effects of an organization's planned actions. Both may be:

- Short term—for capacity loading, information transmission, and control
- Medium term—for the traditional annual planning process
- Long term—for strategic planning, resource planning, and communication

Forecasts need to be dynamic. In other words, changes in the environment require modification of forecasts. From them, budgets may be derived at the sales, production, and profit levels.

Forecasting is based on, and derived from, some other data sources and is conducted at three different levels. Macroforecasts look at total markets and may be derived from national or global data available from the OECD or the U.S. government. However, the most important aggregate forecast for business is at the market or industry level. Microforecasts build on the predictions of individual or group (customer) behavior. Product forecasts may then be split into forecasts by product type and over time.

There are both qualitative and quantitative forecasting methods. Qualitative forecasting is normally employed for long-term forecasts. Techniques include expert opinion, expert panel method, technological forecasting, Delphi technique, decision tree, and scenario.

Quantitative forecasting techniques for short- and medium-term forecasts typically try to isolate the trend, cyclical, seasonal, and random fluctuations. The specific techniques used may be period actuals and percent changes, exponential smoothing, time-series analyses, multiple regression analysis, and more complex econometric modeling. Various leading indicators are also readily available from government sources to forecast the short- to medium-term conditions of the market. Whereas most forecasting techniques ignore the competitors' possible reaction to one company's competitive move, game theory has gained popularity in recent years to address the likely impact of a competitor's move in forecasting.

With the widespread use of personal computers, spreadsheets have become a very useful forecasting tool to model many hypothetical "what-if" scenarios. By developing many scenarios, you can determine which factors are sensitive to changes in the conditions under investigation.

The primary role of forecasting is risk reduction. It should be noted that risk can also be reduced by purchasing insurance against unfavorable events, diversifying into a portfolio of different products and markets, or adopting flexible manufacturing to better cope with unexpected changes in the market. Finally, thanks to Internet use, many companies are emphasizing the needs of the customers through an ability to satisfy and serve them quickly and efficiently by adopting the "build-to-order" model of sales fulfillment with no forecasting error rather than the traditional "build-to-forecast" model.

> # The primary role of forecasting is risk reduction.

QUESTIONS FOR REVIEW

1. What are short-term forecasts used for? What are long-term forecasts needed for?

2. What are the differences between forecasts and budgets? What further budgets may be derived? How may product forecasts be derived from macroforecasts?

3. How may microforecasts be produced? What is the Markov brand-switching model? What may need to be derived from product forecasts?

4. What main qualitative forecasting techniques are available? What elements of judgment do they contain? How does technological forecasting work?

5. Describe the Delphi technique. What other techniques employ similar approaches? How are three structures used?

6. Describe the use of scenarios.

7. What are the four elements that mathematical techniques try to isolate? What techniques are available for this purpose?

8. What are the differences between exponential smoothing and multiple regression analysis?

Questions for Discussion

1. Market intelligence agency Mintel's report, "2010: Marketing to Tomorrow's Consumer," portrays a nation of diverse consumers living increasingly isolated lives and becoming more self-reliant and individualistic. The report blames this on evolving technological trends. Free time will be far more focused on in-home activities. Although this may seem a gloomy prediction of life for consumers in 2010, it is great news for the manufacturers of home-based items, especially leisure-based brown goods. But there will also be losers in this homocentric future. Thus the buzz word for the new era seems to be micromarketing. This means tailoring marketing programs to specific demographics, specific channels, and perhaps even specific stores reducing the effectiveness of mass-market TV advertising and an increase in the effectiveness of targeted niche marketing, such as direct mail, sponsorship, and the Internet. This all points to life being much harder for marketing directors in the year 2010.

   Do you agree with this long-term forecast of the future market? If yes, who will be winners and losers? If no, give your own long-term forecast of the future based on current changes in technology.

2. One marketing authority had forecast there could be 3.8 billion smart cards in use by the year 2000. An all-in-one smart card can serve as a frequent-buyer record, charge card, phone card, stored-value card, ticketless card, or parking card. The Takashimaya Visa Card (TVC) is one such smart card with both a chip and a magnetic stripe that stores customer behavior information. In an interview with *Transactions* magazine, Takashimaya systems manager Leng Chen says: "We know how many shoppers use the card, how often and for what kinds of purchases. We now know the ages and buying habits of shoppers in each of our nine departments."

   Do you think that the accuracy of market forecasting will drastically improve with the prevalence of innovations such as smart cards? Why or why not? Is it ethically acceptable to obtain such market information about particular consumers' behavior?

3. A forecast by a marketing research firm stated that by the year 2000, soft drinks will hit the streets in a big way, with cans and one-shots dispensed from pavement vending machines. Soft drinks will become progressively cheaper in real terms. Carbonates, which account for more than half of all purchases, will do even better with the increasing dominance of age groups that have grown up with them and demand more sophisticated tastes and product positioning. A key driver of the dynamism of carbonates, though, will be the so-called "New Age" drinks revolutionizing the U.S. market, offering benefits beyond mere refreshment. Colas will still look unstoppable and flavor innovations will add value.

   Examine the actual current data from the soft-drink market to check the accuracy of the above forecast. Did you find any major deviation from the forecast? What do you think were the assumptions behind such a forecast?

4. Climate in 100 years' time will be one of greater extremes: summers will be as hot and dry as 1997 every other year, winters will have three times more days with an inch of rain. There will be higher tides, more coastal erosion, and more flooding. Sea levels will probably rise by 4 cm a decade, increasing the risk of flooding, and a

rise in temperature of 3°C can have an enormous effect considering that at the last Ice Age, the temperature fell by only 5°C. The predictions by scientists who no longer believe that past weather patterns are an adequate guide to the future pinpoint that these changes will happen as a result of the rising burden of greenhouse gases in the atmosphere.

By this weather forecast, the number of unusually hot days with temperatures above 77°F is expected to cause a huge surge in demand for air conditioning in offices. How will the energy industry forecast its market demand amidst such desperate demand as well as growing public resentment for being an alleged source of the greenhouse effect?

5. Seasonal or holiday sales forecasts do not often match actual sales figures. For example, the 1998 final tally showed that Christmas '98 sales were robust, slightly beating the forecast for a 5 percent increase in holiday sales that some analysts considered a long shot. Also within the same industry, different firms experience varying sales performance. For example, 1998 Christmas sales for Wal-Mart and Gap were above the forecast, while midline retailers such as Sears Roebuck and JCPenney continued to lose market share to discounters and high-end retailers.

As a marketing executive of Sears how would you forecast your 1999 Christmas sales? What factors will you base it on? How should Wal-Mart plan for its inventory for next year?

6. Long-term forecasts with their opportunities and threats are incorporated into a company's annual budget, depending significantly on its risk-taking capability. In turn, risk taking depends on the financial perspective of firms. Some firms emphasize short-term accounting profits; others treat profit as a byproduct of strategy and not the first order of business. Profit is an accounting abstraction, a snapshot of revenue over expenses at an artificial point in time. That's critical information for old-fashioned firms, some critics argue. Recently, as shares prices surge for money-losing Internet companies, the public awakens to the fundamental truth that short-term profits mean nothing in the quest for long-term value.

How would this forecasted shift in perspective affect annual budgeting by a firm in a rapidly changing high-tech industry?

FURTHER READINGS

Deighton, John. "Commentary on 'Exploring the Implications of the Internet for Consumer Marketing.'" *Journal of the Academy of Marketing Science* 25 (fall 1997): 347–351.

Diebold, Francis X., and Glenn D. Rudebusch. *Business Cycles: Durations, Dynamics, and Forecasting.* Princeton, N.J.: Princeton University Press, 1999.

Flores, Benito E., and Edna M. White. "A Framework for the Combination of Forecasts." *Journal of the Academy of Marketing Science* 16 (fall 1988): 95–103.

Lal, Rajiv, and Ram Rao. "Supermarket Competition: The Case of Every Day Low Pricing." *Marketing Science* 16, no. 1 (1997): 60–80.

Mahmoud, Essam, Gillian Rice, and Naresh Malhotra. "Emerging Issues in Sales Forecasting and Decision Support System." *Journal of the Academy of Marketing Science* 16 (fall 1988): 47–61.

Makridakis, Spyros G., Steven C. Wheelwright, and Rob J. Hyndman. *Forecasting: Methods and Applications.* 3d ed. New York: John Wiley & Sons, 1998.

McMillan, John. *Games, Strategies and Managers.* New York: Oxford University Press, 1992.

Peterson, Robert A., Sridhar A. Balasubramanian, and Bart J. Bronnenberg. "Exploring the Implications of the Internet for Consumer Marketing." *Journal of the Academy of Marketing Science* 25 (fall 1997): 329–346.

Rentz, Joseph O. "Forecasting the Effects of An Aging Population on Product Consumption: An Age-Period-Cohort Framework." *Journal of Marketing Research* 28 (August 1991): 355–360.

Simmons, LeRoy F., and George Wright. *Business and Economic Forecasting: Decision Support System Software.* New York: John Wiley & Sons, 1990.

Wu, L. S. Y., N. Ravishanker, and J. R. M. Hosking. "Forecasting for Business Planning: A Case Study of IBM Product Sales." *Journal of Forecasting* 10 (November 1991): 579–595.

chapter 7

Market Segmentation, Positioning, and Branding

The interface between the consumer and the supplier is the market. The position the supplier chooses in that market for the product or service—relative to consumer needs—defines all of the marketing actions thereafter. Whether determined analytically or by default, this positioning is at the heart of marketing.

The first stage of market positioning is to segment the market itself by dividing the total market into smaller parts based on the key variables chosen by the firm. The firm can then concentrate the organization's resources on a smaller part of the market to gain control over the competitive position. However, the segment has to be viable, and sophisticated marketing research is needed to optimize the segmentation.

> The first stage of market positioning is **to segment the market itself by dividing** the total market into smaller parts

Positioning, or targeting, then places the product or service in the optimal position relative to the competitors on the features most critical to users. The focus for this activity is often a brand, and alternative branding policies are discussed in this chapter. Branding, combined with positioning, usually offers the most sophisticated and powerful application of marketing principles. Because the market is constantly changing, segmentation and positioning strategies require constant vigil over various forces shaping the market (see Manager's Corner 7.1).

Manager's Corner 7.1

Baby boomers versus Generation Y

Today's teens—the biggest bulge since the baby boomers—may force marketers to toss out their old strategies. A host of product labels that have prospered by predicting and shaping popular tastes since the baby boomers were young no longer excite today's children—known as Generation Y—born between 1979 and 1994. Generation Y is 60 million strong, more than three times the size of Generation X.

Marketers have not been dealt an opportunity like this one since the baby boom hit after the second world war. Yet for many entrenched brands, Generation Y poses formidable risks. Baby boomer brands failed in their attempts to reach Generation X, but with a mere 17 million in its ranks, that miss was tolerable. The baby boomer brands appear to be the thing of the past with Generation Y. This generation is radically different from the baby boom generation. Generation Y is more racially and socioeconomically diverse. One in three of them is not white. One in four lives in a single-parent household. Three in four have working mothers. A large majority of Gen Yers are already proficient at computers and are tapping into the Internet as easily as reading the newspaper. They are casually "chatting" and sharing information over the cyberspace across national boundaries.

There is a fundamental shift in values on the part of Gen Y consumers. Some of the biggest, most successfully marketed brands of the past decade are facing a nod of indifference from

Gen Y consumers. Having grown up in a more media-saturated, brand-conscious, computer-connected world than their parents, they respond to advertisement differently, and they prefer to encounter those ads in different places. The marketers that capture Gen Y's attention do so by bringing their messages to the places Gen Yers congregate, whether it is the Internet, a snowboarding tournament, or cable TV.

Table 7.1 is a list of "cool stuff" of interest to baby boomers and Gen Yers.

Source: "Generation Y," *Business Week*, February 15, 1999, 81–88.

WHAT IS A MARKET?

To a producer or service provider, the most practical feature of a market is *where* the product or service is sold or delivered and the profits generated. On the other hand, it can also be defined in terms of the product or service (where the market describes all the buyers and sellers for that product or service—the automobile market, the money market, and so on), and this is the framework favored by many economists. It can also be defined geographically or demographically. The key for a marketer, however, should be that the market is always defined in terms of the customer. Thus, a **market** consists of all the potential customers sharing particular needs and wants who might be willing to engage in exchange to satisfy their needs or wants. Once the potential customers' needs and wants are backed by their purchasing power, an *actual* market is formed.

> a market consists of all the potential customers sharing **particular needs and wants who might be willing** to engage in exchange to satisfy [them]

The market concept applies equally to services. However, in this context, the term *market* can even represent a powerful concept in the nonprofit sectors. Although the word *market* itself might sound strange coming from the mouths of civil servants, the idea of defining the *set of customers* who are the focus of their activities is a powerful one. It helps to concentrate their attention, externally, on the needs that they are meant to address.

Although nonprofit organizations do not refer to the target population they serve as a market, every nonprofit organization has clients or customers. Some, such as the International Monetary Fund, may have just a few very powerful clients; whereas others, such as a government department, may deal with millions of individuals. Defining exactly who these clients are, in relation to the activities of the organization itself, is just as important an exercise for a nonprofit organization as for a commercial organization. This market, albeit not usually complicated by the same competitive overtones as its commercial equivalents, is ultimately just as powerful a force on a nonprofit organization.

WHO IS THE MARKET?

The market is a group of customers. However, in many practical respects it is still defined in the short term by the suppliers who decide what is to be supplied to whom, and hence where the initial boundaries are to be set. After all, consumers cannot make their wishes known if there is no suitable product being offered. This lack of short-term feedback became a major long-term problem for the planned (command) economies of Eastern Europe, hence one of the reasons for the enthusiasm for *perestroika*.

In the long run, it is the customers—with their purchasing power—who will decide what the market really is. They set the boundaries and by their purchases decide what products or services will remain in the market. Thus, to understand

Table 7.1

Cool stuff

According to Boomers	According to Generation Y
Lexus LS400 What to drive when you have your own parking spot. It says you've arrived without the ostentation of a Beemer.	**Jeep Wrangler** Who cares about gas mileage? It looks great in the high school parking lot.
Major League Baseball Mark McGwire and the New York Yankees have made the game hot again.	**Skateboard Triple Crown** Stars compete for glory instead of multiyear contracts.
Gap Those chinos and jeans still look cool. Really.	**Delia's** Definitely not your mother's dress catalog.
ER A worthy successor to *Marcus Welby, MD*.	*Dawson's Creek* High school drama with sizzle.
Superbowl ads Usually they're more entertaining than the game.	**Lilith Fair sponsorship** Supporting the sound of the new voices.
Harrison Ford Tough and fiftysomething. Plus, his action figure is a hot collectible.	**Leonardo DiCaprio** Dashing, sensitive, and irresistible to 12-year-olds.
Esteé Lauder For the way we ought to look.	**Hard Candy** For the way we really look.
L.L. Bean A favorite for the decades, but does anyone actually go duck-hunting in those boots?	**The North Face** Does anyone actually go mountain climbing in that stuff?
Palm Pilot A Rolodex for your pocket, with a high-tech edge.	**Motorola Flex pagers** Stay in touch anytime, anyplace.
Nick at Nite All our favorite reruns in one convenient place.	**WB Network** Creating new favorites and a new look for prime time television.
Political activism Make yourself heard.	**Volunteerism** Make yourself useful.
The Beatles Rock 'n' roll as the signal artistic achievement of a generation.	**Spice Girls** Rock 'n' roll packaged and marketed to children.
Coke Water + sugar + caffeine. Besides, it's the real thing.	**Mountain Dew** Water + sugar + more caffeine. Besides, it's an extreme thing.
David Letterman Late-night TV, slightly mellowed with age. Still among the Top Ten reasons to stay awake.	**Jenny McCarthy** Think Carol Burnett with a bad attitude.
Nikes From Michael to Tiger, no shortage of sports celebs saying Just Do It.	**Vans** No sports celebs allowed. And they're the coolest shoes on skateboards.

Source: "Generation Y," *Business Week*, February 15, 1999, 82–83. Reprinted by permission.

the market, the company must understand the customer. Our concentration on market research in Chapter 5 provides the cornerstone for effective marketing. Remember that the basis of sound marketing practice is the ability to identify with the customer or client and to adopt the consumer's viewpoint.

> **it is the customers —with their purchasing power— who will decide what the market really is**

CHANNELS

The producer may not sell directly to the end user, but may be forced to sell through distribution channels, which act as intermediaries. This is true of some services as well as of products. For example, Commercial Union and Prudential need their brokers to act as intermediaries.

www.cgugroup.com
www.prudential.com

The *producer* thus has consumers who are unseen as well as customers in the distribution chain who are met face-to-face. As we will see later, these customers have different needs from the consumers. Although they are conventionally seen as part of the same market, major differences must be allowed for.

MARKET BOUNDARIES

In earlier chapters, we have seen that consumers of both products and services can be grouped on the basis of a number of factors. Their position against these factors, which may be different for each market, *maps* the true boundaries of that market. The market is defined by the consumers' view of it and in the language (terminology) that is most meaningful to the consumer.

On the other hand, producers, especially those without marketing expertise, tend to have much more *physical* ideas of where markets lie. They want to be able to *touch* them. The practical definitions of markets revolve around the following factors:

- **Product or service category.** This describes what is bought, as defined in the physical terms of the producer. It is the reverse of the example presented in Chapter 1 that the product category is the 2-mm drill, not the 2-mm hole that the end user wants to make.

- **Geography.** Where the product or service is sold or delivered is another factor that defines markets. For example, the location of a shopping mall is determined largely by the geographical area from which customers can be drawn. Also, consumer tastes can vary from region to region. General Foods found that people living to the west of the Mississippi River tend to like dark roasted coffee more than those to the east of the Mississippi.

- **"Physical" customer groupings.** Producers recognize obvious groupings of customers. In industrial markets, for example, suppliers of medical diagnostics recognize that hospitals have different needs from those of corporate health centers.

- **Intangibles.** Although many marketers treat price as a tangible, it is more widely recognized as an intangible that differentiates commercial markets. Thus a *low-end* market refers to a market segment characterized by relatively inexpensive product lines, whereas a *high-end* market is synonymous with a *luxury* market.

CUSTOMERS, USERS, AND PROSPECTS

Marketing myopia is still highly prevalent. Even committed marketers talk about the market for replacement drills—a much easier concept to handle than that of selling the potential for holes. Even so, you need to recognize that it is ultimately the customer who decides where your market will be. Taking this myopia one stage further, producers or service providers mainly see markets in terms of where they themselves are in these markets. This means that they often look at them specifically in terms of their existing customers and potential customers.

- **Customers.** In commercial markets it might seem an easy task to define who your customers are. They are simply the buyers of your brand. The dividing line is often not quite so clear. How do you classify those who have now switched to another brand? Where do you put very loyal users who have most recently bought another brand just for a temporary change? How do you categorize a consumer of a particular durable, when their last purchase might have been half a decade or more ago? In the public sector, the boundaries may be even more blurred. Unemployment benefits are paid to those out of work but are intended just as much to support their dependents. Blockbuster Entertainment's challenges in segmenting its customer base are detailed in Marketing in Action 7.1.

- **Users.** Sometimes users are not the same as purchasers. It may be the children in the family who actually consume the Lucky Charms, and they will usually make their brand preferences very well known, even if it is only because they want to collect the free gifts offered in the cereal boxes. The dif-

www.generalmills.com

www.blockbuster.com

www.youruleschool.com

Marketing in Action 7.1

Blockbuster moves to lifestyle segmentation

A national video specialty chain, Blockbuster Entertainment (www.blockbuster.com) has more than 4,000 video stores in the United States and operates 2,000 international stores. Each of these stores carries anywhere from 7,000 to 10,000 videos. As an entertainment provider, Blockbuster seeks to fulfill its customers' basic desire to have fun. Strategically, Blockbuster views the need to have fun as a chance for repeat business. Thus, the goal is to get potential customers into the store and for these customers to keep returning to Blockbuster to satisfy their desire for fun.

Historically, Blockbuster followed a very basic approach to market segmentation. The company's database was segmented according to active/inactive customers and could provide a breakdown of customers based on recency. With this segmentation approach, Blockbuster was able to identify customers, for example, who had stopped using Blockbuster to fulfill their entertainment needs or

customers who seemed to be making many trips to the store. Unfortunately, in this age of direct marketing, Blockbuster's segmentation approach did not provide any assistance in targeting the company's annual mailings.

The company's marketing group thinks that a lifestyle segmentation approach will enable Blockbuster to increase the precision of its direct marketing initiatives. For example, a lifestyle approach would allow the company to identify customers who increase their video rentals around holiday/school vacation periods or customers who do not rent during the summer months.

Do you agree with the marketing group? Would you expect transactional trends among Blockbuster's membership of 38 million American households? Using your personal knowledge/experience in video rentals, identify four or five "catchall" lifestyle segments that might be appropriate for Blockbuster.

Sources: www.blockbuster.com; Adam Woods, "Blockbuster Edits All Data in Catch-All Segmentation," *Precision Marketing*, June 8, 1998, 3.

ference is most noticeable in the case of newspapers and magazines, where readership figures (the number of those who read a given issue, as determined by market research surveys) can be much higher than those for circulation (the number of copies actually sold).

- **Prospects.** The term *prospects* is most often used in face-to-face selling, and *potential customers* is often used in mass markets. The meaning is the same—those individuals in the market who are not the organization's customers. Again, however, the boundaries are not quite so clear. Are lapsed customers included? Is everyone in the market a prospect, or does it include only those who are likely to buy the particular brand? The concept of prospects may sometimes be just as applicable in the public sector. In the United States, the International Trade Administration has undertaken an advertising campaign to promote its US&FCS (United States and Foreign Commercial Service)—export promotion services—to potential exporters, as most of them are not aware of the services. The government is attempting to convert prospects into customers.

www.ita.doc.gov

PENETRATION. Some individuals in the market buy a particular producer's brand, and some do not. The measure of the difference is known as brand penetration, determined by market research. Penetration is the proportion of individuals in the market who are users of the specific product or service, as in the nonprofit sector it is often used to measure the number of clients receiving help as a proportion of the total population who might need the service.

> Penetration is the proportion of **individuals in the market who are users** of the specific product or service

www.acnielsen.com

BRAND (OR MARKET) SHARE. The most common measure for usage rate is brand (market) share, or the share of overall market sales for each brand. In the consumer field, this is usually measured by audit research on panels of retail outlets, such as that undertaken by ACNielsen. Brand share represents consumer purchases and not necessarily usage, although the distinction is usually not important. In the industrial field, brand share is usually an estimate based on research of a limited number of customers.

But once more there are complications. Brand share can be quoted in terms of volume (the brand has a 10 percent share of the total number of units sold) or in terms of value (at the same time the brand took 15 percent of the total money being paid out for such products, because it was a higher priced brand). This difference can sometimes be dramatic. For example, eMachines, a joint venture between Korea's TriGem and Korea Data Systems, maker of low-cost PCs, captured 10 percent of the retail market in February 1999, ending the month lapping at the heels of IBM, the market leader, with 10.7 percent share of the PC market (in terms of volume). In terms of value, eMachines had much less share than that of IBM.[1]

www.e4me.com
www.trigem.co.kr
www.kdsusa.com
www.ibm.com

The measure of share and the concept of prospects are important because they delineate the extra business that a producer can reasonably look for and where he or she might obtain it. On the other hand, the evidence in many markets is that most business comes from repeat purchases by existing customers.

THE PARETO, OR 80/20, PRINCIPLE. As we have discussed in earlier chapters, the Pareto Principle, or 80/20 Rule, can be applied to a wide range of situations—in mass consumer markets as well as industrial ones—and it applies to groupings of customers (see Figure 7.1). It says that the top 20 percent of customers accounts for 80 percent of sales and that the best-selling 20 percent of products accounts for 80 percent of the volume or value of overall sales. The importance of the principle is that it highlights the need for most producers to concentrate their efforts on the most important customers and products.

MARKET SEGMENTS

As we have seen, producers tend to define markets quite broadly, primarily in terms of the physical characteristics that are important to themselves. These larger markets often contain groups of customers with different needs and wants, each of which represents a different **segment**. This process is called **segmentation**. On the other hand, **target marketing** occurs when the supplier carefully targets a specific group of customers.

If we look at the gasoline retail market, we can see how segmentation works. Mobil Oil is betting that drivers pick cappuccino over low gasoline prices at the pump. At the Mobil gas stations around the nation, the company not only offers what may be the cleanest bathrooms ever but also has added cappuccino in the convenience store and a concierge to assist customers, among other things. The new amenities are part of a major overhaul in Mobil's marketing strategy, based on a conclusion drawn from its segmentation study. The company's gasoline retailing business was losing a huge sum of money year after year, while its competitors were enjoying a healthy profit. Mobil badly needed a change (see Exhibit 7.1).

www.mobil.com

Extensive market research by Mobil, including tapping into the thoughts of more than 2,000 motorists, showed that a strategy of low gasoline prices may be essentially flawed. According to the Mobil study, only 20 percent of motorists buy gasoline based solely on price. Quality and service dimensions seem to be more important. Five different groups of customers have been identified, as follows:

1. Jennifer Lach, "The Price Is Very Right," *American Demographics* 21 (April 1999): 44–45.

Figure 7.1

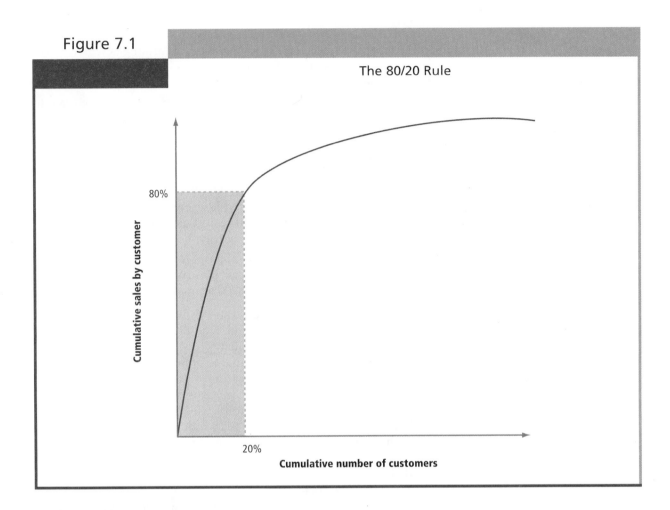

The 80/20 Rule

80%

Cumulative sales by customer

20%

Cumulative number of customers

Exhibit 7.1

Segmentation studies have helped Mobil recuperate market share lost to competitors already pursuing a quality and service strategy. Identifying the segments the company wants to target has resulted in increased amenities—like cappuccino and concierge services. The "Friendly Serve" marketing strategy has increased Mobil's earnings by 30 cents a share.

- *Road Warriors (10 percent of buyers):* Generally higher-income, middle-aged men who drive 25,000 to 50,000 miles a year, buy premium gas with a credit card, purchase sandwiches and drinks from the convenience store, and will sometimes wash their cars at the car wash.

- *True Blues (16 percent of buyers):* Usually men and women with moderate to high incomes who are loyal to a brand, sometimes loyal to a particular gas station, frequently buy premium gasoline, and pay in cash.

- *Generation F3 (27 percent of buyers):* For fuel, food, and fast; upwardly mobile men and women—half under 25 years of age—who are constantly on the go, drive a lot, and snack heavily from the convenience store.

- *Homebodies (21 percent of buyers):* Usually housewife "transporters" who shuttle their children around during the day and use whatever gasoline station is based in town or along their route of travel.

- *Price Shoppers (20 percent of buyers):* Generally not loyal to either a brand or a particular station, rarely buy the premium line of gasoline, frequently on tight budgets, and spends no more than $700 annually at the gas station.

Mobil's less price-conscious marketing strategy, dubbed "Friendly Serve," has proved to be successful. Road Warriors and True Blues want classier snacks from the convenience store, human contact, quality products, top service, privileges for loyal customers, and a nationally available brand. Although they want a reasonably competitive gasoline price, most of them do not worry about a few cents difference in gasoline prices. Road Warriors, True Blues, and Generation F3 are the motorist segments that Mobil targets to please. An extra two cents a gallon at the pump translates into an additional $118 million a year on the 650,000 barrels of gasoline that Mobil sells daily. It amounts to 30 cents a share more in earnings![2]

The value of discovering such segments, each with rather different characteristics, is that they allow producers to offer products that address the needs of just one segment, and hence are not in direct competition with the overall market leaders. Thus segmentation also exists by price.

www.ibm.com
www.compaq.com
www.dell.com
www.packardbell.com
www.e4me.com
www.circuitcity.com
www.staples.com

IBM offers a comprehensive range of products with almost universal applicability, and Compaq, Dell, and Packard Bell NEC are also dominant players in the PC business. However, eMachines has come up in a short time by pricing its machines in the $400 to $600 range in retail outlets like Circuit City and Staples and through online resellers. Rocketing from no market share to fourth place and leapfrogging over players such as Packard Bell NEC, eMachines has captured a low end of the PC market.[3] Despite its aggressive posturing, eMachines is actually avoiding head-on confrontation with Compaq, Dell, and other larger players by concentrating on the specific segment in which it can offer users a better match to their needs.

Once again, although the concept of segmentation is classically described in terms of products, it does apply to services. In the PC market, there are dealers who provide support for the smaller organizations and those who specialize in supporting the large multinationals—each representing different segments of the overall market.

Segmentation can even be a powerful concept in the nonprofit sector, although it tends to be a device for focusing resources rather than dealing with competition. For example, there may be a number of possible segments of the "unemployed." Each of these segments has different characteristics and offers different opportunities for government action.

---

2. "Mobil Bets Drivers Pick Cappuccino Over Low Prices," *Wall Street Journal,* January 30, 1995, B1, B8.
3. "eMachines Gains on PC Market Leaders Company Business and Marketing," *Electronic News,* April 5, 1999, 36.

On the other hand, many industrial firms do not distinguish between industry and market segments. Indeed, the first level of industrial market segmentation is to classify a present or potential user as an OEM (Original Equipment Manufacturer, who buys the product to incorporate it as part of another one) or an aftermarket user. The OEM sale is usually a direct sale, and if there is an aftermarket for the product it is often served through distributors.[4] Beyond that, making use of NAICS (North American Industrial Classification System) codes and identifying applications or buying factors will be useful. The segmentation principle, however, is the same.

www.census.gov/epcd/www/naics.html

SEGMENTATION

In one sense, segmentation is a strategy firms use to concentrate, and thus optimize, their resources within an overall market. In another sense, it is also the group of techniques vendors use for segmenting the market.

One way vendors segment the market is by consumer behavior, which can be divided into consumer characteristics and consumer responses. Consumer characteristics reflect *who buys:*

> One way vendors segment the market
> **is by consumer behavior:**
> characteristics and responses

- **Geographic** (e.g., region—urban or rural)
- **Demographic** (e.g., age, gender, and marital status)
- **Socioeconomic** (e.g., income, social class, and occupation)
- **Cultural** (e.g., lifestyles and culture)

Consumer responses are generally based on *what is bought:*

- **Occasions** when used
- **Benefits**
- **Usage frequency** (heavy or light)
- **Attitudes**, including loyalty

If the emphasis is on the supplier's viewpoint, which it often is, segmentation can be expanded to include elements of the four Ps:

- Price
- Distribution channels (place)
- Physical characteristics of product or service (product)
- Promotion

However, the four Ps are probably unrelated to the customers' own perceptions. For instance, the customer, like a supplier, may genuinely believe that a disinfectant bought in a plastic bottle from a supermarket belongs to a different market segment than one in a glass bottle bought from a pharmacy. On the other hand, the consumer may actually make the choice on totally different grounds. For example, the plastic container, rather than the glass container, appears to offer especially gentle protection for the baby in the family. It behooves a supplier to know what the true reasons are because the promotional message often determines how the consumer perceives the product.

---

4. Kelly E. Fish, James H. Barnes, and Milam W. Aiken, "Artificial Neural Networks: A New Methodology for Industrial Market Segmentation," *Industrial Marketing Management* 24 (October 1995): 431–438.

The characteristics that are important to a specific market may be much more closely defined. The aim of most market research is to identify the exact characteristics that are the most important (conscious or subconscious) delineators of buying behavior. These specific characteristics become the most powerful tools for segmentation.

specific characteristics become the most powerful tools for segmentation

In practice, the picture may be much more complex. The truly meaningful segments may well be based on intangible benefits that only the consumer perceives or based on natural consumer groupings that emerge from much more deep-seated social processes. A conservationist segment seems to exist in an increasing number of industries. For example, there are people who buy small, efficient cars irrespective of their income levels, or who invest their money only in environment-friendly companies such as Ben & Jerry's (the Vermont ice-cream company that has switched the material it uses to make its Best Vanilla pints to a more environmentally friendly unbleached paperboard) and Weyerhaeuser (a forest products company that cuts trees only on the land it owns and reforests the land after the harvest). In some consumer markets, significant amounts of research such as the *factor analysis* and *cluster analysis* techniques may be needed to identify what the key segments are.

www.benjerry.com

www.weyerhaeuser.com

Furthermore, descriptors often overlap from one segment to another and consequently are usually viewed as directional rather than exclusive. For example, an insurance company conducted a segmentation study to better understand the needs and wants of loyal and extremely loyal life insurance customers. An important finding of the study was that extremely loyal customers averaged much higher face amounts of insurance than less loyal ones, preferred to deal with agents, and thought insurance was a great value and that they could always use more. Less-loyal customers did not rank the agents as being so important and did not think they needed more insurance. Although the demographic profiles of these segments were different—extremely loyal customers were usually older, better educated, and held professional and managerial jobs—both groups had their share of what could be termed "average" customers (that is, people between the ages of 35 and 50, married parents earning under $75,000 a year). As a result, although the segments did differ demographically, the fact that both had a significant number of so-called average customers made such differences fuzzy.[5]

The Henley Center for Forecasting has used cross-elasticities of demand as a measure of the separation of segments. This approach is designed to reduce this confusion and to demonstrate the validity of the segments eventually chosen. If reducing the price of one group of products has no effect on the demand for another group of products, the two groups most likely lie in two independent segments. This concept is derived from economics and is simply known as the cross-elasticity of demand (ε):

$$\varepsilon = \frac{\text{percentage change in quantity of commodity X}}{\text{percentage change in price of commodity Y}}$$

The effect will be different if Y is a substitute for X. Notebook computer versus desktop computer is a good example, in which case there will be a positive cross-elasticity; that is, the sales of notebook computers (X) will increase if the price of desktop computers (Y) increases. The effect will also differ if Y is a complement. For example, in personal computers versus Microsoft software, the cross-elasticity will be negative, because the sales of personal computers (X) will decrease with an increase in the price of Microsoft software (Y).

www.microsoft.com

5. George Orme, "Think about an Attitude Adjustment: Using Attitudinal Data to Determine Market Segments," *Direct* 10 (December 1998): 49.

In practice this can become a very sophisticated technique. Removing the effects of the other factors involved, such as promotional activities, typically requires exact sales figures covering an extended period and consumes significant amounts of computing power as various regression analyses are run.

These intangibles, of course, represent the type of characteristic most often used in segmenting consumer markets (services as well as products). The intangibles used in industrial markets may be more directly related to the product or service characteristics (e.g., powerful single-use cleaners rather than general cleaners) or at least to product usage characteristics (floor cleaners rather than upholstery cleaners), but also to *customer set* characteristics (cleaners to be used in industrial workshops, rather than in hospital operating rooms).

BENEFIT SEGMENTATION.   Using general factors as the basis for segmentation has its limitations. It is much more productive to relate segmentation to specific market characteristics for the product or service. Different customers, or groups of customers, look for different combinations of benefits, and it is these groupings of benefits that then define the segments. The producers or service providers can use these differences to position their brands or services where they most clearly meet the consumers' needs in that segment.

As Russell Haley,[6] the father of benefit segmentation, explains in his seminal work:

> The belief underlying this segmentation strategy is that the benefits which people are seeking in consuming a given product are the basic reasons for the existence of true market segments. . . . (Although) most people would like as many benefits as possible, . . . the relative importance they attach to individual benefits can differ importantly and, accordingly, can be used as an effective lever in segmenting markets.

Table 7.2 illustrates this approach by showing an example of various segments in the toothpaste market. Benefit segmentation truly addresses the marketer's fundamental quest for consumer needs—why consumers buy what they buy.

> Benefit segmentation truly addresses the **marketer's fundamental quest for consumer needs** —why consumers buy what they buy.

Table 7.2

Toothpaste market segment description				
Segment name	**The sensory segment**	**The sociables**	**The worriers**	**The independent segment**
Principal benefit sought	Flavor, product appearance	Bright teeth	Decay prevention	Price
Demographic strengths	Children	Teens, young people	Large families	Men
Special behavioral characteristics	Users of spearmint-flavored toothpaste	Smokers	Heavy users	Heavy users
Brands disproportionately favored	Colgate, Aim	Rembrandt, Close-Up, Ultra Brite	Crest, Mentadent	Brands on sale
Personality characteristics	High self-involvement	High sociability	High hypochondriasis	High autonomy
Lifestyle characteristics	Hedonistic	Active	Conservative	Value-oriented

Source: Russell I. Haley, "Benefit Segmentation: A Decision-Oriented Research Tool: Marketing Insight Is Limited Only by the Imagination," *Marketing Management* 4 (summer 1995): 59. Adapted with permission of the American Marketing Association.

6. Russell I. Haley, "Benefit Segmentation: A Decision Oriented Research Tool," *Journal of Marketing* 32 (July 1968): 30–35. Also see his "Benefit Segmentation—20 Years Later," *Journal of Consumer Marketing* 11 (1986).

SEGMENTATION BY CONSUMPTION PROFILE

In recent years, a number of research agencies have started to characterize consumer segments in terms of their consumers' purchasing patterns. Thus, segments are characterized by their purchases of a range of key products and, in particular, by a range of media such as television programs, magazines, newspapers, and radio. The data for this approach may be provided in some depth by MRB's TGI (Target Group Index) or ACNielsen surveys or in less (but still adequate) depth by less wide-ranging surveys. The profile, as described in terms of the bundle of brands purchased, is supposed to be more meaningful to marketers than the relatively esoteric categories offered by lifestyles.

www.mrbcomm.com
www.acnielsen.com

SEGMENTATION ACROSS NATIONAL BOUNDARIES[7]

Global marketers approach segmentation from different angles. The standard country segmentation procedure classifies prospect countries based on a set of socioeconomic, political, and cultural criteria (see Table 7.3). Using statistical algorithms such as cluster analysis and factor analysis, the countries under consideration can be classified into homogeneous groups. The results for a three-group country segmentation are presented in Table 7.4. Note that the United

Table 7.3

	Country characteristics
Characteristics	**Measures**
1. Mobility	Number of air passengers/km
	Air cargo (ton/km)
	Number of newspapers
	Population
	Cars per capita
	Motor gasoline consumption per capita
	Electricity production
2. Health standard	Life expectancy
	Physicians per capita
	Hospital beds per capita
3. Trade Situation	Imports/GNP
	Exports/GNP
4. Lifestyle (Materialism)	GDP per capita
	Phones per capita
	TVs per capita
	Personal computers per capita
	Electricity consumption per capita
5. Tourism	Foreign visitors per capita
	Tourist expenditures per capita
	Tourist receipts per capita
6. Culture	Language
	Religion
	Customs
	Education expenditures
	Graduate education in population

Source: Kristiaan Helsen, Kamel Jedidi, and Wayne S. DeSarbo, "A New Approach to Country Segmentation Utilizing Multinational Diffusion Patterns," *Journal of Marketing* 57 (October 1993): 60–71. Adapted with permission of the American Marketing Association.

7. Masaaki Kotabe and Kristiaan Helsen, "International Segmentation," *Global Marketing Mangement,* 2d ed. (New York: John Wiley & Sons, 2001).

Table 7.4

Country segments based on the country characteristics

	Segment 1	Segment 2	Segment 3
	Holland	Austria	United States
	Japan	Belgium	
	Sweden	Denmark	
	United Kingdom	Finland	
		France	
		Norway	
		Switzerland	
Mobility	Relatively high	Relatively high	Very high
Health standard	Very high	Average	High
Trade situation	Strong in exports	Balanced trade	Dependent on imports
Materialism (Lifestyle)	Conserver society	In between	Material society
Tourism	Low tourist attraction	High tourist attraction	In between
Culture	Not used in the analysis (some factors not quantifiable)		

Source: Kristiaan Helsen, Kamel Jedidi, and Wayne S. DeSarbo, "A New Approach to Country Segmentation Utilizing Multinational Diffusion Patterns," *Journal of Marketing* 57 (October 1993): 60–71. Adapted with permission of the American Marketing Association.

States forms a segment of its own, and Japan is grouped with some of the European countries. In general, country segments seldom match geographic groupings. However, the country groupings do not necessarily correspond to market response measures such as market penetration rate, purchase intention, and willingness to pay. Therefore, from a marketer's perspective, the practical usefulness of country segments may be limited.

To address this shortcoming of the country segmentation approach, the following alternative procedure should be considered.[8]

Step 1: Criteria Development. Determine your cutoff criteria. For example, the convertibility of the local currency for the U.S. dollar is one such criterion. The criteria will be determined by product and company characteristics.

Step 2: Preliminary Screening. Determine which countries meet the thresholds for the criteria set forward in Step 1. Countries that do meet the cutoff will be retained.

Step 3: Microsegmentation. The next stage is to develop microsegments in each of the countries in your consideration set. There are two ways to come up with these segments:

- Derive microsegments for each country individually. Survey data collected from prospect customers in each of the countries are used as inputs. This procedure is similar to the ones used in domestic segmentation. In the next step, the analyst consolidates the microsegments *across* countries based on similarities across the microsegments in the prospective countries, or

- Jointly group individuals in all the prospect countries to come up directly with *cross-border segments.* Marketing practitioners are more likely to benefit from this approach as it is in tune with the marketing concept. Viable cross-border segments, such as "global elites" and "global teenagers," can be identified.

8. Suhdir H. Kale and D. Sudharshan, "A Strategic Approach to International Segmentation," *International Marketing Review* (summer 1987): 60–70.

Behavioral segmentation is particularly useful when firms consider foreign expansion. For new products, they may consider segmenting countries on the basis of the new product diffusion pattern observed in the countries of interest. Diffusion based criteria could relate to country traits such as the speed of adoption, the time-of-sales peak, and the consumer willingness to try new products. Table 7.4 shows the country groupings based on the diffusion patterns observed in each of these markets for three consumer durable products: color televisions, VCRs, and CD players. Note that the respective country groupings have little in common in terms of the number of segments and their composition. In fact, Belgium and Denmark are the only countries that consistently fall into the same grouping for all three consumer durable products.

SEGMENT VIABILITY

One customer-oriented reason behind segmentation is that when designing products or services that are narrowly targeted to the needs of one specific segment, it may be possible to offer consumers in that segment the best match to their needs. For instance, the sellers of PCs below the price of $1,000 have started to target the needs of five distinct segments. The first market segment is supposedly the original target for low-priced PCs, or first-time buyers who have a limited amount of money to spend. The second segment of these buyers is an unlikely crowd populated by knowledgeable buyers purchasing an additional system. The third key segment has just recently started to emerge, and it's business buyers looking for PCs that will be used for only the most basic functions in their companies by undemanding users. Next is the college market. Not only is this a large market segment, but due to the most recent baby boom, it is a segment that is only going to get larger. The final segment is the person just starting a home business. As Americans in increasing numbers take to either augmenting their incomes from traditional jobs or replacing them entirely with their own businesses, the number of computers shipped to this market has exploded.[9] In practice, producers usually target segments rather than the overall market because this allows them to concentrate their resources on a limited group of consumers. In this way, the brand can dominate that segment and gain the benefits of segment leader.

www.microsoft.com
www.hp.com
www.sgi.com
www.sun.com

Similarly, a segment may become less viable by encroaching competitors from adjoining segments. For example, in a growing number of new sales, customers compare high-end PCs running Microsoft's Windows NT operating system with Unix workstations from Hewlett-Packard, Silicon Graphics, and Sun Microsystems. Although there are still a few areas where workstations offer users a distinct performance advantage, there are not as many now as there once were, and the areas of overlap have been increasing. Sun Microsystems recently introduced the Ultra 5 and touted its move to PC-style volume manufacturing. Unix suppliers have been forced to respond to this incursion.[10] Worse yet, the existing segment may shrink in size or even disappear over time. The makers of panty hose are currently experiencing this unfavorable shift in customer taste: More and more fashionable women say that they like the bare-legged look. Indeed, sheer hosiery sales have declined over 20 percent in the last four years.[11]

In the public sector, greater efficiency may justify such concentration, but in the commercial world, the ultimate objective is to make a profit. To be viable, a segment needs to meet a number of broad criteria.

---

9. Aaron Goldberg, "Are You Part of the Sub-$1,000 Market?" *Computer Shopper,* December 1, 1998, 118.
10. Paul Korzeniowski, "High-End PC Vendors Challenge Unix Workstations," *Computer Reseller News,* July 27, 1998, 101–102.
11. Teri Agins, "Sheer Marketing: 'Bare' Pantyhose," *Wall Street Journal,* May 24, 1999, B1.

SIZE.   Is the segment substantial enough to justify attention and will there be enough volume generated to provide an adequate profit? For instance, can multiple producers chasing after one group of consumers all earn a profit? For example, both Gulfstream Aerospace Corp. and Bombardier Inc. are currently chasing after the 950 corporations (e.g., GE and Walt Disney Co.), governments, and individuals (e.g., Bill Cosby) that are likely to buy a large business jet. These two jet makers will spend a combined $1.2 billion to develop long-range jets for this small market. At $30–$40 million for each plane, many CEOs are wondering if it is justifiable to spend this kind of money to fly nonstop to Asia five or six times a year.[12] Similarly, one must also wonder how 400 to 800 Belgian beers are able to all prosper in a country of only 10 million people![13]

www.gulfstreamaircraft
.com
www.bombardier.com
www.ge.com
disney.go.com

As segmentation is a process, at least in the short term, that is largely under the control of the producer, it might be possible to find an increasing number of ever smaller segments that could be targeted separately. In general, however, it is best to choose the fewest number of segments, and hence the largest average size. This allows resources to be concentrated and head-on competition with market leaders avoided.

In part, a viable segment size will be defined in terms of the producer's cost structures. The car market is heavily segmented, with Ford targeting a wide range of separate segments, but even the smallest of these (sharing the same assembly line as others) has to be worth some tens of thousands of cars a year simply to earn its place on that assembly line. On the other hand, Aston Martin, with its custom hand building, can very effectively target a segment that is worth just a few hundred cars a year.

www.ford.com

www.astonmartin.com

IDENTITY.   The segment needs to have unique characteristics that producers and consumers can identify and market research can measure. In the car market there is an identifiable segment for small cars against which Ford targets Escort, and Toyota, its Tercel. Within this segment, and across the larger car segments as well, there is a segment for higher-performance cars. In a high-performance car segment, Chevrolet targets the Corvette brand and Rover uses the otherwise defunct name of MG.

www.toyota.com
www.chevrolet.com
www.rovergroup.com

Producers can segment other markets based on the consumer culture. For instance, large companies such as Colgate-Palmolive, Nestlé, PepsiCo, and Procter & Gamble are increasing the number of products they offer to the Hispanic market in the United States. The U.S. Hispanic population has increased rapidly in recent years, rising from 6 percent of the population in 1980 to 10 percent in 1995. Projections from the Bureau of the Census indicate that the trend will continue for the next several years, with even their "lowest series" projecting that Hispanics will account for 12 percent in 2005.[14] With this growth, consumer spending among Hispanics has become an increasingly important segment of the economy. The same phenomenon is occurring in the publishing industry. For example, Simon & Schuster and HarperCollins Publishers are moving into Spanish-language publishing by translating best-sellers into Spanish and publishing the works of Spanish-speaking authors.[15]

www.colgate.com
www.nestle.com
www.pepsiworld.com
www.pg.com

> The segment needs to have unique characteristics **that producers and consumers can identify** and market research can measure.

www.simonandschuster
.com
www.harpercollins.com

---

12. "A Dogfight over 950 Customers," *Business Week*, February 6, 1995, 66; Anthony L. Velocci, Jr., "Airbus Entry Crowds Field of Large Business Jets," *Aviation Week & Space Technology*, June 23, 1997, 33–34.
13. "A Rich Bouquet of Belgian Brews," *Business Week*, August 15, 1994, 110.
14. Geoffrey D. Paulin, "A Growing Market: Expenditures by Hispanic Consumers," *Monthly Labor Review* 121 (March 1998): 3–21.
15. "How Do You Say Bestseller in Spanish?" *Wall Street Journal*, January 4, 1995, B1, B6.

RELEVANCE. The basis for segmentation must be relevant to the important characteristics of the product or service. For example, the type of pet owned is highly relevant in the pet food market, but will rarely be so in the car market.

Although this seems obvious, much marketing is still undertaken (mistakenly) on the basis of overall population characteristics rather than those directly relating to the specific product or service. For example, in many markets the tacit segmentation has been made in terms of socioeconomic class, yet the major car manufacturers' segmentation of the car market no longer follows these lines.

ACCESS. Finally, the producer must be able to gain access to the segment. If tapping that segment is too difficult, and accordingly too expensive, it clearly will not be viable. For the sake of argument, let us say that there might be a small segment of the general low-priced car market that could be met by a small manufacturer using hand-building techniques. However, if the consumers within the segment were diffused evenly throughout the population, the producer might face difficulties on two levels. The first would be in obtaining national distribution for the low volumes. Setting up a separate dealership network to provide the maintenance facilities would be almost impossible (even some of the smaller existing manufacturers in the United Kingdom for instance, such as Peugeot and Fiat, have incomplete networks). The second difficulty would be finding the means to deliver the promotional message to these potential buyers.

> the producer must be able
> to gain access to the segment

www.peugeot.com
www.fiat.com

All of these criteria apply equally to the segmentation available in the nonprofit sector. If they can be met, segmentation is a very effective marketing device. It can allow even the smaller organizations to obtain leading positions in their respective segments (*niche* marketing) and gain some of the control this offers. It is worth repeating that the most productive bases for segmentation are those that relate to the consumers' own groupings in the market. Marketers should not artificially impose producers' segments. In any case, segmentation is concerned only with dividing customers or prospects (and not products or services) into the segments to which they belong.

THE INTERNET AND SEGMENTATION

The Internet has great potential use for segmentation, but it will not be realized without a focused marketing strategy. Basic concepts such as market segmentation, product differentiation, and determining the right mix of product, price, place, and promotion strategies will be key to using it effectively. For example, one of the most effective uses of the Internet is to sell group insurance products to employees and affinity groups. They can be given online access to product information, price quotes, sales channels, and customer service. Like any advertising medium, the Internet will generate far more indirect sales. The Internet offers a raft of new marketing tools: hyperlinks, banners, click-through measurements, and search engines.

www.datamonitor.com

Datamonitor, a market research firm, predicts that the Internet's share of property casualty sales will be about 7.5 percent in 2001, up from 0.6 percent in 1997. As insurance marketers better understand these tools, they can build in greater sophistication based on experience and customer feedback. Internet users are highly educated, relatively affluent people who work. Although it is tempting to characterize all Internet users as alike, they are not. We still must identify customer needs and perceptions. With this type of information, the market can be properly segmented. In cyberspace, the traditional "sales push" model, in which customers react to information and proposals provided by agents, is replaced by a "market pull" model, where a customer can electronically assess product features and compare prices without personal contact. Internet users still must be offered compelling reasons to buy. Basics like market potential research, customer needs analysis, distinct product design, and, most important, customer communication will still be requisites to success.

> In cyberspace, the traditional **"sales push" model is replaced** by a "market pull" model

The prospect can get a quote by e-mail or by calling a toll-free number. Another approach involves electronic malls such as Insuremarket and InsWeb. Originally designed for term life products, these sites have recently added personal auto coverage. Another company is marketing personal auto coverage on the Autobytel shopping site for new and used cars. A third category of carriers includes those offering direct links to their agencies. Their Web sites have easy-to-use agency directories that let prospective customers hyperlink to the agency site or send e-mail messages. Finally, some insurers are testing the Internet as an information source for curious surfers. These companies, mostly independent agency companies, offer information about themselves to a variety of audiences, including their agents, but are not facilitating contact between the surfing public and their retail agents. They may be interested in establishing an Internet presence while trying to figure out how best to use electronic commerce without agent involvement.

www.insuremarket.com
www.insweb.com
www.autobytel.com

For example, Daniels Insurance Agency, a small agency in Westborough and Shrewsbury, Massachusetts, arranged a sponsored group plan with its Internet service provider, TIAC, to sell auto and home business to TIAC's Massachusetts subscribers. The group plan offers discounted rates on auto policies. TIAC members just click on an icon on the TIAC home page and are linked to the Daniels site, where they can get quotes, submit applications, file claims, and inquire about other types of insurance.

corp.tiac.net

The most promising Internet market segments are characterized by relatively simple, low-cost products, a short sales process, and high customer product awareness and understanding. By placing the right product information in cyber-locations most frequented by target audiences and by taking advantage of bannering and search engines, independent agencies and insurers can attract Internet surfers. Targeting markets that best fit the right cybertemplate will result in the best return on investment.[16]

SEGMENTATION METHODS AND PRACTICAL SEGMENTATION

In order to achieve a genuine consumer-based segmentation, three *technical* problems need to be addressed:[17]

1. Construct a product space, which is a geometric representation of consumers' perceptions of products or brands in a category.

2. Obtain a density distribution by positioning consumers' ideal points in the same space.

3. Construct a model that predicts preferences of consumer groups toward new or modified products.

---

16. Edward F. Ryan, "Cornering the Online Market," *Best's Review* 99 (December 1998): 93.
17. Richard Johnson, "Market Segmentation: A Strategic Management Tool," *Journal of Marketing Research* 8 (1971): 13–18.

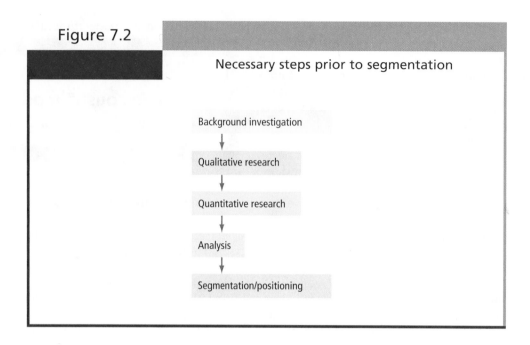

Figure 7.2

Necessary steps prior to segmentation

Background investigation

↓

Qualitative research

↓

Quantitative research

↓

Analysis

↓

Segmentation/positioning

In practice, segmentation is so very clearly tied to market research programs that it often becomes one element of this aspect of marketing activity. To discover and use these *natural segments* requires a number of steps (see Figure 7.2) in market research.

Background Investigation. The first stage is conducting the desk research that will best inform the researcher and the marketer of what the most productive segments are likely to be. This essential stage will lead to the *hypotheses* to be tested, but it must not be the only one used to define the segments. At each stage, the marketer must be prepared to abandon any preconceptions or prejudices, in light of the actual data about the customer's view of such segments.

Qualitative Research. It is vital that all the characteristics that are important to the consumer be measured and that these be described in terms that are meaningful to him or her. The *language* used by consumers should be first investigated in focus group discussions. For example, small-car buyers prefer to appear sophisticated. This consumer psychology is apparent in the following focus group discussion between an interviewer and a respondent.

Respondent: I am concerned about fuel economy.

Interviewer: Why do you want to be concerned about fuel economy?

Respondent: Well, I would like to contribute to reducing our country's dependence on foreign oil.

Interviewer: Your contribution must be very limited.

Respondent: It doesn't matter. I just wish all the people were educated enough to know energy independence is important to our country.

Recall that focus groups are frequently used to pilot major research projects and are best conducted by psychologists who are trained to recognize the important nuances. This research discovers the *dimensions* that are important to the consumer (and that are described in their language) from which later strategies will be developed.

Quantitative Research. Based on the dimensions (the key descriptive words) revealed by the qualitative research, quantitative research attempts to measure attitudes toward the brand and competing brands using various scales. This work may also extend to the consumer's *ideal brand*. The validity of such *idealizations* is questionable, because they are artificial conceptualizations that are not easy for the consumer to articulate, and the results can be ambiguous. In practice, though, the concept of the ideal brand usually appears to work well, especially when the questions are specific, carefully phrased, and *mapped* on the specific dimensions involved in the positioning exercise.

ANALYSIS.   This critical stage is now almost invariably dependent on the use of considerable computing power to undertake the complex analyses involved. Some form of *factor analysis* is usually used to separate those variables that are highly correlated, and hence are almost interchangeable in the consumers' eyes. For example, in some pioneering research in the 1970s, the "motor noise" of a vacuum cleaner was found to be related to its "cleaning power" as perceived by consumers. This allowed Hoover to reposition its vacuum cleaners as more powerful simply by stressing their powerful sound.

www.hoover.com

Only when this factor analysis is complete is *cluster analysis* used to create a specified number of maximally different clusters, or segments, of consumers. The number of such specific clusters should adequately describe the significantly different segments in the market. Each of these consumer clusters is homogeneous within itself, but as different from other clusters as possible. The typical outcome will be a set of prioritized position maps, preferably limited to the five to eight most important dimensions.

As illustrated earlier in Manager's Corner 7.1, Mobil Oil provides an excellent example of consumer segmentation at its gas stations. The company has learned that no more than 20 percent of its customers are price conscious and has begun to emphasize customer service and quality at its gas stations. After all, price competition is what all marketers wish to avoid.

www.mobil.com

SEGMENTATION/POSITIONING.   The marketer must then pore over position *maps* to determine exactly what the strategy should be, taking into account the available resources as well as the competitive and consumer positioning on the map. What will the target groups be? What will the chosen segments be? Where will the products or services be repositioned (if needed) to compete most effectively and/or to be most attractive to consumers? This is probably the most important set of decisions that any marketer makes, and from it most other decisions will emerge naturally. The intellectual effort committed to this process should, therefore, not be underestimated.

Of the thousands of new health and beauty care stockkeeping units introduced each year, few ever really hit it big on supermarket shelves, mostly because manufacturers often misjudge consumers' needs and desires. The product's name, its promise and actual benefits, and its market positioning must all touch a consumer's nerve to stimulate the purchase. For example, Dr. Care Toothpaste was a product that tried to enter the U.S. market from Canada. It was positioned for children and the family, but it was packaged in an aerosol can. Parents were understandably worried by what their young children might do with an aerosol can while unsupervised in the bathroom and shunned Dr. Care.

When Clairol called its new conditioner Small Miracle, it was a major problem for the product. Just about everybody has "bad hair" days. Some have them virtually every day. Consumers move from brand to brand looking for a big miracle. Women had gigantic expectations, and Clairol offered only a small promise. Small Miracle sought a new position with the claim that it was a once-a-week conditioner that would last through three shampoos. Some consumers felt that they did not get one real benefit, much less three, and that it was indeed a small miracle—one they could hardly notice.[18]

www.clairol.com

18. Robert McMath, "New Products Need More than a Small Miracle: An Authority on New Products Reveals Some Truths about Past Successes and Failures," *Supermarket News*, June 29, 1998, 60.

The complexity of this positioning/repositioning process does mean that the marketer and researcher must work closely together. Each must have a sound appreciation of what the other is doing and, most importantly, confidence in the other's ability to handle the complexities. It is a time- and resource-consuming process that reaps tremendous benefits.[19]

PRODUCT/SERVICE POSITIONING

There can be some confusion between **segmentation** and **positioning**, and indeed the two processes often overlap. The key difference is that the former applies to the customers (or occasionally *products*) that are clustered into the *natural* segments that occur in a particular market. The latter relates specifically to the product or service and to what the supplier can do to best *position* its offerings against these segments.

A further complication is that positioning can sometimes be divorced from segmentation in that the supplier can select dimensions on which to position the brand that are not derived from research, but are of his or her own choosing. Indeed, such positioning can be applied (to differentiate a brand, for instance) even when segmentation is not found to be viable. Further confusion can arise when the process is associated with **product differentiation**—the practical "positioning" of products or services so that they are recognizably different from their competitors—as measured in terms of their positions on the *product space,* the "map" of competitive brand positions.

Recall that the most effective segmentation of a market is usually based on sets of characteristics that are specific to that market. As shown in Figure 7.3, the spread of users across these characteristics may, however, differ quite significantly. Both the homogeneous example, where all the users have similar, closely grouped preferences (e.g., a commodity such as sugar), and the diffused example, where users have requirements spread evenly across the spectrum, tend to specify treatment of the market as one single entity (but for very different reasons). Segmentation is not relevant unless competitors in a diffused market have left part of it uncovered.

www.kchealthcare.com

For example, Tecnol Medical Products Inc., now owned by Kimberly-Clark, makes a variety of specialty face masks that can, among other things, protect doc-

Figure 7.3

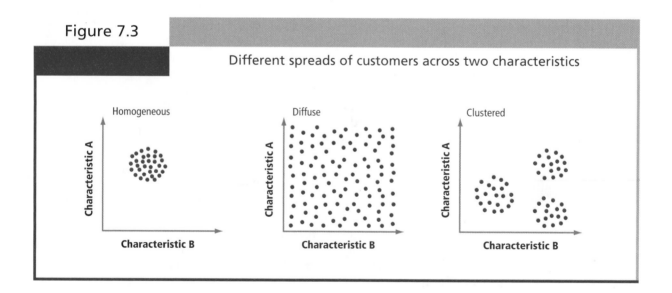

Different spreads of customers across two characteristics

19. Christian Homburg, "Marketing's Influence within the Firm," *Journal of Marketing* 63 (April 1999): 1–17.

tors from micron-sized particles. Tecnol executives found that both Johnson & Johnson and 3M were not responding adequately to health-care personnel's fear over the transmission of AIDS and other diseases. Because Tecnol executives found that their main competitors were "asleep at the switch," they now have 60 percent of the hospital market for face masks as compared to 3M's 21 percent share and Johnson & Johnson's 10 percent share.[20] VTech of Hong Kong provides another example of finding opportunities in uncovered markets. VTech entered the educational toy niche with computer-based offerings and now has more than 60 percent of the electronic educational toy market in the United States and Europe, selling under the VTech name through chains such as Toys "R" Us.[21]

In practice, it is often in the clustered market where segmentation can be most successfully used. Ideally, the marketer will choose to place the product exactly in the center of the cluster for which he or she is aiming (see Figure 7.4). If the clusters are too small to justify a segmentation policy or the marketer simply wants to have a more general product brand that can be correspondingly larger, another approach is to launch the product or service so that it is equidistant from several clusters that the marketer wishes to serve (see Figure 7.5).

Theodore Levitt[22] argues that in an era of global competition, successful companies are shifting from a product policy of offering customized products to that of offering globally standardized ones. According to Levitt, prices tend to be low and product reliability is high as a result of product standardization. Although the product may not exactly match the needs of any one group, it is close to meeting those of several groups and, therefore, customers are attracted to the product. However, such positioning may be vulnerable to attack from a competitor who positions their brand exactly on one of the clusters.

www.johnsonandjohnson.com
www.3m.com

www.vtech.com

www.toysrus.com

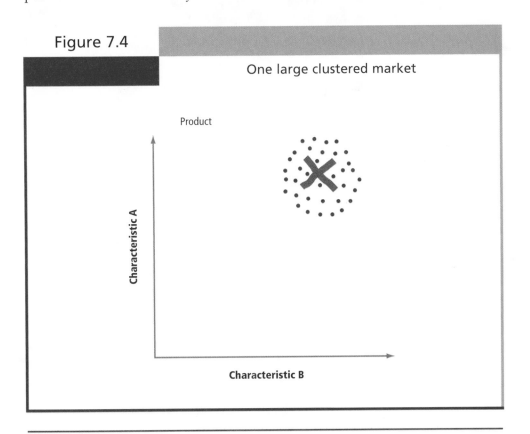

Figure 7.4

One large clustered market

Product

Characteristic A

Characteristic B

20. "Who's Afraid of J&J and 3M?: Not Tecnol. It's a Lesson in How a Small Company Can Win," *Business Week*, December 5, 1994, 66; "Premier Inc. Continues Contract Blitz: Recent Pacts Cover Wide Range of Products," *Hospital Materials Management* 22 (March 1997): 8.

21. Andrew Tanzer, "The VTech Phenomenon," *Forbes*, October 19, 1998, 88–90.

22. Theodore Levitt, "The Globalization of Markets," *Harvard Business Review* 61 (May/June 1983): 92–102.

Figure 7.5

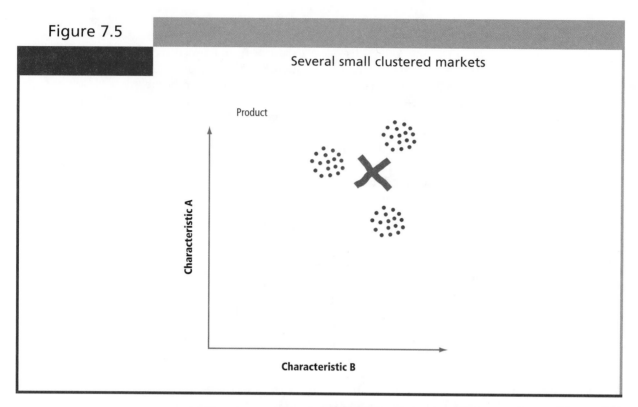

Several small clustered markets

Figure 7.6

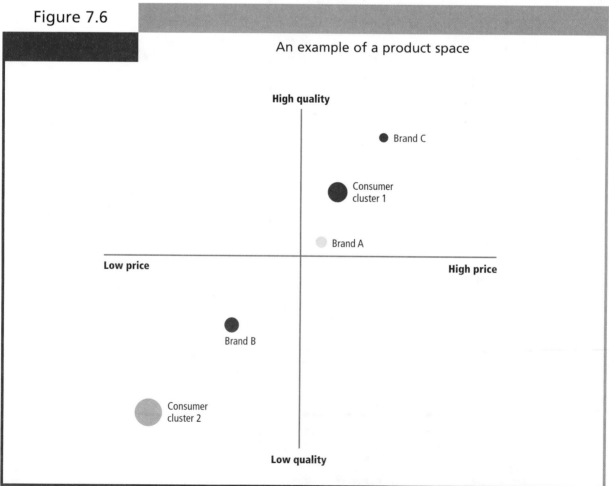

An example of a product space

Conventionally, product positioning (*product space*) maps are drawn with their axes dividing the plot into four quadrants. This is because most of the parameters on which they are based typically range from "high" to "low" or from "+" to "−" with the "average," or zero, position in the center (see Figure 7.6). The value of each product's (or service's) sales, as well as that of each cluster of consumers, is conventionally represented by the area of the related circle.

In Figure 7.6, there are just two clusters of consumers, one buying mainly on the basis of price (and accepting the lower quality that this policy entails) and one on the basis of quality (and prepared to pay extra). Against these segments there are just two main brands (A and B), each associated with a cluster or segment. There is also a smaller brand (C) associated with cluster 1; Brand C offers an even higher quality alternative, but at an even higher price.

Real-life product positioning maps will be more complex, involving a number of such dimensions; they are drawn with less certainty as to where the boundaries might lie. They do, however, offer a very immediate picture of where potential may lie and which products or services are best placed to tap it (see Figure 7.7). They also offer a sound basis for **repositioning** existing products (or launching a complementary new product), so that they better match the requirements of the specific *clusters* they are targeting. In Figure 7.6, Brand C might be content to remain a **niche** product. Alternatively, the positioning map shows that if it were slightly reduced in price (and were backed by sufficient promotion) it might become a very competitive contender for Brand A's market share.

Figure 7.7

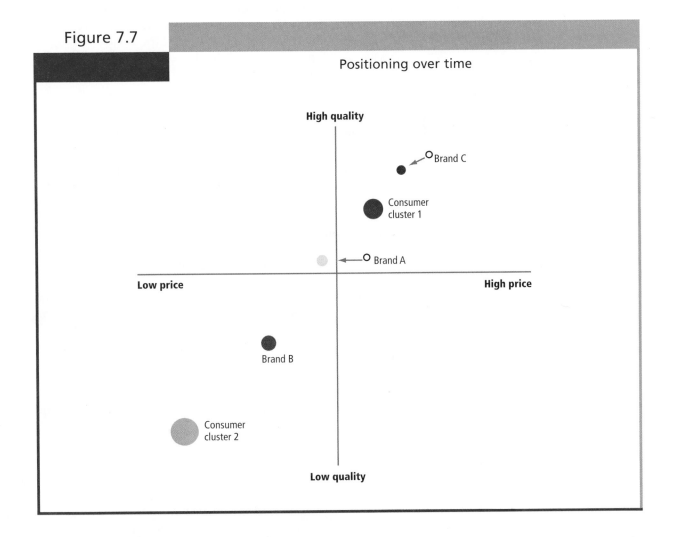

Positioning over time

In theory, it is possible to use promotion to move the consumer ideal closer to the brand rather than the other way around. Equally, the launch of a really innovative product such as the minidisc audio player may change the dimensions of the whole market. Although very effective when they succeed, such approaches are very difficult to achieve.

POSITIONING OVER TIME

So far we discussed the *positions* at one point in time—the *current* position. However, if the positioning research is carried out regularly over time, the map can also show that these positions change, ideally in line with the strategy (see Figure 7.8). In Figure 7.8, we can see that Brand C has moved only slightly (in line with strategy), but in so doing it has improved its competitive position significantly (helped by the fact that Brand A's competitive response, also reducing price, has moved it away from the ideal).

www.cadillac.com
www.gm.com
www.ford.com
www.lincolnmercury.com

www.hyatt.com

The Cadillac Division of General Motors may provide an example of an organization failing to track such market changes over time. Even when it finally revamped its range in 1985, its slimmed-down models actually seemed to move away from where the core of its market was. This gave Ford's Lincoln-Mercury Division, which continued to produce larger cars, a major competitive advantage. Tracking changes in position is thus a very powerful marketing tool.

Like Ford, Hyatt Hotels is also keeping up with changing markets. After an initial slow realization that the "all-frills" approach was not working, Hyatt is now winning high marks for its understanding of "tightened industry economics." The hotel has abandoned its 20-year-long approach of adding services, such as turning down every bed at night, regardless of costs. In response to its changed approach, its revenues are up 13 percent, and profits have climbed 45 percent.[23]

PERCEPTUAL MAPS

Perceptual maps are an alternative graphical approach to the static positioning map. For example, to produce just one diagram containing all the information that would otherwise be contained in the various dimensions (requiring a number of separate maps), a computerized plotting compression technique is used. As most often used, this initially plots the products, say, against the two most significant dimensions (exactly as in the two-dimensional maps that we have already examined). Subsequently, *vectors* are overlaid (from the origin) that show the other, less important dimensions. The direction of these vectors is calculated so that the relative displacement of the products from each other reflects any particular product's position against the others on the original two-dimensional maps (see Figure 7.7).

In Figure 7.8, three dimensions—maturity, nutrition, and refreshment—are found to be most important in representing a beverage market. Using a pair of dimensions, two perceptual maps are developed so that marketing managers can visually see how consumers think of various beverages in their minds. Hot coffee and hot tea are considered mature drinks that are neither refreshing nor nutritious. Bouillon and tomato juice are both considered nutritious drinks, but bouillon is perceived to be a much more mature drink than tomato juice. Naturally, these nutritious drinks are also perceived to be healthful (D), consumed with other food (E), and energy giving (H).

23. "Why Hyatt is Toning Down the Glitz: The Chastened Hotelier Retools for the Cost-Conscious '90s," *Business Week*, February 27, 1995, 92–94.

Figure 7.8

Perceptual maps of a beverage market

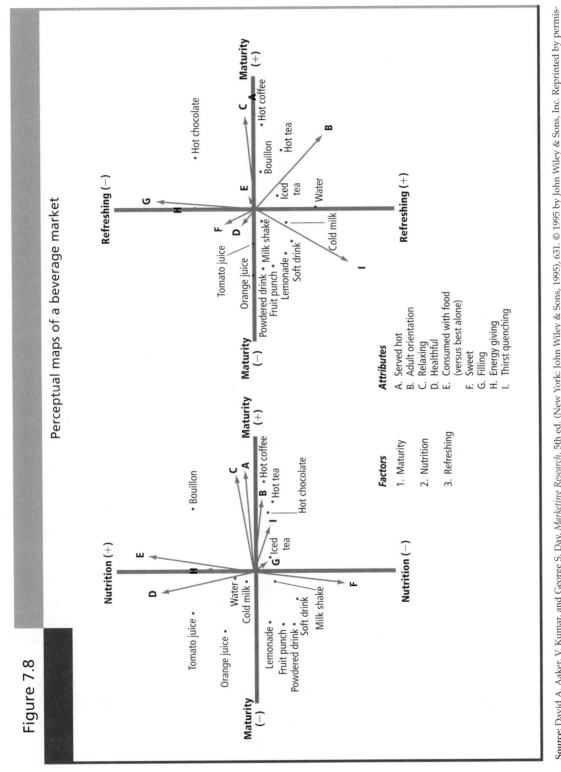

Attributes

A. Served hot
B. Adult orientation
C. Relaxing
D. Healthful
E. Consumed with food
   (versus best alone)
F. Sweet
G. Filling
H. Energy giving
I. Thirst quenching

Factors

1. Maturity
2. Nutrition
3. Refreshing

Source: David A. Aaker, V. Kumar, and George S. Day, *Marketing Research*, 5th ed. (New York: John Wiley & Sons, 1995), 631. © 1995 by John Wiley & Sons, Inc. Reprinted by permission of John Wiley & Sons, Inc.

This type of representation offers a useful shorthand, which is easier for managers to digest. On the other hand, if the manager is capable of digesting the contents of the three or four separate two-dimensional plots (and most are), then the basic approach should offer a better picture, and one that is inherently more useful than the relation to the vectors on the compressed picture, which is often somewhat less than obvious!

The key point to remember, however, is that the dimensions of these product positioning maps must reflect those that are important to the consumer, not just those that the supplier favors. Such knowledge can be worth a great deal of money to the supplier who is able to use it optimally to position the brand where it becomes most attractive to the targeted market segment. It can be almost as valuable to a public service provider, who seeks to position an offering so that it best meets the real needs of the maximum number of recipients.

> the dimensions of . . . positioning maps must reflect **those that are important to the consumer,** not just those that the supplier favors

TARGET MARKETING

The *positioning* process can be developed to most effectively implement the segmentation process. Three steps clearly separate the various activities:

Step 1: Market segmentation. This is the basic activity, which has already been discussed at some length.

Step 2: Target marketing. Knowledge of the segments is not enough. Considerable effort has to be put into selecting the segments that best meet the needs of the organization. As discussed earlier, this involves consideration of the available resources as well as the consumer segments and the competitive positions.

Step 3: Product positioning. This step makes it clear that after selecting the optimum segments, the supplier then needs to choose the optimum position within those segments (as shown, for example, on the brand positioning maps).

Once again, there can be confusion between the ideas generated by positioning and the activities related to its implementation. Thus, the processes of positioning, in terms of the concepts or ideas (deciding *where* the brand should be), are arguably the most important input into the strategy process for some products and services. Indeed, "where the brand should be" largely defines that strategy.

POSSIBLE APPROACHES TO SEGMENTATION

Clearly, there may be a wide range of detailed actions that are suggested by the outcome of a segmentation analysis. As schematically presented in Figure 7.9, there are four main strategies that may be adopted.

SINGLE SEGMENT

The simplest response, often the case where limited funds are available, is to concentrate on one segment and position the product firmly within that segment (sometimes described as *niche* marketing). This is a very effective form of mar-

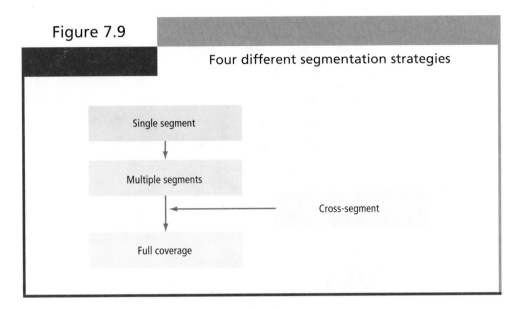

Figure 7.9

Four different segmentation strategies

keting, especially for the smaller organization, because it concentrates resources into a very sharply focused campaign. It is perhaps more risky, as there may be a greater likelihood of the niche disappearing than of the whole market being subject to catastrophic change. On the other hand, it is considerably less risky than spreading resources too thin across a number of segments.

CUSTOMIZED MARKETING.   In recent years two trends have combined to allow for narrower segments or niches:

- **Increasing variety demanded.** Consumers have come to demand more variety from their suppliers, rather than accepting a more uniform product (even if this means that a higher price has to be paid by the consumer).
- **Flexible manufacturing methods.** Microprocessing technology and just-in-time manufacturing enable firms to deliver a greater variety of products without reducing productivity to any significant extent.

The outcome has been that even some *mass marketers* can now provide individually customized products (at least to some degree). With the use of *precision marketing* techniques, described in Chapter 13, the supplier is now able to deliver a product specifically designed for an individual.

NICHES.   A specialized and extreme version of segmentation is that of creating *niches*. This approach is usually practiced by firms pursuing either a low end or a high end of the market. The organization then sets out to capture this segment (and possibly to expand it), confident in the knowledge that no competitor will subsequently be able to follow profitably. On the low end, Ugly Duckling Rent-A-Car, headquartered in Tucson, Arizona, has captured a strong niche for budget-conscious car renters. On the high end, Daimler-Benz has long maintained a strong market niche with Mercedes cars in the automobile market. The danger, as Daimler-Benz discovered, for instance, is that competitors based in other segments, such as Toyota's Lexus Division, may still be able to draw sales from the niche market and in the process reduce the viability of the niche operation itself (see Exhibit 7.2). That is one of the major reasons why Daimler-Benz recently acquired Chrysler to broaden its product lines.

www.uglyduckling.com

www.daimlerchrysler.com
www.mercedesbenz.com

www.toyota.com
www.lexus.com

Exhibit 7.2

Mercedes-Benz has long capitalized on its strength in the niche market of high-end automobiles. A weakness in this niche strategy was revealed by lower-priced competitors able to draw customers out of the high-end niche. Increasing the number of models under $40,000—like the SUVs—can be interpreted as Mercedes-Benz's response to the danger posed by competitors like Lexus and Infiniti.

MULTIPLE SEGMENTS

www.nestle.com

A more complex response is to address several major segments with one brand or to launch several brands targeted against different segments. Nestlé uses this latter strategy by offering brands to meet the "ground coffee," "continental," and "decaffeinated" segments, as well as the main brand itself, which, in line with the former strategy, spans a number of segments. An organization may also use this technique when it intends to achieve full market coverage by invading the market segment by segment.

CROSS-SEGMENT.   Most suppliers resolutely ignore the segments and pattern their marketing on other factors. This is almost invariably the case in the more bureaucratic responses of the public sector, which are based on the demands of the *delivery systems* rather than on the needs of the clients. In the commercial field, this is often a successful strategy. A company may specialize in a particular product that covers a number of segments, with a band of devoted supporters who recognize the specialized expertise embodied. This is a particularly prevalent and successful strategy in the industrial area. For example, DuPont's Teflon, a nonadhesive polymer, is used in tubing, gaskets, bearings, and rollers and as a coating for saw blades and cooking utensils. This approach is based on deliberately targeting across segments that have similar characteristics (such as similar production technologies).

www.dupont.com

FULL COVERAGE ("MASS MARKETING")

www.coke.com

Full coverage is limited to those organizations that can afford the strategy. With the intention of addressing the whole market, it can take two forms:

- **Undifferentiated.** A few organizations attempt to address a whole market with a single product or nonsegmented range. Coca-Cola is arguably such a company.

- **Differentiated.** Where the organization covers the market with a range of products or services (under the one brand) that are more or less individually targeted at segments, the coverage may be differentiated. IBM, for example, covers almost the whole range of computer products and services, but with individual products aimed at each segment.

www.ibm.com

The most sophisticated approach would match the pattern to the market's development stage. In a new market that is typically developed by one supplier, just one brand is launched to cover the whole market. As the market develops and competitors enter (usually targeting specific segments in order to obtain a foothold), the major supplier may move to preempt this competitive segmentation by launching its own new brands targeted at the most vulnerable segments. On the other hand, a competitor seeking to enter a market may initially target a particularly vulnerable segment and then use this as a base from which to grow incrementally by taking in more segments. For example, Kellogg's created a cereal market with cornflakes in the 1920s and has since introduced many other cereals as the market matured. Similarly, Toyota, Nissan, and Honda, respectively, have introduced Lexus, Infiniti, and Acura luxury car divisions as customers traded up from economy to more luxurious cars as their incomes grew over time.

www.kelloggs.com
www.toyota.com
www.nissan.com
www.honda.com
www.lexus.com
www.infiniti.com
www.acura.com

COUNTER-SEGMENTATION

Although segmentation has been a very popular strategic marketing device in recent years, there is an argument that it may have been taken too far in some areas. Toyota and Nissan, for example, have over-segmented the car market, with so many different models and features in search of a better match between consumers' needs and firm offerings. Further aggravated by the appreciation of the yen against the dollar, their costs of maintaining the product lines have gone up precipitously. These Japanese automakers' response is to consolidate several segments by launching a brand (or repositioning a brand or integrating several existing brands) to cover several segments. This may allow economies of scale without major reductions in benefits and, on balance, maintain competitive advantage. This process has been called **counter-segmentation**. Although it may only rarely apply, it should not be forgotten in the enthusiastic rush to segment.

> Although segmentation has been a very popular **strategic marketing device in recent years, . . .** it may have been taken too far in some areas.

SEGMENTATION AND ETHICS

Firms naturally locate their sales outlets where customers have easy access, offer products or services that customers will purchase, and even restrict their supply for an exclusive positioning. Malt liquors such as Anheuser-Busch's King Cobra and Heileman's Colt 45 have been criticized for targeting the poor inner-city segment of the beer market, allegedly emphasizing a high alcohol content for the money.[24] Similarly, the mortgage loan approval rates at banks are found to be much lower for some minority groups than others and cannot be justified on the basis of loan applicants' economic factors alone, implying the existence of some

www.anheuser-busch.com
www.pabst.com

---

24. "Contemporary Cobra," *Beverage World* (July 1993): 12; Gerry Khermouch, "A-B, Long Dogged in Malt Liquor, Readies Three-Tiered Foray into East," *Brandweek*, February 5, 1996, 3.

Manager's Corner 7.2

Targeting credit cards to the gay or lesbian household

For years, credit card issuers have been slow to target gay and lesbian consumers due to fear of controversy and lack of knowledge of how to serve the segment. Now interest in the category is heating up.

Think, for a moment, of a hypothetical two-person household. Both are upper-income professionals; they own their own home; their disposable income exceeds the national average; and they have no children. In addition, the couple belongs to a niche group that is both identifiable as an affinity market and interested in purchasing goods and services from companies that target them specifically. One might think that credit card issuers would beat a path to their doors.

Well, if the household is gay or lesbian, probably not. Although research indicates that an estimated 6 percent to 9 percent of the U.S. population is gay and despite market research showing that self-identified gay consumers are wealthier and more avid spenders than the general populace, the reluctance of most credit card issuers to build relationships with this market segment has been notable.

Perhaps unsurprisingly, much of the banks' resistance to targeting the gay market stems from concerns other than the bottom line. "You couldn't get a more conservative set of institutions" than banks, says William F. Keenan, president of Convergence Group, a Hockessin, Delaware-based card consulting firm. "It simply has to do with the nature of the card industry. It's risk-averse, and if there's any perception of controversy they'll avoid the risk."

Other industry sources agree that societal angst over the acceptance of homosexuality has made banks a bit skittish when it comes to gays and lesbians. "When you've got five different programs that are competing for your time, and they're all worth the same amount of money, and there's one program that's got a potential for controversy, you probably won't choose that," says Scott R. Seitz, a partner and principal in Spare Parts Inc. (www.spare-parts.com), a Westport, Connecticut, market-research firm that surveys gay consumers. In addition, the prejudices that individuals within the card industry might have regarding gays can come into play when it comes to developing gay-focused cards.

The best-known credit card to target the gay and lesbian community directly is the Rainbow Card (www.rainbowcard.com), launched in October of 1995 by Travelers Bank, now part of New York–based financial-services giant Citigroup (www.citigroup.com). The no-annual-fee Visa card, which currently offers an introductory interest rate on purchases of 0 percent for six months and 15.9 percent thereafter, contributes a portion of all transactions to the Rainbow Endowment, a nonprofit organization that donates funds to gay-related causes. "The Rainbow Card has been a very successful product in the gay and lesbian community" in terms of audience penetration, usage, and profitability, says a Citigroup spokesperson, who declined to provide the size of the card program.

Source: Jason Fargo, "Gay Marketing: A Profitable Niche?" *Credit Card Management* (March 1999): 48–54.

customer segmentation across other dimensions.[25] Although their segmentation efforts may be justifiable on the basis of profitability, competition, and risk factors, marketing executives have to be careful that the end result of their segmentation efforts will not go against accepted ethical standards (see Manager's Corner 7.2).

DIFFERENTIATION AND BRANDING

Another technique, which is more normally considered under product strategy, is **product differentiation**. Usually applicable to commercial organizations, product differentiation is used to give products unique identities to distinguish them from their competitors (in particular, between competitors in the same market from the same company).

---

25. "HUD to Test for Mortgage Lending Discrimination," *ABA Bank Compliance* 20 (January 1999): 6.

The epitome of this process is **branding**. The product is given a *character*, an *image*, almost like a personality. This is based first of all on a name (the brand), but then almost as much on the other factors affecting image—the packaging and, in particular, advertising. This all attempts to make the brand its own separate market, or at least its own segment, so that shoppers buy Heinz Baked Beans rather than ordinary baked beans. This sometimes succeeds to the extent that brands (such as Kleenex, Hoover, Netscape, Scotch tape, Vaseline, and Xerox) become almost generic.

> Another technique, normally **considered under product strategy,** is product differentiation.

www.heinz.com
www.kimberly-clark.com
www.hoover.com
www.netscape.com
www.3m.com
www.unilever.ca
www.xerox.com

A firm's branding strategy is to make its products different from its competitors in such a way that customers are convinced that they are superior. This can be done by making the physical product different or by making the way in which the customer perceives the product different. These factors can be achieved by packaging differences; variations in size, shape, or quality; gimmicks; after-sales service provision; or perhaps most importantly by promotional activity usually linked to at least one of the differences. The main aim of media advertising, or "above the line" promotion, is to create a definite and distinct brand image.[26]

Recently, branding has been applied to nonprofit activities. In this case, branding is used as a means of improving awareness of what is available and of differentiating between alternative offerings designed for different segments. Probably the most well-known telephone number for emergency is 911, and it is clearly distinguished from any other number. However, many nonprofit activities are not consolidated into one centralized organization. Therefore, *competition* between charities can sometimes be as cutthroat as any in the commercial sector. It has even reached the stage where major charity organizations, such as the United Way and the March of Dimes, have adopted *logos* in an attempt to differentiate their services.

www.unitedway.org
www.modimes.org

BRAND MONOPOLY

Economically, the **brand** is a device designed to create a *monopoly*—or at least some form of *imperfect competition*—so that the brand owner can obtain some of the benefits that accrue to a monopoly, particularly those related to decreased price competition. Think about brand names like Coca-Cola, Häagen Dazs, Sony, and Perrier. In this context, most branding is established by promotional means. However, there is also a legal dimension, for it is essential that the brand names and trademarks be protected by all means available. The monopoly may also be extended, or even created, by patents and intellectual property (or copyright, as it used to be called in a narrower context).

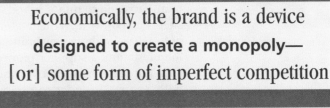

> Economically, the brand is a device **designed to create a monopoly—** [or] some form of imperfect competition

www.coke.com
www.haagendazs.com
www.sony.com
www.perrier.fr

BRANDING POLICIES

Once established in the minds of consumers, brand names can build a strong brand equity.[27] **Brand equity** is considered a powerful asset that has an economic value. There are three levels of branding policies.

26. Trevor Watkins, *The Economics of the Brand: A Marketing Analysis* (New York: McGraw-Hill, 1986).
27. P. Rajan Varadarajan and Satish Jayachandran, "Marketing Strategy: An Assessment of the State of the Field and Outlook," *Journal of the Academy of Marketing Science* 27 (spring 1999): 120–143.

www.ibm.com
www.mercedesbenz.com
www.blackanddecker
    .com
www.cadbury.co.uk
www.sevenup.com
www.mcdonalds.com
www.unilever.ca

www.pg.com

www.generalmills.com

www.victoriassecret.com
www.bathandbody.com

www.mattel.com

www.saralee.com
www.kiwicare.com
www.leggs.com
www.marriott.com
www.fairfieldinn.com
www.ramada.com
www.rodewayinn.com

- **Company name.** Often, especially in the industrial sector, it is just the company's name that is promoted (leading to one of the most powerful statements of branding; the well-known saying "No one ever got fired for buying IBM").
- **Family branding.** In this case a very strong brand name (or company name) is made the vehicle for a range of products (for example, Mercedes or Black & Decker) or even a range of subsidiary brands (such as Cadbury's Dairy Milk, Cadbury's Flake, or Cadbury's Wispa).
- **Individual branding.** Each brand has a separate name (such as Seven-Up or McDonald's), which may even compete against other brands from the same company (for example, Persil, Omo, and Surf are all owned by Unilever).

In terms of existing products, brands may be developed in a number of ways.

BRAND EXTENSION.   An existing strong brand name can be used as a vehicle for new or modified products. For example, after many years of running just one brand, Coca-Cola launched Diet Coke and Cherry Coke. Procter & Gamble, in particular, has made regular use of this device, extending its strongest brand names (such as Ivory Soap) into new markets (the very successful Ivory Detergent, and more recently Ivory Shampoo). General Mills has also adopted the brand extension strategy by introducing variants of its Cheerio brand cereal, including Honey Nut Cheerios, Apple Cinnamon Cheerios, Multi-Grain Cheerios, and, most recently, Frosted Cheerios. Victoria's Secret is rolling out its new cosmetics line; its sister company, Bath & Body Works, just added a glitter line for girls called Art Stuff that includes cosmetics, body care, and accessories. The line was designed "for girls beginning to develop their own personal care routines." Each year, 120 to 175 totally new brands are introduced into America's supermarkets. However, approximately 40 percent of the new brands were actually brand extensions.[28] Brand-extension strategy is designed to capture as wide a shelf space in the retail store as possible in pursuit of *shelf space monopoly*. Marketing in Action 7.2 describes how this strategy may have hurt Mattel.

MULTIBRANDS.   In a market that is fragmented among a number of brands, a supplier can deliberately choose to launch totally new brands in apparent competition with its own existing strong brand (and often with identical product characteristics). This is done simply to soak up some of the share of the market that will in any case go to minor brands. The rationale is that having 3 out of 12 brands in such a market will give a greater overall share than having 1 out of 10 (even if much of the share of these new brands is taken from the existing one). In its most extreme manifestation, a supplier pioneering a new brand that it believes will be particularly attractive may choose immediately to launch a second brand in competition with its first, in order to pre-empt others entering the market. Individual brand names naturally allow greater flexibility by permitting a variety of different products, of differing quality, to be sold without confusing the consumer's perception of what business the company is in or diluting higher quality products.[29]

Once again, Procter & Gamble is a leading exponent of this philosophy, running as many as 10 detergent brands in the U.S. market alone. This also increases the total *shelf space* it receives on supermarket shelves. Sara Lee, on the other hand, uses multibrands from Sara Lee cakes through Kiwi polishes to L'Eggs pantyhose to keep the very different parts of their business separate. In the hotel business, Marriott uses the name Fairfield Inns for its budget chain, and Ramada uses Rodeway for its own budget chain.

Although multibranding has worked very well for many companies in the United States, it is not necessarily the case in other countries. In Japan, consumers

---

28. Byron M. Sharp, "Managing Brand Extension," *Journal of Consumer Marketing* 10, no. 3 (1993): 11–17.
29. C. J. Roberts and G. M. McDonald, "Alternative Naming Strategies: Family versus Individual Brand Names," *Management Decision* 26, no. 6 (1989): 31–37.

Marketing in Action 7.2

How did Mattel go wrong with Barbie?

Founded in 1945, Mattel, Inc. (www.mattel .com) designs, manufactures, and markets family products. In 1959, Mattel introduced "Barbie," the doll that resembled a teenage fashion model and was targeted to the three- to seven-year-old-girl market. Since its introduction, approximately one billion Barbie dolls have been sold.

In 1987, Mattel began implementing a strategy of maximizing its core brands. As a part of this strategy, the company introduced its first "Holiday Barbie" in 1988. Holiday Barbie was Mattel's foray into what it saw as a new segmentation strategy based on designing different professions and activities for Barbie dolls in an attempt to entice girls to want several of the dolls.

The new strategy worked because American girls averaged eight Barbie dolls each by the late 1990s. Additionally, the Holiday Barbie

concept had taken off in the collector's market. This adult market purchased approximately one-half of all 1989 Holiday Barbies. By 1996, collectors constituted a $220-million business.

With collectible Barbies in huge demand by both young girls and collectors, Mattel's operational strategy was one of increased production and expanded distribution. Unfortunately, thousands of the 1997 Holiday Barbie dolls were left on store shelves. By early 1998, the specialty doll was selling for $9.99 at Toys "R" Us. Other exclusive $100 collector Barbie dolls were selling for $29.99 on the Home Shopping Network. By December 1998, Mattel was predicting fourth-quarter sales $500 million below expectations. As such, Mattel's stock dropped 30 percent in one day.

What happened? How did Mattel segment the Barbie doll market? What would you have done differently?

Sources: www.mattel.com; Lisa Bannon, "Goodbye Dolly: Mattel Tries to Adjust as 'Holiday Barbie' Leaves Under a Cloud," *Wall Street Journal*, June 7, 1999, A1+.

tend to associate the quality and reliability of products with the reputation of the company. While maintaining a multibrand strategy, Procter & Gamble became successful in the Japanese market once it began to emphasize its corporate logo more than its brand names.

CANNIBALIZATION. This is a particular problem of a *multibrand* approach, in which an organization's new brand takes business away from its established one. This may be acceptable (indeed to be expected) if there is a net gain overall. Alternatively, it may be the price the organization is willing to pay for shifting its position in the market, the new product being one stage in this process. Some of the alternative scenarios[30] are illustrated in Figure 7.10. However, the cost may sometimes unexpectedly reach an unacceptable level in terms of the attrition of existing profitable business.

COBRANDING. Consumers usually buy a bundle of complementary products. For example, many consumers add raisins, chocolate chips, or peanuts, among other things, when they eat cereal. Noticing this, General Foods and Hershey Foods have teamed up to create a brand of cereal called Reese's™ Peanut Butter Puffs. This **cobranding** strategy helps to fill a market segment not tapped by either company's existing products.

www.hersheys.com

Sometimes, the complementary nature of the products may not be as obvious, yet cobranding may prove to be beneficial to companies. For example, frequent flyer programs encourage people to accumulate mileage by flying with certain airlines. Citibank noticed that many frequent flyers charged their tickets on their credit cards and now offers a MasterCard cobranded with American Airlines' AAdvantage Frequent Flyer Program. Thus its card users can collect mileage for

www.citibank.com
www.mastercard.com
wwwr1.aa.com

---

30. M. B. Taylor, "Cannibalism in Multibrand Firms," *Journal of Consumer Marketing* 3, no. 2 (1986): 69–75.

Figure 7.10

Scenarios of brand cannibalization

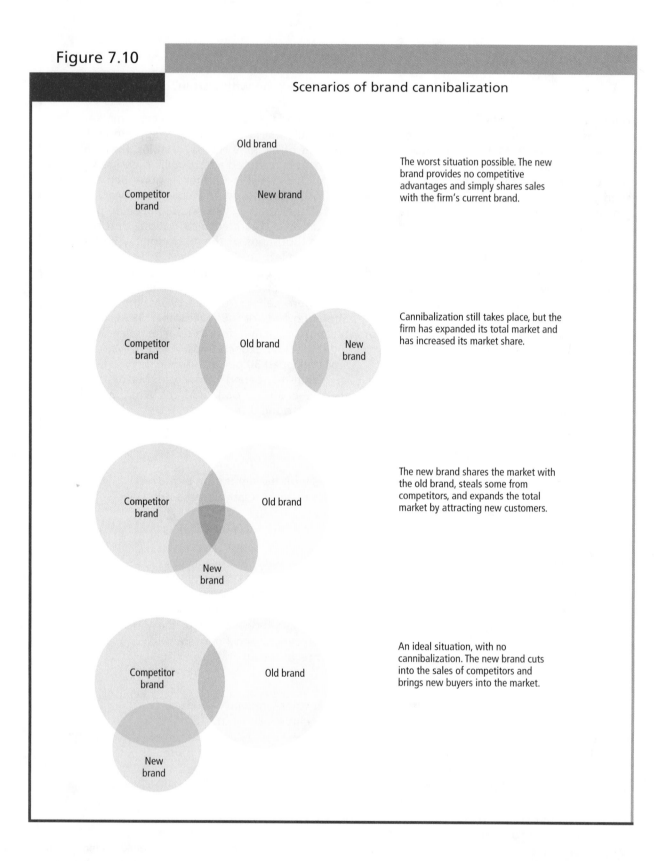

The worst situation possible. The new brand provides no competitive advantages and simply shares sales with the firm's current brand.

Cannibalization still takes place, but the firm has expanded its total market and has increased its market share.

The new brand shares the market with the old brand, steals some from competitors, and expands the total market by attracting new customers.

An ideal situation, with no cannibalization. The new brand cuts into the sales of competitors and brings new buyers into the market.

every dollar charged on their cards. Similarly, recognizing that frequent flyers call home from out of town, MCI has joined American Airlines' Frequent Flyer Program so that MCI customers can collect mileage every time they make long-distance calls.

www.wcom.com

PRIVATE AND GENERIC BRANDS.   With the emergence of strong retailers, the **private brand** has also emerged—the retailer's own branded product (or service). When the retailer has a particularly strong identity (such as Marks & Spencer and Sears), this store brand may be able to compete against even the strongest brand leaders and may dominate those markets, which are not otherwise strongly branded. For example, even though manufactured by Whirlpool, Amana, and others, Sears Roebuck's Kenmore brand of home appliances has a reputation for reliability and durability and competes directly with General Electric and Maytag.

www.marks-and-spencer
.co.uk
www.sears.com
www.whirlpool.com
www.amana.com
www.sears.com
/kenmore/
www.ge.com
www.maytag.com

Companies with national brands became concerned that such private brands might displace all other brands (as they have done in Marks & Spencer outlets), but the evidence is that consumers generally expect to see supermarkets and department stores display something over 50 percent (and preferably over 60 percent) of brands other than those of the retailer. Therefore, the strongest independent national brands such as Kellogg's and Heinz, which have maintained their marketing investments, should continue to flourish.

www.kelloggs.com
www.heinz.com

At the same time, **generic brands** (that is, effectively unbranded goods) have also emerged. These made a positive virtue of saving the cost of almost all marketing activities by emphasizing the lack of advertising and, especially, the plain packaging (which was, however, often simply a vehicle for a different kind of image). The penetration of generic brands peaked in the 1980s, and most consumers still seem to be looking for the qualities that the conventional brand provides. For generics to continue to attract the consumer, they will need to be positioned by the retailer as a sensible value alternative and backed by the retailer's guarantee of acceptable and consistent quality.[31]

DIFFERENTIATION OF SERVICES

Marketers may have difficulty differentiating their own service offerings from those of their competitors. The service company can add innovative supplementary features to distinguish its core service offerings. **Core services** are the necessary outputs of an organization that consumers are looking for, whereas **supplementary services** are either indispensable for the execution of the core service or are available only to improve the overall quality of the service offerings.[32] For example, the core service in the car rental industry is providing customers with safe and well-functioning vehicles for transportation. The facilitating services may include spe-

> a strong reputation gained
> **by providing excellent facilitating services**
> is a key to . . . long-term competitiveness

cial benefits for frequent renters, ease of making reservations, speedy check-in, and availability of maps. Competitive advantage is increasingly determined by a service firm's capability in providing facilitating services to differentiate itself from its competitors.[33] While such *service innovations* are relatively easy to copy, a strong reputation gained early on by providing excellent facilitating services is a key to a service firm's long-term competitiveness.

---

31. B. F. Harris and R. A. Strong, "Marketing Strategies in the Age of Generics," *Journal of Marketing* 49 (fall 1985): 70–81.

32. Christopher H. Lovelock, "A Basic Toolkit for Service Managers," in *Managing Services: Marketing, Operations, and Human Resources,* ed. Christopher H. Lovelock (Upper Saddle River, N.J.: Prentice Hall, 1992): 17–30.

33. Janet Y. Murray and Masaaki Kotabe, "Sourcing Strategies of U.S. Service Companies: A Modified Transaction-Cost Analysis," *Strategic Management Journal* (forthcoming in 2000).

SUMMARY

There are a number of ways of defining markets, but for a marketer the key definition is in defining who the customer is. Even so, there are different categories: customers, users, and prospects. This categorization leads to the concepts of penetration and brand (market) share.

Within markets there may be *segments,* which a producer may target to optimize use of scarce resources. The viability of these segments depends on size, identity, relevance, and access. The identification of market segments requires a number of activities including background investigation, qualitative research, quantitative research, analysis, implementation, and segmentation/positioning. A major aid to positioning is usually offered by two-dimensional maps based on the two most critical dimensions identified by statistical analysis.

Branding is the most powerful marketing device for differentiation, which may, in effect, create a near *monopoly.* Once established, a brand name has a strong *brand equity.* Branding policies may be based on company name, family branding, and individual branding. These may be further developed by brand extensions and multibrands, but this may be limited by cannibalism. *Cobranding* by companies that market complementary products helps fill market segments not met by them individually. *Private brands* and *generic brands* are also becoming increasingly important in price-sensitive markets.

QUESTIONS FOR REVIEW

1. What is the basic element of a market? What are the differences between customers, users, and prospects? What is the difference between penetration and brand share?

2. What are the tests for viability that should be applied to segments within a market?

3. What steps may be involved in practical segmentation?

4. In the process of segmentation, what marketing research techniques may be used, and how?

5. What are the differences between segmentation, market targeting, and brand positioning? How does each work?

6. How may maps best be used to aid positioning?

7. What segmentation strategies may be employed? Where does niche marketing fit in? How may industrial marketing differ?

8. What benefits may be obtained by branding? How may this create a near monopoly?

9. What branding strategies may be employed? How may brands be extended?

QUESTIONS FOR DISCUSSION

1. BMW is easing its all-new X5—which it calls a SAV, or Sports Activity Vehicle—out of the closet. Claiming that it has opened a new market segment, BMW says its X5 will be characterized by its high seating position, coupled with "exceptional handling on roads of any kind throughout the world." The X5—developed from the ground up—will have a unitized body and independent suspension, front and rear. Coupled with the independent suspension will be a four-wheel-drive system that will have four-wheel application of the brakes, plus BMW's All Season Traction and Dynamic Stability Control. Power for all of this will come from three engine choices: a V-8, a straight six, or a six-cylinder diesel engine.

   All of this is packaged in a vehicle with an overall length of 183 inches that has wheel wells designed to handle monster wheels and tires up to 19 inches. Other measurements indicate the X5 will be spacious: Height is 67.7 inches and it's a wide 73.6 inches. Safety will be addressed with a total of 10 inflatable air bags located in front, at the sides, and higher-placed bags for head protection of both front and rear passengers. Comfort features include a multifunction steering wheel, electric rear seat rests, rear climate controls, and a high-line audio system. No prices have been set.

   Write a brief profile of prospective BMW X5 customers in the targeted segment based on the above product description—their lifestyle, values, income, and consumption behavior.

2. Do you think the following market segmentation criteria bring market opportunities to some product marketers? Are these segments viable for certain products? If so, identify them. Also, identify some leading brands currently positioned for people in these segments. Can you think of a few of your own innovative product concepts targeted at these segments?

   - People who are into fitness and into working out and believe in total fitness lifestyle. For them, it is just as important to take care of the outside as the inside.

   - They have the speed bug. The 25- to 30-year-olds save $800 working for three months at a local bar and blow it all on a weekend course in race-car driving. They are tired of recreational vehicles that now clog the showrooms.

   - Online shoppers who tend to be more affluent than average when compared to those who are online but don't shop ($65,000 median annual household income vs. $59,000, respectively). They cut across all ages, although those 50 and over are more likely than their younger counterparts (aged 18 to 24) to make purchases online.

   - Single mothers segment, which includes divorced or never-married women in their 30s who have a child. The single population in general is growing. In 1970, there were 3.4 million single mothers in the United States; now there are nearly 10 million. More important, women with the increased independence for whom husbands are less of an economic necessity.

   - Segregated racial population in the eight largest metropolitan areas in the United States: New York, Los Angeles, Chicago, Washington-Baltimore, San Francisco-Oakland, Philadelphia, Detroit, and Dallas-Fort Worth. In the 1990s, most residences and, often, most workplaces are located beyond big-city boundaries in a new kind of suburbia. These eight metropolitan areas account for one quarter of the total population of the United States. Over this period, while population shifts have occurred, segregated residence patterns remain intact.

3. Anheuser, Miller, Coors, and Stroh's currently control 80 percent of the beer market in the United States. Lately, these brewers have been on a rampage purchasing microbrewers that may produce only 15,000 barrels a year (Anheuser produces 41.4 million barrels of Budweiser every year). What are these major brewers searching for? Once purchased, the majors tend not to apply their massive marketing muscle to promote their new beers. Why is that? Further, why do the majors go to great lengths to hide their ownership of these microbrewers from their customers? What is wrong/right with this marketing and acquisition strategy by the majors?

4. The leading brand of ready-to-eat (RTE) breakfast cereals in the United States has under a 4 percent market share. What kind of branding strategy is this? What challenges would face a potential entrant to the RTE cereal market? How could they be overcome?

5. Positioning maps, which were discussed in this chapter, map products along product characteristics. Discuss why more is not always better; give four real-life examples (Hint: i.e., setting a lower price can decrease sales).

6. Some experts predict that in the near future, most American households will be receiving over 200 television channels. Do you agree or disagree with this prediction? As the management of NBC, ABC, or CBS, what are your long-term positioning strategies? What would be the challenges of a niche player in this market?

FURTHER READINGS

Berthon, Pierre, James M. Hulbert, and Leyland F. Pitt. "Brand Management Prognostications." *Sloan Management Review* 40 (winter 1999): 53–65.

Dubow, Joel S. "Occasion-Based vs. User-Based Benefit Segmentation: A Case Study." *Journal of Advertising Research* 32 (March-April 1992): 32–39.

Helsen, Kristiaan, Kamel Jedidi, and Wayne S. DeSarbo. "A New Approach to Country Segmentation Utilizing Multinational Diffusion Patterns." *Journal of Marketing* 57 (October 1993): 60–71.

Kamakura, Wagner A. "Value Segmentation: A Model for the Measurement of Values and Value Systems." *Journal of Consumer Research* 18 (September 1991): 208–218.

Leclerc, France, Bernd H. Schmitt, and Laurette Dube. "Foreign Branding and Its Effects on Product Perceptions and Attitudes." *Journal of Marketing Research* 31 (May 1994): 263–270.

Lovelock, Christopher H., ed. *Managing Services: Marketing, Operations, and Human Resources.* Upper Saddle River, N.J.: Prentice Hall, 1992.

McDonald, Malcolm, and Ian Dunbar. *Market Segmentation: A Step-by-Step Approach to Creating Profitable Market Segments.* Basingstoke: Macmillan Business, 1995.

Michman, Ronald D. *Lifestyle Segmentation.* New York: Praeger, 1991.

Mitchell, W. W., and Peter J. McGoldrick. "The Role of Geodemographics in Segmenting and Targeting Consumer Markets: A Delphi Study." *European Journal of Marketing* 28 (May 1994): 54–72.

Rangan, V. Kasturi, Roland T. Moriarty, and Gordon S. Swartz. "Segmenting Customers in Mature Industrial Markets." *Journal of Marketing* 56 (October 1992): 72–82.

Rao, Chatrathi P., and Zhengyuan Wang. "Evaluating Alternative Segmentation Strategies in Standard Industrial Markets." *European Journal of Marketing* 29 (February 1995): 58–75.

Srivastava, Rajendra K., and Allan D. Shocker. *Brand Equity: A Perspective on Its Meaning and Measurement.* Cambridge, Mass.: Marketing Science Institute, 1991.

Varadarajan, P. Rajan, and Satish Jayachandran. "Marketing Strategy: An Assessment of the State of the Field and Outlook." *Journal of the Academy of Marketing Science* 27 (spring 1999): 120–143.

chapter 8

So far we have primarily dealt with finding out what the customer wants. But this is not sufficient—the responses of the supplier to these wants are also critical. These responses are delivered through the toolbox of the marketer in the form of the marketing mix, which consists of product, price, promotion, and distribution. Even though all these elements of the marketing mix are important, the product, be it a good, a service, an idea, or a place, is typically the most visible component and serves as the focal point for all marketing mix aspects. In addition, research has shown that a unique, superior product is the most important success factor.[1]

A good product might sell even if the promotion is mediocre. A bad product will rarely obtain repeat sales, no matter how brilliant the promotion is. Of course even a good product might not do well if poorly promoted. Unilever developed a toothpaste dispenser that added stripes to the paste coming out of the tube. In the United States this feature was emphasized with the slogan, "Looks like fun, cleans like crazy." The product was a hit, but repeat sales were dismal, because the "fun" justified only one purchase. In the United Kingdom, however, the company sold the product on the basis that the stripe contained fluoride and was an essential component—and sales are still going strong. Manager's Corner 8.1 shows how automakers have to adjust their products to appeal to customers around the world.

www.unilever.com

Manager's Corner 8.1

Different global strategies by automakers

Automakers around the world are trying to figure out what customers in 200 countries want—and to beat their competitors to the punch. However, they are faced with the most fundamental global marketing challenge in their quest: Although the customer's desire for cost savings drives the automakers' idea for global automobiles, the danger is that the resulting vehicles will be too compromised to appeal to specific markets.

Ignoring local marketing input is a sure way to imperil a marketer's international aspirations. For example, Germany's Volkswagen AG (www.vw.com) operated for years with the philosophy that only one car was good enough for the whole world. VW marketing executives in the United States tried in vain to include items such as cup holders and American-style seat-back release levers in cars destined for the U.S. market. VW is now rethinking its strategy, as are many of its competitors that have seen their sales and profitability slip as a result of not paying enough attention to what customers want.

Nissan (www.nissan.com) determined that it cannot afford to build, design, and market completely distinct models, such as the Infiniti Q45 and J30, just for the U.S. market. Instead, future Infiniti models will be variations of cars designed for affluent Japanese customers as well as for U.S. buyers. Nissan strategists look at the marketing requirements of Japan, the United States, and Europe to determine which customer preferences overlap. Then Nissan's

---

1. Robert G. Cooper, "New Products: The Factors That Drive Success," *International Marketing Review* 11, no. 1 (1994): 60.

export, research and development, and accounting departments decide which car model to manufacture for each market. There is still a strong economic need to manufacture similar products even when working in different markets.

France's Renault (www.renault.com) has taken the middle road between developing a world car and one for a single market. More than 90 percent of the company's sales are generated in Europe. Minor alterations—such as better air conditioning in southern markets and stronger heaters in the Nordic countries—are made, but the body engine, transmission, and chassis are identical for each model.

Ford's (www.fordvehicles.com) approach is best seen in its introduction of the Mondeo in Europe and its sister cars, the Ford Contour and Mercury Mystique, in the North American market. The Mondeo varies slightly for the different European markets. For example, for some markets a sun roof is standard, whereas for others an air conditioner may be included. The Mondeo's image will vary from market to market, because the economies of scale do not carry over to positioning. In Italy, where the Mondeo competes against Fiat (www.fiat.com), the Mondeo is not seen as an upmarket car. But in Germany, where the Mondeo competes with Mercedes (www.usa.mercedes.com) and BMW (www.bmw.com), Ford advertises with the aim of making the Mondeo appear more upscale.

Sources: Ray Serafin, "Auto Marketers Gas Up for World Car Drive," *Advertising Age,* January 16, 1995, 1–16; "Another New Model . . ." *Economist,* January 7, 1995, 52–53; Alex Taylor III, "New Ideas from Europe's Automakers," *Fortune,* December 12, 1994, 159–172.

www.compaq.com
www.ibm.com

The importance of the product was demonstrated in the early days of the market for portable PCs. Compaq, then a small start-up company, and IBM met head on. It should have been no contest. Yet the customers judged the Compaq product to be better. Eventually IBM had to withdraw its product from the market and reorganize its approach.

THE PRODUCT PACKAGE

www.campbellsoups.com

The customer's perception of the good or service is a complex construct. For example, in the case of branded products, such as Campbell's soups, the physical product itself is submerged under layers of image, and emotional involvement build up from childhood, to which decades of advertising and promotion have contributed. Even with industrial goods, such as computers, it is often the intangibles that are most important. One therefore differentiates three product aspects:

- The **core product** is the good or service itself—the bare-bones version.
- The **tangible product** indicates elements such as design, color, packaging, and any other physical dimensions that provide benefits to the customer.
- The **augmented product** is further enriched by including warranty and service benefits, the reputation of the firm, and the psychological benefits conveyed by the product.

Delineating the dimensions of the augmentation may be difficult. For example, confusion may be caused by reading too much into superficial answers by consumers. When asked why they use or prefer a product, consumers may provide strongly rationalized answers or comment mainly on a product's most obvious purposes. When prodded, consumers may then find major differences between products that in reality do not matter to them at all. Similarly, consumers may also be unable to evaluate the true benefits of new or planned products because they do not fully comprehend its purpose and capabilities. For example, few consumers would have been able to understand, much less comprehensively list, the benefits of the introduction of the Walkman radio or the VCR when these technologies were in the planning stage. This is why sophisticated research techniques have been developed to explore consumers' hidden motivations.

THE PRODUCT AUDIT

For existing goods or services, the starting point is to decide exactly what the firm is offering. This is not as obvious as it might seem at first. For example, before Planet Hollywood filed for Chapter 11 bankruptcy protection, CEO Robert Earl stated, "We're not in the restaurant business, we're in the lifestyle and trade-mark business."[2] Therefore all the features of the brand need to be reviewed, per-haps even by outsiders, because the brand manager who has become used to seeing the brand perform—in the way it has always performed—may have overlooked its other potential features.

www.planethollywood
.com

> For existing goods or services,
> **the starting point is to decide**
> exactly what the firm is offering.

The main task of a product audit is to look at goods or services in terms of what benefits the customer derives from them. What counts is what the customer sees. An audit might examine some of these factors, such as:

- What market segment does this brand address?
- Who are the existing and prospective customers?
- What benefits are these customers and prospective customers seeking?
- How does the product fulfill these customer needs and wants?
- How does it compare with competitive products?

These questions can be addressed in the form of a benefit analysis that examines the specific benefits that the products offer in the context of what the customer needs and wants. The list of customer benefits must be very carefully compiled, often by using sophisticated market research, to see it from the customer's viewpoint. The list also needs to be clearly prioritized to show what the customer considers most important. Otherwise the temptation is for the supplier to concentrate on those areas where the organization can excel, regardless of the fact that they are relatively unimportant to the customer. Nevertheless, the differentiating benefits that the supplier can offer, when compared to competitive offerings, may be very important. Equally, the benefits offered by the organization itself should not be ignored, because elements such as service, support, and corporate reputation often have a major influence on the customer's buying decision.

Such a review may be problematic for some organizations in the nonprofit sector. Members of such organizations often have a core product that is considered unchangeable because of beliefs, convictions, training, or the law. However, without a product audit, the value of the organization's activities can be lessened in two ways. First, preoccupation with a core product can blind members of the organization to the overall needs of their customers and obscure ways in which the product can be augmented to increase customer satisfaction. Second, additions and alternatives sometimes become rigidly associated with the core products even though they are not essential to the achievement of the organization's prime goal.[3]

2. Monika Guttman, "Why the Stars Orbit Planet Hollywood," *U.S. News and World Report,* November 27, 1995, 60.
3. K. Blois, "Marketing for Non-Profit Organizations," in *The Marketing Book,* ed. Michael J. Baker (Oxford: Butter-worth Heinemann, 1987), 45.

PRODUCT STRATEGY

A product strategy for reaching long-term product objectives needs to be developed specifically for each product. Market penetration, product development, market development, and diversification are the four basic product strategies for growth in volume and profit, which is what shareholders conventionally demand.

MARKET PENETRATION

The most frequently used strategy is to take the existing product in the existing market and try to obtain an increased share of that market. The two ways in which this can be achieved is by increasing sales to existing customers and by finding new customers in the same market. The first strategy means persuading users to use more of the product on more occasions, perhaps by replacing an indirect competitor—for example, inducing people to drink orange juice rather than coffee at breakfast. Alternatively, the strategy may be to use the product more often without any need to take business from competitors. Arm & Hammer baking soda provides a fitting example. As the firm's advertisements tell us, this versatile product can be used for cleaning countertops, removing burned-on foods in the kitchen, and creating a home spa in your bathroom. It can also keep the refrigerator smelling good, and, most importantly, when the baking soda is poured down the sink, it will keep the disposal fresh smelling. Once that is done, the customer is in need of another baking soda purchase.

www.armhammer.com

The second strategy takes business directly from competitors by increasing both penetration and market share. This can be achieved either by changing the product offering or by changing the positioning of the product offering. On occasion, however, this result is also obtained by serendipity, when the environment changes in favor of the firm. For example, a few decades ago, canned tuna fish in the United States was mainly sold packed in oil. When Japanese firms entered the U.S. market, they decide to occupy a new (albeit very small) niche by selling their tuna packed in water. Over time consumer tastes and preferences have changed, mainly due to dietary considerations. As a result, the segment of consumers desiring tuna packed in water has outgrown the segment preferring the oil-packed tuna.

PRODUCT DEVELOPMENT

This strategy involves a relatively major modification of the good or service, such as quality, style, performance, or variety. An offer of "high-performance" versions of existing car models can be used to extend the ranges to cover additional customers. Similarly, adding vitamins to orange juice will possibly cause some existing users to increase their usage but may also attract new users. Manager's Corner 8.2 shows how a services firm develops its products to cover its current customers and to entice new ones to come on board.

MARKET DEVELOPMENT

This strategy finds new uses for the existing product, thereby taking it into entirely new markets. Apple Computers did so by persuading customers to use its personal computers for desktop publishing and continues to do so with the addition of software. Pharmaceutical firms benefited greatly when it was discovered that one aspirin a day can help prevent heart attacks. Another market development alternative is to aim at a broader market. Going international is an excellent way to implement such a strategy; it offers new markets and new (potential) users. In that sense, any export operation can be viewed as strategic market development.

www.apple.com

Manager's Corner 8.2

Financial powerhouses boost online services

Merrill Lynch (www.ml.com) found out that opposition to cybertrading was a threat to its own health. Its new Internet brokerage strategy is described as a daring bid to get back to the cutting edge of the brokerage industry. The nation's largest full-service securities firm, whose customers pay commissions of up to several hundred dollars per trade, now offers online trading for as little as $29.95 a trade. The company's new online plan will be built on a large-scale, discount-trading operation in which Merrill Lynch adds key features to its computer systems and expands its existing customer-service centers.

Thousands of Merrill Lynch's five million customers are expected to switch to a new fee-based account that offers unlimited online and offline trading, either with a broker, online or over the phone to an order taker, in return for an annual account fee equaling about 0.2 percent to 1 percent of the account's assets. Its minimum fee will be $1,500 a year. This "core relationship account," as Merrill insiders call it, is expected to include free research reports, financial-planning help, and basic banking with free ATM transactions. That discount Internet account will feature Web and telephone trading for the cut-rate fees. The company will also develop systems to let customers open accounts online without a broker and get account updates immediately after they trade.

Sources: Kim James and Rynecki David, "Merrill Lynch Hears Net's Call, Firm Breaks Tradition, Integrates Cyber-trading with Broker Service," *USA Today*, June 2, 1999, 1B; Rebecca Buckman, "Merrill Online: A Bull Enters the Arena—Ambitious Plan Could Result in Lower Fees," *Wall Street Journal*, June 1, 1999, C1.

DIVERSIFICATION

This quantum leap, to a new product and a new market, involves more risk and is often undertaken by organizations that find themselves in markets that have limited, often declining, potential. One obvious example is the tobacco companies that have diversified—often at considerable cost—into areas as varied as cosmetics and engineering. However, diversification can also be a positive move to extend the application of existing expertise. For example, the Disney Corporation diversified from cartoons to theme parks to network broadcasting (see Marketing in Action 8.1). Heinz has steadily and successfully extended beyond its core ketchup business; its Weight Watchers brand is now worth hundreds of millions of dollars. But it should be noted that, like many other similarly successful diversifications, Heinz's strategy was built on a logical extension of the company's existing strengths. Firms must beware of diversification that is undertaken simply because the grass looks greener in the new market. A company needs a systemic analysis of what sets it apart from its competitors. Excelling in one market does not guarantee success in a new or even related one. Managers must ask whether their company has every strategic asset necessary to establish a competitive advantage in the territory it hopes to conquer.[4] Many companies have found out the hard way that diversification without transferable strengths may not pay off. Consider the experience of the Coca-Cola company, long heralded for its intimate knowledge of consumers, its marketing and branding expertise, and its superior distribution capabilities. Based on those strategic assets, Coca-Cola decided to acquire its way into the wine business in which those strengths were imperative. The company quickly learned, however, that it lacked a critical competence—knowledge of the wine business. Having 90 percent of what

disney.go.com
www.heinz.com
www.weightwatchers.com

www.coke.com

> Many companies have found out the **hard way that diversification without** transferable strengths may not pay off.

4. "The Critical Questions for Diversification Success," *Harvard Business Review* (November/December 1997): 97.

Marketing in Action 8.1

Creating new products and services at Disney Imagineering

A \$23 billion conglomerate, Disney's (disney .go.com) 75-year-old corporate mission is to provide quality entertainment to all ages. Worldwide, consumers have experienced Disney's traditional product offerings at Disneyland Resort (Los Angeles, California, USA), Walt Disney World (Orlando, Florida, USA), Disneyland Paris (France), or Tokyo Disneyland (Japan).

While continuing to extend on Disney's traditional forms of theme parks with, for example, Disney's Animal Kingdom and the new Tomorrowland at Disneyland, the company has also ventured into nontraditional entertainment. In 1998, the company began initiatives such as ESPNZone, Radio Disney, ESPN Classic sports channel, and cable's Toon Disney. Additionally, Disney acquired Starwave, created its Go Network, invested in Infoseek, and started the Disney Cruise Line.

Disney has provided its magic for generations. Walt Disney Imagineers is the think tank behind Disney's magic. Disney's Imagineers are over 2,000 creative, technical, and development wizards who bring Disney's entertainment to the consumer marketplace. These experts are constantly on a quest to both develop new product offerings to and improve upon current product offerings. One of the most recent Imagineering examples is Disney's Animal Kingdom. Towering over the Kingdom is the "Tree of Life." This 14-story creation took seven years from concept to completion. DisneyQuest, a family-oriented interactive technology offering, will allow the Imagineers to lead Disney into the future with Internet-related products.

As a creative company, Disney must continue to innovate. What do the Imagineers need to do to take the company into the 21st century? Is high-tech entertainment where these creative wizards should focus their energies? Will the group need to shorten its product development cycle to remain competitive in the vast world of entertainment?

Sources: http://disney.go.com; Ronald Grover, "Disney's Mickey Mensa Club," *Business Week*, March 8, 1999, 108.

it took to succeed in the new industry was not enough, because the missing 10 percent—the ability to make quality wine—was the most critical component of success.[5]

THE ANSOFF MATRIX

The four basic product strategies are often presented in the form of the Ansoff Matrix (see Figure 8.1).[6] The four alternatives are simply the logical combinations of the two available positioning variables of products and markets. In this matrix, the element of risk increases the further the strategy moves away from known quantities (the existing product and the existing market). Thus product development, which requires a new product, and market development, which requires a new market, involve a greater risk than penetration. Diversification, when both the product and market are new, generally carries the greatest risk of all. For this reason, most marketing activity revolves around penetration, which limits the usefulness of the Ansoff Matrix.

Similar to the original Ansoff Matrix, Peter Drucker has identified three kinds of opportunities:[7]

- **Additive.** The additive opportunity more fully exploits already existing resources and does not change the character of the business. In Ansoff's terms, it is the new product in an existing market or the existing product in a new market.

- **Breakthrough.** This typically changes the fundamental economic characteristics and capacity of the business. It is the high-risk extreme of diversification, which Ansoff warns against.

---

5. "To Diversify or Not to Diversify," *Harvard Business Review* (November/December 1997): 97.

6. H. Igor Ansoff, "Strategies for Diversification," *Harvard Business Review* 35, no. 5 (September/October, 1957): 116.

7. Peter Drucker, *Managing for Results* (New York: Butterworth Heinemann, 1964), 36.

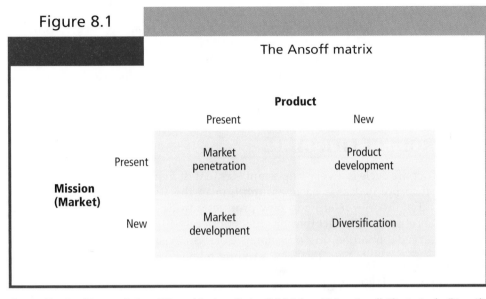

Figure 8.1

The Ansoff matrix

Source: Reprinted by permission of *Harvard Business Review*. Exhibit from H. Igor Ansoff, "Strategies for Diversification," *Harvard Business Review* 35, no. 5 (September/October 1957): 114. Copyright © 1957 by the President and Fellows of Harvard College; all rights reserved.

- **Complementary.** The complementary opportunity will change the structure of the business. It offers something new that, when combined with the present business, results in a new total larger than the parts. But it always carries considerable risk.

Complementary diversification has also been called convergent diversification because it utilizes at least some of the skills and knowledge of the organization.[8] **Conglomerate diversification**, the riskiest diversification of all, moves into completely new areas. For example, British Aerospace decided to apply huge cash flow from its defense business to investments in automobiles, construction, and property. The company never found the expected synergism and either divested the acquisitions or reported large losses.[9] In general, few global conglomerates have been as profitable as organizations focused on a single product category. Mergers and acquisitions of the conglomerate type should not be confused with those of the complementary type, which are frequently undertaken to build more secure trading groups, as insurance to reduce risk by bringing more factors under management control.

www.bae.co.uk

A fourth opportunity that has emerged is **collaboration**. Rather than taking over new business, firms are developing collaborative agreements that ensure their greater competitiveness in the marketplace, together with a broader appeal to consumers and markets. More than 20,000 **alliances** were formed worldwide in the period from 1996 to 1998.[10] For example, airlines increasingly use code-sharing arrangements and alliances to offer broad route coverage to their customers and to save expenses through collaborations such as shared executive lounges and pooled maintenance facilities. Automobile manufacturers offer collaborative product and market coverage by swapping models between themselves and are thus able to round out their product offering without incurring the necessary product development cost. One result of the DaimlerChrysler merger was the scrapping of development plans for a Mercedes-Benz van. The

www.daimlerchrysler.com
www.mercedesbenz.com

8. Robert F. Lusch and Virginia N. Lusch, *Principles of Marketing* (New York: Kent, 1987), 68.

9. "A Tale of Two Conglomerates," *Economist*, November 18, 1995, 20.

10. John Harbinson and Peter Pekar, *Smart Alliances: A Guide to Repeatable Success* (San Francisco: Jossey-Bass Publishers, 1998).

www.boeing.com

new corporation had ample options already developed by Chrysler. Boeing reduced its risk and investment and increased its market acceptance by collaborating with Japanese firms in developing the 777 airplane. Such arrangements are also emerging in the distribution field, where channel members collaborate to improve their product offering and stretch their reach. The risks of such an approach appear to be substantially less than those of diversification. However, the complexity of melding different organizations should not be underestimated.

THE PRODUCT LIFE CYCLE

www.bcg.com

The product life cycle is a very important element of marketing theory. As we will see, it is incorporated as a basic assumption in the **Boston Consulting Group Matrix** and in theories relating to new product introduction which are discussed later in this chapter. The fact that products undergo different life-cycle stages has been observed on numerous occasions. Color televisions replaced black-and-white televisions in the seventies just as, decades later, color computer monitors took over from monochrome ones. Having tested the concept against a selected 140 categories of nondurable consumer products, researchers concluded that the product life-cycle model is valid in many common market situations.[11] The intuitive appeal of analogy with the human life cycle—consisting of introduction, growth, maturity, decline and postmortem—is a crucial aspect of the product life cycle. The concept of the product life cycle thus suggests that any good or service moves through identifiable stages, each of which is related to the passage of time and has different characteristics. A profit level is associated with each stage. Profits are likely to be negative at the beginning and at the end, when there is high initial investment and high closeout costs. Hopefully, however, they will be positive by the maturity stage and more than recoup the losses. Figure 8.2 shows a schematized life cycle.

> The concept of the product life cycle **suggests that any good or service** moves through identifiable stages

Figure 8.2

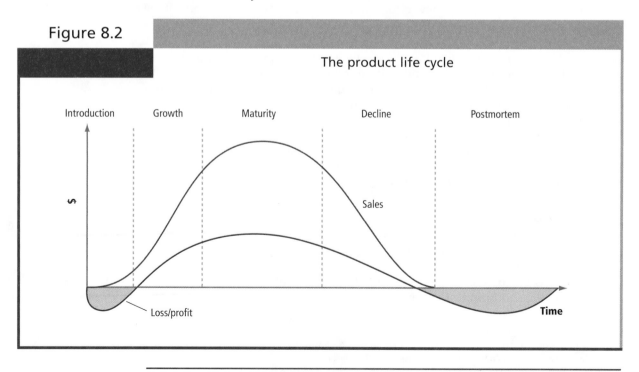

The product life cycle

11. R. Polli and V. Cook, "Validity of the Product Life Cycle," *Journal of Business Management* 42, no. 4 (1969): 28.

LIFE CYCLE STAGES

INTRODUCTION. In this first stage of a product's life, the supplier can choose from a number of strategies ranging from penetration, where the supplier invests through promotion or a low price to gain the maximum share of a new market, to skimming, where the maximum short-term profit is derived, typically by a high price. The speed at which this happens depends primarily on the rate at which the supplier is willing or able to invest. The ideal situation, for both penetration and skimming, is to develop the market as fast as possible. This takes advantage of the lead time before potential competitors can respond. Conversely, if a market develops slowly, **pioneering efforts** may simply pave the way for later suppliers to capitalize on the early investment. In general, though, the pioneer retains the highest market share even after competition enters. It has been shown that such pioneers usually hold double the share of later entrants, even over the longer term.[12] This is why firms increasingly concentrate on enhancing their product's "speed to market," which refers to the time elapsed between product conception and product introduction. An integral part of such speed is the close collaboration between the marketing and production functions within the firm, as well as the development of flexible manufacturing and concurrent engineering. The existence of information systems that tie all corporate functions into the new effort is also crucial in this process.[13] Even though historically it was very difficult to introduce a new product into the market—and even more complex to do so on a global level—the development of Internet technology now makes it possible to carry out such introductions more rapidly and more globally. In consequence, products will be able to succeed and fail on a much larger scale.

GROWTH. In this stage, customers have become aware of the product and its benefits, and usage is growing. It is now in the interest of the innovating firm to achieve rapid market access and penetration to set itself apart from the competition. Therefore firms wish to accomplish maximum sales acceleration (achieved, for example, through product announcements before availability) and constant incremental improvements afterward.[14] During this stage, suppliers often have to increase plant capacity and run promotional campaigns to consolidate and extend their share of the new market. These actions require substantial investments, which usually absorb most profit. As a result, this part of the life cycle may demand further net investment. Because of the increasing volumes, prices usually drop. Attracted by the growth in the market, further competitors may enter, but direct price competition tends not to be a major factor. This growth in sales, number of customers, and number of suppliers can be explosive and is known as the "bandwagon effect." The emphasis on promotion of the brand at this stage may well be to establish consumer attitudes toward the product. In recent years, another feature of this phase has been the battle for distribution, particularly when there has been a concentration of retail distribution in the hands of a few major operators. Because it may be vital to the success of a brand to obtain the widest possible distribution, negotiations with these key distribution players are essential.

MATURITY. No product or market can grow forever; eventually all the significant uses will have been developed. The sales curve will flatten, and the market or product will have reached maturity. The majority of goods and services currently

---

12. W. T. Robinson and C. Fornell, "Sources of Market Pioneer Advantage in Consumer Goods Industries," *Journal of Marketing Research* 22 (August 1985): 305.

13. Joseph T. Vesey, "Time-to-Market: Put Speed in Product Development," *Industrial Marketing Management* 21, no. 2 (1992): 151–158.

14. Thomas S. Robertson, "How to Reduce Market Penetration Cycle Times," *Sloan Management Review* 35, no. 1 (1993): 87–96.

in the marketplace are at this stage, and much of the practice of marketing revolves around this steady state. Sales may continue to grow, albeit more slowly. Suppliers may attempt to stimulate sales by expanding their ranges or by more clearly differentiating themselves from their competitors. There may be an emphasis, in the face of the stagnation of the market, on building groups of loyal users and attracting those from competitors. Price competition may play an increasing role. At the beginning of this phase, profits are likely to be at their maximum, only to decrease as competition increases and prices fall. Some of the minor brands may drop out in the face of this competition, but some new brands may enter as well. At some point there are so many competitors in the market, which is no longer growing, that price wars break out. The product has then reached the saturation level, which is frequently included in the maturity phase.

> ## No product
> ## or market can
> ## grow forever

DECLINE.   Eventually the whole market declines, or other, newer products are introduced that are substitutes for the established product. The good or service goes into a terminal decline, which can last for years. Examples are the mimeograph machine, carbon paper, typewriter, and vinyl record. At this stage, companies often cease to invest and instead milk products by minimizing costs and maximizing price to take the largest profit advantage of the reduced number of loyal customers who still support the brand. Four organizational strategies exist for a market in decline:[15]

- **Leadership.** If the market is still profitable, it may be worthwhile to invest to become one of the few leaders before harvesting profits.
- **Niche.** A segment may be identified that still has high returns and will decay more slowly.
- **Harvest.** This is the "milking" strategy, characterized by cost cutting, no investment, and reduced levels of customer service.
- **Divestment.** The business can be sold early in decline or even at the end of the maturity phase if the symptoms can be accurately detected.

The biggest difficulty is in recognizing that the market or the brand is in decline. It is not unusual for companies with declining products to apply strategies applicable to the maturity phase or even to the growth phase. The reason for such inappropriate corporate behavior lies in the fact that data in real life are never as smooth as the product life-cycle curve would have us believe. Products experience seasonality, temporary lulls, sudden spurts, and sharp drop-offs, particularly when performance is measured on weekly charts. As a result, it becomes very difficult for management to decide exactly where the product is in its life cycle.

> ## The biggest difficulty is in
> ## recognizing that the market
> ## or the brand is in decline.

The major problem of **declining brands** is not the direct losses they bring but rather the distraction of management attention away from the breadwinners and new products. On the other hand, many brands are discontinued early as a result of conscious but misguided marketing decisions. Slavishly following product life-

15. Michael E. Porter, *Competitive Strategy* (New York: Free Press, 1980), 72.

cycle theory poses the considerable danger of a decline being falsely detected. As we will see later, product life cycles are much longer than is generally assumed. A temporary downturn may therefore be mistaken for the onset of decline and resources be withdrawn (and the brand even milked), leading to an inevitable decline of the brand.

POSTMORTEM.   A newly emerging final stage of the life cycle is the post-mortem. It used to be that when management decided to terminate a brand or product, the decision removed the product from the corporate rolls—no more investments, expenditures, sales, revenues, or responsibility. Today, however, for reasons of societal (mainly environmental) concerns, the situation has changed. Even though a product may have been terminated some time ago, its continued existence in the market may require further corporate investment of funds and management attention. In Germany, for example, the manufacturers of automobiles are responsible for the cleanup and recycling cost associated with the disposal of cars even though they may have been produced decades ago. The post-mortem problem also exists for facilities. The worldwide attention paid to the planned disposal of an obsolete oil drilling platform by Shell, which resulted in consumer boycotts, government disputes, and rapid shifts in corporate strategy, highlights how a firm can be affected in the long term by the postmortem stage. Conversely, firms are also faced with the challenge of planning for facilities whose useful lives are much longer than the life cycle of any individual product they manufacture. In such instances, facilities planners need to think early on about flexible facilities that can be put to other uses.[16] Given the growing environmental consciousness permeating society, it would appear that firms increasingly need to plan for the postmortem stage and make appropriate provisions for financial reserves, because there will not be any revenues to offset these expenditures.

www.shelloil.com

LESSONS OF THE PRODUCT LIFE CYCLE

The product life cycle offers a useful model to keep in the back of your mind when making your plans, whether you are marketing a good or a service or are in the nonprofit sector. Indeed, if your product is in the introduction phase, or in decline, it should be at the front of your mind, because in these phases you may be making many life-and-death decisions. Between these two extremes, it is useful to have that vision of mortality in front of you, if for no other reason than to remind you that, if you take no action, product death will come that much earlier. On the other hand, the product life cycle is not without its practical difficulties. Rigid adherence to the product life cycle without consideration of the specifics of a product can lead to erroneous marketing decisions, such as premature withdrawal from markets or insufficient efforts to expand into new markets. If management is mistakenly convinced that the product life cycle is declining and acts as though it is, a self-fulfilling prophecy can occur.[17]

OTHER LIFE CYCLES

The conventional pattern of a life cycle is a gradual rise to a long plateau before a slow decline. However, other patterns may be possible and, in view of their shorter time spans, may be of more practical significance.

16. Cheryl Gaimon and Vinod Singhal, "Flexibility and the Choice of Manufacturing Facilities Under Short Product Life Cycles," *European Journal of Operational Research* 60, no. 2 (1992): 211–223.
17. W. Lazer and E. H. Shaw, "The Product Life Cycle," in *Handbook of Modern Marketing,* 2d ed., ed. V. P. Buell (New York: McGraw-Hill, 1986), 34.

LIFE CYCLE EXTENSION

www.mitsubishi.com

In practice, most products are in the maturity or saturation stage. For example, an analysis of Mitsubishi indicated that among the 40,000 goods and services offered by the corporation, more than 30,000 were faced with a market situation in which supply substantially outstripped demand. Without a careful marketing effort, many products would rapidly reach maturity and then decline. Much of marketing practice is therefore concerned with profitably extending the life cycle of the product by lengthening the growth phase as far as possible. This is why firms introduce "new and improved" products, launch campaigns to explain different uses for products, or attempt to communicate with new customer groups to persuade them to use the product. Nearly 90 percent of the thousands of new consumer packaged goods introduced each year are line extensions—items added to an existing product line under an established brand name. Because line extensions are much easier and cheaper to launch than entirely new products, manufacturers view them as an efficient way to reach untapped markets or to grab greater shelf space.[18]

> Much of marketing practice is therefore concerned with profitably extending the life cycle of the product

Such **product life extension** is also a primary reason that firms go international in search of new users and uses. Only when looking at the global market do firms begin to discover that the life cycles of products, when measured internationally, may slow down substantially. For example, even though telephones have saturated industrialized nations, they have still remained a product for only selected elites in many other countries. It is easily forgotten that more than 50 percent of the world's population has never made a single telephone call.[19]

Figure 8.3 shows the effects of product range development to rejuvenate the product, followed by market extension and then market development. As Manager's Corner 8.3 shows, such market development, particularly in the international arena, can be crucial to the survival of enterprises that are subject to changing domestic market conditions. The overall goal of all these actions is to extend the life cycle, counter the drop in sales, and continue the progress of the sales curve upward. New product development is shown as starting the next product life cycle. A variation on this process is diversification, or moving into a completely new market with a new product range that is either developed in-house or obtained by a purchase or takeover. This process is, of course, analogous to the diversification stages of both Ansoff and Drucker presented earlier, and the same cautions apply. Firms should coordinate the rejuvenation strategies for different products. By arranging such strategies sequentially, improved use can be made of corporate resources, and the cash flow can be enhanced.

FASHION AND FADS

Rapid penetration is an interesting life-cycle pattern that occurs with fashions or fads that come and go very quickly. Almost the whole life cycle is taken up with growth and then rapid decline, with only a very brief period of maturity. Judging these patterns may be a matter of commercial life and death for those in

18. "Why Line Extensions Often Backfire," *Harvard Business Review* (March/April 1999): 19–21.
19. Jagdish N. Sheth and Rajendra S. Sisodia, "Revisiting Marketing's Lawlike Generalizations," *Journal of the Academy of Marketing Science* 27, no. 1 (1999): 71–87.

Figure 8.3

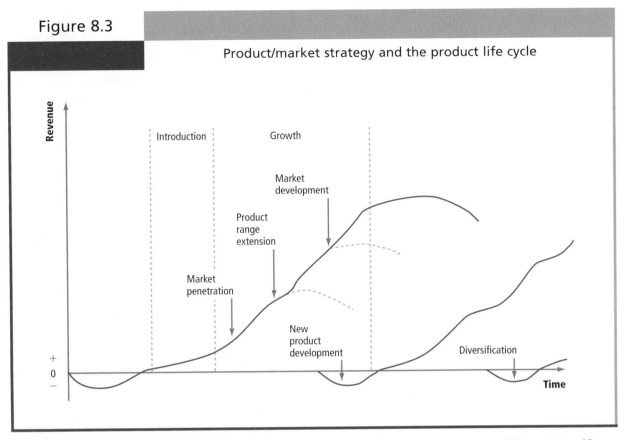

Product/market strategy and the product life cycle

Source: Malcolm H. B. McDonald, *Marketing Plans*, 3d ed. (New York: Butterworth Heinemann, 1995), 102. Reprinted by permission of Butterworth Heinemann Publishers Oxford, a division of Reed Educational & Professional Publishing Ltd.

Manager's Corner 8.3

U.S. hospitals find lucrative clients abroad

The border war between Peru and Ecuador spawned new business—the wounded soldiers or "casualty patients"—for Johns Hopkins Medical Center (www.jhbmc.jhu.edu) in Baltimore, Maryland. Through a network of diplomatic and military contacts, the hospital persuaded the Ecuadorian government to send more than 45 wounded soldiers to Johns Hopkins for artificial limbs. With a price tag of $35,000 per casualty, the hospital was hoping to treat wounded from Bosnia and Turkey, and there was even talk of plans to offer new protheses for soldiers maimed in the Falkland Islands in Argentina 15 years ago.

Soliciting patients from areas of warfare is just one element in the new marketing efforts of U.S. hospitals. Under pressure from empty beds, tighter government regulations, and stricter insurance rules, clinics and medical centers throughout the United States compete to woo more patients from overseas, ranging from soldiers to ailing Asian tycoons and Saudi royals. A growing affluent class in Latin America, Asia, and the Persian Gulf, who lack good medical care in their home contries, are providing a market niche for U.S. hospitals. Hospitals in Florida, for example, lure wealthy patients from South America to stay at resorts for "health vacations," which combine golf and tennis with blood tests.

"Industry has certainly approached international markets as a normal part of their operations, and so why shouldn't hospitals?" said Peter Van Etten, President of Stanford Medical Center, which is building an imaging center in Singapore to provide on-site CAT scans and mammograms and to refer patients to Palo Alto, California, for treatment.

Source: Lagnado Lucette, "Hospital Courts Foreign Patients to Fill Beds," *Wall Street Journal,* October 7, 1996, B1.

www.starwars.com

the fashion businesses. The timing for fashions is very difficult to predict and therefore often results in much more artistic rather than scientific forecasting. Nevertheless, timing is crucial if major sales are not to be lost. For example, toys associated with the release of a major motion picture such as the recent *Star Wars* prequel, *Episode I: The Phantom Menace,* are subject to such a fashion cycle. When the movie is released, the toys may become an instant hit. If the demand is not fulfilled very quickly, the desire for the product may fade just a quickly as it grew. Figure 8.4 illustrates what such a fashion curve might look like. A brief introductory period leads to the product becoming a "hit," whereupon sales shoot up rapidly. The key issue here will be meeting the demand, because after the growth phase there will only be a short maturity stage. After that, the decline phase may also be brief, sometimes spectacularly so, as to be caught with outdated fashion is to invite ridicule.

Many of the most prevalent life cycles relate to **fashions** in design. The television sets of 2000 look very different (at least in detail) to those of the 1950s, although there has been no significant change in function to explain this. Color television, for instance, did not demand a different shape per se. How the product is packaged, the design of the retailer's store, and the outward shape of the product, as much as the packing it comes in, reflect its time and usually date the product far faster than the technology that it contains. **Rejuvenation** is thus often about redesign of features as well as shapes to bring the product in line with current tastes, but without significantly changing its performance. As with technological life cycles, there is therefore a design cycle, but once more, it is largely under the control of the supplier.

An extreme version of a fashion is a fad, such as pet rocks, Rubik's cubes, and Tamagotchi virtual pets. With a **fad**, the rapid growth and decline phases are separated by only a very short maturity phase. There is little consumer resistance and hence no need for investment to overcome it. Those who are quick into the market and just as quick out of it—a much more difficult decision—may do very well.

Figure 8.4

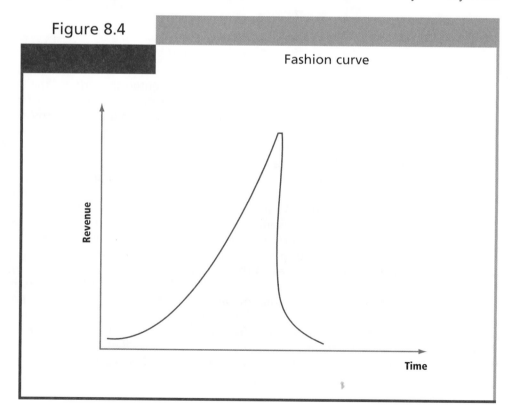

Fashion curve

TECHNOLOGICAL LIFE CYCLE

Perhaps the greatest justification for life-cycle theory lies in the area of technological change, though this topic is seldom discussed in the life-cycle literature. A large number of markets are subject to technological change. Even the laundry detergent market has passed through phases of inclusion of new blue whiteners, biological contents, fabric softeners, deodorants, and nonbiological ingredients. Personal computers now pass through a life cycle in less than a year! Just consider the overlap and then sudden decline in the product life cycles of the computer chips. The effect of these chips has given rise to a component life cycle, which is even shorter than the product life cycle.[20] Chips are the primary determinant of a computer life cycle length, particularly in business conditions in industrialized regions. However, the life cycle of a computer may be extended by exchanging that component or by appealing to different users. For example, in industrialized countries such users can be in consumer markets, but in developing markets they may well yet be firms. Nevertheless, the rapid improvements in technology and the resulting decreases in price make even such an extension increasingly difficult.

The technology processes of balancing cash flow against the competitive advantage offered by having the very latest in technology are somewhat removed from the classically described life-cycle theory. The most important difference from the conventional life cycle is that the brand never changes its place in the market; it is only the version of the product that changes. Sales volumes experience peaks following the new launch and, perhaps unexpectedly, again during the end-of-life price reductions, but these are not the patterns predicted by conventional theory. Almost as important a distinction is that the cycle is under the control of the supplier, not the market. The "technological breakthroughs" achieved by Gillette razors that offer product improvements and keep the product in the foreground of consumers' minds may serve as an example.

www.gillette.com

THE INTERNATIONAL PRODUCT CYCLE

International product cycle theory looks at the production, technology, and cost of products and formulates predictions about their country of production. In addition to the cost aspects, this theory also incorporates demand-side factors—namely, the income levels of consumers. Both the product itself and the methods for its manufacture go through three stages of international maturation as the product becomes increasingly commercialized.[21] These are the new product, the maturing product, and the standardized product.

1. **The new product.** Technical innovation leading to new and profitable products requires highly skilled labor and large quantities of capital for research and development. In general, the product is designed and initially manufactured near the parent firm, usually in a highly industrialized, capital-intensive country. In this development stage, the product is non-standardized. The production process requires a high degree of flexibility (meaning continued use of highly skilled labor), so costs of production are high. The innovator at this stage enjoys all the benefits of monopoly power, including the high profit margins required to repay the development costs and expensive production process. Price elasticity of demand at this stage is low; high-income consumers buy the product regardless of cost. An

20. Robert B. Handfield and Ronald T. Pannesi, "Managing Component Life Cycles in Dynamic Technological Environments," *International Journal of Purchasing and Materials Management* 30, no. 2 (1994): 20–27.
21. Raymond Vernon, "International Investment and International Trade in the Product Cycle," *Quarterly Journal of Economics* 80 (May 1966): 190–207.

www.kodak.com
www.intel.com

example of such innovation is Picture CD, the CD-ROM photo-processing disc developed by Kodak and chip giant Intel Corp. When consumers fill out forms for regular photo processing, they can also check a box to have their film scanned onto a compact disc for a fee of about $9. They can then pop the disc into their personal computers to view, manipulate, or store the images.[22]

2. **The maturing product.** As production expands, processes become increasingly standardized. The need for flexibility in design and manufacturing declines, thereby reducing the demands for highly skilled labor. The innovating country increases its sales to other countries through exports. Competitors develop slight variations, exerting downward pressure on prices and profit margins. Production costs are an increasing concern. Products in this category are Boeing and Airbus aircraft and Microsoft software.

www.boeing.com
www.airbus.com
www.microsoft.com

3. **The standardized product.** In this final stage, the product is completely standardized in its manufacture. With access to capital on world markets, the country of production is simply the one with the cheapest unskilled labor. Profit margins are thin, and competition is fierce. The product has largely run its course in terms of profitability for the innovating firm. The country of comparative advantage has therefore shifted as the technology of the product's manufacture has matured and moved its location of production. But such advantages may be fleeting. As knowledge and technology continually change, so does the country of that product's comparative advantage. Personal computers, televisions, radios, and Nike shoes may serve as examples for products in these categories.

www.nike.com

IMPLICATIONS OF THE INTERNATIONAL PRODUCT CYCLE. Product cycle theory analyzes how specific products were first produced and exported from one country but shifted their location of production and export to other countries over time. Figure 8.5 illustrates the trade patterns that can result from the maturing stages of a specific product's cycle. As the product and its market mature and change, the countries of its production and export shift.

In this example, the product is initially designed and manufactured in the United States. In its early stages (from time t_0 to t_1), the United States is the only country producing and consuming the product, and production is highly capital intensive and skilled labor intensive. At time t_1 the United States begins exporting the product to other developed countries. These countries possess the income to purchase the product while still in the new product stage, although it is relatively high priced. These other developed countries also commence their own production at time t_1, but continue to be net importers. A few exports do find their way to developing countries at this time as well. As the product moves into the maturing product stage, production capability expands rapidly in the other developed countries. Competition begins to appear as the basic technology of the product becomes more widely known, and the need for skilled labor in its production declines. These countries eventually also become net exporters of the product near the end of the stage (time t_3). At time t_2 the developing countries begin their own production, although they continue to be net importers. Meanwhile, the lower-cost production from these growing competitors turns the United States into a net importer by time t_4. The competitive advantage for production and export is clearly shifting across countries at this time. The final stage of the standardized product sees the comparative advantage of production and export shifting to developing countries. The product is now a relatively mass-produced product that can be produced with increasingly less skilled labor. The

---

22. Alec Klein, "Kodak Is Rolling Out Digital Photo Processing on CD-ROM Disks," *Wall Street Journal*, February 9, 1999, A4.

Figure 8.5

Trade patterns and product cycle theory

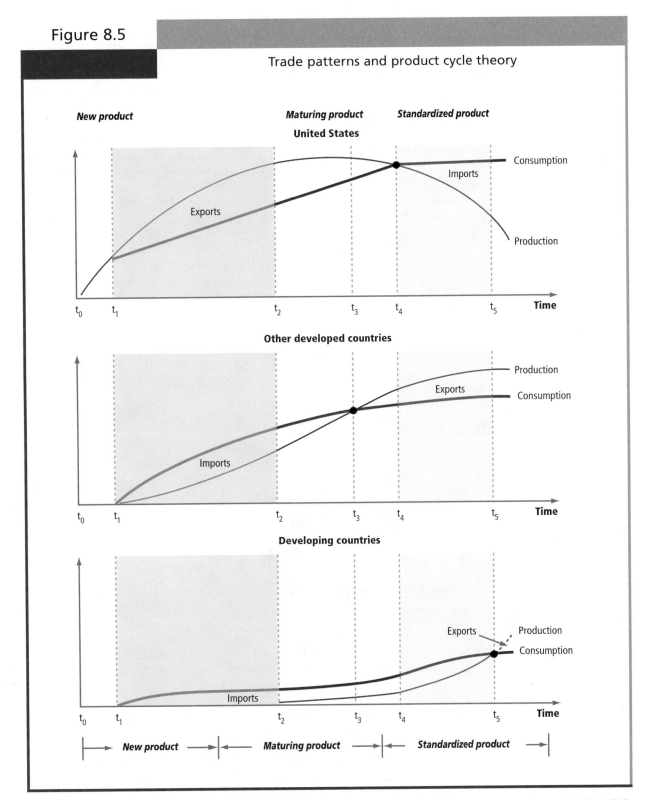

Source: Raymond Vernon, "International Investment and International Trade in the Product Cycle," *Quarterly Journal of Economics* 80 (May 1966): 199. © 1966 by the President and Fellows of Harvard College. Reprinted by permission of MIT Press Journals.

United States continues to reduce domestic production and increase imports. The other developed countries continue to produce and export, although exports peak as the developing countries expand production and become net exporters themselves. The product has run its course, or life cycle, in time t_5.

It is important to note that throughout this product cycle, the countries of production, consumption, export, and import are identified by their labor and capital levels, not by their firms. It could very well be the same firms that are moving production from the United States to other developed countries and to developing countries. The shifting **location of production** is instrumental in the changing patterns of trade but not necessarily in the loss of market share, profitability, or competitiveness of firms. It is the country of comparative advantage that changes.

Of course product cycle theory has many limitations. It is obviously most appropriate for technology-based products. These are the products that are most likely to experience the changes in production process as they grow and mature. Other products, either resource-based (like minerals and other commodities) or services (which employ capital mostly in the form of human capital), are not so easily characterized by stages of maturity. The product cycle theory is most relevant to products that eventually fall victim to mass production and cheap labor forces.[23] In addition, the theory reflects the time of its origin through its principal focus on the United States. Today the innovation can take place in a multitude of European or Asian countries. Nevertheless, the principle of the international product life cycle still appears to hold when one observes, for example, the gradual farming out of production from Japan into other countries of the Pacific Rim such as Malaysia, Indonesia, and China.

PRODUCT LIFE

One aspect of life-cycle theory that is seldom discussed but is vital to the brands involved is the total life span. The life of products, and of markets, can vary dramatically. Life cycles cover a wide range, from the few days of a pop CD to the many years of a Boeing 747; the length of the cycle can vary significantly even in markets that are very similar. The formulation of baked beans has barely changed in generations, but much of the snack market has now become almost a fad market, changing every few months. To reflect these lifestyles, Enis et al. developed a redesigned, extended, product life cycle.[24] They split the conventional maturity stage into maintenance, designed to stabilize sales at a given level, and proliferation, where many more varieties of the basic product are added.

> One aspect of life-cycle theory that is **seldom discussed but is vital to the** brands involved is the total life span.

www.boeing.com

Disagreements about the value of the product life-cycle concept center on its practical use; the predictive rather than descriptive role of the technique is open to question.[25] It has been said that the product life cycle is a dependent variable determined by market actions, not an independent variable to which companies should adapt their marketing programs. Marketing management can alter the shape and duration of a brand's life cycle.[26] Thus, although in the right context the life cycle may be a useful theoretical device, there are frequently significant problems in trying to put it into practice. How, for example, do you determine just where you are in a life cycle when real-life sales or usage curves do not

23. Michael R. Czinkota, Ilkka Ronkainen, and Michael Moffett, *International Business*, 5th ed. (Fort Worth, Tex.: Dryden Press, 1999), 167–170.

24. B. M. Enis, R. Lagarce, and A. E. Prell, "Extending the Product Life Cycle," *Business Horizons* 20 (June 1977): 46–60.

25. T. Watkins, *The Economics of the Brand: A Marketing Analysis* (New York: McGraw-Hill, 1986), 146.

26. N. K. Dhalla and S. Yuspeh, "Forget the Product Life Cycle Concept," *Harvard Business Review* 54 (January/February 1976): 102.

follow the smooth path that the theory shows? How do you predict when turning points will be reached when, again, the picture is "fuzzy" and you need to make decisions well in advance, without the theoretician's invaluable advantage of hindsight? In many markets the prod-uct or brand or market life cycle is signif-

Marketing management can alter the shape and duration of a brand's life cycle.

icantly longer than the planning cycle of the organizations involved. Even if the product life cycle exists for them, their plans will be based upon just that section of the curve where they currently reside (most probably in the "mature" stage), and their view of that part of it will almost certainly not encompass the whole range from growth to postmortem.

LIFE CYCLES AND MARKETING STRATEGY

One of the favorite uses of life-cycle theory is to predict what the strategic mar-keting mix should be at each stage. Once more, the lessons derived from this the-ory are most useful at the beginning and end of the cycle.

INTRODUCTION. At this stage the clear priority is to get the brand established. This generates three main activities. First is the building of distribution, which starts before the brand is formally launched. Emphasis is on achieving the widest distribution through the major distribution channels, or on pilot installations with the major customers in industrial markets. In many sectors, therefore, the sales force spends a disproportionate amount of its time on new brands. The second requirement is to build awareness so that customers know that the brand exists. The classical vehicle for this effort is a heavy television campaign. In industrial markets, where it may take months for the sales force to complete coverage of all potential prospects, the awareness may be built more rapidly by mail cam-paigns or by telemarketing, often backed up by seminars. The third requirement is to obtain trial. In mass consumer markets, door-to-door deliveries of samples or coupons are used to try to achieve early trial of the new product. In industrial markets, or those of capital goods, the free trial is often used as the equivalent.

GROWTH. In the case of mass consumer goods, following a successful intro-duction, distribution is extended further. In other sectors the sales force will can-vass the remaining, smaller prospects. The main task, though, is to develop cus-tomer or consumer sales. The advertising, possibly using longer commercials with more emphasis on features and image, changes to explain the product and create a favorable attitude so that the consumer is persuaded to switch from the existing brands. Coupons and similar promotional devices may be used to extend trial.

MATURITY. This is the maintenance phase occupied by most products. Distri-bution should now be as wide as possible. In the computer industry, for example, products were sold in the introductory stage mainly through the manufacturer's field sales force. In the growth stage, specialized computer retailers were the dominant channel. In the mature stage, distribution shifted to mass merchandis-ers, discount retailers, niche resellers, mail order, and telemarketers. As a result, broader customer groups were reached, and product sales continued to climb.[27] The firm's communication emphasis may now be defensive, consolidating what had been built in the previous phase so that profits can be maximized. At the

27. Norton Paley, "Changing Channels," *Sales and Marketing Management* 146 (November 1994): 30–32.

Exhibit 8.1

Product life is an important product decision, and life cycles vary widely among products. The product life of an airplane can stretch decades, as has been proven by the Concorde. A recent Wall Street Journal article notes that the youngest Concorde is 20 years old and that both British Airways and Air France plan to continue flying the aging planes for at least 10 more years. Has the product life of the Concorde run its course?

Source: Laura Landro, "Pssst: The Concorde's having a sale. Too bad it still costs a fortune, plus aging plane shakes, rattles, roars, scares us silly," *Wall Street Journal*, August 13, 1999, W1.

saturation level, the brand manager eventually faces decreasing prices, so that the profitability per unit sold is reduced. An interesting example of a product moving between stages is the Concorde (pictured in Exhibit 8.1). Still marketed as a fast and chic way to cross the Atlantic, the Concorde is nonetheless losing some credibility as a luxury plane due to recent improvements in first class travel on the major airlines. The Concord planes are noisy, cramped, and shaky compared to their smooth-flying 747 counterparts. In addition, the flying Concorde is still one of the most expensive transatlantic tickets you can purchase. It would seem the airlines need to assess whether or not the product life of the Concorde has run its course. Perhaps it would be advantageous to either re-engineer the plane (remember Figure 6.4, page 166) or shift marketing strategies.

DECLINE. The goal of this stage is to obtain profit by milking the brand. The emphasis moves from marketing to internal factors concerned with productivity—although marketing's key responsibility, that of advising when to terminate the brand, remains. High productivity is of little value when there are few sales, as was found by the owners of highly automated typewriter plants. Yet termination decisions are difficult to make. Research has shown that firms are not consistently removing products from the market at the same rate as they are introducing new products.[28] As a result, declining brands often proliferate, taking management attention and skills away from new and growing brands.

POSTMORTEM. Management must plan for the postmortem expenses that continue after a product is no longer sold by the firm. These costs, which may consist of servicing, environmental cleanup expenses, or other follow-up expenditures, must be budgeted, incorporated into the overall life-cycle planning, and taken into account for product termination decisions. Although the postmortem expenses may sometimes indicate early termination of a product, on other occasions these expenses may lead to a prolongation of its life span, because ongoing staff attention is required anyway.

28. Barry L. Bayus, "Are Product Life Cycles Really Getting Shorter?" *Journal of Product Innovation Management* 11 (September 1994): 300–308.

CASH FLOW

The most important—albeit unwelcome—message that the product life cycle can bring to management is that of cash flow. The model offers a clear reminder that the launch of a new brand requires significant investment that can last from its launch to the end of the growth phase—a longer period than most organizations allow for. What is worse, the more successful the new brand, the greater the investment needed. In new organizations, lack of appreciation of the problems of rapid growth is paradoxically responsible for a number of failures, simply because the owners cannot find the funds to cover the debts that they have incurred to meet the needs of rapid growth. Once the maturity phase is reached, profits must be generated quickly enough to recoup the investments and to fund new products. This was a lesson that EMI learned the hard way. Its development of the CAT body scanner was a technological masterpiece that won its investor a Nobel Prize. Unfortunately, EMI was still investing well into what should have been the maturity phase when its American competitors moved into the next life cycle. The cash drain was such that EMI was forced to offer itself for sale.

PRODUCT PORTFOLIOS

Most organizations offer more than one good or service, and many operate in several markets. The advantage here is that the various products—the product portfolio—can be managed so that they are not all at the same phase in their life cycles. Having products evenly spread out across life cycles allows for the most efficient use of both cash and manpower resources. Figure 8.6 shows an example of such life-cycle management and some of the benefits that can be obtained from a well-managed product portfolio. The current investment in C, which is in the growth phase, is covered by the profits being generated by the earlier product B, which is at maturity. This product had earlier been funded by A, the decline of which is now being balanced by the newer products. An organization looking for growth can introduce new goods or services that it hopes will be bigger sellers than those that they succeed. However, if this expansion is undertaken too rapidly, many of these brands will hungrily demand investment at the beginning of their life cycles, and even the earliest of them will be unlikely to generate profits fast enough to support the numbers of later launches. Therefore the producer will have to find another source of funds until the investments pay off.

Figure 8.6

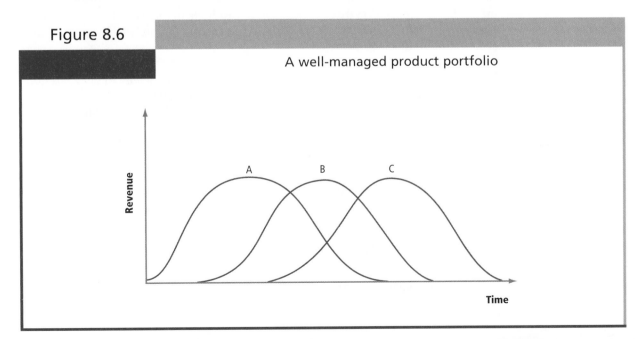

A well-managed product portfolio

Figure 8.7

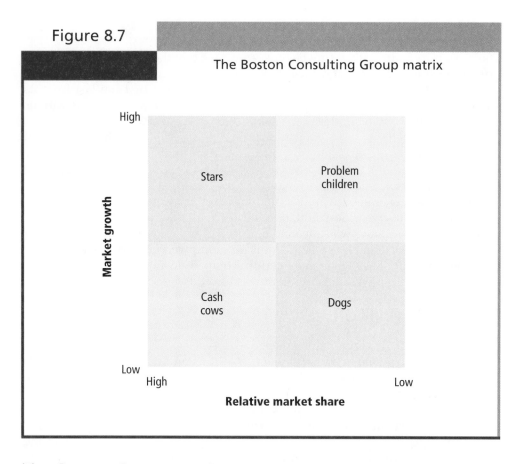

RELATIVE MARKET SHARE.

THE BOSTON CONSULTING GROUP MATRIX

As a visual tool for managing product portfolios, a matrix was developed by the Boston Consulting Group. The Boston Matrix offers a useful map of an organization's product strengths and weaknesses as well as the likely cash flows. What prompted this idea was the need to manage cash flow. It was reasoned that one of the main indicators of cash generation was relative market share, and market growth rate was indicative of cash usage. Figure 8.7 shows the Boston Matrix. It is well worth remembering that one of the key underlying assumptions of this matrix is the expectation that the position of products in their markets will change over time. This assumption is, of course, the incorporation of the product life-cycle thinking discussed earlier.

RELATIVE MARKET SHARE.   A high **market share** indicates likely cash generation, because the higher the share, the more cash will be generated. As a result of economies of scale (another basic assumption of the Boston Matrix), it is assumed that these earnings will grow faster as the share increases. The exact measure is the brand's share relative to its largest competitor. Thus, if the brand had a share of 20 percent and the largest competitor had the same share, the ratio would be 1:1. If the largest competitor had a share of 60 percent, however, the ratio would be 1:3, implying that the organization's brand was in a relatively weak position. If the largest competitor had only a 5 percent share, the ratio would be 4:1, meaning that the brand was in a relatively strong position, which might be reflected in profits and cash flow. The reason for choosing relative market share rather than just profits is that it carries more information than cash flow alone does. It shows where the brand is positioned against it main competitors and indicates where it might be likely to go in the future. It can also show what types of marketing activities might be effective.

www.bcg.com

MARKET GROWTH RATE. Organizations strive for rapidly growing brands in rapidly growing markets. But, as we have seen, the penalty is that such brands tend to be net cash users. High investment buys growth in the reasonable expectation that a high market share will eventually turn into future profits. The theory behind the matrix assumes, therefore, that a higher **market growth** rate is indicative of accompanying demands for investment. Determining the cutoff point above which the growth is deemed to be significant (and likely to lead to extra demands on cash) is a critical requirement of the technique; the chosen cutoff point is usually 10 percent per year. Markets with very low growth rates may make the application of this analysis unworkable. When it can be applied, however, the market growth rate says more about the brand position than just its cash flow. It is a good indicator of that market's strength, of its future potential or level of maturity in terms of the life cycle, and also of its attractiveness to future competitors. The theory is that products lying in each of the quadrants—stars, problem children, cash cows, and dogs—behave differently and require different marketing strategies.

- **Stars** (high market share, high market growth rate). These are typically relatively new products in the growth phase. Because they have high market shares, they may be generating sufficient gross profits to cover their current investment needs. Usually the predominant strategy is to grow stars to the cash cow stage, where the most profit is made. Microsoft Office 2000 software may serve as an example of a star.

  www.microsoft.com

- **Cash cow** (high market share, low market growth rate). Here the brand has maintained its high share and cash generation capabilities, but the market life cycle has moved to maturity and growth is slow. Investment is not required to any significant extent because there is little need to recruit new customers and almost no demand for new plant. A cash cow is therefore the main generator of cash to cover the ongoing investment in new products. The ongoing phone operations of telephone companies are typical cash cows.

- **Problem child** or **question mark** (low market share, high market growth rate). This is a product, typically a recently launched one, that has not yet built its market share. As it does not yet have the share to deliver reasonable profits, it will almost certainly be a net user of cash. Such problem children often absorb most of the cash flow generated by the cash cows, but the organization hopes that this will be a good investment because the problem child could eventually become a winner and a future cash cow. Probably most of today's Internet companies fit into this category.

- **Dog** (low market share, low market growth rate). A product here has few or no prospects. It may not yet be a loss, unless it is demanding a disproportionate use of overhead, but it will probably be one in the not-too-distant future. Hence it should have its future regularly reviewed so that it can be discontinued as soon as it becomes a burden. Some national airlines, particularly those without an international alliance, may be found in this category.

The product life cycle underpinnings of the Boston Matrix indicate that successful products will steadily progress around the quadrants in a counterclockwise fashion, starting as problem children, then moving through stars to cash cows, where hopefully they will dwell for some time, and then on to dogs and eventual extinction. Unsuccessful products will never become cash cows and will probably move from problem children directly to dogs, if they are allowed to survive for that long. The matrix is most useful in markets that show clear product life cycles, such as the pharmaceuticals industry. GlaxoWellcome used at least part of the massive profits from its Zantac antiulcer drug (a cash cow whose life, protected by patents, was running out) to develop two new products,

www.glaxowellcome.co
.uk
www.imgw.com

Sumatriptan (a migraine treatment) and Salmeterol (an asthma treatment). In theory, cash flow is generated almost exclusively in the cash cow quadrant and is transferred in part to the stars, but mainly to the problem children. One can then plot forecasts of future developments to indicate what the related future cash flows may be.

One of the most informative uses of the Boston Matrix is to plot competitors' positions along with the firms's own. This gives a valuable insight into their position (especially their cash position), indicates how they may behave in the future, and shows the relative strengths and weaknesses of the firm's own brands. Figure 8.8 provides an example of different brands, where the size of each circle represents the value of brands sales. The market is maintaining a high rate of growth for Brand A. By increasing its market share, the product has moved from problem child to star. Cash usage should be reduced, and the brand might even become self-supporting. The market growth for Brand B has slowed, but the brand has increased share and has consequently moved from star to cash cow. It has begun to generate the high level of profits that the organization depends on. Despite the fact that Brand C has gained market share and sales volume, the market growth has slowed down while it is still in the star quadrant. Its progress will have to be followed very carefully, for it may absorb disproportionate amounts of cash and could quickly become a dog. The market growth for Brand D has slowed further, but no share has been lost and the product remains a cash cow, still generating healthy profits. Brand E has lost share in a market that is growing and moved over the borderline from cash cow to dog. In view of the lack of precision of the borderline, this may not be as fatal as it sounds, but the future of Brand E must be regularly reviewed so that it can be milked or terminated when the time is ripe.

Figure 8.8

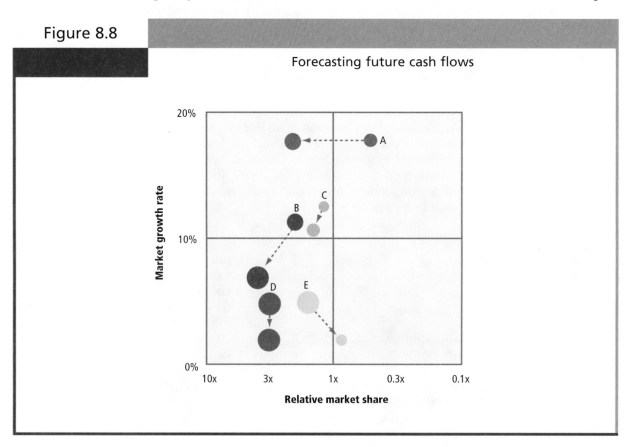

Forecasting future cash flows

www.bcg.com

CRITICISM OF THE BOSTON MATRIX.   As originally introduced by the Boston Consulting Group, the matrix was undoubtedly a useful tool for graphically illustrating cash flows. However, a simplistic use of the matrix can result in at least two major problems: The cash flow techniques are applicable only to the limited number of markets whose growth is relatively high, and where a definite pattern of product life cycles can be observed. Perhaps worse is the automatic implication that the brand-leader cash cows should always be milked to fund new brands. Often the brand leader's position is the one to be defended through corporate investment as brands in this position will probably outperform most newly launched brands. Such brand leaders will generate large cash flows, but they should not be milked to such an extent that their position is jeopardized, particularly because the chance of the new brands achieving similar brand leadership may be slim.

ECONOMIES OF SCALE.   Apart from the general existence of life cycles, one of the major hidden assumptions of the Boston Matrix is **economies of scale**. The more that is sold, the more that is produced, and the lower the unit cost. This is a philosophy that used to be embraced by Japanese corporations in particular. For example, Matsushita strategy gave explicit recognition to the importance of market share. Perhaps the corporation's most outstanding use of economies of scale to dominate a market was seen in the case of its VCRs. Very high volumes enabled Matsushita to offer prices that allowed it to capture almost two-thirds of the world market, which in turn gave it the volumes necessary for massive economies of scale. Such economies of scale are widely believed to apply in many industries.

www.mei.co.jp

More generally, though, experience is now seen as the main source of economies of scale. More production results in more learning. Such learning takes place through improvements in operator or management activities or through process innovations. Simultaneously, more experience makes it possible to achieve economies of scale through procurement economies or reduction of excess capacity.[29] The overall outcome is a reduction in costs, as shown in Figure 8.9. Because economies of scale relate to experience over the total production run, not just the current production levels, the effect is cumulative. This process offers the early leaders a major source of competitive advantage and creates substantial barriers against late entrants. This theory was supported by the Boston Consulting Group when it proposed that the characteristic decline in the unit cost of value added is 20 to 30 percent each time accumulated production is doubled. This decline goes on in time without limit (in constant prices) regardless of the rate of growth of experience. The rate of decline is surprisingly consistent, even from industry to industry.[30]

Today, however, many markets are moving toward a significantly increased variety of goods and services. This requirement imposed by consumer demand does not favor economies of scale. The basis for economies of scale may therefore be of less certain value in the longer term. In fact, it has been shown that at least in the case of stable markets, low market share does not inevitably lead to low profitability. Successful firms are characterized by strategies of selective focus (often described as niche marketing); they do not copy the strategies of market leaders.[31]

Finally, there is growing controversy about additional effects of market share that may influence the future competitive position of the firm. Many believe that market share, growth, and leadership result in improvements in products as well

29. W. W. Alberts, "The Experience Curve Doctrine Reconsidered," *Journal of Marketing* 53 (July 1989): 36–45.
30. Boston Consulting Group, *Perspectives on Experience*, 1970.
31. C. Y. Woo and A. C. Cooper, "The Surprising Case for Low Market Share," in *The Marketing Renaissance*, ed. David E. Gumpert (New York: John Wiley & Sons, 1988).

Figure 8.9

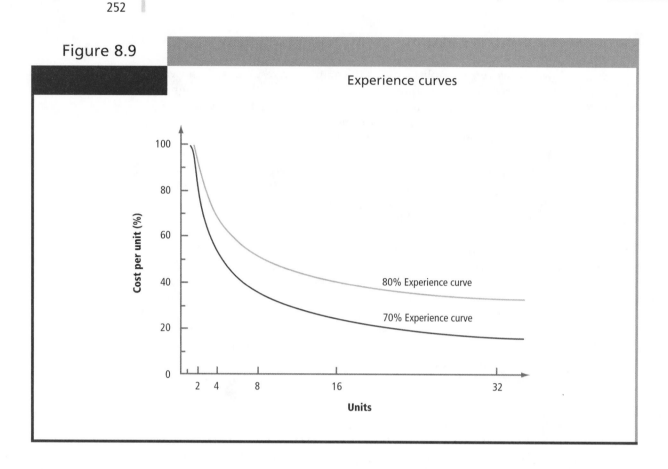

Experience curves

Cost per unit (%)

80% Experience curve

70% Experience curve

Units

as in the level of service obtained by customers. However, growing market share can also strain scarce resources and negatively affect service levels. Systems can become overburdened, and service times can increase. The rash of service outages and inability of customers to connect experienced by America Online is indicative of such a phenomenon. The existence of a negative average effect of market share on quality[32] may then result in growth and profitability patterns that do not fit the expectations raised by the BCG matrix.

www.aol.com

THEORY VERSUS PRACTICE

Having completed our description of two of the most widely taught marketing techniques—product life cycles and product portfolios—some practical cautions are in order. Marketing techniques should be the servants of the marketer. They should be used as an aid to the creative decision-making process and never as a substitute for them. Although they may frequently offer helpful insights, they almost never offer definitive answers in themselves. There is sometimes a desire to look for simple solutions to what are usually complex marketing problems. Solutions that incorporate the expertise of acknowledged masters in the field are particularly welcome. The temptations for the marketer can be severe when the techniques are as elegant, and in their own way powerful, as those we have just described. Indeed, they do frequently offer a valuable insight. In all cases, however, the wise marketer will recognize that such techniques usually offer just one perspective on the problem. The marketer should always consider other perspectives, particularly because, as we have seen, each of these tools typically has a

32. Linda L. Hellofs and Robert Jacobson, "Market Share and Customers' Perceptions of Quality: When Can Firms Grow Their Way to Higher Versus Lower Quality?" *Journal of Marketing* (January 1999): 16–25.

Figure 8.10

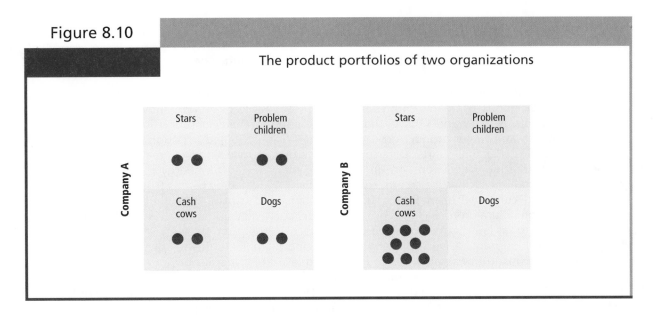

The product portfolios of two organizations

limited range of situations in which it may be appropriately applied. The experienced marketer takes fresh approaches to each new situation. In many ways a blank sheet of paper is the most powerful analytical tool. Only when all the options have been examined should it be decided which of the specific tools available, if any, is most suitable. There is no one tool that offers a universal answer to all marketing problems. Undue attention to any individual tool can distract the marketer from the range of other factors that may apply.

> Marketing techniques should be used
> **as an aid to the creative decision-making process**
> and never as a substitute for them

The myopia this can cause is particularly well illustrated by the dangers inherent in ill-informed use of the Boston Matrix. Review the companies illustrated in Figure 8.10. The chances are that 80 percent of you would choose Company A as being in the best shape because of the evenly balanced spread of products. Even the 20 percent of you that might choose Company B would probably feel nervous about that choice. Yet, as you should now realize, the clear choice has to be Company B. Think of it in terms of the eight cash cows. Which two would you want to downgrade to stars and which to problem children? Which would you want to destroy by making them dogs? Of course, the figure oversimplifies the position. It does not specify the size of the brands, and a star the same size as a cash cow might be preferable because it will presumably grow. The real lesson is that the Boston Matrix is useful as a tool to do a certain job. It should, for example, remind the owners of Company B to invest in some new products so that they may become stars and then cash cows to underwrite an uncertain future. On the other hand, it should not distract attention from the much more important task of maintaining the cash cows so that they do not turn into dogs. The money used to fund new developments should never come at the expense of the future of the existing cash cows.

PRODUCT MIX

The product portfolio can be assessed based on other factors as well, such as the product mix. The product mix refers to the total number of **product lines** carried by a firm, where each line reflects one type of product. For example, Unilever has a

www.unilever.com

Marketing in Action 8.2

Unilever repositions its laundry detergent

Unilever (www.unilever.com) is an Anglo-Dutch consumer goods company with 1998 sales of $44 billion. With around 1,000 brands, the company has four major product groups: Foods, Home and Personal Care, Diversey-Lever, and i-marketing. The Foods group is comprised of products such as ice cream, tea, yellow fats, and culinary frozen foods. The Home and Personal Care group includes product categories such as laundry, personal wash, hair, oral, and deodorants. DiverseyLever focuses upon the institutional and industrial professional cleaning and hygiene marketplace. In 1998, the company created its interactive marketing group by forming strategic alliances with America Online (www.aol.com), Microsoft (www.microsoft.com), and NetGrocer (www.netgrocer.com).

Unilever's Home and Personal Care group had combined 1998 sales of $20 billion. One product, All Free Clear with Allergan Fighter laundry detergent, was introduced in 1991 and targeted to people with sensitive skin. By 1998, All Free Clear held approximately 1.5 percent of the $4 billion worldwide laundry detergent market. In a 1999 move to increase market share, Unilever repositioned All Free Clear. Previously billed as tough on stains but gentle on sensitive skin, All Free Clear is now being marketed as an allergy medication for laundry. Supported by results from internal research, new ads for All Free Clear promise that the product will combat dust mites. Unilever's product is the first to make the allergen-reducing claim, let alone be able to support it. The question is whether or not the shift from stain-fighter to allergy-fighter will be lucrative.

Detergents such as All Free Clear, which do not include dye or perfume, account for around 8 percent of the total detergent market. This 8 percent is a decline from previous years and may be attributed to the onslaught of detergents with bleach and bleach alternatives. Is Unilever making the right move by repositioning its product into a declining submarket? Where should Unilever target its 25 percent projected increase in All Free Clear's ad spending?

Sources: www.unilever.com; Sally Beatty, "Unilever Targets Buyers Bugged by Mites," *Wall Street Journal*, January 6, 1999, B7.

www.birdseye.com
www.lever2000.com
www.snuggle.com
www.coke.com
www.pg.com

very wide product mix, which covers Birds Eye frozen foods as well as Lever 2000 soaps and Snuggle detergents, whereas, for many years, Coca-Cola had a very narrow product mix, based on just one product. **Product line length** refers to the number of products within a product line, such as the different types of laundry detergents offered by Proctor & Gamble. **Product depth** refers to the number of variations of one particular product—for example, a range of package sizes from trial-size to "jumbo economy" that can address the differing needs of the consumers.

The balance of the product mix concerns the volumes achieved by the different lines. What may appear to be a wide and deep portfolio may be an illusion if just one product within it produces 90 percent of the total sales. The same is true—and more frequently found—in relation to profit. A sound product mix shows a balanced profit contribution from a number of lines, although, as predicted by the 80/20 Rule, it is likely even then that a minority of the products will contribute most of the profit. The major overall product decisions are therefore about the type of mix and the product line width and depth. How many items are to be carried, and in what markets and segments? If too few lines are carried, then sales opportunities will be missed. By adding a variation on an existing line—a different package size, for example—additional sales may be created. If the additional revenue created is greater than the additional costs, these extra sales will generate extra profit. On the other hand, there is a tendency for product lines to grow to the point at which some products in the list will actually take a loss. There are, therefore, two types of product mix decisions to be made in this context: (1) **line stretching**, in which additional items are added to tap potentially profitable extra business, and (2) **line rationalization**, in which items are removed to reduce costs and improve profitability. Marketing in Action 8.2 describes an example of expanding product line depth.

REFINING PRODUCT STRATEGIES

So far product strategy has been described as if for just a few products. However, in many organizations there may be many products, perhaps tens of thousands in the case of a superstore operator. In these situations it is impossible to devote the same level of management attention to each individual item. It may be advisable to introduce a **rule-based process** instead. Defining such rules—which determine whether a product line should be promoted, whether it should be stocked widely or only in certain locations, or whether it should be deleted—is a difficult and time-consuming process. However, once these rules are available, they can be rapidly applied to the entire product offering.

A very effective approach is to use simple indices. Each product line is given an index value, calculated from sales and profit levels, growth rates, and market potential, as well as the fit of one product line with others, its importance to customers, and its role in one's relationship with suppliers. Without this additional information, results may be misleading. For example, carrying diapers may be unprofitable, but customers who come to purchase them also buy baby food, which may be highly profitable. Each component is then rated, and the resulting ratings are combined into an overall product score. For example, the value of sales for a given item may justify an index level of 2, profit of 3, importance to customers of 3, and links to other products of 3. The total, 11, can then be compared to rules that say, for instance, that products in the range of 10–20 should be stocked in all locations but not promoted. These indices can also be used in support of other decisions such as customer service levels or shelf space.

The components of these indices are difficult to decide, and their relative weightings are frequently the subject of great debate, which is why making rules absorbs so many resources. But rule making is essential to rational decision making; it yields a well-balanced product mix and a much better understanding of what is really important in terms of the organization's products.

PRODUCT STANDARDIZATION AND ADAPTATION

When expanding its market, the firm is likely to encounter different users, usage conditions, and regulations. Particularly when going international, decisions must be made regarding the product modifications that are needed or warranted. The four basic alternatives are (1) selling the product as is, (2) modifying products for different countries or regions, (3) designing new products for new markets, and (4) introducing a "global" product.

The question of whether to standardize or custom-tailor products and marketing programs in different market areas mirrors the question of whether to practice undifferentiated or differentiated marketing. The key benefits of standardization—that is, selling the same product worldwide—are savings in both production and marketing. Coca-Cola, Levi's jeans, and Colgate toothpaste provide evidence that universal product and marketing strategies can work.[33] Yet the argument that the world is becoming more homogeneous may be true for only a limited number of products with universal brand recognition and minimal product knowledge requirements for their use.[34] Industrial products, such as steel, chemicals, and agricultural equipment, tend to be less culture bound and therefore warrant less adjustment than consumer products. Similarly, marketers in technology-intensive industries, such as scientific instruments or medical equipment, are more likely to find universal acceptability for their products.[35]

www.levis.com
www.colgate.com

33. W. Chan Kim and R. A. Mauborgne, "Cross-Cultural Strategies," *Journal of Business Strategy* 7 (spring 1987): 28–36.

34. "Marketers Turn Sour on Global Sales Pitch Harvard Guru Makes," *Wall Street Journal,* May 12, 1988, 1, 13.

35. S. Tamer Cavusgil and Shaoming Zou, "Marketing Strategy–Performance Relationship: An Investigation of the Empirical Link in Export and Market Ventures," *Journal of Marketing* 58 (January 1994): 1–21.

Exhibit 8.2

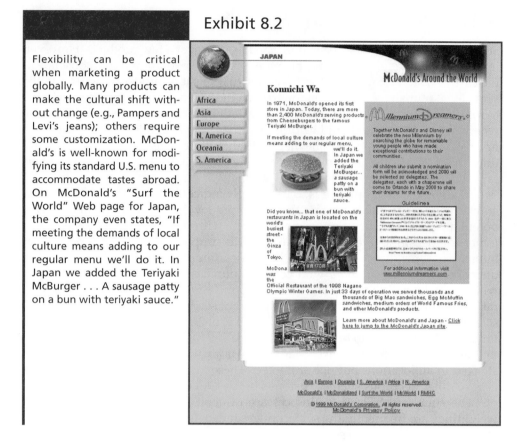

Flexibility can be critical when marketing a product globally. Many products can make the cultural shift without change (e.g., Pampers and Levi's jeans); others require some customization. McDonald's is well-known for modifying its standard U.S. menu to accommodate tastes abroad. On McDonald's "Surf the World" Web page for Japan, the company even states, "If meeting the demands of local culture means adding to our regular menu we'll do it. In Japan we added the Teriyaki McBurger . . . A sausage patty on a bun with teriyaki sauce."

www.mcdonalds.com
www.mcdonalds.com
/surftheworld/

However, in many cases demand and usage conditions vary sufficiently to require some changes in the product. For example, German products are very precise in their performance specifications; if a German product is said to have a lifting capacity of 1,000 kg, it will perform precisely up to that level. Similarly, buyers of Japanese machine tools have found that these tools will perform at the specified level but not beyond them. The U.S. counterpart, however, is likely to maintain a safety factor of 1.5, resulting in a substantially higher payload capacity. Customer usage may take these patterns into account. Consumer goods typically require substantial product adaptation because of their higher degree of culture grounding. For example, McDonald's adjusts its menu to take regional taste preferences into account (see Exhibit 8.2). In the United States, menus in the South carry iced tea, whereas those in the Northeast do not. Internationally, menu additions include beer in Germany and wine in France, while in India, the core product—beef—is deleted from the menu due to local sensitivities. The degree of change needed may depend on economic conditions in the target market as well as on cultural differences. For instance, low incomes in a particular market may suggest a need to simplify the product to make it affordable to those customers.

There is no easy answer to questions of **adaptation**. Certainly in the case of mandatory adaptations, firms must conform to the prevailing economic, legal, and climatic conditions in the market. For discretionary adaptations, firms must resolve the issue of whether the effort is worth the costs involved in adjusting production runs, stock control, or servicing. Such cost factors perhaps accounted for the fact that U.S. carmakers for decades refused to make right-hand driven cars for the Japanese market. At the same time, of course, such a lack of adaptation to local preferences also resulted in low sale of U.S. cars to Japan.

PACKAGING

Packaging is needed to deliver a product to the consumer in sound condition, be it a bottle for shampoo or a box with shock-absorbing padding to protect delicate electronic goods. The requirement here is purely technical: an efficient container designed to hold and protect the product. As self-service has become a dominant feature in most distribution chains, the packaging of a product has become a major element of the product itself. It is often the supplier's only opportunity at the point of sale to present the benefits of the product to the potential consumer who has picked it up to assess its value. Packaging considerations therefore must be broadened beyond the container aspects. One important issue concerns product description. The package must convey to the potential consumer not just what the product is but also what it does. This initial message is conveyed by words, graphics, and the overall design of the package, which the potential buyer is expected to read in a few brief seconds and probably from a distance of three feet or more. **Packaging** must also convey a required **product image**. For example, the boxes for expensive chocolates look expensive in themselves—so much so that one almost hates the waste of throwing the packaging away. Packaging is also linked to product value. Many packages are designed to make their contents look like more than they really are. Liquid laundry detergent bottles, for example, feature large cutouts for use as a handle in order to portray a bigger outline without using extra product. Alternatively, the package may be designed as compact as possible to make the most of the available shelf space. Stackability, so that a shelf can take several layers of product, is another packaging option.

Packaging also needs to harmonize with consumer usage. Thus it delivers pharmaceuticals in tamperproof and childproof containers or with built-in applicators, such as inhalers. Built-in handles allow "economy" packs to be carried. Suppliers must also keep the packaging demands of their customers in mind. In an industrial setting, these may be quite varied. Some large customers, such as Wal-Mart, may delineate precisely how products are to be packaged. In other cases, the development of a packaging strategy that, for example, makes breakbulk of a large shipment at a warehouse easier, may be the winning formula for gaining a competitive edge.

www.wal-mart.com

Packaging in the world market takes on even more importance. An international shipment is subject to the motions of the vessel on which it is carried and to the stress of transfer among different modes of transportation. Differences in climate can also play a major role; special provisions need to be made to prevent damage to the product when the ultimate destination is very humid or particularly cold. Moreover, dramatic changes in climate can take place in the course of long-distance transportation. As a result of heat, for example, grass packaging that is perfectly adequate at the point of shipment may be totally useless at the point of arrival. The weight of packaging must also be considered, particularly when airfreight is used, as the cost of shipping is often based on weight. At the same time, packaging materials must be sufficiently strong to permit stacking in international transportation. Another consideration is that, in some countries, duties are assessed according to the gross weight of shipments, which includes the weight of packaging. Obviously, the heavier the packaging, the higher the duties will be. The supplier must also pay sufficient attention to instructions provided by the customer for packaging. For example, requests that the weight of any one package not exceed a certain limit, that specific packaging dimensions be adhered to, or that bar coding be used may reflect limitations or requirements of transportation and handling facilities at the point of destination.

In addition to these marketing considerations, the formal package description, typically on the label, must conform to any legislative standards for the

www.isetan.co.jp

product category, particularly in terms of the list of ingredients. Packaging must also be responsive to environmental legislation and concerns. As such, it must comply with societal demands for subsequent use, recycling, or disposal. To a growing degree, the ability to reflect such demands is a crucial determinant for market acceptance and profitability. Increasingly customers expect the amount of packaging materials to be minimized and the materials themselves to be environmentally "friendly." For example, Isetan Corporation, one of Japan's leading retail chains, uses simplified wrapping for traditional midyear and year-end gifts rather than the elaborate wrapping used previously.[36]

STRATEGIES FOR SERVICES

So far in our discussions, the term *product* has been used to designate both goods and services. However, services have some different requirements from goods and therefore need to be considered separately. Services also are increasingly part of the global marketplace, as Manager's Corner 8.4 explains.

Manager's Corner 8.4

Service jobs move abroad

If you dial the toll-free reservation number for Jamaica's Wexford Court Hotel, you'll find yourself speaking to an agent with a Jamaican accent. Your call will have automatically become an international one, because the hotel's booking office for American guests is located on the island of Jamaica, and calls are routed there by satellite. Previously, the work had been done by a Miami-based reservation center.

Tom Kelly, who heads a $70 million Eastman Kodak (www.kodak.com) research laboratory, can see Mount Fuji from the lab. He works in Yokohama, where his job requires him to hire Japanese researchers to develop new technology for Kodak. According to Kelly, "If you're serious about staying competitive globally, you've got to be on the ground [in Japan]."

If the buzzword in the 1980s was the "global factory," with American-owned factories opening in lower-cost nations, the new trend is the "global office." Thanks to advances in communications technology and a more sophisticated workforce in many countries, white-collar jobs are increasingly moving around the world. Companies in many industries have taken advantage of the global office. CIGNA Corporation (www.cigna.com), the huge insurer, opened a $5 million center for processing medical claims in the Irish town of Loughrea. A software development facility set up by Texas Instruments in Bangalore, India, is linked by satellite to TI's Dallas headquarters. Editors in Barbados prepare manuscripts for Chicago-based R. R. Donnelley & Sons (www.donnelley .net) to print in the United States. GE Capital (www.gecapital.com) has its business information and financial data from America and Europe updated, reconciled, and corrected in India. And many companies, including Dow Corning (www.corning.com) and IBM (www.ibm .com), have research laboratories in Japan.

In response to the exodus of blue-collar jobs to low-wage countries, many economists downplayed the importance of manufacturing to the U.S. economy's long-term vitality. The enormous growth in the service sector, they say, is more than adequate to make up the difference. However, as white-collar jobs move overseas, they seem to be a less-dependable part of America's economic future. Many developing countries offer tax incentives and start-up assistance to woo service companies to their shores, and workers in these countries earn only one-third the rate paid to comparable U.S. workers. With these advantages, businesses in developing countries are hopeful that they will be able to handle such operations as software development, telemarketing, and data entry. The trend has caused some concern among U.S. labor unions. According to Dennis Chamot, who works for the AFL-CIO's (www.aflcio.org) department for professional employees, "As office work becomes more electronic, it becomes easier to move."

Sources: "Spice Up Your Services," *Economist,* January 16, 1999, 59; John Burgess, "Global Offices on Rise as Firms Shift Services Jobs Abroad," *Washington Post,* April 20, 1990, E1; Susan Moffat, "Picking Japan's Research Brains," *Fortune,* March 25, 1991, 84–86.

---

36. "Think Global, Act Local," *Jetro Monitor* 6 (September 1991): 3.

SERVICE CATEGORIES

"Service" is a general classification that covers both pure services that stand by themselves (such as insurance and consultant services) and services that support goods. Computers, for example, require sophisticated **support services.** In such cases, service elements are ultimately as important and as costly as the physical good itself, although customers typically view the physical good as the dominant element. A home security service is based on physical goods—intruder alarms and smoke detectors—but many homeowners are happy to pay a consultant to design and install them and to pay the people who maintain the service.

The simple knowledge that services and goods can interact is not enough: Successful managers recognize that different customer groups view the service–good combination differently. The type of use and usage conditions also affect evaluations of the market offering. For example, an airline's record of on-time arrivals may be valued differently by college students than by business executives. Similarly, a 20-minute delay will be judged differently by a passenger arriving at the final destination than by one who has just missed an overseas connection. As a result, adjustment possibilities in both the service and goods areas emerge that can be used as a strategic tool to stimulate demand and increase profitability. As Figure 8.11 shows, the importance of service and goods elements varies substantially. The manager must identify the role of each and adjust all of them to meet the desires of the target customer group. By rating the offerings on

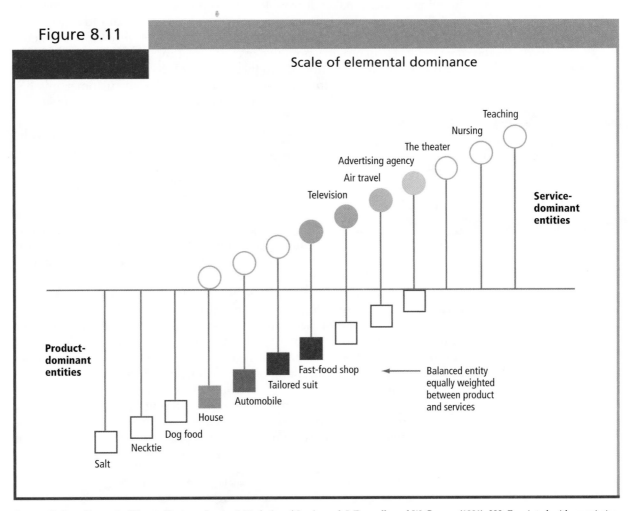

Figure 8.11

Scale of elemental dominance

Service-dominant entities

Product-dominant entities

Teaching
Nursing
The theater
Advertising agency
Air travel
Television

Fast-food shop
Tailored suit
Automobile
House
Dog food
Necktie
Salt

Balanced entity equally weighted between product and services

Source: G. Lynn Shostack, "How to Design a Service," *Marketing of Services,* ed. J. Donnelly and W. George, (1981): 222. Reprinted with permission of the American Marketing Association.

a scale ranging from dominant tangibility to dominant intangibility, the manager can compare offerings and also generate information for subsequent market positioning strategies.

DISTINCTIVE FEATURES OF SERVICES

Services differ from goods most strongly in their intangibility. This inability to hold and touch services has important implications, ranging from difficult competitive comparisons to financing, and makes precise specifications, such as the ones used in manufacturing, almost impossible. Though the intangibility of services is a primary differentiating criterion, it is not always present. For example, publishing services ultimately result in a tangible good—namely, a book or a computer disk. Similarly, construction services eventually result in a building, a subway, or a bridge. Even in those instances, however, the management of the intangible component that leads to the final product is of major concern to both the producer of the service and the recipient of the ultimate output, because it brings with it major considerations that are nontraditional to goods.

Another major difference concerns the storing of services. Services are difficult to inventory. If they are not used, the "brown around the edges" syndrome makes them highly perishable. Unused capacity in the form of an empty seat on an airplane, for example, quickly becomes nonsalable. Once the plane has taken off, selling an empty seat is impossible—except for an in-flight upgrade from coach to first class—and the capacity cannot be stored for future use. Similarly, the difficulty of inventorying services makes it troublesome to provide service backup for peak demand. To maintain constant service capacity at levels necessary to satisfy peak demand would be very expensive. The manager must therefore attempt to smooth out demand levels in order to optimize overall use of capacity.

For many services, the time of production is very close to or even simultaneous with the time of consumption, which necessitates close customer involvement in the production of services. Customers frequently either service themselves or cooperate in the delivery of services. As a result, the service provider often needs to be present when the service is delivered. This physical presence creates both problems and opportunities, and it introduces a new constraint that is seldom present in the marketing of goods. For example, close interaction with the customer requires a much greater understanding of the cultural factors of each market. A service delivered in a culturally unacceptable fashion is doomed to failure. A common pattern of internationalization for service businesses is therefore to develop stand-alone business systems in each country.[37]

> A service delivered in a culturally unacceptable fashion is doomed to failure.

Because of the close interaction with customers, many services are customized; this contradicts the firm's desire to standardize its offering, yet at the same time it offers the service provider an opportunity to differentiate the service. The concomitant problem is that in order to fulfill customer expectations, service consistency is required. For anything offered online, however, consistency is difficult to maintain over the long run. Therefore the human element in the service offering takes on a much greater role than in the offering of goods. Errors may enter the system, and unpredictable individual influences may affect the outcome of the service delivery. The issue of quality control affects the provider as well as

---

37. "Winning in the World Market" (Washington, D.C.: American Business Conference, November 1987), 17.

the recipient of services because efforts to increase control through uniform service may be perceived by customers as the limiting of options and may therefore have a negative market effect.[38]

Buyers have more difficulty observing and evaluating services than goods. this is particularly true when the shopper tries to choose intelligently among service providers. Customers receiving the same service may use it differently. This aspect of service heterogeneity results in services that may not be the same from one delivery to another. For example, the counseling by a teacher, even if it is provided on the same day by the same person, may vary substantially depending on the student. Moreover, the counseling may change over time even for the same student. As a result of all these possible changes, it becomes very difficult to compare services to one another, meaning that for buyers (and often also suppliers) the **transparency** of the services market is low.

Because service quality may vary for each delivery, quality measurements are quite challenging. In response to this challenge, much research work has been carried out in the service quality measurement field. The most visible effort consisted of the SERVQUAL model, which proposed a series of measures to determine the discrepancy between expectations and perceptions of services by customers.[39] Over time, the measures used have been significantly expanded and refined.[40] Most researchers, however, agree that the most important tool for service design and evaluation is **blueprinting**. This refers to a visual definition of a service process that displays each subprocess or step in the service system and links the various steps in the sequence in which they appear. A service blueprint then allows the identification of processes that are visible to the customer, those that are invisible, and the possible failure points. An understanding of these processes and their linkages then allows the firm to design quality into the service.[41]

MARKETING REPERCUSSIONS OF SERVICES

The marketer must first determine the nature and the aim of the services offering, that is, whether the service will be aimed at people or at things and whether the service itself will result in tangible or intangible actions. Table 8.1 provides examples of a classification that will help the marketer clearly determine the position of the services effort. The manager must then consider the tactical variables that have an impact on the preparation of the service offering. For example, the measurement of capacity and delivery efficiency often remains highly qualitative rather than quantitative. Furthermore, the intangibility of the service reduces the manager's ability to provide samples, which makes communicating the service offered much more difficult than communicating an offer of goods. Brochures or catalogs explaining services often must show a proxy for the service to provide the prospective customer with tangible clues. For instance, a cleaning service can show a picture of an individual removing trash or cleaning a window, but the picture will not fully communicate the performance of the service. Because of the different needs and requirements of individual consumers, the manager must also pay attention to the two-way flow of communication. In the service area, mass communication often must be supported by intimate one-on-one follow-up. New technological capabilities to communicate individually with each potential client may presage a host of new opportunities for delivering service information.

38. G. Lynn Shostack, "Service Positioning Through Structural Change," *Journal of Marketing* 51 (January 1987): 38.

39. Valarie Zeithaml, A. Parasuraman, and Leonard L. Berry, *Delivering Quality Service: Balancing Customer Perceptions and Expectations* (New York: Free Press, 1990).

40. Masoud Hemmasi, Kelly C. Strong, and Steven A. Taylor, "Measuring Service Quality for Strategic Planning and Analysis in Service Firms," *Journal of Applied Business Research* 10, no. 4 (1994): 24–34.

41. Zeithaml et al., *Delivering Quality Service*, 159.

Table 8.1

Understanding the nature of the service act

Nature of the service act	Direct recipient of the service	
	People	Things
Tangible actions	Services directed at people's bodies: Health care Passenger transportation Beauty salons Exercise clinics Restaurants Haircutting	Services directed at goods and other physical possessions: Freight transportation Industrial equipment repair and maintenance Janitorial services Laundry and dry cleaning services Landscaping/lawn care Veterinary care
Intangible actions	Services directed at people's minds: Education Broadcasting Information services Theaters Museums	Services directed at intangible assets: Banking Legal services Accounting Securities Insurance

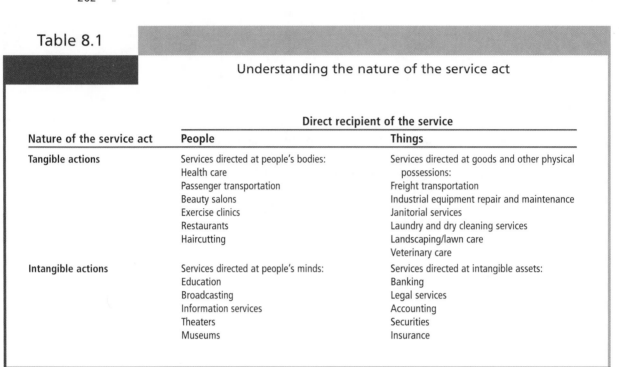

Source: Christopher H. Lovelock, "Classifying Services to Gain Strategic Marketing Insights," *Journal of Marketing* 47 (summer 1983): 9–70. Reprinted with permission of the American Marketing Association.

The role of personnel deserves special consideration in **service delivery**. The customer interface is intense, so proper provisions must be made for training personnel both domestically and internationally. Major emphasis must be placed on appearance. Most of the time the person delivering the service—rather than the service itself—will communicate the spirit, value, and attitudes of the service corporation. This close interaction with the consumer also has organizational implications. While tight control over personnel may be desired, the individual interaction that is required points to the need for decentralization of service delivery. This in turn requires delegation of large amounts of responsibility to individuals and service subsidiaries and demands a great deal of trust in all organizational units. This trust, of course, can be greatly enhanced through proper training and supervision. Sole ownership also helps strengthen this trust. Research has shown that service firms, in their international expansion, tend to greatly prefer the establishment of full-control ventures. Only when costs escalate and the company-specific advantage diminishes will service firms seek out shared-control ventures.[42]

The lack of storage capabilities for services results in the need to aggressively accommodate variations in demand. For example, staff schedules may need to overlap, and part-timers or seasonal staff may be called in to accommodate demand at peak times. Job flexibility may also be essential, so that employees can be redeployed into different functions. For example, line managers in the hotel and catering industries may help with the serving of customers at peak times. Table 8.2 shows some examples of how demand and supply can be balanced in their service system.

The areas of pricing and financing also require special attention. Because services cannot be stored, greater responsiveness to demand fluctuation exists, and therefore greater pricing flexibility must be maintained. As a result, people who book last-minute flights on airlines may be able to get a better price if there

42. M. Krishna Erramilli and C. P. Rao, "Service Firms' International Entry-Mode Choice: A Modified Transaction-Cost Analysis Approach," *Journal of Marketing* 57 (July 1993): 19–38.

Table 8.2

Actions to balance supply and demand in service systems

Supply side	Demand side
1. Inventory wherever possible (e.g., spare capacity, people, etc.).	1. Have customers wait in favorable environments.
2. Schedule workers according to demand (e.g., shift working, part-time employees).	2. Schedule customers (e.g., appointment systems).
3. Subcontract work to other service organizations.	3. Provide substitute goods or services (e.g., automatic tellers).
4. Have peak-time efficiency routines (e.g., only do essential jobs).	4. Diversify demands (e.g., enter counterseasonal markets).
5. Increase customer participation in the production process (e.g., self-service).	5. Turn customers away during peak demand period (e.g., differential pricing).
6. Share service/facilities with other service organizations.	6. Use marketing to shift demand (e.g., advertising campaigns).
7. Improve the service system (e.g., use technology where possible).	7. Change customer expectations of service (e.g., through usage).

Source: Donald Cowell, *The Marketing of Services* (Boston: Butterworth Heinemann, 1984), 42. Reprinted by permission of Butterworth Heinemann Publishers Oxford, a division of Reed Educational & Professional Publishing Ltd.

is a large number of unoccupied seats. Alternatively, someone who is willing to dine in a restaurant during off-peak hours may be able to use a discount coupon. Pricing flexibility is countered by the desire to provide **consistency** for both the seller and the buyer of services in order to foster an ongoing relationship. The intangibility of services also makes financing more difficult. Even financial institutions with considerable experience are often less willing to provide financial support for services than for goods, because the value of services is more difficult to assess, service performance is more difficult to monitor, and services are difficult to repossess. Therefore, customer complaints and problems in receiving payments are more troublesome for a lender to evaluate in the area of services.

Services often require entirely new forms of distribution. Traditional channels frequently are multitiered and long and therefore slow. Often they cannot be used at all because of the perishability of services. A weather-reporting service, for example, either reaches its audience quickly or rapidly loses value. As a result, direct delivery and short distribution channels are required for services. When they do not exist, service providers need to be distribution innovators to reach their market. Increasingly, many services are "footloose," in that they are not tied to any specific location. Advances in technology make it possible for firms to separate production and consumption of services. As a result, labor-intensive service performance can be moved anywhere in the world where qualified, low-cost labor is plentiful. As we read in Manager's Corner 8.4, services such as hotel reservations and insurance claim processing are performed with great ease and at low cost far from the customer. As communication technology further improves, other services such as teaching, medical diagnosis, or bank account management can originate from any point in the world that offers the most cost-efficient service production location and yet can still reach customers in many countries.

The unique characteristics of services exist in both domestic and international settings, but their impact has greater importance for the international manager. For example, the perishability of a service, which may be a mere obstacle in domestic business, may become a major barrier internationally because of the longer distances involved. Quality control for international services may be much more difficult because of different service uses, changing expectations, and varying national regulations. International services are also more sensitive to cultural factors than are goods. Their influence on the individual abroad may be

europa.eu.int

welcomed or greeted with hostility. For example, countries that place a strong emphasis on cultural identity have set barriers inhibiting market penetration by foreign service firms. France is leading a major effort within the European Union to cap the volume of American-produced films to obtain more playing time for French movies.

SUMMARY

The good or service as seen by the consumer constitutes much more than just a physical core product; all the intangibles that accompany the product form the package. The product audit is used to explore what this package comprises. The Ansoff Matrix looks at the four main growth strategies and demonstrates the increase in risk as a company moves from penetration of the known market to diversification into a totally unknown market.

The theory of the product life cycle says that the stages of introduction, growth, maturity, decline, and postmortem that a product goes through are to be reflected in the corresponding marketing mix. Even though most attention is focused on new product launches, most products are in the maturity stage, where they need careful management attention in order to either prolong their life cycle or to lead to graceful retirement.

A popular theoretical tool for structuring product portfolios is the Boston Consulting Group Matrix. Its four quadrants are based on market share and market growth: problem children (or question marks), stars, cash cows, and dogs. Because of its assumption of a significant product life cycle and economies of scale, the Boston Matrix may have less relevance than its advocates suggest. In any event, use of the matrix requires a sound understanding of the complex interrelationship between market growth rate and relative share.

The development of a product mix needs to consider both the width and the depth of product lines and may require line stretching or line rationalization. In doing so, the firm must carefully consider the implications of such product policies on sales, profits, and relationships with customers and suppliers.

When using a strategy of market expansion, the firm must consider whether and how to standardize or adapt its products. In addition, attention must be devoted to packaging. No longer simply driven by product protection, packaging must reflect market requirements, promotional opportunities, and distribution considerations.

Services, whether related to goods or pure services, have distinctive features. In particular, they are more dependent on people, which necessitates more, and higher, standards of management. The intangibility of services means that the associated physical elements may be used for promotion, and strong branding is important. The lack of storage capacity may require new efforts at smoothing out demand fluctuations through personnel management or pricing strategies.

Overall, even though all elements of the marketing mix are equally important, the product is the most visible component and serves as the focal point for all marketing mix aspects.

QUESTIONS FOR REVIEW

1. How do you determine what the goods or service package comprises?

2. What is the Ansoff Matrix? How is it used, and how does it approach risk?

3. What are the stages of the product life cycle? What strategy is employed at each stage?

4. What are the differences between product, market, and technological life cycles?

5. What is the Boston Consulting Group Matrix and how is it used?

6. What are the problems posed for use of the product life cycle? What are the problems posed by use of the Boston Matrix?

7. How can you achieve the requisite width and depth in the product mix?

8. How do services differ from goods? How are these differences dealt with from a marketing standpoint?

9. How does service standardization differ from goods standardization?

QUESTIONS FOR DISCUSSION

1. In the 1960s, American automakers introduced three new cars: the Mustang, the Camaro, and the Firebird/Trans Am. These brands marked the beginning of a completely new product category, the pony car, which was tremendously successful. Recently, however, rising costs of ownership (purchase price, insurance premiums, and fuel costs) and blurred lines of distinction between pony cars and the higher line cars with which they compete have caused sales for all three models to drop dramatically. Ford has adapted by expanding the Mustang product line, thereby expanding the appeal of the product beyond the shrunken pony car segment. Although it will cease production of the current Firebird/Trans Am and Camaro in 2001, GM plans to extend the life of the brand names. The new models would be designed to meet different consumer wants and needs than those of their predecessors. Considering the reactions to shifts in the automotive market by both companies, discuss the differences in the applicability of the product life-cycle theory to product categories (e.g., pony cars) versus brands (e.g., Mustang or Camaro).[43]

2. Levi Strauss' international success can be attributed, in part, to the fact that it creates product lines specific to various countries or regions. Vintage Clothing, All Duty™ and STA-PREST® from Europe, and Crinkle 501® from Japan, are some examples of clothing lines developed specifically for foreign consumption. Mitutoyo is a world leader in the manufacture and sales of industrial measuring equipment such as depth gauges and calipers. In contrast to Levi Strauss, Mitutoyo makes few or no changes to product lines developed in Japan that are sold there and also distributed abroad. Explain why certain companies would adopt a standardization or a customization policy when it comes to marketing their products internationally.[44]

3. Procter & Gamble's recent launch of two new global products marks the beginning of a company initiative to shorten the development, test marketing, and introduction of products designed to be sold worldwide. Dryel home dry-cleaning kit and Swiffer sweeper system spent only 18 months in test marketing performed

43. Steven Cole Smith, "What Does the Future Hold for Pony Cars?" *Car and Driver* 45, no. 2 (August 1999), 52–69.
44. www.levistrauss.com/index_hr.html.

simultaneously in the United States and Europe. P&G will use standardized packaging, brand names, and advertising to pitch the products in American, European, and Asian markets. Standardization will allow P&G to get the two products to market in less than one third of the time required for similar products in the past. Analyze how P&G's ability to take these two new products from development to introduction so quickly might have influenced their decision to market the products globally. How will P&G's marketing strategy affect the international product life cycle for the two products?[45] For more details, see Marketing in Action 9.2 on page 295.

4. In Europe, cellular service often includes more than just phone calls. Sonera cellular service of Finland allows customers to use their mobile phones to charge purchases of commercial products such as vending-machine sodas or car washes and consolidate the charges on their cellular service bill. Omnitel of Italy will soon introduce voice recognition systems that can offer advice about restaurants or relay stock quotes, bank balances, or news and weather information—all through cellular technology. Sonera, Omnitel, and others also plan to make Internet access available through the cellular phone. Americans have not yet embraced such cellular extras for pricing and technological reasons. How can American cellular service providers combat the competitive advantage enjoyed by their European counterparts? How can U.S. companies create domestic demand for the types of supplemental cellular services described above?

45. Tara Parker-Pope, "P&G Cleaning Products Get on Fast Track," *Wall Street Journal*, May 18, 1999, B6.

FURTHER READINGS

Cooper, Robert G., Scott J. Edgett, and Elko J. Kleinschmidt. *Portfolio Management for New Products*. Reading, Mass.: Addison Wesley Longman, 1998.

Kotabe, Masaaki, Arvind Sahay, and Preet S. Aulakh. "Emerging Roles of Technology Licensing in Development of Global Product Strategy: A Conceptual Framework and Research Propositions." *Journal of Marketing* 60 (January 1996): 73–88.

Kurtz, David L., and Kenneth E. Clow. *Services Marketing*. New York: John Wiley & Sons, 1998.

Lovelock, Christopher H. *Principles of Services Marketing and Management*. Upper Saddle River, N.J.: Prentice Hall, 1999.

chapter

9

New Products

New Products
ew Products
New Products
New Products

The first stage in developing new products or services is to undertake a *gap analysis* to establish what the new offering will need to provide. This need may be best met by a feature modification of an existing product or service. Most new product development is, in fact, an incremental development of existing brands, rather than introduction of totally new offerings.

Following the usual (Western) approach, a new development first has to be judged against corporate needs and then against the product factors that the organization can handle. The "creative" steps of developing new products are described in this chapter, as are the subsequent screening and testing stages, to ensure that risk is minimized. Brand stability implies there should be more emphasis on the further development of existing brands than on totally new ones—contrary to conventional teaching. The Japanese approach, however, is to launch many more "new" products without following any of the stages of testing described here.[1]

The one common element of life-cycle theory and portfolio management that is almost universally accepted is that products or services that remain unchanged will sooner or later die. Consumers' tastes or circumstances may change, or the product may be superseded. The Internet is accelerating product development and inevitably shortening the product life cycle (see Manager's Corner 9.1). Inevitably, any

> ## products or services
> ## that remain unchanged
> ## will sooner or later die

organization that plans to be around for more than a few years has to move into the area of new product development, even if it is only to redevelop its existing product or service to extend its life cycle indefinitely.

Manager's Corner 9.1

How does the Internet influence new product development and marketing?

Marketing strategists often assume that marketers should first create a plan on the basis of a careful review of environmental and firm information and then execute that plan. However, in some cases these two occur simultaneously. In the article "The Convergence of Planning and Execution: Improvisation in New Product Development," published in the July 1998 issue of the *Journal of Marketing* (www .ama.org/pubs/jm), authors Christine Moorman and Anne S. Miner define such convergences as "improvisation." They investigated the conditions in which improvisation is likely to occur and be effective.

The results show that organizational improvisation occurs moderately. It also shows

---

1. Michael R. Czinkota and Masaaki Kotabe, "Product Development the Japanese Way," in *Trends in International Business: Critical Perspectives.* ed. Michael R. Czinkota and Masaaki Kotabe (Cambridge, Mass.: Blackwell, 1998), 153–158.

that the frequency of improvised product development decreases as long as the company keeps good track of past product development experiences and increases as market uncertainties and turbulences increase. Although improvisation may reduce new product effectiveness, environmental and organizational factors can reduce negative effects and sometimes create a positive effect for improvisation. This suggests that, in some contexts, improvisation may be not only what organizations actually do practice but also what they should practice in order to flourish.

Electronic commerce puts forward-thinking companies on the leading edge of consumer need identification, helping them to improve new product development and marketing processes. Given the speed and ease of information gathering on the Internet, market intelligence analysis and product development plans proceed increasingly in tandem. The Internet has both upstream and downstream benefits in the corporate value chain. The two most important "downstream" benefits of online marketing are the ability to collect behavioral sales data rapidly and the resulting consumer intimacy. Behavioral data allows marketers to develop relevant marketing campaigns targeting their most valuable customers immediately. Consumer intimacy allows marketers to beat traditional manufacturers to market with successful new products. The important "upstream" benefit of online marketing is that of an information tool that links an original equipment manufacturer with suppliers, distributors, and contract manufacturers to reduce cost, eliminate waste, and speed up new product development.

The Internet opened the gates for manufacturers to sell direct to consumers. Many argue that e-commerce is less intimate than retail, but it actually provides more targeted demographic and psychographic information. Manufacturers that traditionally sell through the retail channel can benefit the most from e-commerce. Furthermore, customer information is no longer held hostage by the retail channel. Instead, marketers have access to robust behavioral data, which allows them to segment best customers and identify trends and customer needs. Most importantly, the data allow for the development of relevant marketing messages aimed at important customers and initiates loyal relationships. Clearly, more interactive, improvised product development and marketing processes are increasingly becoming a mainstay of marketing strategy, which further shortens the product life cycle.

Sources: "Improvisation Can Help New Product Development," *Marketing News,* July 20, 1998, 42; James Carbone, "There's More to E-Commerce Than POS," *Purchasing,* December 10, 1998, S14; Andrew Degenholtz, "E-Commerce Fueling the Flame for New Product Development," *Marketing News,* March 29, 1999, 18.

The most successful new product development typically revolves around the revitalization of existing products. Launches of totally new products generate the drama, but the profit is more likely to come from the more mundane relaunches (see Figure 9.1).[2] About 30 percent of 3M's annual revenues come from products less than four years old, but most of these new products are actually variations on older ones.[3]

www.3m.com

In the service sector, there is a continuing need to develop the offerings that are made to customers or clients

In this chapter, as elsewhere in this book, the term *product* includes services and nonprofit activities. In the service sector, just as in the manufacturing sector, there is a continuing need to develop the offerings that are made to customers or clients, even though there is normally much less new product development activity in the service sector.

2. Roy Rothwell and Paul Gardiner, "The Strategic Management of Re-Innovation," *R & D Management* 19 (April 1989): 147–160.

3. "The Mass Production of Ideas, and Other Impossibilities," *Economist,* March 18, 1995, 72.

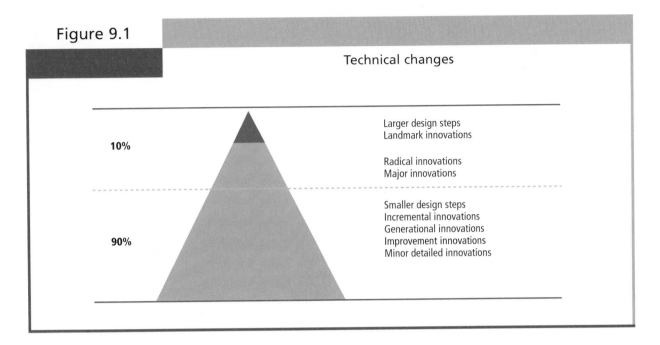

Figure 9.1

GAP ANALYSIS FOR SCANNING AND IDEA GENERATION

The need for totally new products or for additions to existing lines may have emerged from the portfolio analyses, in particular from the use of the BCG Matrix (see Chapter 8). The gaps in the projected cash flow demonstrated by that exercise could have provided sufficient stimulation, but it is more likely that the need will have emerged from the regular process of following trends in consumers' requirements. At some point a gap will have emerged between what the existing products offer the consumer and what the consumer demands. That gap has to be filled if the organization is to survive and grow.

www.bcg.com

To locate a gap in the market the technique of **gap analysis** is often used. In Figure 9.2, the thick descending line shows what the forecasted profits are for the organization as a whole. The rising dotted line shows where the organization (in particular its shareholders) *wants* those profits to be. The shaded area between these two lines represents what is called the **planning gap**: this shows what is needed from new activities in general and of new products in particular.

The planning gap may be divided into four main elements: (1) usage gap, (2) distribution gap, (3) product gap, and (4) competitive gap. The relationship between these gaps is best illustrated in Figure 9.3.

USAGE GAP

The usage gap occurs between the total potential for the market and the actual current usage by all the consumers in the market. Clearly two figures are needed for this calculation:

- Market potential
- Existing usage

Figure 9.2

Gap analysis

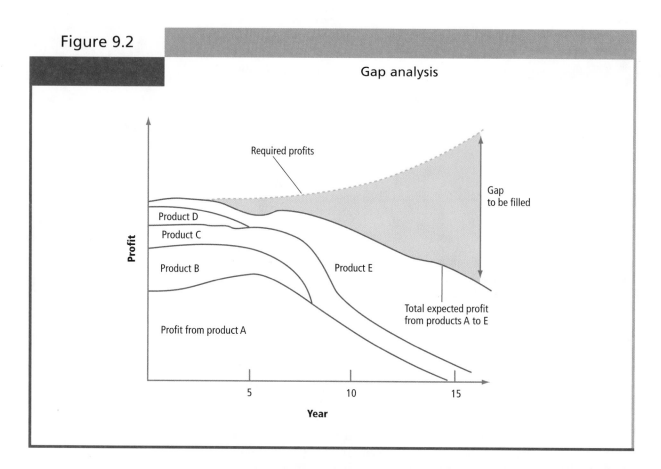

Figure 9.3

Four levels of gaps in a market

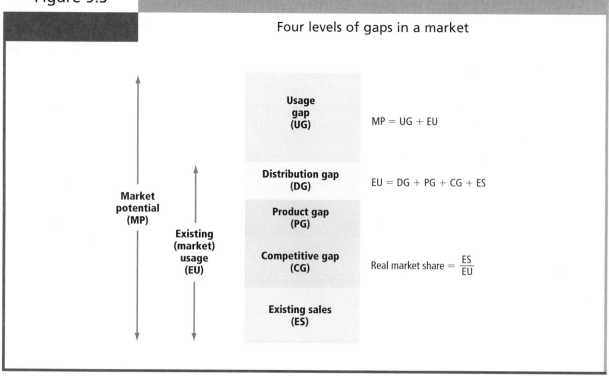

MARKET POTENTIAL.   The most difficult estimate to make is probably that of the total potential available in the whole market, including all segments covered by all competitive brands. It is often achieved by determining the maximum potential individual usage, and then extrapolating this by the maximum number of potential consumers. This is inevitably a judgment rather than a scientific extrapolation, but some of the macroforecasting techniques, which were discussed in Chapter 6, may assist in making this "guesstimate" more soundly based.

The maximum number of consumers available will usually be determined by market research, but it may sometimes be calculated from demographic data or government statistics. Of course, there ultimately will be limitations on the number of consumers. The cosmetics market, for example, is currently limited to most women and girls over the age of 12, but the boundaries of this market may shift in the future. Not so long ago the market's lower age boundary was something over 16 years, and who can say that men will not at some time in the future also purchase cosmetics? After all, they have in recent years purchased perfume, known as men's colognes and fragrances and sometimes even camouflaged as aftershave lotions.

For guidance one can also look to the numbers using similar products. Those wishing to sell the newly developed compact disc would have paid great attention to existing sales of record and cassette decks. Alternatively, a marketer can look to what has happened in other countries. It has often been suggested that Europe follows patterns set in the United States, but after a time lag of a decade or so. The increased affluence of all the major Western economies means that such a time lag can now be much shorter. In fact, in the recent case of the development of a video–CD standard, European and Japanese companies have led the way. One group trying to set the standard is a team led jointly by Philips and Sony, whereas the other is a team of companies led primarily by Toshiba.[4]

www.philips.com
www.sony.com
www.toshiba.com

The maximum potential individual usage, or at least the maximum attainable average usage (there will always be a spread of usage across a range of customers), will usually be determined from market research figures. It is important, however, to consider what lies behind such usage. One consumer panel produced some very high averages when one of the panel members decided to feed her flock of turkeys on a specific brand of porridge oats; the resulting dramatic increase in usage was included in the overall results.

EXISTING USAGE.   The existing usage by consumers makes up the total current market, from which market shares are calculated. It is usually derived from marketing research, most accurately from panel research such as that undertaken by ACNielsen, but also from *ad hoc* work. Sometimes it may be available from figures collected by government departments or industry bodies; however, these are often based on categories that may make sense in bureaucratic terms but are less helpful in marketing terms. The **usage gap** is thus:

www.acnielsen.com

$$\text{usage gap} = \text{market potential} - \text{existing usage}$$

This is an important calculation to make. Many, if not most, marketers accept the *existing* market size, suitably projected over the timescales of their forecasts, as the boundary for their expansion plans. Although this is often the most realistic assumption, it may sometimes impose unnecessary limitations. The original market for video recorders was limited to the professional users who could afford the high prices involved. It was only later that the technology was extended to the mass market. Another ongoing example is the declining coffee consumption as illustrated in Marketing in Action 9.1. Can the existing consumption level be increased?

---

4. "Disc Jockeying," *Economist*, January 28, 1995, 60.

Marketing in Action 9.1

Coffee for the younger generation

Nestlé S.A. (www.nestle.com) may be the world's largest food company, but its coffee products are fighting a drink war with the likes of Coca-Cola and Pepsi. Unfortunately for Nestlé and other large coffee roasters, soft drinks are becoming the drink of choice in America. Because most coffee is purchased in the grocery store, not even the specialty coffee stores have been able to make coffee popular with the younger generation.

The Nestlé Company groups its products into nine categories: baby foods and cereals, milk and dairy products, breakfast cereals, desserts, snacks and ice creams, chocolate and confectionery, convenience and prepared foods, hot and cold beverages, mineral water, and pet care. The hot and cold beverages category includes five roasted coffee products: Bonka, Hills Brothers, Loumidis, MJB, and Zoegas. Additionally, Nestlé markets six brands of soluble coffee and premixed coffee beverages: Nescafé Cappuccino, Nescafé Classic, Nescafé Vending Machines, Nescafé Gold Blend, Nescafé Ice, and Taster's Choice.

While cola companies were hitting the younger generation with advertising that focused on the refreshing aspects of cola, coffee roasters were targeting the older generation with decaffeinated coffee ads. As the older generation began to reduce its coffee consumption, major coffee roasters realized that coffee product interest had declined dramatically. By 1999, coffee ranked below milk, cola, tea, fruit drinks, juices, and alcoholic beverages in popularity.

To recapture the drink market, Nestlé and other major coffee roasters are focusing on new products targeted to today's youth. These new products will likely include flavored coffees laden with milk and sugar. For coffee roasters, are new products and new target markets the key to successfully closing the usage gap in the beverage market? Is coffee simply in the decline stage of the product life cycle, and, if so, should these coffee roasters continue to focus on the older generation?

Source: Nikhil Deogun, "Joe Wakes Up, Smells the Soda," *Wall Street Journal,* June 8, 1999, B1+.

Sometimes the market potential can be grossly overestimated. Approximately $5 billion has been spent on HDTV research and lobbying by companies whose expectations were apparently much greater than what was reasonable. At approximately $3,000 per HDTV set, consumers have not been rushing to showroom floors to purchase the new TVs. Even in Japan, where 10 years of trial broadcasts of HDTV have taken place, a limited number of the sets have been purchased. The recent upgrade of equipment of all of the major American TV networks that did not include HDTV capability and the known preference of most consumers for lower-quality, lower-priced goods (compare demand for laser discs versus VHS tapes), clearly indicates that the $5 billion spent so far is not likely to be recovered anytime soon. Although HBO started HDTV service on March 6, 1999, with only about 45 percent of the network's film titles in true wide-screen HDTV, the diffusion of HDTV into the mainstream household market is slow at best.[5]

www.hbo.com

In the public sector, where the service providers usually enjoy a "monopoly," the usage gap will probably be the most important factor in the development of services, although, as we shall shortly see, the product gap should not be ignored. Persuading taxpayers to pay their income taxes more promptly, for example, should probably be more important to the Internal Revenue Service than opening more local offices and providing free assistance on the phone.

www.irs.gov

The usage gap is most important for the brand leaders. If they have a significant share of the whole market—say in excess of 30 percent—it may become

---

5. "Screened Out," *Economist,* September 24, 1994, 66; Glen Dickson, "HBO Ready to Go with HDTV," *Broadcasting & Cable,* January 25, 1999, 112.

worthwhile for a firm to invest in expanding the total market. The same option is not generally open to the minor players, although they may still be able to profitably target specific offerings as market extensions—as Amstrad and Compaq in particular have in their new extensions to the PC market.

www.amstrad.com
www.compaq.com

All other "gaps" relate to the difference between the organization's existing sales (its market share) and the total sales of the market as a whole. This difference is the share held by competitors. These "gaps" will, therefore, relate to competitive activity.

DISTRIBUTION GAP

The **distribution gap** is imposed by the limits on the distribution of the product or service. If distribution is limited to certain geographical regions, as some draught beers are, it cannot expect to make sales in other regions. At the other end of the spectrum, multinational corporations may take distribution to the extremes of globalization. Equally, if the product is limited to certain outlets, just as some categories of widely advertised drugs are limited by law to pharmacies, then other outlets will not be able to sell them. A more likely outcome is that by not being the market leader, a brand will find its overall percentage of distribution limited. The remedy here is simply to maximize distribution.

Unfortunately, maximizing distribution is not quite as easy as it sounds, except for the obvious market leaders. It is true that additional sales force effort, backed by suitable sales promotional activities, should be able to increase distribution somewhat, although there will still need to be a balance between the benefits gained and the costs incurred. The prime barrier to distribution will probably be the resistance of the distribution chains to stock anything other than the bestsellers. With the power of new computer systems, retailers can more easily tell what they are selling in each of their stores and are now less likely to overstock products that do not sell well or to run out of products that do sell well.[6] This can be partially overcome in the short term by offering better terms and higher margins so that the distributors make more on each sale. The distributors have long since learned that their biggest profits come from concentrating on the main brands. They, above all, live by the *80/20 Rule.*

Again, the Internet may help reduce the distribution gap in many industries. Internet users are becoming more comfortable with the idea of ordering goods over the Web. As a result, the music industry, for instance, is raising the stakes. The big companies want to sell tunes directly to consumers and to transmit the product instantly to personal computers. It is an intriguing vision. Fans would not have to wait in line at a music store for the latest release from hitmakers such as Backstreet Boys, Elton John, Madonna, Whitney Houston, Will Smith, or Britney Spears. Consumers could just click on the right buttons on their PCs, wait about 3 minutes for the download, and boogie (see Exhibit 9.1). The music companies pushed further ahead with a potentially important announcement. Universal Music, Warner Music, Sony, BMG, and EMI—and their partner, IBM—unveiled a technology that makes it easier for companies to track and control music and sales over the Web. Indeed, the distribution gap is disappearing in the music industry.[7]

> the Internet may help
> **reduce the distribution gap**
> in many industries

www.mcarecords.com
www.warnerbros.com
www.sony.com
www.bmg.com
www.emichrysalis.co.uk
www.ibm.com

---

6. "Change at the Check-Out," *Economist*, March 4, 1995, special section, SS3–SS5; Masaaki Kotabe, "The Return of 7-Eleven . . . from Japan: The Vanguard Program," *Columbia Journal of World Business* 30 (winter 1995): 70–81.
7. David Lieberman, "Music Companies Collaborate to Download Tunes," *USA Today*, February 9, 1999, 6B.

Exhibit 9.1

The Internet has created a distribution advantage for new products in many industries, including the music industry. For their 1994 Voodoo Lounge tour, the Rolling Stones broadcast the first five songs of a Texas concert over the Internet. Users with the correct software were able to hear new songs by the Rolling Stones and preview the concert. Future broadcasts of this type could eliminate the need for a record company and perhaps aid bands in their fight against concert promoters like TicketMaster.

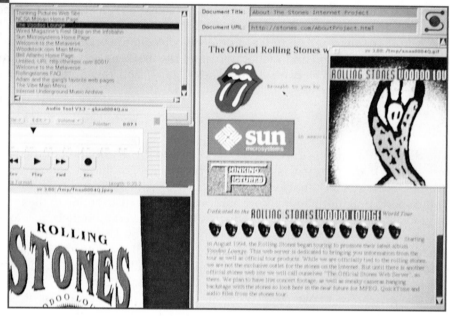

PRODUCT GAP

The **product gap**, which could also be described as the segment or positioning gap, represents that part of the market from which the individual organization is excluded because of product or service characteristics. This may have occurred because the market has been segmented and the organization does not have offerings in some segments. Alternatively, the effective positioning of its offering excludes it from certain groups of potential consumers, because there are competitive offerings much better placed in relation to these groups.

This segmentation may well be the result of deliberate policy. As we have already seen, segmentation and positioning are very powerful marketing techniques, but the trade-off is that some parts of the market may effectively be put beyond reach. On the other hand, this outcome may frequently be by default; the organization has not thought about its positioning and has simply let its offerings drift to where they are now. Because of this product gap, for example, General Motors and Ford still have difficulty competing in the high-end luxury car segment against Mercedes and Toyota's Lexus Division.

www.gm.com
www.ford.com
www.mercedesbenz.com
www.toyota.com
www.lexus.com

The product gap is probably the main element of the planning gap in which the organization can have a productive input, hence the emphasis on the importance of correct positioning in Chapter 7.

COMPETITIVE GAP

The **competitive gap** refers to the differences in effectiveness of a firm's marketing strategy relative to its competitors in the same product market. Again, consider the luxury car segment in the United States. It has been less than a decade since Toyota launched its Lexus models in this segment, once dominated by Mercedes-Benz; Lexus now outsells Mercedes by a large margin. Obviously, Toyota has been more effective in executing its marketing strategy than Mercedes. Manager's Corner 9.2 illustrates the changing concept of Japanese product quality that could widen the competitive gap between Japanese and U.S. automakers.

The competitive gap represents the effects of such factors as price and promotion in terms of the effectiveness of their messages. It is what marketing is

Changing concept of product quality—from "engineering" quality to "feeling" quality

Japanese companies are reeling from the dramatic appreciation of the yen today, and thus are having tremendous difficulty pricing their products competitively in the U.S. market. Consequently—and hastily, however—U.S. business executives as well as MBA students have begun to believe it is the end of the "Japan era" in global competition. Can we really relax? Uh oh, Detroit, watch out. Once again, something extraordinary is happening in Japan. Just as U.S. carmakers have gotten their product quality up to par, the Japanese are redefining and expanding the term. The new concept is called *miryokuteki hinshitsu*—making cars that are more than reliable—that fascinate, bewitch, and delight. In plain English,

it translates into "things gone right." It signals a campaign by the Japanese to engineer unprecedented measures of look, sound, and "feel" into everything from family sedans to luxury models. At the same time they continue to improve reliability.

As Mark Twain once wrote, "If you stand still on the road, you will get run over." You can never relax in an era of global competition. Once the Big Three automakers narrow their competitive gap vis-à-vis their Japanese rivals, they should move on relentlessly to look for a next generation of competitive advantage. That is the only known means of survival in a competitive world.

Sources: "A New Era for Auto Quality," *Business Week,* October 22, 1990, 83; B. Bowonder and T. Miyake, "Creating and Sustaining Competitiveness: An Analysis of the Japanese Robotics Industry," *International Journal of Technology Management* 9 (May–June 1994): 575–601; Mark Magnier, "Japan, While Stronger Than in 1993, Watches Yen Appreciation Cautiously," *Journal of Commerce and Commercial,* March 9, 1995, 8A.

popularly supposed to be about. As we have already seen, the product or service itself will still be the prime focus of marketing activity. Needless to say, the competitive gap is not a factor in the case of the monopoly provision of services by the public sector.

Gap analysis is a tool to help you examine as thoroughly and objectively as possible your current marketing position and the strategies that you could follow to improve and better align them with

> Gap analysis is a tool to help you examine **your current marketing position** and the strategies that you could follow

overall company strategies. It may direct you to fresh product or market strategies—and to the need to develop new and improved products.

MARKET GAP ANALYSIS

In the type of analysis described previously, companies search for gaps in the product range. Another perspective—essentially taking the "product gap" to its logical conclusion—is to look for gaps in the *market* that the company could profitably address, regardless of where its current products stand.

Many proactive marketers would, indeed, question the worth of the theoretical gap analysis described earlier. Instead, they would immediately begin a search for a competitive advantage.

BROADER OBJECTIVES

Gap analysis largely focuses on incremental changes of existing products in existing markets. Even within this most important quadrant, however, the list of possible innovations can be expanded. Peter Drucker,[8] for example, suggests five possibilities:

---

8. Peter Drucker, *The Practice of Management* (New York: Harper, 1954).

1. New products or services that are needed to attain marketing objectives

2. New products or services that will be needed because of technological change that may make present products obsolete

3. Product improvements needed both to attain market objectives and to anticipate expected technological changes

4. New processes and improvements in old processes needed to satisfy market goals—for instance, manufacturing improvements to make possible the attainment of pricing objectives

5. Innovations and improvements in major areas of activity—in accounting or design, office management or labor relations—so as to keep up with advances in knowledge or skill

Despite being more than 40 years old, this list offers sound advice. The last two categories, and in particular the emphasis on innovations in other areas of activity, are often neglected in the "new product" development process. The focus is on the product itself, where changes in how it is manufactured, delivered, or supported may in fact be the main areas where competitive advantage can be gained.

Innovation is important—indeed essential—to the future of most organizations. However, it must be kept in context. Tom Peters and Robert H. Waterman, Jr.'s well-known exhortation[9] still offers sound advice:

Stick to the knitting . . . While there were a few exceptions, the odds for excellent performance seem strongly to favor those companies that stay reasonably close to the businesses they know.

"Focus," as it is now more fashionably known, is a sound policy. Perhaps more important is a keen awareness that the future usually also depends on the existing products (albeit so incrementally changed over time that they would be unrecognizable to today's customers). In this context, it is worth noting the five new product strategy scenarios that were identified based on a study of 140 companies in Canada:[10]

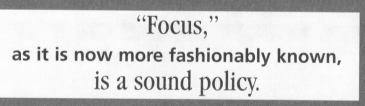

"Focus,"
as it is now more fashionably known,
is a sound policy.

- **Technologically driven strategy** (26 percent of firms). A strategy based on technological sophistication, but lacking marketing orientation and product fit/focus. New products tend to end up in unattractive, low-synergy markets with moderate results; high impact on firm, but low success rate.

- **Balanced, focused strategy** (16 percent of firms). This winning strategy features a balance between technological sophistication, orientation and innovation, and a strong marketing orientation. The program is highly focused, and new products are targeted at very attractive markets, with by far the strongest performance.

- **Technologically deficient strategy** (16 percent of firms). A "nonstrategy": weak technology, with low technological synergy, yet involving new markets and new market needs. Results tend to be very poor.

- **Low-budget, conservative strategy** (24 percent of firms). A low level of R and D spending, involving "me-too" products, but with a "stay-close-to-home" approach—high technological synergy and high product fit/focus. A safe and efficient but undramatic program, with moderate results: good success rate and profitability, but low impact.

9. Tom J. Peters and Robert H. Waterman, Jr., *In Search of Excellence* (New York: Harper and Row, 1982): 292–305.
10. Robert E. Cooper, "Overall Corporate Strategies for New Product Programs," *Industrial Marketing* 14 (August 1985): 179–193.

- **High budget, diverse strategy** (19 percent of firms). A high level of R and D spending, but poorly targeted; new (highly competitive) markets to the firm, no program focus. Results tend to be very poor.

BEYOND THE TRENDS

Even the broader perspective described in the previous section does not, however, cover the major developments in markets that result in quantum leaps and overturn the long-standing positions in those markets. For example, the first steam engine was built in 1705, but it took more than a century to perfect and dramatically improve manufacturing efficiency. Likewise with electricity. Though it was demonstrated in 1876 that small electrical generators could light a lamp, it took decades more of development before electric power generators delivered major productivity gains in factories. And the computer revolution really has been an evolution, with the clunky and expensive mainframes of the 1950s leading to the midsize but still pricey minicomputers of the 1970s and in turn to the small, cheap but far more powerful PCs of the 1990s.[11]

The path of innovation is rarely smooth or predictable. A random discovery can start the whole thing. It may run into numerous blind alleys. Yet a built-in urge—driven by scientific curiosity or commercial gain—can give it momentum. Eventually, one technique spawns an array of unexpected ones. Indeed, even after an idea has emerged, it often cannot be adequately explored by market research because the general public has no understanding (based on previous experience) of what it may mean. Educating the customer is frequently the first objective of such product or service launches.

For instance, consider what happened after 3M's laboratory technician Spencer Silver discovered the glue now used on "Post-it Notes" and his colleague Arthur Fry made the intellectual leap of applying this to the notes themselves:[12]

www.3m.com

> Conventional test marketing still failed, however, until the two executives took a hand. Enthusiasts themselves for the product, they realized its potential indispensability would only be appreciated if it got physically into the hands of potential customers. They gave away wads of little notepads to secretaries, receptionists, bank clerks and businessmen, saying "Here, try this," and watched people becoming literally addicted to the product.

The role of the product champion, the executive who drives the development of the product (often against the odds), is frequently a critical element of new product success.

Dramatically innovative "products" have had major impacts in a number of markets. Although such products are few and far between, their influence on our lifestyle has been vastly greater than that

> The role of the product champion **is frequently a critical element** of new product success.

of the evolving products or services. Think about the notebook computers with built-in modems that became popular in the last five years or so. As a result, we now can work at home or even while vacationing in the mountains of Colorado without going to our offices in Chicago. Similarly, virtual reality, such as "morphing," has changed the excitement of going to see movies forever.

What is more, as we have seen, innovations follow few of the rules of conventional marketing. Even market research is of little use in the basic decisions (although it still is of considerable use in helping to determine the exact details of

---

11. "The Millennium—Ideas: Slow and Steady—The Creation of Some of Our Greatest Products Is Often Unplanned—and Rarely Smooth," *Wall Street Journal*, January 11, 1999, R18.
12. Carol Kennedy, "Planning Global Strategies for 3M," *Long Range Planning* 21 (February 1988): 9–17.

the launch).[13] The main requirement is faith in the new development. The most successful organizations try to create the sort of environment in which such creativity is nurtured. They also foster the mental attitude that will quickly recognize the merits of such outstanding innovations.

> it is the regenerated "cash cow"
> ## that continues to dominate
> even the "development" process in most markets

www.bah.com

As a result of the lack of conventional marketing input to these important new developments, a number of practitioners, as well as some academics, have recently tended to downplay the importance of conventional marketing. That is a mistake. With the distorting benefit of hindsight, we tend to notice the few major developments. We do not see the many hundreds of failures, which were just as sincerely supported by their creators.

Booz-Allen & Hamilton's seminal research[14] offers a very useful classification of new products, based on the newness of the product and its impact on the market. Although many products are considered *new*, the level of their newness varies, and their relative proportions are also indicated, as follows:

New-to-the-world products (entirely new markets) 10 percent

New product lines (new products in existing markets) 20 percent

Additions to existing lines 26 percent

Improvements in/revisions to existing products 26 percent

Repositioning (existing products in new segments/markets) 7 percent

Cost reductions (similar performance at lower cost) 11 percent

Above all, it should be remembered that, despite the glamour of the new product process, it is the regenerated "cash cow" that continues to dominate even the "development" process in most markets (see Manager's Corner 9.3).

PRODUCT MODIFICATION

In practice, most "new" products are modified existing ones. How many times have you seen a television commercial that tells you, "New Brand X now has added Y!"? Such changes are incremental, often barely even that, and follow somewhat different rules from genuine new products. Typical modifications may include the following:

Feature modification. Sometimes called "functional modification," this approach makes changes (usually minor ones) to what the product or service does. Manufacturers of compact disc players added "programming" and remote control to these basic devices to make them marginally more attractive to users (but a margin that gave them a competitive advantage). Frequently, the main element of the modification will simply be a change in packaging. However, it may be expanded into the major message needed to rejuvenate a jaded advertising campaign.

Quality modification. As consumers grow more discriminating, many suppliers (often led by their Japanese competitors) have gradually increased the quality of the basic product. This may be more difficult to convey to consumers, particularly if the product already has a bad image. However, it can be very powerful if successful, as the Jaguar Car Company, now owned by Ford Motor Company, has demonstrated by continually improving its luxury sedan's reliability in the 1990s.

www.jaguar.com
www.ford.com

---

13. John P. Workman, Jr., "Marketing's Limited Role in New Product Development in One Computer Systems Firm," *Journal of Marketing Research* 30 (November 1993): 405–421.
14. Booz-Allen & Hamilton Inc., *New Products Management for the 1980s*, 1982.

Manager's Corner 9.3

Busy-ness of new product development in the computer industry: competing to "compute"

Comdex (www.comdex.com) may be known as the king of personal computer trade shows, but it is always the flood of new personal gadgets that has generated the loudest buzz among event visitors. Every few feet, companies are touting the latest smart phones, identification cards, digital television sets, tiny recording devices, and other computerized products that fall into the catchall category of personal companions. Industry analysts see this push toward mobile appliances as a logical reaction to hypercompetitive conditions in the desktop market. Many companies, both big and small, in search of new growth opportunities are betting that consumers will want more than one digital device to meet their information and communication needs.

A leader in this emerging space is 3Com Corp. (www.3com.com), whose PalmPilot handheld computer has spawned both copycat hardware manufacturers and a rush among software developers to create applications. 3Com sold more than 1 million of the portables in one year alone. The device, which sells for less than $400, allows consumers to store and modify information such as names, addresses, and daily schedules.

Nearly all of these products are light and compact as well as robust and functional. The industry understands that there will never be a single perfect size that will satisfy all consumers. That is why you see everyone experimenting with different designs. As the industry continually strives toward smaller, faster, and more reliable appliances, the look and design of these computers have broadened to fit a myriad of tastes. A laptop is no longer just a laptop. Today, the market consists of everything from the smallest handhelds from Hewlett-Packard (www.hp.com) to ultraslim PCs from Toshiba (www.toshiba.com) to feature-packed machines from IBM (www.ibm.com) and Compaq (www.compaq.com).

Then there are the many vendors who have partnered with Microsoft (www.microsoft.com) around Windows CE, the software king's stripped-down operating system aimed at digital appliances. On display at Comdex were palm-sized PCs that require a penlike stylus for inputting data along with larger devices with bigger screens and more comfortable keyboards.

There were new products, variants, and modifications galore at Comdex. It is, however, the consumers who vote with their pocketbooks and who decide what works and what does not.

Source: P. J. Huffstutter, "Thinking Big by Getting Small: Personal Digital Devices Proliferate at Comdex Trade Show," *Los Angeles Times,* November 19, 1998, 1.

Style modification. This is perhaps the most frequent modification, at least in style-conscious industries. An "old-fashioned" product may be unsaleable in some markets, although it may find a niche in more conservative ones. An annual model change in automobiles is a good example. On the other hand, Volkswagen's famed Beetle, known as the "bug," has found a great niche in Mexico by *not* changing its style as the world's most economical car in the past 60 years. For the United States and other developed markets, Volkswagen has also introduced a modern version of its almost identical-looking, yet souped-up Beetle.

www3.vw.com

Image modification. This may also be associated with style modification (or "perceived quality" changes), but in essence the product or service itself remains unchanged, and some image modifications may actually stress style modification. "Image modification" concentrates on changing the non-product attributes, so that consumers feel that the total package has changed. Image is often the most important element of that package. For example, Pepsi modified the image of its can by making it look more futuristic and "space age."

www.pepsiworld.com

Another good example is national beer producers, which have been battered by the enormous popularity of microbreweries in recent years. In an attempt to keep up with finicky consumers, the national beer companies have undertaken a practice labeled "phantom branding" to lure consumers to their products. Miller Brewing Company now sells its Icehouse beer as a product of the fake Plank Road Brewery. Similarly, Coors Brewing in Golden, Colorado, produces Killian's Irish Red and positions it as an import.[15]

www.millerbrewing.com
www.coors.com

CREATING NEW PRODUCTS

In the 1960s and 1970s, when marketing was a relatively young profession, it was often claimed that the best new products were bound to be those that were specifically created to meet the needs of the marketplace.[16] Ideally, such products originated with the market researcher discovering unsatisfied wants. It is still held to be true that new product ideas, once they have emerged, should be rigorously tested against the needs of the market before the organization's full resources are committed.

> the really creative ideas come **from every direction,** emerging from the least likely places

However, marketing practice has since shown that the really creative ideas can rarely be turned on like a faucet to meet the market researcher's specifications. They come, instead, from every direction, sometimes emerging from the least likely places. They may come from technical developments in the laboratories (e.g., the Sony Walkman was conceived by Akio Morita, Sony's chairman, for his own fun), they may come from the sales force, or they may come from practice in other countries or other industries (e.g., 100 percent alcohol-powered automobiles currently marketed in Argentina and Brazil by Ford and Fiat).

www.sony.com

www.pg.com

Consider Procter & Gamble's Liquid Tide laundry detergent. It was a very innovative product developed in a very innovative way by taking advantage of both the company's technical abilities and various market requirements in the key markets around the world. Germans had been extremely concerned about polluting rivers with phosphate, a key whitening ingredient in the traditional detergent. To meet the German customer demand, Procter & Gamble in Germany developed fatty acid to replace phosphate in the detergent. Similarly, Procter & Gamble in Japan had developed surfactant to effectively remove grease in the tepid water that Japanese use to wash their clothes. In the United States, Procter & Gamble in Cincinnati, Ohio, had independently developed builder to keep dirt from settling on clothes. Putting all these three innovations together, the company introduced Liquid Tide and its sister products around the world.

The secret to finding new products is not to specify them but simply to rec-

> The secret to finding new products is **not to specify them but** simply to recognize them.

ognize them. Keep in mind, "Necessity is the mother of invention." This means, then, that the managers of new products must be constantly scanning the sources available to them, particularly the literature, to find these new ideas. The need, therefore, is for an open mind. The **NIH (Not Invented Here) syndrome** is the worst enemy of new product development.

Perhaps the most common way to build an outstanding brand is to be first into a market. This does not mean being technologically first, but rather being

---

15. Gerry Khermouch, "Coors Puts Killian More at Fore," *Brandweek,* March 11, 1996, 4; Trevor Jensen, "It's Plank Road Time: Hurtling Kegs to Flag Miller's Icehouse Beer in SE," *Brandweek,* February 9, 1998, 54.
16. E. Raymond Corey, *Industrial Marketing: Cases and Concepts,* 2d ed. (New York: Prentice Hall, 1976).

first in the mind of the consumer. IBM, Kleenex, Casio, Boeing, and McDonald's did not invent their respective products, but they were the first to build major brands out of them and bring them into the mass market.[17]

CUSTOMERS

By far the greatest sources of new product ideas are customers. After all, they are the users of the product or service, and the new uses they make of it, or the changes in specification they demand, are both the most potent forces on the product development process and its richest source of ideas.

This customer "information" will normally be received from the sales force (or even through correspondence). This may be in the form of descriptions of what the customer is actually doing with the "product" (which may indicate new uses for it), or requests from the customer for specific new products or services.

Eric von Hippel's research[18] reported that, in 81 percent of all the innovation cases studied, it was the user who perceived that an advance in instrumentation was required, amended the instrument, built a prototype, improved the prototype's value by applying it, and diffused detailed information on the value of the invention. He found that the pattern was repeated in the process equipment industry, but it was not universal (two of his students found that the reverse was true in parts of the polymers industry, where it would have been difficult for users to undertake the development). He continued to make a plea for separating all users into "routine users" and "innovative users."

INNOVATIVE IMITATION

Nothing is wrong with imitating competitors' products. In fact, most so-called innovation in the field of product development is actually imitation. A simple look around us quickly shows that imitation is not only more abundant than innovation, but actually a much more prevalent road to growth and profits. Even in the United States, most successful companies began as imitators. Boeing got into jet aircraft as an imitator of British and German inventions; Texas Instruments and Sony entered transistors as an imitator of Bell Lab's technology; Holiday Inns began a motel business as an imitator.[19]

Peter Drucker[20] explains the advantages of this principle, as follows:

> Like being "Fustest with the Mostest," creative imitation is a strategy aimed at market or industry dominance. But it is much less risky. By the time the creative imitator moves, the market has been established and the new venture has been accepted. Indeed there is usually more demand for it than the original innovator can easily supply. The market segmentations are known or at least knowable. By then, too, market research can find out what customers buy, how they buy, what constitutes value for them, and so on. Most of the uncertainties that abound when the first innovator appears have been dispelled or can at least be analyzed and studied.

Perhaps many Japanese companies are the most successful exponents of this technique. For instance, Matsushita, a global electronics manufacturer of Panasonics, Quasar, Technics, and National brands, deliberately adopts a policy of

www.ibm.com
www.kimberly-clark.com
www.casio.com
www.boeing.com
www.mcdonalds.com

www.ti.com
www.belllabs.com
www.holiday-inn.com

www.mei.co.jp
www.panasonic.co.ip

17. Peter Doyle, "Building Successful Brands: The Strategic Options," *Journal of Consumer Marketing* 7 (spring 1990): 5–20.
18. Eric von Hippel, *The Sources of Innovation* (Oxford: Oxford University Press, 1988).
19. Theodore Levitt, *The Marketing Imagination* (New York: Free Press, 1983).
20. Peter F. Drucker, *Innovation and Entrepreneurship* (New York: Harper & Row, 1985), 222.

www.jvc.com
www.rca.com
www.philips.com
www.sony.com
www.mei.co.jp

"followership."[21] This has most clearly been demonstrated by the company's domination of the video recorder market using its VHS format (together with its Panasonic, JVC, and RCA brands) to displace Philips' V2000 brand and Sony's Betamax, although the latter were considered more technically innovative. Matsushita now has a virtual domination of this market.

Sony learned an important lesson in defense from this experience. Only six months after it launched its revolutionary palm-sized camcorder, Matsushita launched an even lighter look-alike. Within weeks, Sony hit back by launching two new models, one even lighter still and the other with new features. It was able to do this because it had invested in *parallel development*—it had been developing the next generation of product even while it was still introducing the previous one. Succinctly stated, Japanese marketing revolves around the management of product market evolution. They manage not only the product life cycle of individual products, but also the evolution of a complex of product lines and items. They carefully choose and sequence the markets they enter, the products they produce, and the marketing tactics they adopt.[22]

An alternative approach, still based on "imitation," is to find the major problems associated with existing products in a market and to develop a product that resolves them (or at least resolves those that are seen by consumers as having the highest priority). However, this approach will not work against the majority of brand leaders unless marketing managers are alert and informed about their product's performance.

CORPORATE RESPONSE

Assuming that the gap analysis has shown the need for a specific new product or service or for some marketing activity to improve performance in some other area, the next stage will be to determine whether such a product, or service, or activities can be "profitably" developed.

The first consideration will be how it meshes with the existing activities undertaken by the organization. The context for this examination should be that of the formal corporate strategy—the statement of where the organization has decided it is going.

Some of the internal corporate factors that may need to be taken into account in further investigations will be production capabilities, financial performance, investment potential, human factors, materials supply, cannibalism, and time.

PRODUCTION CAPABILITIES

Whether the new product or service can actually be produced will depend on what is available within the organization. Adding extra demand onto equipment that is already being run close to full capacity may either place impossible demands on production or lead to a disproportionately large investment. The existing plant may be unsuitable or may not be ready to handle the expanded demand. General Motors launched a new division, Saturn, with a huge fanfare in 1991. Despite Saturn's prelaunch promotional success, however, various engineering and production snafus prevented Saturn Division from delivering enough cars to meet a sudden increase in demand. As a result, many potential customers were wooed away by competitors such as Honda and Toyota in the first years of production.

www.gm.com
www.saturn.com

www.honda.com
www.toyota.com

---

21. Richard T. Pascale and Anthony G. Athos, *The Art of Japanese Management* (New York: Simon & Schuster, 1981), 41.

22. Philip Kotler, Liam Fahey, and Somkid Jatusripitak, *The New Competition* (Upper Saddle River, N.J.: Prentice Hall, 1985).

The limitations in service sectors might at first sight appear to be less serious, although expansion of local branch premises, if needed, may not be a trivial matter. But the constraints imposed by the availability of human resources, especially those involving specialist skills, may prove to be just as severe a problem as in manufacturing sectors.

FINANCIAL PERFORMANCE

Financial performance is, in large part, what the Boston Consulting Group (BCG) Product Portfolio Matrix is about. The question to be asked is whether the organization can afford the proposed changes. This is not just a matter of potential profits but of cash flow. The extra investments in stock and debt, let alone in plant or promotion, may be too much for a strained cash flow or departmental budget to support.

www.bcg.com

INVESTMENT POTENTIAL

The BCG Matrix relates to cash generation for investment from internal cash flows. This represents the usual form of investment for most larger organizations; the stock market has declined in importance as a primary source of investment funds. On the other hand, in some situations external financing (now more commonly obtained from banks rather than the stock market) will be needed. The standing of the organization with the financial community then becomes an important factor.

This financing of investment is particularly problematic for those medium-sized businesses that are still too small to challenge the major players effectively but have overhead growing. This means that they can no longer survive as small "niche" players. New product policy is particularly important in this situation, as are mergers and acquisitions, which may (at least in theory, but not always in practice) offer a more immediate solution.

HUMAN FACTORS

The available workforce may be a factor and will become an increasingly important one with the demographic changes that are taking place. Chances are that new developments will require skilled personnel, who are becoming increasingly difficult to recruit and keep. It is sometimes possible for the existing workforce to be retrained, but the marketing plans may have to take the organization's training capabilities into account. Such capabilities are in part a function of corporate and societal culture. For example, large Japanese companies, with their custom of lifetime employment for many of their employees, can receive long-term benefits from training them. The Japanese business can undertake expensive training programs without fear that the workers will leave the company. Employees generally remain loyal to the company in anticipation of life-time employment and, by custom, employees that leave a company are generally not considered for hire by other Japanese companies.[23]

MATERIALS SUPPLY

The availability of raw materials, components, or subcontracted services may be critical. Producers increasingly depend on outside suppliers for the greater part

---

23. Paul Sheard, "Japanese Corporate Governance in Comparative Perspective," *Journal of Japanese Trade and Industry* 1 (1998): 7–11.

of the final product or service that they are assembling. Even the insurance broker depends on the underwriters who will do business with him or her, and the fast-food outlet will have a whole range of suppliers, from the wholesale butchers who provide the meat to the employment agencies that constantly cope with the high staff turnover. If suppliers are scarce or erratic, they will pose major problems. This is the primary reason why many Japanese automakers encouraged their Japanese suppliers to follow them to the United States when they located production facilities here. The close relationship between the principal Japanese company and its suppliers is known as a vertical *keiretsu* and is increasingly practiced by U.S. firms.

CANNIBALISM

www.pg.com
www.tide.com
cheer.com

One often-neglected factor is how much of the new brand's business will come from that of existing brands. Such *cannibalism* must be taken into account where there is any degree of overlap. If the organization is building on its strengths, there often will be (and should be) significant overlap.[24] For example, Proctor & Gamble, a company with multibrand strategy, minimizes cannibalism by positioning its laundry detergents, Tide and Cheer, as "dirt fighter" and "effective at any temperature," respectively.

TIME

www.ibm.com

One of the factors often overlooked in any process of innovation is just how long it may take. For instance, IBM may be able to develop a new feature for an existing product and bring it to the market in a few months, but developing and testing even the simplest complete mainframe computer is likely to take between three and five years. Bringing in a new technology (a new "generation" of computers) is likely to need a development period nearer to a decade. Intel normally takes from three to five years from the start of design work on a new microprocessor until its formal introduction.[25]

> One of the factors often overlooked **in any process of innovation** is just how long it may take.

However, these development timescales are rapidly decreasing. The challenges caused by this progressive acceleration in the pace of development is illustrated in Figure 9.4. Despite an ongoing demand for new products, however, marketers in charge of product development tend to go through a spate of "psychological" problems inherent in this process (see Figure 9.5).

MARKETING RESPONSE

At a more detailed level, the *fit* with the existing marketing factors will need to be considered. Elements that affect the marketing response include the product's match with existing ranges, price and quality, distribution patterns, and seasonality.

MATCH WITH EXISTING PRODUCT LINES

New products will be easier to sell if they complement the existing product lines. Then they will be able to build on existing distribution patterns and may even be able to capitalize on existing awareness and favorable consumer attitudes. The

---

24. Kathleen Reavis Conner, "Strategies for Product Cannibalism," *Strategic Management Journal* 9 (summer 1988): 9–26.

25. "Intel: Far Beyond the Pentium," *Business Week*, February 20, 1995, 88.

Figure 9.4

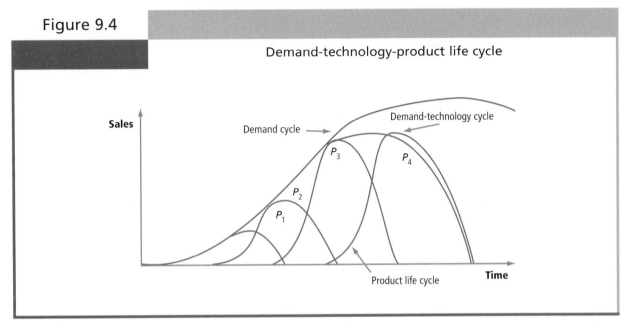

Demand-technology-product life cycle

Source: H. Igor Ansoff, *Implanting Strategic Management*, 1984, 41, published by Prentice Hall International. Reprinted by permission of Pearson Education.

Figure 9.5

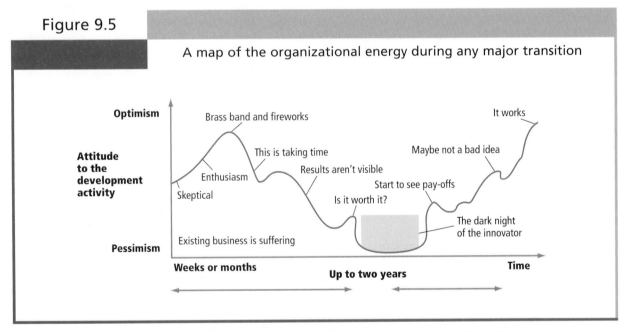

A map of the organizational energy during any major transition

Source: Vincent Nolan, *The Innovator's Handbook* (London: Sphere Books, 1989), 8. Reprinted by permission of Vincent Nolan.

new products may possibly help sell more of the existing ones, because they make the product line more comprehensive. A product line of diet foods will benefit from new additions if these offer a wider choice for the consumer, who may have become bored by the narrower selection previously available. They may also obtain a larger display (shelf space) at the point of sale, up to the point beyond which the retailer will not stock additional items.

PRICE AND QUALITY

There must be some consistency with the existing products or services in terms of consumer perceptions of the price (and quality) range of the organization. This is particularly true when introducing a cheaper product into a high-quality product line. The buyers of the existing product line may see this as reflecting a reduction in the quality of their normal products, and this may have a disastrous effect overall. It may not even help the new product, for consumers in general may assume that, in line with the price, quality has been abandoned. In the 1970s, following a merger, the then very successful line of Rover cars was drowned by the overall mediocrity of the rest of the British Leyland product line—without any noticeable increase in sales of the cheaper product lines.

www.rover.co.uk

At the other extreme, adding a higher-priced product to a cheap product line would probably not be a successful strategy either, as it would be out of line with the overall strategy and unlikely to meet the needs of the existing customers who are, presumably, interested in price. In the 1980s, Honda, Nissan, and Toyota all entered a high-end luxury model segment historically dominated by Mercedes and BMW in the United States. Instead of selling their luxury models as Hondas, Nissans, and Toyotas, the Japanese automakers launched new divisions, called Acura, Infiniti, and Lexus, respectively. Indeed, the Japanese luxury models have successfully taken a market share away from Mercedes and BMW without cannibalizing their own Hondas, Nissans, and Toyotas.

www.honda.com
www.nissan-usa.com
www.toyota.com
www.mercedesbenz.com
www.bmw.com
www.acura.com
www.infiniti.com
www.lexus.com

DISTRIBUTION PATTERNS

Clearly, as we have already seen, if existing distribution channels can be used then costs will be minimized and the product or service can build on existing strengths. If new channels are needed, then their development may pose significant costs and will lead to a learning curve in the handling of those channels, a factor that is not necessarily understood by management.

When launching a new product, particularly in an unfamiliar foreign market such as Japan, use of the existing local distribution channel can be crucial. For example, General Foods has successfully penetrated the Japanese market with its instant coffee products by piggybacking on the well-established distribution channel for seasonings owned by Ajinomoto of Japan. Similarly, Volkswagen has Nissan assemble and distribute its German cars through the Japanese partner's distribution channel.

www.generalmills.com
www.ajinomoto.com
www3.vw.com

SEASONALITY

The ideal organizational trading pattern is an even one, with no seasonal variation, so that resources may be most efficiently utilized, without the unproductive problems posed by having to meet peaks and troughs of sales. Ideally, a new product or service should not be seasonal, or be one that complements existing seasonal patterns—making its peak sales when the others are in a trough, and vice versa. It was reportedly for this reason that the British company Walls decided many years ago to complement its range of ice creams (a summer peak) by starting a hot dog business (a winter peak). Seasonality is also the reason why many refrigeration service firms have added air-conditioning and heating services to their offering.

PRODUCT DEVELOPMENT PROCESS

The complete development process can be conveniently split into a number of stages, as shown in the simplified schematic diagram in Figure 9.6. We have already discussed the first two activities, scanning and idea generation, in the context of gap analysis. Much of the subsequent process comprises steps that are designed to minimize risk. These steps are strategic screening, concept testing, product development, product testing, test marketing, and product launch.

Figure 9.6

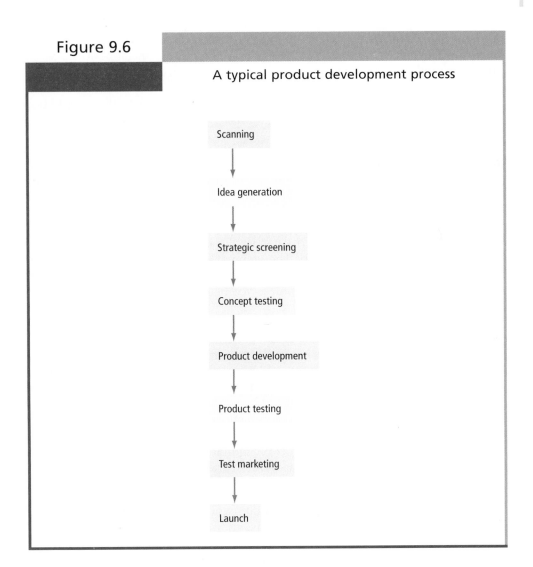

A typical product development process

Scanning

↓

Idea generation

↓

Strategic screening

↓

Concept testing

↓

Product development

↓

Product testing

↓

Test marketing

↓

Launch

STRATEGIC SCREENING

Much of the subsequent process comprises steps that are designed to minimize risk. Indeed, the very next stage is that of the initial screening of these ideas. The contexts for this screening process are the corporate and marketing strategies. We examined the requirements imposed by these in some detail at the beginning of this chapter. The potential new products that have been found are now simply matched against these requirements. This can be handled as a two-stage process.

QUALITATIVE SCREENING. This simply involves qualitative study of the ideas to examine, at the broadest level, whether they conflict with overall corporate or marketing strategies. This need not demand major effort, because the key characteristics of the new product will usually be obvious, as will those of the relevant parts of the strategies—always assuming that the organization takes notice of its own planning documents. A match or mismatch should be fairly obvious.

Make or Buy. The decision either to "make" or "buy out" is likely to be taken at this stage. Traditionally, organizations only offered the products or services that they themselves manufactured. In recent years, many organizations have adopted a wider perspective by marketing products made by other organizations. This is because those other organizations had the special expertise necessary or simply because their costs were lower.

FINANCIAL ANALYSIS. If the qualitative screen reveals no significant problems, the acid test—at this early stage—is to forecast the financial performance of the new brand. The best way to achieve this is to prepare a *pro forma* income statement, together with the associated balance sheet and the traditional further analyses such as cash flow. With the advent of electronic spreadsheets, this should be a relatively simple process.

Sensitivity analysis. The great potential benefit of such spreadsheets, but one rarely capitalized on, is the ability to carry out "What if?" tests (sensitivity analyses) very easily. This means that there should no longer be any excuse for not examining all of the alternatives. For example, a 10 percent change in price will result in a considerably greater than 10 percent change in net profit, and a 10 percent change in volume will also have a disproportionate effect. In a sensitivity analysis, for instance, each of the main variables is altered by 10 percent, and the resulting change in profit is noted. The value of the sensitivity analysis is to see which of the factors has the most effect on net profit. Thus the manager can focus on these variables and perhaps think twice before embarking on a low-price strategy.

The one critical requirement of such a financial analysis is that it must be honest; indeed, as most managers are justifiably enthusiastic about their new products, it should probably aim to be on the pessimistic side. This means that the forecast sales volume in particular should be realistic, and that *all* the costs should be included. Ideally, worst-case scenarios should also be prepared, even if they do not have as wide a distribution.

The danger of building in overly optimistic forecasts can be seen in the experience of the Concorde airliner, as the same development team also carried out this sensitivity analysis. It was not surprising that their optimistic commitment to the new product caused them to considerably underestimate the cost of development and overstate the product's sales potential.

Break-Even Point Analysis. The essential requirement is that the new product should at least break even. In other words, after deduction of both variable and fixed costs, the net operating profit over the projected life of the product or service should at least recover the initial investment. This is demonstrated—and practically calculated—by the use of a simple diagram, as shown in Figure 9.7. The revenue will typically be drawn as a straight line starting at the origin, and this will probably reflect the real situation where the price is unchanged. The variable costs will also be shown as a straight line, but this is more of a simplification because, in practice, there may be steps in the line as new plant capacity has to be added. More importantly, this cost line will start at a height above the origin, which allows for the fixed costs that will occur even if no product is sold, including all the development and launch investments. Assuming that the product does break even, this point will be shown where the two lines cross (and the cumulative revenue covers all the cumulative costs). The shaded area between the lines above this point represents the overall profit. The diagram is a very simple way of demonstrating what volumes are needed to recover all the costs and initial investments.

Marginal Costing. One key concept, which is widely used in marketing and particularly for new products, is that of marginal costing. This says that when considering future plans, any additional (and hence "marginal") business should only bear the **variable** costs incurred. The existing **overhead** costs, which are normally allocated (by a variety of possible methods, but typically by "absorption costing") to the products or services, are *not* included in this case, because it is reasoned that they will be unchanged by the new activity. The aim is to maximize **net**

Figure 9.7

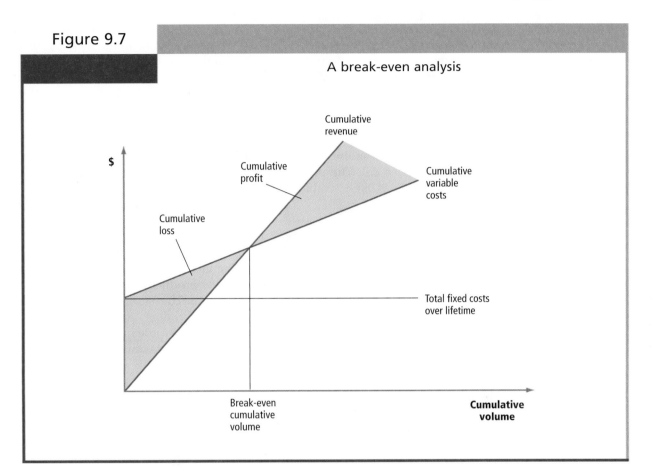

A break-even analysis

profit, or to reach the "optimal" point at which the additional (marginal) costs of the products, services, or activities added are exactly matched by the marginal revenues they generate. Sensible marketers will, however, draw the line somewhat below this point, recognizing that costs are frequently underestimated.

Marginal costing can thus prove to be a particularly valuable accounting technique, which favors growing marketing organizations. However, it should not be allowed to hide the fact that the overhead does eventually have to be picked up by someone. If all the new brands bear no overhead, and the old brands eventually die (perhaps hastened to their grave by the high overhead they have to bear), the marginal profit (conventionally called the **net contribution**) will look excellent, but

> Marginal costing can be a
> **valuable accounting technique,**
> which favors growing marketing organizations.

the overall organization, with no cover for the overhead, may be making a loss.

Marginal costing can also be risky when a company exports its products abroad. A relatively small Korean company manufacturing a certain precision instrument had once received an unexpected purchase order from an American importer. Because it expected just a short-term business relationship with its U.S. importer, the Korean company had set a selling price based on marginal costs plus a reasonable markup, as its overhead cost had been allocated across domestic sales. To its surprise, however, U.S. competitors in the precision instrument industry filed an antidumping charge with the International Trade Commission against this Korean company, alleging that its product was sold at "less than fair value." In other words, the Korean company's overhead cost was not added

www.usitc.gov

on to its selling price. Although the Korean company's marginal costing would have made much marketing sense if sales had occurred in its home market, such pricing might prove to be politically unacceptable for its exports due to anti-dumping laws in the United States.[26] The same could be said for U.S. firms exporting abroad.

CONCEPT TESTING

www.bah.com

Booz-Allen & Hamilton, Inc.'s research has shown that more than 80 percent of new product ideas fail. The proportion that never make it into development is probably at least as high so that, overall, possibly less than 5 percent of new product ideas are successful. Therefore, it is important that the 95 percent of failures be culled as early as possible before large sums are invested in them.[27]

> research has shown that more than 80 percent of new product ideas fail

The **mortality** rates at various stages of the new product process are presented in Figure 9.8. This shows that only one in seven new product ideas resulted in a successful new product introduction. It is perhaps even more interesting that this was a dramatic improvement from an equivalent survey taken in 1968, when the success rate was only one in 58.

This dramatic improvement may have come about because of the improvement in screening procedures at the earliest stage of the new product process—an improvement that may, in part, have been stimulated by the earlier report. Indeed, in the later report it was noted that the success rate of new products once launched had not varied (at 65 percent). Beyond this, Booz-Allen & Hamilton, Inc.'s research showed a number of factors contributing to the success of new products (Figure 9.9). It also found a significant "learning curve" ("experience effect"), where each doubling of the number of new products introduced apparently led to a decline in the cost of introduction by 29 percent.

The **concept test** is the first true consumer filter to be applied. In theory, it should be applied before any significant amount of product development is undertaken, particularly as such development can be very expensive (perhaps hundreds of millions of dollars for a new pharmaceutical). The test is usually undertaken by conventional market research. The aim is simply to find out from consumers what their attitudes to the new product would be and (the acid test) whether they would be likely to buy it. This is easier said than done, because consumers will not usually be able to draw upon existing experiences. They have enough difficulty communicating how they feel about brands that they have actually purchased.

Market researchers use a battery of different techniques to overcome the problem. They may produce dummy versions of the product. However, they are more likely to produce a rough commercial, perhaps just in storyboard form, as this also reflects the difficulty of conveying the concept to the consumers—always a major consideration for a really innovative product. The better finished the vehicle used to carry the concept, the more useful are the responses from the consumers involved likely to be.

Despite the lack of precision in any of these techniques, they are useful in weeding out products or services that have little chance of success. This is potentially very valuable because their creators, who have probably fought many hard battles to reach even this stage, usually can no longer be considered objective.

---

26. Alan M. Rugman and Andrew Anderson, *Administered Protection in America* (New York: Croom Helm, 1987).
27. Booz-Allen & Hamilton Inc., *New Products Management for the 1980s.*

Figure 9.8

The mortality rate at various stages of the new product process

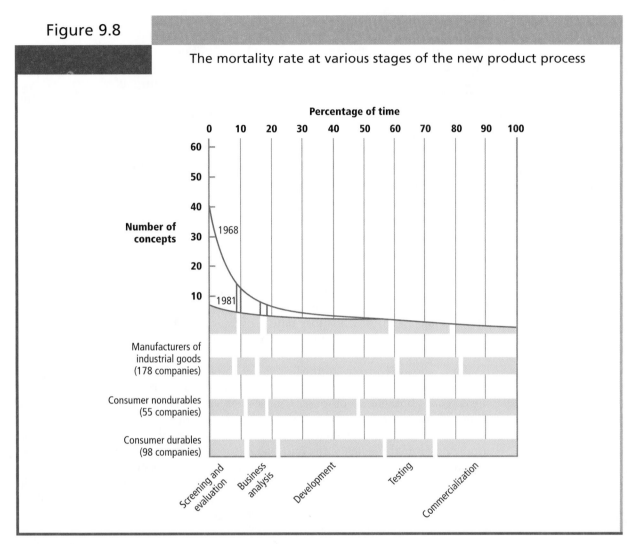

Source: *New Products Management for the 1980's* (Chicago: Booz-Allen & Hamilton Inc., 1982), 14.

Figure 9.9

Factors contributing to the success of new products

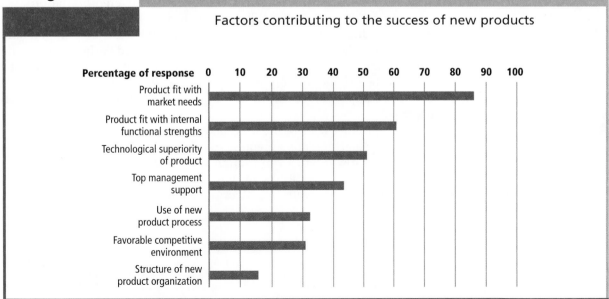

Source: *New Products Management for the 1980's* (Chicago: Booz-Allen & Hamilton Inc., 1982), 16.

PRODUCT DEVELOPMENT

Coming up with a viable concept is one thing, but developing a product is quite another. Between the two may lie a number of years and millions of dollars of research expenditure. Ideally, such development should be driven by the product parameters that were determined by the earlier market research (and, in particular, by the outcome of the concept tests). In reality, though, product development is often more of a creative art rather than a scientific certainty, and what emerges may only be the best possible approximation to what is needed. Indeed, it is probably safe to say that the majority of new products are developed on the basis of creative inspiration *before* any market research is undertaken, and the subsequent market research is only carried out to test their viability (and probably to "justify" their launch).[28]

> product development is often more of a creative art rather than a scientific certainty

Most organizations in the service sector do not have the equivalent of new product development departments. This may be understandable in view of the less-tangible and more transitory nature of their "products." It may, however, also represent an inherent weakness in their marketing armory and leave them very exposed to the developments being explored by their more sophisticated competitors, who are learning *all* the lessons of conventional marketing.[29] One service company that has been incredibly successful with new product development is the discount brokerage company Charles Schwab. Among the major innovations Charles Schwab has brought to its industry are 24-hour, 7-day-a-week order entry for stock trades; an automated telephone order entry system; no-fee mutual funds; no-annual-fee IRA's; fax and pager alerts for its most active traders; a no-fee dividend reinvestment plan; and online trading for its customers to trade via a PC. The reward for Charles Schwab has been impressive. It has increased the customer assets it manages from under $30 billion in 1988 to over $525 billion, including more than $200 billion in Internet accounts, by 1999. Its shares trade at a dizzying 91 times its earnings for the 12 months ending in May 1999.[30]

www.schwab.com

PRODUCT TESTING

With luck, a workable new product or service will be delivered by the product development team. However, there still remains the investment to be made in the launch itself. To reduce the risk, the new product or service is tested on potential consumers in much the same way as the concept was tested earlier. The testing may, however, be more detailed now, because the output of this research can be used to modify the product itself to best match the consumers' needs. An example of product testing as part of the development strategy is described in Marketing in Action 9.2.

Once more, **product testing** must be taken seriously and must be comprehensive; products that are not accepted by consumers and cannot be made acceptable must be discarded. Even though considerable sums may have been spent on development, they will pale in significance against the losses that might be incurred at later stages. Realism is a very precious commodity in the product development business.

---

28. Gordon A. Wyner, "Rethinking Product Development," *Marketing Research* 10 (winter 1998): 49–51.

29. Sundar G. Bharadwaj, P. Rajan Varadarajan, and John Fahy, "Sustainable Competitive Advantage in Service Industries: A Conceptual Model and Research Propositions," *Journal of Marketing* 57 (October 1993): 83–99.

30. Gene G. Marcial, "The Net Gives Schwab its Bounce," *Business Week*, March 22, 1999, 94; Duff McDonald, "Where Will Schwab Go Next?" *Money* (May 1999): 56–58.

Marketing in Action 9.2

Procter & Gamble speeds new product introduction

Procter & Gamble (P&G) (www.pg.com) has provided quality products to consumers since 1837. Entering into the 21st century, P&G has operations in 70 countries, with its consumer products meeting the needs of five billion people in 140 countries. The company employs more than 110,000 people in its global operations.

P&G manufactures products in five major categories: beauty care, food/beverage, health care, laundry/cleaning, and paper. Recently, the company introduced two new products, Dryel and Swiffer, into its laundry/cleaning product line. Popular products within this category include Dawn, Ivory, and Cascade dishwashing products; Comet and Mr. Clean surface cleaners; and Bold, Bounce, Cheer, Ivory Snow, and Tide laundry products.

Historically, P&G spent years test marketing new products. However, the company has brought Dryel and Swiffer into the worldwide market after only 18 months of test marketing. Dryel is a home dry-cleaning kit that responds to consumer frustration with the time and money spent on dry-clean-only clothes. Swiffer is a sweeper system with an electrostatic charge that attracts dust, lint, and hair rather than just stirring them up like traditional brooms, vacuum cleaners, dust mops, and rags.

Implementing its new speed to market strategy, P&G is rolling out the two new products with a worldwide brand name, packaging, and advertising. The company feels that consumer desire for the two products is consistent worldwide so the company does not need to customize the products for each country's market. The impetus behind P&G's new product strategy is the goal of doubling its worldwide annual sales to $70 billion by 2005.

Will speeding new products to market help P&G attain its sales goals? What are the risks associated with such a strategy?

Sources: www.pg.com; Suzanne Vranica, "P&G Puts Two Cleaning Products on Its Marketing Fast Track," *Wall Street Journal,* May 18, 1999, B6.

Ideally, however, this testing process should not be limited to determining the outcome of a single purchase. In order to recoup development and launch costs (and only then to make a profit), products usually need to benefit from repeat purchasing over an extended period. In this context, the researcher needs to estimate four variables—*trial, first repeat, adoption,* and *purchase frequency*—in order to be certain that the product will have a life beyond the first purchase.

The technique suggested to establish this information is **sales-wave research**, where those testing the new product are offered a choice between the product or its competitors (at reduced prices to provide an incentive to purchase a further time, using their own money). This process may be repeated on up to five occasions, over a period of time, to check the repeat-purchase pattern.

> to recoup development and launch costs, **products usually need to benefit from** repeat purchasing over an extended period

The *simulated store technique* attempts to achieve a similar end, by exposing the testers to the promotional material on test (amidst other material) and allowing them to select products from a store; again asking them to demonstrate, by spending their own money, the likely trial purchase rate. They can also be interviewed again later to obtain a measure of their intention to repurchase over time.

On the other hand, the most usual form of product testing still remains that of the single test of acceptability (almost inevitably in comparison with the alternatives, including the existing product and its competitors). It has to be recognized, however, that this may not, as indicated above, be a good measure of long-term performance. In introducing New Coke, Coca-Cola reportedly conducted some 200,000 taste tests before settling on its new formula. It was subsequently rejected by many consumers, and the old formula had to be reinstated under the new name Coke Classic.

www.coke.com

> Service companies have a much
> **more difficult, if not impossible, task**
> in simulating or pretesting a service.

Service companies have a much more difficult, if not impossible, task in simulating or pretesting a service. Prototyping a service is often not a practical proposition and, in any case, side-by-side comparisons with competitive services are typically not feasible. Some of the difficulties found in service development are:

- *Patenting difficulty*—Reduces incentives for large R & D investment. More focus on "me-too" services. Tendency towards improvement rather than innovation. Ease of competitive entry influences viability of new service concepts.

- *Standardization difficulty*—Difficult to develop accurate concept descriptions and concept testing.

This indicates that incremental development might be more widespread in the service sector, resulting in fewer "breakthroughs" but, as we saw earlier, possibly leading to better and more profitable development in general.

Test Marketing

Test marketing ideally aims to duplicate *everything*—promotion and distribution as well as "product"—on a smaller scale. The technique typically replicates in one area what is planned to occur in a national and international launch. The results are carefully monitored, so that they can be extrapolated to projected national and international results. The "area" may be any one of the following:

- **Television viewing area.** In this case the complete campaign, including television commercials and the use of distribution channels, is tested. Sometimes a local radio station may be used in the same way. The cost is lower, but obviously the TV commercials aren't tested.

- **Test city.** It may be possible to duplicate most of the activities in a test city, rather than a complete TV region, at considerably less cost. Clearly, television cannot be used, and the local press will have different characteristics than those of the national press. Typically it carries less authority, and its readership patterns are different. But it can be much cheaper to run and, if the test is a final test of the viability of the product rather than one of the promotional support, it may still provide most of the information needed. Many Japanese consumer electronics companies use the Akihabara district in downtown Tokyo to test out their new products.

- **Residential neighborhoods.** Sometimes just a local area, for instance one served by a single supermarket, can be selected. Here the promotional coverage must be almost exclusively restricted to door-to-door, although this technique may be supplemented by some local press. As a result, such tests move even further away from the realities of a national launch. They can, however, prove to be a useful vehicle for very sophisticated product tests or for workable tests of promotion or pricing alternatives.

- **Test sites.** In the industrial sales (i.e., capital goods) environment the test may consist of recruiting pilot installations with individual customers. These are sometimes referred to as *field trials*. This technique is probably the most suspect of all in terms of grossing the results up to national projections, because it is likely in practice that these will be the best customers, who are unlikely to be typical of the range of customers and prospects as a whole. Even so, it is a very useful device for debugging some of the potential prob-

www.packardbell.com

lems in advance of the launch. Japanese computer companies, such as NEC, are well known to lease their developmental computers free of charge to their *keiretsu* member companies in order to solve all technical problems before national and international launch.

- **Lead countries.** Many multinational companies today are rolling out new products almost simultaneously in all *Triad regions,* including North America (the United States and Canada), Western Europe, and Japan.[31] Those companies identify a set of small *lead countries* in which to test-market their new products. If new products prove successful in lead countries, the companies will roll them out globally. Lead countries preferably should represent a miniature image of the global markets. Singapore, Taiwan, Belgium, and Britain are some favored lead countries.

A number of decisions have to be made about any test market:

- **Which test market?** Where will the test be run? Is it to be economically run in a test city or more comprehensively run in a television area? Which area will be most suitable for the specific needs of the test? Specialist facilities such as retail audits and promotional discounts may be available to support tests, but are the consumers in these test areas then exposed to more new product launches than elsewhere, and are they still typical of consumers across the whole market?

- **What will be tested?** There is a tendency to view test markets as just a "mini national launch." This aspect has to be taken into account, of course, but each "product" has certain factors that are most critical to its success. Special emphasis will need to be placed on measuring these factors.

- **How long a test?** A major decision concerns how long the test will need to run before the repeat purchase patterns can be observed and the all-important long-term future of the product predicted.

- **What success criteria?** What are the levels of performance to be achieved before the test is judged a success and the product deemed suitable for national launch? Part of the design of the test should include "controls" (similar markets that are not exposed to the test "stimuli") to ensure that other factors are not responsible for the results observed.

The decision so far has revolved around a simple go or no-go decision, and this, together with the reduction of risk, is normally the main justification for the expense of test markets. At the same time, however, such test markets can be used to test specific elements of a new product's marketing mix—possibly the version of the product itself, the promotional message and media expenditure, the distribution channels, and the price. In this case, several "matched" test markets (usually small ones) may be used, each testing different marketing mixes. For example, Hollywood movie studios test their new movies with different endings to see audience reaction and to decide on final distributed versions.

Clearly, all test markets provide additional information in advance of a launch and may ensure that the launch is successful. It is reported that, even at such a late stage, half the products entering test markets do not justify a subsequent national launch. However, all test markets suffer from a number of disadvantages:

Replicability. Even the largest test market is not totally representative of the national market, and the smaller ones may introduce gross distortions. Test

---

31. Kenichi Ohmae, *Triad Power* (New York: Free Press, 1985).

market results therefore have to be treated with reservations, in exactly the same way as other market research. See the New Coke fiasco discussed earlier.

Competitor warning. All test markets give competitors advance warning of your intentions and the time to react. They may even be able to go national with their own product before your test is complete. They may also interfere with your test by changing their promotional activities (usually by massively increasing them) to the extent that your results are meaningless. In developing its very successful disc camera, for example, Kodak chose to forgo most of the advantages of test marketing, so they did not alert their competitors to the development. From the "defender's" point of view, incidentally, investing to destroy a competitor's test market may represent a sound use of money, because it can mean that the competitor's full-scale launch has to be undertaken blind—without the lessons learned in a test market (and not a few manufacturers have balked at the prospect of this and pulled out).

www.kodak.com

Cost. Although the main objective of test markets is to reduce the amount of investment put at risk, they may still involve significant costs. It is likely that such costs could easily exceed $1 million. The cost may be much higher where the initial capital demands for the launch cannot be scaled down, for example, where a minimum size of production plant is required to meet national levels of demand. Under these circumstances the costs of a test market may not be too different from those of the national launch. As mentioned above, there is therefore no justification for it, although it might still optimize the marketing mix—and might just avoid a very costly mistake in terms of image.

PRODUCT LAUNCH

It has to be recognized that the development and launch of almost any new product or service carries a considerable element of risk. Indeed, in view of the ongoing dominance of existing brands, it must be questioned whether the risk involved in most major launches is justifiable. In a survey of 700 consumer and industrial companies, Booz-Allen & Hamilton, Inc. reported an average new product success rate (after launch) of 65 percent, although it was noted that only 10 percent of these were totally new products and only 20 percent were new product lines. However, these two, highest risk categories also dominated the "most successful" new product list (accounting for 60 percent).[32]

New product development therefore has to be something of a numbers game. A large number of ideas have to be created and developed for even one to emerge as successful. There is safety in numbers, which once more confers an advantage to the larger organizations.

PRODUCT REPLACEMENT

One form of new product launch is rarely discussed. However, it is probably the most prevalent—and hence most important—of all; it is that of replacing one product with a new one—usually an "improved" version. The risk levels may be much reduced, because there is an existing user base to underwrite sales (as long as the new product does not alienate them—as New Coca-Cola did in the United States, as shown in Exhibit 9.2). Such an introduction will be complicated

> One form of new product launch **that is rarely discussed is that of** replacing one product with a new one

www.coke.com

32. Booz-Allen & Hamilton Inc., *New Products Management for the 1980s.*

Exhibit 9.2

The most common type of new product is the launch of an "improved" version of an existing product. Risk levels for this kind of new product are greatly reduced, but there are some dangers. In launching New Coke in the 1980s, Coca-Cola executives did not count on the staunch loyalty of Coke drinkers to the historical formula. When the product change was announced, consumers snatched up cases of "old" Coke before it was eliminated as a product. As a result, Coca-Cola was forced to re-introduce its historical formula under the name Classic Coke.

by the fact that, at least for some time, there will be two forms of the product in the pipeline. Some firms may opt for a straight cutover; one day the old product will be coming off the production line, and the next day the new product will. Most will favor the products in parallel running for a period of time, even if only because this is forced upon them by their distribution chains. This ensures that the new product really does, eventually, replace the old, and it may reveal that both can run together. One successful example is the sequential improvement of Intel's microprocessors from 286 to 386, to 486, and then on to Pentium over a course of ten years.

www.intel.com
www.pentium.com

RISK VERSUS TIME

Most of the testing stages, which are the key parts of the new product process, are designed to reduce risk to ensure that the product or service will be a success. However, all of them take time.

In some markets, such as fashion, for example, time is a luxury that is not available. The greatest risk here is not having the product available at the right time, and not being ahead of the competitors. These markets consequently obtain less benefit from the more sophisticated new product processes and typically do not make use of them at all.

When to enter a market with a new product should, in any case, be a conscious decision. In relation to competitors there are two main alternatives:

- **Pioneer.** Being first into a market carries considerable risks. On the other hand, the first brand is likely to gain a major, leading, and ongoing share of that market in the long term. Pioneering is often the province of the smaller organizations on a small scale, because their investment can be that much less than that of the majors.

www.ibm.com

www.compaq.com

- **Follower.** This offers the reverse strategy. The risk is minimized because the pioneer has already demonstrated the viability of the market. On the other hand, the related reward, that of becoming the market leader, may also be missed. The solution to this, as practiced by IBM for instance, may be to move into a market as soon as it is proven and then to invest heavily to wrest leadership from the pioneer before it becomes impregnable. This is not a cheap solution, as all the development work has to be undertaken anyway, and the battle for the command of the new market may be very expensive. Even then it may not succeed, as IBM found when Compaq consolidated its position in the portable PC market (and went on to successfully assault the desktop PC market as well).

JAPANESE-STYLE PRODUCT DEVELOPMENT

The product development approach described in this chapter has generally been successful in Western Europe and North America where there may be heavy penalties to brand or corporate image, in particular when backing failures. Japanese companies have challenged this conventional product development approach and taken the reverse tack.

The most important change to the product development process over recent years, led by the Japanese, has been *speed*.[33] Japanese companies have reportedly achieved this with a highly trained workforce, a willingness to build from off-the-shelf components, a persistent effort to develop interchangeable components across product lines and across product generations, a close relationship with their suppliers as well as by such approaches as joint development teams and parallel development.[34] Whatever the reasons, this competitive advantage poses a major challenge to their Western counterparts.

> The most important change to **the product development process** over recent years has been speed.

Furthermore, rather than screening out potential failures, Japanese companies launch *many* new products (as many as 1,000 new soft drinks a year or more than 200 models of Walkman, for example). Those new products are either dropped from the store shelf or improved upon very frequently, such as on a monthly basis, based on input from retailers and customers. Over time, Japanese companies can identify "winning" formulas for a wide range of products. This incrementalist approach to new product development, often called **product churning**, apparently works well in Japan, because their corporations develop new products in a half to a third of the time, and at a quarter to a tenth of the cost, of their Western counterparts.[35] In addition, the Japanese public has been persuaded to accept—indeed to want—new developments at this breakneck pace.

Japanese corporations have led the way in reducing development time dramatically and even to halving it in the very mature car industry. The effects of this

---

33. Ralph E. Gomory, "From the 'Ladder of Science' to the Product Development Cycle," *Harvard Business Review* 67 (November/December 1989): 99–105.

34. X. Michael Song and Mark E. Parry, "The Determinants of Japanese New Product Successes," *Journal of Marketing Research* 34 (February 1997): 64–76.

35. Johny K. Johansson and Ikujiro Nonaka, *Relentless: The Japanese Way of Marketing* (New York: HarperBusiness, 1996).

time-based advantage have been devastating. U.S. automakers have lost leadership of technology and innovation to Japanese competitors. This has led the U.S. government to successfully persuade the Japanese car companies to slow down their product development cycles. Nonetheless, unless U.S. automakers reduce their product development and introduction cycles from 36 to 48 months to 12 to 18 months, Toyota, Honda, and Nissan, among others, will outinnovate and outperform them.[36]

www.toyota.com
www.honda.com
www.nissan-usa.com

www.hp.com

Accordingly, the choice to pioneer or to follow no longer exists in a number of industries. The only way for an organization to even survive may be to shorten development times below those of its competitors. For example, Hewlett-Packard now practices Japanese-style product churning by incessantly improving its laser printer lines even ahead of its Japanese competitor, Canon, and has captured a dominant market position.[37]

www.canon.com

SUMMARY

The theory of new products or new services starts with a *gap analysis*, which looks to the following: usage gap, distribution gap, product gap, and competitive gap. In practice, much organizational development effort is devoted to modification of existing successful products or services by feature modification, quality modification, style modification, and image modification. Potential new products need to be screened against a number of strategic dimensions, including production capabilities, financial performance, investment potential, human factors, materials supply, cannibalism, and time. Market factors, such as a match with existing product lines, price and quality, distribution patterns, and seasonality, also need to be considered.

Sources for generating new product ideas include customers and innovative imitation. In the Western approach, the product development process should then follow a number of formal steps, including gap analysis (for scanning and idea generation), strategic screening, concept testing, product development, product testing, test marketing, and product launch. A test market may take place in a television-viewing area, a test city, or just a residential neighborhood. In industrial markets in particular, it may be restricted to test sites. All of these pose problems of effectiveness and cost and possibly offer competitors advance warning.

It is worth remembering the major caveats mentioned at the beginning of this chapter. Brand stability implies that there should be more emphasis on the further development of existing brands than on totally new ones, contrary to conventional teaching. The Japanese approach is to launch many new products without following any of the stages of testing described here.

36. George Stalk Jr., "Time—The Next Source of Competitive Advantage," *Harvard Business Review* (July/August 1988): 41–51.
37. "How H-P Used Tactics of the Japanese to Beat them at Their Game," *Wall Street Journal*, September 8, 1994, A1, A6.

QUESTIONS FOR REVIEW

1. What are the elements of gap analysis? How are they related to each other?

2. What modifications can be made to existing products or services? Why are such modifications important?

3. What dimensions may be incorporated in a strategic screen? Why is each of these important?

4. What market factors need to be screened for? What is the relevance of each?

5. What practical sources of new product are available?

6. What are the various stages of new product development? What happens at each stage?

7. What types of test market may be employed? What are the advantages and disadvantages of each?

8. How do some Japanese product development processes differ from those in the West?

QUESTIONS FOR DISCUSSION

1. Record labels were horrified when a small company in San Jose, California, came out with the Rio, a $199.95 Walkman-like player in late 1998. As the first widely available portable player of music downloaded from the Internet, the Rio frees people from having to sit at their computer terminals to listen to free tunes. And that threatens to turn the nagging problem of Internet music piracy into serious financial losses for record companies.

   At stake for the technology industry is a lucrative, ground-floor position in the next wave of e-commerce: the digital delivery of media products—music, e-books, and movies—via the Internet. Not all the tech giants are racing in the same direction. Microsoft offers some of the software that makes piracy increasingly easy. Music-industry executives say Microsoft also is quietly considering marketing its own Rio-like device that would play downloaded music.

   What will the new products in the music industry look like in a few decades? Will we see a few large firms or several smaller firms credited for new products?

2. In the United States, two-thirds of consumers who can subscribe to cable do so. Meanwhile, in England, only 20 percent of the consumers do so, and in some areas, the percentage is decreasing. What factors could lead to cable's lower success in England than in the United States?

3. Toshiba's double-sided digital videodisk (DVD-ROM) and the rival system proposed by Sony/Philips competed for global industry standard. In 1995, Toshiba and Sony/Philips decided to reach an agreement on the digital read-only (ROM) videodisk format. Toshiba, Hitachi, and Matsushita—the 3 main Japanese promoters of the rewritable digital video disk (DVD-RAM) format—held a press conference in Tokyo in September 1997 to stress the broad industry support that their proposed standard enjoys. The move followed the surprising announcement late in August 1997 that Sony and NEC would promote their own standard for high-capacity rewritable storage. This battle for industry leadership is similar to the previous battle between VHS and Beta. In what ways is the competition similar? Dissimilar?

4. To be successful, what percentage of a firm's annual revenues should come from products less than four years old? If you were told that 3M (sales $15.1 billion, profits $1.3 billion) had 30 percent of its sales from products less than four years old, what would be your answer? What if 3M's figure were 10 percent?

   Given these new product sales goals, what would be a reasonable return on investment (ROI) target? If 3M's is 20 percent, what would be your answer? What if 3M's figure is 10 percent? Which is more reasonable?

   3M's goal is that 30 percent of sales should be from products less than four years old and its target ROI is 20 percent.

5. You compete in the high end of the market for precision scientific equipment. You increasingly rely upon one of your suppliers, who competes in the low end of your market (not in direct competition with your firm), for a few key

components. You find that you need this supplier to make your next generation of products competitive, yet you are concerned that the supplier may plan to enter your market. Assuming that this supplier's products are superior and technologically complex, how do you respond?

6. Support/dispute the merits of focusing on "new-to-the-world products" versus "additions to existing lines" in high-tech industries. How would segmentation and customer types in particular affect your argument?

FURTHER READINGS

Constantineau, Larry A. "The Twenty Toughest Questions for New Product Proposals," *Journal of Consumer Marketing* 9 (spring 1992): 51–54.

de Bono, Edward. *Lateral Thinking.* Ward Lock Education, 1970.

Jones, Tim. *New Product Development: An Introduction to a Multifunctional Process.* Boston: Butterworth-Heinemann, 1997.

Kuczmanscki, Thomas D. *Managing New Products: The Power of Innovations.* Upper Saddle River, N.J.: Prentice Hall, 1992.

Song, X. Michael, and Mark E. Parry. "A Cross-National Comparative Study of New Product Development Processes: Japan and the United States," *Journal of Marketing* 61 (April 1997): 1–18.

Wheelwright, Steven C., and Kim B. Clark. *Revolutionizing Product Development: Quantum Leap in Speed.* New York: Free Press, 1992.

Wind, Jerry, and Vijay Mahajan. "Issues and Opportunities in New Product Development: An Introduction to the Special Issue." *Journal of Marketing Research* 34 (February 1997): 1–12.

Wind, Yoram. *Product Policy; Concepts, Methods, and Strategy.* Reading, Mass.: Addison Wesley Longman, 1982.

Workman, John P., Jr. "Marketing's Limited Role in New Product Development in One Computer Systems Firm." *Journal of Marketing Research* 30 (November 1993): 405–421.

chapter

10

Pricing Decisions

Pricing Decisions
Pricing Decisions
icing Decisions
Pricing Decisions

The traditional theory of pricing, that of supply versus demand, has developed from economics. As such it offers a useful intellectual framework to consider pricing issues. Unfortunately, most of the parameters needed to apply this theory have been extremely difficult to measure in practice. Customer needs and market factors tend to dominate the more "practical" marketing theory.

New product pricing, whether to skim profits or to penetrate the market, is a particular form of pricing and poses rather different challenges. However, much of this chapter describes the various practical pricing policies adopted from cost-plus and market-based strategies to selective ones. Discounts and competitive pricing are also investigated.

Although fundamentals of pricing remain the same, the proliferation of e-commerce on the Internet is also revolutionizing the relationships between buyers and sellers in the market. Both parties have clearer pictures of the cost and price structures in their market exchange. As Manager's Corner 10.1 suggests, in the new world of the Internet, buyers will probably benefit from lower prices and sellers will also benefit from more fluid pricing to meet the consumer demand more accurately.

> the proliferation of e-commerce on the Internet **is revolutionizing the relationships** between buyers and sellers in the market

Manager's Corner 10.1

The Internet not only permits the consumer easy price comparison but also allows the seller free-market pricing

Electronic commerce on the Internet is killing prices. A whole new world of buying and selling via the Internet is taking shape. Venture capitalists, entrepreneurs, and purveyors of technology have all jumped into the e-commerce fray. The upshot is that many goods and services are cheaper on the Web than off it. It is cheaper to buy and sell stocks. It is cheaper to buy books from Amazon.com, although shipping costs can gobble up much of the savings. Many newspapers are cheaper on the Internet than in print—about 72 percent cheaper in the case of the *Wall Street Journal* (www.wsj.com). Also, Internet coupon sites distribute rebate offerings for a variety of products.

But the story of the Internet's role in pricing goods and services is just beginning to unfold. More than a new way to take orders or delivery, the Internet is emerging as a paradise for comparison shoppers. The past couple of years have brought a slew of Web sites and on-line services that put more information about prices into the hands of buyers. With vastly better data on prices of golf clubs, airline tickets, and cars, consumers are cutting better deals.

It is not only the buyers who are taking advantage of price comparison shopping. The sellers are exploiting vast amounts of information, now readily available on the Internet, about who is buying what at how much, when, and under what conditions. The Internet will make obsolete much of what remains of "list price" convention, developed a century ago for networks of real-world stores that were required to generate some predictable level of sales. Now the sellers can offer flexible "situational" pricing on the Internet.

The idea behind situational pricing on the Internet is that things are worth such different amounts at different times or in different circumstances that price tags need to find their own levels. In perfect markets, people are willing to pay what a product is worth to them. The reason this does not work in the retail world is that the people who set prices are not present at the point of sale to accept or decline an offer. Set prices usually must be honored, and when too-high prices make sales suffer, the price must be lowered in an across-the-board action. This is how books end up on cut-rate racks and massive discounts take place after Christmas. It is an expensive and messy process, particularly when, as in many cases, every product item must be handled to modify its price.

The Internet changes everything, the same as it always does. Already, electronic-commerce software vendors are trying to capitalize on the growing interest in situational pricing by boasting how many kinds of auctions they support. In the future, you may visit a product page at a retailer a few times without buying, and the price will drop. Try to lower the price in this fashion too often, and the site will suspect you are a chiseler and stand its ground. Offer electronic cash and the site will cut you a break on shipping. Post frequently in a users-helping-users support forum and get special just-for-you pricing. If nobody buys a particular product, the price will drop across the board.

The notion of a base price may actually vanish. This will infuriate some consumers, and businesses in particular may demand that fixed prices stay in place to aid them in determining expenses, thus forcing contracts, as many do already, to lock in commodity prices. Elsewhere, such a development will prove revolutionary, especially when a product is inherently scarce. Merchants who see this coming will be able to establish competency in these highly complex economic models and will have a significant advantage in putting things up for sale. The ticket seller who understands how to alter prices as curtain time approaches may fill the house at the most profitable level. Sellers of packaged vacations already offer a break on prebooked packages; now they may offer a break as well to last-minute buyers when not all berths are filled, as airlines already do on the Web.

Sources: Bernard Wysocki Jr., "Internet Is Opening Up a New Era of Pricing," *Wall Street Journal*, June 8, 1998, A1; Whit Andrews, "Net's a Breeding Ground For Free-Market Pricing," *Internet World*, March 16, 1998, www.internetworld.com.

PRICE

Probably the single most important decision in marketing is price. This is partly because price is generally believed to have an impact on sales volumes. If the price is too high and the market is competitive, sales may be correspondingly reduced. Indeed, many economists would see price as the main determinant of sales volume. On the other hand, many of the more sophisticated marketers have found ways to reduce the impact of price—and sometimes have even managed to increase sales by raising the price.

> Probably the single **most important decision** in marketing is price.

In practice, the main reason for the importance of price is that it is one of the three main variables that determine the profit. Thus, the profit per unit is equal to the price less the total cost of producing that unit:

$$\text{profit} = \text{price} - \text{cost}$$

Another important factor is the volume of sales, because the organization's net profit is equal to the number of units sold multiplied by the net profit obtained on each of those units. At this level the mathematics are very simple—but also very important.

Thus, the higher the price can be raised, always assuming that unit costs and sales volume do not change, the greater the profit for the organization. Many of the most powerful marketing techniques have, therefore, been designed to maximize the price that can be achieved. In practice, the calculation of profit is much more complicated than this simple explanation allows. Yet the basic principle still holds—even if it is not necessarily easy to implement! For example, one of the most basic dilemmas every marketing manager in the beverage industry faces is the fundamental choice between a price cut to stimulate sales or a price increase to improve margins. Although both choices are viable depending on the circumstances, too many managers today choose a price cut with little analysis. Even more troubling is the fact that many sales managers rarely give serious consideration to increasing prices, despite tolerating and complaining about pressure on margins. Pricing decisions should be driven by channel strategy. The channel strategy should assess overall sales trends for each channel by package and by brand. It will also define the competitive strategy and identify how the company responds to competitive pricing activity.[1]

SERVICE PRICES

Most pricing theory talks in terms of products, but for services a potential additional complication is that some service providers tend to have different terms for price (admission, tuition, cover charge, interest, fee, point, and so on). However, the result is exactly the same. The consumer has to pay a price, and the mechanisms for determining that price are much the same, with only marginal differences:

- **Negotiation.** In view of the variability of the service being offered, there may be more scope for individual negotiation.

- **Discounts.** Owing to the "perishability" of the service, there may be incentives to use it at unpopular times (off-season air fares, matinée prices for movie theaters, and so on).

- **Quality.** Higher pricing, to demonstrate quality (which is usually much more intangible in a service), may be more prevalent.

For example, in the early 1990s, restaurateurs were not convinced that the charge volume brought in by American Express cards justified the discount rates that often were nearly double the 2 percent average rate charged by Visa and MasterCard acquirers. American Express countered those concerns by reducing merchant fees in selected industries. Today, American Express's average worldwide discount rate is around 2.74 percent. American Express discount rates are still about 25 to 100 basis points higher than those charged by Visa and MasterCard acquirers. Although American Express's rates are higher, it is still perceived as more upscale and can command a little higher discount rate. Because American Express continues to charge higher rates than Visa and MasterCard, American Express must reinforce with its merchant base the value it brings because its card members traditionally spend 20 to 21 percent more per transaction.[2]

www.americanexpress
.com
www.visa.com
www.mastercard.com

PRICE AND NONPROFIT ORGANIZATIONS

Price is an element of the marketing mix that seems, at least on first inspection, largely irrelevant to nonprofit organizations. Even so, there are a number of such organizations that (while having charitable status and, accordingly, are not allowed

1. Kent McSparran and Karl Edmunds, "Don't Be Afraid of Price Increases," *Beverage World*, June 15, 1998, 103.
2. Linda Punch, "Behind AmEx's Merchant Push," *Credit Card Management* (August 1998): 38–50.

to make a profit) still charge for their services. It is frequently the case that the term *surplus* is interchangeable in these organizations with profit, and they behave in exactly the same way as profit-making organizations.

However, there remain a large number of organizations (typically in the government sector) where no money changes hands. There simply is no price. Allocation of the service to the consumer is by other means, such as need (determined by a doctor, for example) or queuing (such as in organ transplant waiting lists). Many aspects of pricing are, therefore, not fully applicable. On the other hand, some of the principles can still be applied if "price" is replaced by the "perceived value" of the consumer (discussed later in this chapter). Thus, the consumer still places a value (often a high value) on the service, and this can be dealt with much as price itself. Certainly, if the service providers are to best match their consumers' needs they should have a good appreciation of the value the consumers place on the service.

DEMAND AND SUPPLY

Much of pricing theory is derived from economics. The basic idea, according to such theories, is that demand will be different at each possible price. Demand is normally assumed to fall as price increases. Similarly, supply is expected to increase as price increases (the reverse of demand). A downward sloping **demand curve** and an upward sloping **supply curve** are represented in Figure 10.1.

The problem posed by this traditional economic approach is that the demand curve is usually almost impossible to determine in practice.[3] However, if we assume that the demand curve is known, then we can determine the **equilibrium price** at

> [At the equilibrium price] **there will be nothing left to sell,** nor will there be any shortage.

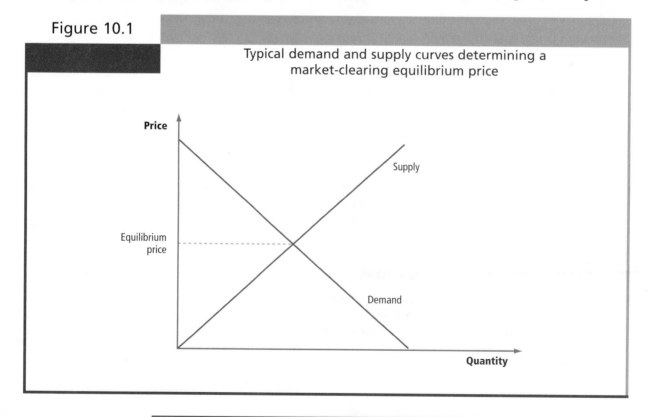

Figure 10.1

Typical demand and supply curves determining a market-clearing equilibrium price

3. W. J. Baumol, *Economic Theory and Operations Analysis*, 3d ed. (Upper Saddle River, N.J.: Prentice Hall, 1972).

which the quantity demanded by consumers matches the quantity supplied by sellers. There will be nothing left to sell, nor will there be any shortage—and it is said that the market has "cleared." This is the price that will, therefore, be set by the market.

In economics, therefore, the basis of price is this balance between supply and demand, and price itself is most often seen as the prime determinant of both supply and demand.

The body of this theory was largely developed in the 19th century, when the economic wealth of nations was still developing. At that time, most of the markets were still almost pure commodity markets, supplying basic essentials, which were undifferentiated. The consumer's choice was accordingly based on price alone. Their purchasing strategy was to use their very limited funds to obtain the maximum amounts of these basic essentials. This simple approach may still work in commodity markets, where professional buyers purchase identical commodities, such as corn and wheat, solely on the basis of price. In addition, this economic model assumes that buyers have near perfect information about the alternatives available to them in the market. It further assumes that competing brands are reasonably close substitutes.[4] Indeed, some of these assumptions are becoming realities as a result of the information revolution in recent years. Now, buyers are able to obtain much more information at a much faster pace and much more cheaply than ever before.

In recent years, however, the majority of the inhabitants of developed nations have moved into a period of affluence, and the basis for their purchasing patterns and the associated economics have changed drastically. In essence, a new view of economics is that most purchasers are no longer restricted to buying essentials, but can indulge in luxuries. The suppliers of these differentiate them, to the extent that some suppliers can achieve almost monopoly powers over their markets. The resulting price theory is, therefore, much more complex. It is in this area of business that most marketing activities take place.

PRICE ELASTICITY OF DEMAND

The degree to which demand is sensitive to price is called **price elasticity of demand**. This is often shortened to "elasticity of demand," although strictly speaking this is incorrect, because economists recognize that demand may also depend on other factors, such as income. The price elasticity of demand refers to the percentage change in the quantity of a good demanded as a result of the percentage change in its price, or:

$$\text{price elasticity of demand} = \frac{\text{percentage change in demand}}{\text{percentage change in price}}$$

This simply recognizes that some products or services are more sensitive to price than others. In the commodities market, for example, the demand for your product will depend on the price you ask. If you set the price above what prevails in the market, you will be very unlikely to sell anything, for the buyers well know that they can buy exactly the same good elsewhere at a lower price. The demand, or even sometimes price itself, here is said to be *elastic*.

At the other end of the spectrum are those products whose demand is very insensitive to price change. For example, Apple Computer has so differentiated its Macintosh line of personal computers with its user-friendliness that it has long enjoyed a virtual monopoly of its segment and has been able to set almost whatever price the company wanted, within limits. This situation is often called *inelastic demand*.

www.apple.com

---

4. Frederick E. Webster Jr. and Yoram Wind, *Organizational Buying Behavior* (Upper Saddle River, N.J.: Prentice Hall, 1972).

However, Microsoft Windows, with its user-friendly features that almost match that of Macintosh, has encroached on Apple Computer's turf. Now that consumers have alternative Windows-based personal computers to switch to, the consumer demand for Macintosh has become less inelastic (or more elastic); that is, consumers have become more sensitive to price changes. Knowing this demand situation, Apple Computer has lowered its Macintosh prices to increase sales, or to keep consumers from switching to Windows-based personal computers.

The above theory assumes perfect markets, in which all consumers and suppliers come equipped with perfect knowledge of all the prices available for products (commodities) that are identical to each other. In addition, the market always clears; that is, all the demand is exactly matched by supply, and vice versa. This may be true of a few money markets, and the pure commodity markets, although even in these cases other factors are often also at work.

As suggested earlier, it clearly is *not* true of most markets in which marketers are plying their trade. Indeed, it is almost impossible, by definition, for a marketer to have any effect in a "perfect market." For example, the U.S. natural gas industry has incredible difficulty predicting prices from year to year. Executives in this industry are accustomed to sudden reversals. Causes of an unexpected decrease in natural gas prices were attributed to an unusually mild summer that lowered the need for air conditioning and depressed natural gas use by electric utilities, more nuclear plants online the past summer, natural gas storage facilities unexpectedly already at near-full capacity, and a large pipeline expansion into the United States from Canada.[5] In economics this unwelcome intrusion of real life is the subject of extensions to the basic theory, to cover "monopolies and imperfect competition"—these extensions are generally rather esoteric.

Even so, an understanding of the basic theories of supply and demand does offer the marketer a useful insight into some of the key factors that may affect the prices that can be obtained. In particular, the concept of "elasticity of demand" is one that is widely discussed and plays a major role in pricing decisions. In some markets, such as the car market, where a long sales history is available and the behavior of the participants has been reasonably consistent and rational, it may even be possible to use regression analysis (described in Chapter 6) to establish what the curves of supply and demand actually are. As always, though, this is a historical process, and future behavior may not be so consistent.

ESTIMATION OF THE DEMAND CURVE AND PRICE ELASTICITY

Three main ways of measuring the demand curve (and the related price elasticity of demand) are suggested by theorists.

- **Statistical analysis of historical data.** This, at least in theory, uses historical data to plot the curve. Unfortunately there are very few situations in which this can be carried out directly, because there are too many variables in the normal complex market situation—and the "environmental" factors, in particular, change over time. Even the use of regression analysis, as mentioned above, may not be able to remove the effects of those other factors.

- **Survey research.** It might seem that market research should be able to find out what consumers would buy at various prices, allowing the curve to be plotted. In practice, the results from such research are generally so inaccurate that the curves cannot be plotted with any certainty.

---

5. Wendy Zellner, "Steamed about Natural Gas," *Business Week*, October 10, 1994, 48.

- **Experiment.** The one successful device is to test prices in a test market. For many manufacturers this may be of questionable value; the costs of the test are significant, and the price effect measured may be relevant for just a short time. Retailers themselves, with the luxury of many branches, are much better positioned to run such trials.

The practical reality is that these techniques are rarely used. The pricing for New York City's Manhattan apartments illustrates the point (see Manager's Corner 10.2). Let us, therefore, look at the factors that can influence elasticity of demand, and thus affect price. As presented in Table 10.1, the main factors can be grouped into those that are almost totally under the control of the organization and those that are out of its control, or can only be partially controlled.

Manager's Corner 10.2

The dynamics of determining optimal pricing

In Manhattan's residential market, pricing has always been used as a strategy to find what the market will accept. But these days, developers of high-end condominiums, capitalizing on the strength of the market, are raising prices more quickly and more frequently than even in the mid-1980s boom. The increases vary among the apartments offered, with price tags on some units increasing several times during the sales period, and other units remaining at their opening prices. For example, at two new East Side condominiums, the Knickerbocker (knickerbocker.nyrealty.com) and the Siena (siena.nyrealty.com), average sales prices for the 147 apartments rose by 10 percent over the sales period. The primary reasons for the frenzy of activity are the lack of product, pent-up demand for large units of two bedrooms or more, and the lack of competition boom.

Pricing newly built apartments is an intricate balancing act. Developers set their starting prices based on market conditions, resales, the competition, and features offered in their buildings and apartments, coming close to what they think is the market value. As buyers react, prices are adjusted upward at different levels and times and by apartment style. As a result, the difference between the opening and final prices in condominiums seems to be, on average, 10 to 15 percent, with price increases ranging from none at all to 30 to 50 percent.

Source: Rachelle Garbarine, "Market's Strength Enables Bigger, More Rapid Price Increases for New Condos," *New York Times*, Late Edition, May 9, 1997, B10.

Table 10.1

Factors affecting the elasticity of demand

Organization factors	Customer factors	Market factors
Product life cycle	Demand	Competition
Product portfolio	Benefits	Economic and regulatory environment
Product line pricing	Value	Exchange rate
Segmentation and positioning	Distribution channel	Geography
Branding		

ORGANIZATION-CONTROLLED FACTORS

Even in a very competitive market, at least some of the factors affecting prices may be under the direct control of the organizations involved.

PRODUCT LIFE CYCLE. We saw earlier that the stage of the life cycle through which the product is currently passing may in theory have an impact on price (see Figure 10.2). At the introduction it may be set high to capitalize on its uniqueness (*skimming*), as the first video recorders were priced. This high price may be carried through to maturity or later, taking skimming to its logical conclusion—as a niche player, such as Mercedes-Benz in the automobile industry might do. More likely, as we will see later, the price might be reduced to maximize *penetration*. It is only at the end of maturity, when the market moves into saturation that, according to this theory, price competition should break out in earnest. Even then, as products decline, prices should rise again as they are milked.

www.mercedesbenz.com

The theory also requires that, to be under the control of the organization, the product have a life cycle that is separate from that of the overall market. That only happens if the organization develops a segment, or "niche," of its own, which is discussed below.

For nonprofit services the life cycle is also important, in that the perceived value of the service will vary in much the same way over the life cycle (and service producers need to recognize this). The concept of "product" portfolio may also be used, based on value, to ensure that the offering to consumers balances the *range* of their needs. For example, a national health service may need to maintain support for a wide range of services, including some "old-fashioned" treatments (which patients still demand), at the same time as bringing in new and exciting services.

PRODUCT PORTFOLIO. If the organization has a portfolio of products, it can follow different pricing policies on each, balancing them against each other, so that the overall impact is optimized. In any case, such pricing may be forced upon

Figure 10.2

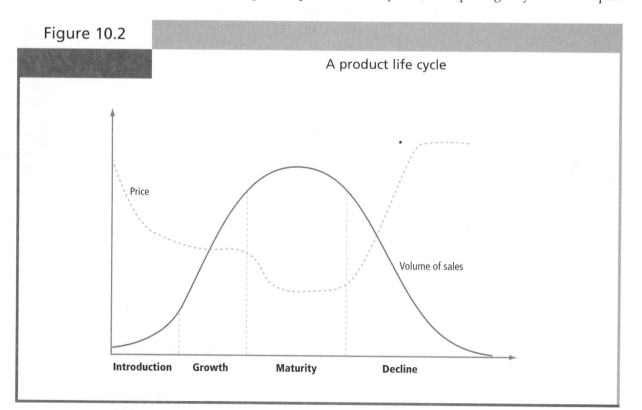

A product life cycle

it. A "problem child" may fail to become a "star," and if it is not immediately discontinued, its price will probably need to be raised so that it can be milked to retrieve some profit cover from the situation.

Looking at the portfolio in more general terms, it may even be possible to run two or more similar product brands with different pricing policies. Thus one can be in the mainstream of the market and at a reasonably high price, as are Toyota's Lexus models, whereas another is quite specifically targeted at a lower price to cover those price-sensitive customers, such as Toyota Camry and Corolla models. This pricing strategy has also been pursued by General Motors for years as evidenced by its range of models produced by Cadillac down to Chevrolet.

www.toyota.com
www.lexus.com
www.gm.com
www.cadillac.com
www.chevrolet.com

The portfolio approach is a powerful one, not in the least because it can underwrite any attempts to set a high-price policy by differentiation, balancing the risk of such experiments against the security offered by the brand remaining in the lower price position. Such a higher-price policy often succeeds, not infrequently against the expectations of most of those involved. The portfolio approach, however, is only available to those who have the financial resources and the position in the market to make it worthwhile.

> The portfolio approach is only available **to those who have the financial resources and** the position in the market to make it worthwhile.

PRODUCT LINE PRICING. The pricing of one product or service may affect others supplied by the organization in one or both of the following ways.

- **Interrelated demand.** The price of one product may affect the demand for another. They may be complementary (for example, the computer and the software that runs on it), so that an increase in one part of the "package" results in demand falling for both parts. Or, they may be alternatives; as already mentioned, Procter & Gamble has a range of detergents, and increasing the price of one may switch demand to another.

www.pg.com

- **Interrelated costs.** Sometimes the products use the same facilities (the same car assembly line may produce a range of models) or may be derivatives of the same process (gasoline and heating oil are different "fractions" of crude oil, and one cannot be produced without the other). In these circumstances, changing sales volumes can obviously have pass-through effects on other costs.

Pricing strategies under these circumstances can be complex and are usually a matter of judgment.

SEGMENTATION AND PRODUCT POSITIONING. The classic techniques for obtaining higher prices are those of positioning and segmentation. By creating a distinct segment that the brand can dominate, the producer hopes that the price can be controlled. Indeed, experience shows that this can often be achieved in practice (Apple, with its own special niche, was able to stay away from the cutthroat pricing that infected the rest of the PC market).

www.apple.com

Most of the techniques involved in this kind of pricing strategy were covered in some detail in Chapter 7. All that need be said at this stage is that a prime benefit of such segmentation and positioning is the reduction in price pressures. If price competition is severe, therefore, the first action should be to see if segmentation can offer a degree of protection.

> If price competition is severe, therefore, **the first action should be to see if** segmentation can offer a degree of protection.

CREATING A BRAND "MONOPOLY."   As already explained, most of the economic thinking that lies behind the theory of price elasticity of demand revolves around "perfect competition" (which, in the economic context, usually means exclusively price-based competition). On the other hand, it can be argued that one of the main objectives of the marketer, as exemplified by the brand manager, is to create a monopoly for the brands that he or she manages.

www.heinz.com

The ideal outcome would be that the brand was so differentiated from its competitors that the customer would not choose these other brands, even if the first choice brand was not available. The marketer wants to see the consumer enter the supermarket determined to buy Heinz Baked Beans, not just a suitable variety of ordinary baked beans.

A variation of this process, in the industrial purchasing sector, is the fact that most supplier selection decisions involve choosing from a limited set of potential vendors. Potential suppliers in this set are "in," while all other potential suppliers are "out." Constraints on the set of possible suppliers can be imposed by any member of the buying organization that has the necessary power. Inertia is the major determinant of buying behavior and stresses habitual behavior. Indeed, buyers are motivated by a desire to reduce the amount of perceived risk in the buying situation to some acceptable level.[6] Something approaching this view surely led to the famous motto "Nobody ever got fired for buying IBM."

www.ibm.com

CUSTOMER FACTORS

The major determinant of prices will, of course, be what the consumer is prepared to pay, which is in turn related to a number of other factors, including benefits, value, and distribution channel.

CUSTOMER DEMAND.   Following from the earlier economic theory and assuming a steady supply—as is often the case—variations in customer demand should result in changes in price. This is most obvious in the commodity markets, such as that in oil. Consumers reduced their demand for oil to such an extent following the massive 1973 price rises that there was eventually a glut, and prices were forced down again. It is also evident in other markets, such as that for housing, which have often seasonally related alternating periods of boom or bust. Holiday markets are closely tied to the seasons, in particular to the school holidays, and the prices reflect this. Telephone companies take a similar approach, but on a daily basis, with high "peak" prices during normal work hours, but "off-peak" bargains during evenings and weekends.

Similarly, big companies are installing "software meters" to help cut the cost of their skyrocketing software costs. New technology allows company offices to share software licenses. Instead of having to purchase 100 copies of a particular software package, the company may only need to purchase 25. If an office in the United States needs the software, it can "borrow" it from its European offices. Likewise, when the Asian office is running short on a particular package, it can borrow it from the U.S. office while they sleep.[7]

In the nonprofit sector, such surges in demand may be controlled, at least to some extent, by allowing waiting queues to lengthen (as happens for charter public school enrollment and museums).

CUSTOMER BENEFITS.   The more important or desirable the benefits, the more the consumer will be prepared to pay. Thus, as we have seen, there is the basic "commodity price" that would be paid for any product of an identical type, assuming that there was perfect competition. Beyond this there is the "premium price" that con-

---

6. R. M. Cyert and J. G. March, *A Behavioral Theory of the Firm* (Cambridge, Mass.: Blackwell, 1992).

7. "The Word Processor Is Ticking," *Economist*, April 8, 1995, 61.

sumers will pay for the additional benefits they believe the specific brand will give them. This emphasizes, yet again, the importance of understanding which are the most important benefits in the eyes of the consumer, because these are the very ones that will justify a premium price. Marketing in Action 10.1 is an example of this.

CUSTOMER VALUE. Benefits are conceptualized as the "value" that the customer sees in the product. In theory, there should be a balance between this value and the price asked.

This "perceived value" can then be matched against the price on offer, to see whether the purchase is worth making. This theory does at least recognize that different buyers—or groups of buyers—may have different motivations. The Volvo buyer probably places a higher value on personal safety than does the Porsche buyer. It is likely that the Porsche buyer will consider the car's value as a status symbol to a greater degree than the buyer of a Hyundai.

> Benefits are conceptualized as the "value" that the **customer sees in the product. In theory, there should** be a balance between this value and the price asked.

www.volvocars.com
www.porsche.com
www.hyundai.com

Paradoxically, price itself is often seen as a measure of quality; the higher the price the higher the quality is presumed to be. Thus, higher-priced cars are perceived to possess (often unwarranted) high quality. High-quality cars are likewise perceived to be higher priced than they actually are.[8]

DISTRIBUTION CHANNEL. In many situations the producer simply *cannot* determine the final price to the end user or consumer. The intermediaries in the distribution channel will apply their own pricing strategies, which may be totally

Marketing in Action 10.1

American safety razor competes on price

With 1998 sales of around $10 billion, Gillette (www.gillette.com) is world renowned for its men's shaving products such as blades, razors, and shaving preparations. One of the company's popular product introductions was the Mach 3 triple-blade razor. The company spent around $300 million to promote the Mach 3 during its introduction. This promotional expenditure was almost equivalent to the total sales of one of its competitors, American Safety Razor (ASR).

American Safety Razor (www.asrco.com) operates out of a manufacturing facility in Verona, Virginia (USA). The company provides products for the consumer, industrial, international, and medical markets. Consumer products include Personna, Bump Fighter, and Burma-Shave. Industrial products include Personna, American Line, and Ardell. Personna International Limited caters to the shaving needs of worldwide consumers. Personna Med-

ical offers surgical blades and medical supplies to the health care market.

With its shaving products for the consumer market, American Safety Razor claims to match the quality performance levels of leading national brands such as Gillette and Schick. However, its products generally sell for 30 to 40 percent less than these leading brands. While Gillette is spending hundreds of millions of dollars promoting its new Mach 3, ASR plans to compete on value pricing. Its low-end promotional efforts (under $3 million) encourage consumers to compare prices. ASR feels that there is a large group of shavers who will not want to spend $7 for a razor. These are the consumers that ASR thinks will comprise its market.

With 6 percent of the U.S. shaving razors and blades market, is value pricing the best strategy for ASR to compete with the likes of Gillette (67 percent U.S. market share) and Schick (16 percent U.S. market share)?

Sources: www.asrco.com; James R. Hagerty, "Concede Defeat to Gillette? Not Just Yet/Burma-Shave," *Wall Street Journal*, June 12, 1998, B1+.

---

8. G. M. Erickson and J. K. Johansson, "The Role of Price in Multi-Attribute Product Evaluations," *Journal of Consumer Research* 12 (September 1985): 195–199.

316

www.ibm.com

unrelated to those of the producer—and may even be contradictory. Thus, the distributor may even choose to absorb any price increases the producer imposes. IBM found itself with a price war on its hands in the PC market, not because that was what IBM wanted—indeed, it was totally in contradiction to IBM's policies—but because that was what its dealers chose to do. On the other hand, the distributor may ignore a price decrease that the producer has introduced (to improve penetration of the product, for instance) to increase the distributor's profit, again with the result that the consumer sees no difference.

MARKET FACTORS

Competition and environment in the market may also have an important impact and may often be the ultimate determinant of prices.

COMPETITION. Apart from the competence of the supplier, in terms of the ability to match price to the consumers' perceived value, the major factor affecting price is probably competition. What the direct competitors, in particular, charge for their comparable products is bound to be taken into consideration by the consumers, if not by the producers. The current situation facing U.S. air carriers illustrates this situation. Few U.S. carriers are regularly profitable, but competition often leads to fare wars that ensure additional years of profitless results.

The framework for the analysis of and response to competition, in general as well as price terms, was covered in Chapter 3. This chapter showed that there were means of managing competition, even price competition, so that its impact on profits could be minimized.

Another response to price competition, therefore, should be to examine if there are ways of "managing" it to reduce its impact, and to signal to competitors that your response is not aggressive.

Direct competition may be rare in the nonprofit sectors, but indirect competition is not, and many of the same techniques can be applied. If, say, you are trying to attract people to fitness classes, you may have to persuade them that the "value" of these is greater than that of an alternative, which may be a session of bingo.

ECONOMIC AND REGULATORY ENVIRONMENT. Whether the economy is booming or in recession may have a direct impact on what consumers can afford to spend. In recent years this effect often seems to have been very selective, mainly hitting those supplying capital goods to industry, whereas consumer sales have continued to rise.

There are also all the various aspects of legislation that constrain freedom to move prices. At the very least, there is often the veiled threat of interest from the agencies that are responsible for monitoring "fair trading" and monopolies hanging over those who are especially effective in managing their price competition. The possibility of such regulatory intervention should never be discounted. Think, for example, about the Clinton Administration's decision to impose a hefty 100 percent punitive tariff on Lexus, Infiniti, and other Japanese luxury cars imported from Japan, which took effect in June 1995. Although it was a politically motivated retaliatory action against Japan's huge recalcitrant trade surplus with the United States, due mostly to its auto and auto parts trade imbalance, it disrupted the price mechanism on the U.S. auto market, hurting many Lexus, Infiniti, and Acura dealers in the United States and probably benefiting other luxury car dealers selling competing models.[9]

www.lexus.com
www.infiniti.com

www.acura.com

9. Clay Chandler, "U.S. Turns Tough on Japan: Administration Renews Pressure in Trade Dispute over Auto, Auto Parts," *Washington Post*, March 30, 1995, D11.

The U.S. court recently struck down the last peak pricing scheme by the Massachusetts Port Authority (MPA) to ration traffic at Logan Airport. Declared discriminatory, MPA halved charges for jumbo jets while boosting fees for commuters, regional airlines, and nonscheduled flights by a factor of eight. Although MPA's peak pricing was rational, given the airlines' demand for facility use, state and federal regulations could intervene in the market mechanism.[10]

www.massport.com

EXCHANGE RATE. In the last decade or so, the exchange rates of major currencies, including the U.S. dollar, the Japanese yen, the German mark, and the British pound, have fluctuated significantly, and so have the prices of imports and exports. For example, as the U.S. dollar has depreciated approximately 50 percent vis-à-vis the Japanese yen and the German mark in just a few years (i.e., the same dollar can buy half as much from Japan and Germany), any components and finished products from Japan and Germany now cost twice as much in dollars. This can be a serious problem for U.S.-based companies, such as Dell and RCA, which rely heavily on components for further manufacture and finished products for sale in the United States. A pricing issue is to what extent those companies *pass through* cost increases to their customers. As presented in Manager's Corner 10.3, successful companies are usually willing to absorb part of the cost increase by reducing their profit margins in order to maintain their market share position.

> successful companies are usually willing to absorb part of the cost increase by reducing their profit margins in order to maintain their market share position

www.dell.com
www.rca.com

On the other hand, as a result of the dollar depreciation, U.S. exports are cheaper now in terms of foreign currencies. However, many U.S. companies also import components for further manufacture in the United States and then export finished products abroad.[11] In other words, the dollar depreciation does not usually help U.S. firms reduce foreign sales prices nearly as much as one might think. Further, a sudden price reduction in foreign markets may even erode the brand image of the U.S. product. For example, although Budweiser beer was considered a premium, or at least high-priced, beer in Japan until a few years ago, it is now one of the least expensive beers in Japan as a result of the steep depreciation of the dollar against the Japanese yen.

www.budweiser.com

Manager's Corner 10.3

> Companies—even domestic companies—should be aware how the foreign exchange rates affect their pricing strategy

The dramatic swings in the value of the dollar since the early 1980s have made it clear that foreign companies charge different prices in the United States than in other markets. When the dollar appreciated against the Japanese yen and the German mark in the 1980s, Japanese cars were priced fairly low in the United States as justified by the cheaper yen, whereas German cars became far more expensive in the United States than in Europe. In the 1990s, when the dollar began depreciating against the yen and the mark, Japanese and German automakers had to increase their dollar prices in the United States. Japanese automakers did not raise their prices nearly as much as German competitors. Obviously, they "price to market." As a result, Japanese carmakers have not decreased their U.S. market share as much as German carmakers.

One of the success factors for many Japanese companies in the U.S. market seems to be in the way they used dollar-yen exchange rates

10. "Peak Pricing Not the Answer," *USA Today*, August 13, 1998, 13A.

11. Masaaki Kotabe and K. Scott Swan, "Offshore Sourcing: Reaction, Maturation, and Consolidation of U.S. Multinationals," *Journal of International Business Studies* 25 (First Quarter 1994): 115–140.

to their advantage, known as the *target exchange rate.* Japanese companies, in particular, are known to employ a very unfavorable target exchange rate (i.e., hypothetically appreciated yen environment) for their costing strategy in order to make sure that they will not be adversely affected should the yen appreciate. Therefore, despite an upwards of twofold appreciation of the yen vis-à-vis the dollar from 240 yen/$ to 85 yen/$ in a decade or so, the dollar prices of Japanese products have not increased nearly as much. Although accurately estimating the average increase in dollar prices of Japanese products is almost impossible, our estimate suggests about a 30-percent price increase over the same period. If this estimate is accurate, Japanese companies must have somehow absorbed more than 70 percent of the price increase! This cost absorption could result from smaller profit margins, cost reductions, or both. According to some estimates, Toyota is now capable of breaking even at 80 yen to the dollar. In other words, as long as the Japanese currency does not appreciate all the way to 80 yen to the dollar, Toyota (www.toyota.com) is still expected to earn windfall operating profits.

Source: Masaaki Kotabe and Kristiaan Helsen, *Global Marketing Management* (New York: John Wiley & Sons, 1998), 68–71.

GEOGRAPHICAL PRICING.   Where transport costs are important, and particularly where there are widely separated populations, as in the United States, then geographical location may become a factor in pricing. There are a range of strategies to cope with this, including the following.

- **Uniform pricing.** The same price is offered at all locations, regardless of delivery costs. This is the most widely applied policy in consumer goods markets, not least because it is easiest to apply, in terms of the paperwork created.
- **FOB (free on board).** The cost of all transport is charged to the customer (this is more likely to be found in industrial markets).
- **Zone pricing.** The price is different for each geographical region, or "zone," to incorporate the average transport costs incurred in shipping to that region.

There are, of course, other possible regional pricing policies. Not least of these are regional variations to allow for the strengths of local or regional competitors.

PRICING NEW PRODUCTS

The time when an organization is most free to determine the price of its products or services is when they are launched. Once the price has been set, so has a precedent. In the event of any future changes, consumers will not only have the competitive prices as a comparison, but they will also have the previous prices as a *very* direct point of reference. This makes it very difficult to make substantial changes to the prices of existing products or services. Consumer reactions may be severe

> The time when an organization is most free to determine the price of its products or services is when they are launched.

if they think they are being taken advantage of by the organization.

If the new product is entering an existing market, then price will be just one of the positioning variables. On this basis, the price will be carefully calculated to position the brand exactly where it will make the most impact—and profit. At a less sophisticated level, the producer of a new brand will decide which of the existing price ranges—cheap or expensive—the product or service should address. A supplier entering a mass consumer market can simply go to the local supermarket, or specialty store, and see what prices are already accepted. In industrial markets it may be much more difficult to obtain competitive prices, even where published price lists are available, because these are often only the starting point for negotiations that result in heavy discounts.

In the case of a totally new product or service, the pricing exercise will be that much more difficult, for there are no precedents to indicate how the consumer might behave, and this is an area where market research is notoriously inaccurate. In the end it will have to be a judgment decision as to what "perceived value" the consumer will put on the offering.

ALTERNATIVE PRICING STRATEGIES

Within these limits, however, there are two main approaches possible for a new product, and to a lesser extent for an existing one: skimming and penetration pricing.

SKIMMING.   One approach is to set the initial price high, to "skim" as much profit as possible, even in the early stages of the product life cycle. This is particularly applicable to new products that, at least for some time, have a monopoly of the market because the competitors have not yet emerged, and it is a pattern often seen in the *introduction* of new technology. For example, when telephone companies entered Russia with cellular phones, they were priced very high at $2,500 for sign-up because they had no competition and appealed to only a handful of wealthy

> [skimming] is a pattern **often seen in the introduction** of new technology

people. Within two years, however, the average price of those cellular phones returned to $200 for sign-up due to a much larger demand than expected and threats of eventual competition.

The price is usually reduced, possibly in stages, by the first entrants to gradually expand demand, until it reaches a competitive level just before the competitors enter the market. However, it is interesting to note that in the case of video recorders, it was the latecomers such as Panasonic and Toshiba, with improved technology and competitive prices, who actually swept the market originally created by Philips and Sony.

www.panasonic.com
www.toshiba.com
www.philips.com
www.sony.com

The rationale behind **skimming** (sometimes called *rapid payback*) is normally quite simply that of maximizing profit. But there may occasionally be another motive—that of maximizing the image of "quality." This is a policy that holds in consumer markets such as the upper end of the perfume trade; for example, sales of Chanel No. 5 would probably not increase dramatically if the price were reduced. But skimming can just as easily apply in industrial markets. It is the foolish consultant who asks for a low price, because the client will probably think that the quality is comparably low.

www.chanel.com

As indicated above, the danger of a skimming policy is that a high price encourages other competitors to enter the market, when they see that sales revenue can quickly cover the expense of developing a rival product. Therefore, as you recover some of your launch costs and as competitors appear—even if your prices are not exorbitant—you may still need to plan for a steady reduction in price. Such a price reduction will normally be helped by economies of scale. For example, Dell began selling sub-$1,000 home PCs and plans to have much more presence and aggressiveness in the lower-priced product segment. Although hardly groundbreaking in an era of $599 machines, Dell's recent embrace of under-$1,000 PCs continues the balancing act of avoiding first-time PC buyers without alienating them from its own line of PCs in its strategy of "skimming the cream" in the low end of the market.[12]

www.dell.com

---

12. Gary McWilliams, "Dell to Boost Its Sales of Low-Cost PCs," *Wall Street Journal*, April 9, 1999, B13.

PENETRATION PRICING. On the other hand, a manufacturer could choose the opposite tactic by adopting a penetration pricing policy; and, indeed, this has

> [penetration pricing] hastens **the growth of demand** and earlier economies of scale

been the very successful policy behind the move of Japanese corporations into a number of existing markets. Here an initial low price might make it less attractive for would-be competitors to imitate innovations, particularly where the technology is expensive, and it encourages more customers to buy the product soon after its introduction, which hastens the growth of demand and earlier economies of scale. The main value of this policy is that it helps to secure a relatively large market share and increase turnover while reducing unit costs, so that the price domination can be maintained and extended. Its major disadvantage lies in lost opportunities for higher profit margins.

In recent years, software companies have been literally giving away their products in order to build market share and to entice buyers to buy their other products. Given the fact that software is easy to copy and cheap to distribute (and hence easy to steal), some software companies have decided to turn these potential negatives into absolute positives. Netscape Communications gives its software to consumers, while charging up to $5,000 to the businesses that use the software to reach the consumers. Giving away the product to consumers is common in consumer goods companies. Companies such as Gillette and Kodak often give away razors and cameras to later make huge profits on blades and film.[13]

Under this broad category, however, there are a number of more specific policies.

www.netscape.com

www.gillette.com
www.kodak.com

- **Maximizing brand/product share.** This justification is sometimes made in terms of maximizing sales growth, particularly in new markets where competitive activity is less evident.
- **Maximizing current revenue.** The assumption is that higher sales automatically lead to higher profits, although in practice most products are more sensitive, in terms of profit, to price than to volume.
- **Survival.** For some organizations, maximizing revenue by price-cutting may be seen as the only way to survive. This is the philosophy of despair.

The circumstances generally favoring the skimming and penetration pricing are summarized in Table 10.2.

Table 10.2

Conditions for skimming versus penetration pricing strategy

Skimming	Penetration
Prices are likely to be inelastic	Prices are likely to be elastic
The product or service is new and unique	Competitors are likely to enter the market quickly
There are distinct segments	There are no distinct segments
Quality is important	Products will be undifferentiated
Competitive costs are unknown	Economies of scale apply

---

13. "Selling Software: Priceless," *Economist*, April 8, 1995, 61.

PRACTICAL PRICING POLICIES

Although the pricing theory that has been described provides managerial insight, it has limited value in practical pricing. Essentially, limitations indicated by Alfred Oxenfeldt[14] over two decades ago apply to this day.

> The current pricing literature has produced few new insights or exciting approaches that would interest most businessmen enough to change their present methods. Those executives who follow the business literature have no doubt broadened their viewpoint and become more explicit and systematic about their pricing decisions; however, few, if any, actually employ new and different goals, concepts or techniques . . . Most authors deal with pricing problems unidimensionally, whereas most businessmen must generally deal with price as one element in a multidimensional marketing program.

Thus, despite the theory described so far, prices are often set by one of a number of more pragmatic "rules of thumb."

COST-PLUS PRICING.   The starting point for most pricing exercises is an examination of the cost of the product or service. In practice, such "cost-plus" pricing is probably the most common approach and may be understandable where the price list contains hundreds of items. Under those circumstances, however, it is highly debatable whether the "cost" for each item represents anything more than an estimate.

Paradoxically, cost-plus pricing seems to suggest that inefficiency (which would lead to a higher unit cost) should be rewarded.

The one area in which cost-plus pricing is possibly justifiable is where the supplier has a long-term relationship—almost a partnership—with a customer (often the government). In these circumstances it is sometimes agreed that a certain level of profit, as a percentage of cost, is acceptable. But even here a question must be asked of whether such a pricing policy is efficient for the customer as well as for the supplier, because profit is supposed to be the main incentive. The legal actions taken by government to recover unwarranted profits made by some defense contractors operating under these pricing policies seem to argue for some dissatisfaction.

> The one area in which cost-plus pricing is possibly justifiable is where the supplier has a long-term relationship with a customer

Exactly what "cost" should be chosen is a matter of debate, although few producers actually do conduct such a debate, often selecting as their "cost"—by default—the first figure thrown up by their accounting system. Choosing what cost to apply and, more importantly, understanding the assumptions that lie behind it is an art, and one in which many marketers are unskilled.

The most critical element in this process is often the most arbitrary—that of the allocation of overheads. The process of absorption of overheads, whereby indirect overheads are allocated on the basis of judgment to production departments and then, combined with direct overheads, absorbed into the individual product costs, is often made on the basis of labor content (see Figure 10.3).

As we saw earlier, "marginal costs," which avoid the problem of overhead allocation, may well be the most favorable approach for new products, but may leave gaps in terms of overhead recovery as the older products die. A judgment also needs to be made as to the period over which any initial investment is to be recovered.

---

14. Alfred R. Oxenfeldt, "The Differential Method of Pricing," *European Journal of Marketing* 13, no. 4 (1979): 199–202.

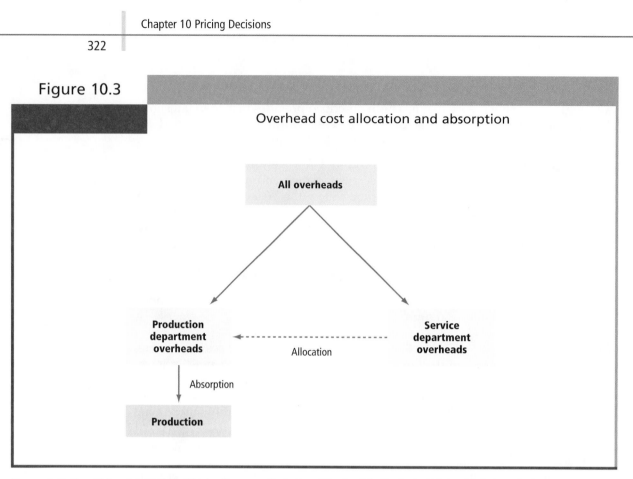

Figure 10.3

Overhead cost allocation and absorption

Source: A. R. Oxenfeldt and A. O. Kelly, "Pricing Consumer Products and Services," in *Handbook of Modern Marketing*, 2d ed., ed. Victor P. Buell (New York: McGraw-Hill, 1986). Adapted by permission of the McGraw-Hill Companies.

A number of fundamental errors committed by business executives in setting price are listed below.[15]

1. **The tendency to think in terms of averages.** This is the assumption that all customers behave in the same way. It ignores the particular and unusual circumstances under which the price move occurs and which call for the use of *marginal* or incremental costs.

2. **The reluctance to "let bygones be bygones."** This mistake lets irrevocable and irretrievable past expenditures enter into the cost computations underlying price decisions. The vital concept to apply here is *sunk costs*. These are outlays already made that cannot be revoked and about which nothing can be done. Such costs must be ignored in setting the price for new products.

3. **The tendency to ignore alternatives.** Businesspeople frequently charge out these elements on the basis of what was paid for them in the past (book costs) rather than what they would yield in alternative use. The concept of *opportunity costs* has been developed to help highlight the constant need to think in terms of alternatives when arriving at the decision.

4. **The tendency to emphasize cost considerations over demand considerations.** This tendency reaches its pinnacle in *cost-plus pricing* where demand considerations are simply ignored.

TARGET PRICING. In this case, the intention is not just to obtain a profit over costs, but is to obtain a reasonable return on investment (ROI). Therefore, the price has to be based on both the variable costs (as in cost-plus) and the fixed

15. Alfred R. Oxenfeldt and A. O. Kelly, "Pricing Consumer Products and Services," in *Handbook of Modern Marketing*, 2d ed., ed. V. P. Buell (New York: McGraw-Hill, 1986), 30-1 to 30-15.

costs. Fixed costs generally include facility, capital equipment, and other overhead, including top management's salaries. The process of trying to consider investment decisions and pricing decisions simultaneously is a very complex one, requiring accurate information.

> ## trying to consider investment
> ### and pricing decisions simultaneously
> ## is very complex

www.gm.com

General Motors used extensively target pricing in the 1980s. Facing intense Japanese competition, General Motors was losing customers. In order to achieve its targeted ROI, the company had to raise prices frequently to compensate for revenues lost to the Japanese automakers and further aggravated its customer losses as a result. Thus, it is not surprising that this is one of the less-popular policies, except where it is used in a theoretical rather than practical context, as part of a justification for a large capital investment program.

HISTORICAL PRICING. The normal extension of cost-plus pricing is to base today's prices on yesterday's. The annual round of price increases, for example, is based on last year's price raised by something approximating the increase in the cost of living or the true increase in costs—whichever is higher.

PRODUCT LINE PRICING. The pricing for a given product may be decided by the range within which it fits. There may thus appear to be an inevitable logic, derived from the rest of the product line. A 12-ounce pack, for example, is expected to have a price somewhere close to the median of the 8-ounce and 16-ounce packs. A premium price on a member of a budget-price product line would pose questions, and, at the other extreme, a budget-price entry into a luxury product line might do severe damage to the quality image of that product line.

A more specific example of product line pricing comes from retailing, where it is often called *price lining*. In this case, there are a limited number of predetermined price points, and all items in a given price category are given a specific price, say $9.99. This also illustrates the psychological aspect of choosing certain price points on the basis that customers will read $9.99 as $9 rather than the $10 it nearly is!

COMPETITIVE PRICING. The most common form of pricing, which is based on evidence from the market, is that where product prices are determined by reference to the prices of competitive products. For example, Advanced Micro Devices (AMD) is struggling to keep up as Intel pushes down prices on its Celeron chip line. The average price of AMD chips has dropped from $88 to $60 in three months, and it is expected to fall further. As a result, Gateway, NEC, and Toshiba have recently begun using AMD chips in machines sold in Japan. Major vendors, including Compaq and IBM, already use AMD chips in some consumer PCs. However, competitive pricing, if unchecked, could lead to price wars.[16]

www.amd.com
www.intel.com
www.celeron.com
www.gateway.com
www.nec.com
www.toshiba.com
www.compaq.com
www.ibm.com

A sound appreciation of competitive actions, especially prices, is necessary for the most effective strategies to be formulated. The most effective marketing manager will, however, try to develop an *understanding* of the various competitive positions based on an appreciation of the customer needs. A market leader should take advantage of the power that position offers, and a niche marketer should be able to use that uniqueness of positioning to gain some control over prices.

> ## A market leader should
> ### take advantage of the power
> ## that position offers.

16. Tom Davey, "Price War Hurts AMD," *Informationweek*, February 8, 1999, 202.

In a "brand monopoly" the marketer may have a significant degree of control over prices. On the other hand, in a commodity market no control at all may be available. Once more, the marketer has to make a judgment as to the price elasticity of demand (in this case in the context of competitors' prices).

The position is usually more complex than participants allow for. Products or services, and in particular brands, are rarely identical. Each will have its special features, presumably developed by its management to meet some market need. Therefore, each may justify a premium, or a degree of differentiation in its pricing. Setting the optimal premium is the subject of considerable skill—and not a little bravery.

> Setting the optimal premium is the subject of considerable skill— and not a little bravery.

The solution chosen by many suppliers is to match or preferably undercut their competitors. The problem is that all the participants can only have the lowest price if they all have the same price. That is usually a commodity-based price, which is significantly lower than the price that should be achieved when products or services are marketed effectively.

In markets where there are many suppliers, the skill is in knowing what premium over the commodity price the chosen marketing mix will justify. In markets in which there are a limited number of major products or services, one could argue that an understanding of the psychology of the competitors is just as important.

A specific example of competitive pricing occurs in the retail sector, in which "loss-leader pricing" is sometimes employed. The prices of certain lines are deliberately set low—perhaps even making a loss. The line then becomes a "loss leader" to attract customers into the store. The intention is that these customers will then also buy other lines on which the real profit will be made. You should note that the practice may be invalidated by customers who realize what is happening, and ethical objections have resulted in the loss-leader approach being made illegal in some states.[17]

MARKET-BASED PRICING. As discussed earlier, market-based pricing it is sometimes called *perceived value pricing*, because the price charged matches the value that the customer perceives that the product or service offers. Clearly it is near ideal, because it is likely to be optimal in terms of obtaining the maximum premium on the commodity price. This is also the ideal price in that it matches the position of the product to the customer's perceptions. Particularly in the luxury goods markets, the price is an element of the overall description of the product, and one

> in the luxury goods markets,
> price is an element of the product description
> seen as reflecting its quality

www.harley-davidson
.com

that is seen as reflecting its quality. There are many examples of luxury products, such as Harley-Davidson motorcycles, which performed badly until the price was increased in line with the quality expected (see Exhibit 10.1).

The problem is, of course, determining just what is the perceived value, or, even more fundamental, finding out what price consumers will be willing to pay. Even in the mass consumer markets, where extensive research is undertaken, establishing optimal prices is difficult. It is not possible to ask market research respondents how much they would be willing to pay, because such research will almost invariably give wildly optimistic results.[18]

---

17. "FTC Aids Wal-Mart in Fighting Oklahoma, Loss Leader Ban," *Discount Store News*, January 7, 1985, 2.
18. C. Hennig Hauf, "Price, Quality, and Consumers' Behavior," *Journal of Consumer Policy* 17 (September 1994): 335–348.

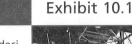

Exhibit 10.1

Pricing is an important decision in the marketing mix. It can establish the product's position in the market and influence consumer perceptions about the product. Harley-Davidson motorcycles is a case in point. Makers of the most sought-after motorcycle in the world, Harley-Davidson had difficulty selling its high-quality product due to low price structure. Once the prices were increased, consumer perception rose to meet the actual product specifications. Sales of the motorcycles increased, as did the product's standing as a luxury purchase.

Price Positioning.   In addition to determining where the "market" price lies, a further decision needs to be made—that of where the brand price is to be positioned in relation to the market price.

Quality Pricing.   Some organizations make a conscious decision to price above the market average. This price is intended to demonstrate the quality, or even the luxury, of the product or service. Rolls-Royce is the example quoted most often, but Hilton Hotels, Sony, and many cosmetic and perfume companies follow the same policy.

www.rolls-royce.com
www.hilton.com
www.sony.com

For these luxury products, the conventional downward-sloping demand curve described earlier in Figure 10.1 does not apply. Although the initial reduction in price may result in increased sales, beyond a critical point any further reduction in price will lead to a *reduction in sales*. In other words, fewer consumers will buy such a luxury product, as its exclusive quality image has been tarnished by lower prices. For this reason it is arguable that the problems being encountered by the Lincoln/Mercury division of Ford have actually been exacerbated by the price cuts that were made to try to restore its competitive position.

www.lincolnmercury.com
www.ford.com

Budget Pricing.   The organizations with the most obvious price positioning are those deliberately choosing to price below the market, since such budget prices are often the main element of their marketing mix. Bic, Hyundai, and Southwest Airlines have all used this approach.

www.bic.com
www.hyundai.com
www.southwest.com

SELECTIVE PRICING.   Some suppliers apply different prices for the same product or service. Marketing in Action 10.2 shows how the Internet is facilitating this for natural gas suppliers.

- **Category pricing.** The supplier aims to cover the range of price categories (possibly all the way from cheap to expensive) with a range of brands based

Marketing in Action 10.2

Is fluid pricing the wave of the future?

Southern California Gas Company (www .socalgas.com) is one of the largest natural gas distribution utilities in the United States. The company services 18 million customers in its 23,000-square-mile territory encompassing central and southern California. The U.S. natural gas marketplace is comprised of 55 million households. Over one-third of U.S. industrial energy use is powered by natural gas. Approximately 5 percent of all gas delivered in the United States is delivered by the Southern California Gas Company.

In 1998, Southern California Gas became a part of Sempra Energy, a global energy services holding company formed by the merger of Pacific Enterprises (parent of California Gas) and Enova Corporation (parent of San Diego Gas & Electric). A Fortune 500 company, Sempra provides integrated solutions to its energy customers' needs through its numerous subsidiaries.

Southern California Gas Company was on the leading edge of gas delivery prior to becoming a subsidiary of Sempra Energy. In November of 1997, the company launched Energy Marketplace (energymarketplace.com). Energy Marketplace is the first Internet-based shopping center providing real-time access that allows industrial customers to shop for the best natural gas prices. Southern California Gas charges a minimal fee to small- and medium-sized gas providers who want to list their gas prices on the exchange. Additionally, the companies can advertise service offerings on the site.

With real-time information on customers and suppliers, the Web provides an opportunity to increase or decrease price instantaneously. As more and more products are offered via the Internet, will uniform pricing give way to fluid pricing? Should Southern California Gas expand Energy Marketplace and offer it to household users?

Sources: www.socalgas.com; Amy E. Cortese and Marcia Stepanek, "Good-Bye to Fixed Pricing?" *Business Week*, May 4, 1998, 71+.

www.bausch.com

on the same product (repackaged, and possibly with some minor changes). This was particularly obvious when Bausch & Lomb marketed Sensitive Eyes 1-oz. eyedrops for $5.65 and Sensitive Eyes 12 oz. contact lens solution for $2.79.[19] It may be less obvious when suppliers run high-priced brands, while at the same time offering low-priced store brands.

- **Customer group pricing.** The ability of various groups to pay prices may be met by having different categories of prices: Entrance fees and fares are often lower for students and senior citizens.

- **Peak pricing.** The price is matched to the demand: High prices are demanded at peak times (the rush hours for transport, the evening performances for theaters, or resort hotel rates for off-season months), but lower prices are offered at off-peak times (to redistribute the resource demands by offering incentives to those who can make use of the services off-peak). Crested Butte Ski resorts in Colorado offer off-peak free lift tickets in one such extreme example.

www.crestedbutte.com

- **Yield pricing.** A variant of peak pricing known as yield management was originally used by airlines to price each seat differently depending on the hourly fluctuating demand conditions. At the Washington Opera Co., located in the nation's capital, the ticket-services manager knew—and his computer system confirmed—that the company routinely turned away people for Friday and Saturday night performances, particularly for prime seats. Meanwhile, midweek tickets went begging. He also knew that not all seats were equal in terms of the view and the acoustics, even in the sought-after orchestra section. So the ticket manager and his staff played with ticket prices until he arrived at nine levels, up from five. In the end, the opera raised prices for

www.dc-opera.com

19. "Eyeway Robbery?" *Business Week*, February 27, 1995, 48.

its most coveted seats by as much as 50 percent but also dropped the prices of some 600 seats. The gamble paid off in a 9 percent revenue increase during the next season. Yield management emphasizes an aggressive micromarket approach to maximizing sales. It assures that companies will sell the right product to the right consumer at the right time for the right price.[20]

- **Service level pricing.** The level of service chosen may determine the price. At its simplest, the buyer may pay for immediate availability rather than having to wait (or may pay more for the guarantee of a seat). This may be extended to levels of "delivery"; the product may be available immediately and gift wrapped in an expensive store—or it may arrive some weeks later by mail from a cheaper mail-order house. There may also be levels of "quality" in delivery; for instance, seats in different parts of a theater may have differing levels of access to the performance, although the basic product may be identical.

The last four of these practices are particularly prevalent in the service industries, where the supplier is in direct contact with the customer.

Above all, the main temptation to avoid is the assumption that price is the most important variable in the marketing mix. Sometimes it may be, and you will obviously need to recognize that. But in *most* situations it is not, and in many it may be a very minor consideration. Under these "typical" circumstances it is important to attend to the other elements of the marketing mix first, and then deal with price in this context.

> Above all, avoid the assumption that **price is the most important** variable in the marketing mix.

DISCOUNTS

Having set the overall price, the supplier then has the option of offering different prices (usually on the basis of a discount) to cover different circumstances. The types of discount most often offered are:

- **Trade discounts.** Members of the supplier's distribution channel (retailers and wholesalers, for example) will demand payment for their services. Trade discounts are covered in more detail in Chapter 11.
- **Quantity discounts.** Those who offer to buy larger quantities of the product or service (again typically as part of the distribution channel, but also the larger industrial buyers) are frequently given incentives. In consumer markets this is more often achieved by larger pack sizes (or by banding together smaller packs) as "family or economy" packs. It is often deemed more cost effective to offer extra product ("30 percent extra free" or "13 for the price of 12") instead of reducing price, because the extra product represents only a marginal increase in cost to the supplier and may push the user into using more (and even finding new uses).
- **Cash discounts.** Where credit is offered, it is sometimes decided to offer an incentive for cash payment or for prompt payment (to persuade customers to pay their bills on the due date, although too often they take the discount anyway and still pay late).

---

20. Susan Greco, "Are Your Prices Right?" *Inc.* (January 1997): 88–89.

- **Allowances.** In the durable goods market, suppliers often attempt to persuade consumers to buy a new piece of equipment by offering allowances against trade-in of their old one. Generally speaking, these are simply hidden discounts targeted at a group of existing competitive users.

- **Seasonal discounts.** Suppliers to markets that are highly seasonal (such as the holiday market) will often price their product or service to match the demand, with the highest prices at peak demand.

- **Promotional pricing.** Suppliers may, from time to time, wish to use a price discount as a specific promotional device. This is discussed at more length in Chapter 13.

- **Individual pricing.** Under certain circumstances, it may be possible for a customer, even in a consumer market, to negotiate a special price. Such haggling is the essence of sales in most Latin American countries. It is also the basis of some industrial and business-to-business selling. Here the pricing decision is left to the sales professional, often with disastrous effects on profit. Control of such processes will be discussed in Chapter 14.

- **Optional features.** The reverse of discounts may be that customers are offered a basic product to which they can add features at extra cost (and often, unlike discounts, with much higher profit margins). Automobile purchases are a good example.

- **Product bundling.** Alternatively, customers might be offered a "bundle" of related products—such as a package of accessories with a camera—at a reduced price, as compared with the prices of the separate items (although sometimes the separate items are not really sold apart from the special promotional bundle).

- **Value package.** Slightly different from product bundling, a value package offers customers a product that automatically comes with a certain package of accessories. In recent years, automakers have adopted value package pricing by selling cars already equipped with such accessories as an air conditioner, antilock brakes, and a CD player. Value package enables automakers to reduce production costs by limiting option packages and to pass on some savings to customers in the form of lower prices.

- **Psychological pricing.** Some suppliers deliberately set very high "recommended" prices in order to offer seemingly very high discounts ("massive savings") against them. However, this policy may backfire when consumers realize what is happening. In any case, such tactics are now often subject to regulation and may even be illegal.

Price Negotiation

The most difficult area of pricing seems to be where the price results from a process of negotiation, typically as part of face-to-face sales activities. There are probably three main reasons why the greatest difficulty arises in this area:

- **Each is believed to be a unique situation.** The buyer and, more importantly, the seller (the salesperson) both believe that each such negotiation starts afresh without any established ground rules—no matter what the seller's policies might be.

- **Negotiation takes place under immediate pressure.** The price is set not by the leisurely processes of the office bureaucracy, but under the severe pressures of "real-time" negotiations with the customer. In this case, the salesperson has to think on his or her feet while keeping all the other sales issues under control.

- **The negotiator is less prepared and motivated.** The negotiator is typically the salesperson, who is not well versed in the factors that should influence any pricing decision. More importantly, he or she is normally motivated in part by the whole ethos of selling and in part (often largely) by actual monetary incentives, to close the sale rather than obtain the highest price.

It is no great exaggeration to state that many sales personnel (at all levels) go into a price negotiation believing that they are in an inherently weak position and, indeed, are bound to lose. Many sales courses on negotiation are largely designed to convince people that this is not true.

In general, then, most sellers put *themselves* in a weak bargaining position, and as a result many, if not most, prices arrived at in such bargaining are lower than they need be. However, the seller can also have a strong position over the buyers. Sellers are in a strong position when:[21]

- Buyers each buy small quantities relative to the total sales of the sellers—the seller can afford to lose the business of individual buyers
- Buyers lack suitable alternative sources—the seller has a quasimonopoly
- Buyers face high "switching costs"—the buyer would have significant costs and problems associated with switching to a new supplier
- The cost of the item is a small part of the buyer's costs—the buyer has more pressing problems
- The cost of the product failing would be high—the buyer needs to play for safety and cannot afford to cut corners
- Cost savings resulting from use of the product are significant—the product more than pays for itself
- Buyers have high-quality images—they cannot afford to buy "cheap" inputs
- Buyers want customer-designed products—the seller again has the potential of a quasimonopoly
- Buyers' organizations are highly profitable—the buyer is not primarily motivated by cost savings
- The buyer is poorly informed—lack of information always undermines a negotiation position
- Large buyers are not necessarily the most price conscious—though they will happily accept the gift of low prices, which many sales personnel, who assume that price is always a function of quantity, hand to them

PROJECT PRICING

Long negotiations—say, for large capital projects—can be the most vicious. By the time the tender is awarded, the sellers may have invested many thousands of dollars or even millions of dollars in the tendering process itself, preparing all the specifications and designs for their submissions. The crucial decision of whether their tender will succeed in being selected is all that stands between the project team and disaster.

PRICING STRATEGY

Whatever the rationale behind the final pricing decisions —from the most elegant of economic theories to the most pragmatic of competitive reactions—it is necessary to consolidate them as a pricing strategy to ensure that what is being

---

21. Michael E. Porter, *Competitive Strategy* (New York: Free Press, 1980).

implemented matches what the participants in the decision actually thought they were agreeing to. Too often major misunderstandings in management decision making are revealed only after the damage has been done. Formalizing these decisions in writing should remove the possibility of such misunderstandings, although it may not always do so.

It is also necessary to ensure that the individual prices are carefully managed and that there is a balance across the whole portfolio.

PRICE WARS

Price competition is seen as the most savage and destructive form of business warfare. It is particularly destructive because at one end of the chain it destroys the profit of the suppliers (and with it the capacity to invest in the future of the market) and at the other because it often destroys the consumer's belief in the quality of offering (and thus in their expectations of development of the market). Volume sales, other stimuli, and minor brands are some of the reasons for indulging in the very risky pursuit of price competition.

> Price competition is seen as **the most savage and destructive** form of business warfare.

The dangers of initiating a price war include the following.

- **Low-quality image.** A low price may be equated with low quality (and may actually represent just that, as the opponents shave quality in order to fund the cost cutting).

- **Temporary advantage.** A price advantage is often held only in the short term, and consumers will be rapidly attracted to the even lower one (which you can be sure will eventually appear).

- **Loss of profit.** Above all, price reductions should be seen as an investment to generate greater sales (for, if they do not, they can only result in reduced profits). It is wise, under these circumstances, to work out which company has the deepest pockets or most favorable cost structure and can invest in such a war of attrition the longest. History tends to show that it is often the initiator of the war who is the first casualty.

The telecommunication market is going through complex price wars of a sort to attract customers with a lower package price for a bundle of various services. Bundling is becoming the byword for data and voice services over upgraded networks. What has long been a confusing rate environment became even more so during the late 1990s as a result of several of developments, including greater competitive pressure on nontariffed voice rates, bundling deals that reduce the ability to pit one carrier against another, and expanded "convergence," which now includes local access as well as long-distance and data. The greatest pricing reductions were in the nontariffed voice market. Now any business paying more than 10 cents a minute for long-distance interstate traffic is considered overcharged. Even five cents a minute under certain circumstances is possible. MCI WorldCom, Sprint,[22] and AT&T are scrambling to hold the pricing fort against newer competitors. AT&T readily admits that lower rates have driven its long-distance revenues down across the board to the tune of 9 to 10 percent.[23]

www.wcom.com
www.sprint.com
www.att.com

---

22. At the time of this writing in October 1999, MCI WorldCom agreed to acquire Sprint. Their merger, however, was struck down by the Federal Communications Commission.

23. Patrick Flanagan, "Voice Service: Confusion Growing, Prices Falling," *Business Communications Review* (February 1999): 23–26.

VOLUME SALES. Not all price reductions are destructive. Some result in such increases in the volume of purchases that absolute profit is increased despite the relative reductions in price (and economies of scale may mean that even the relative profit per unit increases), and the whole market expands rapidly.

The key to making a success of price competition is in ensuring that it reflects a genuine cost advantage. Economies of scale, and hence the justification of lower prices to increase volume, are one aspect. Another is that your own cost structure must offer advantages over those of the competitors. When these factors apply in your favor, then price competition can be very advantageous in exactly the same way that any other "product" advantage would be.

> The key to making a success of **price competition is in ensuring that** it reflects a genuine cost advantage.

Unfortunately, most price competition occurs between companies with very similar cost structures, and, thus, frequently leads to a debilitating price war (e.g., the airline price wars among the major U.S. airlines).

OTHER STIMULI. Apart from a price reduction to reflect a genuine cost advantage, price reductions are often stimulated by the following.

- **Market leadership targeting.** In an "open" market, with a number of similar sized brands (or a new market that has not yet stabilized), a brand owner may decide to make an investment to achieve market leadership (a "penetration" pricing policy in new markets). Price is often the main weapon, particularly where there is a belief (often no more than an unjustified hope) that this may also lead to falling costs per unit.

- **Excess capacity.** Perhaps the most dangerous move is where price is reduced to use up excess capacity, and hence to absorb more overhead. Unfortunately, this often takes place where there is spare capacity in the market as a whole. Competitors are faced with similar problems and will respond similarly.

- **Falling brand share.** Defense of share often involves a more aggressive price position, and hence it may be wise to watch how rapidly share is being taken from competitors by nonprice means (because too rapid an erosion may stimulate a savage price war).

MINOR BRANDS. An exception to the strictures about price competition relates to minor brands in markets that are dominated by major brands. As was discussed earlier (in the section on "Competition" in Chapter 3), minor brands will typically make the largest offer (usually a price reduction) *per unit* (which represents the greatest impact they can make), whereas the response of the leaders is to promote (most economically) across the whole market, usually by advertising. This situation rarely leads to damaging price wars.

REACTIONS TO PRICE CHALLENGES

The first reaction to a price reduction should always be to consider the situation carefully (and metaphorically count to 10 before indulging in self-righteous retaliation). Has the competitor decided on a long-term price reduction, or is this just a short-term promotion? If it is the latter, then the reaction should be purely that relating to short-term promotional activity (and the optimum response is often

> price wars have been started because **simple promotional activities have been** misunderstood as major strategic changes

simply to ignore the challenge). All too often, price wars have been started because simple promotional activities have been misunderstood as major strategic changes.

On the other hand, if it emerges that this *is* a long-term move, then there are a number of possible reactions.

- **Reduce price.** The most obvious, and most popular, reaction is to match the competitor's move. This maintains the *status quo* (but reduces profits *pro rata*). If this route is to be chosen, it is best to make the move rapidly and obviously—not least to send signals to the competitor of your intention to fight.
- **Maintain price.** Another reaction is to hope that the competitor has made a mistake, although if the competitor's action does make inroads into your share, this can rapidly lead to a loss in volume, as well as a loss of confidence in the product.
- **Split the market.** A particularly effective tactic (most notably used by Heublein, the owner of the Smirnoff brand of vodka) is to combine a move to increase the "quality" of the main brand at the same time as launching a "fighting brand" to undermine—by further price-cutting—the competitor's position.
- **React with other measures.** Reducing price is not the only weapon. Other tactics, such as improved quality or increased promotion (to improve the quality image, perhaps) may be used, often to great effect. Coupons may be used to attract price-sensitive customers (see Manager's Corner 10.4).

www.smirnoff.com

AVOIDING PRICE WARS

Avoidance is by far the best policy, but it is advice that may not always be taken if the benefits seem attractive (which, unfortunately, they may also be to competitors). The dangers are summarized in a theory borrowed from the ethics branch of the social sciences.

THE PRISONER'S DILEMMA. The basic, imaginary dilemma (broadly known as *game theory*) has two prisoners accused of a crime. If one confesses and the other does not, the one confessing will be released immediately and the other jailed for 10 years. If neither confesses, each will only be held for a few months. On the other hand, if both confess they will each receive a sentence of five years. The problem for the prisoners is that they are not allowed to communicate with each other. The calculation is that self-interest will be best served for each by confessing, no matter what the other does. But, of course, this is a less-satisfactory solution for them than if they had both held out.

Fortunately, as we saw in Chapter 3, the position in the case of price competition, although sharing some of the features of this dilemma—especially if the participants react without thinking—is somewhat more favorable. The "prisoners" are not held incommunicado. They can exchange signals that indicate their intentions. Under these circumstances, the best outcome can be achieved—and often is. As an example, Ivy Leagues schools used to have occasional meetings to discuss, if not openly fix, tuition and financial aid levels for their students until a class action suit was brought against them.[24]

www.collegenet.com
/geograph/ivy.html

24. Dennis W. Carlton, Gustavo E. Bamberger, and Roy J. Epstein, "Antitrust and Higher Education: Was There a Conspiracy to Restrict Financial Aid?" *Rand Journal of Economics* 26 (spring 1995): 131–147.

Hidden price discounts: coupons go high-tech!

A 1998 study by Professors Ramaswamy and Srinivasan suggests that different segments of consumers place varying emphasis on economic benefits, psychological benefits, effort costs, and substitution costs. Coupons are both a familiar and a useful form of promotion that can create buying patterns and build customer loyalty. They are also an important part of a firm's overall pricing policy as they lower the effective price of products. The researchers predict that coupon and voucher usage may be given a boost by the latest adaptations of information technology to the retail marketplace.

In the 1990s, the use of coupons declined sharply. In 1994, the value of coupons in circulation was $2.6 billion, compared with almost $4.7 billion in 1993 and $8.5 billion in 1992. This was largely due to the retailers/traders whose incentives differed somewhat from those of the manufacturer. These traders adopted the habit of accepting coupons against other brands or any product, even if they did not stock it. In these cases, the manufacturer saw an increase in coupon redemptions and no corresponding sales increase. After falling for three years, the total number of coupons issued by packaged goods marketers in 1998 stabilized at about the 1997 level. However, a decline in redemption rates continued. The stabilized coupon circulation is partially attributed to the Internet.

Coupons have become freely available on the Internet via such Web sites as CoolSavings (www6.coolsavings.com). Some of the innovations include: tailor-made coupons, coupons available on request from coupon Web sites, coupons with a prize drawing or competition, coupons with stricter expiration dates, and significantly improved bar-code technology. Tailor-made coupons can only be redeemed at stores that stock that item. With the increased sophistication at coupon redemption houses this can be more easily monitored. Misredemption could be largely eliminated by matching a bar code on the coupon to the bar code used for that product by a retailer. It is only a question of who will pay to implement this technology: the manufacturer, the retailer, Internet operators, or all of them.

Another alternative involves vouchers. One company, Capital Incentives (www.capital-incentives.co.uk), has come out with the Capital Card, which is a voucher credit card that has gained the participation of 80 retailers and can be used at over 20,000 locations. Under this system, the participants receive a capital card with a zero balance. As they make specific purchases, credit is accumulated and stored on the card. This system is convenient to use and eliminates the need for carrying or storing actual vouchers.

In addition to the positive incentives created through the use of coupons and vouchers, these promotions are linked to overall pricing and brand strategies. They allow manufacturers to price competitively with the in-house brands without appearing overly aggressive. Also, coupons and vouchers do not erode brand image in the way that a price cut can. Furthermore, consumers do not see coupons as a long-term price reduction.

Sources: "Promotions & Incentives: Coupons," *Marketing Week,* October 20, 1995, 59–66; Venkatram Ramaswamy and Srini S. Srinivasan, "Coupon Characteristics and Redemption Intentions: A Segment-Level Analysis," *Psychology & Marketing* 15 (January 1998): 59–80; "Coupon Circulation Flattens Out after 3-Year Slide," *Supermarket Business* 54 (March 1999): 11–12.

PRICE INCREASES

What is less often discussed, but is often more important, is the topic of price increases. The normal reason for these is inflation, which these days appears to be inevitable to at least some degree. The resulting increase in cost has to be passed on if profits are not to be adversely affected. Fortunately, the widespread expectation of inflation usually means that increases can be imposed without too many problems.

Price increases are also often expected (at least by economic theorists) where there is excess demand. Although this is a situation that is very welcome to the suppliers, it is actually a fairly rare phenomenon and even more rarely lasts for any length of time.

On the other hand, where costs rise but price increases cannot be easily imposed, the solution may be to reduce the specification or to produce smaller packs, as many confectionery manufacturers often do.

The following is a six-part practical guide to making price increases.

- Increase the prices when everyone else does. Don't hold back for the sake of competitive edge; you will have to increase eventually and the action will be more noticeable then.

- Don't increase too much at any one time. Incremental increases (around the level of inflation) are less noticeable.

- Don't increase too often. Buyers react against too-frequent changes.

- Look after your key accounts. The 80/20 Rule says that it is the reactions of your key accounts that are most important.

- Provide sound—and true—explanations. Customers understand that prices sometimes have to go up when costs increase.

SUMMARY

Much of the theory is derived from economics, especially from supply and demand theory. This is encapsulated in the famous demand and supply curves. The price is set by the point where the curves intersect. The degree to which demand is susceptible to price changes (*price elasticity of demand*) is another concept borrowed from economics, but very useful to marketers.

Again in theory, but rarely in practice, these curves can be obtained from statistical analysis of historical data, survey research, and experimentation. Rather less theoretically, factors affecting the pricing policies of a specific organization include organization factors, product life cycle, product portfolio, product line pricing, segmentation and positioning, and branding. Factors derived from customers are customer factors, demand, benefits, value, and distribution channel. Of these, *perceived value* is especially important, as it defines what the customer should be prepared to pay.

Pricing new products offers a different set of challenges. In general, two main opposing strategies are seen:

- Skimming—high price, to skim off the short-term profit
- Penetration—low price, to maximize long-term market share

Practical pricing policies for existing brands may include cost-plus pricing, target pricing, historical pricing, product line pricing, competitive pricing, market-based pricing, and selective pricing. It should not be forgotten that price can also be a major factor in determining a product's or service's *image*, ranging from *quality price* to *budget price*.

A wide range of *discounts* may be offered: trade, quantity, cash, and allowances— seasonal, promotional, and individual.

Prices may also be set at levels that are judged to be "psychologically" appropriate ($9.95, for instance). Other ways of achieving a price effect may lie with other parts of the offer, such as *product bundling* at one extreme and charging separately for "options" at the other. Alternatively, price may be *negotiated*, as it often is in capital goods markets.

Organizations may resort to *price competition* for several reasons, including volume sales, other stimuli, and minor brands. On the other hand, the dangers of initiating a price war include low-quality image, temporary advantage, and profit loss.

QUESTIONS FOR REVIEW

1. How does the equilibrium price come about? What is the price elasticity of demand?

2. How may supply and demand curves be established in practice?

3. What organizational factors, derived from related marketing theory, might influence price? How may positioning or branding be used to raise prices?

4. What customer-related factors might, in theory, affect price? Why may perceived value be important?

5. What opposing pricing policies may be applied to new products, and how do they work?

6. List the pricing policies used in practice. What are the drawbacks of cost-plus pricing?

7. How is competitive pricing different from market-based pricing? What selective pricing policies may be employed?

8. What discounts may be offered? What is psychological pricing? What are the differences between product bundling and charging for options?

9. Why might price competition be employed? When can it be justified in terms of volume sales? What are the dangers posed by price wars?

10. What responses to price competition may be available? How may they be successfully employed?

QUESTIONS FOR DISCUSSION

1. If a new airline began operating in your area and offered everyday fares that were only 90 percent of the price of its nearest competitor, how likely would you be to fly on that airline regularly? What if they were 50 percent of the price? What if they were 10 percent of the price?

2. What would you think about a car manufacturer that placed coupons in the paper to be cut out and brought into a local car dealership for redemption? Compare your reaction to a situation where a breakfast cereal manufacturer placed coupons in the paper to be brought into your local grocery store for redemption. In which case are you more likely to value the coupon? Why?

3. The dollar depreciated about 20 percent against the Japanese yen in a few months. How much could or would Dell Computer be willing to lower the yen prices of its U.S.-assembled PCs in Japan? Consider the company's reliance on Japan for computer chips, motors, and flat panel displays. Also consider two marketing objectives: profit maximization versus market share.

4. Your firm's position is third in a durable goods market, and the number two competitor has initiated a 9 percent price cut. You find that you must announce/decide your prices before

knowing what the market leader's reaction will be. What factors would cause you to raise, lower, or maintain prices?

5. Many firms enter a market as price leaders, but their strategy changes as they dominate the lower end of the market. What are some of the challenges these firms face? What strategies have/have not been successful?

6. Most Western tobacco companies see Russia as a lucrative new territory. Indeed, Russians smoke 250 billion cigarettes a year, and there are few restrictions on smoking. Russian companies sell their cigarettes for two to three rubles—10 to 13 cents—a pack. The cheapest local brands made by Western manufacturers sell for six to seven rubles, but the same companies' import brands sell for 20 to 30 rubles. Evaluate the commercial and the ethical aspects of marketing Western cigarettes in Russia. Why is the pricing different for imported and locally produced cigarettes?

7. Buy.com Inc., among other Internet retail Web sites, is offering bargain-basement prices on computer products. Some small and midsize resellers say they find it disconcerting that customers can buy certain products from Web-based retailers at a lower cost than these same value-added retailers (VARs) can secure them

from many distributors. Other VARs say the existence of this new retail channel reaffirms that they must offer quality services to effectively compete in a climate of cutthroat hardware pricing. Buy.com scans the Web on a daily basis in an effort to beat the competition by at least a dollar. Although Buy.com is positioned as a site mostly for consumers, small and midsize businesses account for more than 80 percent of sales. Ingram Micro provides much of the back office functions for Buy.com. Can you paint a scenario a few decades from now when e-commerce is expected to dominate the mode of market transaction? How will the prices in product groups such as grocery be affected? Will certain product groups be immune to such changes? If so, why?

8. Some PC resellers that have lost corporate accounts to direct marketer Dell Computer are battling to win back business through an assortment of pricing, marketing, and service tactics. One of the strategies resellers are deploying is regularly dispatching their salespeople to Dell accounts to keep customers informed of current product pricing from Compaq Computer, Hewlett-Packard, and IBM. Although Dell often wins large accounts based on the pricing of its products, resellers are arguing to customers that Dell's contract pricing is not as competitive in the long term because the agreements do not accurately predict industry price drops. Although Dell admits that resellers sometimes do win business back, the company contends that its pricing policies are not the reason. How does the cost structure of a direct marketer differ from that of a reseller? Can the resellers through their assortment of pricing, marketing, and service tactics compete with the direct marketer who in most cases adopts pricing alone as its focus?

FURTHER READINGS

Begg, David, Stanley Fischer, and Rudiger Dornbusch. *Economics.* 3d ed. New York: McGraw-Hill, 1991.

Devinney, Timothy M., ed. *Issues in Pricing: Theory and Research.* Lexington, Mass.: Lexington Books, 1988.

Holden, Reed, and Thomas Nagle. "Kamikaze Pricing." *Marketing Management* 7 (summer 1998): 30–39.

Lowell, Julia, and Loren Yager. *Pricing and Markets: U.S. and Japanese Responses to Currency Fluctuations.* Santa Monica, Calif.: Rand Corp., 1994.

Morris, Michael H., and Gene Morris. *Market-Oriented Pricing: Strategies for Management.* New York: Quorum Books, 1990.

Ratchford, Brian T., and Pola Gupta. "On the Implementation of Price-Quality Relations." *Journal of Consumer Research* 13 (December 1990): 389–411.

Rayport, Jeffrey F. "Case Study: Information on a Silver Platter." *Journal of Interactive Marketing* 13 (spring 1999): 29–48.

Simon, Hermann, and Robert J. Dolan. "Price Customization." *Marketing Management* 7 (fall 1998): 11–17.

chapter **11**

Distribution and Supply Chain Management

This chapter covers the "place" element of the marketing mix by addressing the location and movement of goods. In doing so, we will examine the institutional linkages between suppliers, known as channels, which comprise retailers, wholesalers, and distributors. The discussion of supply chain management will then address the processes underlying these linkages, such as warehousing, transportation, and inventory management. Both areas are of a fundamental strategic nature for the firm, both because they have long-lasting impact and because decisions, once made, are difficult to change. At the same time, market-driven channels and supply chain management will determine the level of customer service, which is crucial to a firm's success. Customer service is therefore addressed in the final part of this chapter.

THE DISTRIBUTION CHANNEL

In the ideal sales situation the supplier and the customer meet face-to-face for a dialogue. However, for many goods and services the value of the individual sale does not justify such an approach. Imagine if each toothpaste producer tried to sell directly to consumers—the result would be cost and relationship nightmare. With intermediaries, marketing activities can be consolidated and costs spread across a range of products. Figure 11.1 illustrates the beneficial effects of channel geometry. Even with only a few producers and retailers, the number of contacts grows very quickly. By introducing an intermediary—a wholesaler, for example—the number of contacts is much smaller, and the distribution task becomes more manageable. The most obvious examples of such intermediaries are the retailers from whom we buy our consumer goods.

Before a product reaches the consumer or end user, it must frequently go through a chain of intermediaries, each one passing the product down to the next organization. This process is known as the distribution chain or channel. Channels are important because "consumption is a function of availability . . . one can only consume products that are available."[1] Each element in the chain has specific needs and performs different functions, which the producer must take into account, along with the requirements of the all-important end user. Table 11.1 gives an example of the functions performed by the channel of Japan's cosmetics industry, with each member concentrating on a different set of activities.

---

1. M. J. Baker, *Marketing Strategy and Management* (New York: Macmillan, 1985).

Figure 11.1

Channel geometry effects on the distribution system

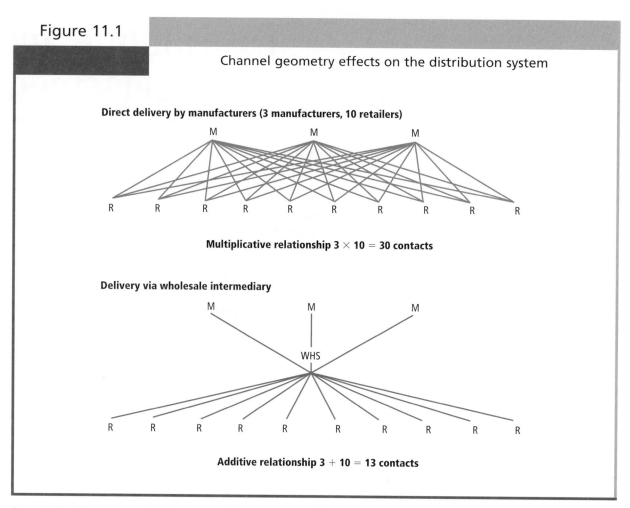

Direct delivery by manufacturers (3 manufacturers, 10 retailers)

Multiplicative relationship 3 × 10 = 30 contacts

Delivery via wholesale intermediary

Additive relationship 3 + 10 = 13 contacts

Source: Michael R. Czinkota and Jon Woronoff, *Unlocking Japan's Markets*, 2d ed. (Rutland, Vt.: Charles E. Tuttle, 1993), 83. Reprinted by permission of Probus Publications (Richard D. Irwin, Inc.).

Table 11.1

An example of function performance in the channel system

Cosmetics industry channel members		
Manufacturer	**Intermediary**	**Retail**
Production	Order taking	Selling
Advertising	Inventory maintenance	Organizing consumers
National sales promotion	Space control at the retail level	In-store promotion
Dealer aids	Product assortment	
Education of dealers	Dispatching of sales support personnel	
Financing	Area of marketing	
	Financing	

Source: Michael R. Czinkota and Jon Woronoff, *Unlocking Japan's Markets*, 2d ed. (Rutland, Vt.: Charles E. Tuttle, 1993), 85. Reprinted by permission of Probus Publications (Richard D. Irwin, Inc.).

Exhibit 11.1

Bluefly.com is only an online department store with no other outlets or channels. Barely two years old, Bluefly .com has been a successful entrant in the Internet retailing market. By using what has now become a standard personalization format, Bluefly .com allows its customers to create a profile that helps generate a personalized on-line catalog of new offerings every time a user connects to the site. This kind of electronic customization has become the hallmark of many Internet retailers, and may be how they leverage the unique power of the Internet as a distribution channel.

tuesday, 11:15 p.m.
buying a new dress.

bluefly

www.bluefly.com℠
the outlet store in your home℠

Women's, men's and kid's designer fashions
Save up to 75%.   90-day money-back guarantee.

CHANNEL MEMBERS AND LEVELS

Distribution channels include retailers, wholesalers, and agents, or direct distribution via a sales force or mail order. Channels are not restricted to physical products; they may be just as important for moving a service from the producer to the consumer. Hotels, for example, may sell their services directly or through travel agents, tour operators, airlines, or centralized reservation systems.

Distribution channels have a number of levels. The simplest is the zero-level channel, in which the contact between the manufacturer and the end user is direct and no intermediaries are involved. Traditionally, this type of channel is most frequently encountered in an industrial or business-to-business setting where few customers acquire big-ticket items. For consumer goods, channels typically have two levels, leading from producer to wholesaler and retailers. At the extreme end of the spectrum are the very elaborate distribution systems in Japan, with many levels of channels even for the simplest of consumer goods. Such differences in channels are typically the result of tradition, geography, culture, and consumer purchasing patterns. For example, during the feudal period of Japan, the country consisted of many small provinces that were largely self-contained. As a result, each province developed its own distribution system. Because Japan consisted of about 500 regions, many manufacturers needed to develop wholesalers for each territory, some of which survive today.

In recent years the channel picture has been complicated by rapid changes driven by technological capabilities and the emergence of new power structures. The traditional channels of distribution have become scrambled. Some distribution processes, so essential when information and quality control were poor, are being bypassed and eventually eliminated. The increasing ubiquitousness of Internet Web sites is promising to significantly alter the way large parts of our

www.amazon.com

distribution system are managed[2] (see Exhibit 11.1 on page 341). Internet merchants like Amazon.com are engaging in head-to-head battles with conventional retailers and seem to be gaining in advantage. They are unencumbered by the overhead of physical stores, have larger trading areas, carry less inventory, work closely with producers, and can offer an almost unlimited selection of merchandise. Internet merchants are also increasingly sophisticated in leveraging customer information. As a result, products and promotions can be targeted much more efficiently than through conventional media.[3] In many ways, the Internet empowers firms, often through automation, to regain the one-on-one relationship with their customer, without having to bear prohibitive cost. In addition, Internet merchants can offer the benefits of speed, which increasingly differentiate firms. As stated by Larry Carter, chief financial officer of Cisco Systems, a company that sells most of the routers that power the Internet, "It's no longer about the big beating the small, it's about the fast beating the slow."[4]

www.cisco.com

Both in industrial as well as in consumer marketing, electronic business is accepted with great speed in the United States, but it is also growing rapidly internationally, as Manager's Corner 11.1 shows.

CHANNEL DECISIONS

In evaluating the various levels of distribution, one must consider the relationship between channel members.[5] These relationships can be conventional, in which a range of intermediaries passes the goods on to the end user. They can also be geared to a single transaction, in which case a temporary channel is set up for one transaction only, such as the sale of property or a specific civil engineering project. Channels can also be integrated, in that different intermediaries work closely together.

Manager's Corner 11.1

Switching from paper to electronic orders

Electronic commerce is growing rapidly in the United States and is expected to grow into an inevitable international trend as U.S. businesses are trying to push overseas vendors into electronic communication. Although at present three-fourths of the purchase orders sent to vendors overseas are still sent in paper form, electronic order filing and processing are believed to be poised for takeoff.

The benefits are potentially huge: Electronic commerce eliminates paperwork, which is costly and error-prone, and can speed up the whole order-filing and processing procedure. Electronic filing also allows management an effective information system to plan business better. With electronic communication, importers can take various measures to force foreign vendors to provide accurate and timely information on shipments. For exam-

ple, importers will impose a "charge-back" to the foreign wholesaler if they need to relabel or recount the contents of a shipment because the documentation contained inaccurate information on the quantity, size, or color of the merchandise. These charge-backs can be high enough to wipe out the entire profit of a shipment.

However, the switch can be a herculean task. Large U.S. retailers had to struggle for five years before they could achieve electronic compliance from their domestic vendors. This e-commerce strategy is likely to meet with even fiercer resistance from overseas vendors, especially those in developing countries, given the poor state of electronic infrastructure there and vendors' unwillingness to invest even a modest amount in electronic facilities.

Source: "Importers Push Overseas Vendors to Communicate Electronically," *Journal of Commerce*, January 27, 1999, 17A.

2. Alan Greenspan, as quoted in "Fed Chief Indicates Belief in Sustainability of Economic Growth," *Washington Post*, May 7, 1999, A15.
3. Raymond Burke, "Marketing in the 21st Century," *Journal of the Academy of Marketing Science* (fall 1997): 352–360.
4. "Cisco@speed," *Economist*, June 26, 1999, Special Survey, 12.
5. G. Lancaster and L. Massingham, *Essentials of Marketing* (New York: McGraw-Hill, 1988), 249.

The Body Shop foresees changes in its retail store concept

The Body Shop International PLC (www.the-body-shop.com) has established a worldwide reputation with its naturally-based skin and hair care products. By 1999, the company operated over 1,500 retail outlets in 47 countries. The company reported a 1998 loss of $25 million on sales of $497 million. In a move to improve the bottom line, the company has decided to focus on becoming a brand retailer. Historically, the company operated as manufacturer, distributor, and retailer. Although the company will continue developing new products, it will outsource manufacturing.

Early efforts at implementing the brand retail strategy have resulted in considerable changes. One major change is the flagship store concept. The Body Shop will open two flagship stores in the United States. These flagship stores will be twice as big as the average Body Shop store. Additionally, the company is refurbishing 400 stores in 28 markets. Along with the refurbishing, the company will begin streamlining the number of stockkeeping units in each store. The streamlining, combined with an effort to have 40 percent new products each year, resulted in the company opening its first outlet store as a way of disposing of discontinued inventory.

Looking ahead, the company's CEO is considering additional strategies. One possible strategy is partnering with other retail stores to promote and sell Body Shop products. Another idea is that of utilizing e-commerce as a means of retailing its product lines.

What do you think of The Body Shop's changes in its traditional store format? Are large flagship stores in conflict with the company's move to reduce its stockkeeping units? Will outlet stores further reduce the company's in-store sales? What about the strategies still under consideration?

Sources: www.the-body-shop.com; Julie Naughton, "Body Shop Digs In," *Women's Wear Daily*, June 18, 1999, 10.

Choosing a channel traditionally is a major decision for most organizations, because once an option is selected, it becomes very difficult and expensive to make major changes. If one chooses to use intermediaries, the amount of control that a producer has over the relationship with the end user can be significantly reduced. The factors determining the decision are corporate strategy, product cost, and consumer location. The characteristics of the channel must be in line with the overall requirements of the marketing strategy; for example, packaged food products are unlikely to be offered in banks. At the same time, the existence of new channels can offer new distribution opportunities. For example, banking services could well be offered in the future by retail giants such as Wal-Mart, which has a "branch" advantage and the available cash quantities together with the cash management capabilities to carry out banking tasks.

www.wal-mart.com

For the channel decision, the characteristics of the product itself also come into play; for example, if it needs to be kept refrigerated, then a very specialized distribution chain is required. Where the end users themselves are located and where they do their shopping has a major influence. Finally, the comparative cost of the alternative channels is an important criterion. Marketing in Action 11.1 is an example of the challenges facing companies needing to rethink their channel strategy.

CHANNEL COMPENSATION

The various members of the distribution chain take over some of the producer's responsibilities. In general, their primary value-added activity is the wider distribution that they offer, as well as their on-location inventory, which may increase the overall penetration of the brand. These intermediaries also provide service support and may act as information gatherers and business consultants to the producer. The exact relationship depends in part on the contractual conditions.

For example, a **dealer** may be totally independent of the producer, whereas an **agent** acts on behalf of that producer. In return for their services, the members of the distribution chains receive payments, mostly in the form of various discounts:

- **Trade discounts.** These are usually of a fixed percentage. However, the percentage may vary according to the priority category into which the producer places the intermediary. Textiles and apparel as well as books are examples of industries using trade discounts.

- **Quantity discounts.** By offering higher discount levels as the volume increases, this discount offers an incentive for all intermediaries to try to sell the maximum volume. Electronic and white goods such as refrigerators, washers, and dryers are often distributed with such discounts.

- **Promotional discounts.** The producer may also attempt to "push" the good or service by offering promotional discounts, which are designed to persuade the intermediary to substitute the brand in question for another. Alternatively, the intention may be to persuade the retailer to overstock, thus creating inventory pressure, which forces additional display space for the brand. Canned goods in supermarkets are typically associated with promotional discounts.

- **Cash discounts.** Most producers normally offer trade intermediaries payment terms that require settlement in 30 days or later. This is of considerable value to some retailers who have managed to reduce their inventory to less than 5 days. The extra 25-days' credit can in effect be used as a free loan. However, the producer may want to provide an incentive for retailers or wholesalers to pay earlier by offering a discount for immediate or prompt payment.

There are other, more hidden discount offers as well. For example, wholesalers may offer special financing to their retailers where promissory notes require payment only in 120 days. This way, retailers are encouraged to take on more, and often new, items. Extended return privileges act as indirect discounts and again encourage a greater willingness for experimentation within the channel. Other discounts can come in the form of bonuses when sales thresholds are surpassed or channel members have been particularly loyal to a producer. The key aim of all discounts or bonuses is to motivate channel members to carry out actions supportive of the producer's strategy, which they might not otherwise have done.

> The key aim of all discounts is **to motivate channel members** [to support] the producer's strategy

CHANNEL MANAGEMENT

Channel management refers to the different degrees of control that channel members can exercise. However, channel control can be expensive and time consuming. Therefore, a firm needs to decide how much control is necessary. For example, when the producer is large, the product is expensive, the customers are few, and linkage to the customer is very important, then intermediaries may be eliminated. That is why airplanes are typically sold directly by manufacturers. Sometimes, the ease of switching is so great that manufacturers decide to own or otherwise tie down the retail level to ensure that there will be no switching away from their product. That accounts for so many pubs being owned or financed by beer-brewing companies.

Lack of control can be highly detrimental to business strategy. Exporters often discover that a lack of channel control means that exchange-rate-based price changes are never passed through to customers abroad—and therefore their distribution strategies are not successful. In many instances, however, control is less important, and companies use multiple intermediaries.

The Internet's ability to fundamentally change the reach of firms has empowered companies small and large to achieve high levels of accessibility and to establish two-way information flows directly with end users almost immediately and at low cost. As firms deal more directly with their customers, they are placing major pressure on their intermediaries. Companies can now sell directly without the sales force and offer technical support on a one-on-one basis.[6]

> **As firms deal more directly with their customers, they are placing major pressure on their intermediaries.**

The Internet also allows suppliers to continue the supportive activities for their customers once their product has been sold into the channel. The sale itself does not finish the job, because the distribution chain is merely assuming a part of the supplier's responsibility. To be market oriented, the supplier needs to manage all the processes involved in that chain, until the product arrives at the end user. Even at that point, the channel management task is not complete, because the entire distribution chain needs to stand ready to further communicate with the customer, be it for additional information, for a recall or return, or in preparation for the next purchase of the channel's products. Doing so involves a number of decisions, including the management of channel membership, channel motivation, and channel monitoring.

CHANNEL MEMBERSHIP

The supplier has some control over which organizations participate in the distribution chain and what the structure of that channel might be. At one extreme, in mass consumer goods markets, such as canned soup, the supplier's main concern may be to maximize distribution levels so that a large number of outlets stock the product. At the other extreme, where dealers, for example, take over some of the supplier's responsibility for supporting sophisticated technical products, the supplier may be primarily concerned about the quality of the individual dealer. Generally, there are three different levels of distribution intensity.

In the case of *intensive* distribution, the majority of resellers stock the product. This method is used mostly for convenience products and particularly for the brand leaders in consumer goods markets. Price competition may be very important here. Under conditions of *selective* distribution, only specially chosen resellers stock the product, with the selection being a function of location, image, or other reseller attributes important to the product. Specialty watches may be an example. Under an *exclusive* distribution approach, only a few resellers (typically only one per geographic area) are allowed to sell the product, in order to ensure that the product is properly supported. Such exclusive distribution is used most often where products are unique, expensive, or complex and where the resellers add distinctive value to the product through their highly specialized activities and knowledge. Desire for such exclusivity is why Toyota developed an entirely new set of dealerships for their Lexus cars rather than simply having them sold by existing dealers. Of course, distribution does not always go according to plan. For

www.toyota.com
www.lexus.com

6. Jagdish N. Sheth and Rajendra S. Sisodia, "Revisiting Marketing's Lawlike Generalizations," *Journal of the Academy of Marketing Science* 27, no. 1 (1999): 71–87.

example, if large price differentials exist across national borders, new sources of unauthorized distribution or gray markets can emerge. Manager's Corner 11.2 explains how gray markets offer both advantages and disadvantages.

CHANNEL MOTIVATION

It is difficult enough to motivate employees to provide the necessary sales and service support; motivating the owners and employees of the independent organizations in a distribution chain requires even greater effort. Profit is the most frequently used motivator to entice a channel member to push one product over its competitors. Some suppliers offer a better margin (which is the price minus manufacturing and marketing cost) or more frequent turnover of the product. Others offer an incentive to the distributors' sales personnel, such as a competition, so that they are tempted to push the product. Alternatively, producers can supply their own personnel to the channel in order to retain full control over the presentation and sale of their products.

Manager's Corner 11.2

Gray markets: advantages and disadvantages

Manufacturers and retailers tend to shy away from gray markets, where products are sold at cut-rate prices outside their authorized distribution channels. Manufacturers fear that these markets will undercut margins and tarnish brand names. Retailers fear that they will siphon away customers and erode prices. Gray marketing is a form of arbitrage—exploiting differences in the prices for which branded goods sell in different markets. Gray marketers buy a product in the low-price market and then transport it to the high-price market, where they can sell it at a discount and still net a profit. Many scholars claim that gray markets actually do more good than harm to both manufacturers and authorized distributors. In order for this to be true, two criteria must be met by the market: First, sharp differences must exist in consumers' price sensitivity; second, large numbers of consumers are price insensitive. In such markets, the low prices of the gray market will attract the most price-sensitive customers. The authorized channels will then compete only for the remaining customers—those who are insensitive to price but are sensitive to service.

The following example from the cigarette industry shows the good and bad points of gray markets. Spurred by a 50 percent increase in domestic cigarette prices over the past two years, many "made for export" Marlboros, Winstons, and Camels have appeared for sale in the U.S. stores and on the Internet at huge markdowns—as much as 25 percent off market prices. Here's how it works: Philip Morris (www.philipmorris.com) makes cartons of Marlboros in the United States earmarked for foreign markets, where prices are lower. Some of the cigarettes may then steam offshore, only to return; others may never actually leave. They will find their way into stores in the United States at cut-rate prices. Each week Cigarettes Cheaper!, a California-based discount store, sells more than 45,000 cartons of cigarettes made for export by R. J. Reynolds (www.rjrnabisco.com). There a carton of Winston costs $24.89 instead of the regular price of $30.39. Tobacco companies strongly deny that they participate in or benefit from the diversion, noting that the practice damages multibillion-dollar brands. From a marketing standpoint the tobacco companies invest a lot of time and money building brand loyalty. These products do not meet consumer expectations of U.S. brands. Philip Morris, for example, has fielded as many as 200 calls a month from irate smokers who purchased export Marlboros and couldn't find their "miles" insignias on U.S. packs that are collected and redeemed for promotional items like T-shirts and duffel bags.

Sources: David Champion, "Marketing: The Bright Side of Gray Markets," *Harvard Business Review* (September/October 1998): 19–22; Suein L. Hwang, "Tobacco: As Cigarette Prices Soar, a Gray Market Booms," *Wall Street Journal*, January 28, 1999, B1; "When Grey Is Good," *Economist*, August 22, 1998, 17.

Monitoring Channels

In much the same way that the organization's own sales and distribution activities need to be monitored and managed, so do those of the distribution chain. For example, the supplier needs to know which products sell, how they are displayed, and what promotional plans the intermediaries have in order to be able to respond to their needs. Traditionally, monitoring has implied a one-way flow of information. For example, firms like Holiday Inn would send employees unannounced as "mystery sleepers" to different locations to monitor the performance of franchisees.[7] Increasingly, however, as we will see in this chapter's section on supply chain management, success requires close collaboration and intensive information exchange. Only through a two-way interaction can higher levels of efficiency in channel management be achieved.

www.holiday-inn.com

One very direct form of channel management takes place through channel integration. For example, the supplier can form one unified system with wholesalers and retailers. Such an approach may arise when one member of the chain owns the other elements. When a supplier owns its own retail outlets, as is often the case with gasoline stations, we speak of **forward integration**. If a retailer owns its own suppliers—for example, a department store with its own dedicated textile producers—we refer to it as **backward integration**. Integration can also be accomplished through franchise operations, such as those offered by Domino's Pizza. An alternative approach is the administered marketing system, in which one (dominant) member of the distribution chain uses its position to coordinate the other members' activities. This has traditionally been the form favored by manufacturers. Increasingly, however, retailers develop such systems as well. For example, Wal-Mart has developed an information system through which the firm can prescribe delivery quantities and schedules to its suppliers. This system represents a unique strategic advantage, as it allows the firm to devise product and pricing policies with much greater efficiency.

www.dominos.com

www.wal-mart.com

The intention of integration is to give those involved (and particularly the supplier at one end and the retailer at the other) control over the distribution chain. This removes one set of variables from the marketing equation. Research indicates that integration is a strategy that is best pursued at the mature stage of the market or product; at earlier stages it can actually reduce profits. Some argue that it also diverts attention from the real business of the organization. Suppliers rarely excel in retail operations, and in theory, retailers should focus on their sales outlets rather than on manufacturing facilities. The most successful retail operator in the United Kingdom, Marks & Spencer, which sells clothing, food, and nonfood products, deliberately provides considerable technical assistance to its suppliers but does not own them. If integration, whether through ownership or simple market power, is successfully accomplished, however, it can lead to a substantial competitive advantage in the market place.

> integration is a strategy that is **best pursued at the mature stage** of the market or product

www.marks-and-spencer.co.uk

Another approach to channel management is collaboration. In this situation, two or more competing organizations agree to a joint marketing operation because the tasks to be competed are either beyond the capacity of each individual organization alone or they are greatly strengthened by such collaboration. The Internet vividly illustrates this trend. For example, Excite, a leading search engine company, has cooperative agreements in place with Netscape Communications,

www.excite.com
www.netscape.com

---

7. Gary L. Frazier, "Organizing and Managing Channels of Distribution," *Journal of the Academy of Marketing Science* 27, no. 2 (1999): 226–240.

Table 11.2

The world's top retailers, by sales

	Home country	1998 sales (in $ billions)	% of sales overseas	No. of countries	Market capitalization ($ billion)
Wal-Mart	United States	150.7	17	10	199.7
Royal Ahold	The Netherlands	37.1	71	17	22.0
Promodes	France	36.2	54	12	12.6
Carrefour	France	36.0	44	20	30.5
Home Depot	United States	30.2	Negligible	4	84.5
Tesco	Britain	28.4	13	9	19.5
Marks & Spencer	Britain	13.3	16	34	16.8
Toys "R" Us	United States	11.2	27	26	5.3
Pinault Printemps	France	10.0	30	23	19.3
Hennes & Mauritz	Sweden	3.4	82	12	17.9

Source: "Shopping All over the World," *Economist*, June 19, 1999, 60. © 1999 The Economist Newspaper Group, Inc. Reprinted with permission. Further reproduction prohibited. www.economist.com

www.aol.com
www.intuit.com

America Online, and Intuit, even though it competes with all of those companies in trying to become a "portal," or first stop on the Internet. The agreements involve sharing technology, customers, and advertising revenue.[8]

RETAILING

Retailing represents a large part of the service sector and includes all the activities involved in selling goods or services directly to final consumers for their personal, nonbusiness use.[9] In the past few decades retailers have grown both domestically and internationally to become some of the world's largest companies. As Table 11.2 shows, Wal-Mart has become the world's top retailer, with an annual turnover of more than $150 billion.[10] Retailers can be categorized in a variety of ways, the most obvious of which are by type of product or service sold, type of customer service, type of organization, and location.

www.wal-mart.com

Type of Product or Service Sold

Consumers categorize retail outlets by what they find in them. Specialty outlets typically handle just one type of merchandise. Some, such as shoe and fashion shops, are the major providers of a type of good; others, such as butchers, duplicate what can now be found elsewhere. In marketing terms, such stores typically have a narrow product line. In fashion, for example, specialty outlets aim not just at women, but at women in a relatively narrow age range or size. Within that narrow product line, however, these outlets usually have a deep assortment of products offering a wider range and greater expertise than their more generalized rivals. They also tend to offer a greater degree of personal service.

Supermarkets have become the source of most consumers' general needs. They have gown in floor area and product range: A typical store now occupies

8. Sheth and Sisodia, "Revisiting Marketing's Lawlike Generalizations."
9. Kotler, *Marketing Management* 8th ed. (Upper Saddle River, N.J.: Prentice Hall, 1994), 558.
10. "Shopping All over the World" *Economist*, June 19, 1999, 59–61.

20,000 square feet and offers up to 10,000 product lines, sometimes including fashion and furniture items. The increasing number of superstores multiply these levels. The supermarket concept revolves around five basic principles.[11]

1. Self-service and self-selection displays
2. Centralization of customer services, usually at the checkout counter
3. Large-scale, low-cost facilities
4. A strong price emphasis
5. A broad assortment of merchandise to facilitate multiple-item purchases

Department stores were once the flagships of the retail sector, with separate departments covering a wide range of products. They have in recent years suffered from the competition offered by supermarkets and category-killer specialty stores (particularly those in fashion, toys, and office materials).

Discount outlets specialize in high turnover at low cost ("stack it high, sell it cheap") on the basis of the 30-days' credit from their suppliers; indeed, they often obtain most of their corporate funds from their suppliers. They usually specialize in one field, such as consumer electronics, furniture, or clothing.

TYPE OF CUSTOMER SERVICE

Three service options are self-service, self-selection, and personalized service. Under the self-service concept, customers select their own goods and take them to the checkout in the supermarket or to a cash point in other retail establishments such as bookshops and fashion outlets. The sole contact with the staff of the retailer is the act of payment. Self-selection means that customers still select items from the shelf, but they may ask for and receive assistance from sales staff. Personalized service offers advice and counseling to customers and is particularly valuable where expert advice is needed, as in high fashion or investment banking. To offer such service, however, retailers must invest in training and long-term retention of staff. As shoppers are becoming increasingly disenchanted by complex merchandise and insufficient advice, this type of service may see a resurgence. Leading department stores are already experimenting with all three levels of service in the same store. The service-level variations depend on the merchandise offered and the location within the store. For example, there may be a bargain basement that offers shoes based on self-selection, while on the second floor the latest shoe fashions are presented with substantial service support. Other stores provide a self-service format but offer specialized customer service on request.

TYPE OF ORGANIZATION

The key original purpose of retailing was to serve the local clientele. As a result, most retailers were small stores owned by individuals or families. In many countries in Asia and Europe, retailing is still characterized by independent "mom-and-pop" stores.

Information technology is changing the retail structure. Due to improved management capability and greater purchasing power, corporate chain stores are becoming the dominant form of retail stores. Electronic point-of-sale data provide the information that enables detailed assessment of branch performance, improved store management, a decrease in cost structure, and an increased focus on customer demand and satisfaction. This information advantage, together with

---

11. R. F. Lusch and V. N. Lusch, *Principles of Marketing* (Boston: Kent, 1989).

Manager's Corner 11.3

Computer-dating the customer

Because of astute database management, retailers may know consumers' names and addresses, what they buy, what they have stopped buying, and even how they respond to a rise in the price of dog food. For retailers this is the equivalent of going back to the days of the individual store owner who knew and greeted each customer personally. The benefits are potentially huge: Instead of spending millions on advertising beamed at people who may be indifferent or even hostile to it, retailers can use databases to help them hang on to their existing customers and persuade them to spend more. This is important, because typically 20 to 35 percent of customers generate 70 to 80 percent of a retailer's profit. But it is not trouble-free: Databases are expensive to develop and analyze, and customers may expect big discounts in return for their loyalty. Some may also see such individual marketing as an invasion of privacy.

Here is an example of database benefits accruing to retailers. Talbot's (www.talbots.com), a 385-store women's clothing chain based in Massachusetts, has compiled a database of 7 million names that includes information about customers' sizes. This has enabled the firm to forecast more accurately which sizes will sell in particular stores. Talbot's also asks all customers for their zip codes when they pay, to help it plan new store openings. The effort seems to be paying off. For the past five years the company has been opening around 50 new stores per year.

Source: "Computer-Dating the Customer," *Economist*, March 4, 1995.

economies of scale and bulk buying, gives chain stores a major advantage over their smaller competitors and their suppliers. Manager's Corner 11.3 provides some more details of the benefits of information in retailing. Even though these stores are more efficient, they also lead to a certain degree of homogeneity in the retail sector, and, perhaps, to a reduction of consumer choice. For example, in Eastern Europe, the newly arriving Western chain food stores have mostly brought with them their own suppliers. As a result, it is nearly impossible to obtain locally grown fruit or locally baked bread, much to the chagrin of customers who would like to be offered a combination of efficiency and traditional products.[12]

An increasing number of retail outlets are run by franchisees who personally own the outlet. The format for the franchise, how it is run, its products or services, its technical and management expertise, and its promotion are the responsibility of the franchisee. The franchisor owns the format and typically receives a commission on sales or a margin on supplies. In the United States, with about 600,000 units operating under more than 2,500 franchisor banners, the franchising industry accounts for about $1 trillion, or one-half of all retail sales.[13] Going far beyond fast-food outlets, franchising is improving all areas of retailing. Take Country Visions Inc., a chain based in Vacaville, California, that operates and franchises Country Clutter stores. Although the outlets themselves present the ambience of a small country general store, everything "behind the curtain" is driven by technology. The company's Web site, administered in-house, presents product offerings and other news for customers, an intranet for franchisees that offers operations manuals, an e-mail system, and a bulletin-board and discussion area.[14]

www.countryclutter.com

---

12. Michael R. Czinkota, Helmut Gaisbauer, and Reiner Springer, "A Perspective of Marketing in Central and Eastern Europe," *The International Executive* 39, no. 6 (1997): 831–848.
13. International Franchise Association, 1999, www.franchise.org.
14. Dale D. Buss, "New Dynamics for a New Era," *Nation's Business* (June 1999): 45.

LOCATION

The traditional hubs of retailing are the shopping mall and Main Street, but other locations must also be considered. The central shopping area is the province of the chain stores—and the location with the highest property costs. The high rents are paid because traditionally location, above all, determines a retail outlet's turn-over, hence the old adage that the three most important elements of retailing are location, location, and location. Chain stores use surveys of where consumers shop to determine where to place an outlet. Obtaining the best location (balancing pedestrian traffic against property cost) is a skill that retailers justifiably rate highly. The value of each location can shift, however, because of changing customer patterns or other environmental dimensions. For example, with the advent of electronic banking, which permits customers to do most of their bank transactions via automated teller machines, telephone, or even the Internet, the value of stately bank buildings in city centers is likely to decrease.

Sites outside of cities but with good road links have become the preferred location of the warehouse stores and no-frills discount operations. Increasingly, such sites are also the chosen location for super-stores—very large supermarkets of up to 80,000 square feet—and are rapidly taking share from the smaller, more conventional supermarkets. Hypermarkets are similar, but typically of 100,000 to 200,000 square feet and carrying a product range similar to that of a department store. In Europe, Carrefour is a well-established chain of hypermarkets, whereas in the United States Wal-Mart is a primary developer of the concept.

> One key desire of retailers **is to be footloose** and location independent.

www.carrefour.com
www.wal-mart.com

One key desire of retailers is to be footloose and location independent. They desire to serve customers without the need to create a retail establishment close to them. Technology increasingly enables retailers to take such direct marketing approaches.

The most obvious manifestations of direct marketing are the large, lavishly illustrated catalogs mailed to consumers. Some of them offer a range of goods that matches that of a department store. The advantage to the supplier is reduced cost, as there are no expensive store locations to maintain, while the advantage to the consumer is convenience. For example, Williams-Sonoma is a marketer of kitchenware and home and garden products both through brick-and-mortar stores and direct mail. In 1999 the company launched a "Pottery Barns Kids brand," sold exclusively in catalogs, which featured children's bedroom furniture, rugs, and other tasteful kids furnishings. The initial mailing of 500,000 catalogs was so successful that the company mailed out additional batches a few months later.[15]

www.williams-sonoma.com
www.potterybarn.com

Another form of nonstore retailing is door-to-door selling, which has reached new global heights with firms like Avon and Amway. Both catalog and door-to-door marketing are effective, but are limited by their need to target specific customers and can only present a one-way dialogue with their merchandise. The catalog needs a detailed address; the Avon lady needs to find a customer at home. Both approaches offer merchandise that is already in existence.

avon.avon.com
www.amway.com

Operating without the restraint of advance targeting are television shopping networks, which are growing successfully in many countries. Even more open and, most importantly, able to engage in a two-way dialogue is the rapidly growing form of electronic retailing. Dell Computer and Gateway, Inc., two of

www.dell.com
www.gateway.com

15. Amy Hughes, "Catalog Firm Likely to Post Modest Profits—Internet Helps Firms Cut Costs, Gain Customers in the Recent Quarter" *Wall Street Journal,* July 9, 1999, www.wsj.com.

the largest direct marketers of personal computers, are excellent examples of how to capitalize on the unique benefits of Internet retailing. These firms use the Internet to communicate detailed, up-to-date information on their fast-changing lines of products to a computer-literate audience of customers. Shoppers can custom-design a computer by selecting options from an on-screen form and see the immediate impact on price. Concurrent with the shopper's input, feedback can be provided on the quality of choices made. When the shopper is satisfied with the configuration and places an order, the company builds the computer to specification and ships it to the customer's home. The customer receives the latest technology, and the manufacturer avoids obsolete inventory.[16] Due to all its advantages, it can be expected that electronic retailing may well become one of the most important retailing methods in the next decade.

> electronic retailing may well become **one of the most important** retailing methods in the next decade

WHOLESALING

Sandwiched between producers and retailers may be a layer of wholesalers, distributors, and agents. Their role is to provide a link between the extremes of the distribution chain. The number of independent retailers, for example, may make it uneconomical for the producer's own sales force and distribution network to work with each one of them.

Wholesalers service retailers and are usually independent. They stock a range of items from different suppliers and market these either through their own sales force or through self-service cash-and-carry warehouse facilities exclusively for retailers. A **distributor** is a wholesaler that deals with industrial establishments and business-to-business marketing. Agents differ from wholesalers in their relationship with the producer. **Agents** typically represent one or more suppliers on the basis of a formal agreement. They operate as extensions of a supplier, following established terms of business and quality standards, but they do not take title to goods. Rather than making a profit from reselling merchandise, they earn a commission on their sales.

Wholesale intermediaries vary also in the levels of support they offer. Cash-and-carry wholesalers offer the most basic level of support, mimicking the self-service element of supermarkets. The customers, typically small retailers and caterers, service themselves and pay at a checkout counter, just as supermarket customers do. At the other extreme, the wholesaler's representative may visit the retailer to take the order, which is then delivered. This is the traditional—but declining—form, now increasingly limited to specialist markets. However, many countries in Asia and Europe still have distribution systems characterized by multiple layers of wholesalers deeply involved in the sales process. Between those two extremes are various forms of cooperative relationships between channel members. One example is category management, in which a leading supplier manages shelf space allocation and arranges for shelf stock replenishment. This approach has been widely used in the tobacco industry and in supermarkets. For example, rather than tracking inventory and ordering replenishments itself, Wal-Mart has handed over the management of in-store inventories of items such as Tide and Crest to its producer, Proctor & Gamble. The firm has direct access to point-of-sale data, and it is up to P&G to manage inventory and assure that there are no out-of-stock conditions in stores. Also used are service merchandisers

www.wal-mart.com
www.tide.com
www.cresttoothpaste
    .com
www.pg.com

---

16. Burke, "Marketing in the 21st Century."

("rack jobbers"), who manage and service an assigned department or category such as periodicals, greeting cards, or recorded music. This approach is often found in department stores, discount department stores, and drugstores. Finally there are leased departments, in which an independent contractor manages a section of a department store.[17] Cosmetics and jewelry are frequent examples of this "store-within-a-store" concept.

Strategically, it is important for wholesalers to find new ways of adding value to the marketing process. Without such additions, both retailers and suppliers have a great incentive to circumvent the wholesale level. The typical way to add value is to perform distribution processes more efficiently. A wholesaler may offer better and more efficient inventory management, better transportation or break-bulk service, more efficient restocking practices, or more complementary product assortments. Alternatively, a wholesaler may specialize in an information-gathering role, to facilitate the planning and management of retailers and suppliers. If wholesale intermediaries cannot perform functions better and more efficiently than other channel members, the functions will be taken on by other channel members and the intermediary will be eliminated.

PURCHASING

The purchasing function is dealt with here because it concerns the relationship with the firm's buyer and is particularly relevant to wholesalers and retailers. Purchasing is still generally seen as the "poor cousin" of the marketing discipline and, as such, has been insufficiently researched. This is despite the fact that bought-in elements usually account for more than half the total cost of goods and sometimes of services too. Inefficient or ineffective purchasing can easily lose far more value than the best possible management can add in the remaining processes under its control. Therefore, firms should put a great deal of effort into working with their suppliers, particularly because the increase in global sourcing makes the tasks increasingly complex.[18]

> Inefficient or ineffective purchasing can **easily lose far more value than the** best possible management can add

There are several elements to successful purchasing. First, the buying department has to appreciate the needs of the internal customers, those departments that will be the users of the purchased goods and services. Second, the buyer must understand the product to be bought. Third, the buyer must know the supplier. The culture of buying is still dominated by the "master-servant" relationship. However, it is very much in the buyer's interest to treat the supplier as a partner in order to optimize purchases. In essence the buyer should deal with suppliers as if they were in another department within the organization. After all, both the supplier and the buyer organization have the same key objective: to please the customer and thus to increase their market share. By working together, both parties can improve their overall operations, leading to lower costs, better products, and higher profitability.

It is also important that the buyer be part of the product specification process. Insufficient understanding of specifications can result in inefficient buying, inadequate specifications can lead to very expensive modifications later on (not to mention the costs of recalls or lawsuits), and overspecification inevitably causes inflated product costs. One of the most important activities in purchasing is the

17. Robert D. Buzzell and Gwen Ortmeyer, *Channel Partnerships: A New Approach to Streamlining Distribution* (Cambridge, Mass.: Marketing Science Institute, Report 19-104, April 1994): 6.
18. Masaaki Kotabe, *Global Sourcing Strategy* (New York: Quorum, 1992), 25.

www.iso.ch

supplier selection. This activity requires judgment as to the suitability of the prospective suppliers, including their ability to meet requirements over the long term. The starting point is the identification and evaluation of suppliers through desk research. Often, buyers will insist that suppliers meet certain certification standards. For example, ISO certification, issued by the International Standards Organization, provides the buyer with assurance about a firm's internal processes. The ISO 9000 series of international standards represents quality management and the practice of quality assurance. Its aim is to give organizations guidelines on what constitutes an effective quality management system, which in turn can serve as a framework for continuous improvement.[19] On many occasions the evaluation will include a formal inspection visit. The outcome of the visit may be the inclusion of the supplier on the "approved list," with the tacit implication that the firm has a good chance of receiving an order at some time in the future.

When it comes to supplier choice, there are two extremes. The most efficient approach, making the best use of any economies of scale, is to concentrate all purchases on a single supplier. This also allows the best chance of developing a close partnership. Alternatively, several suppliers may be chosen, to ensure continuity of supply. A buyer may even place business in several countries in order to assure local supply and to reduce the effect of exchange rate changes. For example, for imported supplies the devaluation of a country's currency may dramatically affect production and pricing, whereas for domestically sourced supplies the effect may be minimal. Multiple suppliers are expected to recognize the existence of these competitors and accordingly offer more competitive prices. However, this approach may have an adverse impact on the supplier partnership.

Once an order is received, the supplier should be evaluated against the specific order. This can be done by developing a rating system based on quality and service as well as price. Doing so avoids purchasing systems in which business is conducted solely on the basis of personal relationships. Such an evaluation must be conducted on a continuing basis in order to monitor changes at the supplier level. One important service the buyer can provide for suppliers is the development of a global industry benchmarking system. Through such a system, which can be administered by neutral third parties such as the International Trade Centre in Geneva, suppliers anywhere in the world can check how they measure up in terms of international competitiveness. By obtaining detailed comparative information, they can also take steps to improve their activities, which leads to greater competitiveness and in turn provides for better supplies to the buyer. The buyer needs to assure itself that, in addition to product standards, production process standards are being met. Production processes need to be reviewed in terms of cost and quality, but also in terms of human rights, child labor laws, and wage levels. Basically, the firm needs to determine whether the conditions of production meet standards that are acceptable to its management, stockholders, and stakeholders. Manager's Corner 11.4 provides some insights about the problems that can be encountered.

www.intracen.org/itc

Manager's Corner 11.4

Supplying product with dignity

One of those $20 T-shirts in your drawer could have been made by a Central American teenager who says she regularly labors for 18 hours a day in a garment factory. The bargain dress on your back might have been made by kids who couldn't go to the bathroom without a pass from their boss. Those inexpensive pants may have been assembled in Los Angeles by Thai workers imprisoned behind barbed-wire fences.

19. Suchalee Ponprasert, "IBM Thailand Bags ISO 9002 Certification," *The Nation* (Thailand), June 15, 1999, Technology section.

Sweatshops are a part of doing business in the garment industry—particularly for those involved in inexpensive to moderate merchandise, where price is all that matters. Purchasers are trying to fight inhumane treatment in the production process. Gap (www.gap.com), Levi Strauss (www.levis.com), and Phillips-Van Heusen (www.vanheusen.com), for instance, all have corporate codes of conduct addressing issues of minimum wages, humane working conditions, hiring practices, and more. But getting suppliers to adhere to these codes is not easy. Since Levi Strauss instituted its "terms of engagement" in 1991, it has ceased business with about 5 percent of its suppliers and has required improvements by another 25 percent. Those improvements ranged from clearing the path to a fire exit to actually creating one. The company has about 600 contractors worldwide. "In many respects, we're protecting our single largest asset: our brand image and corporate reputation," says spokesman David Samson.

Phillips-Van Heusen, which includes Geoffrey Beene, Gant, Jantzen, Izod, and Bass, makes its ethics guidelines clear to suppliers up front. To prevent violations, the company regularly dispatches a team of employees to make surprise inspections of suppliers' factories. "We have zero tolerance for anyone violating our policy," says CEO Bruce Klatsky. "As soon as we find out about violations, we're not going to be doing business anymore." But sometimes there are contractors who, when unable to fill an order in the time allotted, turn to subcontractors. Those subcontractors, in turn, may be running a sweatshop.

Source: Robin D. Givhan, "A Stain on Fashion," *Washington Post,* September 12, 1995, B1, B4.

SUPPLY CHAIN MANAGEMENT

In supply chain management the firm uses a series of value-adding activities to connect the company's supply side with its demand side. This approach views the supply chain of the entire extended enterprise, beginning with the supplier's supplier and ending with consumers, or end users. The perspective encompasses all products, information, and funds that form one cohesive link to acquire, purchase, convert/manufacture, assemble, and distribute goods and services to the ultimate consumer.[20] The implementation effects of such supply chain management systems can be major. Efficient supply chain design can increase customer satisfaction and save money at the same time.[21] On an industry-wide basis, research conducted by Coopers and Lybrand, before its 1998 merger with Price Waterhouse, indicates that the use of such tools in the structuring of supplier relations could reduce operating costs of the European grocery industry by $27 billion per year, with savings equivalent to a 5.7 percent reduction in price.[22] Clearly, the use of such strategic tools is crucial to develop and maintain key competitive advantages. An overview of the supply chain is shown in Figure 11.2; Manager's Corner 11.5 explains how McDonald's uses its global supply chain.

> Efficient supply chain design can **increase customer satisfaction and** save money at the same time.

www.pwcglobal.com

www.mcdonalds.com

Underlying effective supply chain management is the development of a logistics system that controls the flow of materials into, through, and out of the corporation. Due to the systems approach, the firm explicitly recognizes and coordinates the linkages among the traditionally separate logistics components within the corporation, which are production, transportation facility, inventory, and communication decisions. By recognizing the logistics interaction with outside organizations and individuals, such as suppliers and customers, the firm is able to create a mutual purpose for all partners in the areas of performance, quality,

20. Michael R. Czinkota, Ilkka A. Ronkainen, and Michael H. Moffett, *International Business, Update 2000* (Fort Worth, Tex.: Dryden Press, 2000), 541.
21. Tom Davis, "Effective Supply Chain Management," *Sloan Management Review* (summer 1993): 35–45.
22. Coopers and Lybrand, "The Value Chain Analysis," *Efficient Consumer Response Europe,* London, 1995.

Figure 11.2

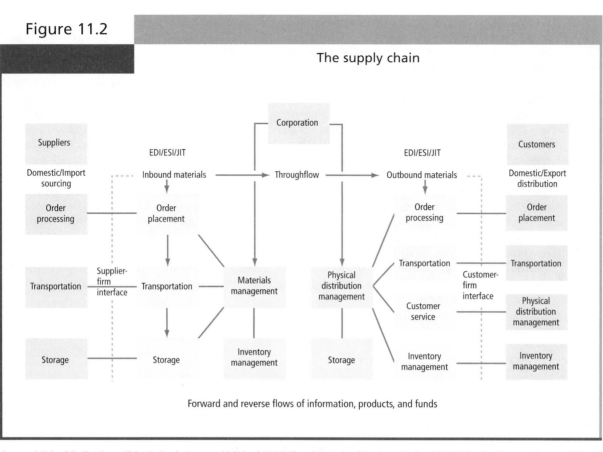

The supply chain

Forward and reverse flows of information, products, and funds

Source: Michael R. Czinkota, Ilkka A. Ronkainen, and Michael H. Moffett, *International Business, Update 2000* (Orlando: Harcourt Brace and Company, 2000), 542. Copyright © 2000 by Harcourt, Inc. Reprinted by permission of the publisher.

Manager's Corner 11.5

Global supply chain management at McDonald's

Except for Saudi wheat, Big Macs sold in Saudi Arabia are all made from foreign ingredients: beef patties from Spain, sauce from the United States, Mexican onions and sesame seeds, Brazilian oil and sugar, and packaging from Germany. How can the world's giant fast-food chain McDonald's (www.mcdonalds.com) do that? The answer is consolidated global warehousing and distribution so that all the materials of the uniform Big Mac can come together from producers and distributors however far flung they may be.

The company "cracks the global supply chain to create a borderless environment" said its global logistics manager, Raymond Cesca.

In order to keep McDonald's restaurants in 115 countries worldwide with an estimated 40 million customers per day in continuous supply, the company is one of the world's largest buyers of beef and other ingredients for its products. In large markets, the company sources its ingredients locally, whereas in small markets like Saudi Arabia McDonald's uses its distribution system so that items like beef patties can be supplied almost anywhere in the world. The benefits of this type of supply chain management for global retailers like McDonald's is assurance of a stable source of supply and protection against fluctuations in the value of local currencies.

Source: Aviva Freudmann, "Supplying Big Macs: A Lesson in Logistics," *The Journal of Commerce*, May 19, 1999, 3A.

and timing. As a result of implementing a logistics system, the firm can develop just-in-time (JIT) delivery for lower inventory cost, electronic data interchange (EDI) for more efficient order processing, and early supplier involvement (ESI) for better planning of product movement. The logistics effort has two parts: materials management and physical distribution management.

Materials management controls the movement through the production processes. It takes in raw materials and schedules them through the various processes until the final product is placed into the finished goods warehouse. Physical distribution management deals with the inflow of products from suppliers and the movement of the firm's finished product to its customers. In both phases, movement is seen within the context of the entire process. Stationary periods (storage and inventory) are therefore included. The basic goal is the effective coordination of both materials and physical distribution management to result in maximum cost-effectiveness while maintaining service goals and requirements. In the words of the director of international logistics operations at General Motors, the purpose of logistics is "to plan cost-effective systems for future use, attempt to eliminate duplication of effort, and determine where distribution policy is lacking or inappropriate. Emphasis is placed on consolidating existing movements, planning new systems, identifying useful ideas, techniques, or experiences, and working with various divisions toward implementation of beneficial changes."[23]

www.gm.com

Next we will examine the five decision areas for logistics management.

PRODUCTION DECISIONS

In the context of the distribution function, production decisions concern issues such as the quantity in each production batch and the lead time required for production. Production of a good can be continuous, as in an oil refinery or on a car assembly line. In these cases the whole production process has to be matched to demand. Very expensive mistakes can be made if the capacity installed turns out to be greater than demand; this results in frequent shutdowns.

Production is typically "batched" into specific production runs. The size of the production order, and the frequency with which the order is placed, is a matter for calculation on two separate fronts. The first refers to economies of scale. There is a cost overhead involved in placing every order, so the number of orders placed should be minimized. At the same time there is an ongoing cost involved in holding stock, and thus the amount of stock should also be minimized. Needless to say, these two factors work in opposition, as the graph in Figure 11.3 demonstrates. The equation that determines the EOQ (economic order quantity) is

$$EOQ = \sqrt{2\,AT/C}$$

where A is the cost of placing the order, T is the expected throughput in the time to the next order, and C is the unit cost of storing an item over the period until the next order is received.

The second major consideration in determining batch size and frequency concerns the buffer stock to be held to cope with variations in demand. Depending on the known pattern of demand, the optimal size of this buffer stock can be statistically calculated, although the calculations are beyond the scope of this book.

---

23. Rex R. Williams, "International Physical Distribution Management," in *Contemporary Physical Distribution and Logistics,* 10th ed., ed. James C. Johnson and Donald F. Woods (Tulsa, Okla.: Penwell Books, 1981), 150.

Figure 11.3

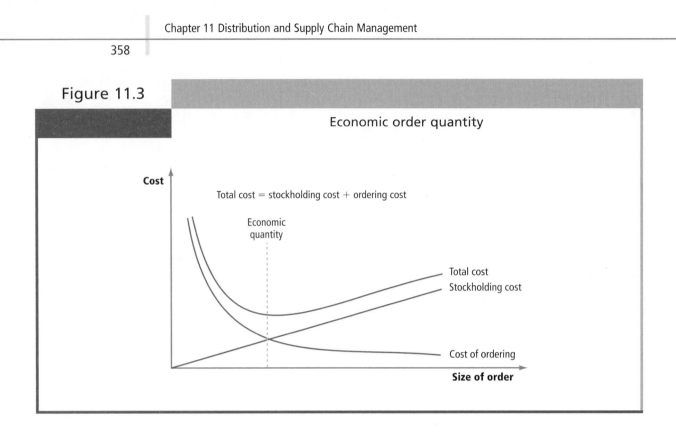

Economic order quantity

Total cost = stockholding cost + ordering cost

Economic quantity

Cost

Total cost
Stockholding cost

Cost of ordering

Size of order

www.wrangler.com

All these considerations, however, deal only with the status quo and do not address the distribution processes. That is where the coordination of activities with suppliers and customers can play a major role. For example, because the Wrangler jeans company receives precise, ongoing information about purchase levels (in terms of quantity, style, and sizes) from its major retail clients, the firm can plan its own purchasing and production more efficiently and thus offer a better price. Similarly, if customers provide real-time information on their needs, the producer can be more efficient in scheduling production. In both instances, the degree of uncertainty is reduced, and the extent of mutual trust is increased.

To achieve these benefits, the firm has to invest substantially in building a system relationship and providing for information exchange. Clearly such investment is viable only if it is driven by a long-term perspective. However, the results show that the investment may well be worthwhile, as its benefits can far exceed the results of efficient internal management alone. For example, typical savings from integrating the supply chain include the liberation of 50 percent of working capital, a 30 percent reduction in operating costs, and a sizable reduction in fixed assets.[24] UPS Aviation Technologies, a subsidiary of United Parcel Service, used

www.upsat.com
www.ups.com

EDI to reduce the administrative time necessary for creating and sending purchase orders by 67 percent and reduced order processing time by 30 percent.[25] With the Internet offering a lower-cost alternative to the development of private value-added networks, such collaboration is expected to increase markedly.

TRANSPORTATION DECISIONS

Coordinating the transportation of products is a major operation. The investment is substantial, and the specialized management of the personnel and resources involved can be just as important. The main tasks of transportation management traditionally are those of scheduling—once more a balance between prompt ser-

24. Bernard LaLonde, Kee-Hian Tan, and Michael Standing, "Forget Supply Chains, Think of Value Flows," *Transformation* 3 (summer 1994), 24–31.
25. Philip Wintermyer, "EDI Saves Partners Cost and Time," *Electronic Buyer's News,* July 19, 1999, 46.

vice and the cost of providing it most economically—and routing, which focuses the classic linear programming problem of achieving the minimum distance (and time) to reach all the delivery points. In addition, the transportation flow must be coordinated between the different links in the supply chain. Transparency of information flow is crucial here. If the precise transportation status of orders can be tracked at any time, it becomes possible to expedite or reroute shipments to meet emergencies, to consolidate shipments in order to reduce costs, and to minimize the time that shipments simply sit and await further instructions. It must be remembered that transportation is the by-product of the need to get the product to the customer. Every action that can be taken to reduce movement and handling will improve the process and reduce costs.

> **transportation is only the by-product of the need to get the product to the customer**

The marketer must also make the appropriate selection from the available modes of transportation. This decision is, of course, heavily influenced by the needs of the firm and its customers. The manager must consider the performance of each mode in three contexts: transit time, predictability, and cost.

TRANSIT TIME. The period between departure and arrival of the carrier varies significantly. For example, between ocean freight and airfreight the 45-day transit time of an ocean shipment can be reduced to 24 hours if the firm chooses airfreight. The length of transit time has a major impact on the overall logistic operations of the firm. A short transit time may reduce or even eliminate the need for an overseas depot, and inventories can be significantly reduced if they are replenished frequently. As a result, capital can be freed up and used to finance other corporate opportunities. Transit time can also play a major role in emergency situations. For example, if the shipper is about to miss an important delivery date because of production delays, a shipment normally made by ocean freight can be made by air.

Perishable products require shorter transit times, and rapid transportation prolongs their shelf life in the market. For products with a short life span, air delivery may be the only way to successfully enter distant markets. For example, international sales of cut flowers have reached their current volume only as a result of airfreight. Manager's Corner 11.6 shows how effective transport management can be crucial in the development of new markets for products.

Manager's Corner 11.6

The challenge of short shelf life

Chiquita (bananas) (www.chiquita.com) and Dole (pineapples) (www.dole.com) are experts at the logistics of international shipping. The success of their businesses depends on getting the product to the stores as quickly as possible, while the product is still ripe. Bananas, exported primarily from Latin American countries, are the most popular fruit consumed in the United States. Although Chiquita enjoys a high demand for its product, the firm faces significant logistics challenges. Specifically, Chiquita had to develop an international system to ship the product fresh, keep the price low, and

provide efficient and reliable delivery. With this in mind, a Chiquita researcher discovered that packing bananas in corrugated boxes and storing them at a temperature of 58° would greatly extend the ripening period. Although a 1950s advertisement featured a singing banana warning listeners that you should never put bananas in the refrigerator, nearly all bananas shipped today are packed in carefully monitored refrigerated holds on ocean freighters.

But if ocean shipping is acceptable for bananas, Hawaiian pineapple growers have been increasingly turning to airfreight. Discontented with the length of shipping time and the difficulty of getting fresh product to stores on the East Coast of the United States when shipping by ocean carrier, pineapple companies now fly their product. Although it was economically impossible to ship pineapples by air before deregulation, the new and intense competition among airlines has brought down shipping prices significantly. Still, perishable low-margin products often cannot support independent airfreight services alone. Clever managers, like Sylvia Nam of Dole Fresh Fruit, solve the problem by identifying 747s with extra cargo space and now regularly use the commercial airlines for shipping fresh pineapples. Because these bookings take up otherwise unused space, the airlines often provide special rates.

Sources: "Carriers, Ports Savor Growing Volumes," *Global Trade* (June 1992): 10; "Air Freight Makes Pineapples Fast Food," *Journal of Commerce,* June 29, 1990, 11B.

RELIABILITY. All providers of transportation services wrestle with the issue of reliability. Modes are subject to the vagaries of nature, which may impose delays. Yet because reliability is a relative measure, the delay of one day for airfreight tends to be seen as much more severe and "unreliable" than the same delay for ocean freight. However, delays tend to be shorter in absolute time for air shipments; as a result, arrival time via air is more predictable. This attribute has a major influence on corporate strategy. For example, because of the higher predictability of airfreight, inventory safety stock an be kept at lower levels. Greater predictability can also serve as a useful sales tool for distributors, who are able to make more precise delivery promises to their customers. If inadequate port facilities exist, airfreight may again be the better alternative. Unloading operations from ocean-going vessels are more cumbersome and time consuming than from planes. Finally, merchandise shipped via air is likely to suffer less loss and damage from exposure of the cargo to movement. Therefore, once the merchandise arrives, it is ready for immediate delivery—a facet that also enhances reliability.

COST. Transportation services are usually priced on the basis of both cost of the service provided and value of the service to the shipper. Because of the high value of the products shipped by air, airfreight is often priced according to the value of the service. In this instance, of course, price becomes a function of market demand and the monopolistic power of the carrier.

The marketer must decide whether the clearly higher cost of airfreight can be justified. In part, this depends on the cargo's properties; the physical density and the value of the cargo affects of the decision. Bulky products may be too expensive to ship by air, whereas very compact products may be more amenable to airfreight transportation. High-priced items can absorb transportation cost more easily than low-priced goods because the cost of transportation as a percentage of total product cost is lower. As a result, sending diamonds by airfreight is easier to justify than sending coal by air. To keep costs down, a shipper can join a shippers' association, which gives the shipper more leverage in negotiations. Alternatively, a shipper can decide to mix modes of transportation in order to reduce overall cost and time delays. For example, part of the shipment route can move by air, while another portion can move by truck or ship.

Most important, however, are the overall logistic considerations of the firm. For example, the marketer must determine how important it is for merchandise to arrive on time. The desire to be at the cutting edge of trends results in the latest clothing fashions always being shipped by air. The need to reduce or increase inventory must be carefully measured. Related to these considerations are the effect of transportation cost on price and the need for product availability. For example, some firms may wish to use airfreight as a new tool for aggressive market expansion. Airfreight may also be considered a good way to begin operations in new markets without making sizable investments for warehouses and distribution centers.

Although costs are important, the marketing manager must take an overall perspective when deciding on transportation. The manager must factor in all corporate activities that are affected by modal choice and explore the total cost effects of each alternative. A useful overall comparison between the different modes of transportation is provided in Table 11.3. The marketer's choice will depend on the importance of the different transportation dimensions to the market under consideration.

Increasingly, though, organizations are subcontracting their entire transportation operation to outside operators; indeed, this has become the classic make or buy decision. Contract, or third-party, logistics is a rapidly expanding industry. The main thrust behind the idea is that individual firms are experts in their industry and should therefore concentrate only on their operations. Third-party logistics providers, on the other hand, are experts solely in logistics, with the knowledge and means to perform efficient and innovative services for those companies in need. The goal is improved service at equal or lower cost.

Logistics providers' services vary in scope. For instance, some use their own assets in physical transportation whereas others subcontract out portions of the job. Some providers are not involved with the actual transportation but develop systems and databases or consult on administrative management services. In many instances, the partnership consists of working closely with established transport providers, such as Federal Express or UPS. These firms happily provide their self-service parcel boxes by the entrances for stores and firms. This way, a customer desiring overnight delivery does not have to expend energy trying to find a carrier willing to perform the service.[26]

www.fedex.com
www.ups.com

The concept of improving service, cutting costs, and unloading the daily management onto willing experts is driving the momentum of contract logistics. One of the greatest benefits of contracting out the logistics function is the ability to take advantage of an in-place network complete with resources and experience. The local expertise and image are crucial when a business is just starting up. The prospect of newly entering a region as confusing as Europe with different regulations, standards, and even languages can be frightening without access to a seasoned and familiar logistics provider.

Table 11.3

Evaluating transportation choices

Characteristics of mode	Mode of transportation				
	Air	Pipeline	Highway	Rail	Water
Speed (1 = fastest)	1	4	2	3	5
Cost (1 = highest)	1	4	2	3	5
Loss and damage (1 = least)	3	1	4	5	2
Frequency* (1 = best)	3	1	2	4	5
Dependability (1 = best)	5	1	2	3	4
Capacity** (1 = best)	4	5	3	2	1
Availability (1 = best)	3	5	1	2	4

* Frequency: number of times mode is available during a given time period.

** Capacity: ability of mode to handle large or heavy goods.

Source: Ronald H. Ballou, *Business Logistics Management*, 4th ed. (Upper Saddle River, N.J.: Prentice Hall, 1998), 146. Reprinted by permission of Prentice Hall, Inc., Upper Saddle River, N.J.

26. Joseph C. Andraski and Robert A. Novack, "Marketing Logistics Value: Managing the 5 P's," *Journal of Business Logistics* 17 (Issue 1): 23–34.

One of the main arguments leveled against contract logistics is the loss of the firm's control in the supply chain. Yet contract logistics does not and should not require a firm to hand over control. Rather, it offers concentration on one's specialization—a division of labor. The control and responsibility to the customer remain with the firm, even though operations may move to a highly trained outside organization.

FACILITY DECISIONS

After deciding *what* product or service to provide, the organization must decide *where* to provide it. The questions that follow are how these chosen markets can best be served and how the best possible service can be offered for the lowest cost. Unfortunately, once again, these two factors are usually in opposition. Service tends to improve with the number of warehouses or branches. At the same time, more warehouses require more buildings, higher inventory, and more staff—in short, higher cost.

The location of any particular central or regional plants can be mapped by calculating the weighted distribution costs for each part of the market to be served. But distribution times and costs are also affected by the pattern of natural barriers, such as rivers and mountains, and by the quality of the road systems. In addition, trade-offs to building warehouses can be found in better modes of transportation and closer collaboration with customers and suppliers, who, for example, may be asked to preposition product for rapid delivery. This is particularly the case in industrial marketing. For example, when it comes to crucial parts on an assembly line, even an eight-hour delivery delay may be unacceptable because it means shutting down the line. Location models increasingly rely on the use of computer simulations to deal with these considerable complexities. Marketing in Action 11.2 describes the facilities decisions facing Pepsico in its attempt to gain greater international market share.

INVENTORY DECISIONS

Decisions about how much inventory to hold as raw materials, work in progress, or finished goods; where to hold it; and in what quantities are vital. Inventory levels largely determine the level of service that an organization can offer to its customers or clients. The level of inventory is almost totally dependent on the accuracy of the sales forecasts described earlier. The vagaries accompanying such forecasts have led to the need for large inventories to be held (as buffers) to maintain customer service levels, and there is usually a clear trade-off between the cost of stockholding and customer service.

INVENTORY CONTROL.   For most organizations control of inventory is a crucial activity. If a product is not available when the customer wants it, the sale may be lost, and the dissatisfied customer may take the business elsewhere. For example, it has been estimated that under low promotion conditions, retailers lose 6 to 9 percent of sales due to out-of-stock situations. Under conditions of heavy promotion, the losses typically amount to 12 to 15 percent of sales.[27] For example, in the supermarket industry, stockouts are probably the worst for heavily promoted items on Sunday evenings—just before the restocking takes place. On the other hand, if too much

> For most organizations **control of inventory is** a crucial activity.

27. Thomas J. Blischok, "Supply Chain Reinvention," *AT&T Global Information Solutions*, 1994.

Marketing in Action 11.2

Are U.S. bottlers the international answer for Pepsi-Cola?

Headquartered in Purchase, New York (USA), PepsiCo (www.pepsico.com) is comprised of three powerful consumer products companies: Pepsi-Cola Company (beverages), Frito-Lay Company (www.fritolay.com) (snack chips), and Tropicana Products (www.tropicana.com) (branded juices). PepsiCo reported 1998 revenues of over $22 billion. Unfortunately, Pepsi-Cola's international beverage sales are not contributing to PepsiCo's revenues.

Pepsi-Cola began selling its products in the international market in 1934, with products now available in 170 countries. Whereas Pepsi, Diet Pepsi, Pepsi-One, Mountain Dew, Slice, and Mug brands account for around one-third of total soft drink sales in the United States, Pepsi-Cola's worldwide market share is only around 20 percent. This worldwide market share compares to Coca-Cola's (www.coke.com) worldwide share of almost 50 percent. Coca-Cola's success in the international marketplace can be attributed, in part, to its reliance on large regional bottlers

in various countries. In addition to having strong local ties, these large regional bottlers also have the capital to invest in operations.

In a move to bring its international beverage sales up to par with its domestic sales, Pepsi-Cola is thinking about following in Coca-Cola's footprints. Historically, Pepsi-Cola has relied on company-owned bottling facilities and small, international partners. Now, Pepsi-Cola is considering the creation of several large regional bottlers in key territories throughout the world. To accomplish this, Pepsi-Cola is asking several of its large United States bottlers to take control of many of its international markets. Pepsi feels that these U.S. bottlers have the managerial and operational expertise to make its international operations a success.

Can Pepsi successfully mimic what Coca-Cola has done with its regional bottlers? Why would a United States bottling company invest millions of dollars in Pepsi's international bottling operations?

Sources: www.pepsico.com; Nikhil Deogun, "Pepsi's Domestic Bottlers May Expand to Run Overseas Franchise Territories," *Wall Street Journal*, February 21, 1997, A3.

inventory is held, the cost can be exorbitant; in most industries annual inventory holding costs (physical warehousing, financing, administration, shrinkage, and deterioration) can easily exceed 30 percent of the total value of the stock.

Methods of inventory control vary widely in sophistication. One of the simplest methods is to have two "bins" of a product. When the first bin is empty it is replaced by the second (full) one, and another bin of product is ordered. An alternative is computerized inventory control, which in most cases is just a form of stock recording. The record merely states what the balance of stock is—or should be. More sophisticated versions also make provision for on-order and back-order items. All of these are records of what has happened. The decisions of when and what amount to reorder are the responsibility of the human operator, but the computer helps by providing a reminder when the stock falls below the minimum or reorder point and provides assistance with some of the calculations (such as the EOQ). In service industries it usually also shows the slots available at some time in the future.

One important development in inventory management, pioneered by Toyota, is the just-in-time (JIT) approach. Here components are delivered from the suppliers directly to the production line just as they are needed (or at least only a few hours before). This way, very little stock is held by the manufacturer. It is accordingly a very efficient method of planning inventory.

www.toyota.com

However, JIT does have hidden disadvantages, the most important of which is its lack of flexibility. It demands flat scheduling, which means that the production runs must be forecast exactly several weeks in advance, because the comparable production runs by the suppliers will take place some time in advance of the final assembly. Changes in plan are not possible in the short term; although if the key components are produced in-house and flexible manufacturing (especially reduced setup times) is employed, this disadvantage may be minimized. Equally, the much vaunted inventory savings by the manufacturer may sometimes come about simply because the suppliers are holding buffer stocks instead. Yet the discipline of meeting JIT demands has improved the performance of many organizations.

It should be noted that JIT is not a technique, but the outcome of a very rich package of measures, including zero defects (or total quality management, TQM) and flexible manufacturing, as well as the traditional workforce dedication involving quality circles and multifunctional workers. It is the practical combination of these techniques, along with the support of sophisticated management information systems providing details on production schedules, vendors, parts, buyers, and transportation, that offers the greatest reward.

> JIT is not a technique, but the outcome of a very rich package of measures

www.gm.com

Finally, it needs to be considered that a shift to a just-in-time system makes a company and its production processes much more vulnerable. For example, during the 1996 strike at a brake-pad plant of General Motors, most of the firm's assembly plants around the nation had to be shut down very quickly due to a lack of product flow and the lack of any inventories. Thus a narrowly focused strike can have major corporate repercussions. In consequence, a total commitment to just-in-time systems will be particularly successful if management and labor agree not to use this corporate vulnerability as a bargaining chip.[28]

INVENTORY AS A STRATEGIC TOOL

Inventories can be used by the international corporation as a strategic tool in dealing with currency valuation changes or to hedge against inflation. By increasing inventories before an imminent devaluation of a currency instead of holding cash, the corporation may reduce its exposure to devaluation losses. Similarly, in the case of high inflation, large inventories can provide an important inflation hedge. In such circumstances, the international inventory manager must balance the cost of maintaining high levels of inventories with the benefits accruing from hedging against inflation or devaluation. Many countries, for example, charge a property tax on stored goods. If the increase in tax payments outweighs the hedging benefits to the corporation, it would be unwise to increase inventories before a devaluation.[29]

COMMUNICATIONS DECISIONS

Logistics management is not concerned only with the flow of materials through the company and its distribution channels. It also deals with the flow of information, including order processing, invoicing, records of each customer's past usage, forecasts of demand, and stockholding. The logistics system needs to handle the information effectively in order to provide satisfactory customer service at acceptable cost. It also needs to offer effective communication and information systems so

> The flow of information has become as important to the success of a company as the flow of physical products.

28. Michael R. Czinkota, "GM Strike Requires New Industrial Covenant," *Chicago Tribune,* April 4, 1996, 27.
29. Czinkota, Ronkainen, and Moffett, *International Business,* 556–557.

that management can make better day-to-day and long-term decisions. The flow of information has become as important to the success of a company as the flow of physical products. It is information that ensures that the right goods are in the right place at the right time to meet customer needs.

LOGISTICS AND THE ENVIRONMENT

The logistician plays an increasingly important role in allowing the firm to operate in an environmentally conscious way. Environmental laws, expectations, and self-imposed goals set by firms are difficult to adhere to without a logistics orientation that systematically takes these concerns into account. Because laws and regulations differ around the world, the firm's efforts need to be responsive to a wide variety of requirements. One new logistics orientation that has grown in importance because of environmental concerns is the development of reverse distribution systems. Such systems are instrumental in ensuring that the firm not only delivers the product to the market but also can retrieve it from the market for subsequent use, recycling, or disposal. The ability to develop such reverse logistics systems is becoming an essential determinant of market acceptance and profitability.

Society is also beginning to recognize that retrieval should not be restricted to short-term consumer goods, such as bottles. Rather, it may be even more important to devise systems that enable the retrieval and disposal of long-term capital goods, such as cars, refrigerators, air conditioners, and industrial goods, with the least possible burden on the environment. The design of such long-term systems around the world may be one of the most important challenges—and opportunities—for the logistician and will require close collaboration with all other functions in the firm, such as design, production, and marketing. On the transportation side, logistics managers need to expand their involvement in carrier and routing selection. For example, shippers of oil or other potentially hazardous materials need to be involved in choosing the route that the shipment will travel and select those that are far from ecologically sensitive zones.

In the packaging field, environmental concerns increasingly lead to expectations that the amount of packaging materials used is minimized and that the materials used are environmentally "friendly." Companies need to learn how to simultaneously achieve environmental and economic goals. Esprit, the apparel maker, and The Body Shop, a British cosmetics producer, screen all their suppliers for environmental and socially responsible practices. ISO-14000 is a standard specifically targeted at international environmental practices by evaluating companies both at the organization level (management systems, environmental performance, and environmental auditing) and product level (life-cycle assessment, labeling, and product standards).[30] From the environmental perspective, those practices are desirable that bring about fewer shipments, less handling, and more direct movement. Such practices are to be weighed against optimal efficiency routings, including just-in-time inventory and quantity discount purchasing. This means that even though a JIT inventory system may connote highly desirable inventory savings, the resulting cost of frequent delivery, additional highway congestion, and incremental air pollution must also be factored into the planning horizon. Despite the difficulty, firms will need to assert leadership in such trade-off considerations in order to provide society with a better quality of life.

www.esprit.com
www.the-body-shop.com

---

30. Haw-Jan Wu and Steven C. Dunn, "Environmentally Responsible Logistics Systems," *International Journal of Physical Distribution and Logistics Management* 2 (1995): 20–38.

CUSTOMER SERVICE

All the distribution and supply chain activities discussed so far have a common goal: to provide delightful customer service. Goods and services need to be available when and where the customer wants them; they need to be distributed efficiently so that the customer can afford them; and the process should delight customers so that they will come back. Even though all marketing functions aim for customer service and satisfaction, it is becoming more difficult for firms to differentiate themselves from the competition. Product performance is becoming similar, and prices are adjusted rapidly in response to competitive activity. However, high levels of channel capabilities and supply chain performance are not easily copied and are sometimes ignored as a competitive tool. They can be successfully used to develop a sustainable competitive advantage.[31] This section presents some details on the important dimension of customer service by discussing its various components, which are service levels, customer complaints and satisfaction, and the organization necessary to provide customer service.

SERVICE LEVELS

The percentage of product availability is described as the service level. It might seem that the simple goal would be to achieve 100 percent availability, but the cost of achieving this level rises very steeply as the service level approaches 100 percent, as the diagram in Figure 11.4 shows. There is a very clear trade-off here

Figure 11.4

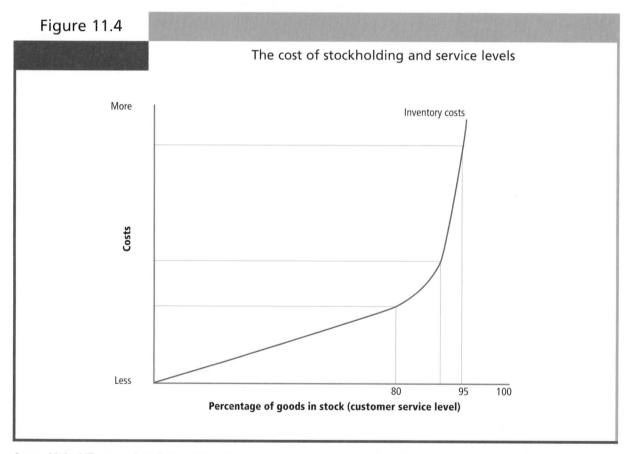

The cost of stockholding and service levels

Source: Michael Thomas and W. G. Donaldson, "Customer Service/Customer Care," in *Marketing Handbook*, ed., Michael Thomas (Aldershot, England: Gower, 1989), 199. Reprinted by permission.

---

31. Arun Sharma, Dhruv Grewal, and Michael Levy, "The Customer Satisfaction/Logistics Interface," *Journal of Business Logistics* 16, no. 2 (1995): 1–21.

between customer service (level) and cost. Marketers must therefore decide on the implications of service levels. Typical issues to explore are whether customers understand and appreciate the different service levels and whether they are willing to pay for higher service levels. It may will become necessary to offer different degrees of service in order to permit more customer choice. For example, Federal Express offers delivery of packages on the next morning, the next afternoon, or after two days. Each one of these services is priced differently, of course, and appeals to different consumer uses.

www.fedex.com

CUSTOMER COMPLAINTS

In order to keep a good benchmark of one's customer service and to learn how to improve performance, it is essential to record all complaints and the manner with which they are dealt. This may seem obvious, but it is often not done. Customer complaints are one of the most important aspects of business operations that need management control, yet they are often neglected and treated as a nuisance by many organizations. Nevertheless they have considerable value for several reasons.

Although there will always be a small number of "frivolous" complaints, a complaint usually highlights something that has gone wrong with a part of the overall marketing operation. Whatever the reason, the sensible marketer will want to know exactly what went wrong so that remedial action may be taken. As is shown in Exhibit 11.2, the way in which a complaint is handled is often seen by customers, and their many contacts, as the litmus test of the true quality of support. What is more, it is also a powerful reminder to the organization's own staff of just how important quality is. Customers who complain are usually loyal customers (those who are not loyal tend to switch to another supplier) and will continue to be loyal and valuable customers—particularly if their complaint is handled well. Ritz Carlton, FedEx, and Xerox are all known as service quality leaders, partly for their internal specification for the speed and convenience of the complaint procedure, as well as in their concern for appropriate customer compensation delivered by caring employees.[32]

> The way a complaint is handled is often seen by customers as the litmus test of the true quality of support.

www.ritzcarlton.com
www.xerox.com

The first rule is that complaints should be positively encouraged. One of the surest signs of a bad or declining relationship with a customer is the absence of complaints from the customer. Nobody is ever that satisfied, especially over an extended period of time; the customer is either not being candid or is not being contacted.[33] This is not the same as saying that the reasons for complaints should be encouraged. But assuming that problems have occurred despite your best efforts, you should put nothing in the way of any customer who wants to complain. The main problem lies with the many customers who do not complain and instead change to another supplier rather than the few who abuse the complaint system.

Many businesses have established toll-free numbers so that customers can report problems easily and at the company's expense. American Express has installed such lines and estimates that it achieves responses more quickly and at 10 to 20 percent of the cost of handling correspondence.[34] General Electric has gone further still, by providing a round-the-clock, centralized, expert, general support service: Anyone who has a query—not necessarily a complaint—about

www.americanexpress
.com
www.ge.com

32. Tax Stephen, Stephen Brown, and Murali Chandrashekaran, "Customer Evaluations of Service Complaint Experiences: Implications for Relationship Marketing," *Journal of Marketing* (April 1998): 60–76.

33. T. Levitt, "After the Sale Is Over," *Harvard Business Review* 61, no. 5 (September/October 1983): 87–93.

34. C. W. L. Hart, J. L. Heskett, and W. E. Sasser Jr., "The Profitable Art of Service Recovery," *Harvard Business Review* 68, no. 4 (July/August 1990): 148–157.

Exhibit 11.2

Carnival Cruise ship *Tropical* was stranded at sea in September 1999. Carnival maintained that there were very limited plumbing problems during the period, but many passengers claim to have been without water and toilets for two days. Some even reported raw sewage rising into the sinks. Carnival promised all passengers full refunds, free tickets for a future cruise, and new flights home. Despite these customer service concessions, Carnival's earnings were off 1 cent a share for the quarter.

www.jiffylube.com

www.microsoft.com

any of GE's products may call free of charge. Jiffy Lube, the world's largest fast-lube franchisor, has information about each individual customer, with each service center boasting a database of 8,000 to 50,000 customers. The firm knows about customer driving habits and oil change requirements and has performance data to determine which Jiffy Lube outlet is not as effective as it might be.[35] Microsoft established beta sites to seek customer knowledge in all important phases of new software development, from generating product specifications to alpha (verifying that the software conforms to specifications) and gamma (final checking of the product before its release) testing. Microsoft attributes its continued market success to its vigorous pursuit of customer knowledge in new product development.[36]

The second rule is that all complaints should be carefully handled by painstakingly controlled and monitored procedures. Complaints must be handled well—and must be seen to be handled well by the complainer and by the organization's own staff. The third and most important rule is that the complaint should be fully investigated and the cause remedied. Complaints are only symptoms; the disease needs to be cured! There may be an understandable temptation to overlook complaints until they reach a significant level, but holding off until the complaints reach this pain threshold usually means that they have already become damaging to the organization's image. It is far better to take the position that even one complaint is too many.

CUSTOMER SATISFACTION

Up to 97 percent of dissatisfied customers do not complain, but they do tell their friends (a survey showed that 13 percent complained to more than 20 other people).[37] The threat of such negative word-of-mouth publicity alone should encourage every organization to develop an ongoing focus on customer satisfaction particularly because the Internet has dramatically raised the number of people one can complain to—or share praises with. Rather than appealing only to a few

35. Bill Gates, *Business @ The Speed of Thought* (New York: Warner Books, 1999): 201–205

36. Tiger Li and Roger J. Calantone, "The Impact of Market Knowledge Competence on New Product Advantage: Conceptualization and Empirical Examination," *Journal of Marketing* 62 (October 1998): 13–29.

37. K. Albrecht and R. Zemke, "Service America," *Harvard Business Review* 68 (July/August 1990): 148–157.

dozen friends, active Web participants can now easily complain to hundreds if not thousands. All it takes is a well-visited Web site or chat room.

But there are other powerful implications to customer satisfaction. Customer satisfaction leads to increased corporate profitability,[38] as seen by the track record of Nordstrom department store, which consistently obtains the highest levels of customer satisfaction in U.S. retailing. Satisfied customers are less sensitive to price than either dissatisfied customers or new customers.[39] they are more willing to pay for the services they receive. It is also far less expensive to maintain an existing account than to develop a new one.[40] Satisfied customers tend to purchase more frequently and in greater volume than less satisfied ones.[41] Data from a report from the Office of Consumer Affairs, shown in Figure 11.5, demonstrate that even for dissatisfied customers the repurchase rates vary substantially, depending on whether and how their complaints are addressed. It is therefore essential that an organization monitor and assess the satisfaction level of its customers. The results should be analyzed to produce overall satisfaction indices and should also be provided to field managers so that they can rectify any individual problems.

There are a number of advantages to conducting satisfaction surveys (particularly when any individual problems highlighted can subsequently be dealt with):

- Like complaints, they indicate where problems lie.
- If they cover all customers, they allow 96 percent of noncomplainers to communicate their feelings and vent their anger.

www2.nordstrom.com

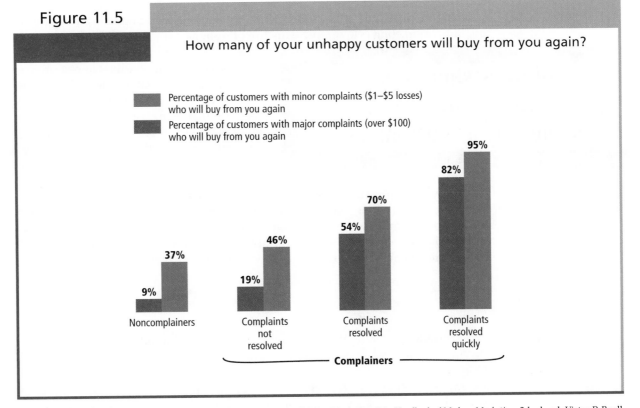

Figure 11.5

How many of your unhappy customers will buy from you again?

Source: J. A. Goodman and A. R. Malech, "The Role of Service in Effective Marketing," in *Handbook of Modern Marketing*, 2d ed., ed. Victor P. Buell (New York: McGraw-Hill, 1986), 68. Reprinted with permission of the McGraw-Hill Companies.

38. Eugene W. Anderson, Claes Fornell, and Donald R. Lehman, "Customer Satisfaction, Market Share, and Profitability: Findings from Sweden," *Journal of Marketing* 58 (July 1994): 53–66.
39. Davis A. Garvin, *Managing Quality: The Strategic and Competitive Edge* (New York: Free Press, 1988), 49.
40. Sharma, Grewal, and Levy, "The Customer Satisfaction/Logistics Interface."
41. Fredrick F. Reichheld and W. Earl Sasser, "Zero Defections: Quality Comes to Services," *Harvard Business Review* 68 (September/October 1990): 105–111.

- They show even the satisfied customers that the supplier is interested.
- They help to persuade the supplier's staff to take customer service more seriously.

www.mcdonalds.com

The importance of very high standards of customer service can be demonstrated by McDonald's marketing philosophy, which is encapsulated in its motto "QSC&V" (Quality, Service, Cleanliness, and Value). The standards, enforced on its franchisees and managers at the Hamburger University, require that the customer receive a good-tasting hamburger in no more than five minutes from a friendly server in a spotless restaurant. It is instructive to observe how few of their competitors manage even the simple task of keeping their premises clean.

www.xerox.com
caterpillar.com

Technology allows firms to learn about the possibility of failure before the customer even notices a problem. For example, Xerox and Caterpillar are already implementing information systems that allow service technicians to diagnose problems before customers realize they need help. Computer systems at district service centers continually monitor firms' equipment by remotely reading sensors on each machine. When a pending problem is spotted, an electronic alert is sent to the portable computer of the local field technician, specifying exactly which parts and tools will be needed to make the repair. Onsite, an interactive computer then guides the service technician through the best and most efficient practices for making the repair. [42]

ORGANIZING FOR CUSTOMER SERVICE

By definition, marketing is concerned primarily with the world outside the organization. But if marketing is to optimize the use of resources, it has to be concerned with

> **Employees should be marketed to in exactly the same way as customers.**

what lies inside the organizational perimeter as well. The most valuable resource of any organization is its people and the skills that they possess. Many of the traditional tools of marketing can be used to great effect in the very important areas of internal communication and motivation. Employees should be marketed to in exactly the same way as customers. Such internal marketing is as much about finding out what the employees want as it is persuading them to do what the organization wants.

Marketing research conducted on the organization's own employees should be used to determine where they stand in relation to their perception of the customer and of the customer service programs. It should explore the attitudes and motivations of employees by asking questions such as these:

- Is the customer seen as a friend or foe?
- Does anyone do anything more than pay lip service to customer research programs, and why?
- Do employees really want to offer a good service? If not, why?
- How can they be persuaded to change their views?

MANAGING SERVICE ATTITUDES. Perhaps the most important but least appreciated aspect of internal marketing is that it is a process of managing change; the marketing department needs to adopt the role of change agent. The aspects to be imbued in an organization are as follows.

- **Adopting an (internal) customer perspective.** Find out how the "internal customer" (the employee) feels about the changes.
- **Investing in education.** Stimulating change takes considerable, extended effort.

---

42. Stephen W. Brown, "Service Recovery through IT," *Marketing Management* (fall 1997): 25–26.

- **Planning for change.** Work out the complex relationships that need to be addressed and modified.
- **Using conviction marketing.** Changing the culture is the most powerful change that can be made, but it takes a considerable investment over a number of years.

The last two objectives represent areas in which internal marketing diverges most from conventional marketing. The techniques may be closer to those of education and indeed may require significant amounts of retraining.

The culture of the company is often what conditions this customer service. Customers see customer service in terms of all their contacts with the company. They do not restrict their view to the narrow confines of product availability or to just those members of the sales force who are supposed to be the ambassadors of the company. Being told that "your call is important to us" provides them with very little solace when they continue to remain on hold. They are even less influenced by

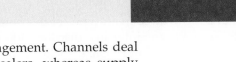

It is essential for **customer service thinking** to permeate the organization

advertisements that tell them how good the customer service is if their own experiences tell them otherwise. It is therefore essential for customer service thinking to permeate the organization so that the customer encounters a service orientation at every level of contact.

SUMMARY

Distribution comprises channels and supply chain management. Channels deal with institutional linkages such as retailers and wholesalers, whereas supply chain management addresses the processes underlying these linkages, such as warehousing, transportation, and inventory management, and connects them from the supplier to the end user. The objective of both components is to provide a high level of customer service at a manageable cost.

Distribution channels take on various functions of the manufacturers because they can perform them more efficiently. Depending on the type of product and type of consumer, they can range from the zero level, where the contact between manufacturer and end user is direct, to multiple levels, from producer to wholesalers and retailers. The choice of channel is an important one because it has major strategic implications and is difficult to change. Within the channel choice, decisions also need to be made about channel compensation and control. To a large degree, effective channel management is dependent on close information linkages. The use of information analysis on the retail level increasingly makes other channel members dependent on these information sources. Overall, channel members need to add value to the distribution process—or be eliminated. This also applies to the purchasing process, which is an integral part of distribution, albeit an internally focused one.

Supply chain management benefits from a systems view of corporate activity and includes the development of close relationships with both suppliers and customers. Effective coordination between parties reduces cost and provides for competitive advantage through approaches such as just-in-time (JIT) delivery, electronic data interchange (EDI), and early supplier involvement (ESI). Production, transportation, facility, inventory, and communication decisions are the key areas within logistics, all of which require trade-offs and collaborative action among participants. Even though the optimizing activities of a firm provide for some benefits, competitive differentiation occurs mainly through coordination with other companies.

The firm may evaluate transportation based on transit time, reliability, and cost and achieve operational improvements, but a strategic collaborative approach with customers and suppliers can deliver even greater benefits. Such collaboration can include the use of third-party logistics providers. Logistics can also play a major role in making the firm more environmentally responsive by designing reverse distribution systems for the recycling of merchandise and by devising distribution processes that minimize risk and damage to the environment.

All channel and supply chain efforts are designed to increase customer service. The intent is to delight the customer. It is therefore important to understand the importance of customer complaints. Such complaints should be encouraged so that the firm learns early on about potential problem areas. In addition, they need to be resolved quickly so that customers are willing to return. Good customer service requires the orientation and commitment of the entire corporate culture so that the customer notices at each point of contact with the firm that customer service thinking is a part of the organization.

QUESTIONS FOR REVIEW

1. What are the roles of the different levels of distribution channels?

2. What are the main decisions to be made in logistics management? What are the most important production decisions?

3. What are the three main types of distribution intensity? Why is intensive distribution more difficult to control and channel members harder to motivate?

4. What are the main retail product decisions? Why is location important?

5. How should complaints be handled, and why? What can be done about customer satisfaction?

6. What are the main decisions to be made in purchasing?

QUESTIONS FOR DISCUSSION

1. The advent of the Internet seemed to sound the death knell for distributors. As e-commerce became ever more popular, it was expected that products would be obtained directly from manufacturers. Yet there are still several steps in the online retail supply chain. Some predict that rather than the distributor going the way of the dinosaur, it will ultimately be the online retailer that disappears.[43] How can information technology affect the channel structure of an industry? Provide examples of such changes.

2. Both General Motors and Ford Motor have parts-producing operations that are seeking to spin off from their parent companies. In the case of GM's Delphi unit, the goal is to make Delphi more competitive with nonunion rivals.[44] With a historic trend in industrialized nations tending toward channel integration, are these efforts at channel disintegration an anomaly? Provide examples to support your position.

---

43. William Gurley, "Why Online Distributors—Once Written Off—May Thrive," *Fortune,* September 6, 1999, 270–271.
44. Joann Muller, "Labor Could Back This GM Spin Off," *Fortune,* August 2, 1999, 62–63.

3. In 1998, Barnes & Noble had more bookstores than any of its competitors. After a series of acquisitions, the company moved away from the mall-based strategy that carried it through the late 1980s and began building superstores. But its new hope lies in the success of barnesandnoble.com, a retailer with as many locations as there are Web users.[45] New forms of retailing are said to dramatically affect the importance of location. What are the implications for city centers and real estate values? Are these shifts inevitable?

4. To date, there have been no wildly successful Internet hardware stores. In fact, Wall Street analysts are bullish on Home Depot and Lowe's because of the seeming inability of the industry to translate well to online retailing. Nonetheless, the Web is enabling suppliers of hardware superstores to sell directly to consumers. Home Depot responded with a letter that states its intolerance of vendors that began to compete with it through online ventures.[46] Is this an example of channel control or channel imperialism? Will the end result be customer satisfaction?

5. In the wake of the health scare that plagued Coca-Cola Europe in the summer of 1999, CEO Doug Ivester was slow to make a public relations announcement to Belgian consumers. Despite the PR fiasco, Ivester was quoted as saying, "In ten years, we'll sell twice the volume we do today. The turmoil of the last 18 months will be history, just like New Coke is history."[47] Do you think Ivester is right? Because measuring customer satisfaction deals only with the current environment, are such measurements a waste of time and money? Why or why not?

FURTHER READINGS

Ballou, Ronald H. *Business Logistics Management.* 4th ed. Upper Saddle River, N.J.: Prentice Hall, 1999.

Brown Stanley A., ed. *Breakthrough Customer Service: Best Practices of Leaders in Customer Support.* New York: John Wiley & Sons, 1998.

Ernst, Ricardo, Panos Kouvelis, Phillippe-Pierre Dornier, and Michel Fender. *Global Operations and Logistics: Text and Cases.* New York: John Wiley & Sons, 1998.

Koppelmann, Udo. *Procurement Marketing: A Strategic Concept.* Berlin: Springer Verlag, 1998.

Kotabe, Masaaki. *Global Sourcing Strategy: R&D, Manufacturing and Marketing Interfaces.* New York: Quorum Books, 1992.

Martin, Christopher. *Logistics and Supply Chain Management.* 2d ed. London: Financial Times Management, 1999.

Monczka, Robert M., Robert J. Trent, and Robert B. Handfield. *Purchasing and Supply Chain Management.* Cincinnati: South-Western Publishing, 1998.

Rosenbloom, Bert. *Marketing Channels: A Management View.* 6th ed. Fort Worth, Tex.: Dryden Press, 1999.

Wood, Donald F., Daniel L. Wardlow, Paul R. Murphy, Mae Johnson, and James C. Johnson. *Contemporary Logistics.* 7th ed. Upper Saddle River, N.J.: Prentice Hall, 1999.

45. Nina Munk, "Title Fight," *Fortune,* June 21, 1999, 86–94.
46. Katrina Brooker, "E-Rivals Seem to Have Home Depot Awfully Nervous," *Fortune,* August 16, 1999, 28–29; Rheka Balu, "Stocks the All-Stars Favor Now: Retail: Specialty," *Wall Street Journal,* June 29, 1999, R13.
47. Patricia Sellers, "Crunch Time for Coke," *Fortune,* July 19, 1999, 72–78.

chapter
12

Designing Effective Promotion and Advertising Strategies

In earlier chapters, we defined marketing as a dialogue. Specifically, we explained how market research is used to *listen* to customers. In this chapter, we come to the other half of the dialogue—that of *talking* to customers.

The promotional mix consists of a wide variety of specific techniques that may be used to communicate with customers. Broadly speaking, it can be grouped into three main categories in terms of decreasing impact on the customer: personal selling (direct contact), advertising (indirect contact), and sales promotion and publicity (complementary support). The ideal form of promotion is the conversation that takes place between the sales professional and his or her customer. It is ideal because, in addition to being interactive, the communication in each direction is specific to the needs of both. However, it is the most expensive form of promotion. Other forms of promotion can only hope to approximate this ideal.

In this chapter, we examine advertising practices in terms of both the overall promotional mix and media, with a review of the main media types. Advertising offers an indirect contact with the customer. We will examine promotional methods involving direct contact with the customer and complementary support in Chapters 13 and 14.

DIALOGUE

Promotion is only one half of a dialogue. If the promotion does not respond to customer needs, which should have been discovered from marketing research, it will probably fail, no matter how creative the treatment.

Effective promotion is thus inextricably linked to sound market research, in one form or another. This is also an ongoing dialogue, because the promotion itself will change what the customer thinks and needs.[1]

> Promotion is only
> **one half**
> of a dialogue.

ENCODING AND DECODING

The traditional model of the communication process stresses the elements of **encoding** and **decoding**, as shown in Figure 12.1. Simply put, human-to-human communication is a very complex process with plenty of room for misinterpretation. Considerable skill is needed to create the messages that the receiver (the consumer) finds persuasive, hence the justification for highly paid advertising agency copywriters.

---

1. Demetrios Vakratsas and Tim Ambler, "How Advertising Works: What Do We Really Know?" *Journal of Marketing* 63 (January 1999): 26–43.

Figure 12.1

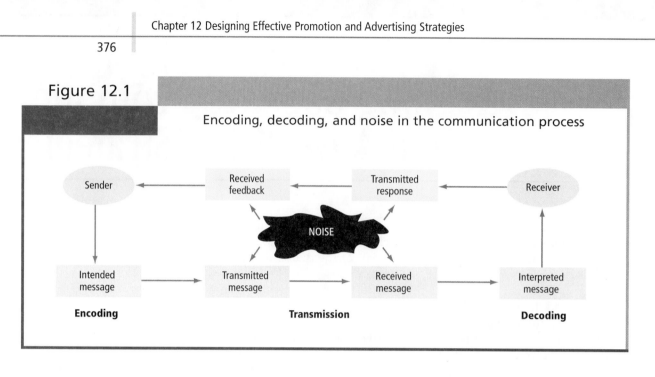

Encoding, decoding, and noise in the communication process

The fact that the medium (newspaper or television) can also change the message further justifies the need for the copywriters and media buyers.

This electronic metaphor does, however, illustrate the point that "noise" is a major problem for any promotional message. The message itself may be distorted in transmission during the few seconds the reader spends on it before the page is turned or before the viewer is distracted from the message of the commercial. The recipient may, accordingly, obtain a very fragmentary message (hence the emphasis on simplicity in advertising messages). Worst of all, though, will be the torrent of other noise, the potentially more interesting editorial matter surrounding the advertisement, or just the distractions of the everyday life through which the advertiser's messages have to be heard. Hence, advertisers rely on multiple opportunities to see (OTS), to "turn up the volume," or to break through the noise barrier. There is also a need to invest in creative talent to optimize the impact of the individual message.

MARKETING MIX

The final caveat, before we discuss promotion itself, is that all promotion must be seen in the context of the *whole marketing mix*. Promotion is just one of the four Ps. Price and place may be just as important and certainly have their own impacts on any promotion. A high-priced product sold through specialist outlets will demand a very different form of promotion to that of a cut-rate brand sold through supermarkets.

> all promotion must be seen in the context of the whole marketing mix

In addition, the most important element of the marketing mix must always be the product or service itself. Consumers will not buy—at least not more than once—a product or service that does not meet their needs, no matter how persuasive the promotion. In a way, a one-term presidency for the Oval Office epitomizes this hard fact.

At the same time, the form of the promotion itself, the message, and even the medium may be largely determined by the specification of that product or service. Thus, by defining the product, you largely define the entire marketing mix, which explains the heavy emphasis on the product in earlier chapters. In this way, then, all the elements of the marketing mix contribute to the overall promotion of a product, service, or company, and the "input" into promotion may come from areas even further afield.

CORPORATE PROMOTION VERSUS BRAND PROMOTION

Most advertising, along with other forms of promotion, relates to specific brands and is very direct in attempting to increase sales of that product or service. However, a growing element is that of **corporate advertising**, which promotes the overall organization rather than its individual brands (this type of promotion is particularly important in Japan, where consumers often buy based on the overall reputation of the organization). This rationale may be that the support to be obtained from the organizational umbrella ultimately sells the brands. Such a case can certainly be made for Marks & Spencer (whose corporate name is better known than its "St. Michael" brand name) or IBM. It may well be due to a degree of nervousness induced by the increasing possibility of even very large corporations falling to hostile takeovers. The principles of corporate advertising follow those of brand advertising very closely; in this context, the corporation is the brand name.

www.marks-and-spencer
.co.uk
www.ibm.com

The example of corporate advertising does, however, illustrate a more general point. An organization may conduct a number of promotional campaigns, often aimed at different audiences. That target on consumers is usually obvious, but there may also be a significant amount of promotion—often in the form of direct mail—directed at shareholders and other members of the financial community to protect the share price and reduce the risk of takeover activity.

Another good example is Intel, a manufacturer of microprocessors for IBM-compatible personal computers. Traditionally, components manufacturers sell their component products to manufacturers of finished products on an OEM (original equipment manufacturer) basis. However, as shown in Manager's Corner 12.1, Intel began to emphasize its component products—486, Pentium, and now Pentium Pro microprocessors—in personal computers with its "Intel Inside" slogan. Intel's corporate advertising is designed to achieve a dominant product design status for its microprocessor-based personal computers (see Exhibit 12.1).

www.intel.com

Manager's Corner 12.1

Technobranding!

Brand identity is being recognized as increasingly important to firms manufacturing or selling high-tech products. A brand encompasses the "visual, emotional, rational, and cultural image" that buyers associate with a company or product. The most significant difference between technology and consumer branding is the level of *complexity* of the product or service. The messaging process for simple versus complex products differs in two ways: (1) simple, commodity products and services attempt to "magnify small differences" (i.e., Ivory Soap is marketed as "99.4 Pure") and (2) complex, technological products and services attempt to "simplify the message to reduce buyer confusion" (i.e., Intel simply states "Intel Inside").

One reason why branding should be important to technology firms is that these products and services are essentially more differentiated than typical consumer products. Thus, there is more substance to their claim that their product offering is unique. Brands are

unlikely to be effective unless they are perceived as minimizing one's exposure to risk. This is a challenge that can be effectively met and maintained in a high-tech product scenario, especially given the functional and proprietary differentiation.

Technobranding Processes

The goal of creating the brand identity is to increase overall sales. Thus, in creating a brand the focus of the research should be firmly on discovering the most important factors motivating a product purchase. The following steps discuss the whole branding process:

1. Define objectives and what questions need to be answered
2. Conduct qualitative and quantitative research
3. Define the brand—create the brand identity
4. Develop the brand strategy and communications plan

5. Execute an integrated marketing communications plan—use the brand identity
6. Manage the brand and track it to build brand equity

Intel's Success

The reasons for the success of Intel's "Intel Inside" campaign is that it communicates its message clearly, reduces the buyer's anxiety, and relates its message wholly to the customer's buying criteria. "Intel Inside" conveys the message of state-of-the-art technology and upgradability that are perceived as protecting the customer's investment in the product. Also, these branding benefits are realized both by Intel and the PC vendor. Valued at $17.8 billion, Intel's brand name is now ranked by *Financial World* as number three among all brands for total brand value. Should this trend continue, we would expect that big-money brand management would no longer be identified only with consumer products.

Sources: "Brand ID's Importance to High-Tech Direct Marketing," *DM News*, March 27, 1995; "Brands Are Back; Saturn's Example; Cyberbrands Live," *Advertising Age*, May 8, 1995, 1–3.

Exhibit 12.1

Many of Intel's competitors have been inspired by the successful campaign to launch television and magazine advertising of their own component parts. This is an unusual move by an industry that typically does not implement consumer advertising strategies. But the success of "ingredient marketing" in other industries, such as clothing and food products, has transitioned into the computer industry, where "host" brands risk becoming a commodity.

PUSH VERSUS PULL

Where a supplier uses any form of distribution channel, as most of those in the mass consumer markets do, he or she is faced with two extremes in terms of promotion:

1. **Push.** In this case the supplier directs the bulk of the promotional effort at selling the product into the channel (into the various organizations that make up the chain of distribution) in order to persuade the members of the

channel to "push" the product forward until it reaches the final consumer. It thus tends to revolve around sales promotion and is sometimes referred to as "below the line." This term is derived from the days when advertising agencies managed all promotional activity, and the items on the accounts that did not relate to advertising were put below the line that divided off the agency's main activity on the expenditure reports. This technique is particularly favored by organizations without strong brands that are involved in price competition.

2. **Pull.** Here the supplier focuses the promotional effort (typically advertising) on the consumer, in the belief that he or she will be motivated to "pull" the product through the channel (by demanding it from retailers, for example). Due to its association with advertising, it is sometimes referred to as "above the line." This technique is usually favored by the owners of strong, differentiated brands, such as Procter & Gamble or Nestlé.

www.pg.com
www.nestle.com

In practice, most suppliers choose a route somewhere between these two extremes, blending both elements to obtain the optimum effect, and thus an optimum blend of the overall marketing mix. Which type of promotion to emphasize must also be decided in light of the economic development of the target nation. Oftentimes the ability to reach consumers in developing countries may be limited by the availability of suitable media. In these markets, a push strategy is often more effective.

CONSUMER VERSUS INDUSTRIAL ADVERTISING

Whereas **consumer advertising** has to handle almost all of the contact with the end-user audience, **industrial advertising** (often called business-to-business advertising) typically forms only part of the overall communication. It is often designed just to create the initial awareness and to generate leads (frequently based on postage-paid reply forms with advertising) before the face-to-face sales process conducted by the producer's own sales force (or, perhaps more likely, by its agent's and dealer's sales forces) takes over.

Much of industrial advertising is therefore designed to elicit responses leading to a sales visit. It also often needs to convey more information than equivalent consumer advertising; capital goods, for example, are significantly more complex than repeat-purchase consumer goods. The advertising campaigns may also have to work over much longer periods, because purchases may be more infrequent; the purchase process itself may be extended.

The average advertising budget is usually much lower for consumer goods—normally less than seven figures and often less than six figures, even for relatively large organizations (as compared with Nike, McDonald's, and Coke, which have advertising budgets in the hundreds of millions of dollars). The average target audience is also much more specifically selected, and this has led to the emergence of a specialist group of media, particularly the trade journal. In this context, media buying has become a correspondingly specialized activity, frequently focusing on identification of the few publications that can reach the specialized target audience, rather than producing a balanced schedule for reaching them most economically, as is the task with consumer goods campaigns.

www.nike.com
www.mcdonalds.com
www.coke.com

The main differences between industrial and consumer advertising are listed in Table 12.1.

Table 12.1

Differences between industrial and consumer advertising

Industrial advertisers	Consumer advertisers
Complex and multitiered buying influences.	Simple one-person or family influence.
Advertising is "support" to the sales influence.	Advertising is the major sales influence.
Purchase decisions are long range and considered; immediate, measurable sales results rarely occur.	Purchase decisions are more spontaneous (i.e., if you need it, buy it); immediate, measurable sales results often occur.
Product usage cycle is long.	Product usage cycle is short for most items.
If purchase is not satisfactory, buyer is challenged—his job is on the line.	If purchase is not satisfactory, repercussions are minimal.
More advertising planning—less "marketing" planning—so less result oriented.	Product management (marketing) systems are based on results.
"Test" marketing is not common.	"Test" marketing is the norm.
Advertising budgets are based on last year's sales—and historical spending levels.	Advertising budgets are based on *task* or *need* from test results.
Reliance on "readership scores" and "did you buy?" to evaluate success of advertising.	Communications, recall, and image measurements.
Advertising is technical/factual in copy content. Often very potent, informative, and persuasive.	Advertising emphasis is on brand image. Sometimes even *dumb* versus *smart* sell—often persuasive.
Editorial environment is naturally business oriented.	Editorial environment tends to be personal fulfillment/ entertainment environment.
Attitude of "catching up" to marketing world.	Great confidence. "Know everything" attitude.

Source: Yolanda Brugaletta, "What Business-to-Business Advertisers Can Learn from Consumer Advertisers," *Journal of Advertising Research* 25, no. 131 (June/July 1985): RC8+. Reprinted by permission of the Advertising Research Foundation.

CREATING THE CORRECT MESSAGES

Clearly, the prime objective of any promotional method—whether direct, indirect, or supportive—is to make the sale (in the case of a nonprofit organization the sale might be to persuade the target audience to adopt a different behavior pattern— say, give up smoking). To achieve this result, though, it will almost certainly need to communicate one or more messages (whether the promotion consists of face-to-face selling or advertising on television). The objectives of these messages— awareness, interest, understanding, attitude, and buying decision—are illustrated in Figure 12.2.

AWARENESS

The first task, awareness, is to gain the attention of the target audience. According to David Ogilvy, one of the great gurus of advertising, "On average, five times as many people read the headlines as read the body copy. It follows that unless your headline sells your product, you have wasted 90 percent of your money."[2]

Achieving awareness means, therefore, that the messages must first of all be seen and "read." They must grab the audience's attention. Advertising agencies

---

2. Cited in Axel Anderson and Denison Hatch, "How to Create Headlines that Get Results," *Target Marketing* 17 (March 1994): 28–30, or see David Ogilvy, *Ogilvy on Advertising* (London: Pan Books, 1983).

Figure 12.2

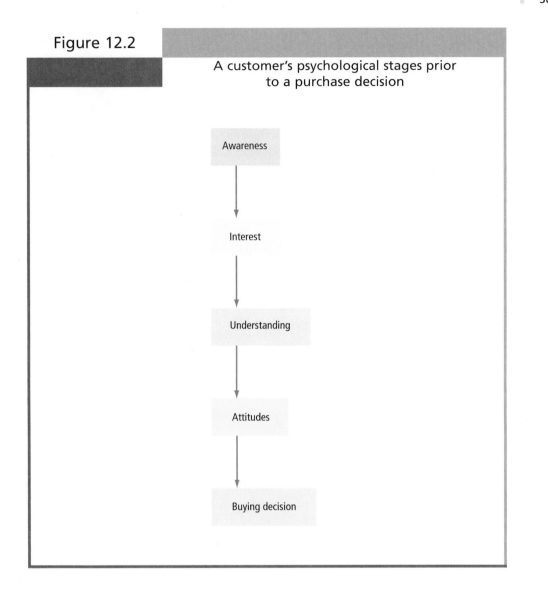

A customer's psychological stages prior to a purchase decision

have spent decades honing the techniques involved; from challenging headlines (like the famous Avis line, "We try harder") in the newspaper to memorable images on television (such as the Coca-Cola "I'd like to teach the world to sing"). One of the most successful campaigns of recent years has been Taco Bell's ad featuring a Chihuahua with the signature line, "Yo quiero Taco Bell."[3]

Getting attention is critical to success and is in part a function of size. A full-page advertisement is more likely to command attention than a quarter-page, a two-minute commercial more than a 15-second one. What helps is having some feature that breaks through the apathy of the reader or viewer, such as an extraordinary image or a provocative headline. But this has to be achieved in an environment in which every other advertiser is attempting the same task. A unique example of creating and reshaping awareness is presented in Marketing in Action 12.1.

www.avis.com
www.coke.com
www.tacobell.com

---

3. "Taco Bell Named PMA Promotion Marketers of the Year," *Potentials* 32 (May 1999): 16–17.

Marketing in Action 12.1

Gateway's new campaign drops the "2000"

In 1987, Gateway's CEO recognized a direct-selling opportunity and began designing, assembling, and shipping fully configured personal computers to end users. By the mid-1990s, Gateway (www.gateway.com) had expanded its service operations to include retail outlets, called Gateway Country, where customers could learn about Gateway's products before buying direct.

The first company slogan was "Gateway to the Future," and "2000" was added to the Gateway name to imply that the company's products would take users into the next millennium. Thus, the marketplace began referring to the company and its products as "Gateway 2000." Fearing that this brand tag no longer adequately communicates the company's direction, however, Gateway is investing in a new branding campaign.

The new campaign, implemented by McCann-Erickson Advertising, drops the "2000" from the Gateway name because the year 2000 is no longer in the future. The company plans to do business under its true corporate name, Gateway. In addition to dropping the 2000 from its name, the company also has a new logo that combines a hand-drawn representation of a cow-spotted box with the name Gateway in a green font. The green coloring is supposed to represent growth, momentum, and vitality. The logo also includes the company's 1-800 telephone number and Web address.

With above-average earnings, did Gateway need to worry about the use of the Gateway 2000 name? Estimate the impact of the name and logo change on each step of the promotional model. Will dropping the "2000" allow Gateway to better position itself among business buyers?

Sources: www.gateway.com; Sally Beatty and Evan Ramstad, "Gateway 2000: Pleasing Profit, Short Name," *Wall Street Journal*, April 24, 1998, B6.

INTEREST

It is not sufficient to grab the reader's attention for only a second or so, until it wanders again. In that brief time the message must *interest* that reader and persuade him or her to read on. The content of the message(s) must be meaningful and clearly relevant to the target audience's needs.

This is where marketing research can come into its own as the basis for effective advertising. In the first instance, the advertiser needs to know exactly *who* the audience is. Then the advertiser has to understand the audience's interests and needs, which must be addressed, and the exact benefits (in the consumer's own terms) that the product or service will provide. In short, the message must be in the language of the consumer in the target audience and must make an offer that is of real interest to the specific audience. For example, the increase in the Hispanic population in the United States has not only made Ricky Martin, a Grammy Award–winning Latino musician singing in Spanglish (a mixture of Spanish and English), very popular, but also has encouraged advertisers to develop ads in Spanglish targeted at Generation N (Latin Generation X—12- to 19-year-olds—who are currently rediscovering their roots and inventing a new, bicultural identity).[4]

This may mean that the message may not be interesting at all to other audiences (including those who are commissioning and creating the advertisement), but that is not the point; it has only to be of interest to the specific target audience. The messages that are of interest to Generation N teenage pop CD buyers are very different from those aimed at middle-aged buyers of Volvo station wagons.

This second stage, therefore, largely depends on an excellent appreciation of the results of marketing research.

www.volvocars.com

---

4. Helene Stapinski, "Generacion Latino," *American Demographics* 21 (July 1999): 62–68; John Leland and Veronica Chambers, "Generation N," *Newsweek*, July 12, 1999, 52–58.

UNDERSTANDING

Once interest is established, the message needs to explain the product or service and its benefits in such a way that readers can understand them and can appreciate how well the product or service may meet their needs, again as revealed by marketing research. This is no small achievement when the copywriter has just 50 words—or 10 seconds—to convey the entire message. That is one reason why complex capital goods sales are the province of the sales professional who may take many hours to explain the product fully. This is also the reason why there is such a demand for good copywriters who can actually describe consumer goods— in meaningful terms—in just a few words. In the case of Taco Bell, its copywriters condensed the message to very few words indeed! On the other hand, "long copy—more than 300 words—actually attracts *more* readers than short copy," for print ads that try to create awareness, arouse interest, and build preference.[5] German companies, in particular, tend to provide very technical, detailed descriptions of their products. Thus, this stage is a mix of sound marketing research mediated by professional copywriting skills.

www.tacobell.com

ATTITUDE

The message must then persuade the reader to adopt such a positive attitude toward the product or service that he or she will purchase it, albeit as a trial. There is no adequate way of describing how this may be achieved. Often it comes down to the creative magic of the copywriter's art, based on the strength of the product or service itself.

BUYING DECISION

All of the above stages might happen in a few minutes while the reader is considering the advertisement in the comfort of his or her favorite couch. On the other hand, the final decision to buy may take place some time later, perhaps weeks later, when the prospective buyer actually tries to find a shop that stocks the product. This means that the basic message will probably need to be reinforced, by repeats, until the potential buyer is finally in the position to buy. Above all, the product or service must be distributed widely enough for the prospective buyer to be able to find it.

OTHER MODELS.   There are other models similar to the one illustrated in Figure 12.2. For example, the **AIDA**[6] (Attention, Interest, Desire, Action) model is frequently advocated as a structure for the selling process. Similar stages are also described in the "hierarchy of effects"[7] model (in which interest and understanding are paralleled by knowledge, liking, and preference). After AIDA, the most often quoted model within the advertising industry is **DAGMAR** (Defining Advertising Goals for Measuring Advertising Results), which splits the process into the four steps of awareness, comprehension, conviction, and action. These models all tend to describe the same processes from differing viewpoints.

---

5. John L. Naccarato and Kimberly A. Neuendorf, "Content Analysis as a Predictive Methodology: Recall, Readership, and Evaluations of Business-to-Business Print Advertising," *Journal of Advertising Research* 38 (May/June 1998): 19–33.

6. E. K. Strong, *The Psychology of Selling* (New York: McGraw-Hill, 1925).

7. R. J. Lavidge and G. A. Steiner, "A Model for Predictive Measurements of Advertising," *Journal of Marketing* 25 (October 1961): 59–62.

These models are all limited by certain factors. Although they may work in a cold sales call, in other complex real-life marketing situations they do not take into account time and experience. Attitude changes are likely to be more gradual, and much of advertising succeeds by virtue of marginally increasing the frequency of purchase of the brand among consumers who already have experience with it.[8]

Thus, one of the major weaknesses of most promotion theory is that it fails to take into account the history of the brand. Buying decisions are rarely made in isolation. They are an accumulation of months, even years, of experience on the part of the buyer. According to a study by Abraham and Lodish, on average, 76 percent of the difference observed in the test year persisted one year after the advertising was rolled back. Over a three-year period, the cumulative sales increase was at least twice the sales increase observed in the test year. Their study further indicates that, if advertising changes do not show an effect in six months, they will not have any impact, even if continued for a year.[9]

THE MESSAGE

The main message will usually be based on the specific benefit that the advertiser has identified as the main advantage the product offers over its competitors. This may not be the main benefit the buyer will receive from the product, for that may also be offered by all the competitors. It is a foolish advertiser who does not realize that the consumer is aware that many products are identical in offering the main benefit.

The advertiser will aim to find a unique selling proposition (USP) or an important benefit unique to the product or service in one of three ways.

1. **Product feature.** This USP may be based on physical or intangible product features associated with the product, ranging from what it actually does to the quality of the support services. Most advertising follows this route, and it is particularly easy to target, communicate, and monitor messages of this type.

2. **Psychological feature.** The USP may occasionally be based on a psychological appeal, such as on fear (e.g., financial services and condoms), guilt (educational toys), love (the mini soap operas in the Taster's Choice campaign), or humor (Budweiser). In the case of humor, the viewer or reader who shares the joke will develop a positive attitude toward the product; unfortunately, if the joke is not shared—and humor is a notoriously difficult art form—it is likely to alienate the potential customer.

3. **Association.** The message may be communicated by association with a well-known personality either in person (e.g., Nike's use of Tiger Woods) or in a voice-over (e.g., James Earl Jones for Bell Atlantic Yellow Pages commercials).

www.nestle.com
www.anheuser-busch
   .com
www.budweiser.com

www.nike.com
www.bellatlantic.org

MESSAGE CONSISTENCY

One factor that is often ignored by marketers, and in particular by agencies, is the need for successive campaigns to be consistent with their predecessors. Too often, campaigns are seen in isolation, with just the current task to carry out. To

8. Mark Lovell, "Advertising Research," in *Consumer Market Research Handbook*, eds. R. Worcester and J. Downham (New York: McGraw-Hill, 1986).

9. M. M. Abraham and L. M. Lodish, "Getting the Most Out of Advertising and Promotion," *Harvard Business Review* (May/June 1990): 50–60.

achieve the maximum effect, campaigns must be consistent with their previous messages or, at least, justify the inherent investment in consumer image built up by these messages.

> **To achieve the maximum effect, campaigns must be consistent with their previous messages**

For example, Nike has poured millions of dollars into making its brand one of America's most powerful. "Nike" is the Greek goddess of victory. In the late 1970s and 1980s, Nike created an image of itself as an athlete's company, a winning company, and has stuck to this message because consumers, mostly teenagers, like to associate themselves with winning companies and winning products. The brand is successful from Taiwan to Tivoli, and the reason is because the company's advertising message as remained strong and consistent throughout its history. Until recently, when the company faced lagging athletic gear sales in the United States, Nike never even ran product-related ad campaigns. What Nike did run was clever, edgy advertising that grabbed consumers' attention. More important, the ad campaigns spoke directly to the consumer, appealing to an athlete's need to win. The strategy was that high-profile, successful athletes would build a winning brand for consumers to associate with. Such world-class endorsers as Michael Jordan, John McEnroe, Andre Agassi, and Joan Benoit Samuelson built Nike in the 1980s. Star athletes still drive its advertising, but the company has added some product spots to counteract a saturated sneaker market in the United States. Yet, whether the campaign is pushing a new running sneaker or is simply an image spot featuring Tiger Woods, the strategy always remains consistent.[10]

OPINION LEADERS

It is often argued that in the case of a new product the effect of promotion may occur in two stages. The promotion itself (usually advertising) persuades the more adventurous **opinion leaders** in the population to try the product or service. These opinion leaders then carry the message to those who are less exposed to it. In the mass markets this often means those who are less exposed to the media. Most personal influence is transmitted within a network of peers who possess similar demographic characteristics.[11]

WORD OF MOUTH

A more generalized aspect of communication within the community as a whole is **word of mouth**. Much of advertising theory concentrates on the direct receipt of these indirect communications. It assumes that the consumer receives the message directly from the media and only from the media. In practice, as we have seen in the preceding section, the message may well be received by word of mouth from a contact (who may have either seen the advertising or in turn have received it from someone else). Even if the consumer had previously seen the advertising, word-of-mouth comments may reinforce (or undermine) what this has achieved directly.

Some manufacturers have embraced the importance of word of mouth by embarking on an "antimarketing marketing strategy." Particularly Converse, Adidas, and Puma have decided not to advertise many of their old-style athletic shoes. They are targeting their shoes at Generation Xers who "don't like being

www.converse.com
www.adidas.com
www.puma.com

10. Andy Cohen, "A Consistent Brand Message," *Sales and Marketing Management* (October 1998): 140.
11. Hubert Gatignon and Thomas S. Robertson, "A Propositional Inventory for New Diffusion Research," *Journal of Consumer Research* 11 (March 1985): 849–867.

www.adidas.com
www.nike.com
www.reebok.com

overmarketed to, don't like hype, and are wise to paying a premium for celebrity-endorsed shoes." One Adidas marketing executive said that "the best advertising strategy is, you don't." Considering that Nike and Reebok spent $120 million and $70 million, respectively, on advertising in one year, the strategy pursued by the antimarketers may seem risky. However, all three of the antimarketers report great success. The success of their shoe sales "was sparked entirely by word of mouth, executives say." The shoes became popular with skateboarders, at hip-hop dance clubs, with Madonna, and with Elle Macpherson. As one reporter has observed about the success of the antimarketers: "Sometimes, it seems, the best way to be heard is to whisper."[12] Marketing in Action 12.2 considers Nike's Alpha Project in the light of message consistency and recapturing market share among younger consumers.

MESSAGE SELECTION

The advertising messages used, usually created by the advertising agency's creative department, need to be evaluated carefully. Experts recommend that an effective advertisement should concentrate on just one central selling proposition. Complicating advertisements by adding further messages will generally dilute the main message as well as the overall impact.

Marketing in Action 12.2

Is advertising the name of the game for shoe manufacturers?

Consumers are inundated with various options when selecting a sneaker. Nike (www.nike .com), for example, offers options such as Monkey Paw, Ball Control Materials, N-Site, Tensile Sockliner, Abrasion Resistant Materials, and Footform. Many of the options appear in shoes targeted at particular athletic events. Monkey Paw is for basketball players, Ball Control Materials and Tensile Sockliner are for soccer players, N-Site and Footform are for runners, and Abrasion Resistant Materials is for tennis players.

Over the past two decades, Nike's innovative product development process has become the industry standard. In the late 1970s, Nike began the development of shoes with air bag cushioning, and "Nike Air" was born. A few of the Nike shoes built on this air technology were called Tailwind, Pegasus, Epic, and Air Max. The introduction of Air Max started the market trend of see-through openings that allowed consumers to see the shoe's air-cushioning system. Throughout the company's history, technological development has been the cornerstone of the brand's success. Although Nike will continue to follow a strategy of continual product innovation, however, changes in the traditional footwear market are driving Nike and other shoe manufacturers to rethink their strategies.

For Nike this has meant the creation of the Alpha Project. The Nike Alpha Project is an attempt to focus on the broader needs of an athlete—footwear, apparel, and equipment. Alpha will focus on a particular sport and market the entire line of Nike products to the players of this particular sport. The company will have Alpha Athletes with targeted ads featuring the athlete clad solely in Nike products. Perhaps Nike hopes this shift in focus—from footwear technology to complete athletic outfitting—will help recapture the attention of younger consumers who are leaving the sneaker market for the hiking boot/walking shoe market. Is the Alpha Project consistent with Nike's historical brand message? Why or why not? What are the implications for Nike if the shift to complete athletic outfitting is perceived by the market as a departure from the company's historic image and positioning? Will the use of Alpha Athletes bring younger buyers back to sneakers?

Sources: www.info.nike.com; Bill Richards, "Tripped Up by Too Many Shoes, Nike Regroups," *Wall Street Journal*, March 3, 1998, B1+.

12. "Sneakers That Jump into the Past: The 'Retro' Look Is All the Rage—and without Big Ad Campaigns," *Business Week*, March 13, 1995, 71.

The most effective method of message selection is that of pretesting the advertisement on a sample of the target audience. This is a specialized form of marketing research, which is usually the province of specialized research agencies. An audience is typically shown a new commercial (sometimes in storyboard form, although this is a very difficult approach to use) and questioned to determine its impact (before seeing it, as well as after, to detect shifts in opinion).

In their messages, most companies seem to place too much emphasis on the product itself and not enough on individuals' values or perspectives. For example, women are often portrayed as frazzled and out of control in advertisements. In actuality, female consumers are stressed and busy. To better cater to female consumers, Kellogg's discontinued a long-running ad campaign for its Special K cereal showing slender women consuming the product. The company admitted that the creative elements did not accurately portray women or their attitudes about health. Kellogg's discovered that female consumers are "maxed out" on the representation of photogenic, model-like women in ads. The new Special K theme is "Reshape Your Attitude." The new Reshape campaign chides the stereotypical complaints women have about maintaining a perfect figure. One man sitting at a bar asks about his slacks, "Do these make my butt look big?" Kellogg's then asks, "Men don't obsess about these things, so why do we?"[13]

www.kelloggs.com

COGNITIVE DISSONANCE.   One perhaps unexpected feature of audience behavior, reported by Leon Festinger, is that interest in all forms of promotion, particularly advertising, reaches a maximum *after* the consumer has made his or her purchase.[14] The usual explanation for this apparently illogical behavior is that the consumer is then searching for proof to *justify* his or her recent decision. The consumer seeks out flaws, in comparison with the chosen product or service, to obtain reassurance that his or her decision was correct.

The importance of this is that there is still a job to do even after the sale has been made. In addition, the messages needed to address cognitive dissonance may be subtly different; they will provide reassurance, and will allow for the fact that these purchasers will also represent the main source of future sales.

MEDIA SELECTION

Media selection is the process of choosing the most cost-effective media to achieve the necessary coverage and number of exposures among the target audience. Performance is typically measured in terms of coverage and frequency.

COVERAGE

To maximize overall awareness, the maximum number of the target audience should be reached by the advertising. This is known as coverage. Coverage is limited, however, because a small percentage of the general population is not exposed to the main media used by advertisers and is thus difficult (and accordingly very expensive) to reach. Indeed, the cost of cumulative coverage typically follows an exponential pattern. Reaching 90 percent can cost double what it costs to reach 70 percent, and reaching 95 percent can double the cost yet again. The coverage decision is, in practice, a balance between the desired coverage and the cost of achieving it. A large budget will achieve high coverage, whereas a smaller budget will limit the ambitions of the advertiser.

13. Steve Dwyer, "Ad Spots Aim for Cyberspace," *Prepared Foods*, March 1, 1999, 25.
14. Leon A. Festinger, *A Theory of Cognitive Dissonance* (New York: Row, Peterson & Co., 1957).

In some markets, such as China, the cost to reach even 50 percent of the market could be extremely expensive. The variety of languages and dialects, the low incomes, and for most the lack of televisions limits the effectiveness of any one advertising message. In China, there are 600 television stations, 9,000 newspapers, and 4,500 magazines. Whereas elsewhere in the world advertisers expect $20 to $30 of sales for every dollar spent on advertising, in China the expected sales are half of that and falling. The effectiveness of advertising in China may have already reached a point of diminishing return.[15]

In spite of the problems faced by advertisers in countries like China, the use of global ad campaigns is increasing. Globe-trotting companies are increasingly employing either pattern standardization or globally standardized ads to develop a global image for their products as well as to reduce advertising costs. Pattern standardization refers to synchronizing advertising messages in different countries while using their respective locally popular features such as movie stars and sports.[16] Coca-Cola, Anheuser-Busch, McDonald's, and American Express are but a few examples. Global standardization is an extreme and relatively rare case in which one ad is developed for many different countries.[17] For example, Unilever has one ad for its Dove soap that it uses in a number of countries. The ad features a succession of thirtyish women—of Australian, French, German, Italian, and other nationalities—each praising Dove in their own language. An increasing number of companies have begun such standardized global ad campaigns. As another indication of the growing use of these global campaigns, Saatchi & Saatchi reports that half of its $1.35-billion annual revenue is generated from ad campaigns that span five or more countries; five years ago, only 10 percent came from such campaigns.[18] Despite increased use of pattern standardization or standardized ads, however, advertisers should take special care *not* to violate local customs and cultural mores and taboos, such as showing an animal wearing eyeglasses in certain Asian countries where animals are considered lowly creatures, or showing a chunk of ham in a refrigerator in Muslim nations where eating pork is prohibited.

The European Commission is also working to find agreement between member states on all forms of cross-border communications. What is likely to emerge is a system of "mutual recognition," in which companies can carry out sales promotion activities in the target country as long as they are legal in the company's country of origin. This would allow European consumers to be presented with sales promotions across all media, including more of the spam practices we have seen from Internet promoters.[19]

www.coke.com
www.anheuser-busch
.com
www.mcdonalds.com
www.americanexpress
.com
www.unilever.com
www.saatchi.com

FREQUENCY

Even with high coverage, however, it is not sufficient for a member of the target audience to have just one opportunity to see (OTS) the advertisement. It is generally reckoned that around five OTS are needed before any reasonable degree of impact is achieved, and significantly more may be needed to build attitudes that lead to brand switching. To achieve five OTS, even across a coverage of only 70 percent of the overall audience, may require 20 or 30 peak-time transmissions of a commercial or a significant number of insertions of newspaper advertisements

15. "Advertising in China: Hard Sell," *Economist*, March 4, 1995, 67.
16. Michael Colvin, R. Heeler, and J. Thorpe, "Developing International Advertising Strategy," *Journal of Marketing* 44 (fall 1980): 73–79.
17. Robert E. Hite and C. Fraser, "International Advertising Strategies of Multinational Corporations," *Journal of Advertising Research* 28 (August/September 1988): 9–17.
18. "Global Ad Campaigns, after Many Missteps, Finally Pay Dividends," *Wall Street Journal*, August 27, 1992, A1.
19. Allyson L. Stewart-Allen, "Cross-Border Conflicts of European Sales Promotions," *Marketing News*, April 26, 1999, 10.

in the national media. As these figures suggest, most consumers simply do not see the commercials that frequently. The point is that the life of advertising campaigns can often be extended far beyond the relatively short life that is usually expected of them. Indeed, as indicated above, the research shows that advertisements need to achieve a significant number of exposures to consumers before they even register.[20]

The more sophisticated media planners will also look at the *spread* of frequencies. Ideally all of the audience should receive the average number of OTS (because those who receive less are insufficiently motivated, and the extra advertising is wasted on those who receive more). Needless to say, it is impossible to achieve this ideal. As with coverage, the pattern will be weighted toward a smaller number of heavy viewers, for example, who will receive significantly more OTS, and away from the difficult remaining percent. However, the good media buyer will manage the resulting spread of frequencies so that it is weighted close to the average, with as few as possible of the audience away from the average.

Frequency is also complicated by the fact that it is a function of time. A pattern if 12 OTS across a year may be scarcely noticed, whereas 12 OTS in a week will be very evident to most viewers. This is often the rationale for advertising in "bursts" or "waves" (sometimes described as *pulsing*), with expenditure concentrated into a number of intense periods of advertising, but with these bursts spread throughout the year so that brands do not remain uncovered for long periods.

One advertising campaign that has an extremely long period between bursts is the one run by Oscar Meyer. Only once in every few years do we see the now famous Oscar Meyer bologna ad featuring the small boy singing the company's jingle. Another company, Apple Computers, has run a widely expensive and memorable ad on only one occasion. The ad featuring IBM as Big Brother in an Orwellian setting being destroyed by the Apple Macintosh was shown only once.[21]

www.kraftfoods.com

www.apple.com
www.ibm.com

In the end, it is the media buyers who deliver the goods, by negotiating special deals with the media owners and buying the best "slots" to achieve the best cost (normally measured in terms of the cost per thousand viewers, per thousand household "impressions," or per thousand impressions on the target audience). The growth of the very large, international agencies has been partly justified by their increased buying power over the media owners.

TYPES OF MEDIA AND THEIR CHARACTERISTICS

In terms of overall advertising expenditures, media advertising is dominated by newspaper and television, which are of comparable size in terms of sales. Billboards and radio follow some way behind, with cinema representing a specialist medium. Although the Internet sales still constitute a small fraction of the total sales, the role that the Internet plays as a new medium has been growing rapidly.

Effective media selection depends on having an in-depth understanding of each target audience and then matching their characteristics with the different attributes offered by each medium. Because consumers have different wants, needs, and habits, there are few products and services that can be effectively marketed via only one medium. However, this does not mean that resources should be equally divided among all media. Rather, marketers must test each medium on an ongoing basis to ensure that financial resources are utilized in the most productive manner possible. The proportion of broadcast to mail to print will vary by product, market segment, and many other variables. For example, seniors tend

20. David Ogilvy, *Ogilvy on Advertising* (London: Pan Books, 1983).
21. "Advertising Mergers," *Economist*, February 4, 1995, 61.

to rely more on print and mail. They're used to reading to gather the information they need. Generation Xers, on the other hand, are less likely to be suspicious of what they see on television or on the Internet.[22]

NEWSPAPER/MAGAZINE.   In this medium, spending is dominated by the national and local newspapers, the latter taking almost all the classified advertising revenue. The magazines and trade or technical journal markets are about equal in size to each other, but are less than half that of the newspaper sectors.

TELEVISION.   This is normally the most expensive medium, and as such is generally only open to the major advertisers, although some cable and specialized channels offer more affordable packages to their local advertisers. Television offers by far the widest coverage, particularly at peak hours (roughly 7 to 10:30 P.M.) and especially of family audiences. Offering sight, sound, movement, and color, it has the greatest impact, especially for those products or services where a demonstration is essential, because it combines the virtues of both the storyteller and the demonstrator. However, to be effective these messages must be kept simple—and have the impact to overcome the surrounding distractions of family life.

www.cnn.com
www.mtv.com
www.aande.com

Because of the explosive growth of cable TV channels with specialized programs, such as CNN News, MTV, and the Arts and Entertainment Channel, it has become possible to "narrowcast" messages to more targeted audiences.[23] Many channels offer local advertising time slots for regional trials or promotions (including test marketing). In Europe, TV transmission may reach far beyond national borders. To the delight of West (now western) German producers right after the German unification, many of their products were well known in east (now eastern) Germany, even though they were unavailable there. Everyone in eastern Germany had seen them on TV from western Germany.

Price structures for television advertising can be horrendously complicated, with the "rate card" (the price list) offering different prices for different times throughout the day; this is further complicated by a wide range of special promotional packages and individual negotiations. It is truly the province of the specialist media buyer.

Satellite television is now considered to be the medium of the future in many developed countries, just as cable television represented the future a decade ago. The promise of satellite television has been largely fulfilled in the United States, where the average household can now tune in to 31 channels. However, it has yet to achieve comparable levels of penetration in other countries. Advertisers in Hong Kong report problems with reaching their intended Chinese target audience. Hong Kong advertisers in the past were confident that they could reach millions of Chinese viewers in the south of China. Now, however, many Chinese stations are "illegally retransmitting the Hong Kong stations' programs and inserting their own advertising slots."[24]

www.apple.com
www.bankofamerica.com
www.ford.com
www.texaco.com

Another increasingly popular use of television is the infomercial. Featuring such celebrity hosts as Dionne Warwick, Jane Fonda, and others, small companies and Fortune 500 companies such as Apple Computer, Bank of America, Ford Motor Company, and Texaco have begun using infomercials in record numbers. Sales from infomercials reached $1.5 billion in 1998. Infomercials are unparalleled in their ability to generate consumer demand, qualified leads, and immediate sales for a fraction of the budget needed to create an advertising campaign around a 30-second commercial spot.[25]

22. Jay Klitsch, "Making Your Message Hit Home: Some Basics to Consider When Selecting Media," *Direct Marketing* (June 1998): 32–33+.
23. Owen McDonald, "Channel Surfing; Teleshopping; Airwave," *Sporting Goods Business* 27 (July 1994): 76.
24. "Advertising in China: Hard Sell."
25. Tim Hawthorne, "When & Why to Consider Informercials," *Target Marketing* 21 (February 1998): 52–53+.

Rapidly changing advertising landscape

Ragu spaghetti sauce, Volvos (www.volvocars.com), IBM (www.ibm.com) PCs, and Hyatt Hotels (www.hyatt.com) are just a few of the products being promoted on the Internet these days. Corporate America's interest in this medium stems from the awareness that approximately 25 million Americans have access to the Internet and about 6 million of these use the World Wide Web.

On the technical side, such firms as Sun Microsystems (www.sun.com) and Silicon Graphics (www.sgi.com) are designing software to improve the overall appeal and graphic capabilities of this media, including three-dimensional imaging, expanded animation, and other computerized special effects. Large advertising agencies are also catching the Internet "wave" by setting up in-house project teams focused solely on Internet marketing. These traditional firms are meeting stiff competition from newer technically based specialty firms that are hoping the Madison Avenue crowd "wipes out."

Marketing Advantages

The reason companies are so interested in Internet advertising is not the size of the market, but the *precision* of the medium in reaching a particular segment. Traditional broadcasting (television, radio, or print) is essentially one-way mass marketing. Only a percentage of the people exposed to such broadcasts are actually interested in the advertising. Internet advertising, on the other hand, has the potential for interactivity. Messages are activated by the potential consumer who shows an interest in the product/service. In this view, interactive marketing is not advertising by *intrusion*, but advertising by *invitation*. Even more important is the potential for "individual marketing," whereby the marketer learns about the tastes of individual consumers. By maintaining this information on digitized databases, the marketer can develop customized promotions and product/service offerings.

What's New?

Following are some of the more interesting approaches to Internet advertising:

The Ragu spaghetti sauce (eat.com) ad shows a cartoon spokeswoman, "Mama," who walks the audience through the kitchen and provides viewers with the options of product information, recipes, sights/sounds of Italy, or a brief Italian lesson.

Volvo has an electronic service center that allows question/answer communication through e-mail between the consumer and a Volvo technician.

Oldsmobile (www.oldsmobile.com) sponsors an evening "chat show" on America Online featuring different celebrities every night.

Source: "Selling Moves to the Internet," *San Francisco Chronicle*, June 12, 1995, Final Edition.

THE INTERNET.   Internet advertising—which began in 1994 when the first banner ads were sold on Hotwired—is coming of age. Online audiences are growing, often at the expense of other media. The technology is advancing rapidly, and many major advertisers have realized that the Internet should form a key part of their advertising strategies. Banner ads are the most popular Internet advertising format (see Manager's Corner 12.2).

www.hotwired.com

> many major advertisers have realized that the Internet should form a key part of their advertising strategies

Online advertising is expected to make up more than 8 percent of advertisers' total marketing efforts by 2004, accounting for about $22 billion in spending in the United States. Currently, advertisers' devote about 1.3 percent of their overall advertising budgets to Internet ads, for a total of about $2.8 billion. Based on interviews with 50 companies, most of which have a significant Web presence and include companies such as America Online and Yahoo! that have a big stake in the growth of Internet banner advertising, marketing executives expect their Internet spending to leapfrog Yellow Pages

www.aol.com
www.yahoo.com

and magazine advertising spending, trailing only television, newspapers, and direct mail in popularity for advertising spending.[26]

Although the advertisers believe that cyberspace advertising is effective, the major challenge is how to measure the results. Furthermore, ethical issues concerning liquor and cigarette ads have reemerged.[27] Cyberspace advertisers have begun to track how computer users interact with the cyberspace messages. For example, Nielsen Media Research, Yankelovish Partners, and ASI Market Research have a strategic partnership, called ANYwhere Online, to develop research service online. This online service will measure the use, appeal, and impact of advertising and commercial ventures on the Internet.[28]

In 1996, research by Millward Brown Interactive found that exposure to Internet banner ads generated greater awareness than television or print advertising. However, their impact on consumers' purchase decision is not well known. As Internet advertising budgets grow, the pressure is intensifying for advertisers, media owners, and agencies to identify and develop formats, technologies, and creative approaches that will deliver the results. To boost the effectiveness of Internet advertising, new formats, including pop-up signs and microsites, are being deployed. Rich media—the combination of high-grade graphics, audio, and interactive capabilities—are being used to create more engaging, memorable, or intrusive advertising. But greater use of rich media does not mean that the standard banner is redundant. Banners can be effective as signals. They can be a first step into advertising in this medium. Advertisers, agencies, and media owners must consider whether the audience is able to download and view rich media.[29] (See Manager's Corner 12.3.)

RADIO. The use of radio has increased greatly in recent years, with the granting of many more licenses. It typically generates specific audiences at different times of the day—for example, adults at breakfast, housewives thereafter, and motorists during rush hours. It can be a very cost-effective way of reaching these audiences (especially as production costs can also be much cheaper), although the types of message conveyed will be limited by the lack of any visual elements and may have a "lightweight" image.

MOVIE AND RENTAL VIDEO. Although the numbers in the national audience are now small, this may be the most effective medium for extending coverage to the younger age groups, because the core audience is aged 15 to 24. Additionally, a captive audience, boredom, and lack of suitable alternatives create a tendency to watch the ads. Similarly, thanks to the explosive growth of rental movie business, such as Blockbuster, rental movie videos are also used increasingly as a mobile advertising tool.

BILLBOARDS. This is something of a specialist medium, which is generally used in support of campaigns using other media. On the other hand, some advertisers, particularly those in brewing and tobacco, have successfully made significant use of the medium, although, to achieve this, they have developed the requisite expertise to make efficient use of its peculiarities.

www.nielsenmedia.com
www.yankelovich.com
www.asiresearch.com

www.mbinteractive.com

www.blockbuster.com

26. Yochi Dreazen, "Online Ad Spending Is Expected to More Than Triple by Year 2004," *Wall Street Journal*, August 12, 1999, B12.

27. Michael B. Mazis, "Marketing and Public Policy: Prospects for the Future," *Journal of Public Policy & Marketing* 16 (spring 1997): 139–143.

28. "News Digest," *Marketing News*, June 19, 1995, 1; and "Honomichl '99 Top Fifty," *Marketing News*, June 7, 1999, 33+.

29. Matthew Reed, "Going Beyond the Banner Ad," *Marketing*, April 29, 1999, 25.

Manager's Corner 12.3

How do we measure the effectiveness of ads on the Internet?

Knowing how effectively an advertisement on different media reaches potential customers is very important to any advertiser. Boasting the popularity of the electronic version of *Penthouse*, General Media International claims that it gets about 14 million "hits" a week from computer users tapping into the magazine on the Internet. Microsoft gets some three million hits a week. Does the number of "hits" mean that millions of Internet cruisers are tapping into these ad sites? The answer is no. The so-called "hit" is the unit of measure most commonly cited by companies that have set up Web sites on the Internet, but it does not mean how many people visit a Web site.

Hits count files, not people. Because one file is required for every chunk of text and every graphic element on a Web page, and also because most Web sites contain more than one page, one mouse click may count as a dozen or more "hits" depending on how complex the page is. Therefore, to estimate how many "visits" are made, the number of hits to a page must be divided by the number of files on that page. Based on this, Penthouse is estimated to have received 100,000 visits a day. This could be a significant number if—and only if—it meant 100,000 "people" a day. Unfortunately, however, there is no way of knowing how many "people" actually visited the *Penthouse* Web site.

According to a new survey of 1,000 adults conducted by Eisner & Associates, most Internet users ignore the ads they see online. More than 80 percent of regular Internet users said they either pay no attention to ads or spend only a few seconds on the advertised Web site. Even worse, those belonging to affluent households—a choice market segment for most advertisers—are the least likely to pay attention to online advertising. Some other evalua-

tions, including one by Jupiter Communications (www.jvp.com), show that "click-through" rates are falling. That means people are clicking on an ad and visiting the ad site less frequently than they were in years past.

But there are some encouraging signs for the future of online advertising. Namely, big corporations are continuing to pour money into the effort. Total online ad revenues leaped from $55 million in 1995 to $940 million in 1997 and $1.9 billion in 1998. Although that is a relatively tiny portion of overall ad spending—which is somewhere in the $200 billion ballpark—it is growing rapidly. Total online ad revenues are expected to hit $7.7 billion by 2002. According to Procter & Gamble (www.pg.com), successful online advertising must have the two Rs—richness and reward. It must have the richness of presentation to draw consumers in, and it must reward them with added utility such as extra product information.

Fortunately, the effectiveness of mass media is evaluated by professional rating agencies. Television has Nielsen (www.acnielsen.com) ratings. Radio has Arbitron (internet.arbitron.com) ratings. Now, a joint venture between Nielsen and NetRatings has begun rating the Internet advertising. In 1999, Nielsen and NetRatings recruited a panel of 9,000 U.S. home Internet users. The Nielsen-NetRatings (www.nielsennetratings.com) reports go beyond simply enumerating and profiling a Web site's audience. Enhanced ad-banner tracking capabilities also provide competitive analysis. An advertiser can run reports on the most-viewed banner ads for a given week, the specific sites on which they ran, the demographic profile of the viewers of those banners, and even the way that profile varied for a competitor's campaign or sale.

Sources: Julie Chao, "Tallies of Web-Site Browsers Often Deceive," *Wall Street Journal*, June 21, 1995, B1, B7; Greg Hassell, "Online Advertisers Seeking Attention," *Houston Chronicle*, January 20, 1999, Business Section, 1; Maryann Jones Thompson, "Nielsen Rates the Web," *Industry Standard*, March 29, 1999, 20.

The best sites are typically reserved for the long-term clients, mainly the brewers and tobacco companies (hence one reason for their success in the use of the medium), so that new users may find this a relatively unattractive medium. One interesting public policy question regarding billboards is the large number of alcohol, particularly beer, companies that use billboards to advertise. The billboards could be interpreted as encouraging drivers to drink while driving.

PROMOTIONAL MIX

In the United States, manufacturers spent 11 percent of sales on trade promotions in the 1990s, as opposed to 4 percent in the 1970s.[30] The increased promotional spending suggests increased competition over the years. Allocating the promotional budget in an optimal manner has become increasingly important. The ideal promotional mix (advertising, personal selling, and sales promotion) will be specific to an individual product or service, and to the marketing objectives that have been set for it. In deciding that optimal mix, however, a number of general factors may need to be taken into account.

www.pepsico.com

- **Available budget.** The prime practical determinant of the promotional mix, and one that is often ignored by theory, is usually the amount of money available. For example, if you do not have a budget running well into six or seven figures then you need not consider television. If your budget is below six figures you will need to look at newspapers.

- **Promotional message.** The chosen message will also largely determine the medium to be used. A demonstration of the product will demand either face-to-face selling of some form or television (or movie). A coupon response will only work in the newspaper or by direct mail (or door-to-door). Certain types of promotion can also incur risks for the firm. PepsiCo is facing numerous lawsuits from a botched promotion in the Philippines. In its promotion, Pepsi offered a grand prize of one million pesos (equal to $36,000 U.S. at that time) to the person who found the number "349" printed on a Pepsi bottle cap. As a result of a computer glitch, more than 500,000 bottle caps had the winning number! That number of winners meant that Pepsi potentially owed $18 billion. When Pepsi announced there was an error, rioting took place at its bottling plant near Manila. Pepsi offered a compromise of $19 per winning bottle cap. As a result, $10 million has been paid to 500,000 Filipinos. Nonetheless, 6,000 Filipinos have filed more than 600 civil suits seeking damages, and approximately 5,000 criminal suits have been started by 16,000 others. In addition, anti-Pepsi rallies have taken place in various Philippine cities, and Pepsi plants and trucks continue to be attacked. Although the financial impact of all the suits and attacks was not expected to result in significant financial losses, the impact on Pepsi's image was notable.[31]

- **Complexity of product or service.** Sometimes the product or service will determine the medium. If, as often happens in industrial and capital goods markets, the product is complex or requires significant amounts of service support, then face-to-face selling may be the only route open.

- **Market size and location.** Where the target audience is located will be a determinant of the media chosen. If the audience covers a large part of the population and the budget can afford it, television will usually be the best choice. If it is very specialized, but spread throughout the whole population, then relevant newspapers or even direct mail may be most suitable.

- **Distribution.** Obtaining distribution, in particular through retailers, may often be the key to success. The promotional mix chosen may, therefore, be designed as much to sway the buyers in the distribution chain as the end users.

- **Product life cycle.** The life-cycle stage may be critical. If the product or service is in the introductory stage, building awareness is the main aim, whereas

30. George S. Low and Jakki J. Mohr, "Setting Advertising and Promotion Budgets in Multi-Brand Companies," *Journal of Advertising Research* 39 (January/February 1999): 67–78.
31. "PepsiCo Is Facing Mounting Lawsuits from Botched Promotion in Philippines," *Wall Street Journal*, July 28, 1993, B2.

Exhibit 12.2

Despite the celebratory tone of this photo, taken for the Home Shopping Network's 20th Anniversary in 1997, the company had just settled charges with the Federal Trade Commission of making unsubstantiated advertising claims for four of its therapeutic products. In 1999, HSN received the fifth largest fine ever metted out by the FTC—$1.1 million—for ignoring provisions of the 1996 settlement.

if it is in the growth stage, the requirement is to persuade potential consumers to switch their buying patterns.

- **Competition.** Any marketer needs to consider what the competitors are doing. If the main competitor launches a high-spending television campaign, and you have a low-spending newspaper campaign, then you will have to make some serious decisions. Do you also move into television and probably increase costs to the extent that your profits will be hit? Or do you stay where you are and possibly accept a reduced market share? When advertising abroad, multinational companies must also be aware that they may need to spend more to keep up with local competition. In China, local media owners discriminate against foreigners by charging them up to five times more for ads than they do for local companies.[32]

- **Government regulations.** Although advertising is a form of constitutionally protected free speech in the United States, a state government may restrict truthful advertising about lawful products, such as alcohol and cigarettes, to reduce consumer demand. As Exhibit 12.2 demonstrates, if societal welfare is deemed to outweigh the virtue of free speech, the government may step in to control certain types of advertisement.[33] Advertising regulations vary across the states in the United States and across national boundaries. For example, Sweden, which has a ban on all TV advertising to children under the age of 12, is hoping that it can introduce the same legislation throughout the European Union (EU) when it takes the EU presidency in 2001.[34]

europa.eu.int

- **Ethical issues.** Over and above the government regulations, advertisers should be aware of societal norms for advertising. Is it ethical to promote high-alcohol-content beers in poor neighborhoods? How about an automaker showing its car model cruising at a speed in excess of 80 miles an hour on a road, when in fact driving at that speed is obviously illegal? In particular, recent Calvin Klein jeans ads featuring undressed young models in sexy and suggestive

32. "Advertising in China: Hard Sell."

33. "Liquor Ad Curb Reaches High Court: Law Pits Free Speech Rights, Economic Theory," *Chicago Tribune*, November 2, 1995, 15.

34. Allyson L. Stewart-Allen, "Rules for Reaching Euro Kids Are Changing," *Marketing News*, June 7, 1999, 10.

www.rjrnabisco.com

poses have raised the eyebrows of many observers, including President Bill Clinton.[35] Similarly, R. J. Reynolds announced that it is retiring Joe Camel, ending one of the cigarette industry's most criticized advertising campaigns. The cartoon character, who projected hipness and was accused of luring teenagers to the Camel brand, is being dropped from future print and billboard advertisements and will no longer be emblazoned on T-shirts and hats.[36] While our society tolerates a certain degree of sex and immoral behavior in entertainment and advertising, advertisers' ethical consideration is necessary even if their ads do not violate government laws.

PROMOTION OF SERVICES

Despite the fact that services follow much the same pattern of promotion as products, there may be some differences.

- **Personal selling and employees.** We have already seen that services are usually produced and consumed at the same time, and frequently this is also the time of the sale itself. This means that the sale is often made personally by the staff providing the service. In this way, perhaps the majority of the staff in effect becomes sales personnel. To persuade them to provide the requisite quality of service, "advertising" may have to target them as much as the external customers.

- **Word of mouth.** Because of the problems of demonstrating quality and value and the customer's need to build up trust, word-of-mouth recommendations by loyal customers may be more important, particularly for those services such as personal services, that are based on local branches with relatively small market areas.[37]

www.mcdonalds.com
www.prudential.com

- **Tangibility.** The promotional campaign needs to make the intangible tangible, possibly by the use of symbols such as McDonald's Golden Arches or Prudential Securities' Rock of Gibraltar logo.

www.ibm.com

- **Consistency.** As trust can easily be destroyed by a single bad experience, it is important that the service and its promotion maintain consistency. It must continue to offer and deliver what was promised to the customer. As evidence of the importance of consistency, and in a break from its past, IBM decided in the early 1990s to cease individually tailoring its ad campaigns to each of the European countries. The company tailors the language to the country, but uses the same image and text with its broadcast and print media.

PROMOTION IN NONPROFIT ORGANIZATIONS

Service providers in general have the same promotional needs as manufacturers of physical products, although the detailed messages may be very different. However, employees at nonprofit organizations may fail to see any requirement to sell or promote their products or organizations. A national health service, for example, does not need to advertise for customers, although its private-sector competitors do.

One thing is clear: Such organizations still have to communicate with their customers. They need to let their consumers know that the organization exists, what it offers, and how they can use it, hence the plethora of promotional booklets that social services departments offer to the unemployed. The requirements

35. Kirk Davidson, "Calvin Klein Ads: Bad Ethics, Bad Business," *Marketing News*, November 6, 1995, 11.
36. David Segal, "Joe Camel Fired: Cigarette Ads Were Accused of Luring Youth," *Washington Post*, July 11, 1997, A1.
37. Christopher H. Lovelock, *Product Plus: How Product + Service = Competitive Advantage* (New York: McGraw-Hill, 1994).

imposed by these communications are often indistinguishable from conventional service industry promotions. Indeed, government information campaigns, such as those to combat cigarette smoking and drug addiction, or United Way campaigns for charitable contributions, can dominate the mass media.

www.unitedway.com

ADVERTISING PLAN

As with all marketing activities, objectives must be set for advertising and should include the following:

- **Who and where.** It is critical to define the target audience as exactly as possible. Defining the target audience allows the media buyers in the advertising agency to plan for an economical coverage and build up the media schedule to give a cumulative coverage of the desired audience. It is also important to agree what percentage coverage of this desired audience will be acceptable.

- **When.** Timing needs to be balanced with the requirement for each separate campaign to have sufficient impact. Also, it is important to note the difference in seasons between the northern and southern hemispheres. In the northern hemisphere we enjoy a cold December, whereas people in the southern hemisphere celebrate their "green" Christmas in the midst of their summer.

- **What and how.** The message that the agency's creative team will encapsulate has to be the right message for the product and the audience; thus, the impact required may also determine the medium used.

The most important aspect of an advertising plan is that it should be quantified as much as possible so that the subsequent performance of the advertising itself can be measured. If affordable, both awareness and attitude should be measured after each campaign. Unless awareness was already very high, the advertising should have achieved a measurable increase; it should also have brought about the planned attitude shifts.

ADVERTISING BUDGETS

The average cost for 30 seconds of airtime during the Super Bowl is $1.3 million. Budweiser, Coke, Toyota, and GTE logos ring the stadium. They also appear everywhere a logo can fit. Sprint logos are on coaches' headsets. Nike logos are on players' shoulders. Overhead is the Budweiser blimp. Even at $1.3 million per 30-second slot, advertisers jostle for the opportunity to be seen. The big players are Pepsi, Budweiser, Visa, and Nike. There are also the usual assortment of walk-ons—companies such as Autobytel, Tabasco, and Iomega, which try to leap into the national consciousness with one outrageous investment.[38] Advertising can be very expensive.

Ideally, advertising should be set on the basis of profit maximization models. Thus, in theory, the demand curve for a product or service against advertising expenditure is plotted, in much the same way as is that of the more traditional demand against price. Needless to say, however, there are very few products or services for which this ideal can be achieved. Where it is an option, where there are lengthy series of historical data, and where competitors are consistent in

www.budweiser.com
www.coke.com
www.toyota.com
www.gte.com
www.sprint.com
www.nike.com
www.pepsiworld.com
www.visa.com
www.autobytel.com
www.tabasco.com
www.iomega.com

advertising should be set
on the basis of
profit maximization models

---

38. Mark Johnson and Tom Nelson, "Super Bowl: The Real Winners," *Campaign*, February 6, 1998, 28.

their actions, it is sometimes attained by sophisticated (computerized) "regression analyses." Sometimes, more pragmatically, the shape of the curve is guessed, judgmentally, by the experts involved. Then marginal analysis (the same principle as marginal costing) can be applied, and advertising can be increased just up to the point at which the additional income offsets the additional costs. Unfortunately, due to the inherent complexities of promotion (and its long-term investment impact), such calculations are rarely possible.

More generally, the advertising budget is determined by even more basic means, such as:

- **Affordability.** The management may decide on what they think is a reasonable figure, often based on last year's budget or on whatever is left over when the expected revenue is offset against the projected costs and the required profits.

- **Percentage of sales.** This is virtually the classic method, where a fixed percentage of sales revenue is allocated. It is fast and easy to calculate, but does not take into account any changes in market conditions—and perhaps implies that sales create advertising, rather than the other way around. It is essentially the same problem as found in new product development.

- **Competitive parity.** In competitive markets, the share of the advertising budget is often equated with the share of the market. There is evidence from the U.S. automobile industry, for example, that advertising shares do broadly follow market shares. It is advertising that creates the market share, rather than the other way around.[39] As a result, large-share competitors may end up allocating more to their advertising budget than necessary, while small-share companies may underinvest in advertising.

- **Objective and task.** This simply asks what needs to be done (although with carefully calculated and quantified objectives), and then costs it. Although this method is most logical, it is not extensively used.

As suggested earlier, it would be ideal if a general model could be found that allowed advertisers to forecast the sales outcomes of their advertising expenditure, but in most markets the complexity of the other factors involved precludes this. So there is, perhaps, some excuse for the rules of thumb previously described. In practice, many marketers use all of these techniques, weighting the budget by the one that seems most applicable to the task in hand.

One survey[40] shows that only three approaches are in common use:

Percentage of sales	44 percent
Affordability	21 percent
Objective and task	18 percent
All others	17 percent

The approach may be more subversive, as Thomas Bonoma reports:

The egalitarianism in resource allocation creates "global mediocrity"; marketing that is excellent at nothing. Because the company spreads its resources thinly over many programs, the most vital marketing projects don't get the funding and attention they need. The creative marketing manager subverts this parody of equality by allocating resources on the basis of merit, often through budget switching of loose "shoe-box" money.[41]

39. David W. Schuman, Jan H. Hathcote, and Susan West, "Corporate Advertising in America: A Review of Published Studies on Use, Measurement, and Effectiveness," *Journal of Advertising* 20 (September 1991): 35–54.
40. Keith Crosier, "Promotion," in *The Marketing Book*, ed. M. J. Baker (Butterworth Heinemann, 1987).
41. Thomas V. Bonoma, "Marketing Subversives," *Harvard Business Review* 64 (November/December 1986): 113–118.

The wise marketer also monitors what is happening throughout the year, as the various campaigns progress, to see if the budgets need reviewing. In any case, marketers will conduct formal reviews on a quarterly basis.

RESEARCHING ADVERTISING EFFECTIVENESS

The marketing research process is frequently used to test individual pieces of advertising, newspaper advertisements, and (in particular) commercials before they are used to ensure that they actually meet the objectives that have been set for them.

The coverage achieved by the advertising will almost certainly be tracked directly if television commercials are used, as ACNielsen research monitors the performance of all television advertising. In the case of newspaper advertising, it is sometimes considered worthwhile to conduct separate research to measure the proportion of the target audience that has actually seen the advertisement and, more importantly, can remember seeing it. The same techniques can also be used for commercials (whereas the Nielsen results are limited to which television sets are switched on and who is in the room at the time, which may not always give the result that the advertiser is seeking). It is normal to monitor any advertising campaign's performance against the objectives set for it.

www.acnielsen.com

In general, there are three main advertising objectives: building awareness, creating favorable attitudes, and maintaining customer loyalty.

1. **Building awareness (informing).** The first task of any advertising is to make the audiences appreciate that the product or service exists and to explain exactly what it is. *Spontaneous awareness* is measured as the proportion of those who can remember the brand without an prompting. *Prompted awareness*, which is usually much higher, measures the proportion who can recognize the brand when a prompt card (listing its name amongst other competitive brands) is shown to the respondents. *Recall tests* explore what consumers can remember about the elements within the advertising (in the case of aided recall, with the benefit of being shown the advertisement).

2. **Creating favorable attitudes (persuading).** The next objective, and the one that preoccupies most advertisers, is to create favorable attitudes toward the brand that will eventually lead the customer to switch their purchasing patterns. Most advertisements are normally designed to have an impact on specific attitudes. Ideally, in the most sophisticated approaches, the research should check that the brand has achieved the new position that was set as the objective.

3. **Maintaining customer loyalty (reinforcing).** One of the tasks that is often forgotten is maintaining the loyalty of existing customers, who will almost always represent the main source of future sales. It is known that maintaining loyal customers is more profitable than gaining new customers. The acid test of advertising is the additional sales generated. Due to the multitude of other factors usually involved, this is normally a difficult, if not impossible, causal measurement to make. However, it is an exercise that should be undertaken, no matter how approximate the results may be.

> maintaining loyal customers **is more profitable** than gaining new customers

The question "Just how effective is advertising?" is an age-old pursuit of any business organization. Lord Leverhulme, the founder of Unilever, had made the famous comment that he was sure that half of his advertising did not work—but

www.unilever.com

the problem was that he did not know which half. This view is reinforced by Abraham and Lodish, whose research showed that only 46 percent of advertising campaigns for established brands showed a positive impact on sales, while this ratio was slightly higher at 59 percent for new products.[42]

One researcher took the 200 most-praised ads from around the world for the years 1992 and 1993 to see whether they had increased sales, market share, or brand awareness. Overall he found that 80 percent of the ads were successful by using one of those measures. However, it should be noted with caution that most of the data from the study came from the ad agencies themselves.[43]

Similarly, there is an increased public distrust of both the entertainment and news media, media that receive billions of advertising dollars every year. Parents are highly concerned about sex and violence on TV and in movies. An alarming 70 percent of the public think that those who control the TV industry do not share their moral values. And 63 percent said news reporting is often improperly influenced by the media's desire to make a profit. The big question that cannot be dodged by marketers is: How can trust be nurtured via media that are becoming saturated by mistrust? Marketers first need to think about how well the content of their advertising responds to consumer demand for honesty and impartiality. As it stands, few measure up: Airline ads headlining one-way fares rather than round trips; car leasing deals where the catch is in the details of hidden costs and restrictions; telecommunications companies that sometimes steal our business without even telling us. Marketers are well advised to choose a medium based on its ability to reinforce the reliability, honesty, and integrity of the message.[44]

COUPON RESPONSE.   One particularly useful measure of the effectiveness of newspaper advertising, along with that of direct mail, can be implemented where the purpose of the advertising is to elicit a direct response, typically in terms of motivating the reader to ask for further information through a coupon included in the advertisement or mailed material.

Each such advertisement or mailing can then be given a code, the usual means being to include a dummy department number (which corresponds to, say, the publication used) as part of the mailing address. The response obtained from each of the publications (or each of the mail packages) can then be measured accurately, at least in terms of the percentage coupon response rate. Of course, that may not be an appropriate measure if what is primarily being attempted is a shift in attitudes.

This technique can also be used to test, and directly compare, two or more advertisements where the media owner offers split runs: The overall print run is split geographically or the television is run by regions. Comparison of the results for each part of the test may give a good indication of performance, although geographical variations will need to be allowed for (an may even be partly compensated for by "flip-flop testing," where the test is repeated with the regions reversed). Coupon response my not always be the best measure of the performance that you want to gauge. For example, long-term image building and brand loyalty will not be demonstrated. Despite such a limitation, many package and consumer durable goods companies, such as Procter & Gamble and Panasonic, frequently use this method.

www.pg.com
www.panasonic.com

42. Abraham and Lodish, "Getting the Most out of Advertising and Promotion."
43. "Scientific Moonshine," *Economist*, June 25, 1994, 65.
44. John Bissell, "How Much Do We Trust the Messengers?" *Brandweek*, March 16, 1998, 18.

SELECTING AN ADVERTISING AGENCY

We have seen that many promotional activities, especially those in the area of advertising, demand specialized skills. In the United States and the United Kingdom, few suppliers are likely to find these specialist skills in-house. In France and Japan, however, it is reported that almost half of all advertising is handled within the advertiser's own organization. The choice of an advertising agency represents a major strategic decision for any organization because that agency will be almost solely responsible for a number of key marketing activities. The success of the organization will thus come to depend on the success of that agency and on the relationship with it.

There are directories that list advertising agencies, the most generally available being the *Standard Directory of Advertising Agencies* (Skokie, Ill.: National Register Publication Co.) for domestic advertisers and the *Standard Directory of International Advertisers and Advertising Agencies* (Skokie, Ill.: National Register Publication Co.) for international advertisers. The equivalent for direct mail organizations are the *Directory of Mailing List Sources* (Chicago: Dartnell Co.) and the *Direct Marketing List Source* (Wilmette, Ill.: Standard Rate & Data Service). Probably the wisest move is to find someone who has had firsthand experience of a particular agency. If all else fails, you should consider contacting some of their existing clients, but beware—for legal and other reasons, few clients will criticize their suppliers, even if they are so dissatisfied that they are about to move to another agency.

The next step depends on the size of your budget. If you have one of the relatively few multimillion dollar accounts, then you can expect half a dozen agencies to compete for your business (although it its normally recommended that you limit the number, finally making a formal presentation to three or four). Each will put considerable effort, and possibly thousands of dollars of investment, into producing their idea of what your new advertising platforms should be, although the client may well be expected to fund the direct costs of such presentations. The client's role in this scenario is to examine the material, and the personnel involved, and determine which package best meets the marketing needs of the organization, as well as which group the client's marketing staff will be happiest working with.

A client with a smaller budget may find that the burden is on him or her to persuade an agency to take an interest. Anything less than $80,000 per year (of which $30,000 will go for service charges alone) may be almost impossible to place. Given that the business is minimally attractive, most smaller agencies will be prepared to send the potential account team along to deliver a standard presentation, which will typically cover what they have achieved, especially in terms of creative treatments, for their existing clients. Again it might be wise, and fairer to the contenders, to limit the number, committing their resources to such a presentation to just three or four agencies. In this case, the match of this "house style," along with the rapport with the account team (and, hopefully, the reports from other clients contacted) will form the basis of the selection.

One important element in any discussions will be, of course, exactly what charges will be incurred. Many agencies now charge on a fee basis, as well as receiving their traditional media discounts, so it is well worth spelling out exactly what these will be. Will there be an overall service charge? There will almost certainly be charges for the production of the blocks for newspaper advertisements and sometimes even for the finished artwork. Understandably, the cost of commercials (which may run in to six figures) will almost always be passed on. A typical breakdown of where the money goes is shown in Table 12.2.

Table 12.2

A typical advertising agency account

Total billed to clients	$67,000,000
Less:	
Paid to media and suppliers	57,000,000
Gross income	10,000,000
Expenses:	
Payroll—principal owners	800,000
Payroll—staff	4,472,000
Nonpayroll expenses	2,728,000
Gross profit	2,000,000
Less:	
Bonus—principal owners	250,000
Bonus—staff	950,000
Profit sharing—principal owners	50,000
Profit sharing—staff	250,000
Profit before taxes	500,000
Less:	
Taxes	75,000
Net profit	425,000

The cost of the creativity is small compared with the cost of the media and minute compared with the rewards you hope the advertising will bring. It is, therefore, very worthwhile indeed to buy the best creativity that money can buy. The main practical advice must be to invest the time and effort necessary to make the best choice, and to learn, if necessary, exactly how each of the agencies on the short list operates. After all, they may largely determine your own marketing success.

The following six stages are suggested for agency selection:[45]

1. *Define the need*—summarize (in one page) what is needed and what tasks are to be performed
2. *Desk research*—check the opinions of others, including existing clients (as well as trade organizations and references in the advertising trade journal)
3. *Formulate a short list*—eliminate those agencies handling competitors' business or not offering the services wanted
4. *Evaluation*—decide on the checklist (detailing the key questions to be asked) to be used in the evaluation
5. *Narrow the selection*—assess each agency and reduce the short list to two or three before visiting each agency several times
6. *Final selections and appointment*—agree to terms with the agency chosen

---

45. John Winkler, "Marketing and the Function of Advertising Within It," in *The Practice of Advertising*, ed. N. A. Hart and J. O. O'Connor (Oxford: Butterworth Heinemann, 1983).

SUMMARY

Advertising represents the *talking* part of the dialogue referred to at the beginning of the book. In practice, it is a much more complex process, as is hinted at by the encoding/decoding model.

However, it is just one element of the promotional mix; which includes personal selling and word of mouth, particularly in the case of services. It may be just as applicable to many nonprofit organizations. It is also, increasingly, a vehicle for corporate promotion. In all these cases it is a pull technique (persuading consumers to pull the product through retailers), rather than push (selling, by sales promotions, for instance, into the channels).

Promotion provides a message to create awareness, interest, understanding, attitudes, and purchase decisions. The message should ideally contain a unique selling proposition, although it should also be consistent with past campaigns. It may be advisable to recognize that this message is also passed by word of mouth, with opinion leaders playing an important role.

Media selection and buying require specialized knowledge and skills, and essentially aim to achieve satisfactory (cumulative) coverage with the requisite opportunities to see (OTS) at an economic cost. Whereas different markets may require different kinds of media to accomplish the same advertising objective, globally minded companies are increasingly employing pattern standardization or globally standardized ads to develop a global image for their products and to reduce advertising costs.[46]

Like other budgets, advertising budgets are determined by a number of means, based on affordability, a percentage of sales, competitive parity, and objective and task. Advertising effectiveness can be measured against its objectives, including building awareness, creating favorable attitudes, and maintaining customer loyalty.

Advertising budgets determine whether or not a company should use an advertising agency. Use of an advertising agency represents a strategic decision because the success of the organization will depend largely on the success of that agency. Therefore, careful agency selection is important.

QUESTIONS FOR REVIEW

1. What are the main elements of the promotional mix? Which elements may be push and which pull? What are the advantages and disadvantages of personal selling?

2. How does advertising on the Internet affect other forms of promotion?

3. What is meant by encoding? What are the main functions of advertising? What does the advertising message need to do to carry out these functions?

4. Is a USP compatible with consistency? What role do opinion leaders play?

5. What are the main measures of media performance? Why are the important? What are the differences between the two most popular forms of media?

6. How may advertising budgets be set? How may performance be measured?

46. Dana L. Alden, Jan-Benedict E. M. Steenkamp, and Rajeev Batra, "Brand Positioning through Advertising in Asia, North America, and Europe: The Role of Global Consumer Culture," *Journal of Marketing* 63 (January 1999): 75–87.

QUESTIONS FOR DISCUSSION

1. Deregulation is forcing many natural gas utilities to take a good look at every aspect of their business, including customer communication. Gas companies will be hard pressed to maintain their customer base without paying serious attention to when, why, and how they communicate with customers. Customer communication used to mean providing consumer information, sending utility bills, and making announcements in times of emergency. These functions are still important, but they have been joined by a new need: building relationships. Now customer communication includes marketing, brand promotion, image enhancement, and—perhaps most important—eliciting information from customers themselves. What media can utilities use to deliver the right messages to the right audiences? What combination of old and new techniques do you suggest they use in an environment of advancing technology and exciting changes in vehicles?

2. An experiment was conducted in which subjects were exposed to a special shopping section of a newspaper in the Buffalo, New York, area containing news stories, ads, and coupons for more than 30 area retailers. News stories outperformed the marketer-dominated sources of information (ads and coupons) in recall and amount read. Can you suggest a few factors that can account for this?

3. Procter & Gamble is changing the advertising strategy for its Pantene Pro-V with a new TV campaign. Breaking away from using supermodels, the commercials feature "everyday" young women with no professional modeling experience. The 22-year-old star of the campaign, who is now the regular face of Pantene, was found in a nationwide model search competition. The first commercial she stars in also features the runners-up. P&G's idea is to use real people to prove that anyone can become the star of a Pantene commercial because everyone's hair has the potential to shine. Do you think that this switch in the advertising strategy of P&G to break away from using supermodels will improve sales of Pantene Pro-V? Provide your reasons one way or the other. You may want to use the concept of brand positioning to check the consistency of the advertising message.

4. What international cultural taboos can you think of that may influence the uniformity of advertising content? If it was possible for an advertisement not to offend any culture's sensitivities, would it still be an interesting or effective ad?

5. Why is it that sometimes you can remember the ad but not the product, service, or company being advertised? What can advertisers do to limit this occurrence?

6. Part of the way in which a firm adds value for the customer is by keeping costs and prices as low as possible. Unfortunately, advertising can be quite expensive. What is the proper trade-off to the firm in terms of keeping costs and prices low and advertising sufficient to increase product awareness?

7. Assume you make a product or service with a fairly complex message and your media choices are limited to newspaper, television, radio, billboards, and cyberspace. What percent of your advertising budget would you allocate for each medium if your product is in its (a) introduction, (b) growth, (c) maturity, or (d) decline stage.

8. As a PR person or salesperson for a pharmaceutical company, you market your wares to hospitals, doctors' groups, HMOs, and so on. Assuming that (1) each potential customer (the health professional) will purchase the same amount of product from your company for his or her own clientele, and that (2) you cannot visit every health professional, who would you target and why? What is the marketing term for such a group?

9. The number of new users of your consumer product has been consistently high over the five-month period of your new ad campaign. However, the overall level of sales has not increased much. Can you be certain from this information whether the problem is with the ad campaign or the product? What are your hypotheses? How urgent is the situation, and how much of your resources should be allocated to it? What steps would you consider?

FURTHER READINGS

Alden, Dana L., Jan-Benedict E. M. Steenkamp, and Rajeev Batra. "Brand Positioning through Advertising in Asia, North America, and Europe: The Role of Global Consumer Culture." *Journal of Marketing* 63 (January 1999): 75–87.

Bly, Robert W. *Advertising Manager's Handbook*, 2d ed. Upper Saddle River, N.J.: Prentice Hall, 1998.

Cunningham, Peggy. "Ethics and Manipulation in Advertising: Answering a Flawed Indictment." *Academy of Marketing Science Journal* 27 (winter 1999): 107–108.

Czerniawski, Richard D., and Michael W. Maloney. *Creating Brand Loyalty: The Management of Power Positioning and Really Great Advertising.* New York: AMACOM, 1999.

Hoque, Abeer Y., and Gerald L. Lohse. "An Information Search Cost Perspective for Designing Interfaces for Electronic Commerce." *Journal of Marketing Research* 36 (August 1999): 387–394.

Low, George S., and Jakki J. Mohr. "Setting Advertising and promotion Budgets in Multi-Brand Companies." *Journal of Advertising Research* 39 (January/February 1999): 67–78.

Ogilvy, David. *Confessions of an Advertising Man,* rev. ed. New York: Atheneum, 1988.

Murray, George B., and John R. G. Jenkins. "The Concept of 'Effective Reach' in Advertising." *Journal of Advertising Research* 32 (May/June 1992): 34–42.

Shapiro, Arthur. "Advertising vs. Promotion: Which Is Which?" *Journal of Advertising Research* 30 (June/July 1990): 13–17.

Vakratsas, Demetrios, and Tim Ambler. "How Advertising Works: What Do We Really Know?" *Journal of Marketing* 63 (January 1999): 26–43.

chapter

13

Direct Marketing, Sales Promotion, and Public Relations

A firm can make use of other forms of communication and promotion besides advertising. Some are established, whereas others are newly emerging as part of the revolutionary growth of information technology. Direct marketing, sales promotion, and public relations complement advertising and personal selling. The most important objective for these complementary promotional activities is to identify and approach prospective customers with a promotional message as precisely as possible. Direct marketing activities are substantially increasing with the arrival of new data collection techniques and available computing power for analyzing the massive amount of customer data. Direct mail and telemarketing are such examples. At the same time, many traditional sales promotion efforts that support members of the distribution channel continue to flourish. Sales promotion includes various forms of promotional pricing, such as discounts and coupons, and nonprice promotional techniques, such as free gifts and sampling. Other promotional activities, such as sponsorships and trade shows, also provide broad marketing support. The press and public relations are also of growing importance in an era in which the firm's relationship to society at large becomes an increasingly relevant factor in the acceptance of its products. The importance of the relationship between the firm and the customer becomes even more clear in Manager's Corner 13.1, which illustrates that the success of firms increasingly depends on effective database marketing.

Manager's Corner 13.1

Precision marketing is the future

Several experts in the area of database marketing contend that companies without a marketing database will be going out of business within a few years. Says Tracy Emerick, president of Taurus Direct Marketing (taurus.receptive .com), "With a finite number of business sites and households out there, you can't afford not to have a lock on your customers." The CEO of a small industrial company, who remains anonymous so that competitors won't catch on, believes that "you're an idiot if you don't at least use some databasing techniques. It's an easy way to access and segment information about your customers." The CEO argues that databasing is not just for megacorporations: "It makes more sense for small companies, because the president or owner is likely to be the company's chief salesperson as well." Backed by reliable information about people genuinely interested in the company's product, the president can concentrate on the prospects and customers most likely to buy.

Despite the strategic advantages, a considerable number of firms lack databases. "I'm shocked at how much bad marketing is going on," says one consultant referring to this problem. "It's still a wasteland out there." Even high-tech companies that presumably should be leading the way haven't gotten to first base in databasing. What, then, is this concept that, while seeming to embody the right stuff for success in a customer-focused era, has thus far failed to capture the fancy of top management at most small and medium-sized companies? According to Arthur M. Hughes, author of *Strategic Database Marketing*, it means "managing a computerized relational database system that collects relevant data about customers and prospects, which enables you to better service and establish long-term relationships with them." Done right, says Hughes, databasing helps build loyalty, reduce attrition, and increase customer satisfaction and sales. "The database is used to target offerings to customers and prospects, enabling you to send the right message at the right time to the right people."

Few people have a handle on who the company's best customers are and, even more important, why they buy. "If you want to develop long-term relationships, you've got to know how you acquire customers," remarks Frederick Timmerman, executive director of corporate research for United States Automobile Association. Timmerman believes that developing trust is a gradual process. Once someone feels comfortable talking to a rep, it's possible to ask open-ended questions that truly enrich a database. "We ask members who else they're doing business with, who's their banker," says Timmerman, "to see how we compare with them." Knowing where cus-

tomers are coming from is a big step toward knowing where they are going, which, its advocates proclaim, is the destiny of database marketing.

Randall Bean, a vice president with database builder Harte-Hanks Data Technologies, points out that as technology makes it possible to communicate with likely buyers on a one-on-one basis, people are referring to the process as "database-driven marketing." A few years ago, marketers might have recoiled at the thought of digitized information driving them to do anything, but Bean says that where he once dealt entirely with banks and other financial services marketers, he now has clients in 15 major industries. "It's much more than just people climbing on a bandwagon," he says. "Databasing enables management to measure the effectiveness of the entire business. This could involve anything from examining how a company creates a new business to looking at opportunities for cross-selling and identifying the best prospects for new products."

Source: Martin Everett, "Know Why They Buy," *Sales & Marketing Management* 146 (December 1994): 67.

PRECISION MARKETING

Until recently suppliers in mass markets were unable to communicate one-on-one with their customers. The cost of employing a direct sales force was, and still is, prohibitive. What has changed is the increasing availability of much more detailed information on large numbers of individual customers—together with the processing power to handle these data. By using data management, firms can now adapt their marketing efforts to individual customers without face-to-face contact. Although such direct marketing does not provide for personalized interaction, it can achieve the benefits of personalization by precisely tailoring the sale to the individual's specific needs. The key to such precision marketing is detailed information about individual customers. The firm can obtain such information by making use of the increasing availability of secondary data and combining those with specific data collected at the point of sale.

AVAILABILITY AND CONSOLIDATION OF SECONDARY DATA

More data are becoming available from existing sources. Summary census data are now available in computerized form. Many organizations are making their own databases and membership lists available for sale. In addition, new techniques and tools have been developed to consolidate various databases and to provide a multidimensional picture of current and prospective customers. For example, the market information provided by consumers who return warranty cards to different suppliers constitutes a useful database to identify the profile of purchasers, and it can be used to predict the purchasing behavior of prospective customers. In the longer term, the consolidation of very large databases will likely provide quite detailed information about many activities of most individuals in the population.

Indeed, many businesses are commissioning research and gathering information from a broad spectrum of companies within the marketing services industry. Buyers of research now have a wide choice of suppliers, from traditional market research agencies to management consultants, advertising agencies, media planners, direct marketing agencies, field marketing companies, database specialists, and universities. At the same time, many companies are investing more in their own databases and in-house expertise. Market research firms no longer have the monopoly on research.

The fast-growing database sector is enticing research buyers with in-depth lifestyle and demographic data and access to large numbers of consumers. Experian, for example, allows companies such as Procter & Gamble, Coca-Cola, and Tetley Tea to pose questions to hundreds of thousands of consumers through its quarterly Canvasse Lifestyle survey. It is a cost-effective way to locate niche consumer groups.

www.pg.com
www.coke.com
www.tetleygroup.com

This approach recognizes that research—no matter how in-depth and exact—has to be usable in a business context to be of value. We all have as much information as we need. Through the Internet, we can gain access to information that previously would have taken us a long time to obtain. Information itself no longer provides marketing executives any measurable advantage. It is marketing executives' ability to use that information effectively that provides a powerful advantage.[1]

POINT-OF-SALE DATA

One powerful tool has been the introduction of electronic point-of-sale (EPOS) systems by major retailers. Using EPOS, details of an individual transaction, but not the identity of an individual purchaser, can be tracked. By linking EPOS data with payment information (credit card or electronic funds transfer data), it becomes possible to relate these transactions to specific individuals. This way retailers in particular can build up a very detailed picture of the buying habits of individual customers. A number of organizations, ranging from direct mail houses to domestic appliance retailers, already have detailed customer information available in their existing records. For example, Sears, Roebuck and Co. uses the computerized database information on its 40 million customers to promote special offers to specific target segments.

www.sears.com

The next step is the conversion of such "passive" databases into active real-time ones that reflect the latest in purchasing trends. Food and department stores have developed customer loyalty cards. These cards, which are used at the checkout counter, provide a small discount to customers and allow the store to meticulously track what products are purchased when, together with customer preferences and behavior. The Seiyu chain in Japan, for example, uses this information to determine most of its stocking policy.[2] Of equal importance is that this information allows retailers to understand what customers did *not* buy. Retailers can then take steps to persuade customers to buy something new and different.[3] Overall, such precision marketing approaches result in the mass customization of markets, where a large number of customers can be reached and treated individually.[4] The result is a different perspective of markets, as shown in Figure 13.1.

www.seiyu.co.jp

1. Rachel Miller, "Tailoring Data to Get the Real Story," *Marketing,* June 10, 1999, 23.
2. Michael R. Czinkota and Jon Woronoff, *Unlocking Japan's Markets* (Chicago: Probus, 1991), 137.
3. Penelope Ody, "Many Happy Returns from Loyalty Schemes?," *Super Marketing* (October 1992): 32.
4. S. M. Davis, *Future Perfect* (Reading, Mass.: Addison Wesley Longman, 1987), 168–169.

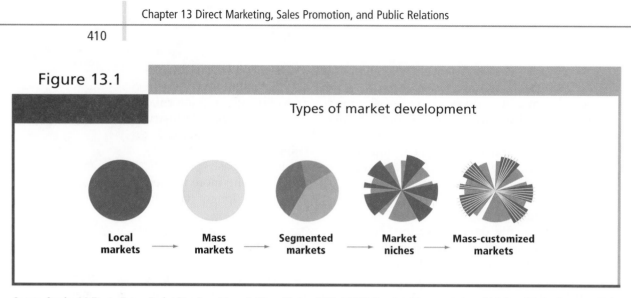

Figure 13.1

Types of market development

Local markets → Mass markets → Segmented markets → Market niches → Mass-customized markets

Source: Stanley M. Davis, *Future Perfect* (Reading, Mass.: Addison Wesley, 1987). © 1987. Reprinted by permission of Addison Wesley Longman Publishing Company, Inc.

MANIPULATION OF DATA

www.firstunion.com

www.ibm.com

The theory of precision marketing is simple: One matches the requisite marketing approach to the individual. For example, First Union has decided to triple the capacity of its customer data warehouse to 27 terabytes, enabling the company to deliver customized marketing to its 16 million customers. By upgrading its system to one of the largest commercial installations of an IBM supercomputer of its type in the world, First Union will add customer information from its five 1998 acquisitions and expand the warehouse to include small business and commercial customers. First Union is able to use the information it collects on both its individual and business customers and their needs to precisely target its banking services as well as to check on their credit status.[5] A salesperson, in face-to-face contact, follows much the same process. Until recently precision marketers found manipulation of the vast quantities of data to be an impossible task, but now computers can easily handle the amount of information. Unfortunately, computers cannot make decisions without a very elaborate set of rules to govern every possible situation. The main solution to this problem lies in the development of expert systems. Expert systems teach computers how to make the necessary decisions by learning from experience and by using artificial intelligence-based approaches. Through such approaches, patterns can be recognized, and deviations from these patterns can be highlighted. For example, American Express assesses the spending habits of its customers on an ongoing basis. For routine expenditures, computerized authorization can be granted. If a request comes for an atypical expenditure, such a request can be flagged and questioned by a representative. Scrutiny does not need to confine itself to unusually high expenditures but can also be exercised in instances where the type of purchase reported does not match the previous purchasing pattern of the client. As a result, clients can be better protected from unauthorized card use, and the number of claims can be reduced. A few weeks after his return from Rio de Janeiro, Brazil, one of the coauthors of this book received a surprise call at home (in the United States) from Citibank about a possible misuse of his credit card. The card was being used to purchase expen-

> The theory of precision marketing is simple: One matches the requisite marketing approach to the individual.

www.americanexpress.com

www.citibank.com

---

5. Craig McGuire, "First Union to Boost Warehouse Capacity," *Wall Street & Technology* 17 (July 1999): 14.

sive furniture on one day and to pay for a hospital bill the following day in Niterol, a city across the bay from Rio de Janeiro. Obviously, someone in Brazil obtained a credit card carbon copy and started using the credit card number for payment. The continued illegal use of the credit card was fortunately suspended.

DIRECT MARKETING DELIVERY SYSTEMS

A precision marketing system also needs to be capable of delivering the promotional effort where it is needed. Many forms of media claim to deliver tightly defined audiences, and some of the specialist and trade magazines do exactly that. However, the traditional minimum group size that can be targeted is often no smaller than an individual town. Such a general targeting is still far too diffuse for precision marketing. Yet technology makes it increasingly possible to target the individual customer or subscriber, for example, by including magazine text designed for one specific person. Significant progress in this area has been made in the field of direct mail.

DIRECT MAIL COMMUNICATION

Direct mail is a large part of the overall direct marketing effort and can make an important contribution to targeted precision marketing campaigns. Direct mail has become very popular as personal data have become easily available, thanks to proliferation of electronic transactions, including cash register scanner data, use of credit cards, magazine subscriptions, and purchases on the Internet. Much coveted information about consumers' purchase patterns, preferences, habits, and purchasing power is readily available and marketed to companies that want to use such information. Direct mail has become an important personalized means of advertisement, particularly in a business-to-business environment. According to research by Hewlett-Packard, however, the average manager has a backlog of around 12 hours' work, so it is little wonder that agencies attempting to get the attention of busy marketers or suppliers hoping to influence agency decision makers still face an uphill struggle in their direct mail activity.[6]

www.hp.com

At the heart of most direct mail campaigns is the idea of making better use of time for the sales force. By providing sales personnel with more and better-qualified leads, they will be able to make more and higher-value sales.[7] One effective way to generate prospects for the face-to-face industrial sales force is to undertake mass mailings. A response rate of 1 or 2 percent for such mailings is considered good; when mailing to specialized markets with a particularly powerful message, the response rate can reach almost 10 percent. Whatever part of this very wide range a mailing falls into, direct mailers typically distribute large quantities to obtain reasonable numbers of prospects—it is a numbers game with a vengeance. As with all forms of promotion, one has to be clear about specific objectives before conducting any mailing. Most mailings are designed to produce immediate sales inquiries. One may decide to set specific objectives, such as attracting people to a free seminar or offering a free sample in order to "buy inquiries." Alternatively, a mailing may be from a local florist to customers reminding them of an upcoming anniversary or

> As with all forms of promotion, **one has to be clear about specific** objectives before conducting any mailing.

---

6. Holly Acland, "Putting Direct Mail through its Paces," *Marketing*, August 26, 1999, 27.
7. Dean Rieck, "How to Get Leads," *Target Marketing* 18 (April 1995): 14–15.

birthday, or from a shoe store that lets its big-footed customers know about a new shipment that includes extra-large sizes. There are many ways of achieving results, but it is important to know exactly what is to be achieved.

ADVANTAGES AND DISADVANTAGES OF DIRECT MAIL

www.porsche.com

Like all other marketing tools, direct mail has advantages and disadvantages, as summarized in Table 13.1. The most important advantage of direct mail is that it can be directed at a specific, individual customer. For example, Porsche was able to target the 300,000 Americans most likely to spend $75,000 on a German car. Direct mail can also address the customer personally. If the full benefits of precision marketing are exploited, it can be directly tailored to his or her needs and modified based on prior experience, as recorded on the database. Needless to say, the Porsche mailing was elaborately personalized. Because of its direct response nature, the marketing campaign can also be tested and varied to obtain optimal results.

> A direct mail campaign . . .
> **can circumvent barriers**
> to market entry.

Responses can be added to the database, allowing future mailings to be even better targeted. A direct mail campaign can be mounted quickly on a wide variety of topics within an overall promotional campaign. In addition, it can circumvent barriers to market entry. Particularly during international expansion, firms may encounter uncooperative distribution channels that are unwilling to carry their merchandise. By using direct mail, such as catalog sales, distribution roadblocks can be circumvented and direct consumer acceptance secured.

www.foliomag.com

A prime disadvantage of direct mail is its cost. For example, according to the 1999 Consumer Magazine/Circulation Management survey conducted by *Folio*, continuing declines in both direct mail response and newsstand sales—all coupled with increases in costs—are hurting the consumer magazine subscription business. The current direct mail average gross response rate is 4 percent and is down from 6.8 percent in 1997. Furthermore, sending larger mail volumes to lists that pull lower response rates naturally translates into higher acquisition costs. The cost of acquiring a new customer by direct mail shot up by 60 percent, from $15.66 in 1997 to $25.16 in 1998.[8]

The problem is exacerbated if one uses mailing lists that contain old or duplicate names. Lists are expensive to "clean" and may even offend customers. Perhaps

Table 13.1	Advantages and disadvantages of direct mail

Advantages	Disadvantages
Specific targeting	Cost
Personalization	Poor-quality lists
Variation	Image problems
Accumulation of information	
Flexibility	
Circumvention of barriers	

---

8. Karlene Lukovitz and Joanna Lowenstein, "Rising Costs, Poor Response—And Promise," *Folio: The Magazine for Magazine Management* 28 (May 1999): 49–56.

the greatest disadvantage, certainly in terms of consumer marketing, is the poor image that direct mail currently holds. It is commonly described as *junk mail*. Mailings have too often been poorly planned, poorly targeted, and poorly presented. As a result, many recipients see direct mail as an invasion of their privacy. In the United States, for example, more than 430 bills have been introduced in federal and state legislatures to limit direct mail, access to names, and the perceived invasion of privacy. Each month about 50,000 people join the Mail Preference Service, which already boasts 3.5 million members and has as its objective the removal of its members' names from mailing lists.[9]

> Perhaps the greatest disadvantage **is the poor image that** direct mail currently holds.

consumer.net

STRUCTURING THE DIRECT MAIL CAMPAIGN

The first question to ask is to whom you wish to mail. A key group is probably your own database of customers and prospects. Even though you may have a great many names in your files, it may be worthwhile to be selective, choosing just those who will be responsive to the mailing. This saves on cost and also protects the investment in the database by not exposing recipients to mounds of irrelevant junk mail.

Without a suitable list of prospects in one's database, one can use the services of a specialist mailing house that maintains such lists. These are often compiled from customer and prospect lists bought from other suppliers. Mailing houses usually sell a list for one-time use, providing labels or computer readable data or even a complete mailing service. The most important questions to ask in buying such a list concern its accuracy. The source of many lists may be suspect. Lists may be derived from subscribers to magazines, for example, or respondents to free offers, who may not be the ideal prospects. Lists may also be out of date and may need "cleaning" to remove duplicate entries or to update contacts within organizations. Usually the only satisfactory way of finding out how useful they are is to run a test mailing, although that represents an investment of time and money.

Sometimes mailing lists are not available, particularly for new products and customers, and frequently in the international marketing arena. In those instances, the firm must build its own mailing list from scratch. The most productive mailing list is usually the one that was built in-house. Tragically, in-house data are often neglected. For most direct marketing companies, they are the single most precious asset—the one whose loss could put them out of business. It is also usually the most responsive list to a company's additional offers.[10] In all organizations, the data obtained as a result of inquiries, face-to-face selling, exhibitions, and direct mail should be regarded as precious. These data should be consolidated and protected so that they are usable and useful as a direct input to all marketing activities—especially precision marketing.

THE DIRECT MAIL OFFER.   The basis for a mailing list has to be a clear-cut offer, whether simply a statement about the products or services or a specific promotion. Despite the opportunity to convey large amounts of material, the offer should be kept as simple as possible. The material will almost inevitably arrive in the prospect's mailbox with half a dozen other similar mailings. Thus, as with all advertising, the direct mail message will have just a few seconds to grab the recipient's attention. The much quoted sales acronym KISS ("Keep It Simple, Stupid!")

---

9. Denison Hatch, "An Alternative to 'Do Not Mail,'" *Target Marketing* 18 (March 1995): 80–87.
10. E. L. Nash, *Direct Marketing: Strategy, Planning, Execution*, 2d ed. (New York: McGraw-Hill, 1986).

is nowhere more applicable than in mailings. In addition, there must be a clear action associated with the message, such as a suggestion to the recipient to return the reply card or to be prepared for a telephone call from a salesperson.

THE LETTER.   It is, of course, possible to send out a mailing without a letter, but the evidence suggests that enclosing a letter improves the response rate. Enclosing a personalized letter improves it by up to a factor of four. Market research among personal computer buyers showed that between 60 and 80 percent of them read a letter addressed to them by name, fewer than 40 percent read one addressed to them by title, and just over 20 percent read it when it was addressed to the company. There is some controversy as to the best form of letter. Clearly a simple price promotion will benefit from a short, punchy style, whereas technical information on a sophisticated new product might be better suited to a longer format. The one point that most commentators seem to agree on is that the areas at the top and end of the letter receive the most attention from the recipient. The top should encapsulate the overall message in a punchy headline, immediately followed by the hottest offer. The best way to use the area at the end is to include an important postscript. Research has also shown that 79 percent of all people who open a direct mail piece will read the P.S. first before reading anything else in the letter. Several studies have indicated other parts of a letter may be read more thoroughly, yet no one disagrees that a P.S. plays an important role in successful direct mail.[11]

Because of the powerful effect of personalization, direct mailers are very creative when it comes to finding new ways to express the personal touch. Examples are envelopes that are addressed by hand (or by computer script that looks like it) and return addresses form the recipient's city. The attachment of mock handwritten stick-on notes with remarks like "I really think you would like this, J." has also proven to be very successful. In all these instances, the direct marketer only tries to sell the impression of personalization—which evaporates once the recipient has received a sufficient number of messages using the same technique. Using the full power of information, however, allows the marketer to adapt the content of the message to the customer, which will result in a much stronger and longer-lasting personalization effect.

TIMING.   The timing of mailings can influence their impact. Clearly they have to be integrated with the overall campaign. There are some times of year, particularly July, August, and the holidays, when it is traditionally considered unproductive to mail. Even the day of the week can have an effect. For example, one should avoid reaching an executive's desk on any day following a holiday, when there is likely to be a large accumulation of letters needing attention.

RESPONSE RATES.   The great advantage of direct mail advertising is that every aspect of the promotion can be tested by measuring the resulting response rates. All that is required is that the reply card be coded to the campaign being tested. The most frequently used technique is to include a mock department number in the address. This way every element of direct mail promotion may be optimized and the letter and other promotional material designed to have the greatest response impact. This technique has been honed to a fine edge by large-scale users, such as *Reader's Digest*. These firms test every part of a mailing and select

---

11. "All about Post and Post Post Scripts: A Key Element in Direct Mail," *Direct Marketing* 59 (January 1997): 44–45.

those components that are most effective in terms of generating responses. This testing is often carried out using split runs, in which some randomly selected customers receive one version of a mailing and other customers receive another one; the effectiveness of both can then be compared.

INTERNET-BASED COMMUNICATIONS

Increasingly, organizations use the fax and computer in the same way as direct mail. The use of the Internet as a marketing communications medium is already well established. This is understandable because, for the majority of Internet users, Web use has become a daily habit. Recent research from Cyber Dialogue shows that 35.3 million, or 63 percent of U.S. adults, use the Web daily. These users account for 87 percent of all Web ad clicks and 90 percent of all dollars spent online. Nielsen NetRatings' data show that portals and financial services sites are the best at keeping Internet users coming back.[12] Consequently, marketers have kept up with their investment in online advertisement. Internet Advertising Bureau figures showed that Internet advertising spending in the first quarter of 1999 reached $693 million, a 97 percent increase over the same period the previous year. Analysis forecasts predict that U.S. Internet advertising spending will grow four-fold from $5 billion in 2000 to $22 billion by 2004. In particular, consumer goods advertisers are expected to increase their share of Internet media dollars. More than half of marketers surveyed by Forrester Research have indicated that their online advertising spending will come on top of current media budgets. Only 33 percent of them are planning to prune their TV advertising budget to reallocate additional funds to Internet advertising.[13]

www.cyberdialogue.com

www.nielsennetratings.com
www.iab.net

www.forrester.com

Corporate Web sites can provide a valuable—and cost effective—customer care marketing and information tool. These sites are basically electronic catalogs or brochures. However, they usually provide a simple level of interaction via the ability to move from Web page to Web page. Some sites provide customer request mechanisms for information via online form fill-in or e-mail options. Web sites can also act as a great way of capturing customer data. Some sites are utilizing "push" technology to e-mail specific information to specific customers.[14]

Furthermore, the relatively low cost of developing a Web site allows smaller firms and even individuals to compete head-to-head with larger firms. As a result, direct communication via the Internet has become a crucial component of marketing outreach efforts. Internet communication is also evolving into direct selling, as Marketing in Action 13.1 shows.

> direct communication via the Internet **has become a crucial component** of marketing outreach efforts

DOOR-TO-DOOR

Another approach is to employ a door-to-door distribution company to deliver unaddressed mailings to all addresses in a specific area. This technique loses many of the advantages (e.g., specific targeting, personalization, and wide coverage) of direct mail, but where the area is tightly defined it can still offer a high degree of precision. In particular, it now offers a very good vehicle for sampling new users on a tightly targeted basis that, once again, can be optimized by testing.

---

12. "Web Devotees Are the Best Online Consumers," *Industry Standard,* August 30–September 6, 1999, 110.
13. "Marketing Spotlight: Internet Ad Spending Keeps Climbing," *Industry Standard,* August 30–September 6, 1999, 112.
14. "Relationship Management Environments," *Credit World* 87 (November/December 1998): 14–21.

Marketing in Action 13.1

Can Bank One direct-sell banking and tap into a new market?

Bank One Corporation (www.bankone.com), headquartered in Chicago, Illinois (USA), has assets of $256 billion. The bank's U.S. statistics are impressive: largest online credit card issuer, second largest ATM distribution network, third largest corporate bank, fourth largest bank-affiliated leasing company, and fifth largest bank holding company. The bank is structured around national lines of business (e.g., retail, commercial, investment management, and credit card).

Bank One's corporate mission is to maintain at least a number-three position in all major markets served. To fulfill this mission, the company offers innovative, high-quality products to a diverse customer base. In 1999, Bank One launched a "new" bank called Wingspan Bank (wingspanbank.com), which is only accessible via the Internet. Bank One historically has offered Internet banking as a service to its existing customers. The goal of Wingspan Bank is to attract new customers.

WingspanBank.com has been established as a division of First USA Bank (a subsidiary of Bank One). First USA Bank, the largest issuer of VISA credit cards in the United States, cross-sells Bank One products. WingspanBank.com offers access to all of Bank One's traditional line of products and is able to utilize the direct marketing systems in place at First USA Bank. Additionally, credit card members at WingspanBank.com have access to a free service that includes online travel bookings, entertainment ticket purchases, and a product locator. The motive behind all of WingspanBank.com's products and services is that the users of online banking are busy people.

Did Bank One need to establish a separate bank to offer its online services? How can WingspanBank.com tap into the direct marketing efforts of First USA Bank to gain access to new markets?

Sources: www.bankone.com; Joseph B. Cahill, "Bank One Establishes Internet Unit as Part of Plan to Use Web to Expand," *Wall Street Journal*, June 25, 1999, A10.

PUBLICATIONS

www.farmjournal.com

It is also possible for publications mailed to readers to produce tailored versions to suit even relatively small groups of consumers. *Farm Journal,* for instance, uses computer-collated binding to send out 8,896 different versions to its 825,000 readers. Advertisers are similarly matched to readers on the basis of computerized subscriber profiles.[15]

TELEMARKETING

www.ford.com

www.directline.net
www.rbs.co.uk

Somewhere between direct mail and the face-to-face sales call lies telemarketing. To a degree this is a personal technique because it can be interactive, whereas a mailing cannot. It is the medium most often used in the industrial goods sector, where the relatively high cost per call can be more easily justified. However, telemarketing can also be useful in the consumer sector. For example, Ford once made 20 million calls to produce leads for its sales personnel. In Europe the most spectacular success in telemarketing was achieved by Direct Line, a telephone sales service set up in Britain by Royal Bank of Scotland. By 1995 Direct Line had come from nowhere to become Britain's biggest auto insurer, by doing away with traditional brokers. It reasoned that customers would not need the hand-holding and emotional comfort that brokers traditionally provide if the company did a better job of, for example, paying claims rapidly and eliminating complicated paperwork. So instead of using brokers and regional branch offices, Direct Line substitutes information technology to improve claims handling, and it passes on

15. S. Rapp and T. Collins, *The Great Marketing Turnaround* (Upper Saddle River, N.J.: Prentice Hall, 1990).

some of the cost savings to customers in the form of lower insurance premiums.[16] Telemarketing sales have also been growing in the United States. More than 80 million Americans bought from telemarketers, with consumer sales totaling $186 billion and business-to-business transactions reaching $239 billion in 1997.[17]

The great advantage of telemarketing over face-to-face selling is the rate at which calls can be made. It is quite realistic for even untrained sales personnel to make more than 50 telephone calls in a day, compared to as few as 300 face-to-face calls in a year. With specialist telesales personnel, the call rate can rise to hundreds per day. An advantage over direct mail is the success rate of telemarketing, which is estimated to be as much as ten times as high. It is not unusual to achieve a 10 percent response rate when, for instance, the intention is to invite contacts to a seminar for face-to-face selling. The clear disadvantages are that teleselling is limited in comparison with face-to-face calls; there are no visual stimuli for either side; and the calls have to be much shorter. It is considerably more difficult to be persuasive as a disembodied voice, which is why the technique is often used only as a first step toward achieving a face-to-face call. This technique is several times more expensive than direct mail, but much less expensive than a face-to-face call. Researchers quote a cost of $17 per hour for telemarketers compared with $300 per hour for face-to-face representatives.[18] As Manager's Corner 13.2 shows, telemarketing can be accompanied by a host of ethical and privacy problems. Nevertheless, its effectiveness will continue to make it an important communications tool.

> The great advantage of telemarketing over face-to-face selling is the rate at which calls can be made.

Manager's Corner 13.2

Privacy and ethics in direct marketing

Privacy is one of the hottest topics discussed by direct marketers, consumers, and legislators, and, not surprisingly, it was listed as a top external challenge by nearly one-third (32.2 percent) of direct marketers surveyed. Unfortunately, it is disheartening that few direct marketers were acting to stave off the criticism against them. Only 56 percent of those who rent their telemarketing lists give an opt-out option, and only 53 percent maintain an in-house suppression file. More surprisingly, only 7 percent and 14 percent of respondents subscribed to the Direct Marketing Association telephone and mail preference services, respectively.

Consumers are concerned with privacy, and direct marketers need to pay more attention. Martha Rogers, influential author of *Marketing 1 to 1* and cofounder for Marketing 1 to 1

(www.1to1.com) consulting and training group, sees the situation as more dire, warning, "If direct marketers don't take care of privacy inside the industry, it's an open invitation to get the Feds involved. I just spent two weeks in Europe, and it taught me a good lesson on privacy. They are way, way more paranoid than we are, way ahead of us in terms of privacy regulations, and they're already paying the price."

Indeed, the European Union (europa.eu.int) put into effect a law in 1998 prohibiting American-style buying and selling of personal data, a move that could interrupt electronic commerce with the United States if the two sides fail to resolve deep philosophical and legal differences over protecting privacy. The law was adopted three years earlier by the European Union after a majority of its 15 member nations agreed to issue what is known as

16. W. Chan Kim and Renee Mauborgne, "Creating New Market Space," *Harvard Business Review* 77 (January/February 1999): 83–93.

17. Catherine Romano, "Telemarketing Grows Up," *Management Review* 87 (June 1998): 31–34.

18. R. T. Moriarty and U. Moran, "Managing Hybrid Marketing Systems," *Harvard Business Review* 68, no. 6 (November/December 1990): 146–155.

a directive. Under European law, each member nation is required to implement the directive by enacting its own law. Six nations have drafted or passed such laws so far.

Beyond its impact on Europe, the directive has the potential to disrupt electronic commerce with the United States. A key provision of the new measure would prohibit any company doing business in the European Union from transmitting personal data to any country that does not guarantee comparable privacy protection. Foremost among them is the United States.

Sources: Kelly J. Andrews, "State of the Industry," *Target Marketing* 22 (January 1999): 36–40+; Edmund L. Andrews, "European Law Aims to Protect Privacy of Data," *New York Times,* October 26, 1998, A1.

TELEMARKETING AGENCIES

Maintaining a telemarketing team is expensive, so many organizations use specialist agencies or call centers to handle the difficult task of controlling and motivating their personnel. As evidenced in Manager's Corner 13.3, some firms have established effective, albeit perhaps unethical, methods to control high labor costs with the use of prison labor. Motivation in particular is very important when one spends all day making "cold" telephone calls. The basis for such calls is usually a script produced in cooperation with the client. Script writing requires a high degree of skill, because it must take the telesales staff through the various levels of conversation with their contacts and the wide range of possible responses.

INBOUND TELEMARKETING

A telemarketing team can also *receive* calls from customers and prospects. Many of these calls are inquiries regarding product use or complaints about the product. The handling of such calls is often a weak link in the marketing operations of organizations. Far too few organizations have formally planned and carefully monitored incoming call systems. It is very difficult to demonstrate quality when the customer cannot find anyone to handle an inquiry. Complaints are definitely exacerbated when nobody seems willing to listen.

> It is very difficult to demonstrate quality when the customer cannot find anyone to handle an inquiry.

For executives, a simple but often enlightening test is to call their own organizations with inquiries and see just how well—or how disastrously—they are handled. Companies should view such self-initiated calls as an opportunity to both strengthen the loyalty of the customer and to learn from complaints. However, such learning will take place only if the content of the calls is carefully recorded and routed to decision makers within the organization who can remedy the cause of the problems.

www.llbean.com

Inbound telemarketing has another major use: It can be part of a promotional campaign that elicits a direct consumer response. For example, L. L. Bean, the outdoor clothing catalog firm, has established a toll-free line from the United Kingdom to Portland, Maine, in order to support the catalogs mailed to UK prospects and customers.[19] When using such inbound telemarketing, it is important that consumers can actually reach someone and get responses when calling. There are many instances in which expensive promotional efforts successfully trigger consumer calls, only to disappoint when telephone lines are always busy or the representatives reached either don't have any information or cannot take orders. Call centers can be instrumental in overcoming some of these problems, by providing an extensive telephone network for peak loads. They can also be of great value in multilingual environments. In Europe, for example, many television advertise-

---

19. Matthew Rose, "L. L. Bean Opens Toll-Free Line to Main HQ," *DM News/Global Direct Marketing,* October 9, 1995, 3.

Manager's Corner 13.3

Prison labor and telemarketing

When most of us think of convicts at work, we picture them banging out license plates or digging ditches. Those images are now far too limited to encompass the great range of jobs that America's prison workforce is performing. If you book a flight on Delta (www.delta-air.com), you will likely be talking to a prisoner at a California correctional facility that the airline uses for its reservations service. Microsoft (www.microsoft.com) has used Washington State prisoners to pack and ship Windows software; Honda (www.honda.com), for manufacturing parts; and even Toys "R" Us (www.toysrus.com), for cleaning and stocking shelves for the next day's customers. And AT&T (www.att.com) has used prisoners for telemarketing.

During the past 20 years, more than 30 states in the United States have enacted laws permitting the use of convict labor by private enterprise. The growth in prison population in the United States and the attendant costs of incarceration suggest that there will be strong pressures to put more prisoners to work. And it is not hard to figure why corporations like prison labor: It costs a meager 10 percent of free labor. Prison employers pay no health insurance, no unemployment insurance, no payroll or Social Security taxes, no workers' compensation, no vacation time, no sick leave, and no overtime. Prison workers can be hired, fired, or reassigned at will. Not only do they have no right to organize or strike, they also have no means of filing a grievance or voicing any kind of complaint whatsoever. They have no right to circulate an employee petition or newsletter, no right to call a meeting, and no access to the press. Prison labor is the ultimate flexible and disciplined workforce.

Do you see any ethical dilemma?

Source: Gordon Lafer and Nicholas Confessore, "Captive Labor: America's Prisoners as Corporate Workforce," *The American Prospect* (September/October 1999): 66–70.

ments have a footprint that far exceeds any single nation. Often an advertisement encourages the audience to call to order a product. Although many people may enjoy watching a program in a nonnative language, they may not be able to order merchandise in that language. The advertisement can overcome these obstacles by displaying different phone numbers for each country. Whereas communications technology makes it possible to route all responses to the same call center, which may be located in, say, Ireland, these individual numbers ensure that the operator taking the call is knowledgeable in the particular language. However, care must be taken in designing such systems to ensure system responsiveness to customer requirements. For example, operators need to be aware of major events in a country, just in case consumers refer to them. Therefore, many call centers require their operators to read a major newspaper from the country they are handling. Similarly, the call must be structured according to the customers. Calls from Scandinavia, for example, are likely to be short and to the point. From Italy, however, they are likely to be longer and much more involved. Therefore operators cannot be measured by the same performance standards (such as length of time to close a sale) if they are handling different regions.

NETWORK MARKETING

A direct sales force is ideal but very expensive. This problem has been nicely sidestepped by some organizations that have recruited part-time agents at low pay (see Exhibit 13.1). Network marketing refers to retail selling channels that use independent distributors not only to buy and resell product at retail, but also to recruit new distributors into a growing network over time.[20] Avon Cosmetics and

avon.avon.com

---

20. Anne T. Coughlan and Kent Grayson, "Network Marketing Organizations: Compensation Plans, Retail Network Growth, and Profitability," *International Journal of Research in Marketing* 15 (December 1998): 401–426.

Exhibit 13.1

Mary Kay Cosmetics is known for its "Pink Army." The 1999 International Convention brought 40,000 businesswomen from around the world to the Dallas Convention Center. A very clear system of rewards and advancements unites the members of this expansive network and ensures its peak efficiency. To see more on how well organized the Mary Kay sales network is, go to www.marykay .com/marykay/Look/Rewards /Rewards.html.

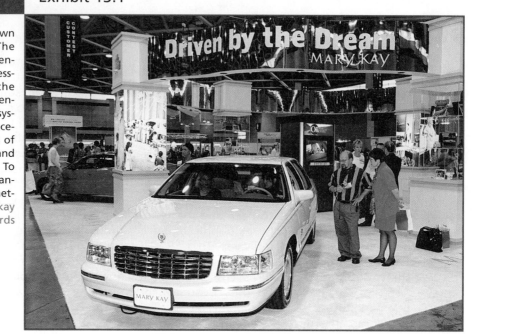

www.amway.com

Amway have developed this network marketing approach successfully, with reportedly a million representatives worldwide. The friendly relationship between seller and buyer, who often know each other socially, reinforces the sale and also motivates both parties. These techniques can be considered precision marketing in that they involve a very direct—and often a very knowledgeable—approach to the customer. On the other hand, because the organization employing the seller does not have access to this knowledge, but depends on the informal relationship of its agents, it encounters some problems in terms of applying the other techniques of precision marketing.

SALES PROMOTION

Sales promotion is normally an adjunct to personal selling or advertising. It can be directed either at consumers, the sales force, or the channel members carrying a product. Typically such promotions are a relatively short-term activity used to stimulate some specific action. Because of the cost and clutter of media advertising, better targeting capabilities, and easier tracking of its effectiveness, sales promotion budgets have overtaken advertising budgets in both the United States and Europe. Table 13.2 lists the wide range of possible sales promotion activities.

ADVANTAGES AND DISADVANTAGES OF SALES PROMOTION

Despite its widespread use as the most important element of communication campaigns, at least in terms of money spent, the essence of sales promotion is that it is intended as a very short-term influence on sales. It typically has an insignificant long-term effect, but may be a powerful additional factor to sway short-term sales in the supplier's favor or to advance sales that would have been made later.

> the essence of sales promotion is that it is intended as a very short-term influence on sales

Table 13.2

Types of sales promotions

Money		Goods		Services	
Direct	**Indirect**	**Direct**	**Indirect**	**Direct**	**Indirect**
Price reductions	Coupons	Free goods and samples	Stamps	Guarantees	Cooperative advertising
Cash refunds	Vouchers	Premium offers	Coupons	Group participation events	Vouchers for services
Loyalty schemes	Money equivalent	Free gifts	Vouchers	Free services	Contests
Incentives	Contests	Trade-in offers	Money equivalents	Risk reduction schemes	
Bonuses	Extended credit	Tied offers	Contests	Training	
Commissions	Delayed invoicing			Demonstrations	
	Return policies				

The advantages of sales promotion are as follows:

- **Sales increase.** This is the main short-term benefit.
- **Defined target audience.** Sales promotion can be targeted to specific groups, especially selected retailers and their customers.
- **Defined role.** It can be targeted to achieve specific objectives, such as increasing repeat purchases.
- **Indirect roles.** Other objectives include wider distribution and shelf space.

These are the disadvantages:

- **Short term.** Almost all of the effect is immediate. There is rarely any lasting increase in sales.
- **Hidden costs.** Many costs, not least the management and sales force time and effort, do not appear in the direct costs.
- **Confusion.** Promotions can conflict with the main brand messages and confuse the customer as to what the image really is. For example, during the health and fitness craze of the 1980s in the United States, turkey was aggressively promoted as a low-fat meat with various forms of sales promotion including in-store coupons and loss-leader pricing before Thanksgiving. Sales promotions were intended to encourage consumers to eat more turkey year round, but unfortunately strengthened turkey's image as a Thanksgiving meal. Now in the post-health-craze era of the 1990s and beyond, turkey consumption has dropped, as many consumers consider turkey as a health food. The National Turkey Federation always promoted it as a low-fat meat, but it is consumers who have redefined it as a health food.[21]   www.turkeyfed.org
- **Price cutting.** This can cause users to expect a lower price in the future and damage quality perception.
- **Postponement effect.** Too many sales promotion efforts in a product category can result in customer refusal to purchase a product at full price and the willingness to defer purchases until the next promotion.

21. Hilary Stout, "Can Turkey Scallopine Transform Selling of Bird?" *Wall Street Journal Interactive Edition*, September 10, 1999.

- **Significant governmental regulation.** Much sales promotion is regulated by governments. As a result, a particular incentive may be permissible in one market but illegal in another. In Scandinavia, for example, every promotion has to be approved by a government body. In France, a gift cannot be worth more than 4 percent of the retail value of the product being promoted, subject to a maximum of 10 francs. The maximum prize value in the Netherlands is 250 guilders, making certain promotions virtually impossible.[22] All these differing regulations make it very difficult to carry out global sales promotion efforts.

Perhaps the greatest disadvantage of sales promotions is their lack of effectiveness. Researchers have reported that only 16 percent of the trade promotion events studied were profitable, based on incremental sales of brands distributed through retailer warehouses. For many promotions the cost of promoting an additional dollar of sales was greater than one dollar.[23] Yet promotions have become so popular that they now account for more than 65 percent of typical communication budgets.

In line with its essentially short-term impact, a promotion may be expected to achieve certain limited objectives. Some promotions are expressly planned to induce consumers to make a trial purchase of the product or service. Examples include money-off coupons or samples of the product, possibly linked as a free gift with a related product. Other promotions are designed to achieve extra volume by stimulating the user's decision at the point of sale; on-package coupons are the obvious example. Another alternative is to offer more of the product (e.g., 20 percent more free) for the same price. Promotions can also be designed to build repeat business. A good example is a coupon for money off the next purchase. Competition among retailers or the sales force may lead to a better display at the point of sale, but it is the extra shelf space that sells the product rather than the promotion itself.

www.att.com
www.ibm.com
www.hp.com

Sales promotion and advertising should be complementary. The most effective campaign often includes an integrated mix of several types of promotion. Although such an effort may be expensive, corporations such as AT&T, IBM, and Hewlett-Packard have found that by synchronizing their advertising, direct mail, telemarketing, and field sales force, they can increase response and customer satisfaction.[24]

Customer satisfaction is important, as it costs five to seven times more to find new customers than to retain the customers a company already has. Most dissatisfied customers never complain; they just switch to other competitors. The bright side is that totally satisfied customers are six times more likely to repurchase a company's products over a span of one to two years than merely satisfied customers.[25]

PROMOTIONAL PRICING

One of the most frequently used sales promotion techniques is offering promotional discounts to buy extra sales—albeit only in the short term. These can be grouped into a number of main categories.

---

22. Michael R. Czinkota and Ilkka Ronkainen, *International Marketing,* 4th ed. (Fort Worth, Tex.: Dryden Press, 1995), 621.
23. M. M. Abraham and L. M. Lodish, "Getting the Most out of Advertising and Promotion," *Harvard Business Review* 68, no. 3 (May/June 1990): 50–63.
24. Ernan Roman, "The Media Mix," *Target Marketing* 18 (April 1995): 30–32.
25. Jeremy Galbreath, "Relationship Management Environments," *Credit World* 87 (November/December 1998): 14–21.

PRICE REDUCTIONS.   The simple money-off promotion imprinted on the packaging is the most direct method and may have the most immediate impact on sales levels. Because it is shown on the package, it is nearly impossible for any retailer to avoid passing it on to the consumer. It is the most expensive technique, because to be effective it usually needs to represent 15 to 20 percent off the regular retail price. It may also prove difficult to restore the price to its original level at the end of the promotion, as consumers may decide to stockpile in order to hold off on additional purchases until the next promotion. It may also do considerable damage to the image of quality products or services, especially where the price-off sticker visually dominates the label. Even though there are many drawbacks to price reductions, researchers have found that in spite of the success of the everyday low pricing scheme of Wal-Mart and other retailers, a high-low pricing scheme works more profitably for most firms. At the same time, however, they concluded that price is not a defensible point of differentiation for a firm unless it is driven by an existing advantageous operating cost structure.[26]

www.wal-mart.com

FREE GOODS.   The offer of more products for the same price (e.g., two for the price of one) has several advantages. It forces the customer to buy more than usual for the same price during the sale. However, it clearly signals what a normal price is and that such a discount is temporary. Therefore, it has less impact on the image of the product and its established price.

TIED OFFERS.   Two or more kinds of products, often shrink-wrapped together and offered at a lower price (e.g., a Microsoft Windows 2000 manual that comes with a Rand McNally's Trip Routing Software on a CD-ROM and its instruction brochure). This packaging requires retooling of the assembly process and changes to the production and assembly lines with considerable reductions in productivity. In addition, larger or different shelf space may be required at the retail store. It could be a dangerous promotional campaign if cooperation was not assured in advance from the retailer.

www.microsoft.com
www.randmcnally.com

COUPONS AND VIRTUAL COUPONS.   Coupons are often used when the aim is to extend the penetration or trial of the product to new customers. These are most effectively delivered door-to-door, where they achieve high redemption rates. Increasingly, coupons are also delivered via freestanding inserts, which are books full of coupons. Coupons can also be incorporated in press advertisements, which are cheaper to run but have a considerably lower redemption rate. Depending on the generosity of the offer, the coupon is supposed to tempt consumers away from the brands they use to try a new one. This can be a very effective type of promotion if coupon redemption levels are high enough and may be more cost effective than sampling.

The use of traditional coupons, along with other forms of sales promotion, has not been without controversy. Procter & Gamble, probably the most successful package goods marketer with a wide array of sales promotions in the United States, came to realize how difficult the company had made it for consumers over the years to make a purchase decision. In 1996, the company began standardizing product formulas, eliminating marginal brands, cutting product lines,

www.pg.com

---

26. Stephen J. Hoch, Xavier Dreze, and Mary E. Purk, "EDLP, Hi-Lo, and Margin Arithmetic," *Journal of Marketing* 58 (October 1994): 36.

www.spicnspan.com

www.pg.com

www.acnielsen.com

and reducing complex deals and coupons. Gone are 27 types of promotions, including such outlandish tactics as goldfish giveaways to buyers of Spic & Span (unfortunately, many froze to death during midwinter shipping). Although it is not possible to attribute the results solely to reduced use of coupons, the company has increased its business by a third. P&G executives attribute it to the power of simplicity. Obviously, the reduced use of coupons has not hurt sales at all.[27]

Coupons can also meet with cultural resistance. When ACNielsen tried to introduce money-off coupons in Chile, the firm ran into trouble with the nation's supermarket union, which notified its members that it opposed the project and recommended that coupons not be accepted. The main complaint was that an intermediary such as Nielsen would unnecessarily raise costs and thus the prices charged to consumers. Also, some critics felt that coupons would limit individual negotiations, because Chileans often bargain for their purchases.[28]

However, emerging forms of coupons permit more precise targeting and therefore result in less waste. Advanced Promotions Technologies, for example, has developed a unit with a small color touch screen and a printer that sits on the check-writing stand in supermarkets. The customer can watch the screen to see coupons that are applicable to the purchases made and touch the screen to request a printout.[29] Other technology prints out coupons at the checkout counter that either highlight complementary products that the customer has not bought or products competitive with ones that have been purchased. Similarly, consumers can sign up on various Internet-based coupon offering Web sites by providing their residential and other personal information so that the Web-based companies can show on the screen various coupons on goods and services that they may be interested in purchasing. A study by NPD Online Research shows that 46 percent of Internet users who have downloaded coupons have used coolsavings.com, 41 percent have used valupage.com, 12 percent have used valpak.com, 12 percent have used hotcoupons.com, and 10 percent have used directcoupons.com. Obviously, coupons are alive and well on the Internet.[30] With such greater precision, the coupon tool becomes less expensive and more efficient and is therefore likely to be used more. It can be problematic, however, for some industries, as Marketing in Action 13.2 describes.

CASH REFUND.   A cash refund (from the retailer or by mail), usually on the basis of a coupon that is part of the packaging, is another way of offering a controlled price reduction. However, the redemption procedures may be complex and unwelcome to the trade, because proper monitoring is required to ensure that cash refunds are issued only for sales that have actually been made. Unless there is a matching of inventory held, products sold, and refunds issued, manufacturers may expose themselves to the possibility of retailers claiming cash refund reimbursements without having sold the merchandise. Cash refunds can also be expensive. Sometimes the refund may be as much as the whole purchase price.

MONEY OFF NEXT PURCHASE.   This method may be used to extend buying patterns and build customer loyalty. Such offers are often part of the product label and require some effort to use. For example, the label may have to be soaked off the bottle, or the packaging may have to be preserved. Sometimes, the hassle of such requirements can result in customer dissatisfaction rather than promotion.

---

27. Jack Trout and Steve Rivkin, "The Future of Marketing? It's Simple," *Marketing News,* December 7, 1998, 23.
28. Czinkota and Ronkainen, *International Marketing.*
29. Ody, "Many Happy Returns from Loyalty Schemes?"
30. "Electronic Coupon Clipping," *USA Today,* May 11, 1999, 1B.

Marketing in Action 13.2

Ford mails coupons to prospective customers

Attempting to attract prospective automobile purchasers, both Ford Motor Company (www .ford.com) and General Motors (www.gm.com) have started mailing coupons to customers. These coupons, valued anywhere from $500 to $1,000, are the automobile manufacturers' response to price pressures from Japanese companies, stagnant demand, and excess capacity. Demand in the U.S. market for cars and small trucks has stabilized at 15 million units a year. However, production capacity is at almost 20 million units a year. Combining excess capacity with a weak yen, automobile manufacturers have begun using coupon incentives to entice potential buyers into their showrooms.

Using coupons in conjunction with low interest rates and/or dealer incentives, automobile buyers should expect incentives totaling around $1,500 per vehicle purchase. Some industry experts think, however, that auto manufacturers should just cut prices instead of having to administer incentive programs. Even the automobile manufacturers are not certain that incentive programs are good for the companies' brand images.

Do coupons, rebates, and various other consumer promotions tarnish an automobile company's brand image? Will automobile coupons become as popular as traditional grocery store coupons?

Sources: www.ford.com; Emily R. Sendler and Fara Warner, "Ford Matches Coupon Mailing by GM, and Offers to Honor Rival's Discounts," *Wall Street Journal*, April 24, 1998, B7.

LOSS-LEADER PRICING. A product may actually be priced below cost in order to attract customers into a store, in the hope that they will buy other products or services that are profitable. This pricing strategy was discussed in detail in Chapter 10.

CHEAP CREDIT. If credit is offered, lower-priced or even free credit may be used instead of a simple price reduction. This may be cheaper to the vendor who has access to lower-cost credit, although the cost of bad debts must also be covered. Such offers are often seen in the furniture business (e.g., 90 days same as cash; pay nothing until January 2001), where low financing rates are advertised. Low-cost credit and delayed invoicing can also be used as important tools to get retailers to carry a new product. By offering payment terms of 120 days, for example, many Japanese manufacturers and wholesalers achieve high acceptance levels from their retailers, who can keep the funds for some time after the sale and earn interest.[31] Low-cost credit may also introduce the consumer to the use of the supplier's credit facilities.

NONPRICE PROMOTIONS

Other forms of promotion offer added value but are not directly price related.

CONTESTS. In this case the purchaser receives the right to one or more entries in a competition. Because the size of the top prize reportedly determines the interest of the customer, a large prize can be a very attention-getting form of promotion. Contests can be easy and cheap to mount and have a guaranteed fixed maximum cost. They can also be used as incentives for retailers for the sales force in the form of bonuses or prizes, such as participation in special top-production meetings in a desirable resort area.

---

31. Michael R. Czinkota and Masaaki Kotabe, *The Japanese Distribution System* (Chicago, Ill.: Probus Publishing, 1993).

FREE GIFTS. Such offers can be designed to lure customers and channel members from the competition or to build loyalty. Banks, for example, offer home equity loans without charging financing points or advertise that they will pay for any legal expenses of the closing costs. Customers are thus encouraged to change banks. The use of frequent flyer miles by airlines is an example of a customer loyalty builder. Here customers are encouraged to fly regularly on a specific airline in order to receive, after a number of flights, a free ticket. On the Internet, there is now a ubiquitous virtual gift. For example, InternetPerks' IncentiveWare is an Internet promotional piece that companies can use to keep their names in front of customers while giving them free desktop applications. As the use of sales forces declines, the Internet becomes a valuable tool with which to reach customers. IncentiveWare consists of applications for the desktop called droplets that can be sent as virtual gifts attached to e-mail, downloaded free from a Web site, or put on disks to be handed out at trade shows and sales calls. IncentiveWare is meant to replace promotional gifts, such as hats, coffee mugs, and T-shirts bearing the corporate logo, that companies frequently use.[32]

www.internetperks.com

SELF-SUPPORTING OFFERS. In this case, the offer is not free, which is why it is also called a premium offer. The impression is usually given that the supplier is subsidizing the offer so that the customer will obtain a good deal on the item. In practice, the intention is usually to cover the cost with the amount paid by the customer, in effect offering the customer only the benefit of the supplier's buying power. Marlboro sweatshirts is one example. Such offers can be difficult to administer, and the forecasting of inventory levels can be problematic.

MULTIBRAND PROMOTIONS. In this case a number of brands, typically from one supplier, share a single promotion in order to maximize impact for given costs. This technique can be used to recruit new users to these brands. For example, Taco Bell promotes Six Flags amusement parks with a "Buy One Get One Free" discount ticket. Taco Bell has booths and restaurants at Six Flags parks to boost its sales as well.

www.tacobell.com
www.sixflags.com

GUARANTEES AND SERVICES. Trade promotion can also take the form of special guarantees or services, either to consumers or to channel members. For example, in order to increase sales for online retailers, much emphasis has been placed on network and referral programs, as seen in Manager's Corner 13.4. Consumers can also be offered a 30-day trial period. Frequently such promotions are used for magazine subscriptions, allowing customers to cancel the subscription after trying out one or more issues. However, similar guarantees are emerging in many other sectors, where customers can return merchandise liberally. The same tool is also applied to channel members, where manufacturers may desire that retailers stock up in expectation of large demand. Liberal return privileges facilitate such overordering. Offering special services, such as restocking assistance, cooperative advertising, or providing display stands can also be used as enticements.

SAMPLING

Sampling is generally the most powerful form of promotion in the early stages of a new product launch, the immediate aim being to obtain trial by users. Sampling is most appropriate for products that offer some unique feature other than price.

---

32. "Virtual Gifts Offer Internet Perks," *AS/400 Systems Management* 26 (May 1998): 30–32.

Manager's Corner 13.4

A frequent "surfer" program on the Internet

Is there a way to apply the frequent-flyer model and thus reward loyalty on the Internet? Roughly 56 percent of online consumers reported in a survey that they would be more likely to purchase from a given e-commerce site if a loyalty program was available. That is good news for online retailers fed up with dismal returns on banner ads and struggling to drive traffic and sales to their home page.

Today's online consumers can hoard free merchandise, frequent-flyer miles, and cash rebates. Of course, they have to do something to get these rewards. At Cybergold (www.cybergold.com), a network incentives program, members earn cash by filling out surveys, reading ads, trying out a particular product or service, and purchasing items from affiliated merchants. The company tailors e-mails about new incentives based on a member's past activities in the program. Willing to sign up for a 30-day trial membership with the American Homeowners Association (www.ahahome.com)? Cybergold will pay you $5 if you do.

But network programs can get expensive. Compare the variable costs of a network program to that of a referral program. Associates of a referral program display a link to the merchant on their Web sites; whenever a customer accesses the merchant through an associate's page, the associate receives a commission from their purchase. Sparks.com associates receive a 20 percent commission. It is usually a one-time commission, because the next time that customer wants to shop at Sparks.com, he will go there directly. You can give a 100 percent commission if you think you can keep that customer for life. Customers who are members of a network program, however, cost the merchant every time they buy something because of the incentives attached to the purchase.

Source: Jennifer Lach, "Carrots in Cyberspace," *American Demographics* 21 (May 1999): 43–45.

The experience of a new taste or different product performance can best be communicated by sampling. For example, when Ocean Spray decided to introduce its cranberry juice internationally, the company quickly discovered that it was introducing an unknown fruit and an unknown brand into unfamiliar foreign markets. Lots of samples had to be given away to help people acquire a taste for cranberries.[33] Most consumers who receive a free sample will try it, which accounts for the fact that about 11 percent of U.S. consumer promotion budgets are spent on sampling.[34] In fact, some sampling programs even become events in themselves. One such effort involved nacho cheese-flavored Doritos, in which more than six million bags and coupons were distributed through 100 special events and 10,000 supermarkets in a single day—the largest one-day sampling effort ever undertaken by a snack marketer.[35]

www.oceanspray.com

> Sampling is generally the
> **most powerful form of promotion**
> in the early stages of a new product launch

www.doritos.com

Sampling is a very expensive promotional device, but it is the most effective, direct, and immediate way of obtaining consumer trial. Retailers also recognize its power to pull in customers and may accordingly help to achieve distribution. Sampling is often combined with a money-off voucher to ensure that a successful trial is rapidly followed by a purchase.

---

33. Joseph Pereira, "Unknown Fruit Takes on Unfamiliar Markets," *Wall Street Journal*, November 9, 1995, B1.
34. Suzanne Bidlake, "Sampling's New Dawn," *Marketing*, September 1, 1994, 24.
35. "Free for All," *Food & Beverage Marketing* 14 (May 1995): S5.

Most forms of promotion have a cumulative effect in the long run and can therefore be thought of as an investment. Sales promotions, however, are almost always developed to have a direct and immediate effect, so the extra sales should be linked to the promotion. Each sales promotion effort should have specific performance objectives. The performance should be monitored both to ensure that these objectives are attained and to judge the usefulness of similar promotions in the future.

> Most forms of promotion **have a cumulative effect** and can be thought of as an investment.

SPONSORSHIP

This very specialized form of promotion can be very expensive and is typically found in the arts or in sports. It requires careful justification and is all too often based solely on the private interests of the members of the board. However, sponsorship can be very productive for those organizations, such as tobacco companies, that have limited access to the media or those that have more complex objectives, such as arranging events in order to meet customers. For the 1996 Olympics in Atlanta, for example, Coca-Cola reached a $60-million sponsorship agreement with NBC. As part of the agreement, Coca-Cola received exclusive sponsorship rights for NBC's coverage of the games in all nonalcoholic beverage categories.[36] Given the worldwide dissemination of the Olympics, this investment ensured that the Coca-Cola name attained wide visibility. Coca-Cola also signed on as the first worldwide corporate sponsor and official soft drink of the Paralymics, the international games for the disabled, by paying $7 million in cash and products. Although this event does not have the broad coverage of the Olympics, the sponsorship implies the firm's strong support of the disabled, even though the firm views its sponsorship as a business activity rather than a philanthropic one.[37]

www.coke.com
www.nbc.com

www.olympics.com

TRADE SHOWS

Marketing goods and services through trade fairs is a European tradition that dates back to A.D. 1240. At a trade show manufacturers, distributors, and other vendors display their products or describe their services to current and prospective customers, suppliers, other business associates, and the press. The firm can achieve the two benefits of demonstration and personal contact, because prospective buyers can see and handle the product, try it out for themselves, and ask questions. Shows can target the consumer market or, more often, the business-to-business market. Generally, the more sophisticated the product, the more sales depend on trade shows, where the product can be thoroughly explained in person. Many companies overlook the cost of human resources committed to planning and participating in a show. Besides sales personnel, experts such as engineers, designers, and project managers should be present at trade shows to provide immediate answers to the questions of serious prospects, who will buy a company's products or services as a direct result of its trade-show participation. Add to this the cost of direct mail promotion, free gifts or samples, catering, accommodations, and follow-up, and it becomes less surprising that the exhibit space fee accounts for only 10 to 15 percent of the total budget for participation.[38]

36. "Coke Celebrates Olympic Victory," *Mediaweek,* July 25, 1994, 4.
37. "Coca-Cola Co. Gives Paralympic Games a Boost," *Atlanta Journal and Constitution,* November 9, 1993, D9.
38. Sherrie Zhan, "Trade Shows Mean Big Business," *World Trade* 12 (September 1999): 88.

There are powerful benefits but, like any other promotional activity, trade shows demand careful planning—and not a little expertise—in order to reap rewards. The main considerations in planning a trade show are as follows:

- **Objectives.** One of the most important and frequently neglected activities relating to exhibitions is deciding the objectives. Why are you there? Figure 13.2 provides a range of possible objectives across a matrix that compares prospects with current customers and direct selling objectives with more indirect ones.[39] Carefully plotting your objectives is the necessary first step for measuring the success of your trade-show exhibit.

- **Selection.** Every exhibition organizer thinks that his or her offering is essential, but few of them really are. Most organizations need to select very carefully those trade shows they must attend. Clearly the organizers should be able to provide statistics of attendance at previous events, and the exhibitor list for the forthcoming one should convey the best flavor of that show. If the main vendors in the industry are not attending, then ask yourself why.

- **Booth location and design.** The main requirement, whatever the chosen size and shape, is to obtain the best position. As with retail outlets, the three main priorities at a trade show are location, location, and location. The best positions are typically along the central aisles, as close as possible to the largest, most spectacular booths.[40]

Figure 13.2

Trade shows and market constituencies

	Selling objectives	Nonselling objectives
Current customers	Maintain relationship Transmit messages to key accounts Remedy service problems Stimulate add-on sales	Maintain image Test products Gather competitive intelligence Widen exposure
Potential customers	Contact prospects Determine needs Transmit messages Commit to call back or sale	Contact prospects Foster image building Test products Gather competitor intelligence

Source: Reprinted by permission of *Harvard Business Review*. Exhibit from Thomas V. Bonoma, "Get More Out of Your Trade Shows," *Harvard Business Review* (January/February 1983). Reprinted in *The Marketing Renaissance*, ed. David F. Gumpert (*Harvard Business Review* Executive Book Series), published by John Wiley & Sons, 1985. Copyright © 1983 by the President and Fellows of Harvard College; all rights reserved.

39. T. V. Bonoma, "Get More out of Your Trade Shows," *The Marketing Renaissance*, ed. D. E. Gumpert (New York: John Wiley & Sons, 1985).
40. J. Fenton, *How to Sell Against Competition* (New York: Butterworth Heinemann, 1984).

THE PRESS AND PUBLIC RELATIONS

Face-to-face selling, advertising, and sales promotion can all be described as primary sources of communication. They are under the firm's direct control and are paid for. But there are also secondary sources of communication, including world of mouth, editorial comment, and personal recommendation. These secondary sources may not be under the firm's control but can still be influenced by promotional activities. In turn, because of their supposed impartial nature, they may carry considerable weight with consumers, possibly even more so than direct primary sources. The most important secondary source of communication is the media: newspapers, magazines, radio, and television. They can be a very effective part of the marketing mix, particularly because it is through the media's characterizations that the public develops an understanding and an image of the company. Often an investment into secondary communication can be many times more productive than that spent on other types of promotions. In spite of this importance and effectiveness, secondary sources of communications are often neglected by firms.

Public relations (PR) is a particularly valuable promotional device for services, because the authority offered by independent recommendations in editorial matter can add vital credibility to an intangible service. It is also an easy promotional device for nonprofit organizations to use. Next we will explore the wide range of vehicles available to PR professionals.

Media Contact

One of the most important PR tasks is to maintain contact with the key journalists in the relevant media. This is a two-way process: The PR professional learns about, and can contribute to, features that will appear in the media, while journalists become more receptive to news stories from the PR professional. It is an investment process in which the relationship with the media—and especially with individual journalists—has to be cultivated until a mutual trust has been earned. A survey revealed that more than 90 percent of U.S. journalists rated candor as the primary quality they required in an executive responsible for public relations; the same percentage said they were more likely to deal with PR people whom they knew personally.[41]

News Stories

The backbone of PR is the interesting and entertaining news item that shows the client or product in a good light. Such stories are best placed by personal, professional contact. For more general distribution, carefully written press kits also demand expert attention. Public relations handbooks stress good writing skills in delivering such stories, but that is only the starting point. PR is like any other form of marketing. You must know the customers—here the journalists—and provide the right product: the story they want. For example, KFC's "All-American Salute to Mothers" promotion and announcement, "A 12-year-old girl from Fargo, North Dakota, won $5,000, and Kosovo refugees will receive up to $10,000 in aid from KFC" caught a lot of attention from media journalists in 1999. A sixth-grader was chosen from thousands of students as the winner of the nationwide

> The backbone of PR is the **interesting and entertaining news item** that shows the client or product in a good light.

www.kfc.com

---

41. R. Haywood, *All About PR: What to Say and When to Say It* (New York: McGraw-Hill, 1984).

promotion, in which children designed cards for Mother's Day. Her card was placed for sale in Hallmark Gold Crown stores. For every one of the Mother's Day cards sold, KFC agreed to donate $1, up to a maximum of $10,000, to the Kosovo relief effort sponsored by the relief agency, Save the Children. It was KFC's great public gesture.[42]

www.hallmark.com
www.savethechildren.org

THE PRESS OFFICE

It is important that a firm be able to react to press inquiries. A press office, which can handle any level of questioning from journalists, and is almost effusively enthusiastic to help, is essential if PR is to be taken seriously. It is worthwhile to ensure that all senior executives who come into contact with the media are trained in handling such interviews. Many executives wish to shy away from contact with the press, yet in this era of increased public scrutiny of corporate actions, it is part of executive responsibility to work with the press. It is also a sound investment to have suitable executives who are professionally trained in the techniques of handling radio and television interviews, because doing so requires some skill.

CORPORATE PUBLIC RELATIONS

PR is often used as a term to cover a wide range of activities. Of these, perhaps the most important one may be the corporate interface with both internal and external stakeholders. This aspect of PR is much more likely to be the province of corporate PR personnel. Some of the routine tasks include communications to shareholders, such as annual reports, newsletters, company magazines, and sponsored journals. These communications not only let shareholders know what their company is doing but also, and perhaps more importantly, help the diverse members of the workforce share in the corporate culture. In order to be part of an organization, employees must receive additional information on issues not necessarily related to their jobs, but important to the firm. The better the communications vehicle can satisfy the information needs of employees, the less they will have to rely on informal sources, rumors, and the grapevine. The corporate PR function also supplies the various speeches and presentations in which senior management becomes involved and acts as the channel for the "corporate citizen" activities that organizations believe, usually with some justification, will help their image in the community.

There are two types of corporate public relations. One deals with anticipating and countering criticism of the corporation and is often called defensive, or reactive, PR. The second tries to enhance the image of the firm and its products and is labeled proactive PR.

DEFENSIVE PUBLIC RELATIONS. Organizations are often exposed to the activities of large, effective external pressure groups. For example, Greenpeace, an environmental interest group, employs 1,200 people in more than 30 countries around the world.[43] Such groups can cause significant problems for a corporation if they believe that the firm's activities violate or inhibit their goals. Their actions can result in boycotts of the firm's products and in damage to the firm's image and its employees' morale. The corporate PR department defends the organization against these onslaughts and handles the external interface with such groups. Indeed the corporate PR group may be the source of the organization's knowledge of such groups. It is the responsibility of the PR adviser to understand the position of all important external groups—particularly those trying to exert pressure for change,

www.greenpeace.org

42. Gregg Cebrzynski, "KFC's Mother's Day Promotion also Benefits Kosovo Refugees," *Nation's Restaurant News*, May 24, 1999, 46.
43. "Hardly a Greenhorn," *Financial Times*, June 21, 1995, 25.

such as a campaigning consumer body or a group of dissident shareholders. What is their case? Is it factually based? Who are they trying to influence? How are they attempting this? If the PR adviser feels there is validity in their claims, then it becomes his or her responsibility to advise management and to try to institute appropriate policy changes within the organization.[44]

Good defensive PR does not just consist of circling the wagons but also of acknowledging and understanding the other side's position. In times of crisis the instinctive reaction may be to seek shelter and wait for the noise to die down, but any organization should think very carefully before refusing to communicate in sensitive areas. Openness about corporate activity, preparedness to utilize the reach and power of the firm to swiftly counter criticism, a reputation for integrity, and clarity in communication go a long way toward diffusing difficult situations.[45] Research has shown that the side getting to the news media first tends to be believed more. But such early action also needs to be accompanied by past efforts at building credibility with the media and important constituencies and even adversaries.[46] When the makers of Tylenol learned about possible outside contamination of their product, a swift and open public response helped preserve much goodwill and market share. Conversely, when Mercedes-Benz's A-Class car failed in a rollover test, the carmaker publicly ridiculed the results by issuing the sarcastic statement, "You can tip any car in the world if you really want to." In continuing with its disbelief, the company officially announced that the A-Class was absolutely secure and started to blame its wheel producer, Goodyear, for the car's apparent failure. Clearly, Mercedes was unable to admit its own failures in the production and engineering of the A-Class. By resorting to such tactics, Mercedes counteracted to save its reputation, but brought about a strong disapproval reaction from the media and consumers alike. Its initial reaction added considerably to the public disapproval and negative attitude towards the German carmaker.[47]

> Good defensive PR does not just consist of **circling the wagons but also of acknowledging** and understanding the other side's position.

tylenol.com

www.mercedesbenz.com

www.goodyear.com

PROACTIVE PUBLIC RELATIONS.   Few organizations use PR to influence external activities to their advantage. However, those that do may gain considerable benefits. For example, when Microsoft introduced its new Windows 95 product, the press reported:

www.microsoft.com

> You can hide under a bridge, row a boat to the middle of the ocean or wedge yourself under the sofa, cover your ears and then hum loudly. But get near a newspaper, radio, television or a computer retailer today, and you will experience the multimillion-dollar hype surrounding the launch of Windows 95. Microsoft has succeeded in generating a buzz that has landed the new product on the cover of national news magazines and made it a topic of conversation even among computer illiterates.[48]

44. Haywood, *All About PR.*
45. Oliver Williams, "Who Cast the First Stone?" *Harvard Business Review* 62 (September/October 1984): 151–160.
46. William C. Adams, "Helping Your Organization Triumph over Negatives," *Public Relations Quarterly* 37, no. 1 (1992): 12.
47. "Mercedes Topples Its Critics," *Daily Telegraph,* January 31, 1998, 5.
48. David Segal, "Software's Glitz Blitz," *Washington Post,* August 24, 1995, A1.

But proactive PR need not confine itself to short-term promotions. It can also be used to achieve market success against overwhelming odds, as in the case of Ben & Jerry's ice cream (see Exhibit 13.2). Early in the life of the company, Ben & Jerry's was confronted with a distribution problem. As it attempted to enter larger metropolitan markets in the Northeast, Pillsbury, which markets Häagen-Dazs ice cream, threatened to withdraw Häagen-Dazs from those distributors that agreed to carry Ben & Jerry's ice cream. Of course, the foreclosure of distribution is illegal because it is a restraint of fair trade. But how was a tiny company like Ben & Jerry's going to fight a huge corporation like Pillsbury with its large staff of lawyers? The answer was found through proactive PR.

Printed on each Ben & Jerry's carton was a toll-free number with the provocative question, "What's the doughboy afraid of?" When a customer called the 800 number, he or she was played a message describing the particulars of the problem. They were then sent a bumper sticker (also with the question "What's the doughboy afraid of?") and a form letter that they could sign and send to their member of Congress protesting the actions of Pillsbury. Needless to say, the effective use of the PR weapon got the attention of Pillsbury's lawyers, who suggested that Ben & Jerry's be "allowed" to expand distribution of their ice cream in the Northeast if Ben & Jerry's agreed to stop the doughboy campaign! For a small company, the use of publicity was an effective weapon against a large corporation. Intensive personal effort on the part of the owners of Ben & Jerry's overcame the vast marketing resources of a much larger competitor.

www.benjerry.com

pillsbury.com
www.haagendazs.com

Exhibit 13.2

Ben & Jerry's fight against rBGH (recombinant bovine growth hormone) is both reactive and proactive. Since settling a 1997 Illinois lawsuit that allows the company to use cautionary labels on its products, Ben & Jerry's has regularly mounted the offensive against the use of rBGH. The Illinois packaging, depicted here, is a compromise between the state and Ben & Jerry's. The state objected to the previous labeling—"rBGH-free"—because it implied something was wrong with products containing rBGH milk.

SUMMARY

precision marketing is likely
to expand significantly because of the
explosive growth of the Internet

As a method of promotion, precision marketing is likely to expand significantly because of the explosive growth of the Internet and data collection techniques needed to drive it. Precision marketing is best evidenced by direct mail activity and telesales.

Sales promotion should be used almost exclusively in support of other promotional activities, because it offers essentially short-term gains, whether or not it takes the form of price-based promotions. Despite its limited effectiveness, however, this form of promotion accounts for a greater proportion of the overall spending than advertising.

Trade shows and sponsorships are specialized activities that may have much to offer to some organizations because of their dual benefit of demonstration and interaction.

Public relations is a neglected resource in most organizations. In terms of press relations it offers a very cost-effective vehicle for promotion. In terms of corporate relations, it is the vehicle for dealing with many of the contacts with the external environment, in both a reactive and a proactive way.

QUESTIONS FOR REVIEW

1. Why is precision marketing growing in importance?

2. What are the main advantages and disadvantages of direct mail? How is it used?

3. What are the main elements of a direct mailing? How may they be optimized?

4. What are the advantages and disadvantages of sales promotions? How are they best used?

5. What price promotions and nonprice promotions are available? How is a sampling used?

6. What are the main elements of public relations? How can its effect be optimized?

7. What are the defensive aspects of corporate PR? What are the proactive elements?

QUESTIONS FOR DISCUSSION

1. Database marketing builds and maintains a fruitful and voluntary consumer base. Conversely, careless or aggressive database marketing efforts come across as intrusive and unwelcome, raise the hackles of furious customers, and send them running. Take, for example, the case of CVS Corp. and Giant Food Inc., two of the country's largest pharmaceutical chains. The companies hired Woburn, Massachusetts, database marketer Elensys to send refill reminder letters to pharmacy patients and, in some cases, suggest other products for their conditions. When word of the deal made it onto the pages of the *Washington Post,* consumers nationwide angrily complained to the corporate offices of both stores, calling the program an unauthorized release of private prescription records. As a result, the situation spurred at least one lawsuit. Elensys explained its program as more patient compliance than marketing, but was fired anyway.

   Then there is the case of the Nevada woman who, according to a recent story in the *Wall Street Journal,* bought a used computer and discovered personal records of thousands of patients with mental illness and AIDS still on the hard drive. The pharmacy from which the computer came forgot to erase the information from the computer before selling it. Many people were appalled.

   What are some ethical implications of maintaining customer databases for the purpose of precision marketing? Can companies acquire fuller and more accurate customer information and uphold an ironclad standard of privacy at the same time? Would you agree with the notion that the more privileged information a company can acquire about a consumer's need for a product, the more value the company can provide in meeting the long-terms needs of that person? Provide your reasons.

2. Marjorie Thompson, a director of Cause Connection, Saatchi & Saatchi's cause-related marketing arm, suggests the way to counteract bad publicity is to go on the offensive by using advertising showing the benefits of financial contributions to charities, such as after-school care for children. She adds, "It's not just about marketing the brand, but marketing what the brand believes in." Another company that could have used good works in an advertising campaign to counter bad publicity is McDonald's, claims writer Hamish Pringle. He says, "If more people had known about Ronald McDonald House Charities for underprivileged children, I doubt the company would be suffering as much from McLibel now."

   Pringle, who has written a book with Thompson on cause-related marketing called *Brand Spirit,* thinks the market is in the "third wave of branding," having been through the promotion of practical product-related benefits in the 1950s and the emotional aspects of brands in the 1980s. He says, "Consumers want a brand that works, that gives them thoughts and feelings, but they also want to know what it believes in."

   Should companies embark on cause-related and ethical programs and embrace the activists' suggestions on business practice to improve their public image?

3. Database marketing allows us to do precision marketing, to find out what the audience tends to respond to, and to find out what kinds of ads draw them in. Coaxing information from wary or indifferent customers for use in a marketing database requires skills of its own. A common point of contact between potential consumers and pharmaceutical companies is the toll-free number—the phone numbers through which readers or viewers can ask for more information on a free offer. The goal at that point is keeping potential customers on the phone. Respecting the person's privacy and time is important. Too many questions will make the consumer on the other end hang up. To prevent that, keep the person on the line only long enough to get their most critical marketing information.

A call center is a term for the automated capture of a caller's number and address. From that information, a company can deduce general demographic profiles based on the census and other public records, such as the caller's estimated educational level, age, household income, and approximate family size. By using that process, companies can focus on asking for the information they can't get anywhere else. For example, pharmaceutical companies can focus on information like prescription use and medication attitudes. There is a trade-off for making demographic generalizations about callers. But you can lose the customer if you ask too many questions. It's more important to keep them on the phone.

Pick a branded product of your choice marketed by a reputable company and design a questionnaire for soliciting information from consumers through a call center. Discuss the success potential and ethical aspects of your questionnaire.

FURTHER READINGS

Annual Survey of Promotional Practices. Stamford, Conn.: Donnelley Marketing, 1999.

Kasulis, Jack J., Fred W. Morgan, David E. Griffith, and James M. Kenderdine. "Managing Trade Promotions in the Context of Market Power." *Journal of the Academy of Marketing Science* 27 (summer 1999): 320–332.

Miller, Steve. *How to Get the Most Out of Trade Shows.* Lincolnwood, Ill.: NTC Business Books, 1999.

Schultz, Don E., William A. Robinson, and Lisa A. Petrison, *Sales Promotion Essentials: The 10 Basic Sales Promotion Techniques . . . and How to Use Them.* Lincolnwood, Ill.: NTC Business Books, 1997.

Shimp, Terence A. *Advertising Promotions, and Supplemental Aspects of Marketing Communications,* 5th ed. Fort Worth, Tex.: Dryden Press, 1999.

Sinha, Indrajit, Rajan Chandran, and Srini S. Srinivasan. "Consumer Evaluations of Price and Promotional Restrictions: A Public Policy Perspective." *Journal of Public Policy & Marketing* 18 (spring 1999): 37–51.

Selling and Sales Management

The most important elements of marketing for the majority of organizations in building and maintaining the dialogue between the company and its customers is selling and sales management. In all cases, the customer sees only the salesperson and the product, and through the salesperson develops an opinion of the company. The success or failure of the company rests largely on the ability of the sales force. The importance of making good decisions when those decisions affect the quality and ability of the company's sales force cannot be overstated. As illustrated in Manager's Corner 14.1, the role of salespeople is also changing as the nature of the product changes over time. An understanding of sales—in its widest sense—and of sales management is, therefore, an essential requirement for most managers.

Manager's Corner 14.1

The new breed of salespeople

Could the new manufacturing signal the end of the traditional salesperson—the product-oriented, territory-based representative carrying a sample case or product catalog and earning commissions on sales volume? For most leading manufacturers, the answer is, increasingly, yes. The role of the salesperson has evolved dramatically, reflecting changes in purchasing practice and in the competitive environment, and is supported by rapid advances in information technology.

According to Michael Hammer, coauthor of *Reengineering the Corporation*, the pressure on sales comes from both increasing commoditization and increasing complexity in terms of product choices and product applications. Manufacturers could not say that their product is different. The customer base is also consolidating in many industries. The customer relationship is changing such that sales is no longer a matter of selling products, but is rather a matter of selling solutions, of solving problems, and of helping customers get value out of a product.

The new breed of salesperson has to be a problem solver who can identify and define customer needs, problems, and inefficiencies and offer solutions that will solve those problems and eliminate those inefficiencies. The features-and-benefits approach to sales, a model that served manufacturing companies well when business was product driven, will no longer work in a customer-focused marketplace. The sales force at Hewlett-Packard's manufacturing industries business unit in Cupertino, California, provides a good illustration. Six years ago HP's (www.hp.com) sales force was territory focused, calling on technical specifiers and technical decision makers. Today, operational executives are much more knowledgeable and involved in information technology. That has necessitated a change in HP's sales message from one of bits, bytes, and bandwidths to a deep focus on supply chain management issues. Similarly, at Kimberly-Clark (www.kimberly-clark.com), information technology helps make its sales force smarter, particularly in terms of its focus on cost-in-use positioning. The computer-based approach has also helped Kimberly-Clark salespeople refine their new consultative role with their customers.

Source: Bill Keenan, "Selling's New Breed," *Industry Week*, September 21, 1998, 40–42.

The sales role itself revolves around a variety of management processes. The basic building block is territory management, the territory being in many respects a small business in its own right. This involves a considerable degree of resource management, but the most important element is that of managing customers and prospects, though project management is also required. The heart of the sales process, which will be explained in some detail, is the **sales call**. However, this often has more to do with myth than reality, particularly in **industrial sales** where **relationship marketing** and **account management** come to the fore.

At the sales management level, people management skills are most important, if little recognized in practice. Recruitment, motivation, control, and training all have their part to play in an area of management that poses considerable challenges.

In most organizations more money is spent on personal selling than on advertising and sales promotions combined. Accordingly, many organizations are prepared to spend a high proportion of their communications budget on personal selling (which also indicated just how expensive it is). IBM, for example, spent $800 million training and recruiting 1,000 new reps for its database division in 1998. IBM lures sales personnel with salaries topping out at $90,000. In addition, the database division offered salespeople unlimited incentive earnings, with total compensation equaling approximately 150 percent of base salary.[1]

Personal selling is qualitatively different from almost all other aspects of marketing, being much more dependent on relationships between sales personnel and customers, and between sales management and its sales personnel. It is generally the management of these human relationships, communications, and information flows, rather than the logistics, that is most important. Therefore, sales and sales force management tend to be culture-bound activities and can vary from country to country.

For example, international marketers are beginning to understand that the difficulty of making inroads into the Japanese market may have little to do with its trade barriers. Japan does not impose any tariffs on foreign cars and has eliminated nearly all nontariff barriers to automobile trade. Rather, the difficulty is attributed to how cars are sold in Japan. Unlike the United States, where customers visit car dealerships, a majority of the cars sold in Japan are peddled by door-to-door salespeople, much the same way Avon representatives sell personal care and beauty products in the United States.[2]

As with most other management tasks, the management of selling process (at the sales management level) starts with a definition of how the sales activities are to be organized. Although different sales and sales force management may be needed in different countries or regions of the world, sales management *procedures* are generally transferable across national boundaries.

TERRITORY MANAGEMENT AND PLANNING

The most important decision in sales management is how to allocate responsibilities within the sales team. The traditional basis for this allocation decision uses the building block of the individual territory. In fact, the concept of sales professionals being entitled to their own territories is a relatively recent one. It was only just before World War I that John Patterson instituted the concept of territories as a fundamental aspect of the NCR sales operation; shortly afterward Thomas J. Watson, then at NCR, took it to IBM and used it as a basis for building that company's legendary sales force. Prior to that time, there had been no "territories": All prospects were fair game for all salespeople, and their main competitors could just as easily be from the same company as they were.

www.ibm.com

avon.avon.com

www.ncr.com

---

1. Michele Marchetti, "The New Gold Rush," *Sales and Marketing Management* (September 1998): 42–52+.
2. "In Japan's Car Market, Big Three Face Rivals Who Go Door-to-Door," *Wall Street Journal*, September 28, 1994, A1, A11.

Although such territories are normally thought of as geographical areas, there can be a number of other bases for the way territories are structured, such as by industry and by product.

GEOGRAPHICAL TERRITORIES

Most territories are based on a geographical area, ranging from a whole country all the way to a single ZIP code. One advantage of such an approach is that the areas are relatively easy to define, and hence should avoid unnecessary contention. On the other hand, very few sales professionals rigorously check what their territories are. This situation may be complicated by the fact that such territories are often split along main roads, with one sales professional calling on the businesses on one side and another on the opposite side.

An alternative geographical approach may be to explore which parts of these purely geographical territories have the most potential and allocate sales territories on that basis. This potential may be immediately evident in the form of large residential areas, shopping centers, or office complexes. But it may also require considerable research in terms of searching through the various lists and directories to determine where individual large prospects are located. At the end of the day, however, no such system can beat the exploratory eye of the individual salesperson walking or driving along every street of his or her territory, particularly as this is the only way of finding the new business that is just moving in—normally some of the hottest prospects.

However, other factors can complicate the picture considerably. For example, traffic patterns can mean that physical distances are much less important than traveling times, and it is the latter that the salesperson must take into consideration, by drawing contours of equal traveling time, just like the altitudinal contours on a map.

BY INDUSTRY. A territory split that is used much less frequently than geography is industry, but this can be a very powerful choice. For example, IBM is organizing sales staffs into 14 industry groups, such as banking and retail, rather than by region or country. This structure has two great benefits. First, the sales professionals dedicated to each industry are steeped in the knowledge and folklore of that industry, even though their geographical range is wide. Second, for globetrotting companies like IBM, this structure helps break down national barriers inside the company, moving it toward a global organization.[3]

BY PRODUCT. This approach is often necessary because it may be time consuming to get to know the products in sufficient depth, and sales personnel may not have the personal resources to apply equal expertise to all products in the range. This is the case, for example, with General Electric, whose product lines range from home appliances to jet engines. Sales professionals specialized in a certain product line have a broad geographical coverage. For highly specialized, high-tech products such as jet engines and power-generation turbines, sales professionals may have a responsibility around the world.

www.ge.com

TERRITORY PLANS

Once these territory decisions have been made, management should be in a position to plot those areas of highest potential on their maps to give the true shape of the territories. Based on the sales potential of each territory, sales managers need to determine the resources that will be required to tap it and what is actually available. The essential resource is, of course, sales personnel.

---

3. "Borderless Management: Companies Strive to Become Truly Stateless," *Business Week*, May 23, 1994.

In order to manage this resource plan, sales management needs to first of all know how much its sales personnel cost per hour, which is usually far more than sales management thinks, hence the reason for expanding on it at this stage. Sales activities are *very* expensive. The following factors are included in sales personnel cost:

1. Salary
2. Commission
3. Bonuses
4. Direct expenses
5. Indirect expenses
6. Overhead costs[4]

Overhead costs cover the cost of support staff and management and can typically double the costs attributed to individual salespersons. Thus, the total cost of maintaining a salesperson is much higher than one may think. A typical cost of face-to-face selling time for account managers is estimated at up to $500 per hour and for direct sales representatives at an average of $300 per hour.[5]

Most managers, who have little practical experience of selling, are surprised by just how short a time is actually spent with the customer. Table 14.1 shows a breakdown of a salesperson's daily workload in one consumer goods company. It indicated that less than one-third of his or her time is spent on a customer's premises, and only one-twentieth of the overall time is spent waiting on the customer. Obviously, it is crucial for salespeople to plan their time effectively.

In recent years, however, the computer revolution has ushered in a more flexible working environment for many sales professionals with the aid of laptop computers, modems, and faxes. This allows sales professionals to allocate more time to traveling and visiting their clients and new prospects. For example, the 600 sales representatives based in IBM's new sales office in Cranford, New Jersey, do not have offices. They come in to pick up mail and see associates once or twice each

the computer revolution has ushered in a more flexible working environment for many sales professionals

www.ibm.com

www.rubbermaid.com

www.wal-mart.com

www.marketsoft.com

week, and their tasks are computer-assigned and communicated with their office via modems and laptop computers.[6] Lagging behind in this computer revolution can be costly. Rubbermaid has lagged behind in computer systems and communications with its sales force and had difficulty replenishing supplies based on actual sales rather than on forecasts for major retailer customers such as Wal-Mart.[7]

Recently, several software programs have been designed to support sales efforts within companies. For example, MarketSoft Corp. is introducing eLeads, a software that helps businesses pass leads to internal salespeople and channel partners. It can track the leads, letting managers see what a salesperson has done with them and which salespeople are most effective. Sales leads, such as those garnered from trade shows, are wasted because no one follows up quickly enough and the leads become stale. A company can spend a large amount of money for a trade show booth, and find the list of leads generated still sitting there a month

4. Alan Gillam, *The Principle and Practice of Selling* (Oxford: Butterworth Heinemann, 1982).
5. R. T. Moriarty and U. Moran, "Managing Hybrid Marketing Systems," *Harvard Business Review* (November/December 1990).
6. "The New World of Work," *Business Week*, October 14, 1994.
7. "The Revolving Door at Rubbermaid," *Business Week*, September 18, 1995.

Table 14.1	Breakdown of a salesperson's daily workload	
		% of time spent
Travel		50
Making the call		24
Selling		6
Administration		20

Source: Malcolm H. B. McDonald, *Marketing Plans*, 3d ed. (New York: Butterworth Heinemann, 1985), 275–276. Adapted by permission of Butterworth Heinemann Publishers Oxford, a division of Reed Educational & Professional Publishing Ltd.

later. The software is designed to help salespeople get those leads almost instantaneously and contact potential customers within 24 hours. It lets companies transmit leads electronically to the appropriate salesperson via front-office and contact-management packages such as Siebel 99, Symantec Act!, and Microsoft Outlook, rather than through slower telephone, mail, and fax services.[8]

www.siebel.com
www.symantec.com
www.microsoft.com

ANNUAL CALLS AVAILABLE

In preparing these resource plans, perhaps the most important calculation is determining how many calls the sales force will be able to make in a year. The basic element of this measurement is the day. For many sales professionals, at least for those in the area of capital goods such as workstations and earthmoving equipment, it may be difficult to book more than two or three calls a day; it is also difficult to predict exactly how long they will last. Depending on industry structure, however, it should be possible to supplement this by ad hoc or "cold" calls, and to at least double this rate. Some retail salespeople can easily achieve rates of 10 times this level.

This rate assumes an ideal sales day, which rarely happens. Many sales professionals have to spend a great deal of time preparing for calls, supporting customers, and writing proposals. In the past, sales professionals used to spend about half of their work hours at their desks in the branch office. Today, thanks to notebook computers, modems, and various communication software that create a virtual office, sales professionals are no longer confined to their traditional offices. This flexibility has enormously improved sales professionals' productivity.

In calculating annual calls, allowance must be made for holidays, training, and so on. In general, it can be assumed that any staff member will be available for only 200 days a year. Therefore, if 50 percent has been allowed for office work, a simple calculation shows that the effective time available for face-to-face selling can be reduced to as little as 100 days a year. At perhaps two calls a day, this equals only 200 possible calls a year. It is a sobering experience for most sales managers when they first come face-to-face with the true figures. It makes them much more aware of how important *each* call is. They realize that they cannot afford to let their sales personnel miss any calls or to achieve anything less than their optimum performance in each call they do make.

8. Jeff Sweat, "Sales-Lead Management," *Informationweek*, May 24, 1999, 30.

avon.avon.com

SALES PERSONNEL PLAN

The most important decision for any sales manager to make (and then to justify to the board) is how many sales personnel are needed. Avon has established a 400,000-person sales force just for Brazil![9] The complex decision of how many sales personnel are needed can be based on a number of different approaches.

RESOURCES NEEDED TO EXPLOIT POTENTIAL. The amount of sales time needed to support the projected number of customers and prospects will need to be calculated. This may be done on the basis of experience, allowing for the fact that customers should, against most salespersons' natural inclinations, be given a greater amount of support than prospects—and large accounts considerably more. Alternatively, the calculation may be based on the resources needed to support the specific accounts (although this is rare, except where account planning is implemented).

The resulting total sales time is then divided by the realistic sales time available per person to give the number of salespeople needed. A number of alternative models (based on market penetration or sales response factors, for instance) attempt to provide more accurate estimates.

One of these alternative models is *marginal analysis*, which follows the same principles as marginal costing. Extra salespeople are added to the payroll until the profit generated by the marginal salesperson exactly matches the cost of this person. In view of the difficulties of determining what the cost of an individual salesperson is, let alone what his or her profit might be, this approach is rarely practiced, no matter how attractive it is in theory.

Few sales forces are ever allowed to recruit to the levels deemed necessary by such calculations. This may not necessarily be a bad thing, depending on the scale of the underresourcing. It is better—in terms of morale and management control— to have a sales force that is overworked by a small margin than one that has too little potential for its members to work toward.

RESOURCES NEEDED TO MEET TARGET. This is the most popular technique among the few organizations that actually produce a sales plan. It may follow the calculations above, but it is more likely to be based on experience—for instance, how many salespeople, in the organization's experience, will be needed to meet next year's targets.

As extension to this process involves negotiations (for example, as division justifying its sales plan to the group headquarters) for extra sales personnel in return for increased targets.

Affordability. Following the same principles as those for the overall promotional budget, the organization decides—usually on the basis of historical precedent— how much it can afford to spend on a sales force after all the other costs and the planned profit have been deducted from revenue.

Percentage of revenue. Alternatively, sales can once more be allocated on a (often arbitrary) percentage of the planned revenue.

NEGOTIATED LEVELS. Negotiation is, by default, the most widely used technique for making changes to the numbers in the sales force. The sales manager negotiates with the board (or sells his or her "package" to it, usually on the basis of emotional rather than rational arguments) to increase the numbers of sales personnel. We have yet to hear of a sales manager who has proposed a reduction in the size of his or her overall sales force.

---

9. "Perfuming the Amazon," *Economist*, October 22, 1994, 74.

Marketing in Action 14.1

Daewoo's college student sales force

Daewoo Motor Company (www.dm.co.kr.com) was established in 1972 by a joint venture between Shinjin Motor Co. (Korea) and General Motors (www.gm.com). However, by 2000, as a result of a vital bankruptcy of its parent company, Daewoo Motor is struggling to keep its growth momentum. Now in the midst of various takeover rumors, the ailing Korean car maker is trying to make a comeback.

The combination of a weak currency and sluggish Korean automobile sales (forcing manufacturers to operate at 40 percent of capacity) has prompted Korean car makers to focus on the export market. With a first-year sales target of 30,000 cars, Daewoo has launched an ambitious effort in the U.S. market. Entering the United States with three models priced at $8,999, $12,000, and $18,600, Daewoo plans to initially open 15 factory-owned dealerships in California, Florida, and the Northeast. These dealerships will sell directly to the public.

In addition to traditional dealerships, the company has hired 2,000 Daewoo Campus Advisors on 200 college campuses to promote the cars and to direct potential buyers to showrooms. These campus advisors are 18 to 20 years old, predominantly male, and marketing/business majors. The advisors earn $300 to $500 per car sold, a company sponsored seven-day trip to Daewoo's facilities in Korea, and the use of a Daewoo car for three months (which can then be purchased at a reduced price).

With college students as salespeople, Daewoo appears to be targeting the college student crowd—a crowd without a steady income, little savings, and a lack of credit history. Will Daewoo be reaching the purchaser of its automobiles? Do you think salesperson turnover will be a problem? Evaluate Daewoo's organization of territories. Do campus divisions ensure the greatest coverage? Why or why not?

Sources: www.dm.co.kr.com; Joseph Siano, "Daewoo, of Korea, Gives America the Old College Try," *New York Times*, July 19, 1998, section 12, 1; "General Motors Wants to Take Over Daewoo Motor," http://cnn.com/ASIA NOW, accessed December 6, 1999.

BUSINESS AS USUAL.   In most cases no change is proposed. There is a fixed pattern of territories, and sales personnel are simply replaced when they leave. The only exception is those territories that have moved so far out of line that they have to be split or combined. The main force for sales force planning, therefore, is that of inertia.

Marketing in Action 14.1 raises issues not only about the number of sales personnel but also about the type of sales personnel recruited.

THE SALES PROFESSIONAL

The actions of the individual sales professional will produce the overall sales impact. The next part of this chapter will, therefore, look at individual sales activities. Conventionally these are not treated as management activities, but they are as much marketing tools as any of the other techniques we have described. Accordingly, you should appreciate that they imply, and thus understand what lies behind one of the most important operations of almost all commercial organizations and many nonprofit organizations as well.

> The actions of the individual sales professional **will produce the overall sales impact.**

INDIVIDUAL MANAGEMENT OF SALES

The traditional view of selling has been that it is a professional role rather than a managerial one (very few sales professionals manage teams of subordinates).

In practice, however, much of the sales professional's role is actually concerned with management. The typical competent sales professional should manage a number of resources and processes:

- **Territory.** Typically, the sales professional is solely responsible for his or her territory. He or she is responsible for everything that happens in this territory and for all activities, with the range of responsibilities comparable with those normally assumed by a brand manager, or even by the chief executive of a subsidiary.

- **Sales plan.** Within that territory a sales plan has to be created that is usually a simplified version of the marketing plan. Performance will have to be monitored against that plan and tactics changed to allow for deviations from target, just as in the overall organizational plan.

- **Organizational resources.** Every sales professional will have some organizational resources available, including service support, marketing support, and, possibly, even budgeted amounts of territory-based promotional funding. All of these resources will have to be managed.

- **Support personnel.** Most sales professionals do not manage people; indeed, as mentioned earlier, very few actually have formal responsibility for subordinates. Yet many indirectly control the activities of support personnel. What is more, they often have to achieve this management control under difficult circumstances on customer premises and without any formal authority.

- **Customer interface.** Above all, the sales professional manages the customer interface, or goodwill, which is the most important asset of any organization. This demands a great deal of skill and is a role that contains many of the key elements of management.

TERRITORY SALES PLAN

The sales plan for an individual sales territory should define the customer and prospects and contain sales forecasts.

DEFINING THE CUSTOMER AND PROSPECT SETS.

At this stage the customer and the prospect databases will usually be constructed, because each group will be approached differently.

Without a doubt, the most important split within almost all territories is between customers and prospects. Customers are almost universally more productive than prospects and indeed more productive than many sales professionals (or their management) allow for. Assuming that the organization has previously offered good service, customers are already loyal to it. Competitors will have to justify breaking these links before they can even begin their selling process. For such customers the organization already has an existing base on which it is natural to build. A contemporary business philosophy is that it is easier and thus more profitable to maintain existing customers than to try to increase market share. Indeed, it costs five times more to get a new customer than to keep a current one.[10]

> it costs five times more
> **to get a new customer**
> than to keep a current one

---

10. Joshua Levine, "Relationship Marketing," *Forbes,* December 20, 1993, 232–233.

However, many—if not most—sales professionals devote little time to customers. The "macho" stereotype, discussed later in this chapter, persuades them to spend their time unproductively, touting for new business, when common sense should tell them to spend at least adequate time defending and developing their customer base.

This problem was particularly evident in the earlier days of the personal computer market. All of the research showed that the one group almost guaranteed to buy a new system consisted of existing customers who had already bought a previous system—typically within the past year. On the other hand, cold prospects were unlikely to show a better than 10 percent chance of buying a system. Yet most sales professionals sadly neglected their customers, and the industry had an appalling reputation of poor customer service.

Therefore the first priority of any sales professional must be to allocate resources to the customer set, and to differentiate between customers according to what they are worth. Some will be "bankers" and will bring in a large part of the easy 80 percent of business and these investments must be cosseted. On the other hand, some will be totally unproductive, demanding resource for little return, and in these cases the plan must be to "stop the bleeding."

"A" prospects.   The sales team should know its customers well enough to predict the sales performance of each, but the real skill comes in being able to separate the sheep from the goats among the prospects. The question of which are the 10 percent or so who will bring in more than 50 percent of the new business is partly a function of their size (in terms of potential business) and partly of the sales professionals' probability of closing deals. These are the prospects who should have first claim on the resources left after the planned support of customers.

"B" prospects.   Similarly, the sales team will have to determine which prospects bring in the remaining 50 percent of new business. This needs careful planning and a ruthless determination to control expenses in order to ration the small amount of resource remaining after customers and "A" prospects have been catered to.

Losers.   All other prospects have to be treated as outcasts. No matter how much certain prospects plead, the productive sales force will have to be ruthless and refuse to fritter away resources on unproductive areas. The true sales professional must insist that customers *prove* their good intentions. This sounds like the reverse of good salesmanship, but at times good salesmanship is as much about managing scarce resources as it is about winning friends and influencing people.

As indicated earlier, husbanding resources for the 20 percent of accounts that will bring in 80 percent of business is a critical aspect of all territory and account planning. It is one of the management aspects of professional salesmanship that many sales professionals find most difficult to implement; they more naturally rush to the account that demands immediate attention, without considering the long-term implications. The old saying, "The squeaky wheel gets the grease," summarizes this pitfall. Planning is often the activity that distinguishes the senior sales professional from less-professional juniors.

SALES FORECASTS.   The most productive phase of any planning usually starts with the forecasts of where future business will come from.

The easiest part of any forecast should be to deal with the "bankers"—those major accounts that the sales personnel know will soon complete the formality of signing the order. Even then, forecasting exactly when they will sign is not necessarily that easy. Paradoxically, it is somewhat more difficult to control if they have already stated that they will be placing the order. As far as they are concerned, they have already given their sales contact the order and see their formal signature as a petty administrative detail. Nevertheless, bankers are still the easiest to predict and should form the core of any forecast.

"Probables" and "possibles" fall into three main groups. Those accounts labeled "80 percent chance of closing" can usually be regarded as genuine "probables"; sales professionals tend to be unduly optimistic, but a more than 80 percent confidence level is usually indicative of a good chance of success.

Below 50 percent, however, the "possibles" that most sales professionals would hope for are likely "losers." The main question to be asked of this category is whether it is worth putting any more resource into them. The experienced sales professional (and, in particular, his or her manager) will usually include in the overall forecast only the business rated to have a better than 50 percent chance.

In any event, the wise sales manager will then still divide the aggregated forecasts of the sales team by a factor of two when making his or her own submission to senior management.

SALES OBJECTIVES

The specific sales objectives should be derived in part from these investigations, but they will also emerge from the overall marketing plan, which will be discussed later. They should include at least three major elements:

- **Total shares to be achieved.** This is quoted in terms of volume, value, or possibly both; for example, 400 cases (volume) or $2,000,000 (value).

- **Product mix.** This is the relative contribution of each product to total sales; for example, 80 percent of sales to be product A, 15 percent to be product B, and 5 percent to be product C.

- **Market mix.** This is the proportion of total sales in each market; for example, 10 percent in New York, 20 percent in Pennsylvania, and 70 percent in Ohio; or 80 percent to the financial services sector, 15 percent to retailers, and 5 percent to the rest of the industry.

CALL TARGETS.　　The basic building block of any sales campaign has to be its calls. Generally speaking, a number of calls are needed to secure the business, and it is certainly true that the more calls that are made, the more business will be booked. This is often described in sales circles as the "numbers game."

For example, for every 1,000 promotional flyers sent out there will be a certain percentage of returns that justify a sales call. Telesales and cold calling will also generate proportional results. From these subsequent calls a proportion will turn into serious prospects (some of whom will progress to demonstrations and proposals), and out of these serious prospects a proportion will place orders. Finally, a proportion will place those orders with the organization undertaking these activities rather than with its competitors.

At each stage, therefore, there is a conversion ratio. It is clearly the sales professional's personal skills (backed by sound account management) that ensure that this conversion ratio is as high as it can be. Converting a good prospect into a customer requires all the skills that a sales professional possesses (as does converting a return postage-paid card from a promotional flyer into a prospect). It is a basic fact of the sales game that providing the numbers of prospects to feed into the "machine" that eventually converts them into business is just sheer hard work.

INDUSTRIAL SALES

The sales professional is most likely to come into contact with industrial sales, in which a number of individuals are involved in the buying decision and the sales campaign extends over a number of calls.

In industrial sales, salespeople have short-term and long-term objectives. In the short term, they must close as many individual deals as they possibly can, as quickly as possible. In the long term, salespeople want to maintain healthy relationships with the customers signing the deals, so the customers will be willing to make purchases in the months and years to come.

In many ways this environment is very different from that of the single-call sale, which has been the staple diet of many sales trainers, though it is a rapidly declining aspect of selling. Because most sales-training programs emphasize tactical rather than strategic skills, even very good salespeople sometimes find themselves cut out of a sale at the last minute because they failed to locate or cover all the real decision makers for their specific sale. 3M takes the novel approach of surveying its customers to have them specify what training the 3M salespeople require.[11]

www.3m.com

INDUSTRIAL BUYING SITUATIONS

Some researchers identify different industrial buying decisions:[12]

- **Straight rebuy.** This is the repeat purchase of an existing product or service that has given satisfactory performance. No new information is needed for the buying decision. The existing supplier is usually difficult to displace in such situations, because buyers favor existing (known risk) suppliers and much of their buying is routine.

- **Modified rebuy.** The buyer may be dissatisfied with the existing product or service. In this case, the buying decision has to be reevaluated. This is the occasion when new suppliers are most likely to make changes to a buyer's existing purchasing patterns. However, in many markets it is the incompetence or inattention of the existing supplier—not the attractiveness of the new one—that triggers this change.

- **New task buying.** In this situation there is no previous history, so the buyer has to start from scratch, and all suppliers begin with the same chance of winning a job contract.

Naturally, new task buying requires the most effort by both buyers and sellers. Buyers have to assess their corporate needs accurately and get purchase approvals from a layer of decision makers before soliciting business from prospective sellers. Product quality and reliability, credit terms, and postpurchase service contracts are some of the issues that industrial buyers have to deal with. Accordingly, sellers need to be able to handle the high-level technical aspects of buyers' inquiries and specifications. Once their business relationships get established over time, then the industrial buying process will become routinized from modified rebuy to straight rebuy.

---

11. William Keenan, Jr., "Getting Customers into the A.C.T.," *Sales and Marketing Management* (February 1995): 58–63.
12. P. J. Robinson, C. W. Farris, and Y. Wind, *Industrial Buying and Creative Marketing* (Boston: Allyn and Bacon, 1967).

DECISION MAKERS AND INFLUENCERS

Regardless of the buying situation in industrial sales, it is no longer sufficient to persuade just one buyer. Instead, sales professionals have to convince a whole range of individuals, all with different (and often contradictory) requirements.

The first problem that this poses is quite simply that of identifying who the various buyers are. In industrial sales it is no longer an easy task; the "buyers" involved can range from the Chief Executive Officer to members of the various departments.

The convention is to split these buyers into **decision makers** and **influencers**; with the clear implication that the small group of decision makers should be the prime target, although influencers should not be neglected. This is a useful distinction, in that it correctly focuses the sales professional's attention on the key decision makers, and forces him or her to contact them, whereas too many sales personnel remain bogged down among the influencers. It was certainly true, in the early days of the personal computer market, that dealers rarely contacted more than one person in their prospect (even in larger corporations). Generally, that person was a buyer in the purchasing department and was usually only an influencer. The real decisions were made elsewhere, though, because the only sales message was price; the lack of face-to-face contact with the decision maker was not really a critical factor.

The problem with this two-way split is that both decision makers and influencers are very general categories, probably too general (and too confined within the sales perspective) to best help the sales professional to home in on the exact decision-making structure. In their book, Heiman and Sanchez[13] identify four buying influences, the first three of which relate to the more conventional structure.

ECONOMIC BUYERS.   The economic buyer is the ultimate decision maker. This person—or group, such as a board—holds the purse strings and *must* approve the decisions. Clearly this buyer is the most important person in the whole structure. However, almost by definition salespeople cannot reach the decision maker far up on the corporate ladder who gives final approval.

USER BUYERS.   User buyers are the people who are going to use whatever is being offered. In the more conventional model they would lie between decision makers and influencers. A virtue of the more complex model is that it allows sales professionals to handle this important group most effectively. As someone who will actually use (or supervise the use of) a product or service, the role of the user buyer is to make judgments about the impact of that product or service on the job to be done.

TECHNICAL BUYERS.   Technical buyers are the true influencers of the simpler model, but with a powerful ability to veto that could still be fatal for the sale. They examine the specification for technical conformance. In many industrial sales situations (certainly in the case of machine tools) the purchasing department staffed with quality engineers falls into this category.

COACH.   The sales professional should identify a contact who is willing and able to serve as a guide through the complexities of the sale. The **coach** gives the salesperson the information that he or she needs to manage it to a close, thus guaranteeing not only the order but satisfied customers and repeat business as well. This contact could be anyone who is aware of the purchasing process in that company.

13. Stephen E. Heiman and Diane Sanchez, *The New Strategic Selling* (New York: Warner Books, 1998).

These categories are not a function of the titles on the doors; they are a result of specific relationships to the purchase. Even more important, the structure is not fixed. The relationships change for different purchases, and people move from one category to another.

In practice, the decision-making process is normally deeply embedded in the user process. Users have a great deal of delegated power. Although the final decision may have to be approved by higher authority, in many cases it is in reality only a power of veto (any board that saddles its user departments with unwelcome choice is asking for trouble).

PROJECT MANAGEMENT

Perhaps the most important skill in handling industrial sales customers is that of project management. Customer sales tend to run as a series of projects, and each sales campaign can be thought of as a separate project and managed as such. But after an order is won, the next project—the installation—is the most complex of all and requires the highest management skills. In addition, there are other smaller projects, such as training or the extension of product or service use into new areas, that can also benefit from project management skills.

PROPOSALS

Proposals often form a major element of the industrial sales process. The skills needed for producing proposals are similar to those needed for project management and, in particular, relate to those of surveying; a good survey is almost a prerequisite for a proposal.

However, the first question the sales professional or manager has to ask is, "Does this sale (or proposed management action) need a proposal?" Often the answer is "No," because proposals are time and resource consuming. It is much better to confirm the agreements with a short letter or memo and use the time saved to build the prospect base or continue the project.

Occasionally, it is necessary to produce a full proposal, particularly if the sale is competitive or, for management, if approval for an internal project is difficult to obtain. A well-prepared, well-presented proposal is very impressive; it is unlikely that the competitors will have produced one (or at least not one as effective), so it may well give a competitive edge. It also serves as a very useful record of all the agreements.

The content of the proposal should directly reflect the sales campaign. If that sales campaign has a sound structure, so too will the proposal. The one rule, however, is that all the main material in a proposal should have been previously agreed to by the prospect or, in the case of managers, with the others involved in the project. Nothing should come as a surprise. A suggested format is as follows:

1. Summary
2. Prospect or senior management requirements (in brief)
3. Summary background (including a review of the problem to be solved)
4. Proposed solutions (in summary)
5. General benefits
6. Financial justification and costs
7. Appendices
   A. Detailed background (survey results)
   B. Detailed solutions (including flowcharts)

C. Product or concept descriptions

D. References (descriptions of similar systems with customers or—for internal proposals—use of similar approaches by other organizations)

INTERORGANIZATIONAL RELATIONS

Selling has traditionally been seen as a confrontational activity, with the salesperson "hierarchically" subservient to the buyer, with the former trying to persuade the latter to buy something not wanted or needed. It is seen as a zero-sum game in which each of the participants can gain only at the expense of the other. A new approach to selling, known as relationship marketing, attempts to change this pattern to a win-win situation. As David Ulrich puts it,

> in the turbulent and increasingly competitive 1990s, firms need to go beyond customer satisfaction. Firms earn customer satisfaction in the short term by assessing and meeting needs; they earn customer commitment in the long term through hundreds of small, heroic acts that create loyalty and devotion . . . committed customers look beyond short term pleasures and develop an allegiance to the firm . . . committed customers become interdependent with the firm through shared resources and values.[14]

Relationship marketing is gaining acceptance as a valuable tool for many firms, as it helps build an opportunity share in the future, if not a market share immediately.[15] Because this type of relationship requires a higher level of personal support, from a more skilled sales professional (a "relationship manager"), it will typically be limited to the 5 or 10 most important customers.

RELATIONSHIP MARKETING

www.bose.com
www.compaq.com
www.motorola.com

In the past 20 years, an increasing number of U.S. Companies, such as Bose, Compaq, and Motorola, have been influenced by Japan's vertical *keiretsu* (a closely knit group affiliation among the principal company, upstream suppliers of components and other materials, and downstream retailers for its finished products along the value chain). As a result, they have begun to station their engineering personnel in their independent parts suppliers for more effective product development and to station their sales personnel work in the retailer's offices. The principal companies can track demand directly at store levels and place orders on a just-in-time basis. Both upstream and downstream involvements by the principal companies along the value chain can manage information flow from the retailers and customers more effectively and step up the pace of new product development.[16]

This type of buyer-seller relationship is a win-win situation because both sides gain from the deal (albeit in a different ways). Thus, they start out with the intention of producing a mutually beneficial arrangement. An increasing number of organizations have, indeed, come to see the relationship as one of interdependence; the two sides adopt a peer-to-peer relationship.

---

14. David Ulrich, "Tie the Corporate Knot: Gaining Complete Customer Commitment," *Sloan Management Review* (1989).

15. Joel R. Evans and Richard L. Laskin, "The Relationship Marketing Process: A Conceptual Application," *Industrial Marketing Management* 23 (December 1994): 439–452.

16. Michiel R. Leenders and David L. Blenkhorn, *Reverse Marketing: The New Buyer-Supplier Relationship* (New York: Free Press, 1988).

Indeed, the relationship between a seller and a buyer seldom ends when the sale is made. In an increasing proportion of transactions, the relationship actually intensifies subsequent to the sale. This becomes the critical factor in the buyer's choice of the seller the next time around. How good the seller-buyer relationship is depends on how well it is managed by the seller.[17] Again, many companies are finding that adoption of personal computer technology in maintaining product, pricing, and technical data for effective customer relationships is crucial for their success.

> the relationship between a seller and a buyer seldom ends when the sale is made. . . . [it] actually intensifies subsequent to the sale.

It is almost a decade since management consultancy Bain & Co. carried out its groundbreaking research into the key differences between customer acquisition and customer retention. By considering the real costs and long-term returns, it found that acquisition costs were often understated by most companies, while cross-selling to an existing customer cost one-sixth of the price of making a sale to a prospect. Bain introduced one of the most famous equations on marketing: A 5 percent increase in customer retention would increase the value of each customer by between 25 and 100 percent. The potential implied in that finding led directly toward customer relationship marketing.[18]

www.bain.com

Table 14.2 illustrates the point by comparing the typical reactions of the seller versus those of the buyer at the time of the purchase. Regular contact is essential in order to maintain rapport, to maintain the partnership. It is also very productive in terms of developing the account. The investment in a satisfied customer may not show immediately on the balance sheet, but it creates commitment and trust relationships and contributes handsomely to the bottom-line profit.[19]

Let us take a look at Safeway, a supermarket, as an example. Exactly what does Safeway do with the data collected on its customers? Safeway offers its ABC card, a loyalty card for discount purchase, to its customers (see Exhibit 14.1). On the condition that its customers sign up for an ABC loyalty card, surrendering certain information about themselves and putting themselves in line to receive mail shots, they will be offered 10 percent off their grocery bills. Safeway now has 10 million ABC cardholders, with between six and seven million cards in regular use.

www.safeway.com

Table 14.2

Seller	Buyer
When the sale is first made	
Seller	**Buyer**
Objective achieved	Judgment postponed; applies test of time
Selling stops	Shopping continues
Focus goes elsewhere	Focus on purchase; wants affirmation that expectations have been met
Tension released	Tension increased
Relationship reduced or ended	Commitment made; relationship intensified

Source: Reprinted by permission of *Harvard Business Review.* From Theodore Levitt, "After the Sale is Over," *Harvard Business Review* 61 (September/October 1983): 87. Copyright © 1983 by the President and Fellows of Harvard College; all rights reserved.

17. Barton A. Weitz and Kevin D. Bradford, "Personal Selling and Sales Management: A Relationship Marketing Perspective," *Journal of the Academy of Marketing Science* 27 (spring 1999): 241–254.
18. David Reed, "Great Expectations," *Marketing Week*, April 29, 1999, 57–58.
19. Robert M. Morgan and Shelby D. Hunt, "The Commitment-Trust Theory of Relationship Marketing," *Journal of Marketing* 58 (July 1994): 20–38.

Exhibit 14.1

In November 1999, PowerGen LPC (UK) purchased Safeway's ABC frequent shopper list in hopes that the 10 million loyalty card users would become loyal PowerGen customers. Safeway cardholders purchasing PowerGen utilities receive 100 ABC points and £15 (pounds sterling) in supermarket vouchers for each fuel they switch from their existing utilities providers. This overt sale of a loyalty list for distinctly marketing purposes may cause consumer privacy advocates to escalate efforts at regulation.

Its database boasts 12 billion rows of product-specific data from every customer and every transaction they make, and Safeway's head office was the first supermarket headquarters to set up a dedicated relationship marketing team. Around 40 percent of Safeway's budget for communications is now spent on sending out 13 million mailing contacts a year. For example, although women starting a family are just the shoppers Safeway wants to develop a relationship with, the supermarket is also using relationship marketing to gain feedback from all kinds of customers deemed important for the business.

In a bid to find out what can be done to make these shoppers more loyal, Safeway targets them with questionnaires. The various responses that make their way back to the head office then allow Safeway to generate closely tailored letters giving information or promotional incentives to these shoppers. Safeway targeted 100,000 people from its database over the last 12 to 15 months and sent out questions asking customers if they thought they were spending less in Safeway stores. Safeway is able to use the data to create a highly targeted conversation with its customers and to convert that into information that is useful to them when they shop at the supermarket. The company is confident that its relationship marketing effort can make a real difference in the long-term purchasing trends of customers that receive regular contact from the supermarket.[20]

ACCOUNT PLANNING

The most important activity in developing relationship accounts is creating a sound account plan. Unlike the overall sales plan that will deal with groups of customers, each account plan concerns just a single customer.

An account plan should match (at least in its scope of content) the overall marketing plan. It should detail the specific objectives, which will be individually related to the customer's needs and wants and the activities that are planned to meet these objectives and to build the relationship.

---

20. Susie Whalley, "ABC of Relationship Marketing," *Supermarketing*, March 12, 1999, 12.

If such a plan is produced within the selling organization it will be a productive exercise. If it is produced in cooperation with the customer so that the resulting plan becomes a shared plan, it may make a major contribution to the development of a genuine peer-to-peer relationship. Key account management is gaining popularity. For example, in 1998, both IBM and Compaq established direct relationships with certain large corporate accounts. Under the IBM and Compaq initiatives, channel service partners are brought into the deals as service subcontractors, and the vendors act in general contractor roles. Hewlett-Packard now works more closely with global account customers seeking more vendor accountability. HP's strategy is designed to free the vendor to work with certain customers while keeping the channel involved in key accounts.[21] Given the rapid information revolution of the 1990s, many other companies are also accumulating the capability to better maintain seller-customer relationships.

www.ibm.com
www.compaq.com

www.hp.com

Major account management is a team effort. The ideal team would consist not only of dedicated sales and marketing people, but financial, MIS, logistics, manufacturing, customer-service, technical-support, and international contract coordinators. The account manager must be the leader and point person of the cross-functional support team assigned to the customer. More often, a customer will measure satisfaction on the total efforts of the team rather than the individual performance of the account manager. Therefore, strong interpersonal and organizational skills are must-haves for successful account management.[22]

As we have already stressed, account management (covering prospects as well as customers) is the essence of professional salesmanship. Customer account management, in particular, is probably the most important single skill (apart from selling itself) required of a sales professional, yet it is almost entirely neglected by sales trainers.

Not surprisingly, however, banks are at the forefront of this trend for customer account management, particularly as they merge with other financial institutions. The very nature of financial services requires that banks always have a lot of information about their customers. Selling products like loans requires an ability to understand risk and the ability to assess it. All that ties back to understanding customers and their likelihood of being able to make payments. But telecommunications, retail, and media—highly competitive industries with a lot of customers in which brand differentiation can be difficult—are also becoming proponents of this strategy.[23]

SALES TEAM MANAGEMENT

In many respects, sales team management has been a neglected element of management training, yet the sales manager's responsibility—managing the entire interface with the customer—is probably the most critical of all in terms of ultimate success for the organization. Because it is a very complex role, we will look at those aspects that are the province of sales management alone.

MARKETING MANAGEMENT

In many organizations, the sales manager is responsible for all marketing activities. Even in those where there is a parallel marketing structure, he or she is usually responsible for a range of marketing activities beyond those of simply managing

21. Edward F. Moltzen and Craig Zarley, "HP's Platt Outlines New Enterprise Account Strategy," *Computer Reseller News*, October 19, 1998, 1, 10.
22. Ray Holley, "Major Account Management: Not Just Another Job," *Computer Reseller News*, May 3, 1999, 125.
23. Erika Rasmusson, "Wanted: Profitable Customers," *Sales and Marketing Management* (May 1999): 28–34.

the sales force. In this context, therefore, the sales management role often requires an appreciation of the range of techniques described throughout this book. Marketing in Action 14.2 describes a situation where a changing marketing strategy may greatly affect successful sales management.

The struggle between sales and marketing departments for mutual respect and proper credit has been waged constantly. Despite such a struggle, sales and marketing departments depend on each other. And now, with globalization and e-commerce beginning to take hold at many companies, this reliance is especially important. The market is moving so fast that if marketing and sales organizations aren't communicating, then a company could be in real trouble. As Marketing in Action 14.2 describes, an internal system of constant communication is required to avoid such a situation. For example, Eastern Transport Corporation, a shipping and logistics company based in Quebec, Canada, ensures this type of communication in a couple of ways. First, all sales meetings include every member of the company's marketing department. When the company's salespeople see marketing reps in sales meetings, it sends the message that they are involved in the sales process and in how their ideas are implemented. Second, the company also sets this tone by having nine salespeople each go to lunch with a marketing employee at least once a month. This gives them a chance to exchange ideas.

Technology has enhanced the need for a cooperative relationship between salespeople and marketing representatives. With Web sites, database marketing, and electronic data interchange (EDI) all becoming major parts of companies' business processes, leads and sales are coming from many directions. If an organization's salespeople are not in tune with everything that marketing is putting out,

> Technology has enhanced the need **for a cooperative relationship between** salespeople and marketing representatives.

www.d-a-stuart.com

they can easily be caught off guard and miss out on deals. For example, D. A. Stuart Company uses an intranet to keep salespeople up to date in promotional material or other projects that marketing is developing. Any time a change is made to its Web site or a promo piece is mailed out, a memo is put up on the intranet so salespeople have access to the information.[24]

CULTURAL GENERALIZATION

In general, the company's human resource practices closely follow the local practices of the country in which it operates.[25] The age-old saying, "When in Rome, do as Romans do," generally applies to sales management. For international sales executives, some understanding of cultural differences is crucial (see Manager's Corner 14.2). These human resource practices include time off, benefits, gender composition, training, executive bonuses, and employee participation in management. Human resource practices also depend on the strategy desired, the culture of the company, and even the country from which the company originated. Although we can say that the sales management process *should* adapt to the local environment, we acknowledge the difficult give-and-take involved in adapting a U.S. Company's culture and procedures to the sales and management practices of a foreign country.

When host country standards seem substandard from the perspective of the home country (manager), the manager faces a dilemma. Should the multi-

---

24. Andy Cohen, "Sales and Marketing Separate but Equal? How Interaction between Sales and Marketing Departments Can Improve Performance of Both Departments," *Sales and Marketing Management* (September 1998): 15.
25. Philip M. Rosenzweig and Ritin Nohria, "Influences on Human Resource Management Practices in Multinational Corporations," *Journal of International Business Studies* 25, no. 2 (1994): 229–251.

Marketing in Action 14.2

Avon goes to the mall

Founded in 1886, Avon (avon.avon.com) is the world's premier direct seller of beauty and related products. Although Avon divides its products into four major categories (cosmetics, fragrances, and toiletries; apparel; fashion jewelry and accessories; and gift and decorative products) it is the category of cosmetics, fragrances, and toiletries that accounts for over one-half of Avon's revenues. And until just recently nearly all of the company's revenues were generated by a direct sales force operating in 135 countries worldwide.

However, despite annual revenue of $5.2 billion for its worldwide direct-selling effort, Avon is expanding on its tried-and-true independent sales network with retail outlets. Meant to service women who either do not know an Avon representative or who do not want to be serviced by one, the retail outlets are positioned to capture the estimated 20 to 30 million women who fall into either of these categories.

Retail outlets and shopping mall kiosks are only one part of Avon's growth strategy, which also includes geographic expansion and the use of market analysis software, Tactician, to finely tune its direct mail and recruiting efforts (among others). The entire re-engineering plan is underpinned by information provided from the field by an army of Avon ladies. The data that the network shared with the marketing department was invaluable in the company's plan to meet its goal of 8 to 10 percent sales growth per year.

Increasing the effectiveness of Avon's direct mail business, its one-on-one generated business, and its geographical expansion all hinge on leveraging the direct-selling channel, and Avon executives feel that there is even more potential to further leverage this successful channel to sell more of its non-beauty-related products. Expanding access to its products through strategically placed retail outlets will enable Avon to go beyond the traditional one-on-one sales call and reach those 20 to 30 million potential American customers.

How will expanded access methods such as retail kiosks in shopping malls, direct mail catalogs, and online ordering affect the company's relationships with its direct sellers? Could such outlets adversely affect the salesperson's profitability?

Sources: http://avon.avon.com; Cathleen Egan, "Avon Opens Retail Outlets to Lure Buyers," *Wall Street Journal*, September 21, 1998, B11.

---

national corporation (MNC) implement home country standards and so seem to lack respect for the cultural diversity and national integrity of the host (country)? Or, should the MNC implement seemingly less optimal host country standards?[26]

It would be wonderful to provide a diagram that could help managers plot the appropriate solutions for each country. Although such a diagram is too much to hope for, we can take a look at some common generalizations and categorizations of cultural traits and think how they might affect our sales approach. We must take care, though, not to imply that any culture can be described accurately in a few words or categories.

As an example of a cultural generalization with both helpful insights and misleading oversights, consider the foreign view of Germans. Germans are typically viewed as scientifically exacting and industrious people. We might therefore approach sales in Germany by building a small core of technically trained, independent sales agents to deal with technically exacting German customers. But if we think Germans look at work the same way Americans do, we will be misguided! The typical German manufacturing work week is only 30 hours. And Germans jealously guard their free time and show little interest in working more to earn more.[27]

---

26. Thomas Donaldson, "Multinational Decision-Making: Reconciling International Norms," *Journal of Business Ethics* 4 (1985): 357–366.

27. Daniel Benjamin and Tony Horwitz, "German View: You Americans Work Too Hard—And For What?" *Wall Street Journal*, July 14, 1994, B1.

Manager's Corner 14.2

Cultural sensitivity is all the more important in an era of global competition

You don't need a Harvard MBA to figure out that many of today's opportunities for growth lie overseas. However, when it comes to developing a global workforce, most managers feel lost. Therefore, what does it take to be a global manager?

Particularly, selling at a retail level is a very local activity. French salespeople will be selling to customers in Paris. Similarly, Indonesian salespeople will in all likelihood be selling in Jakarta. It does not mean that sales take place only at a retail level. Many U.S. sales managers engage in "selling" to corporate clients in other countries, as is well illustrated by the country's export boom in recent years.

A global mind-set is the capacity to appreciate the beliefs, values, behaviors, and business practices of individuals and organizations from different regions and cultures. Generally, European and Asian executives tend to be better at developing global workforce than U.S. executives. According to one study, some 25 percent of the U.S. managers who take on foreign assignments fail in their tasks and are sent back home prematurely, whereas the failure rate for European and Asian executives is about 6 to 7 percent.

So what should you do? First, globalize your career path. If you have an opportunity to be assigned to an overseas position (which usually lasts for three years) in your company, take it now and don't wait until you become a 45-year-old manager. Make sure that you take some language and cultural training before the foreign assignment. Cultural sensitivity is very important.

Before any business negotiation, the Japanese typically go through an elaborate litany of rituals involving dinners and parties with their business partners, which seems never ending to many U.S. executives. In the actual negotiation setting, then, the Japanese go through another ritual of exchanging business cards with their business partners. To Japanese, their business cards represent their status and dignity at a negotiation. To U.S. executives, business cards are just pieces of paper with names and addresses on them. Not liking the slow pace of business card exchange, one American executive tossed (without any malicious intent) some of her business cards across the negotiation table to Japanese "would-be" partners. This act stunned the Japanese executives, and of course the deal never went through.

Second, now as a globally-minded manager, you should make sure that you share your expertise with the rest of your organization. Unilever (www.unilever.com), for example, has 25,000 employees using Lotus Notes (www.lotus.com) to exchange their international business experiences over a global personal computer network. Even anecdotal stories will help sensitize people.

Source: "Don't Be an Ugly-American Manager," *Fortune*, October 16, 1995, 225.

We must also be careful not to group people from cultures that may appear to us as very similar but who consider themselves and their reactions to situations in a very distinct manner. Consider, for example, South Korea and Japan. We may think that Koreans would be accustomed to the same bottom-up consensual decision-making approach the Japanese are known for. Korean workers, however, tend to work within a top-down, authoritarian leadership structure[28] and require a higher level of definition in their job structure to avoid suffering from role conflict. A Korean salesperson might accept as normal a short-term position with a few prospects for long-term progress, whereas a Japanese salesperson would not dream of it.[29]

Another example is the difference in the orientation of salespeople in Australia and New Zealand. Most of us tend to think that their cultures are very similar.

28. Hak Chong Lee, "Managerial Characteristics of Korean Firms," in *Korean Managerial Dynamics*, ed. K. H. Chung and H. C. Lee (New York: Praeger, 1989), 147–162.

29. Alan J. Dubinsky, Ronald E. Michaels, Masaaki Kotabe, Chae Un Lim, and Hee-Cheol Moon, "Influence of Role Stress on Industrial Salespeople's Work Outcomes in the United States, Japan, and Korea," *Journal of International Business Studies* 23 (First Quarter 1992): 77–99.

Table 14.3

Five cultural dimensions

Dimension	Definition	Examples
Power distance	The concentration of power (physical and intellectual capabilities, power, and wealth) in certain groups and the acceptance of it.	*High power distance:* Korea, India, Japan, Mexico *Low power distance:* Australia, United States, Germany
Individualism versus collectivism	The importance of the individual versus the group. Or the pursuit of self-interests versus subordination to group interests (i.e., "I" versus "we" orientation).	*High individualism:* United States, Australia, Great Britain, Canada *Low individualism:* Japan, Venezuela, China, Pakistan, Thailand, Mexico
Masculinity versus femininity	The need for achievement, assertiveness, and material success versus the need for relationships and modesty. Masculine cultures have segregated roles, consider big beautiful, and need to show off. Feminine cultures care more for quality of life and environment than money.	*Feminine:* Sweden, France, Netherlands *Masculine:* Japan, Mexico, Great Britain, Germany
Uncertainty avoidance	Extent of ability to cope with uncertainty about the future without stress.	*High uncertainty avoidance:* Japan, France, Mexico *Low uncertainty avoidance:* United States, Hong Kong, Great Britain
Long-term versus short-term orientation	Values oriented toward the future, thrift, and perseverance.	*Long-term orientation:* Hong Kong, Japan *Short-term orientation:* United States, Great Britain, Germany

Source: Geert H. Hofstede, *Cultures and Organizations: Software of the Mind* (New York: McGraw-Hill, 1991). Reprinted with permission of the McGraw-Hill Companies.

However, salespeople in New Zealand tend to be more committed to, and generally more satisfied with, their work than their Australian counterparts. Additionally, there are differences in compensation (Australians preferring greater security in the form of larger salaries) and special incentives (New Zealanders having a much higher preference for travel with other sales contest winners and supervisory staff).[30] In a way, salespeople in New Zealand share more similarities in their value system with their Japanese counterparts than their Australian neighbors.

One of the most widely used tools for categorizing cultures for managerial purposes is Hofstede's scale of five cultural dimensions (see Table 14.3) Hofstede's scale uses a large number of questions to determine where countries stand on each dimension.

PEOPLE MANAGEMENT

The most obvious, and crucial, role of any sales manager is managing the sales professionals. The same applies almost as forcefully to the managers of service and support personnel (including the very large numbers in the service industries). A successful sales manager *must* have the following qualities:[31]

---

30. William H. Murphy, "Hofstede's National Culture as a Guide for Sales Practices across Countries: The Case of a MNC's Sales Practices in Australia and New Zealand," *Australian Journal of Management* 24 (June 1999): 37–58.
31. John Strafford and Colin Grant, *Effective Sales Management* (Oxford: Butterworth Heinemann, 1993).

- Desire to be a manager
- Ability to lead and motivate others
- Good organizing and planning skills
- Capabilities of control and administration
- Full understanding of the implications of finance
- Skills to recruit, train, motivate, and develop those who will form part of the team
- Acceptance of the fact that the computer is here to stay!

Apart from the rather idiosyncratic emphasis on the last item, this list is fairly typical of what many sales management writers also recommend. It is significant that, in common with those others, this list lacks *any* direct reference to marketing skills. On the other hand, it is even more significant for its emphasis on people management, which accounts for five out of the six main categories.

> **sales managers must inspire teamwork and cooperation while motivating salespeople to achieve**

To be successful, sales managers must inspire teamwork and cooperation while motivating salespeople to achieve their own peak performance. Table 14.4 lists 10 skills needed for effective sales managers.

Table 14.4

Ten skills needed for effective sales managers

1. *Treat your salespeople the same as you would treat your best client.* Salespeople treat their best clients very well, listening to their needs and responding to them. Make your salespeople feel special. Give them your undivided attention when talking to them.

2. *If you have to do something that is unpopular with the salespeople, explain why you are doing it.* Let the salespeople see the overall picture. They need to feel they are a part of the whole organization and see how their efforts impact the growth of the company.

3. *Give salespeople immediate recognition for sales made.* Ring bells, write memos, make announcements. People are not working just for money, but for the rewards, challenge, and excitement of winning. Show confidence in your people. If you expect them to win, they will.

4. *Praise in public, but reprimand in private.* Give the salesperson a chance to explain before you criticize. You may have the facts wrong. Begin with a question, not an accusation. Show your concern for their welfare. Express your appreciation. When you give praise, be specific.

5. *Hold short sales meetings often and focus on the positive.* Talk about sales made. This inspires confidence. Remain positive. Your attitude is contagious.

6. *Encourage your salespeople to set their own goals.* Often salespeople will set goals for themselves that are higher than you would set for them. And, people work harder to make their own goals.

7. *Hit the streets with your salespeople once a week.* They will respect you for it. Also, you will see what they are doing, right and wrong. Give them feedback. You will motivate them by taking an honest interest.

8. *You need to role-play.* Sales meetings should be for learning and practicing sales techniques. Role-playing involves everyone and promotes team spirit as it instructs.

9. *In handling disputes, don't talk to each person separately.* Bring them into your office together so they each tell his or her side in front of the other person.

10. *Have your salespeople listen to motivational tapes in meetings or in cars.* They face rejection daily and need the boost. Maintain an appreciation for their perspective. Salespeople respond to a teacher, team builder, and coach. Assume those roles, and your billings will soar.

Source: Pam Lontos, "10 Laws for Sales Managers," *Executive Excellence* 16 (March 1999): 12. Reprinted by permission.

RECRUITMENT.   This is a particularly difficult process where sales personnel are concerned because quality sales skills are all-important. Yet there are relatively few good sales professionals, and considerably more mediocre ones, many who hamper their performance even more by an unnecessary (and often enthusiastic) commitment to the stereotype. The success of a sales team is therefore almost entirely dependent on the number of high-quality sales personnel who can be recruited. Fortunately, for college students, "many sales managers who recruit at colleges say they found their best salespeople on campus."[32]

The recruitment process is probably the single most important task for sales management, yet it is often the most neglected. The first requirement for successful recruitment is that it must be taken seriously by being given the resources, including sales management time, that it deserves.

Recruitment can be broken down into a number of stages: (1) generation of prospects, (2) creation of a short list, (3) final selection, and (4) persuasion. Recruitment is also a sales process; the candidate will be buying an organization just as much as a customer, and for him or her it is a very important decision. Therefore, the whole recruitment process should entail continuously selling the organization and the job. In fact, continuous recruiting may be costly but it costs less than constant high turnover.[33]

MOTIVATION AND COMPENSATION.   Even the above average salesperson rarely works at more than 60 percent of capacity.[34] This problem is very different from that of "managing" teams of other employees, for a number of reasons, including (1) lack of contact, (2) complexity of role, and (3) entrepreneurship. These challenges are dealt with (or perhaps, more accurately, evaded) by the traditional tools of sales force motivation, which concentrate almost exclusively on the single task of motivating sales personnel to achieve their narrow short-term targets. Examples are commission payments (often seen as the basic motivator behind overall sales performance), sales competitions (used to stimulate short-term interest), and leadership.

Financial compensation is one of the key motivators for employees in all cultures. However, successful sales programs make use of a wide variety of motivators. The sales manager will want to adapt the incentive structure to best meet local desires, regulations, and situations. For example, the recent devaluation of the Mexican peso posed problems for many sales compensation plans. Electrolux's 250-person-strong Mexican sales force is being switched from a pure commission system to a combined salary-commission plan as a result of the 45 percent decrease in sales resulting from the devaluation.[35]

www.electrolux.com

Unlike in the United States, the use of commissions to motivate salespeople is not publicly acceptable in many countries. Commissions reinforce the negative image of the salesperson benefiting from the sale, with no regard for the purchaser's well-being. Salary increases may substitute for commissions to motivate salespeople to consistently perform well. However, under certain circumstances, large salary discrepancies between employees are also not acceptable. Strong unions may tie a company's hands in setting salaries. The "collectivist" culture of a country like Japan may not accept that one person should earn substantially

32. "Finding Top Reps on Campus," *Sales and Marketing Management* (March 1995): 38.

33. Saul W. Gellerman, "The Tests of a Good Salesperson," *Harvard Business Review* (May/June 1990).

34. Walter Vieira, *The New Sales Manager: Challenge for the 21st Century* (New York: Research Periodicals & Book Publishing House, 2000).

35. "Compensating during Crises," *Sales and Marketing Management* (May 1995): 84.

www.konica.com

more than another in the same position. Koreans, for example, are used to working under conditions where compensation is not directly contingent on performance, but rather on seniority.

When financial rewards are not acceptable, the company must rely more heavily on nonfinancial rewards, such as recognition, titles, and perquisites for motivation. Foreign travel is another reward employed by international companies. For example, in order to encourage its more than 350 dealers to sell four of its high-ticket copiers, Konica, based in Windsor, Connecticut, gave the top seller for each month of the five-month program a choice of 16 trips—including such adventurous activities as dogsledding and skiing, as well as more traditional tennis and golf excursions. To promote the program, each month Konica sent dealers oversized postcards promoting that month's vacation package offer and announcing the previous month's winner. Reps used an 800 number to report the model, price, and customer each time they made a sale. The system also helped Konica track the success of the program. Sales of the targeted copiers increased by 26 percent during the months of the program.[36]

LEADERSHIP.   Their personal characteristics—in particular, leadership qualities—of the sales manager are probably the most important motivator. Some oft-cited qualities that make an effective leader are enthusiasm, courage, self-confidence, integrity, interest, and a sense of humor. Charisma, ability to delegate, and communication ability are also often mentioned.

CONTROL.   Controlling sales personnel is complicated by the same factors as discussed in the last section. There is one further complication: time. Most sales campaigns now take a number of calls over several months. The sales manager has to manage this process by controlling the interim stages without the measure of the final result by which to judge the effectiveness of these actions. But sales management does have, in the final outcome (the sales itself), the ultimate measure of performance. The performance of sales personnel, more than that of almost any other employees, can be measured with some degree of accuracy—at least in the long term.

The salesperson's performance is typically measured by numbers, and in particular by sales volumes. These numbers may be compared with (1) past sales, (2) performance of other sales personnel, and (3) sales targets. In practice, many other judgments are qualitative. The sales manager judges his or her subordinates on the basis of what they seem to be doing and how they are doing it. This is particularly true of those involved in the sale of capital goods, where long periods may elapse between orders, and management becomes almost an act of faith. However, such subjective judgments are notoriously unreliable.[37]

The manager may define the employee's roles explicitly and require a standardized sales pitch. Alternatively, the manager may set broad, general goals that allow each salesperson to develop his or her own skills. A number of studies have found that the best management approach varies by culture and country. For example, Dubinsky and associates[38] found that role ambiguity, role conflict, job satisfaction, and organizational commitment were just as relevant to salespeople in Japan and Korea as in the United States, and that role conflict and ambiguity have deleterious effects on salespeople in any of the countries. However,

---

36. "Technologies Inc.," *Sales and Marketing Management* (December 1998): 78.

37. R. F. Hartley, *Sales Management* (Boston: Houghton Mifflin Co., 1979).

38. Dubinsky, Michaels, Kotabe, Lim, and Moon, "Influence of Role Stress on Industrial Salespeople's Work Outcomes in the United States, Japan, and Korea."

specific remedies for role ambiguity, such as greater job formalization (or more hierarchical power, defined rules and supervision), have a distinct effect on the salespeople in different countries.

One generalization is that greater formalization invokes negative responses from the sales force in countries in which the power distance is low and the individualism is high (such as in the United States). Greater formalization invokes positive responses from the sales force in countries in which the power distance is high and the individualism is low (such as in India).[39] For example, Kraft Foods' sales reps visit fewer stores than before its restructuring, and most will serve a single retail chain rather than different retailers in the same area. They have more freedom to set up more displays and build better relationships with store managers on their own. This incentive program is expected to generate some 30 percent more time that Kraft sales reps will spend at each store.[40]

www.kraftfoods.com

ETHICAL PERCEPTIONS. Culture, or nationality, also influences salespeople's beliefs about the ethics of common selling practices and the need for company policies to guide those practices. Why is this important? Salespeople need to stay within the law, of course. More important, in order to maintain the respect of customers, salespeople must know what is ethically acceptable in a culture. For example, in the United States, giving a bribe is tantamount to admitting that your product cannot compete without help. However, in many cultures, receiving a bribe is seen as a privilege of having attained a position of influence. An understanding of the ethical norms in a culture will help the company maintain a clean image and will also help the company create policies that keep salespeople out of tense and frustrating situations where they feel they are compromising their ethical standards.

As an example of differences in ethical perceptions, consider the results of a study by Dubinsky and associates.[41] The study presented salespeople in Korea, Japan, and the United States with written examples of "questionable" sales situations. Such examples were:

- Having different prices for buyers for which you are the sole supplier
- Attempting to circumvent the purchasing department and directly reach other departments when it will help sales
- Giving preferential treatment to customers who management prefers or who are also good suppliers

The salespeople were asked to rate the extent to which it was unethical to take part in the suggested activity. The results indicated that, in general, American salespeople felt the situations posed fewer ethical problems than did the salespeople from Japan and Korea. The study also disproved the assumption that Japanese gift giving would extend into the sales realm. In fact, the Japanese felt it was more of an ethical problem to give gifts to a purchaser than did U.S. salespeople. For Koreans, however, gift giving was less of an issue.

Paradoxically, U.S. salespeople indicated that they wanted their companies to have more policies explicitly addressing these ethical questions! Why? Apparently, they feel more comfortable when the ethical guidelines are explicitly stated, whereas in Korea and Japan, the cultural exchange of living in a more community-oriented society provides the necessary guidelines.

39. Sanjeev Agarwal, "Influence of Formalization on Role Stress, Organizational Commitment, and Work Alienation of Salespersons: A Cross-National Comparative Study," *Journal of International Business Studies* 24 (Fourth Quarter 1993): 715–740.

40. "Will So Many Ingredients Work Together?" *Business Week*, March 27, 1995.

41. Alan J. Dubinsky, Marvin A. Jolson, Masaaki Kotabe, and Chae Un Lim, "A Cross-National Investigation of Industrial Salespeople's Ethical Perceptions," *Journal of International Business Studies* 22 (Fourth Quarter 1991): 651–670.

SUMMARY

In most organizations the main marketing resource is the sales force. This resource is qualitatively different from almost all other marketing activities, because of its dependence on relationships between individuals. The role of the sales force mainly covers prospecting, selling, and supporting.

The building block of a sales organization is the territory, which may be defined by geography, by industry, or by product. Territory plans should, at least in theory, take into account annual costs (including direct and indirect expenses/overheads, which may be high, as well as salary and commission) and annual calls available, which may be as low as 200 per year.

The overall sales personnel plan may, however, be derived in a number of ways:

- *Resources needed to exploit the potential:* equivalent to objective and task
- *Resources needed to meet target:* usually based on affordability or percentage of revenue
- *Negotiated level:* a major selling task for the sales manager
- *Business as usual*

The whole of the selling operation revolves around the individual sales professional, whose role holds many similarities with management in general:

- Territory management
- Resource management
- Management of support personnel
- Management of the customer interface

The last aspect, the customer interface, may represent the major investment of the organization; although this may be unrecognized.

The territory sales plan will include:

- *Identification of customer and prospect sets:* "A," "B," and losers
- *Sales objectives:* including product and/or market mix
- *Sales forecasts:* totals, with bankers, probables, and possibles
- *Call and activity targets:* for example, mailings

Prospecting (generating new customers) is a numbers game; the more mailings that are sent out the more prospects, and ultimately customers, that will be generated. On the other hand, much of the work of sales professionals revolves around industrial sales. This employs long-term sales campaigns to multiple personnel in an organization. Accordingly, relationship marketing and account planning are important activities—and with them project management skills.

Sales team management is a specialized form of human resource management, but it differs in terms of recruitment, motivation, control, and training. Motivation is usually linked to compensation (commission), although other factors, such as leadership, may be the main requirement for a sales manager. Sales managers should also be aware that as sales activities are local activities, they tend to be strongly affected by cultural differences (e.g., shopping habits, negotiation styles) around the world, making it difficult, if not impossible, for the international marketing manager to integrate overseas sales operations. The development of an effective sales organization requires sales force objectives and sales force strategy adapted to local differences and calls for careful recruiting, training, supervising, motivating, and compensating of local salespeople.

Two major forces are reshaping sales management. First, a recent trend of downsizing and restructuring across corporate America, and increasingly around the world, puts mounting pressure on sales personnel to perform more effectively. Second, the computer revolution has ushered in an officeless working environment for many sales professionals with the aid of laptop computers, modems, and faxes. Although this allows sales professionals to allocate more time to traveling and visiting their clients and new prospects, managing them effectively has increasingly become an important issue.

QUESTIONS FOR REVIEW

1. What are the main roles of the sales force? What are the main differences between prospecting and selling/supporting?

2. How may territories be organized? What should territory plans take into account? Under what circumstances should the sales force be organized into territories? What are some of the alternatives to territories as a basis of sales force organization? What may be the bases for the overall manpower plans?

3. What are the main management aspects of the sales professional's role? What is the investment in the customer interface?

4. Who may be the parties involved in industrial sales? What categories of individual sales may be involved? What are the differences between industrial and consumer goods purchases?

5. How does account planning support relationship marketing? What skills does this require? How does the salesperson stereotype impact the process?

6. What people management skills are necessary in the sales manager's role? Do compensation plans alone provide the necessary motivation?

7. What factors should the sales manager take into consideration when managing a sales organization abroad?

8. If your firm is considering changing the shape of certain territories, what actions would you take to lessen the protests of the sales force who may be upset about this type of change?

QUESTIONS FOR DISCUSSION

1. "The Japanese market is quite different from the U.S. Market," says Mr. Eiji Iwakuni, who was appointed president of Ford Motor Co. (Japan) Ltd. in March of 1998. He is an engineer who spent 32 years with Honda in marketing, sales planning, and production control. "With 9 or 10 attractive Ford models (such as the Ka, a 1.3L, three-door compact hatchback produced in Valencia, Spain, and 1.6L Ford Focus sedans and wagons), we can sell 60,000 to 100,000 vehicles a year in Japan within five years," he says.[42]

To reach that goal, his priority is an overhaul of the dealer network in which possibly 10 percent of Ford Japan's 248 outlets will have to close. A rival foreign car executive, pointing out that some of these outlets sell only four or five vehicles a month, says scornfully, "They're a hobby, not a business." Mr. Iwakuni is embarrassed that Ford Japan salespeople currently average fewer than 20 cars a year each, not even half that of competitors. Too many of them, he says, "are ignorant about product, don't keep proper records, forget who they sold to and treat new car customers like used car customers."

New training is planned to change attitudes and improve performance, and "students" will have to shape up or ship out. The break-even point for Ford Japan's 107 dealers is 250 to 300 sales per outlet per year. Although most are losing money, Mr. Iwakuni is confident that new products, properly marketed,

---

42. "Tapping Honda's Talent Pool," *World's Auto World*, May 1999, 21–23.

will turn them into profitable businesses. In time, he aims for 300 outlets.

Japan's sales of imported Fords, never significant, plummeted 50 percent in 1999 to 6,997. Even when Ford-badged cars made by Mazda Motor Corp. were lumped in, a practice Mr. Iwakuni uses to reach his 0.5 percent share, the total was only 21, 995, a decline of 37.5 percent from 1997.

In this challenging Japanese car market, evaluate the strategy of Mr. Iwakuni to overhaul the dealer network for selling Ford cars.

2. It can be tough to get a sales team going early in the year. If reps have just finished a strong push to hit the past year's targets, and the next big goal is still 12 months away, it should not be a surprise when January fatigue sets in.

Curt Tueffert, vice president of sales for JBS, a computer distributor, says motivating a staff early in the year requires setting intermediate goals, and then clearly communicating them. He uses January to announce a quarterly bonus and to preview the president's club incentive. To keep reps' interest, he periodically sends small gifts related to the prize. If it's a trip to a tropical location, he'll send sunglasses, suntan lotion, and beach towels, for instance. Tueffert also sends gifts to salespeople's spouses to get them into the spirit.

How effective are these "extrinsic" ways to motivate salespeople as opposed to "intrinsic," which, according to some theories of management, may require enrichment of the sales job itself? In contrast to the system of extrinsic compensations, can you think of ways to make selling creative and challenging to ensure performance?

3. Within the next three to five years, the size of many sales forces may be reduced by as much as 40 to 50 percent. Dick Canada, director of the Center for Sales Studies and Market Intelligence, Indiana University, Bloomington, says perhaps the single biggest factor influencing this change is being directed by the way people buy. "For example, copiers, long-distance carriers, and financial services are now being purchased based on price. Why? The customer doesn't perceive a value difference between these products due to heightened competition and product commoditization." Tomorrow's sales forces will have to create value for customers, rather than just communicate value, he argues.

Pick a specific product area (such as the personal computer market) to identify ways that a salesperson can create value for customers in the given new environment of heightened competition and product commoditization.

4. A sample of National Association of Purchasing Management buyers reported their perceptions of salespeople who called upon them on overall sales performance, buyer trust of the salesperson, product expertise, and sales presentation ability, and so on. Males were evaluated more highly on two performance dimensions and one specific sales behavior, but not on overall performance, and were paid more. There is some evidence that buyers use a different evaluation criterion for men and women. The results were consistent across both male and female buyers. Overall, results indicate that gender bias remains a part of the industrial sales environment.

Can you identify some specific product markets where the gender bias may be more prominent? Can you suggest some remedies to overcome such bias if you as a sales manager had several saleswomen in your sales team?

FURTHER READINGS

Carnegie, Dale. *How to Win Friends and Influence People*, rev. ed. New York: Simon & Schuster, 1981.

Churchill, Gilbert A., Jr., Neil M. Ford, Orville C. Walker, John F. Tanner, and Mark W. Johnston. *Sales Force Management*, 6th ed. New York: McGraw-Hill, 2000.

DeCarlo, Thomas E., Raymond C. Rody, and James E. DeCarlo. "A Cross National Example of Supervisory Management Practices in the Sales Force." *Journal of Personal Selling & Sales Management* 19 (winter 1999): 1–14.

Dubinsky, Alan J., Marvin A. Jolson, Masaaki Kotabe, and Chae Un Lim. "A Cross-National Investigation of Industrial Salespeople's Ethical Perceptions." *Journal of International Business Studies* 22 (Fourth Quarter 1991): 651–670.

Hill, John S., and Arthur W. Allaway. "How U.S.-Based Companies Manage Sales in Foreign Countries." *Journal of Business Research* 22 (February 1993): 7–16.

Jolson, Marvin A., Alan J. Dubinsky, Francis J. Yammarino, and Lucette B. Comer. "Transforming the Salesforce with Leadership." *Sloan Management Review* 34 (spring 1993): 95–106.

Pilling, Bruce K., Naveen Donthu, and Steven Henson. "Accounting for the Impact of Territory Characteristics on Sales Performance: Relative Efficiency as a Measure of Salesperson Performance." *Journal of Personal Selling & Sales Management* 19 (spring 1999): 35–45.

Sharma, Arun. "Who Prefers Key Account Management Programs? An Investigation of Business Buying Behavior and Buying Firm Characteristics." *Journal of Personal Selling & Sales Management* 17 (fall 1997): 27–39.

Weitz, Barton A., and Kevin D. Bradford. "Personal Selling and Sales Management: A Relationship Marketing Perspective." *Journal of the Academy of Marketing Science* 27 (spring 1999): 241–254.

The Future of Marketing

Marketers

are constantly faced with change. This is neither a new situation, nor one to be feared, because change provides the opportunity for the emergence of new marketing activities and market positions. Recognizing the importance of change and adapting creatively to new conditions are the daily bread of marketing professionals. Recently, however, changes are occurring more frequently and more rapidly, with more severe impacts. As a result, the past has lost much of its value as a predictor of the future. The very source of what defines a

> **changes are occurring more frequently and more rapidly, with more severe impacts**

company's value is much different today than it has been in the past, as Manager's Corner 15.1 illustrates.

To assist in forward thinking, this chapter discusses possible future developments in the marketing environment. It highlights the implications of these changes for marketing management and offers suggestions for a creative response.

Manager's Corner 15.1

Knowledge is power

The value of firms no longer comes from physical or financial assets shown on the balance sheet, but from intangibles like brands, patents, franchises, software, research programs, ideas, marketing, and management expertise. These soft assets, rooted in human qualities, will increasingly overtake hard assets as the most important sources of a company's value. Microsoft's (www.microsoft.com) former boss, Bill Gates, said, "Our primary assets, which are our software and our software development skills, do not show up on the balance sheet at all."

There is a growing gap between firms' stock market value and the book value of their assets. This is best illustrated by the boom in high-tech shares. The biggest difference is found in companies that have the highest spending on R & D. A recent study indicates that the share price of U.S. multinationals spending heavily on R & D rises when they acquire foreign subsidiaries, but it falls when an MNC with a low R & D budget buys abroad. Investors understand that firms in knowledge-based businesses benefit from rising returns to scale. Once a pill or a software program is developed, each extra sale brings in more money at little additional cost. Thus, the bigger the market, the greater the profits.

The preservation of a firm's intangibles as its competitive advantage is highly complex because they differ from normal assets in a crucial way: Most of a firm's intangible assets are locked in the brains of its employees, who can come and go. Many of those who developed Disney's (disney.go.com) Internet business have left to join start-ups where they can make more money. It is therefore more important for firms to understand the value of their employees, who carry so much of the firm's knowledge capital in their heads, than of other intangible assets.

Source: "Measuring Intangible Assets, a Price on the Priceless," *Economist*, June 12, 1999, 61–62.

ENVIRONMENTAL CHANGES

Although the environment of firms is composed of many interacting elements, we will focus here on just some of the changes occurring in the technological, financial, regulatory, and societal environment, because it is in these areas where the impact of change has its most profound effects on marketers.

THE TECHNOLOGICAL ENVIRONMENT

The concept of the global village is commonly accepted today and indicates the importance of communication in the technological environment. Globally, society is rapidly reaching a watershed in terms of individual technology orientation. Just consider: In the United States the number of adults with Internet access in 1999 was 83.7 million. In fact, 42.2 percent of the total U.S. adult population over 18 were regular Internet users, up 20 percent from the previous year. The number of women online is growing: Of the entire online population, 51.4 percent are male and 48.6 percent are female.[1] The number of people who have made purchases online has jumped to 31 percent of users, up from 19 percent in 1997.[2]

In Japan, the estimated number of Internet users during the fiscal 1998 reached nearly 17 million, up 47 percent from the previous year, meaning 11 percent of that nation's households are now connected to the Net.[3] Internet access among households broke the 10 percent figure in just five years since it became commercially available in 1993. Internet use has proliferated at a much faster pace than personal computers and cellular phones, which took 13 years and 15 years, respectively, to break the 10 percent barrier. The rapid transformation of the telecommunications infrastructure, combined with a rabid appetite for the communications and commerce applications offered by the Internet, are propelling an online explosion in Mexico and Central and South America. Various studies estimate that in 1999, the number of Latin American Internet users totaled about 8.5 million—a 49 percent increase over a year ago—and it is projected to increase to 30 to 34 million, including business users, by 2003.[4] Overall, the global number of Internet users is expected to grow to more than 700 million by 2001.[5]

For both consumer services and business-to-business relations, the Internet is democratizing global marketing. It has made it easier for new global retail brands— like Amazon.com and CDnow—to emerge. The Internet is also helping specialists like Australia's high-sensitivity hearing aids manufacturer Cochlear to reach target customers around the world without having to invest in a distribution network in each country. The ability to reach a worldwide audience economically via the Internet spells success for niche marketers who could never make money by just servicing their niches in the domestic market. The Internet also allows customers, especially those in emerging markets, to access global brands at more competitive prices than those offered by exclusive national distributors.[6]

www.amazon.com
www.cdnow.com
www.cochlear.com

the Internet is democratizing global marketing

Starting a new business will be much easier, allowing a far greater number of suppliers to enter a market. Small- and medium-sized enterprises, as well as large multinational corporations, will now be full participants in the global market-

1. "More Than 42% of US Online," *New Media Age*, May 20, 1999, 16.
2. Roger O. Crockett, "A Web That Looks Like the World," *Business Week*, March 22, 1999, EB46.
3. "1999 White Paper Sees Rapid Growth in Internet Users," *Daily Yomiuri*, June 19, 1999, P3.
4. Joanne Cleaver, "Online Explosion," *Marketing News*, June 21, 1999, 13.
5. Jagdish N. Sheth and Rajendra S. Sisodia, "Revisiting Marketing's Lawlike Generalizations," *Journal of the Academy of Marketing Science* 27, Issue 1 (winter 1999): 71–87.
6. John Quelch, "Global Village People," *World Link Magazine* (January/February 1999), www.worldlink.co.uk.

place. Businesses in developing countries can now overcome many of the obstacles of infrastructure and transport that limited their economic potential in the past. The global services economy will be a knowledge-based economy, and its most precious resource will be information and ideas. Unlike the classical factors of production—land, labor, and capital—information and knowledge are not bound to any region or country but are infinitely mobile and infinitely capable of expansion.[7] Changes in technology will also make available vast amounts of data worldwide.

With the availability of this huge amount of data, the management of information becomes as important as the information itself. The premium is on the organization, maintenance, and use of huge, current, and accurate databases on customers, other vendors' products, regulations, and standards.[8] Mark Twain put it succinctly: "There is a road ahead of us. If we stand still, we will get run over." This analogy still holds true in today's competition. Technological developments are crucial for firms. Through their investments they can make technology more valuable, but technology itself also makes investments more valuable.[9] Firms therefore cannot afford to rest on the laurels of their temporary technological advantage, but rather must continue to invest in order to preserve their edge. They must also invest to restructure their processes in order to reflect new consumer capabilities and desires that will affect the ways products are developed, advertised, priced, distributed, and serviced. (Exhibit 15.1 reflects the difficulty of anticipating such future market demands.)

Because many of these investments require large amounts of capital, often beyond the internal capabilities of the firm, the dependence of firms on worldwide financial markets will continue to increase. In light of rising global competition for funds, one of the prime occupations of corporate executives will be to position their firm as a market leader and worthy of attracting funds. Marketing in Action 15.1 gives an example of how data management through software innovations is increasing in value.

Exhibit 15.1

Do you know what she will want to buy in 2020? As all environments are experiencing rapid change, it will become increasingly critical—and difficult—to predict future spending habits and consumer needs and wants. This is true not only of technological products, but of other goods and services as well.

7. Renato Ruggiero, "The New Frontier," *World Link Magazine* (January/February 1998), www.worldlink.co.uk.
8. "Preparing for a Point-to-Point World," *Marketing Management* 3, no. 4 (1995): 40.
9. Peter Robinson, "Paul Romer," *Forbes*, ASAP, June 15, 1995, 67.

Marketing in Action 15.1

The right marketing effort, the right customer, the right time

Founded in Dulles, Virginia (USA), MarketSwitch Corporation (www.marketswitch.com) is the industry leader in enterprise marketing optimization (EMO). EMO helps marketers use multidimensional analytical tools to fully implement one-to-one marketing campaigns. Two major components of the EMO system are data-mining and decision support systems.

MarketSwitch Corporation's software product in this new category of products is called MarketSwitch Workstation. The MarketSwitch Workstation is comprised of four integration components that analyze a firm's customer database: (1) Cross-Selling Optimizer identifies which offers to send to which customers based on the predicted return on marketing investment, (2) Targeting Optimizer denotes market segments that will profitably respond to the firm's marketing efforts, (3) Real Time Offer Optimizer focuses on the targeting of Internet advertising, and (4) Strategy Optimizer identifies which customers to invest in due to their individual value to the company. With these compo-

nent tools, users of MarketSwitch Workstation can provide the right marketing effort to the right customer at the right time—optimizing the value of each customer relationship.

Insurance and financial services firms have been the primary users of these new data-mining and data-warehousing tools. EMO has allowed these firms to identify trends earlier than ever before, find the most profitable customers, and better understand the composition of individual customers. The ultimate key to success has been the development of targeted customer-acquisition campaigns that proactively initiate communications with the customer.

The price for software packages such as MarketSwitch Workstation depends on the software's marketing capability, with prices ranging from $50,000 to $800,000. Are data-mining and customer data-analysis tools the key to future marketing success? Where should companies such as MarketSwitch target their marketing efforts?

Sources: www.marketswitch.com; Joanne Cleaver, "Marketing in the New Millennium," *Business and Management Practices, Responsive Database Services, Inc.*, February 1999, 34–36.

THE FINANCIAL ENVIRONMENT

Because of improved communication flows and a decrease in government regulations, financial flows have begun to take on a life of their own. No longer is capital confined to the narrow borders of a nation, forced to select only from domestic investment choices. Today financial markets have become thoroughly globalized, moving capital with lightning speed to those areas where the expected return is highest. Through the actions of thousands of participating money managers around the globe, exchange rates can fluctuate substantially in very short time periods and exercise major, often unforeseen influences on trade and investment flows. Private-sector financial flows vastly outnumber the finances that can be marshaled by governments, even when acting in concert.

As a result, governments will have to carefully measure the effect of their actions on global financial markets or risk depriving domestic firms of capital and creating domestic as well as international financial dislocations.

THE REGULATORY ENVIRONMENT

Influenced in part by financial flows, governments are increasingly recognizing the limits of their power in shaping the business environment. Many financial influences on business emanate from offshore activities, such as the Eurodollar market, which are not under the regulatory control of any government. Major changes of fiscal or monetary policies can quickly extract a hefty price due to the resulting

governments are increasingly recognizing the limits of their power in shaping the business environment

movement of capital. Shifts in regulations that are unwarranted and onerous can precipitate the exodus of firms into other countries that present a more desirable competitive platform or can place domestic firms at a significant disadvantage to their competitors from abroad. For example, U.S. legislation that created the Environmental Superfund requires payment by chemical firms based on their production volume, regardless of whether the production is sold domestically or exported. As a result, U.S. firms are at a disadvantage internationally when exporting their commodity-type products, because they must compete against foreign firms that are not required to make such a payment in their home countries and therefore have a cost advantage.

When foreign competition is entering domestic markets and exerting pressure on domestic firms, governments often discover that traditional tariff and nontariff measures, which have been successfully used in the past to protect domestic firms, are no longer available. International trade agreements that are enforced through the World Trade Organization often restrict such actions. As a result, governments individually have become less powerful in taking effective policy measures, even when they know what to do. Consequently, a closer collaboration between governments and businesses in the regulatory domain is likely to emerge, which will try to reconcile domestic regulatory needs with global competitive requirements. In addition, closer coordination of regulations between governments will be attempted in order to neutralize the competitive effects of necessary regulatory shifts.[10]

www.wto.org

THE SOCIETAL ENVIRONMENT

Many societies are undergoing major transformations. In some, rapid population growth is a major issue; in others, population decline is a peril that has many implications for the number of workers available to firms. In many countries the aging of its society also poses particular problems. For example, in most European countries and Japan, the next few decades will see a large number of retired individuals who will depend on a shrinking base of workers to support them.

Both immigration and migration also have distinct effects on society and on the marketing task. Immigration can affect the composition of society. For example, during the past decade, immigration to the United States has risen to its highest point since the beginning of the century. As a result, the face of America today is vastly different than it was in 1900. Hispanics make up 11 percent of the population, African Americans make up 12 percent, Asians make up 4 percent, and non-Hispanic whites make up 72 percent. Unlike the immigrants who arrived in the United States at the beginning of the 20th century, most who came from Europe, today's immigrants come primarily from Asia and Latin America.[11]

As a result of these immigration shifts, the marketer must understand that Latino teens are the fastest-growing youth segment in the United States, and they are redefining mainstream American culture. Currently 4.3 million strong, Hispanic youth ages 12 to 19 account for more than 14 percent of the total Hispanic population in the United States, and 13.6 percent of all teens. By the year 2020, the number will grow by 62 percent, according to Census Bureau projections. In fact, by 2005, Hispanic youths will be the largest ethnic youth population in the United States, and the trend will only keep growing, affecting marketing in terms of customer value systems, communication, media, and language.[12]

www.census.gov

The effects of migration are most clearly visible through urbanization. In many nations, large migration movements bring ever-growing portions of the population to urban centers while abandoning rural areas. The increasing number of megacities of more than eight million inhabitants illustrates the change. In 1950, only two cities, London and New York, were that size. In 1975, there were 11 megacities,

---

10. Michael R. Czinkota and Ilkka A. Ronkainen, "International Business and Trade in the Next Decade: Report from a Delphi Study," *Journal of International Business Studies* 28, no. 4 (1997): 827–844.
11. "Immigration and Diversity Still Controversial at Century's End," *Population Today* (June 1999): 1–2.
12. Helene Stapinski, "Generacion Latino," *American Demographics* (July 1999): 62–68.

including six in the industrialized countries. In 1995, there were 23, most of them (17) in the developing countries. In 2015, the projected number of megacities is 36; 30 of them will be in the developing world and most (22) in Asia.

Urbanization is taking place at different speeds on different continents. In North America, the number of city dwellers overtook the rural population before 1940. In Europe, this happened after 1950, and in Latin America, at the beginning of the 1960s. Today, these three continents are almost equally urbanized (according to UN estimates, 75 percent of Europeans and Latin Americans and 77 percent of North Americans are city dwellers). A similar process is occurring in Africa and Asia, which are still mainly rural. Their proportion of city dwellers rose from 25 percent in 1975 to 35 percent in 1995, and to a little more than 37 percent in 2000.[13] The turning point, when the figure will top 50 percent, is predicted for around 2025. Such movements and concentrations of people are likely to place significant stress on economic activity and the provision of services, but will also make it easier for marketers to direct their activities toward customers.

In many countries, a key societal change results from a reprioritization of values. The aim for financial progress and an improved quantitative standard of living may be giving way to other priorities based on newly resurging core values such as religion or societal relations. For example, it has been argued that in Japan, firms put people instead of profits first. Firms do their best not to fire workers; government protects weak firms and industries, even if this hurts the overall efficiency of the economy.[14] This clash of values has been exacerbated since the disappearance of the Iron Curtain. The demise of the Soviet system has again united the world into one global market. However, the central values of market economies, such as competition, risk, profit, and property, are not universally shared. The marketer must therefore consider new approaches in such economies in transition, fully cognizant of the limits to change and the many societal constraints that result from decades of ideological pressures fundamentally opposed to the core aspects of marketing. Marketers should be challenged by the potential to nourish the emergence of a new and better world order. By working with these societies, marketing can become a true change agent for society.[15]

> Marketers should be challenged **by the potential to nourish** the emergence of a new and better world order.

Globally, business decisions are increasingly evaluated based on their impact on specific population groups and may be challenged when they are seen as too selectively detrimental. Furthermore, a wider ethnic distribution of consumers in the market will require more fine-tuned target marketing to diverse ethnic groups (see Exhibit 15.2). For example, a 1995 increase in New York City subway fares had to be rescinded when a judge decided that poor black people would be disproportionately affected by the increase.

The emergence of new orientations, together with easy ways of communicating, has also given rise to a more activist societal environment. Greenpeace can now mobilize thousands of loyal supporters in a matter of days in order to protest corporate actions. Consumer boycotts of corporate products can be developed and implemented quickly, to the major detriment of firms. Dubious corporate actions can no longer be hidden even in the farthest corners of the earth. The bright light of public scrutiny can rapidly expose labor exploitations or unethical practices worldwide. This risk of exposure, combined with the rising capacity of

www.un.org

www.mta.nyc.ny.us

www.greenpeace.org

---

13. "The Urban Explosion," *Unesco Courier* (June 1999): 20–21.
14. "The New Nationalists," *Economist*, January 14, 1995, 20.
15. Reiner Springer and Michael R. Czinkota, "Marketing's Contribution to the Transformation of Central and Eastern Europe," *Thunderbird International Business Review* 41, no. 1 (1999): 29–48.

Exhibit 15.2

Already part of our global awareness and expected to continue into the future is the issue of human rights. This part of the societal environment will challenge the business sector as more and more multinationals move operations to developing nations in an effort to drive down the cost of goods sold. Some companies, like Royal Dutch Shell, have already taken a proactive stance on this issue.

individuals to manifest their displeasure with unacceptable practices through decisive actions, is likely to make firms more cautious and more ethical in their activities.

Closer ties between individuals and better methods of communication also work to the advantage of firms. Just as public outrage can depress sales or block permits for new facilities, public approval of a company's association with good causes can create customer and public goodwill and can even allay local concerns about foreign companies. British Airways raises change for UNICEF on international flights. Timberland has created City Year Gear, casual clothing reflecting its support of City Year, a youth service corps. EDS, a large systems integration company, has run a Global Volunteer Day (GVD) since 1993; in India the new relationships and positive aura created by GVD was a main factor in successful market entry. IBM's Reinventing Education initiative puts IBM engineers, systems integrators, and consultants on significant projects in partnership with public schools, such as developing new voice recognition technology to teach reading. In Brazil, IBM teams up with local companies to improve education. These activities bear no resemblance to traditional charity; they apply a company's skills and innovation processes to increase quality of life.[16] The result is new opportunities for both customers and firms.

www.british-airways
.com
www.unicef.org
www.timberland.com
www.cityyear.org
www.eds.com
www.ibm.com
www.ibm.com/ibm
/ibmgives

THE COMPETITIVE ENVIRONMENT

All the above factors shape the competitive environment of firms. Three additional dimensions, however, directly affect the ways firms compete. These are changes in corporate structure, shifts in corporate location, and the emergence of new leadership premiums.

CORPORATE STRUCTURE. One key restructuring strategy employed by firms in the services as well as the manufacturing sector is that of mergers and acquisitions. The merger of Citicorp and Travelers created the world's largest financial

www.citicorp.com

---

16. Rosabeth Moss Kanter, "Six Strategic Challenges," *World Link Magazine* (January/February 1998), www.world link.co.uk.

www.daimlerchrysler.com

services group. Daimler-Benz's takeover of Chrysler created a new global automotive giant. The rush of worldwide mergers and acquisitions is accelerating. In 1995 the volume of U.S. mergers and acquisitions reached well over $360 billion, with a worldwide volume of more than $800 billion.[17] In America, deals worth $570 billion were completed in the first half of 1999, compared with $528 billion for the same period in the previous year. European deals, fueled by monetary union, were worth $346 billion in the first half of 1999, whereas the total for all of 1998 was $541 billion.[18]

Through these activities firms attempt to buy market dominance via the acquisition of distribution presence, manufacturing prowess, customer contacts, or knowledge primacy. In addition, the synergy between the merging institutions brings higher competitive efficiency—mainly through the elimination of jobs. In reality, such synergies are often difficult to implement or fail to materialize altogether, as Manager's Corner 15.2 shows. Also, the departure of key personnel often reduces the hoped-for benefits. However, the fact remains that marketers, particularly in the industrial field, are witnessing a decline in the number of their large customers due to these mergers, and are learning that competition from larger firms is often harsher and fought with deeper pockets.

Many firms are also shrinking themselves to what is considered a "lean and mean" level. Again, such reductions are focused mainly on the personnel side, with the consequence that some corporate functions are either no longer performed or are delivered differently. For example, the installation of voice mail systems will eliminate the need for personal assistants or secretaries; the restructuring of corporate hierarchies will reduce the demand for middle management. Such steps tend to have direct marketing implications. Voice mail will serve the

Manager's Corner 15.2

Will marriage failures stop merger mania?

In 1998, there were mergers worth $2.4 trillion worldwide, a 50 percent increase over the previous year. The merger mania, no longer a mere American affair, is now spreading to Europe, with cross-border deals taking a growing share as more firms go global. However, studies of past mergers have shown that two out of every three deals have failed, and there is no lack of stories of unsuccessful marriages in this new merger wave. The reasons for merger failure are many. Bosses jump into speedy deals without paying attention to integration obstacles. These range from hard pitfalls like the linking of disparate distribution systems to soft issues such as personnel and other corporate culture differences, which had been blamed for disastrous mergers, like the one between AT&T (www.att.com) and NCR (www.ncr.com), bought for $7 billion in 1991 and sold for $3 billion four years later. In many cases, a merger was the product of weakness rather than strength.

The conventional cultural differences in mergers are even harder to manage with cross-border mergers and the growing importance of intangible assets. DaimlerChrysler (www.daimlerchrysler.com) is a good example of differing corporate cultures in a cross-border marriage in which egalitarian Germans dislike big wage differences, whereas Chrysler managers may quit their jobs if their pay is cut. Mergers as a way of cutting costs have also been blamed for unsatisfactory performance of firms, like Boeing (www.boeing.com), which reported a loss for the first time in 50 years. The company said part of the reason were difficulties stemming from its disastrous merger with McDonnell Douglas.

Successful integration of two companies requires advance planning and principally relies on the combined companies' ability to add value, something which only happens after the deal is concluded.

Source: "How to Merge—After the Deal," *Economist*, January 9, 1999, 21.

---

17. "1995's Merger Mania Continues with a Big Day of Dealmaking," *Washington Post*, November 7, 1995, C1.
18. "French Dressing," *Economist*, July 10, 1999, 7.

customer less directly and personally. Although routine calls can indeed be handled more efficiently through automated equipment, the treatment of nonroutine cases is likely to suffer. Similarly, the elimination of middle management is apt to reduce the extent of corporate memory and the firm's ability to draw on an inventory of human capital for innovation, creativity, and adaptation to change. As a result, the firm's reservoir of capability to respond to future change is diminished.

Many firms also attempt to lengthen their reach either by forming strategic alliances or by developing new outsourcing relationships. Strategic alliances are a form of business agreement between companies to exchange their respective strengths in pursuit of mutual benefits. They may or may not involve equity participation. A Toyota-GM joint venture in Fremont, California, involved equity investment in which Toyota could learn about management of American labor and GM could learn Toyota's JIT production know-how. Similarly, IBM and Apple Computer, threatened by Microsoft's encroaching domination of operating standards and software applications, agreed to enter into a joint-venture alliance in order to develop a dominant operating system that will work on both systems.[19] Corporations also increasingly form temporary ventures to manage large projects and to develop overwhelming competitive power. It has been predicted that the corporation of tomorrow will be less a physical, localized entity than a network-based consortium, with an ad hoc–oriented rather than a hierarchical culture, constant redeployment of its professionals, and semipermeable boundaries with its partners and competitors.[20] Such an approach allows a firm to significantly increase its geographic reach and to participate in projects that would have been too resource-intensive for one firm alone to carry out. In addition, it minimizes investment into areas that are not considered central to the firm's mission and maximizes the capital available for core activities. Conceptually, there appear to be few limits to the emergence of virtual corporations. For example, Alpha 1 Biomedical of Bethesda, Maryland, conducts major medical research with only five employees. They are the ones who coordinate all the activities provided by outside suppliers, such as research labs, testing facilities, and research teams. In essence, the firm acts as an idea broker and research coordinator.[21]

www.toyota.com
www.gm.com
www.ibm.com
www.apple.com
www.microsoft.com

At the same time that some firms head in the virtual direction of short, fluid, tangential relationships, others are banking on the development of close, long-lasting partnerships to achieve efficiency. One recent example is 7-Eleven convenience stores. The Southland Corporation's 7-Eleven stores lost millions of dollars every year in the 1980s and were eventually acquired by Ito-Yokada of Japan in 1991. Since then, Ito-Yokada has introduced its JIT inventory management and combined distribution center system into U.S. 7-Eleven store chains. Under Southland's leadership, McLane independently owns and handles combined distribution of nonperishable items and CaterAir provides JIT delivery of fresh food items for 7-Eleven stores. Southland now has begun to show profits that have eluded the company for so many years.[22] Similarly, grocery chains are creating seamless partnerships with manufacturers via efficient wholesalers, distributors, and other marketing intermediaries by automating the supply system with allied vendors. Ford announced a wide-ranging plan to reduce its supplier list by about 90 percent over a two-year period, whittling 52,000 firms down to about 5,000. Ford plans to develop formal purchasing partnerships with the remaining organizations and save $1.6 billion annually in the process.[23] These firms believe that long-lasting partnerships benefiting from close exchange of information and joint strategic planning are the route of competitive excellence.

www.7eleven.com

www.ford.com

19. Masaaki Kotabe, *Global Sourcing Strategies* (New York: Quorum, 1992), 207–208.
20. "Preparing for a Point-to-Point World," 40.
21. Kathleen Day, "Now, the 'Virtual Company,'" *Washington Post*, October 29, 1995, H1, H5.
22. Masaaki Kotabe, "The Return of 7-Eleven . . . From Japan: The Vanguard Program," *Columbia Journal of World Business* 31 (winter 1996).
23. Eugene H. Fram, "Purchasing Partnerships: The Buyer's View," *Marketing Management* 4, no. 1 (1995): 49.

The two vastly different approaches to corporate efficiency have major implications for the marketer. Fleeting joint ventures will require quick response to opportunities in many different areas, demanding a broad orientation with few core activities. Long-lasting partnerships will compel firms to deepen efforts and to concentrate on the synchronization of activities between partners. Clearly, such a strategy will affect the dependence relationships between firms. In addition, the focus on the long term is likely to lead to a broader definition of the firm's core activities, including manufacturing and logistics processes, which may well be neglected in short-term ventures.

CORPORATE LOCATION.   The new competitive environment also offers varied location opportunities for firms and their production activities. Never before has it been so easy to manufacture different car components in countries around the world, assemble the vehicle in yet another country, and then market it globally. Former Secretary of State George Shultz highlighted the issue when he remarked:

> A few months ago I saw a snapshot of a shipping label for some integrated circuits produced by an American firm. It said "Made in one or more of the following countries: Korea, Hong Kong, Malaysia, Singapore, Taiwan, Mauritius, Thailand, Indonesia, Mexico, Philippines. The exact country of origin in unknown." That label says a lot about where current trends are taking us.[24]

Such mobility of production also applies to services—perhaps even more so. Consider that only 3 percent of the cost of a typical semiconductor is sand and other raw materials. The remainder of the costs are attributed to service workers such as design engineers, research scientists, computer programmers, investment bankers, and lawyers who provide problem-identifying, problem-solving, and strategic brokering activities. In an increasing number of industries, management must ask itself regularly whether work can be moved to countries with a highly skilled workforce and favorable wage levels.[25] In their global operations, firms are likely to increasingly seek only the right to operations, rather than the right to establishment, because of their ability to serve markets without any physical presence in them.

As a consequence of these new location alternatives, unskilled and unmotivated workers in industrialized nations face growing employment difficulties. On a regional, national, and even international basis, the opportunities for these workers are shrinking, and their standard of living is in decline. If the fiber of society is not to be wrung dry by transfer payments to welfare and unemployment funds or threatened to be torn apart by ever-rising inequity, learning will have to assume a major role.[26] For the individual, learning will need to focus on an improvement in the acquisition of skills and knowledge, primarily at the technical level. From a corporate view, learning must focus on reducing the complexity of processes and bringing them into closer harmony with the existing capabilities of large portions of the workforce. In addition, new decision and implementation processes must be learned that bring together the craft skills on the shop floor and the engineering and design skills of management.[27]

---

24. Walter B. Wriston, "The Information Revolution and the New Global Market Economy," speech given at Dartmouth College, September 1993.
25. Blake Ives, Sirkka L. Jarvenpaa, and Richard O. Mason, "Global Business Drivers: Aligning Information Technology to Global Business Strategy," in *Information Technology in a Global Business Environment*, ed. C. Deans and J. Jurison (Danvers, Mass.: Boyd & Fraser, 1996), 143–167.
26. Peter R. Dickson and Michael R. Czinkota, "How the U.S. Can Be Number One Again: Resurrecting the Industrial Policy Debate," *Columbia Journal of World Business* 31 (fall 1996).
27. William Lazonick, *Business Organization and the Myth of the Market Economy* (Cambridge, England: Cambridge University Press, 1991).

Leading companies increasingly distinguish themselves by recognizing the importance of people and of the informal processes that can quickly disseminate new ideas and best practices throughout the firm. Education by companies is already a $55-billion-per-year industry in the United States, and it will grow elsewhere, reflecting the need for lifelong learning. In-house education is related not to company size but to its market complexity and to its use of new workplace practices such as team-based work, cross-functional integration, and supplier partnerships—hallmarks of world-class companies. The most sought-after resource will be human capital, not financial capital. Silicon Valley is awash with capital eager to fund new ventures, but short on talent to run them. John Doerr, the venture capitalist behind Netscape, has said that the product of Silicon Valley is not silicon but networking, and its scarcest resource is technical ad managerial talent. The more desirable that talent, the more it will be sought in a world labor market—especially as professionals are educated to common world standards—facilitated by information technology.[28]

www.netscape.com

LEADERSHIP PREMIUM.   A third major change in the competitive environment is, particularly in the United States, an emerging "winner takes all" effect[29] Corporate leadership is honored and reinforced by markets through the payment of a premium, which, by itself, often reinforces the leadership. For example, the best opera singer, football player, professor, or surgeon commands a premium compensation when compared to more mediocre colleagues. The best product in its category is likely to command a higher price than the also-ran products. However, rather than being linear, this premium is likely to be disproportionately higher than the increase in performance. A 10 percent higher performance level may result in a 100 percent higher price. Simply put, being the best is likely to pay off handsomely. The marketing consequences of this dictum are dramatic. Particularly in light of the capital requirements needed to stay ahead, being the best may be instrumental in laying the cornerstone for future excellence or even survival. It will therefore be necessary to engage in that extra effort that elevates a firm's activities to a level of superiority. By understanding the customer and making proper use of the marketing tools available, the marketing function can make the crucial difference to corporate success.

EFFECTS ON MARKETING MANAGEMENT

Each of these environmental changes has major effects on marketers. However, by recognizing and adjusting to changing conditions, marketers are able to bring into play their capability to perform their tasks better and in a more responsive fashion. In light of high investments into the development of capabilities, processes, knowledge, and equipment, firms will need to have access to customers globally in order to achieve the economies of scale that permit an amortization of the investments. The importance of domestic markets will also increase because of the borderless reach of competition.[30] Within this world of global competition, marketers will need to focus on their marketing mix with renewed vigor and from new perspectives.

28. Rosabeth Moss Kanter, "Six Strategic Challenges," *World Link Magazine* (January/February 1998), www.world link.co.uk.
29. Robert M. Frank and Philip J. Cook, *The Winner-Take-All Society* (New York: Free Press, 1995), 42.
30. Kenichi Ohmae, *The Borderless World: Power and Strategy in the Interlinked Economy* (New York: Harper Business, 1990), 22.

PRODUCT POLICY

A key issue affecting product planning will be environmental concern. Dramatic growth in public attention paid to the deterioration of the natural environment, pollution, and global warming will provide many new product opportunities and affect existing products to a large degree. Consumers in most industrialized nations will require products that are environmentally friendly but at the same time do not require too much compromise on performance and value. Manufacturers, in turn, will increasingly be expected to take responsibility for their products from cradle to grave and be intimately involved in product disposal and recycling.

> Manufacturers will increasingly be expected to take responsibility for their products from cradle to grave

In light of the global competitive challenge, firms will also need to introduce their products more quickly and into more markets simultaneously. Due to rapidly accelerating international product life cycles, firms can no longer afford to spread worldwide product introduction over several years. Firms now must prepare for global product introduction periods that can be measured in months or even weeks.[31] To delay or to stop further product development means placing the entire product at risk. For example, Totes developed slipper socks, a pair of heavy socks with rubbery treads. Shortly after its introduction, this very successful product sold 14 million pairs a year. Within two years, however, other producers had developed a similar product that sold for less, knocking Totes from the shelves of its major customers.[32] Firms must realize that there are millions of skilled people around the world willing to work for low wages and ready to imitate innovation.

www.totes.com

Global product introductions force firms to reconsider how to develop products. No longer is it sufficient to develop them for domestic markets and to gradually make changes to adapt them to the international market. Rather, product development must incorporate the international dimension at the earliest stages. For example, Procter & Gamble believes that if the company does not think through the concept of a new product on a global basis from the very beginning, it will not be able to enter additional markets until it sees the results from its initial country introduction. Global development from the beginning has almost certainly saved years in the firm's global product introductions.[33] Such early incorporation of the global market dimension, however, does not point toward increasing standardization. On the contrary, companies will have to be ready to deliver more mass customization. Customers are no longer satisfied with simply having a product: They want it to precisely meet their needs and preferences. Mass customization requires working with existing product technology, often in modular form, to create specific product bundles for a particular customer. For example, Dell Computer's plant in Limerick, Ireland, supplies custom-built computers to all of Europe. As orders come into the factory via Dell's Web site and call centers, the company relays to its suppliers details of which components it needs, how many, and when. All these hard drives, motherboards, and modems then roll up in vans to big bays at the back of the building and roll out again as complete computers just a few hours later. Dell sells $15 million worth of computers from its Web site each day. Because Dell's suppliers have real-time access to its orders via its corporate extranet, they can plan their production and delivery to ensure that there are always just enough of the right parts to keep the production line

www.pg.com

www.dell.com

---

31. Michael R. Czinkota and Masaaki Kotabe, "Product Development the Japanese Way," in *Trends in International Business: Critical Perspectives,* eds. Michael R. Czinkota and Masaaki Kotabe (Oxford: Blackwell Publishers, 1998), 153–158.

32. Stan Rapp and Thomas L. Collins, *Beyond MaxiMarketing: The New Power of Caring and Daring* (New York: McGraw-Hill, 1994), 14–15.

33. Kotabe, *Global Sourcing Strategy,* 210.

moving smoothly. By plugging its customers into its supply chain via its Web site, Dell enables them to track the progress of their order from the factory to their doorstep, thus saving on telephone and fax inquiries. The Internet's global connectivity has enabled the company to form a three-way communication partnership with its suppliers and customers by treating them as collaborators who together find ways of improving efficiency across the entire chain of supply and demand and then share the benefits.[34]

Overall, product development and introduction will become more complex, more expensive, and more risky, yet the rewards to be reaped from a successful product will also accumulate more quickly.

PRICING POLICY

In light of global competition, many products are taking on commodity characteristics where price differentials of one cent per unit may become crucial in making the sale. In addition, the many newly emerging products and technologies will be faced with substantial pricing problems. Marketers will need to set forward prices by distributing very high development cost over an anticipated volume of sales. This task will become increasingly difficult and controversial, because demand levels for totally new products are impossible to predict with accuracy. Because the type of forward pricing system used will have a major effect on demand structure, the system itself will influence its own validity. The problem will become even more complex because new product development will require increasing amounts of investment into research, resulting in very high fixed costs, while demanding only very low variable cost for actual production. Under such conditions, high levels of (predicted) sales can magnify the competitive price advantage of firms, as Table 15.1 shows.

It is therefore crucial for the marketer to concentrate on differentiating the offering in the market on a nonprice basis. Major efforts need to be undertaken to appeal to the market on service, quality, or other special aspects rather than on price. By accomplishing this objective, the firm can buy itself freedom from short-term fluctuations in its business relationships, which will enable it to perform even better in the future.

DISTRIBUTING STRATEGY

Distribution systems may become the deciding factor in whether markets can and will be served. Innovative distribution will also determine new ways of serving markets. For example, television shopping through QVC has already created a $2.2 billion shopping mall available in more than 60 million homes. Marketing in Action 15.2 describes how CBS is trying to strengthen the ties between television viewing and online retailing. As a next step it can easily be envisioned that self-sustaining consumer-distributor relationships emerge through, say, refrigerators that report directly to grocery store computers that they are running low on supplies and require a home delivery billed to the customer's account.[35] Firms that are not part of such a system will simply not be able to participate in the transaction.

www.qvc.com

www.cbs.com

The link to internal distribution systems will also be crucial to marketers on the business-to-business level. As large retailers develop increasingly sophisticated inventory tracking and reordering systems, only the firms able to interact with such systems and to respond to them will remain eligible suppliers. Therefore, firms will need to create internal systems that are able to respond to JIT and direct order entry requirements. At the same time, however, firms need to remain

34. "You'll Never Walk Alone," *Economist*, June 26, 1999, 11–21.
35. Vic Sussman and Kenan Pollack, "Goldrush in Cyberspace," *U.S. News & World Report*, November 13, 1995, 77.

Table 15.1

Changing price advantages

The old economy

In the typical manufacturing industry, a widget maker's fixed costs—upfront, one-time expenditures for land, buildings, machinery—typically account for 30 percent of production costs. Variable costs—labor, materials, energy, shipping—depend on how many widgets are produced.

Imagine two companies, Smith and Jones, that sell widgets for $1.00 apiece. Jones sells 25 percent more widgets.

Smith		Jones	
Annual production:	1 million	Annual production:	1.25 million
Fixed costs:	$300,000	Fixed costs:	$300,000
Variable costs:	$700,000	Variable costs:	$875,000
Total costs:	$1,000,000	Total costs:	$1,175,000
Cost per widget:	$1.00	Cost per widget:	$0.94

Because Jones sells more widgets, it has a modest 6 percent cost advantage.

The new economy

In a high-tech industry such as computer chips, the ratios are reversed. Fixed costs—much of them for research and development—are 70 percent, and variable costs are 30 percent.

Smith and Jones sell computer chips for $1.00 apiece. Again, Jones outsells Smith by 25 percent.

Smith		Jones	
Annual production:	1 million	Annual production:	1.25 million
Fixed costs:	$700,000	Fixed costs:	$700,000
Variable costs:	$300,000	Variable costs:	$375,000
Total costs:	$1,000,000	Total costs:	$1,075,000
Cost per widget:	$1.00	Cost per widget:	$0.86

This time, Jones has a formidable 14 percent cost advantage.

Source: *Washington Post*, November 13, 1995, A10. © 1995, *The Washington Post*. Reprinted by permission.

alert to the implications of such new regimes. For example, a JIT system will reduce the firm's error robustness: Only a few things need to go wrong for the firm to run out of product.

Another key to success will consist of the successful combination of different pieces of information and using them to form new distribution alternatives. Each piece of knowledge one has about a customer represents potentially valuable intelligence. Its value, however, is only realized once the pieces are put together to form a mosaic of the customer, which one can then use to serve the client better. For example, an airline ticket will soon be as much an entree for selling hotel bookings, car rentals, and travel insurance as the right to a seat on a plane. If an airline collects more information about a customer's preferences, it can suggest a theater performance to a traveler to New York, make all the bookings, provide a limousine for pickup, have flowers delivered, and reserve a table at a favorite restaurant 15 minutes after the end of the show. If the customer's schedule (or the airport's arrival) changes, the airline can change all other arrangements as well.[36]

Firms must also consider the future in their distribution planning. The need for tracking distributed products—at least to the intermediary level—in order to facilitate recalls has already become evident. The same rationale can support the extension of such tracking to the ultimate user level. However, the incentive to do so becomes much more powerful if one broadens the perspective of postpurchase

36. "Survey Business and the Internet," *Economist*, June 26, 1999, 20.

Marketing in Action 15.2

CBS promotes bracelet via soap opera plot

Based in New York City, CBS Corporation (www .cbs.com) provides broadcast television programming through 14 company-owned stations and 200 affiliates. Cable television coverage is offered through ownership of The Nashville Network and Country Music Television. Holding 82 percent in Infinity Broadcasting provides CBS with radio coverage in 34 United States markets. In addition to its extensive television and radio offerings, CBS owns close to 40 percent of MarketWatch.com and 20 percent of SportsLine USA.

Now the company is adding a new twist to its Tiffany Network nickname. In the summer of 1999, CBS began implementing plans to spotlight jewelry on one of its most popular soap operas. The plan, to accessorize the "Humanity Bracelet" into *Guiding Light*'s plot, should generate viewers' interest and leave them wondering about the bracelet's mysterious origin.

The real goal is to generate demand so that viewers will buy the bracelet at the CBS Web site. This merchandising effort comes at a time when CBS is at the top of the television ratings. Unfortunately, CBS viewers tend to be older than viewers of rival television stations, resulting in lower ad revenues per show.

With decreasing ad revenue and increasing programming costs, CBS is seeking new ways to raise the network's revenue. Disney and Warner Brothers are proof that consumers will purchase program-related merchandise. However, the new twist at CBS is that the promoted product must be purchased at CBS.com.

Is CBS entering new territory with its link among shows, merchandise, and Web-based purchasing? *Guiding Light*'s Web page at the CBS Web site collects information about site visitors and their interest in CBS e-commerce opportunities. What might CBS do with this information?

Sources: www.cbs.com; Sally Beatty,"Latest Soap-Opera Starlet? CBS Casts a Bracelet," *Wall Street Journal*, June 11, 1999, B1+.

customer distribution contact by recognizing such contact as a new opportunity to continue the dialogue with the customer, which can include product updates, product servicing, and cross-product marketing. Such a broader perspective will strengthen the marketers' capabilities and reach. By expanding the effort beyond mere tracking, which is a unidirectional activity, it can become a two-way distribution exchange. Thus the development of reverse distribution systems may take on an importance equal to traditional outward distribution.

COMMUNICATIONS STRATEGY

The communications function is likely to take on increasing importance, easily outdistancing the pricing dimension and at least on a par with product and distribution policies. Internally, communication will provide the firm with new opportunities of linkages and efficiency. For example, Ford provides the designers in all   www.ford.com
its design centers with a global database of vehicle safety regulations, which makes global product design possible. Internal communications will also have major effects on corporate hierarchies and decision-making processes.[37]

Externally, communication is the crucial interface with both the supply chain and the customer. On the supply chain side, communication leads to collaboration, efficiency, and productivity. Closer cooperation will facilitate planning and delivery. Communication's most important role, however, will be with the customer. Customer loyalty, measurable as retention, persistence, and repeat purchasing, is crucial for corporate profitability. Research has found that a decrease of 5 percentage points in customer defection rates can increase profits by 25 to 100 percent in terms of the net present value of profit streams.[38] Customer involvement transforms the relationship between firm and customer from an exchange into a partnership, leading to shared interests, goals, and long-term interaction. Only through effective communication can such involvement be generated.

37. Ives, Jarvenpaa, and Mason, "Global Business Drivers," 153.
38. Frederick F. Reichheld, "Loyalty and the Renaissance of Marketing," *Marketing Management* 2, no. 4 (1994): 10–21.

www.lego.com

www.shiseido.co.jp

www.carmax.com

Customer pleasure, finally, is the ultimate objective of the marketer. It is no longer enough to do one or two things right. Rather, one has to do everything right, and do so more frequently. The LEGO company has 12 different contact points for interaction with the market, such as the LEGO Builders Club, LEGO-Land theme parks, and LEGO Imagination Center. Shiseido offers monthly mailings to the home, a full-sized beauty magazine, specialty catalogs, and beauty counselors.[39] By focusing on the customer and delivering the best in all marketing dimensions, firms can transform entire industries. Just look at the emergence of CarMax: the Auto Superstore in the used car market. By offering a broad selection and full information to customers, by positioning salespersons as knowledge providers rather than as hagglers, and by providing full-service programs and a linkage to financial institutions, the chain is quickly redefining the market.[40]

The old era of marketing was one of satisfying the customer. The environment of the new millennium, of new forms of global competition, and of heightened customer expectations now demands customer delight. It is true that this new objective requires harder work, intensive customer dialogue, a broader perspective, and greater alertness. But with the new tools available to the marketer these demands can be met. Fulfilling them offers greater rewards than ever before.

This brings us to the end of the last chapter. We authors, together with a large team of reviewers, researchers, assistants, editors, designers, and printing and publishing executives, have produced this book to educate, inform, and delight you. We are looking forward to learning about your conclusion through your comments and suggestions sent to us at czinkotm@msb.edu and mkotabe@sbm.temple.edu.

FURTHER READINGS

Baldock, Robert. *Destination Z: The History of the Future*. New York: John Wiley & Sons, 1999.

Brown, Stephen. *Postmodern Marketing*. London: International Thomson Business Press, 1998.

Dertouzos, Michael L., and Bill Gates. *What Will Be: How the New World of Information Will Change Our Lives*. New York: Harper Business, 1998.

Downes, Larry, Chunka Mui, and Nicholas Negroponte. *Unleashing the Killer App: Digital Strategies for Market Dominance*. Boston: Harvard Business School Press, 1998.

Drucker, Peter F. *Management Challenges for the 21st Century*. New York: Harper Business, 1999.

Friedman, Thomas L. *The Lexus and the Olive Tree*. New York: Farrar, Straus & Giroux, 1999.

Neef, Dale. *A Little Knowledge Is a Dangerous Thing: Understanding Our Global Knowledge Economy*. Boston: Butterworth Heinemann, 1999.

Schiller, Dan. *Digital Capitalism: Networking the Global Market System*. Cambridge, Mass.: MIT Press, 1999.

Tolman, Jay W. *Marketing for the New Millennium: Applying New Techniques*. Central Point, Ore.: Oasis Press, 1998.

Winkler, Agnieszka. *Warp-Speed Branding: The Impact of Technology on Marketing*. New York: John Wiley & Sons, 1999.

Zyman, Sergio. *The End of Marketing as We Know It*. New York: Harper Business, 1999.

39. Rapp and Collins, *Beyond Maximarketing*, 309.
40. Howard Rudnitsky, "Would You Buy a Used Car from This Man?" *Forbes*, October 23, 1995, 52–54.

case 1

Amazon.com opened its virtual doors in July 1995 with a mission "to use the Internet to offer products that educate, inform, and inspire." By early 1999, Amazon.com was the largest Internet-based seller of books and music and operated one of the most frequently used Web sites on the Internet, offering over 4.7 million discounted books, as well as CDs, DVDs, computer games, audio books, and videotapes. The company had an 85 percent share of online book sales, with over six million customers in more than 160 countries.

Customers use Amazon.com's interactive Web site both to select and to purchase products. Specifically, customers are able to use the site to search for titles, browse selections, read and post reviews, register for personalized services, make a credit card purchase, and check order status. Most orders are shipped to customers directly from Amazon.com's warehouses, usually within 24 to 72 hours. If a customer needs to return a product, complimentary return postage is provided.

Amazon.com communicates with its customers electronically throughout the order process. A confirmation e-mail is sent to the customer when the order is received, and another when the order has been processed. Customers can then track the delivery status of orders online by using a key code number. Customers who prefer not to use a credit card on the Internet may fax or telephone in the credit card number using Amazon.com's toll-free numbers.

Amazon.com's headquarters are located in Seattle, Washington, with distribution facilities in Seattle, Delaware, Nevada, the United Kingdom, and Germany. In 1999, the firm had over 2,100 employees and was expanding rapidly. Since May 1997, Amazon.com has been publicly owned, with common stock shares traded on the NASDAQ National Market exchange in the United States. Despite persistent operating losses, Amazon.com's stock was trading at $209 a share, or 23 times its initial public offering price of $9 in December of 1998.

MAJOR EVENTS AND PLAYERS IN ITS DEVELOPMENT

The most significant player in Amazon.com's short history is its founder and chief executive officer, Jeff Bezos. With a background in computer science and finance, including fund management at Bankers Trust, Bezos decided in 1994 that the Internet could provide customers with services unavailable through traditional retailers, including discounted prices, wider selection, and greater product information.

Source: Georgetown MBA candidates Sarah Knight, Harry Kobrak, and Paul Lewis prepared this case study under the direction of Professor Michael R. Czinkota ©. Reprinted by permission.

In a November 1998 interview with the *Washington Post*, Bezos explained that he sees the success of electronic retailers as depending on their ability to analyze each customer's tastes. "If we have 4.5 million customers, we shouldn't have one store," he said. "We should have 4.5 million stores." Using its proprietary personalization technology, the Amazon.com Web page greets customers by name and, through mathematical formulas that analyze a customer's purchase history, provides instant recommendations for other products to consider for purchase.

Bezos oversees seven vice presidents, a chief financial officer, a chief information officer, and a chief logistics officer (CLO). The CLO, Jimmy Wright, was hired in July 1998 after retiring from Wal-Mart. Wright is responsible for all global supply-chain activities, including management of distribution centers, product purchasing, distribution, and shipping.

Since its founding, Amazon.com has undergone frequent and significant changes to maintain its leadership position as an Internet firm. Among the most notable developments are:

- May 14, 1997 — Initial public offering of three million shares of common stock. The capital generated from going public was used to pay existing debts and to make future systems investments.

- July 1997 — Multimillion-dollar advertising and promotional agreements finalized with America Online and Excite. Similar agreements have been made with Yahoo!, Netscape, @Home, GeoCities, and AltaVista.

- June 10, 1998 — Expanded product line to include music. Amazon.com now offers more than 125,000 CD titles. Through its Web site, Amazon.com's customers can listen to song samples before purchasing. As of December 1998, Amazon.com stood as the Internet's largest music retailer.

- August 1998 — Purchase of Junglee Corporation for its comparison-shopping technology, and PlanetAll, an address book and scheduler program for customers, for $270 million.

- September 1998 — Amazon.com established local Internet presence in Germany and the United Kingdom by purchasing two existing online book companies. In just three months, Amazon.com became the leading online bookseller in these markets.

SALES AND PROFIT RECORD

In its four-year existence, Amazon.com has experienced explosive sales. In 1998, sales jumped to just under $610 million, a 312 percent increase from 1997 sales of $147.8 million (see Table C1.1 for details). Amazon.com's customer base has been building at a similar rate. In 1998, customer accounts stood at 6,700,000, a 343 percent increase from 1,510,000 in 1997.

Despite rapidly growing sales, Amazon.com continues to generate multimillion-dollar operating losses ($111.9 million in 1998, compared with $32.6 million in 1997). According to the company's 1998 10-K: "the company will continue to incur substantial operating losses for the foreseeable future and these losses may be significantly higher than our current losses." These persistent losses are due primarily

Table C1.1

Amazon.com financial history

	1998	1997	1996
Net sales	$609,996	$147,787	$15,746
Cost of sales	476,155	118,969	12,287
Gross profit	**133,841**	**28,818**	**3,459**
Operating expenses:			
Marketing and sales	133,023	40,486	6,090
Product development	46,807	13,916	2,401
General and administrative	15,799	7,011	1,411
Merger and acquisition-related costs	50,172	—	—
Total operating expenses	**245,801**	**61,413**	**9,902**
Loss from operations	**(111,960)**	**(32,595)**	**(6,443)**
Interest income	14,053	1,901	202
Interest expense	(26,639)	(326)	(5)
Net interest income	(12,586)	1,575	197
Net loss	**(124,546)**	**(31,020)**	**(6,246)**

Figures in thousands of U.S. dollars.

Source: Amazon.com 1998 10-K report.

to low product gross margins. The company is also making significant investments in its technological and distribution infrastructure, as well as on building brand recognition.

THE AMAZON.COM BUSINESS MODEL

The Amazon.com business model creates value for customers by offering:

1. Shopping convenience (from home or office)
2. Decision-enabling information
3. Discounted pricing
4. Ease of purchase
5. A wide selection
6. Speed
7. Reliability of order fulfillment

No single aspect of Amazon.com's business model is sufficient to create a competitive advantage. Locational shopping convenience, ease of purchase, and wide selection are clearly not sources of sustainable competitive advantage. Customers have long been able to order books from wide selections available through catalogs or by telephone. Furthermore, decision-enabling information is available at a plethora of online sites and most public libraries. Finally, speed and reliability are clearly superior at a "real" bookstore, where one can receive the product immediately (as long as it is in stock). Thus, it is the combination of some or all of these characteristics that comprise Amazon.com's competitive advantage.

As a pure retailer, which does not engage in the physical customization of the products it sells, Amazon.com creates value for customers through a series of information services and logistical processes.

SOURCES OF COMPETITIVE ADVANTAGE

LOGISTICAL PROCESSES

Maintaining and improving operational efficiencies is absolutely essential for Amazon.com. The ability to offer a wide selection, discounted prices, speed, and reliability are all tied directly to the company's logistical competencies.

In a bid to simultaneously improve its margins and increase price discounts, Amazon.com is attempting to purchase more product directly from publishers. The firm hopes to increase the mid-40 percent discounts received from wholesalers to the mid-50 percent rates available from publishers. Circumventing wholesalers would also enable the company to shorten shipping times.

Between 1996 and 1998, Amazon.com increased its Seattle warehouse space by 70 percent and built a new warehouse in Delaware. It also began leasing a highly mechanized distribution facility in Fernley, Nevada. These recent investments in material handling systems, together with the increases in warehouse capacity, are expected to result in a six- to eightfold improvement in throughput within one year. Currently, Amazon.com ships 20 percent of books on the day they are ordered and aims to raise that rate to 95 percent. This is a staggering logistical challenge, as the company stocks over 700,000 copies of approximately 200,000 titles.

Despite Amazon.com's focus on improving operational efficiencies, industry analysts are sharply divided on whether the company's logistical processes are truly competitive. J. Cohen at Merrill Lynch Capital Markets observed that:

> [Amazon.com] is not large enough (in terms of order volumes and distribution infrastructure) to generate the economies of scale necessary to compete effectively with large physical-world retail chains. At the same time, Amazon.com is far too large in terms of the cost structure (associated with its proprietary inventory and distribution systems) to compete effectively with companies that forego that structure and provide a linkage with existing distributors.

Amazon.com's disadvantages in scale relative to traditional booksellers, such as Barnes & Noble, are apparent. It is important to note that in 1998, Internet book sales accounted for approximately $300 million, slightly less than 1 percent of the U.S. market. Despite the expectation that Internet book sales were to double in 1999, national retailers will retain massive scale economies. Furthermore, both Borders and Barnes & Noble have Web sites, which are expected to grow with the market (or faster). Barnes & Noble, which formed a strategic alliance with the German media conglomerate Bertelsmann, has direct relationships with some 20,000 publishers and distributors. In addition, Barnes & Noble's state-of-the-art distribution center has roughly 750,000 titles available for same-day shipping. It is interesting to note that despite these gains, Barnes & Noble, barnesandnoble.com, and Borders combined have only 10 percent the market value of Amazon.com (as of the first quarter of 2000).

BUILDING BRAND EQUITY

Amazon.com has steadily increased its spending on advertising and promotion both in absolute terms and as a percentage of revenue. Between 1996 and 1998, Amazon.com spent roughly one-quarter of sales on advertising and promotion. The company invested in promotional relationships with both the domestic and international sites of America Online, Excite, and Yahoo!

Amazon.com's efforts to build brand equity through its extensive advertising and promotion has received mixed reviews from industry analysts. One Merrill Lynch analyst criticized Amazon.com's attempt to develop brand equity, questioning its value for the distributor of commodity products, such as books:

> We do not believe that online commodity product sales produce the sort of brand equity generated by the distribution of proprietary information or media products. The implication here is that while it may make economic sense for Yahoo! to lose money while building a user population, it probably does not make sense for Amazon.com to follow the same path.

Although advertising and promotion are extremely important to a growing business, it is doubtful brand equity alone will be enough to gain new customers and retain old ones if competitors with superior logistical systems and identical products enter the market. This increases the importance of Amazon.com's value-added information services to customers.

VALUE-ADDED INFORMATION SERVICES

Amazon.com is strongly focused on achieving value-added differentiation through customer-oriented information services. Perhaps the most important information service Amazon.com provides is a comprehensive online catalog, which enables customers to search for books or CDs. Amazon.com's proprietary software will also track individual customer orders and subsequently recommend titles of a similar genre or related subject matter. Thus, Amazon.com's site provides automated customization for users. Jeff Bezos, the founder and CEO, has a vivid vision for how this technology will be used:

> Personalization is like retreating to the time when you have small-town merchants who got to know you, and they could help you get the right products. The right products can improve your life, and the wrong products detract from it. Before the era of mass merchandising, it used to be that most things were personalized. The promise of . . . customization is . . . you get the economies of mass merchandising and the individuality of 100-years-ago merchandising.

In addition to retaining customer preferences, the system retains customer purchase information, eliminating the need for repeat customers to reenter the same address and billing information. This is an extremely powerful tool and may represent a strong incumbency advantage. For example, in the fourth quarter of 1997, Amazon.com's automated system captured information for over 1.5 million customers, including e-mail address, mailing address, credit card number, and the products they purchased (including various classifications such as genre or topic). Unless a customer objects, Amazon.com reserves the right to utilize—or even possibly sell—this information.

Repeat customers account for approximately 60 percent of Amazon.com's orders, and this proportion appears to be growing. This statistic *may* indicate a high level of customer satisfaction. However, it could merely indicate customers' lack of awareness of Amazon.com's new online competitors, such as barnesandnoble.com. In the Barnes & Noble and Bertelsmann joint venture announced in late 1998, both companies pledged to invest $100 million in expanding barnesandnoble.com's U.S. sales (compared to $20 million for the Barnes & Noble superstores). This will lessen the incumbency advantage of brand awareness. Amazon.com will be under pressure to provide a higher level of value-added differentiation in customer service. Ultimately, Amazon.com's market success depends on its ability to maintain and grow its customer base by knowing and serving its customers better than its competitors.

INTERNATIONAL ACTIVITIES

Amazon.com began direct exporting almost immediately after its inception in 1995. Preliminary exports could be described as reactive, as the company's first international customers sought out Amazon.com rather than vice versa. Early on, international orders were more concentrated in nonfiction technological and computer-oriented publications, although that customer base soon diversified. Amazon.com's international orders now follow a similar pattern to domestic orders, with customer interest in a wide range of subject matter.

Amazon.com currently sells in over 160 countries and is aggressively pursuing international sales through direct exporting as well as local overseas presence. In 1998, Amazon.com established a local presence in the United Kingdom and Germany by purchasing two existing online book companies, Telebook and BookPages. Amazon.com is currently the largest online retailer in these markets. The European subsidiaries have been set up to serve the entire EU market and have currency and shipping procedures in place. These efforts, as part of Amazon.com's international strategy, appear to be paying off; in 1998, about 20 percent of Amazon .com's sales were from international customers.

Despite the fact that Amazon.com exports to such a high number of countries, the company is still in the process of establishing an international presence. Amazon .com is continually increasing its efforts to reach out to international customers. As the company explained in its 1997 annual report:

> [Amazon.com] has only limited experience in sourcing, marketing, and distributing products on an international basis and in developing localized versions of its Web site and other systems. The Company expects to incur significant costs in establishing international facilities and operations, in promoting its brand internationally, in developing localized versions of its Web site and other systems, and in sourcing, marketing, and distributing products in foreign markets.

Amazon.com's use of regional interfaces adds a "third layer" to its international business activities. The cornerstone of Amazon.com's approach to international business is to leverage its existing systems and routines to serve all of its customers, regardless of location. The regional interfaces allow most of Amazon.com's customers to use their own language. Standardized algorithms and routines provide the same automated personalized services to international customers.

Continuing to expand local overseas operations, according to CEO Jeff Bezos, is the only way Amazon.com can stay competitive in the face of growing international competition. As in the U.S. market, Amazon.com has strong, albeit relatively new, competitors in the international marketplace. This competition increased considerably when in the fall of 1998 Bertelsmann—the German media conglomerate—agreed to purchase half of the interest in barnsandnoble.com for

$200 million. Both Bertelsmann and Barnes & Noble plan to invest heavily in expanding barnesandnoble.com's international business.

The partnership between Bertelsmann and Barnes & Noble thus far does not appear to be hurting Amazon.com's international or domestic sales. Nonetheless, Media Metrix, a company that measures traffic on the Internet, calculates that the number of people visiting barnesandnoble.com's site is skyrocketing. As research shows that online customers like to browse for six months or longer before buying, Barnes & Noble is hoping that its domestic and international sales will soon pick up.

Amazon.com uses global merchant agreements with other Internet-based companies to promote the company internationally. In September 1998, Yahoo! Inc. agreed to place Amazon.com merchant links on its international sites, including those in Asia, the United Kingdom and Ireland, France, Germany, Denmark, Sweden, Norway, Canada, Australia and New Zealand, Japan, and Korea. According to David Risher, senior vice president at Amazon.com, "This agreement with Yahoo!, combined with our local presence in Germany and the United Kingdom, strengthens our position around the world as a leading global book merchant." Similar agreements have been established with other popular Internet Web sites including Netscape, @Home, GeoCities, and AltaVista.

Like its domestic customers, Amazon.com's international customers select and purchase products through the company's U.S. or European Web pages. There are several foreign-language versions, including Japanese, Dutch, French, Italian, Portuguese, German, and Spanish. The majority of Amazon.com's international customers pays with a credit card, such as Visa, MasterCard, and JB. International customers are required to bear all customs and duties charges.

For shipping, Amazon.com gives its customers a choice of international mail (estimated time of 7 to 21 business days, with a minimum shipping and handling charge of $12.95) or DHL Worldwide Express International (1 to 4 business days, with a minimum charge of $35.95). Amazon.com has been actively working to reduce the delivery times and shipping costs for its international (as well as its domestic) customers. The establishment of local distribution centers in Germany and the United Kingdom significantly reduces both delivery lead times and shipping costs for customers, and thus brings Amazon.com closer to its customers, both physically and psychologically.

TRAINING FOR CUSTOMER SATISFACTION

Training is vital to ensure Amazon.com can run a highly responsive customer service program. Jeff Bezos, the founder and CEO, emphasizes the importance of developing people with the term *people bandwidth*. Bezos describes people bandwidth as "smart people, working hard, passionately and smartly." With huge numbers of investors eager to purchase a stake in Amazon.com, Bezos claims that the real constraint on the company's growth is not capital, but people. The CEO's comments provide insight into the strategic importance the company places on training. Amazon.com's Customer Service Manager described how the training process certifies representatives at different levels on an ongoing basis to respond quickly to customer needs:

> Classroom and on-the-job training and mentoring are all utilized. There is follow-up training to advance to the next skill/task level and review training on any new products or business processes. We also keep a pretty extensive intranet for reference.

Within the standard training curriculum, Amazon.com's customer service representatives also receive special training in how to correspond with international customers.

COMMUNICATING WITH OVERSEAS CUSTOMERS

As its business is based on the Internet, the majority of Amazon.com's international customers communicate via e-mail. Some customers choose to complain by telephone, although toll-free numbers are only offered domestically. The benchmark for answering e-mails is 100 percent within 24 hours or less. Customer service response routines are designed to be predictive, automated, and efficient.

Most international customers complain in English or Spanish, but customer service representatives are equipped to handle complaints in other languages. In fact, Amazon.com claims to have representatives conversant in nineteen languages. These include all the major European languages, as well as Japanese, Chinese, Korean, Vietnamese, Thai, Hebrew, Zulu, Swazi, and Hausa.

EXPORT COMPLAINT MANAGEMENT

Amazon.com prides itself on superior service for both its international and domestic customers. The company has seen superior customer service and in particular complaint management as a key point of differentiation and therefore a source of competitive advantage. Amazon.com believes its international customers are "quite happy" with the level of service they have received.

One key to the quality of service is a high degree of responsiveness from Amazon.com's customer service department. Customer service representatives in the Seattle, Washington, headquarters handle complaints from both domestic and international customers. These representatives are given a great deal of authority to resolve customer complaints. As Amazon.com's Customer Service Manager explained, complaints are rarely elevated to higher level managers:

> Most things are caught on the first shot. Escalations occur if a customer is not satisfied with a response, or if there is a complex issue such as large quantities or a complex billing issue like suspected fraud. Non-English phone or e-mail messages are escalated—e-mail is escalated mostly for tracking purposes since [it is usually] obvious what the customer needs from the e-mail message. Obviously, phone calls are more difficult if English is not spoken at all.

EXPORT COMPLAINTS AND RESOLUTION POLICIES

The most frequent complaints from international customers center on distribution problems. This is not surprising, given the long lead times and high shipping costs Amazon.com's international customers must endure. As a result, customers are dissatisfied if their purchases arrive later than expected, or if their order is never received. According to Amazon.com's customer service department, the quantity of complaints are similar for domestic and overseas customers.

There is no separate department at Amazon.com to deal with overseas complaints. Within this organizational structure, customer service representatives must rely largely on standardized routines and protocol for interacting with customers. As a heuristic, customer service representatives are taught to mirror the tone and formality of their e-mail to the complaint they receive. Amazon.com's standard methods for placating dissatisfied international customers include a range of remedies that are designed to cost-effectively maintain customer goodwill. These remedies include:

1. Upgraded or complimentary shipping
2. Free replacements for lost or damaged items

3. Allowing customers to donate a book delivered late or incorrectly where return shipping is not cost effective

Amazon.com tracks customer complaints through regular internal management reports. Complaints are routinely used to make continuous improvements to the shipping, billing, and order-taking processes. Also, other departments, including Web site software, product development, and marketing, use customer service reports to make continuous improvements to their operating processes.

QUESTIONS FOR DISCUSSION

1. Approximately a quarter of Amazon.com's sales are to overseas customers. How could Amazon.com structure its customer service department to better serve an increasingly international and culturally/linguistically diverse customer base? Should Amazon.com have "country specialists" for markets where it lacks an overseas presence? Why or why not?

2. How should Amazon.com address the two key areas of export complaints—long distribution times and high shipping costs? Although Amazon.com's existing international expansion strategy has emphasized in-house ownership of warehousing and inventory, potential arrangements with specialized third parties are an alternative model. Is the outsourcing of warehousing and inventory management consistent with their existing business model?

3. How could Amazon.com better measure customer service? How could the customer service manager implement a continuous improvement process? What companies would you benchmark and how?

Anheuser-Busch International, Inc.
Making Inroads into Brazil and Mexico

case 2

HISTORY

In 1852, George Schneider started a small brewery in St. Louis. Five years later, the brewery faced insolvency. Several St. Louis businessmen purchased the brewery, launching an expansion largely financed by a loan from Eberhard Anheuser. By 1860, the enterprise had run into trouble again. Anheuser, with money already earned from a successful soap-manufacturing business, bought up the interest of minority creditors and became a brewery owner. In 1864, he joined forces with his new son-in-law, brewery supplier Adolphus Busch, and eventually Busch became president of the company. Busch is credited with transforming it into a giant industry and is therefore considered the founder of the company.

Busch wanted to break the barriers of all local beers and breweries, so he created a network of railside icehouses to cool cars of beer being shipped long distances. This innovation moved the company much closer to becoming one of the first national beers in the United States.

In the late 1870s, Busch launched the industry's first fleet of refrigerated cars, but the company needed more than that to ensure the beer's freshness over long distances. In response, Busch pioneered the use of a new pasteurization process.

In 1876, Busch created Budweiser, and today it brews Bud the same way as in 1876. In 1896, the company introduced Michelob as their first premium beer. By 1879, annual sales rose to more than 105,000 barrels, and in 1901 the company reached the one-million barrel mark.

In 1913, after his father's death, August A. Busch, Sr., took charge of the company. With the new leadership came new problems: World War I, Prohibition, and the Great Depression. To keep the company running, Anheuser-Busch switched its emphasis to the production of corn products, baker's yeast, ice cream, soft drinks, commercial refrigeration units, and truck bodies. They stopped most of these activities when Prohibition ended. However, yeast production was kept and even expanded to the point where Anheuser-Busch became the nation's leading producer of compressed baker's yeast through the encouragement of Adolphus Busch III, who became the company's new president in 1934.

August A. Busch, Jr., succeeded his brother as president in 1946 and served as the company's CEO until 1975. During this time, eight branch breweries were constructed and annual sales increased from three million barrels in 1946 to more than 34 million in 1974. The company was extended to include family entertainment, real estate, can manufacturing, transportation, and major-league baseball.

August A. Busch III became president in 1974 and was named CEO in 1975. From that time to the present, the company opened three new breweries and

Source: This case was prepared by Professor Masaaki Kotabe with the assistance of John Graham of Temple University (1999). Reprinted with permission.

acquired one. Other acquisitions included the nation's second-largest baking company and Sea World. The company also increased vertical integration capabilities with the addition of new can manufacturing and malt production facilities, container recovery, metalized label printing, snack foods, and international marketing and creative services.

CORPORATE MISSION STATEMENT

Anheuser-Busch's corporate mission statement provides the foundation for strategic planning for the company's businesses:

> The fundamental premise of the mission statement is that beer is and always will be Anheuser-Busch's core business. In the brewing industry, Anheuser-Busch's goals are to extend its position as the world's leading brewer of quality products; increase its share of the domestic beer market 50% by the late 1990s; and extend its presence in the international beer market. In non-beer areas, Anheuser-Busch's existing food products, packaging, and entertainment will continue to be developed.

> The mission statement also sets forth Anheuser-Busch's belief that the cornerstones of its success are a commitment to quality and maintaining the highest standards of honesty and integrity in its dealings with all stakeholders.

BEER AND BEER-RELATED OPERATIONS

Anheuser-Busch, which began operations in 1852 as the Bavarian Brewery, ranks as the world's largest brewer and has held the position of industry leader in the United States since 1957. More than 4 of every 10 beers sold in the United States are Anheuser-Busch products.

The company's principal product is beer, produced and distributed by its subsidiary, Anheuser-Busch, Inc. (A-BI), in a variety of containers primarily under the brand names Budweiser, Bud Light, Bud Dry Draft, Michelob, Michelob Light, Michelob Dry, Michelob Golden Draft, Michelob Gold, Draft Light, Busch Light, Natural Light, and King Cobra, to name just a few. In 1993, Anheuser-Busch introduced a new brand, Ice Draft from Budweiser, which is marketed in the United States and abroad as the preferred beer because it is lighter and less bitter than beer produced in foreign countries. Bud Draft from Budweiser was first introduced in the United States in late 1993 in 14 states, with a full national rollout in 1994 in the United States and abroad.

SALES

Anheuser-Busch's sales grew slowly after a sales decline in 1994. The company's principal product, beer, produced and distributed by its subsidiary, A-BI, sold 96.6 million barrels of beer in 1997, an increase of 1.05 percent compared to 1996 beer volume of 95.1 million barrels. The gross sales for Anheuser-Busch Companies, Inc., during 1997 were $12.83 billion, an increase of $820 million over 1995 gross sales of $12.01 billion. Net sales for 1997 were $11.07 billion and were still lower than a record net sales of $11.51 billion in 1993.

ANHEUSER-BUSCH INTERNATIONAL, INC.

Anheuser-Busch International, Inc. (A-BII), was formed in 1981 to explore and develop the international beer market. A-BII is responsible for the company's foreign beer operations and for exploring and developing beer markets outside the United States. Its activities include contract and license brewing, export sales, marketing and distribution of the company's beer in foreign markets, and equity partnerships with foreign brewers.

A-BII has a two-pronged strategy: (1) build Budweiser into an international brand, and (2) build an international business through equity investments or leading foreign brewers. In seeking growth, A-BII emphasizes part ownership in foreign brewers, joint ventures, and contract-brewing arrangements. These give the company opportunities to use its marketing expertise and its management practices in foreign markets. The success of these growth opportunities depends largely on finding the right partnerships that create a net gain for both companies. Other options for international expansion include license-brewing arrangements and exporting.

A-BII is currently pursuing the dual objectives of building Budweiser's worldwide presence and establishing a significant international business operation through joint ventures and equity investments in foreign brewers. Anheuser-Busch brands are exported to more than 60 countries and brewed under Anheuser-Busch's supervision in five countries. A-BII has experienced international growth in all operating regions with a 9 percent market share worldwide and has the largest export volume of any U.S. brewer. Anheuser-Busch had more than 45 percent of all U.S. beer exports and exported a record volume of more than 3.4 million barrels of beer in 1998.

MARKET SHARE

The top 10 beer brands for 1998 in worldwide market share are as shown in Table C2.1. Most recently, Anheuser-Busch has announced several agreements with other leading brewers around the world, including Modelo in Mexico, Antarctica

Table C2.1

Top 10 beer brands in 1998

Brand	Company	Share of world beer market
Budweiser	A-BI	4.4%
Miller Lite	Miller Brewing Co.	1.7
Kirin Lager	Kirin Brewery	1.7
Bud Light	A-BI	1.5
Brahma Chopp	Companhia Cervejaria	1.4
Coors Light	Coors Brewing Co.	1.4
Heineken	Heineken NV	1.3
Antarctica	Antarctica Paulista	1.3
Polar	Cerveceria Polar SA	1.2
Asahi Super Dry	Asahi Breweries	1.2

in Brazil, and Tsingtao Brewery in China. These agreements are part of A-BII's two-pronged strategy of investing internationally through both brand and partnership development. Through partnerships A-BII will continue to identify, execute, and manage significant brewing acquisitions and joint ventures, partnering with the number one or number two brewers in growing markets. This strategy will allow A-BII to participate in beer industries around the world by investing in leading foreign brands, such as Corona in Mexico through Modelo. A-BII's goal is to share the best practices with its partners, allowing an open interchange of ideas that will benefit both partners.

LATIN AMERICA

The development of Budweiser in Latin America is one of the keys to long-term growth in the international beer business, as it is one of the world's fastest-growing beer markets and is a region with a growing consumer demand for beer. Anheuser-Busch products are sold in 11 Latin American countries—Argentina, Belize, Brazil, Chile, Ecuador, Mexico, Nicaragua, Panama, Paraguay, Uruguay, and Venezuela—with a total population of over 350 million consumers. Particularly, the three countries showing the fastest growth in total beer consumption in the 1998–1999 period are Brazil (over 200 percent), Colombia (over 130 percent), and Mexico (over 100 percent).

BRAZIL

Anheuser-Busch International recently made an initial investment of 10 percent in a new Antarctica subsidiary in Brazil that consolidates all of Antarctica's holdings in affiliated companies and controls 75 percent of Antarctica's operations. Anheuser-Busch will have an option to increase its investment to approximately 30 percent in the new company in the future. The amount of the initial investment was approximately $105 million. The investment has established a partnership that gives Antarctica a seat on the board of A-BI and gives A-BII proportionate representation on the board of the new Antarctica subsidiary. The two brewers will also explore joint distribution opportunities in the fast-growing South American beer market.

According to Scott Bussen (South American representative for A-BII), A-BII is currently in the process of signing a deal that calls for an establishment of an Anheuser-Busch-controlled marketing and distribution agreement between the two brewers to support sales of Budweiser in Brazil.

The deal makes Anheuser-Busch the first American brewer to hold an equity stake in the Brazilian beer market, which is the largest in Latin America and the sixth largest in the world. In 1998, the Brazilian beer market grew by more than 15 percent. Its potential for future growth markets make it one of the most important global beer markets.

The second component of the partnership will be a licensing agreement in which Antarctica will brew Budweiser in Brazil. The joint venture will be 51 percent owned and controlled by Anheuser-Busch, 49 percent by Antarctica. Antarctica's production plants will produce Budweiser according to the brand's quality requirements. Local sourcing of Budweiser will allow more competitive pricing and increased sales of the brand in Brazil. The agreement is expected to be signed sometime before the end of summer.

Antarctica, based in São Paulo, controls 35 percent of the Brazilian beer market. Its annual production in 1998 was about 20 million barrels of beer. Antarctica has a network of close to 1,000 Brazilian wholesalers. Prior to its investment in Antarctica, Budweiser had achieved a distribution foothold in the Brazilian beer market through cooperation with its distributor, Arisco. Brazil has a population of 161 million people with per capita beer consumption in Brazil estimated to be 40 liters per year. With Brazil's population growing by 1.7 percent a year, reduced import duties, and free market reforms, Anheuser-Busch is expected to do well over the next decade in the Brazilian market.

The combined strengths of Anheuser-Busch and Antarctica in the booming Brazilian environment will lead to increased sales for both companies' products, resulting in a more competitive beer market, which benefits consumers, suppliers, and distributors in Brazil over the long term.

MEXICO

DEMOGRAPHICS.   Mexico's overall population in 1998 was estimated at 92.7 million people. Based on 1998 statistics, the age breakdown is as follows: under 15, 38 percent; 15 to 29, 29 percent; 30 to 44, 17 percent; 45 to 59, 9 percent; 60 to 74, 5 percent; and 75 and over, 2 percent. The average age of the Mexican population was 23.3 years.

Between 1970 and 1990, the ratio of the population living in localities with between 100,000 and 500,000 inhabitants grew from 12 to 22 percent. This was largely due to rural-urban migration. More than 71 percent of the population lives in urban areas of Mexico. In 1990, 22 percent of the national population lived in Mexico City and the State of Mexico. The Mexican population is expected to rise to 112 million in the year 2010.

OPPORTUNITIES.   Mexico offers the U.S. exporter a variety of opportunities encompassing most product categories. Mexico is continuing to open its borders to imported products. Mexico's population of approximately 92 million is the eleventh largest in the world and the third largest in Latin America (after Brazil and Argentina). Mexico is a young country, with 69 percent of its population under 30 years of age. In addition, the Mexican government has adopted new privitization policies decreasing its involvement in the country's economy. As a result, private resources, both local and foreign, are playing a greater role in all areas of the Mexican economy.

The North American Free Trade Agreement (NAFTA), which aims to eliminate all tariffs on goods originating from Canada and the United States, is expected to create a massive market with more than 360 million people and $6 trillion in annual output.

In a further move to strengthen its international capabilities, Anheuser-Busch Companies purchased a 37 percent direct and indirect equity interest for $980 million in Grupo Modelo (located in Mexico City) and its subsidiaries, which thus far are privately held. Modelo is Mexico's largest brewer and is the producer of Corona, that country's best-selling beer. The brewer has a 51 percent market share and exports to 56 countries. In connection with the purchases, three Anheuser-Busch representatives have been elected to the Modelo board, and a Modelo representative has been elected to serve on the Anheuser-Busch board.

Additionally, the agreement includes the planned implementation of a program for the exchange of executives and management personnel between Modelo and Anheuser-Busch in key areas, including accounting/auditing, marketing, operations, planning, and finance. Modelo will remain Mexico's exclusive importer and distributor of Budweiser and other Anheuser-Busch brands, which have achieved a leadership position in imported beers sold in Mexico. These brands will continue to be brewed exclusively by Anheuser-Busch breweries in the United States. Currently, Anheuser-Busch brews beer for Mexico at their Houston and Los Angeles breweries, which are not very far away but add to the markup of A-BI brands.

All of Modelo's brands will continue to be brewed exclusively in its seven existing Mexican breweries and a new brewery in North Central Mexico. U.S. distribution rights for the Modelo products are not involved in the arrangement. Corona and other Modelo brands will continue to be imported into the United States by Barton Beers and Gambrinus Company and distributed by those importers to beer wholesalers.

Modelo is the world's tenth-largest brewer and, through sales of Corona Modelo Especial, Pacifico, Negra Modelo, and other regional brands, holds more than 51 percent of the Mexican beer market. Its beer exports to 56 countries in North and South America, Asia, Australia, Europe, and Africa account for more than 69 percent of Mexico's total beer exports.

Modelo is one of several companies that distribute Budweiser besides Antarctica in Brazil and other local import-export companies in other Latin American countries. Modelo is the exclusive importer and distributor of Anheuser-Busch beers in Mexico. The newest brand, Ice Draft, will be the fourth A-BI brand distributed in Mexico by Modelo, joining Budweiser, Bud Light, and O'Doul's.

The Modelo agreement is significant because beer consumption has grown 6.5 percent annually in Mexico in the past few years. Mexico's beer consumption is the eighth largest in the world but is still only half of U.S. consumption. The per capita beer consumption rate in Mexico is estimated at 44 liters, compared to 87 liters per person in the United States, which is high given that Mexico's per capita income is one-tenth that of the United States. The Mexican market is expected to grow at a rapid rate.

Anheuser-Busch does not have control over foreign pricing. The local wholesalers and retailers set prices for Budweiser. A-BII also does not have plans to set up a full-scale production facility in Mexico at this time.

Right now Budweiser is imported, which makes it two to three times higher in price than local beers. Therefore, it is largely an upscale, niche market brand at this time. An equity arrangement in another brewery or an agreement with Modelo could lead to local production and make A-BI brands more competitive with the local beer brands.

Besides the 11 Latin American countries mentioned, Anheuser-Busch has signed agreements with the largest brewers in Costa Rica, El Salvador, Guatemala, and Honduras to distribute and market Budweiser in their respective countries. Local breweries (Cervecerma Costa Rica in Costa Rica, La Constancia in El Salvador, Cerveceria Centroamericanas in Guatemala, and Cervecerma Hondureqa in Honduras) distribute Budweiser in 12-ounce bottles and 12-ounce aluminum cans.

These distribution agreements will allow Budweiser to expand its distribution throughout the rest of Central America. These countries have an extensive national distribution network and, more important, have local market expertise to develop Budweiser throughout the region.

Under the agreements, the Central American brewers will import Budweiser from Anheuser-Busch plants in Houston, Texas, and Williamsburg, Virginia. Anheuser-Busch will share responsibility for Budweiser's marketing with each of its Central American partners, supported by nationwide advertising and promotional campaigns.

ADVERTISING

EVENT SPONSORSHIP

Given that Budweiser's advertising approach is traditionally built around sports, the decision to hold the 1994 World Cup tournament in the United States gave

A-BII a perfect venue to pitch Budweiser to Latin Americans. The company signed a multimillion-dollar sponsorship deal with the World Cup Organizing Committee, making Budweiser the only beer authorized to use the World Cup logo. "The World Cup has become a vehicle for us to reach Latin America," said Charlie Acevedo, director of Latin American marketing for Anheuser-Busch International.

For 10 months, soccer fans in South America saw the Bud logo on everything from soccer balls to beer glasses. Soccer fans received a World Cup bumper sticker when they purchased a 12-pack of Bud. When they watched the game on television, they saw Budweiser signs decorating the stadiums and got a glimpse of the Bud blimp hovering overhead. According to Charlie Acevedo, the goal is to make Budweiser a global icon, like McDonald's golden arches or Coca-Cola.

Anheuser-Busch just signed its second two-year agreement with ESPN Latin America. "Being able to buy on a regional basis gives a consistent message that is very reasonable in terms of cost," said Steve Burrows, A-BII's executive vice president of marketing.

Latin America offers promise with its youthful population and rising personal income (Figure C2.1 illustrates the GDP of selected Latin American countries). Half of Mexico's population is under 21, and other Latin American countries have similar profiles, offering opportunities for advertisers to reach the region's 450 million population.

The biggest new advertising opportunities in the Latin American market are cable channels (see Table C2.2) such as Fox Latin America, MTV Latino, Cinemax Olé (a premium channel venture with Caracas cable operator Omnivision Latin American Entertainment), USA Network, and Telemundo (a 24-hour Spanish-language news channel). Marketers will have yet another panregional advertising

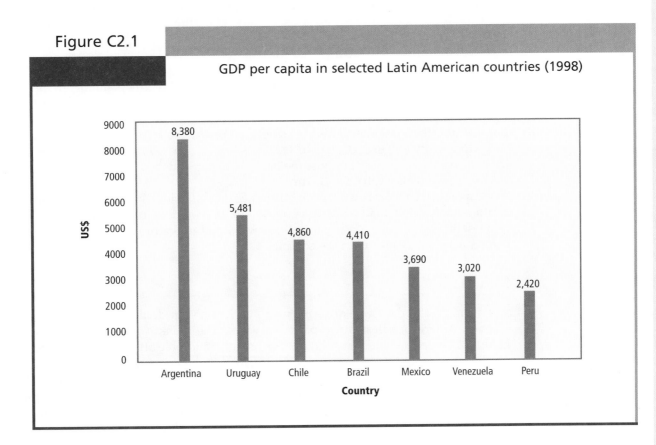

Figure C2.1

GDP per capita in selected Latin American countries (1998)

Table C2.2

Location	TV households (in millions)	Paid subscribers	Penetration rate
		Penetration of paid cable TV channels	
Brazil	30.0	3,300,000	15%
Mexico	14.0	1,700,000	12
Argentina	9.0	4,300,000	47
Chile	3.4	200,000	6
Venezuela	3.3	90,000	3
Uruguay	0.7	35,000	5
Ecuador	0.5	25,000	5
Paraguay	0.5	45,000	9

option. Hughes (the U.S. aerospace company) and three Latin American partners—Multivision in Mexico, Televisao Abril in Brazil, and the Cisneros Group in Venezuela—launched a $700 million satellite that will beam programs in Spanish and Portuguese into homes across the continent. The service is called DirecTV. Because of this satellite, Central and South America have added 24 new channels; with digital compression technology, its capability could reach 144 cable channels.

In the past, Anheuser-Busch used CNN International as its only ad vehicle, but with all the new opportunities, "the company will begin adding a local media presence throughout Latin America," said Robert Gunthner, A-BII's vice president of the Americas region.

Anheuser-Busch will be using ads originally aimed at U.S. Hispanics, most of which were created by Carter Advertising of New York. A-BII will let local agencies pick its messages, customize advertising, and do local media planning. In the past, there has been much criticism toward A-BI's ethnocentric approach toward marketing Budweiser; however, because of the world obsession with American pop culture, they feel they don't need to tone down their American image. In Costa Rica, A-BII will use JBQ, San Jose; in El Salvador, Apex/BBDO, San Salvador; in Guatemala, Cerveceria's in-house media department; and in Honduras, McCann-Erickson Centroamericana, San Pedro.

Imported beers cost two or three times as much as locally brewed beers in South America, but thanks to cable television and product positioning in U.S. movies, Budweiser was already a well-known brand in South America when the company began exporting to the continent.

STRATEGY

According to Charlie Acevedo, Anheuser-Busch has seen double-digit increases in Latin American sales in the past five years. The gains came from both an increase in disposable income and an increasingly favorable attitude toward U.S. products, especially in Argentina, Brazil, Chile, and Venezuela. Because Latin America has a very young population, Anheuser-Busch expects this market to grow at 4 percent annually. Furthermore, with NAFTA and a free trade zone, the company expects to see a significant rise in personal income in Latin American countries, which translates to great growth potential for Anheuser-Busch brands.

North American products and lifestyles are very much accepted in South America, but beer consumption still lags far behind U.S. levels. Argentines consume about 30 liters annually per capita, Brazilians 40 liters, Chileans 50 liters, and Venezuelans 65 liters, compared to nearly 90 liters per person annually in the United States.

"The international focus will be almost completely on Budweiser because there is a worldwide trend toward less-heavy, less-bitter beers," said Jack Purnell, chair and CEO of A-BII. They're counting on the American image to carry their beer, therefore opting for a universal campaign with American themes as opposed to tailoring Budweiser's image for local markets.

In the past, A-BI has tinkered with its formula and marketed Budweiser under different names to give a local flavor to their beer, but had absolutely no success. Purnell said, "What the market does not need is an American brewery trying to make up from scratch new European-style beers. Bud should be Bud wherever you get it."

AT&T

AT&T

AT&T

The Threat of Internet Telephony

case 3

It is September 15th, 1999, at the semiannual Voice On the Net (VON) conference in Washington, D.C. The warm weather and slowly turning leaves have put the city in a hiatus of sorts, basking in the clear days of the present but expecting the cold winter to come. Similar thoughts came to the mind of Ted Hurty, as he listened to yet another speaker make predictions about the future of telecommunications. Ted Hurty, a Network Infrastructure Manager at AT&T, has been working on various projects aimed at improving the company's overall communications infrastructure in preparation for that same future. In the past few months, AT&T has been gearing up for a slew of mergers and alliances aimed at establishing its presence in emerging technologies and new markets. In the months to come, AT&T will hold talks with British Telecom, IBM, Telecommunications International, and many small cable television companies.

As of right now, Ted Hurty is not worried about what his company is doing to ensure its leadership in the years to come, but rather whether it is doing enough to survive the technological revolution that is looming ahead. The biggest threat comes from an emerging technology that is redefining the concept of voice communication, IP telephony, a technology that uses the Internet, instead of the telephone network, to connect callers anywhere on the planet. It promises a cheaper (if not free), more efficient way for people anywhere to talk to each other, without using their telephones or paying hefty long-distance fees.

A BRIEF HISTORY OF TELEPHONY

Traditionally, the packet switched telephone network (or PSTN) and the Internet were viewed as separate entities, each designed for a specific purpose. As such, telephone companies and long-distance carrier companies (LDCs) worked with each other to connect calls from end to end (see Figure C3.1). In the last few years the popularity of home-based Internet access has increased dramatically, with millions of computer users logging on to the Internet to communicate, to find information, and to seek entertainment. The Internet itself relied upon the high bandwidth data "backbones" of LDCs like MCI, AT&T, Sprint, and so on.

Then came the "voice on the net" revolution and the possibility of listening to music, news shows, and other recorded sounds over the Internet. Software

Source: This case was prepared by Ketan Bhatia, Deepak Mehrotra, and Nitin Putcha of Temple University under the supervision of Professor Masaaki Kotabe, September 1999. Reprinted by permission. Names have been slightly altered to protect identities.

505

Figure C3.1

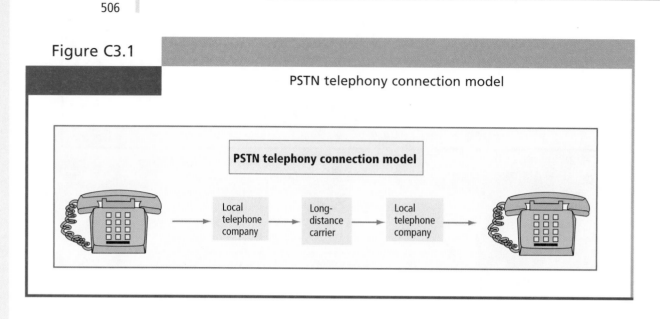

PSTN telephony connection model

developers began to realize that it might be possible for people to talk to each other in real time. The first Internet Protocol (IP) telephony software began to appear, allowing people with a computer and an Internet connection to engage in very low quality but real-time voice conversation for almost no cost. The only costs incurred were that of the Internet connection and the use of the computer. The software, from companies such as iPhone, Voicenet, and Microsoft, was distributed free of charge.

HOW IP TELEPHONY WORKS OUT CHEAPER

When a person using a regular telephone wishes to make a call from Philadelphia to Chicago, the person essentially requests to be connected to another phone by dialing its number. The local telephone company—in this case, Bell Atlantic—handles this request. Bell Atlantic in turn connects to a long-distance carrier (say, AT&T), who carries the connection across the country to Chicago. AT&T then connects to another local telephone company (say, Ameritech) in Chicago. Ameritech completes the call, connecting to a phone at the other end. This system works fine, but it is expensive. At each point in a call where one company connects to another, an access fee is charged. In the above example, Ameritech charges AT&T an access fee to complete the call, Bell Atlantic charges AT&T for using its subscriber line, and so on. These charges are passed down to the caller, who ends up paying between five cents to one dollar per minute for the call.

IP telephony makes things much cheaper. An IP telephone call requires an Internet connection on either end and some equipment for converting analog voice into digital data. The caller does one of two things—connects to the Internet using a computer and IP telephony software or uses the phone to call an 800 number (essentially uses the phone to call a mainframe computer that is connected to the Internet). The caller supplies the IP address[1] or the phone number of the person being called. The call is then routed from origin to destination via the Internet, directly to the phone or computer of the receiving party (see Figure C3.2). This whole process costs little or nothing for the caller, because the Internet connection costs about $20 per month (e.g., dial-up connection service from AOL, Compuserve, or another provider) and the software is free.

---

1. IP address: a unique identification number assigned to each computer on the Internet.

Figure C3.2

IP telephony connection model

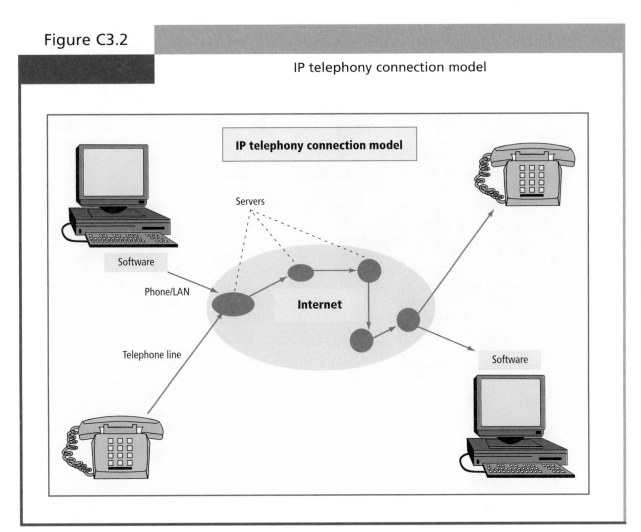

The biggest parts of this model are the high-speed Internet connections and the switches and servers that route the call from origin to destination. Because there are no access fees of any kind for routing data through the Internet, an IP telephone call becomes very cheap. Currently these servers and switches are mostly owned and operated by long-distance carriers, but the IP telephony providers and the callers use these switches and servers for free. Essentially, they are piggybacking on the Internet public domain.

AT&T

Global communications giant AT&T is the world's premier communication and related services service company with annual revenues of more than $52 billion. It is spread through more than 200 countries and has a customer base of 90 million. This includes consumers, business, and government. Moreover, the company has more than 130,000 employees around the world.

AT&T has operating assets of $55 billion, and with such high stakes it seems not to have made any mistakes so far. As a foray into global consolidations of industries of all kinds, it has formed a strategic alliance with British Telecom. The primary purpose of this $10-billion joint venture of their overseas operations is to prepare the battlegrounds for the new generation of technology shaping the industry today. AT&T's other two overseas alliances—with Unisource and World Partners—have been dismal failures. They amounted to little more than clumsily executed reselling arrangements. This time around, AT&T is happy to let BT shape its international strategy. The BT alliance is not, however, the only strategy AT&T is implementing to supplement falling domestic long-distance revenues. The company's recent $32-billion deal to buy the largest cable TV operator in the United States could be the much-needed battering ram into local telecommunications markets. And AT&T is now concentrating on satisfying the next generation of customers. On December 8, 1998, AT&T announced its decision to acquire IBM's Global Network business for $5 billion, with outsourcing agreements between the two companies. IBM will outsource a significant portion of its global networking needs to AT&T, and AT&T will outsource certain applications processing and data center management operations to IBM. The IBM Global Network business serves the networking needs of several hundred large global companies, tens of thousands of midsized businesses and more than one million individual Internet users in 59 countries. The acquisition boosts AT&T's strategy to rapidly increase the company's revenue, especially at its fast-growing networking services unit, AT&T Solutions. About 5,000 IBM employees will join AT&T as part of the acquisition.

"These strategic agreements are all about growth," said AT&T Chairman and CEO C. Michael Armstrong. "Growth in revenue, growth in technology, and—most important—growth in what AT&T can do for customers. For AT&T, today's announcement supports four areas we've targeted for growth: global services, data networking, Internet Protocol technology and network outsourcing through our AT&T Solutions business," said Armstrong. "The acquisition of IBM's global data network will accelerate our ability to deliver IP-based services to global customers. It will give us a sophisticated new platform for revenue growth."

THE PLAYERS

The total telecom market is estimated at $1,200 billion, with $300 billion in investments made through 1999. It is quite interesting to examine who the long-term players in this potential key market of the future are, particularly as related to the threat of IP telephony (or IT). With so much at stake, the major telephone companies are no doubt going to be affected, but there are a number of other companies that are also influenced by this revolution in telecommunications.

LOCAL TELEPHONE COMPANIES

These are the companies that provide regional service and local calling facilities in our homes and offices. Overall, local calls contribute to a very small percentage of the profits. The reason is this: Although local calls outclass long-distance calls in both frequency and sheer number, immense competition and the presence of a large and complex regulatory governing framework prevents local calls from being primary revenue generators. Large chunks of the profits come from the **last mile service** that local telephone companies provide to long-distance carriers. These phone companies charge a comparatively high rate from the long-distance carriers for the last mile of network access that they provide right to the customer's phone. For example, Bell Atlantic would charge AT&T a last mile service charge for any long-distance calls made to a customer having Bell Atlantic as their local telephone company.

Another potential money-maker for a local telephone company that may be threatened by IP is the access price that they charge the telephone companies of developing and underdeveloped economies in return for permission to use their sophisticated telephonic networks. IP telephony threatens to eliminate all these profit centers, as it involves dialing up only to the local service providers, bypassing long-distance carriers and the chain of access charges (profits) they demand, as is the case with Internet access.

LONG-DISTANCE CARRIERS

IP telephony poses the largest threat to long-distance carriers such as AT&T, MCI Worldcom, U.S. Sprint, and others. However, a couple of interesting factors in favor of these long-distance carriers may prove to be a tremendous advantage for them in the future. Over a period of many years, these companies have earned healthy profits and have managed to build an established and sophisticated reserve of financial, research and development, and infrastructure capabilities. These capabilities, if properly utilized, may enable them to retain their current position and also to expand their current market share in the future. The markets are changing dramatically, however, and no one is safe in the long run.

IP TELEPHONY SERVICE PROVIDERS (IPTSPs)

The IPTSPs have a lot going for their product, as they are providing an essential service at extremely low prices, basically dealing with a marketing team's dream product. However, so far the development of IP telephony has been extremely haphazard, with a lot of new companies entering the market for a short time and then dying away. It is estimated that, at present, there are approximately 5,000 Internet service providers and several hundred IPTSP software and hardware developers.

The industry is still considered to be in its teething stage, and a major boom is predicted that makes it potentially inviting to a large number of new entrants, pouring oil on troubled waters and making the market even more chaotic. Irrespective of the competition, all the companies that enter this market must invest a great amount of resources into large scale R&D, which is essential until the product reaches a certain level of maturity in technical as well as in marketing terms.

INTERNET SERVICE PROVIDERS (ISPs)

ISPs already provide an existing and rapidly growing service to the public at large—that of providing access to the Internet and the World Wide Web. These companies consider IP telephony to be a supplementary function of the services that they provide—a mere extension of their existing product offerings.

GOVERNMENTS

IP telephony is a product of the future, and it involves the complete restructuring of the telephony industry and long-distance voice communication as we know it today. It involves the dissolution, or at least a major redistribution, of a traditional "cash cow" industry that may not be an easy thing to convince anyone to give up. Governments also want to control this industry for strategic and political reasons. This is especially true in case of traditionally protectionist governments, especially considering the pressures that would arise from the threat of great losses in revenues and in customers.

Countries like Pakistan and India have banned IP telephony due to the major loss of revenue for state-owned telephone companies, which adversely affects their developing economies. But these state-run telephone companies are also experimenting with IP telephony. The Federal Communications Commission (FCC) in the United States has imposed no regulation on Internet and IP telephony service at present. This is believed to be due to the industry's minimal market size. As this scenario changes so will the regulatory climate surrounding this industry.

This simple idea of allowing people to talk to each other for little or no cost over the Internet is stirring up a hornet's nest of activities and new players, all jostling for better seats in the communications show of the new century.

AT&T UNDER FIRE

It all started with the data-com market. New entrants into the superior economies of IP networks will dominate this $60-billion market by 2001. Evidence is growing that this transition from proprietary networks to IP-based networks will increase much more than expected. There are more than 5,000 Internet service providers, and they are making progress in new areas such as EDI, fax services, and anywhere else they have a price advantage. The Internet segment of the data communication market will grow at a rate of about 58 percent per year versus 20 percent per year for propriety networks. Now that the newer players have established themselves via IP-based networks, the voice service sector seems to be increasingly attractive to them—mostly because it has high profit margins and is nearly 20 times larger than the data communication market in volume terms. The migration of users from conventional voice networks to IP-based networks has already started in international consumer calls and in domestic and international fax traffic. Call it the battle of telecom networks. In one corner are the telecom companies who have invested upwards of $300 billion in building extensive proprietary phone networks, and in the other are new entrants with their new technologies and superior economies of IP networking. This battle is being hastened by a boom in voice and data traffic and the inexorable transition from a circuit to a packet switched telecom infrastructure.

Companies like UUNET (now a part of Worldcom), BBN (now part of GTE) and Ascend/Crescend are using the Internet and its open standards to pick off horizontal slices of the telecom industry's value chain, such as hosting and redundancy. The attempt now is to hijack the voice traffic currently routed through propriety networks. As a leader, AT&T has the most at stake. The question is: How will AT&T protect its sizable investments in these networks?

Lessons from other industries demonstrate that both incumbents and attackers can be winners in the battle for the value. These lessons also show that during the transition to open standards and products, the risks of making wrong bets on technology or markets escalate, but then so does the risk of making no bets at all!

NEW BATTLEGROUNDS, NEW RULES

Less than a decade ago, U.S. customers were served by three autonomous propriety networks: The phone networks carried voice, the LAN/WAN systems carried data; and the broadcast networks carried video. Each network was a vertical pipe, a closed system in which a single vendor provided all the software, hardware, and services to more or less captive end users. That orderly world has become a chaotic place, thanks to the digital revolution of the Internet, which has enabled the disintegration of the three pipes and created opportunities for many new entrants to participate. The 1996 U.S. Telecom Act ensures that customers are no longer tied to a single service provider. The mandate for open competition is similar in Europe.

SO WHAT WILL HAPPEN?

Consumers, at least the technology-friendly ones, have already started to make calls on the Net through their computers, with the help of software such as Microsoft's NetMeeting. Now, there are videoconference kits available on the market for as low as $80 that enable users to place a videoconferencing call on the Net. Some companies that provide prepaid calling cards that allow customers to place calls over the Net using a standard phone and an 800-number line to an Internet server. All this is extremely cost effective and is killing propriety networks in call rates. Once this starts to happen on a large scale, which is sure once technology and voice quality improve, the next wave of adopters will be corporations that will adopt this technology for its cost savings and superior technology. A single port will allow them to access information and data, make commercial transactions, and most of all make both audio and video calls. With the new technology requiring more customization and extremely high levels of service, smaller companies will mushroom and provide complete solutions. How will companies like AT&T manage such fragmented competition?

SITUATION ANALYSIS—A TASTE OF THINGS TO COME

It has become clear that IP telephony will be the communications medium of the future. Within the next five to seven years, we will see high-speed, data, and voice-capable networks coming into our homes at very low prices. The average computer-illiterate consumer will be able to make IP telephone and video calls using simple equipment. Ted Hurty recalled a strategy meeting in October, where his superior summed up AT&T's position in the business. "Its obvious that our ultimate goal is to have an end-to-end hybrid (data and voice) network." He went on to discuss the IP telephony projects that were underway in Japan[2] and Europe and the ongoing process of conversion and installation of new networks around the world.

AT&T is building advanced IP telephony–capable networks, but AT&T serves as an international telecom carrier to many customers around the world who still require access to the older network technology. These customers are foreign country telephone companies and carriers and users who rely on AT&T to connect them from point to point around the world. For AT&T to retain this global connectivity and continue to serve international and long-distance calling needs, it has to maintain its older voice-only networks. This will be a very expensive position for AT&T to hold, as it will have to incur costs in the upkeep of two types of networks. Although AT&T's existing networks are capable of IP service, the bandwidth required to conduct IP telephony and live video will quickly consume their capacity. Also, maintaining global connectivity means that AT&T will still have to pay access charges to other networks (egress fees) and maintenance costs.

FREE OR FEE?

The nature of the Internet is that it is a freely accessible network. Although no one organization "owns" the Internet, parts of it operate on the network of backbones (very high capacity network links) owned by companies such as AT&T, Sprint, MCI, and UUNET. These companies support the cost of their networks by charging customers for accessing them. The customers are business firms, ISPs, and local and regional telephone companies as well as retail customers. AT&T supports

---

2. AT&T has deployed a phone-card-based IP telephone system between Japan and the United States.

its networks by charging firms and individual customers a fee for accessing its network for long-distance and international calling, as well as for Internet connections. Although voice calling is charged on a per-minute basis, Internet service is charged on a flat rate, per month, or year basis. Based on the forecast that 25 percent of international calling will be over IP networks by 2003, we can safely predict that by 2010 virtually 100 percent of all international and domestic long-distance calls will be IP based. If this prediction comes true, it will spell the end of AT&T's lucrative retail international and long-distance service. AT&T stands to lose its entire customer base. AT&T's networks have so far been supported by the high per-minute rates it charges customers. Now, the company will have to make do with the low profit margins of Internet access. There even exists an opportunity for AT&T to deploy telephone-based IP telephony services (as it has done in Japan) worldwide. This would still allow it to charge per-minute rates for phone calls. But this business will not last very long; as Internet access becomes cheaper and faster, any competitor can set up a similar service and charge lower rates, as they do not own the network.

So, what can be done? In 7 to 10 years from now, the communications business will be characterized by the following:

- Inexpensive, high-speed Internet access for individuals and companies
- Drastic improvement in IP telephony technology, raising sound quality and connection reliability beyond that of the telephone
- Exponential adoption rates by customers, as they cut off their long-distance calling services and place calls via IP
- A shake-up of the traditional slices of the communications market

In the current model of an Internet telephone call, the participants are:

- The end user, who provides the hardware and software
- The local telephone company, which provides the phone line or network cable connection
- The IPTSP, who provides a gateway server, used to log on to the Internet and then contact a similar gateway at the destination
- The Internet itself, providing access from one point to another
- At the other end, another local telephone company, providing the line that reaches the receiving party

COST STRUCTURE

Right now, the end user pays either a monthly Internet access fee (approximately $20) and connects through a computer, or pays a per-minute charge (approximately 10 to 50 cents) and connects using a standard phone. The end user pays this fee to the ISP or the IPTSP. The end user also pays a small fee for the phone/LAN connection from the local telephone company. The ISP or IPTSP also pays a local telephone company or other ISP a fee for high-speed Internet access at both the origin and destination. At the other end, the end user usually pays nothing, except for Internet access.

It is plain to see that long-distance carriers have been cut out of this new model completely. In this situation, AT&T can only earn revenues if it can provide the Internet access needed by the IPTSP or ISP and the end user, but the profit margins on this service are meager. Within five to seven years from now, Internet access will become much cheaper and faster for end users, eliminating the need for an exchange, as users will be able to contact each other directly over the Internet. That will soon put the local telephone companies out of the business of providing local access services, except for that of providing the physical wire that reaches the customer. Here, they will face their toughest competition—from cable TV companies, which have already put in place high bandwidth cable wires, and from long-distance carriers like AT&T, who are trying to enter the local access market. Thus, the crucial question for AT&T is this: What will its business be 10 years from now? Will it be relegated to the position of a lowly network provider, building an IP network and charging small fees for access? Can AT&T become a local service provider (perhaps through its acquisition of cable TV companies)? Or will it have to become a full-service provider once again?

THE IMMEDIATE CRISIS

The big threat at the moment is the cost advantage that the IP-based carriers provide to the user. Already, long-distance carriers have started slashing their calling charges, so the margins are coming down. But then, with the hundreds of smaller IPTSPs that will use the backbones of companies like AT&T, paying them virtually nothing, there could be a time when such calls could be virtually free! Where will AT&T gets its revenue? It's already predicted that 25 percent of international calls will be made over IP networks by 2003. This challenge will again strain profit margins. As AT&T enters the race full bore, which it has to, its problems are just starting. It has recently acquired IBM's networking business for a sum of $5 billion, which is 10 percent of its existing assets. Also, it has plans for improving its technological backbone with high-capacity lines and for taking over cable companies in order to enter local markets. All these investments are just the beginning. To widen its customer base, it will have to make many more deals like these, and the amount to be invested will be astronomical. What happens to AT&T's return on investment (ROI) then? Although AT&T is trying to enter local markets, local telephone companies like Bell Atlantic have already entrenched their assets in these markets and will be in a stronger position to offer better deals. With such enormous investments and low profit margins, there seems to be no escape for AT&T. Whatever AT&T may charge, the competitors, or the free riders, will always charge less, and so AT&T has to walk on the tightrope.

As of 1999, AT&T has a few things going for it. Management seems to have awakened, and in its planning and preparing for AT&T's future the company has been making profits and caching reserve funds for a while. And IP telephony is still a couple of years away from worldwide acceptance and adoption. AT&T has a two- to three-year deadline to come up to speed in the IP network world of the future, to lose some weight, and to take a shot at remaining the biggest communications company in the world. In the meantime, Ted Hurty and his colleagues continue to strategize and revise their plans for dominating an industry that is, literally, moving at the speed of light.

QUESTIONS FOR DISCUSSION

1. What will be the future of AT&T after this communications revolution? Where in the value chain can AT&T add value to its customers? How can marketing executives contribute in defining the company's strategic direction?

2. How will the merging of voice communication and Internet networking industries affect AT&T's overall organization?

3. AT&T has been making investments into the creation of a fully digital voice/data/video network that still has to be freely accessible by the public domain. Is this investment wise?

Citibank N.A. in Japan

case 4

JAPANESE BANKING SCENE

In 1986, when Citibank began opening branches in Japan to offer retail-banking services, Japanese banks could be forgiven for yawning. They had a reason to do so, as until 1997 almost 7 of the top 10 banks in the world were from Japan. Citibank, the largest bank in the United States, was seventh on the list. With just a handful of branches, Citibank was the financial equivalent of a bonsai tree in a forest of rosewoods. Moreover, xenophobic Japanese consumers tended to regard foreign banks as less-safe places to park their savings. "When I first came here four and one-half years ago, the bank was very quiet," says Hiroshi Yoshioka, a Citibank customer who works for a Japanese chemical company. "I had to summon up some courage to step in."[1]

Times have changed now, and the tables are turned. With the Japanese economy in recession and the domestic banks burdened with about $1 trillion of nonperforming loans, Citibank is making some serious inroads into the Japanese market. Citibank's spurts of growth have coincided with successive Japanese financial disasters, ranging from the 1995 bond-trading scandal that led the Federal Reserve to expel Daiwa Bank from the United States to the triple collapse in 1998 of Sanyo Securities, Yamaichi Securities, and Hokkaido Takushoku Bank. "You have seen a 180-degree turn in the way Japanese are thinking," says Robert Berardy, Citibank Vice President in charge of "virtual banking," or telephone and computer banking services. "The negative (of being a foreign bank) has become a positive."[2] Consumer confidence in the domestic banks has eroded, and people are looking for new options.

CITIBANK WORLDWIDE

Citibank N.A. is significantly more international in scope than its international competitors. In 1997, it operated more than 3,400 locations in 98 countries and derived some 60 percent of its net income from foreign operations. The bulk of that income came from its emerging market franchise. Presently Citibank is a part of Citigroup, which is a result of the merger of Citicorp and Travelers Group in October 1998. As a result of this merger, Citigroup displaced Bank of Tokyo and Mitsubishi ($691 billion in assets) from the first position to become the largest financial company ($698 billion in assets) in the world. The group earned a net income of $5.8 billion in 1998 (see Figure C4.1).

Citibank had not always been a world-class success story, however. The bank suffered through a very difficult period in the late 1980s and early 1990s as a result

Source: This case was prepared by Rajat Khanna and Sizhen Jiao of the University of Hawaii at Manoa under the supervision of Professor Masaaki Kotabe of Temple University, August 1999. Reprinted by permission.

1. Steven Butler, "Japan's Down, Citibank's Up," *U.S. News & World Report*, September 7, 1998, 34–37.
2. Ibid.

Figure C4.1

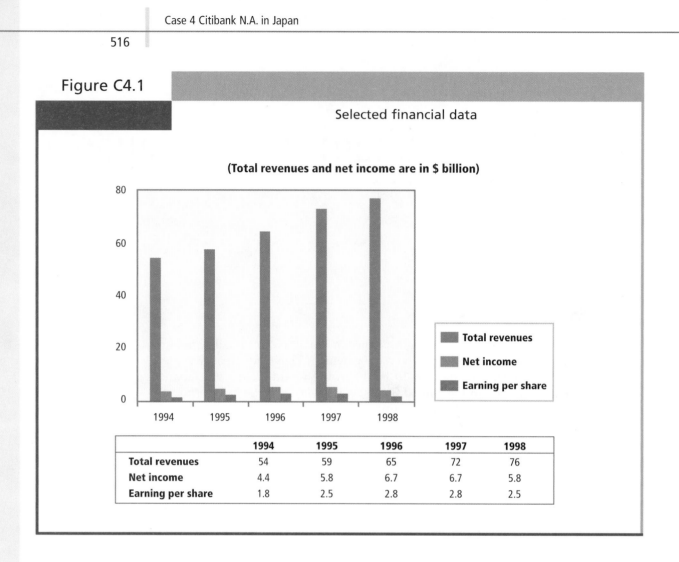

Selected financial data

(Total revenues and net income are in $ billion)

	1994	1995	1996	1997	1998
Total revenues	54	59	65	72	76
Net income	4.4	5.8	6.7	6.7	5.8
Earning per share	1.8	2.5	2.8	2.8	2.5

of its decentralized decision-making structure and what *Euromoney* called a "near fatal brush with commercial real estate lending" in the United States. It was due to the present Co-CEO John Reed's (Chairman and CEO until 1998) reengineering efforts that the decision making was centralized, the balance sheet was repaired, tier-one capital was rebuilt, and the credit ratings were restored by 1996.

CITIBANK'S GLOBAL NETWORK

Citibank's global presence can be judged by the following comment from Mr. Shaukat Aziz, head of Asia/Pacific global finance operations: "When a multinational company wants to enter an emerging market it calls its lawyers, its accountants, the embassy, and Citibank."

Citibank has a wide network of branches all over the world. Its presence in the emerging market economies is very strong, and in 1995 almost 50 percent of the total profits came from the bank's operations in these economies. The Asia/Pacific region (including Japan) brought 23 percent of the bank's net profit in 1996.

Long Presence and Local Market Experience

Citibank is a strong believer in the first mover advantage and always tries to be among the first foreign banks to enter a foreign market. In some of the countries Citibank has maintained its presence for almost a century. In Japan, Citibank started its first office in 1902. Even if it is not able to provide all the services due to government regulations, it stays to provide corporate services to the multinationals. In Japan also it maintained its presence without offering full-scale services and began offering retail services only in 1986. The bank's experience in the foreign markets gives it the operational expertise that, in times of turbulence, is difficult for other banks to match. This experience is advantageous for Citibank to keep important multinational accounts.

LOCALIZATION COMMITMENT

"We want to be totally global and totally local," said John Reed, Co-CEO, Citigroup. From this statement, Citibank's commitment to local markets is clear. Citibank tries to develop strong ties with the local community and with the local central bank. In 1997, locally hired staff held 95 percent of Citibank's jobs outside the United States. Technology is transferred, and local staff is trained. Citibank enters a market with a long-term objective and does not leave when profits are slow to materialize. The bank's long-term commitment approach makes it very popular with the local governments. In Japan, after opening its retail banking operations in 1986, it operated profitably for only three years and then ran into losses for eight straight years, but it stayed on to wait for the right opportunity in the long run.

TECHNOLOGICAL ORIENTATION

Citibank was "ahead of the curve" with respect to technology and financial innovation in the mid 1990s. The strong focus on technology and innovative financial services have won Citibank many awards. Citibank has established technology development centers, which build global platforms to support customer needs from any location. Citibank aims to use technology not only for improving customer services but also to reduce costs. Citibank is currently exploring how biometrics technologies like iris scanning might unobtrusively and reliably verify customers' identities, which could make bank cards and PIN numbers things of the past. In Japan, Citibank also wants to focus on technology in order to bring down the operating and transaction costs. Services such as telebanking and Internet banking are good examples of this. Besides opening new branches, Citibank plans to expand by installing thousands of ATM machines.

TRAINING AND DEVELOPMENT

Citibank has one of the best training and development programs for its employees. The employees are trained in general operations of the bank and also in their area of specialization. The employee's career path is well defined, and the progress is monitored. Mentor programs help in grooming future managers. In fact, Citibank people are in great demand by other banks and are often poached by them.

RISE OF CITIBANK IN JAPAN

For Citibank, it has been a long and at times bumpy road. Although it has maintained its presence in Japan since 1902, it became active in a small way in 1986 with retail banking operations. The true dynamism in Citibank's life in Japan materialized in the 1990s. The dormant existence in the early years was a result of government regulations, powerful Japanese banks, and the unsafe image of foreign banks. Citibank's success in Japan in the 1990s can be attributed to several factors, the chief ones being the weakened Japanese banks (nonperforming loans of approximately $1 trillion), the collapse of the security companies and other financial institutions (mentioned earlier), and the "Big Bang" (a major overhaul of Japan's financial regulations) in the Japanese financial sector. It is interesting to see how Citibank became the beneficiary of Japan's mounting financial turmoil.

The series of disclosures of the financial problems by Japanese banks eroded consumer confidence, and the safe image of these banks took a big blow. Consumers were now looking for alternatives. At the same time, Citibank—true to its image of being innovative—came up with services that were an instant hit with consumers. An example of its innovative services is multicurrency accounts. When the value of the dollar plunged below 100 yen in 1995, many Japanese consumers understood that their currency was being priced into a stratosphere from which it would eventually descend, and Citibank offered the most convenient way for small-time savers to play the currency market. The multicurrency accounts attracted customers who could shift money into dollars and earn higher interest rates but switch the money back into yen with a phone call—at any time of day or night. In one day, Citibank logged a record 315,000 calls from prospective and current customers; the next day, people mobbed the bank's 19 branches in a scramble to buy dollars that were suddenly cheap. Seeing this success, Citibank has developed ambitious plans for Japan. It hopes to reach 35 million accounts by the year 2010 from its present 1 million accounts. That pace of growth will launch Citibank into the mainstream of Japanese banking giants.

According to Berardy, customers do not come to Citibank just because of its safe image. Instead, he says, customers are now looking at Citibank positively and evaluating its products on their own merit. With just 19 branches, compared with many hundreds managed by its Japanese competitors, Citibank has earned the reputation as the country's most innovative bank by offering services such as 24-hour ATMs and telebanking. These services are taken for granted in the United States but are a novelty in Japan. The bank has also become popular among customers and gained tremendous free publicity by swallowing some of the fees that other banks charge when customers access their Citibank accounts on a rival bank's ATMs. By doing this, Citibank has in effect added thousands of ATMs using their rivals' infrastructure.

STRATEGIC ALLIANCES

To have a better customer reach and to provide more services, Citibank has entered into several strategic alliances in Japan. In a widely publicized deal that seemed to stamp Citibank with an official seal of approval, it became the first bank of any kind to reach a cooperative business deal with Japan's mammoth Post Office Savings System, which most Japanese believe is the safest place to put their money. The deal will add thousands of remote-access points for Citibank customers, making it more practical for the majority of the Japanese who live far from a Citibank branch to open accounts. Citigroup also has bought 25 percent equity in Nikko Securities, which is the third largest brokerage house in Japan. In addition, Citibank is thinking about entering into alliances with Asahi Bank and the Tokai Bank. These alliances will increase Citibank's access to huge savings amassed by Japanese savers estimated to be around $9 trillion.

FINANCIAL RECORD

Citibank's trading volume has been increasing these years even though the total trading volume for all banks has not been increasing worldwide. Citibank's net income and earnings per share have been stable, as it has focused not only on total revenues but also on cost reduction for the customers as a way to add more value to bank services (see Figure C4.1). Citibank's loans and deposits have also been increasing steadily. The average growth rates are 8.1 percent for loans and 9.8 percent for deposits (see Figure C4.2). Citibank is very aggressive in expanding its market share globally, and at the same time it is maintaining the loan to deposit ratio at above the industry average. Its ratios for 1997 and 1998 were both 89 percent (see Figure C4.3).

Figure C4.2

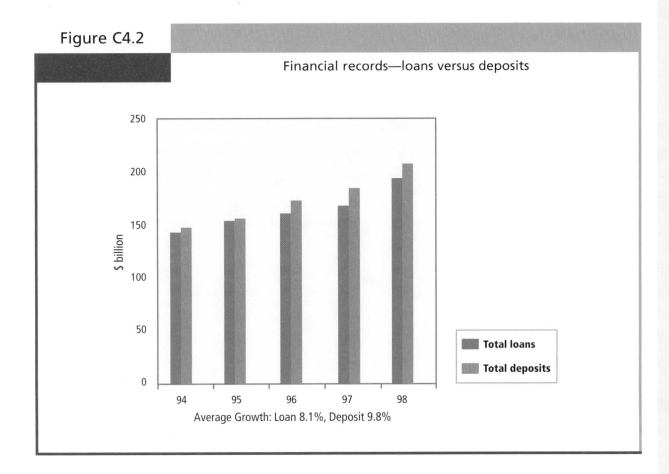

Financial records—loans versus deposits

$ billion

- Total loans
- Total deposits

Average Growth: Loan 8.1%, Deposit 9.8%

Figure C4.3

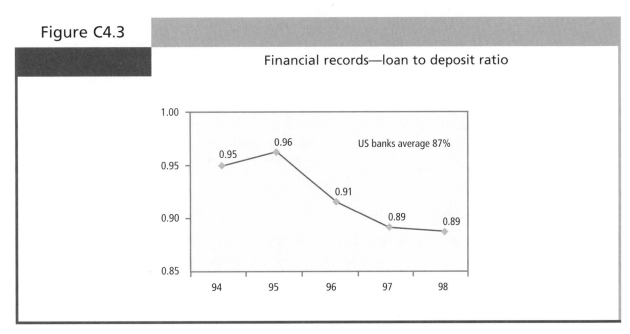

Financial records—loan to deposit ratio

US banks average 87%

0.95 0.96 0.91 0.89 0.89

Figure C4.4

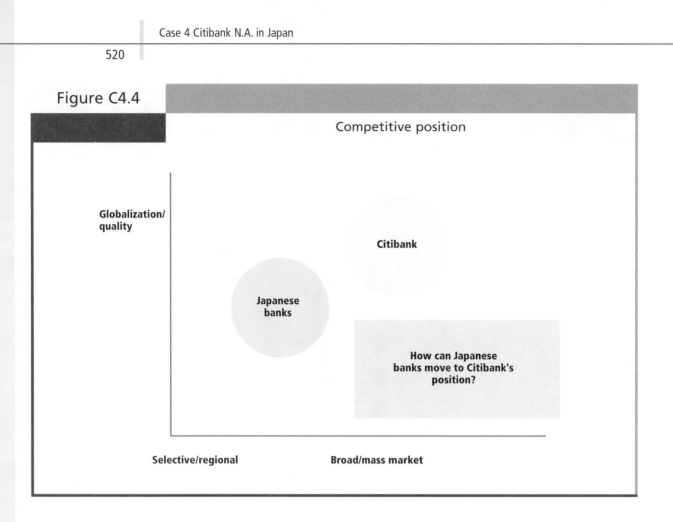

Competitive position

Globalization/quality

Citibank

Japanese banks

How can Japanese banks move to Citibank's position?

Selective/regional   Broad/mass market

MAJOR COMPETITORS

The major competitors include domestic banks and foreign banks. Major domestic competitors are Bank of Tokyo–Mitsubishi, Dai-Ichi Kangyo Bank (DKB), and Sanwa Bank. The foreign banks mainly include ABN Amro, HSBC, and Deutsche Bank, among others. At present, none of the foreign banks, except Citibank, has retail banking operations. Thus Citibank Japan has many competitive advantages: strong brand equity, globalized operations, innovations, and localized staff of very high quality. On a competitive positioning map Citibank can be seen as having a broader product range and better quality of service (see Figure C4.4).

MARKETING STRATEGY

The market may be getting smaller, but the top players are taking bigger slices in Japan. The largest foreign-exchange firms are having to work harder to carve out a point of difference in a mature market with thin margins. Given that the banks cannot distinguish themselves from their competitors on the grounds of better interest rates (controlled by the government), the only area where the banks can make a difference is in their services and product (financial product) innovation. Citibank is doing a good job differentiating itself along these lines by (1) product strategy designed as "one-stop shop" concept or financial supermarket in a global setting and (2) developing unique services and innovations.

PRODUCT

Under the umbrella of Citigroup, Citibank plans to provide several financial services. The "one-stop shop" will offer retail banking, corporate banking, investment banking, insurance, project financing, currency transactions, and a host of other products. To offer these services, Citibank will use the different arms of Citigroup. Special services like credit advice and research are being provided to add more value.

PRICE

It is widely recognized that in pricing terms there is no difference between what Citibank can provide and what other banks can do. Therefore, Citibank is trying to maximize the value added to its customers by providing more unique and creative services while at the same time minimizing the costs and expenses of customers by providing telephone banking, Internet banking, and direct mail for opening an account.

PROMOTION

Citibank, in its effort to build strong brand equity and in its pursuit to become the "Coca-Cola of finance," is using strategies such as cobranding, cross marketing, and "Citibanking" as an experience. The Sony Citibank Card launched in the United States is an effort to be associated with the top names in the world. In the past, Citibank has solicited the services of former president of the United States George Bush to promote its global image. Although criticized as being discriminatory, Citibank has efficiently and profitably used an unusual approach toward its wealthy customers. In April 1998, Japan began deregulating its banks. Koichiro Kitade, head of Citibank's private banking division in Tokyo, knew it was time to try a new marketing approach to expand its market share. Through newspaper advertisements, Citibank exclusively targeted rich people having more than $750,000. Although discriminatory, Citibank succeeded with this creative and unique approach.

PLACE

Citibank is constantly and actively expanding all kinds of distribution channels, such as new branches, Internet banking, low-cost nationwide network of ATMs, and telephone banking. With services like telebanking and Internet banking, Citibank has in effect expanded the distribution channel to its customers' homes. According to Robert Berardy, although Citibank is adding 10 more branches in Japan this year, an expensive high-density branch network that matches those of its Japanese rivals is not a part of the strategy. "The proliferation of branches that made these Japanese banks successful will be the thing that kills them in the future," says Berardy. "They can't cut costs. Even if they closed the branches what would they do with the people?" Even after seven years of economic stagnation, layoffs remain socially unacceptable in Japan.

CHALLENGES FOR CITIBANK

On its road to success Citibank faces several challenges. One of the foremost challenges is from within, that is, the question of the smooth amalgamation of Citicorp and the Travelers Group, which merged to form Citigroup. If managed and coordinated properly, their merger can give the new company the synergy to be a front runner in world banking. On the contrary, bad management and lack of coordination can lead to a fiasco. Problems can arise due to the different cultures of the two organizations. Already there are reports of differences and conflict of opinion between the two co-CEOs, John Reed and Sanford Weill. John Reed is known to have long-term objectives and favors market share over profits, whereas Sanford Weill is a hard-core profit-oriented executive. His main focus is on quarterly profits and maximization of shareholder wealth. For this reason, he is very popular on Wall Street.

The other challenge is in the form of the competitors, both domestic (Japanese) and foreign. Even now the Japanese banks have formidable strength, and with their government's help and successful alliances, these banks can give their competitors a run for their money. Taking clues from the 1980s domination of U.S. competition by Japanese manufacturing companies, the banks may also follow the same course.

QUESTIONS FOR DISCUSSION

1. One of the questions that comes to mind when talking about the rise of Citibank in Japan is whether it can maintain the same rate of growth and popularity as it has done in recent years. Japanese banks may be down now, but it would be a serious mistake to discount their power. Japanese companies have overtaken the West in the manufacturing industries and are known to be effective in managing distribution channels. Can Japanese banks also do the same in financial services?

2. What have been the market expansion strategies of Citibank? Will these strategies help it to achieve the "one-stop shop" objective?

Direction for the 21st Century

case 5

HISTORY AND BACKGROUND

In 1887 Tomiro Nagase opened a very modest shop in the heart of Tokyo selling soap and other pharmaceutical products. He named his store *Kao*, or the King of Flowers. Always focusing on the welfare of the consumer, Nagase used this motive as a way to get to the people of Japan. Then, in 1890, he introduced the first product to be manufactured by Kao, called Kao Soap. By 1923, Kao opened its first manufacturing plant in Tokyo and began to produce Kao Soap there. From this period forward, other products began to enter into the expertise of Kao, with the introduction of Kao's own shampoo, laundry detergent, scouring powder, and liquid detergent.

During the war, like many other manufacturers, Kao felt the brunt of the conflict. However, in 1949, Kao marked its way into a new era with its listing in the Tokyo Stock Exchange. From that point on, Kao made many aggressive moves in this industry by acquiring and merging with other chemical companies and by expanding abroad. In 1964 Kao moved into Taiwan and Thailand, marking its move to expand into Asia. Subsequent acquisitions and moves include Dino Indonesia, Infosystems Canada Inc., Andrew Jergens' in the United States, and Goldwell in Germany. By 1990 Kao's market share in the Japanese cosmetics market was 16 percent (see Figure C5.1), and their products were distributed through many channels (see Figure C5.2). Currently Kao is the largest household product manufacturer in Japan and boasts over 550 different products worldwide, in 27 different countries. The product family overall includes personal care products, cosmetics, laundry and cleaning products, hygiene products and bath additives, food products (edible oils), floppy disks, information technology, and chemical products (see Figure C5.3).

Even though most Japanese companies had difficulties sustaining growth and profitability due to the collapse of the bubble economy and decreased consumption of Japanese consumers, Kao continues to grow while earning profits up to the 1999 fiscal year (see Figure C5.4). Moreover, Kao's stock price has soared despite the overall decline of the Japanese stock market (see Figure C5.5). Analysts in the stock market have a favorable impression of Kao because it emphasizes profitability as one of the major concerns for management, unlike the typical Japanese firms that mainly focus on the growth rate and market share.

In 1998 Kao decided to withdraw from the floppy disk business, because top managers of Kao judged that the market had too many players, and thus was no longer a prospective business for growth. Before the decision, Kao had a 15 percent market share in the floppy disks market in Japan. Following the withdrawal from

Source: This case was prepared by Jamie Kaku and SeokHo Lee of the University of Hawaii at Manoa, under the supervision of Professor Masaaki Kotabe of Temple University, August 1999. Reprinted by permission.

floppy disk business, Kao is discussing the future of its Information Technology (IT) division as well. Top managers of Kao felt that the company may not have a competitive advantage in the IT business. In addition to the positive response to Kao's own concerns on profitability, analysts have also responded very favorably to Kao's cash flow–oriented management.

Figure C5.1

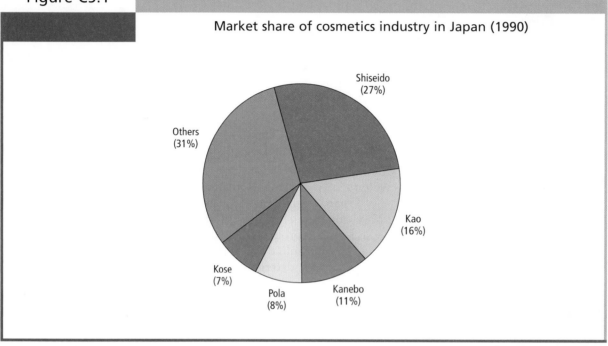

Market share of cosmetics industry in Japan (1990)

Shiseido (27%)
Others (31%)
Kao (16%)
Kose (7%)
Pola (8%)
Kanebo (11%)

Figure C5.2

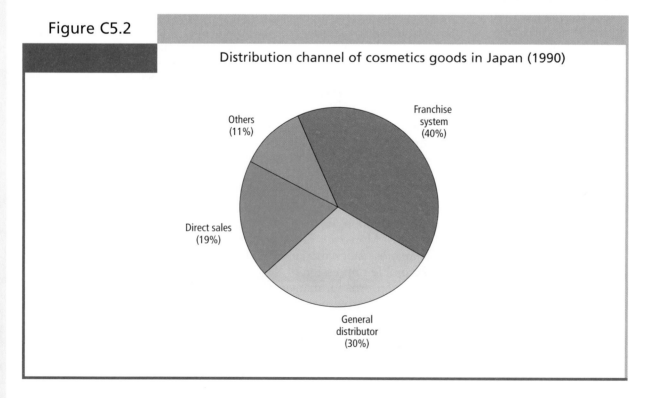

Distribution channel of cosmetics goods in Japan (1990)

Others (11%)
Franchise system (40%)
Direct sales (19%)
General distributor (30%)

Figure C5.3

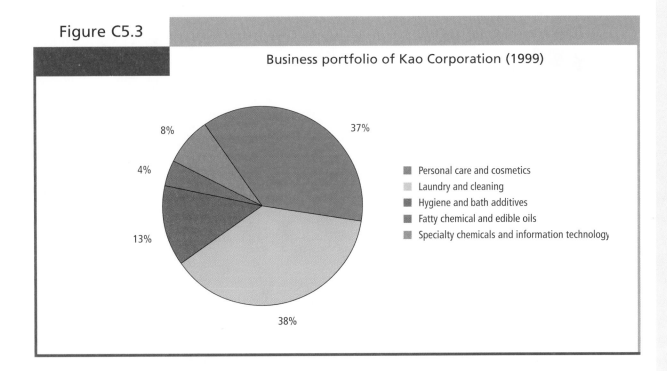

Business portfolio of Kao Corporation (1999)

- Personal care and cosmetics
- Laundry and cleaning
- Hygiene and bath additives
- Fatty chemical and edible oils
- Specialty chemicals and information technology

Figure C5.4

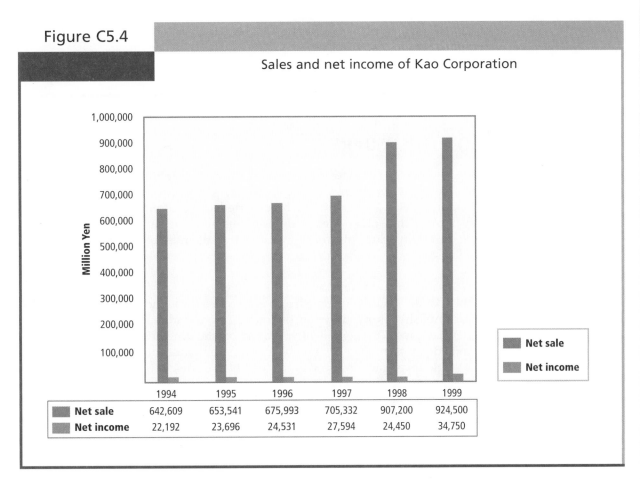

Sales and net income of Kao Corporation

	1994	1995	1996	1997	1998	1999
Net sale	642,609	653,541	675,993	705,332	907,200	924,500
Net income	22,192	23,696	24,531	27,594	24,450	34,750

Figure C5.5

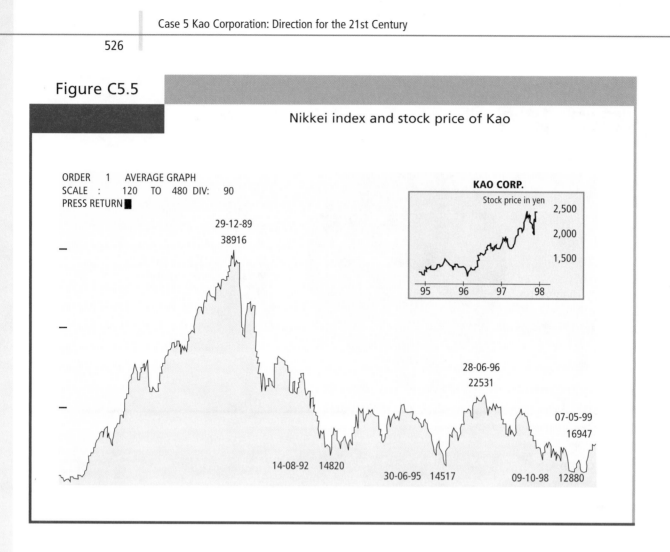

Nikkei index and stock price of Kao

ORDER   1   AVERAGE GRAPH
SCALE   :   120   TO   480 DIV: 90
PRESS RETURN ■

29-12-89
38916

KAO CORP.
Stock price in yen
2,500
2,000
1,500
95   96   97   98

28-06-96
22531

07-05-99
16947

14-08-92   14820

30-06-95   14517

09-10-98   12880

KAO'S PHILOSOPHY

Living by the idea that satisfying consumers will bring the company success in the market, Kao has lived by a simple slogan, "Create products of superior quality that provide consumers with wholehearted satisfaction." This ideal has obviously moved into other areas of Kao's business in ways that have directly affected the corporate culture, so much so that the mission statement is quoted as follows:

> Kao's mission is to contribute to the wholehearted satisfaction and the enrichment of the lives of customers and employees throughout the world. We will accomplish this by drawing on our creative and innovative strengths to develop products of excellent value and outstanding performance. Fully committed to this mission, all members of Kao companies are working together as a single corporate force to win the loyalty and trust of their customers.

From the time when Nagase opened up his own pharmaceuticals store to now, this philosophy of always satisfying the customer has become his credo. Using this as the guiding principle for business, the philosophy has filtered down to other areas of the company as well.

MANAGEMENT PRINCIPLES

There are five basic principles that Kao's management uses as a guide in devising business strategies in the industry. These principles are as follows:

1. Ensure customers' wholehearted satisfaction worldwide.
2. Create innovative products based on original ideas and technologies.
3. Sustain profitable growth and respond to the trust of stakeholders.
4. Leverage the abilities of individuals into a powerful corporate force.
5. Encourage close harmony with the environment and the community.

All of these principles are based on the premise of Kao's slogan and mission statement and its focus on the customers. The mission extends out into these principles, which help to shape it in the minds of the employees and other stakeholders that Kao would have.

PRODUCT DEVELOPMENT AND R&D

As part of Kao's goal to continually satisfy its customers, product innovation is a key focus. The current president of the Kao group, Takuya Goto, stated that "a strong brand needs to be supported by R&D" (annual report). To ensure product innovation and development, there are four basic guidelines that this department follows:

- Base all new developments through scientific discovery.
- Always seek to improve on products.
- Become the first in the market with an innovative product.
- Create a product that will bring the most satisfaction to the customer.

With these guidelines as a basis, Kao also uses a product developmental format, in which all departments are in contact with each other, thus focusing on an aggregate company product innovation, and customer satisfaction (see Figure C5.6). This format also helps all departments keep in touch with the importance that Kao places on environmental issues when producing their product as well.

As Kao continues to uncover the needs of the consumer, marketing research becomes the focus for corporate activities. For this purpose, Kao operates a consumer information center, called the "Echo system" (see Figure C5.7). This system allows the company to do marketing research systematically as a product is being produced. Kao's consumer center has pools of consumer inquiries and constantly receives comments from them on a daily basis. The collected information gathered by the center is accessible to all sections within the company. In addition, through establishing an information network system that functions online between the head office of Kao and *Hansha* (sales companies exclusively handling Kao products), Kao can get timely market information on current trends. This marketing research system has allowed Kao to trace and respond to market trends quickly.

Uncharacteristic of a Japanese corporation, Kao has a lot of local-based R&D divisions. This is primarily due to the different features that are required in different areas of the world. For Kao, it is important to ensure that the production and marketing of its products are both attractive and beneficial to each of its local consumers.

Figure C5.6

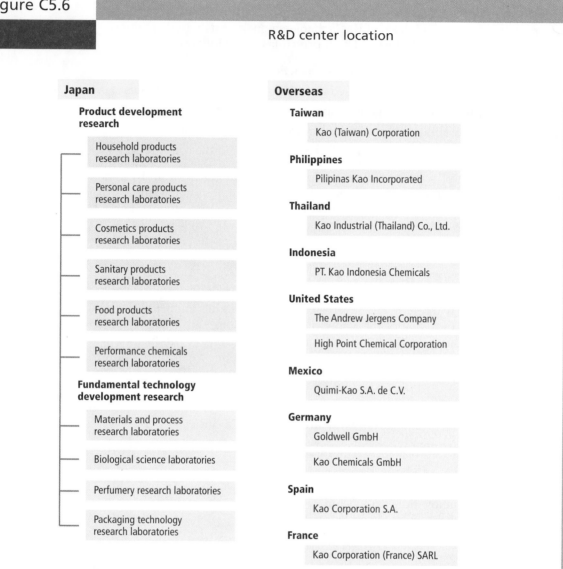

R&D center location

Japan

Product development research

- Household products research laboratories
- Personal care products research laboratories
- Cosmetics products research laboratories
- Sanitary products research laboratories
- Food products research laboratories
- Performance chemicals research laboratories

Fundamental technology development research

- Materials and process research laboratories
- Biological science laboratories
- Perfumery research laboratories
- Packaging technology research laboratories

Overseas

Taiwan
- Kao (Taiwan) Corporation

Philippines
- Pilipinas Kao Incorporated

Thailand
- Kao Industrial (Thailand) Co., Ltd.

Indonesia
- PT. Kao Indonesia Chemicals

United States
- The Andrew Jergens Company
- High Point Chemical Corporation

Mexico
- Quimi-Kao S.A. de C.V.

Germany
- Goldwell GmbH
- Kao Chemicals GmbH

Spain
- Kao Corporation S.A.

France
- Kao Corporation (France) SARL

BRAND POWER

Probably one of Kao's greatest strengths lies in its "brand power." According to the Nikkei Research Institute of Industry and Markets (operated by Nihon Keizai Shinbun), brand power is determined by a power-ranking survey of consumers' opinions. This survey takes a look at the 170 leading brands in the Japanese market in 19 different product categories and examines factors like brand recognition, perceptions of the product's quality, and feelings of loyalty to those brands.

According to this survey, Kao's laundry detergent Attack had the highest rating (see Table C5.1). Launched in 1987, Attack was considered to be a breakthrough product that combined compact packaging with extra cleaning power. In addition to Attack, Kao had four other brands that were listed in the top 20 of the "Brand Power Ranking." These products range from shampoos and conditioners, dishwashing detergents, sanitary napkins, and cosmetics.

Figure C5.7

"Echo system"

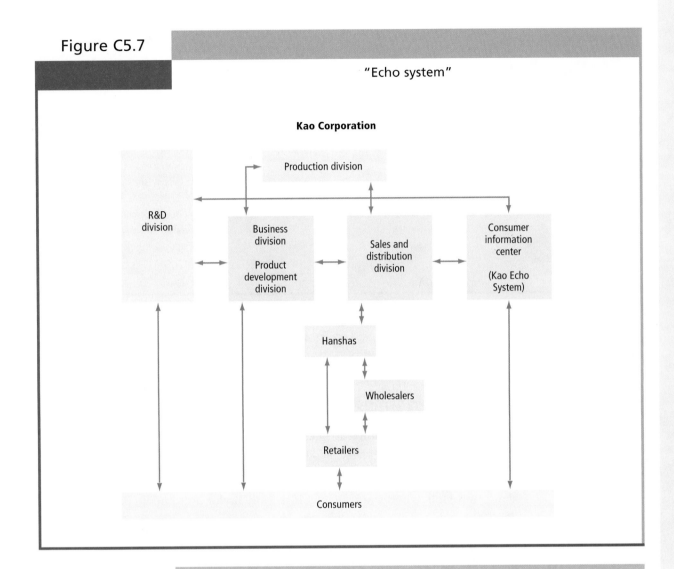

Kao Corporation

Table C5.1

"Brand Power Ranking" (top 20 brands in Japan)

Rank	Brand name	Product category	Points	Company name
1	Attack	Laundry detergent	83.0	Kao Corporation
2	Kleenex	Tissue paper	78.3	CRECIA Corporation
3	Cup Noodle	Instant cup noodles	75.0	Nissin Food Products Co., Ltd.
4	Whisper	Sanitary napkin	73.2	Procter & Gamble Far East, Inc.
5	Asahi Super Dry	Beer	69.6	Asahi Breweries, Ltd.
6	Pabron	Cold medicine	68.6	Taisho Pharmaceutical Co., Ltd.
7	Handycam	Video camera	67.2	Sony Corporation
8	Meiji Milk Chocolate	Chocolate	67.0	Meiji Seika Kaisha, Ltd.
9	Merit	Shampoo-conditioner	66.9	Kao Corporation
10	Kirin Ichiban Shibori	Beer	66.8	Kirin Brewery Company, Ltd.
11	LuLu	Cold medicine	65.7	Sankyo Co., Ltd.

(continued)

Table C5.1

"Brand Power Ranking" (Top 20 brands in Japan) (cont.)

Rank	Brand name	Product category	Points	Company name
12	Family Fresh	Dishwashing detergent	65.2	Kao Corporation
12	Laurier	Sanitary napkin	65.2	Kao Corporation
14	Kirin Lager Beer	Beer	64.4	Kirin Brewery Company, Ltd.
15	Georgia	Canned coffee	64.3	Coca Cola (Japan) Ltd.
16	Aisaigo	Washing machine	63.8	Matsushita Electric Industrial Co., Ltd.
17	Kirigamine	Air conditioner	63.2	Mitsubishi Electric Corporation
17	Sofina	Cosmetics	63.2	Kao Corporation
19	Scottie	Tissue paper	62.4	CRECIA Corporation
20	Elleair	Tissue paper	61.8	Daio Paper Corporation

Source: Courtesy of the *Nikkei Marketing Journal,* September 6, 1997.

EXPANDING INTO THE U.S. MARKET

Andrew Jergens has been a household name in the United States for decades. Founded with $5,000 as "The Andrew Soap Company" in 1882 and headquartered in Cincinnati, Ohio, Jergens' has become one of the most recognized brands in skin care in the United States. Jergens' products are sold in 56 countries around the world, with the majority of sales in North America. Jergens' has led the U.S. market with innovations such as Jergens' Body Shampoo and Pore Perfect. Its cherry-almond smell is synonymous with the company and is comfortingly familiar to most Americans. In the 1950s, the company enjoyed a 70 percent market share, and Hollywood stars such as Elizabeth Taylor and Lucille Ball advertised its products.

In 1970, the family-owned company was sold to American Brands, becoming a part of a huge conglomerate that also sold tobacco, alcohol, and food. The company was run purely for profit and suffered a lack of capital investment, but bumbled along until the late 1980s. At that point, American Brands decided to diversify and put Jergens' up for sale.

At about the same time, Kao was looking for an American distributor for its skin care products. Kao produced nearly 600 consumer products from laundry detergent to floppy disks, with its gross sales hovering around approximately 4 billion yen. Kao succeeded in the Asian market but had difficulties establishing itself in the United States. Because Kao was without a distribution arm in the United States, it set up an office in New York, hired consultants, and started looking for a company to work with. Coincidentally, Jergens' came into the market at about the same time. George Sperzel, Andrew Jergens' CFO, stated, "Kao had developed the first concentrated laundry detergents, which were a huge success in Asia and Japan. But it hadn't expanded globally beyond Southeast Asia, and its products were copied and quickly developed by other companies in Europe and the United States." Being fully aware of this, finding a local partner became even more of an imperative to Kao.

Interestingly, Jergens' expertise in skin care was largely irrelevant to Kao at the time. What mattered was that it had a sales and distribution system. In fact, the two companies complemented each other better than either could have imagined. Thus far, Jergens' has had success with both the Bioré line and Kao's liquid body cleansers, while Kao has launched the Jergens' skin care products in Japan, hence tapping into a whole new market.

GEORGE SPERZEL

George Sperzel, who joined Jergens' about five years after the purchase, previously spent most of his career with General Electric (GE). It was GE's rigorous training and management style that Jergens' particularly sought in its new CFO.

> I met with the Japanese president of the company at that time, and he talked for about two hours. At the end of it I said, "Don't you want to hear about me?" and he said no, because he knew GE's reputation and just wanted to be sure that I would fit in. The parent company is "supportive but hands off," with the minimum of corporate bureaucracy. They rely more on the judgement of the management team when it comes to decision-making due to my experience with U.S. companies. As far as processes and policy, I'm completely free to do what I want, which is how it should be.

As it turned out, there was plenty to do upon his arrival. Finance had a very small role in the company—mainly just a reporting role—and was not even represented on the executive committee. They stayed on their floor of the administration buildings, producing reports that they then threw over the wall to someone else. Mr. Sperzel stated, "The idea was that I would bring the finance function into the 1990s." He immediately set about upsetting the company's habit of operating in "functional silos" (a term derived from the farming community around Cincinnati, where the company is based).

> The sales, marketing and other functions didn't really talk to each other except at the very top. So if someone in finance had a marketing question, they would go up the line to the VP (Vice President) of finance, over to the VP of marketing, and down the line to whoever knew the answer. Within the first two weeks, I took the best two finance people and said, "Starting Monday you're working in marketing." The marketing people really liked it. The finance people were unsure. But from my experience with GE I knew that it worked better than anything. The company is now organized into production teams, with marketing, sales, and R&D and finance all represented and seated together. We've also sent finance people into the manufacturing and IT systems operations. The end result is that we are able to contribute at the beginning of a project. Before, finance only had a chance to comment at the end, when it was too late and it came across as nit picking, or hindsight. We're now viewed as a support member of the team rather than an observer.

He has also taken pains to foster an atmosphere of what he calls "constructive conflict."

> A lot of people were uncomfortable with people questioning what they were doing. Arguing was encouraged at GE because people come up with a better answer than if you go for a consensus, which is of course the traditional Japanese way of doing things. There was no interaction, but now everyone challenges everything, in a cooperative rather than a hostile way.

The company underwent another transformation in 1995, when Bill Gentner was brought in from Unilever as president, replacing the Japanese president, who became the Managing Director of Kao. One of Gentner's first moves was to essentially restructure the entire management team. George Sperzel ended up the only one left in an executive role when all the changes were said and done. Sperzel explained the situation as such:

Bill Gentner has brought in a lot of people from big companies. Although Jergens' is very small, we know what a big company looks like. We have a clear goal of where we want to go, but because we're small we can be fast and flexible about getting there. We also get our hands a lot dirtier than we did at the bigger companies.

BIORÉ STRIP

The biggest event in Jergens' recent history, though, is the Bioré strip. This skin-cleansing strip of paper was first launched by Kao in Japan. There are many differences between the Japanese market and its U.S. counterpart, particularly so in the skin care business. (As it is very humid in Japan, dry skin isn't an issue.) Bioré, marketed as a midpriced family brand in Japan, was repackaged for the U.S. market and directed to an entirely different audience. Jergens' seized the opportunity to develop an entirely new brand under the Bioré name, which would draw in a much younger audience than its products had in the past.

> We wanted to use the strips as a way to develop a new category—facial care—that we weren't in already. Andrew Jergens' is seen more as a product targeted towards women of 35 and above, but this was a way of getting to the younger age group, which is a neglected territory.

The strips were patented, but it was still only a matter of time before similar products were launched by rival companies. Unilever's Ponds brand, for instance, a major rival, has already launched its own version. Jergens' lack of size compared to Procter & Gamble and Unilever makes it difficult to compete on any grounds other than constant innovation. Sperzel went on, stating, "We won't get into an advertising war because they have resources that we don't. The business is pretty cut-throat, but if you have good products it doesn't matter how big or small you are." Jergens' sales amounted to a 24 billion (US$180.4 million) yen in the 1996 financial year and 30.5 billion yen (US$229.2 million) in 1997. Much of that increase can be attributed to Bioré. Sales of the Bioré products alone reached 22.5 billion (US$169.1 million) yen in 1998. Jergens' has also recently bought two established brands, Curel and Soft Sense, from Bausch & Lomb, which it hopes to add to the skin care line's profitability. There is a strong sense of making the most of Bioré while the market is still somewhat active. So far the strips continue to sell, and the range of new Bioré-branded facial products launched on the back of its success show every sign of continuing its high profile. "This was a once in a lifetime, a once in a career product," Sperzel said. "But we're not going to wait and find out how long this will last. We are constantly looking for new products."

ISSUES

Kao is an extremely innovative Japanese company that Procter & Gamble, a much larger U.S. competitor, uses as a benchmark for its product development in areas of personal care products, cosmetics, and laundry and cleaning products, among other things. Kao's foreign expansion, albeit aggressive, has not yet produced results of the kind that Sony and Honda, two comparable Japanese companies, enjoy (see Figure C5.8). Tables C5.2 and C5.3 show that the majority of sales are still in the household products line in Japan. According to Kao's recent annual report, there are six areas the company would like to focus on in the 21st century: (1) concentrating on core businesses, (2) continuing to develop innovative products, (3) increasing brand power, (4) pursuing cash flow–oriented management, (5) developing new businesses, and (6) continuing to improve operations.

Figure C5.8

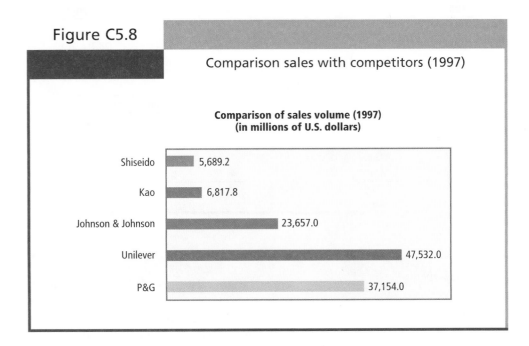

Comparison sales with competitors (1997)

**Comparison of sales volume (1997)
(in millions of U.S. dollars)**

Shiseido	5,689.2
Kao	6,817.8
Johnson & Johnson	23,657.0
Unilever	47,532.0
P&G	37,154.0

Table C5.2

Sales by industry

	Billions of yen					
	Sales			Operating income		
Year ended March 31	1999	1998	% change	1999	1998	% change
Household products	730.6	696.7	4.9	85.7	77.5	10.7
Chemical products	193.9	210.4	(7.8)	5.8	(4.6)	N/A
Total	924.5	907.1	1.9	91.5	72.8	25.8

	Millions of U.S. dollars					
	Sales			Operating income		
Year ended March 31	1999	1998	% change	1999	1998	% change
Household products	6,060.9	5,780.2	4.9	711.7	642.9	10.7
Chemical products	1,608.9	1,745.7	(7.8)	48.7	(38.5)	N/A
Total	7,669.8	7,525.9	1.9	760.4	604.4	25.8

Table C5.3

Sales by region

Billions of yen

Year ended March 31	Sales			Operating income		
	1999	1998	% change	1999	1998	% change
Japan	672.1	674.6	(0.4)	80.9	71.6	12.9
Asia	104.6	101.7	2.9	5.3	7.4	(28.3)
Europe and Americas	178.9	162.0	10.4	5.3	(6.2)	N/A

Millions of U.S. dollars

Year ended March 31	Sales			Operating income		
	1999	1998	% change	1999	1998	% change
Japan	5,575.5	5,596.4	(0.4)	671.4	594.5	12.9
Asia	868.5	843.8	2.9	44.5	62.1	(28.3)
Europe and Americas	1,484.3	1,344.6	10.4	44.7	(51.9)	N/A

QUESTIONS FOR DISCUSSION

Given Kao's corporate objectives, address the following issues:

1. Is the company's current strategy with Jergens' sufficient for its expansion and building its brand recognition in the U.S. market?

2. Kao's Attack is the most innovative laundry detergent with unparalleled cleaning power introduced in the world. However, it has not yet been introduced in other major markets such as the United States and Europe. Why is Kao slow in introducing such an innovative product around the world?

3. Was the company's decision to pull out of the profitable disk business a wise one despite its admirable market share position? How about other information technology areas where it has invested?

Marketing and the Environment: Tuna versus Dolphins

case 6

In the eastern tropical areas of the Pacific Ocean (a major tuna-fishing area), schools of yellowfish, skipjack, and bigeye tuna often swim beneath schools of dolphins. To catch quantities of tuna, fishermen look for the leaping dolphins and cast purse seines (nets pulled into a baglike shape to enclose fish) around both tuna and dolphins. When tuna is harvested with the purse seine method, fishermen can efficiently and reliably catch a high number of good-sized tuna. Unfortunately, dolphins are also trapped in the nets. Because they are mammals, dolphins must surface to breathe oxygen. Entangled in the net, they can asphyxiate and die unless they are released.

In the late 1960s and early 1970s, the "incidental" catch of various species of dolphins by tuna fishers in the eastern tropical Pacific (ETP) was in the hundreds of thousands. Because of society's growing and vociferous concern for these senseless deaths, new fishing techniques were developed to reduce dolphin mortality.

Perhaps the most important new technique is the "backdown operation." After "setting on" dolphins to catch tuna—that is, encircling both tuna and dolphins with the purse seine—the ship backs away, elongating the net, which submerges the corkline in the back, and pulls the net out from under the dolphins. If the operation works correctly, the tuna remain in the bottom of the net and the dolphins swim free. However, if the operation is flawed, dolphins are injured or killed and discarded from the catch as waste.

Rather than relying on this imperfect correction of the purse seine method, some environmental groups think that entirely different methods of fishing for tuna should be employed. Alternatives could include using a pole and line or setting on tuna not associated with dolphins. However, according to marine scientists and fishermen, the alternative methods have serious drawbacks as well.

Some catch many sexually immature tuna, which for some reason don't associate with dolphins. Juvenile tuna often are too small to be marketed. If too many are caught, the sustainability of the population could be jeopardized. In addition, alternative methods frequently catch high numbers of other incidental species, such as sharks, turtles, rays, mahimahi, and many kinds of noncommercial fish. Finally, all fishing methods expend energy. The practice of setting on dolphins uses the least amount of energy per volume of tuna caught.

According to many of the experts involved, including the Inter-American Tropical Tuna Commission, the U.S. National Marine Fisheries Service, and the scientific advisor to the American Tunaboat Association, the most efficient method for fishing tuna, in terms of operational cost yield and the conservation of tuna population, is to set on dolphins with a purse seine. From the canning industry's point of view, only purse seine fishing provides the volume of catch necessary for the growth of the industry.

Source: This case was written by Professor Michael Czinkota © with George Garcia and Kristen M. Mehlum. Reprinted by permission.

535

Many experts also believe that with current technology, it is not possible to abandon the practice of setting on dolphins without falling into other, more grave problems. Although research to develop better techniques continues, positive results are not expected in the near future.

THE TRADE IMPLICATIONS

This tuna-dolphin problem has been the source of serious friction on the international level. The United States and Mexico, two countries sensitive to marine mammal protection and with solid laws in place for many years, have come head-to-head over the issue. The conflict between environmental concerns and free trade for the United States and Mexico is further complicated by the existence of the North American Free Trade Agreement.

In 1988 the United States amended the U.S. Marine Mammal Act to prohibit the incidental killing of dolphins during commercial tuna fishing. The amendment required the banning of tuna imports from any country that did not implement several specific measures to reduce dolphin mortality and achieve a kill-per-set rate (the number of dolphins killed in each casting of the fishing net) of no more than 1.25 times the U.S. rate.

In February of 1991, a U.S. trade embargo was imposed on tuna caught by foreign fishing fleets using the purse seine method in the ETP, with Mexico as a prime target. This harsh step was seen as necessary, because over the previous 15 years, an estimated seven million dolphins died in tuna nets. The embargo cost tuna-exporting countries such as Mexico, Costa Rica, and Ecuador hundreds of millions of dollars. To avoid future losses, the embargoed nations met with U.S. officials in 1992 to determine ways in which they could improve their fishing methods, end the embargo, and regain access to the lucrative U.S. market.

Several changes in fishing methods were introduced after these negotiations. Although foreign fishers did not abandon the purse seine method, they learned to dip their nets deeper to allow dolphins to escape. Dolphin safety panels were installed in many nets, serving as escape hatches for the dolphins. Divers are now deployed to assist dolphins unable to find their way out of the nets. A biologist is assigned to every ship to observe fishing methods and to record dolphin mortality. The participating governments also adopted a vessel quota system in which the overall yearly quota for dolphin mortality is equally divided among the boats fishing in the region. This way, each boat is individually held responsible for its dolphin kill. Otherwise, a few careless ships could destroy the entire fishery's attempts to meet lower mortality rates for the year.

The effect of these changes on dolphin survival were major. Figure C6.1 shows that in 1986 over 20,000 dolphin mortalities were caused by U.S. vessels in the ETP. By 1998, the estimated amount was 738. The amount of dolphin mortalities caused by non–U.S. vessels also dropped drastically from 112,482 in 1986 to a preliminary estimate of 2,000 for 1998.

As of the mid-1990s, the total yearly mortality for each dolphin species was under 1 percent of its population, an amount that can be sustained without reducing the total number; in fact, the dolphin population was increasing. Thus, concern for dolphin conservation started to diminish. Most scientists started to view the mortality of dolphins incidental to tuna fishing not as an environmental problem but as one of avoiding unnecessary killing. In fact, a National Marine Fisheries Service scientist stated that if Mexico had money for research, it would be better invested on behalf of the Vaquita, a species in real danger of extinction, than in the tuna-dolphin issue, because there is no danger to the dolphin population as a whole.

Figure C6.1

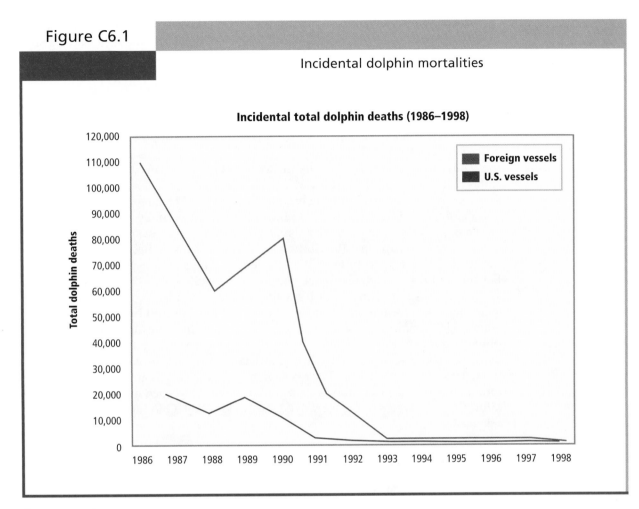

Incidental dolphin mortalities

Incidental total dolphin deaths (1986–1998)

Foreign vessels

U.S. vessels

Source: www.cnie.org.

In November of 1996, President Clinton promised that a revision of U.S. tuna/dolphin legislation would be a priority for the next convening Congress. A revision was necessary in order to appease Mexican discontent about restrictions on their tuna imports to the United States. The International Dolphin Conservation Program Act (IDCPA) was the result and became law in August 1997. This act served to weaken the U.S. Marine Mammal Act of 1988. The legislation called for the lifting of the U.S. embargo on tuna imports from countries that continued to use the purse seine during fishing operations. However, these nations had to be certified by the U.S. State Department as having joined a binding international program and having domestic legislation in place to enforce international dolphin protection efforts. The program consists of nations working together through having international observers on board when the purse seine nets are tossed, to see if any dolphins are killed.

The IDCPA also allowed "dolphin-deadly" tuna (or tuna caught by purse seine method) to be sold in the U.S. market. Eventually, such a catch would even be allowed to use a "dolphin-safe" label. However, until a study could be completed by the U.S. Department of Commerce concerning the positive or negative impact of purse seines on dolphin populations, "dolphin-safe" labels were still restricted to non–purse seine tuna. This was to ensure that consumers knew which brands of tuna use fishing methods that threaten dolphin conservation efforts.

In April of 1999 the U.S. Secretary of Commerce decided that "catching tuna by chasing and ensnaring dolphins in large encircling nets does not cause a significant adverse impact on the dolphin population." This decision enables the enactment of new dolphin-safe standards under the IDCPA. Thus, "dolphin-safe" labels can now be used for purse seine tuna, provided that an international observer and a captain do not see dead or injured dolphins in the nets.

A number of environmental organizations, including the Center for Marine Conservation, Greenpeace, and the World Wildlife Fund, support the change. Greenpeace believes the U.S. Department of Commerce decision reflects the success of the IDCPA to reduce dolphin kills in the ETP. Gerald Leape of Greenpeace also states that it is "appropriate for the U.S. to now modify the definition of dolphin-safe . . . since 1992, the nations fishing for tuna in the ETP have reduced the number of dolphins killed from 27,000 to fewer than 2,100 annually . . . this is an undeniable improvement in the way we manage the marine ecosystem."

But other groups feel the dolphin-safe label will now become meaningless. Representatives from countless environmental groups and organizations such as Earth Island Institute, the Humane Society of the United States, Dolphin Safe/Fair Trade Campaign, and Sierra Club say the decision was made contrary to all available scientific information. David Phillips of the Earth Island Institute states "Scientists, U.S. tuna companies, and the public know that chasing and netting dolphins is not safe for dolphins . . . the decision is consumer fraud and a death warrant for thousands of dolphins." Patricia Forkan, executive vice president of the Humane Society, states, "The decision by the Secretary is an outrageous attack on environmental protection laws in order to allow Mexico and other dolphin-killing nations access to the lucrative U.S. tuna market. Once again, trade trumps science."

THE ONGOING DEBATE

On August 19, 1999, a coalition of environmental groups including Earth Island Institute filed a lawsuit against Secretary of Commerce William Daley and the National Marine Fisheries Service (NMFS). They alleged that the federal government decision to relax dolphin-safe standards wrongly weakened the protections guaranteed by the dolphin-safe label on cans of tuna. Mark Palmer, a spokesman for Earth Island Institute, states that "the research done so far by the National Marine Fisheries Service (NMFS) staff scientists and the Inter-American Tropical Commission already shows that the [dolphin] populations are not rebounding and in some cases are still declining." Others also argue that "some dolphins that are not observed to die in the nets die later from stress." The suit, filed in the U.S. District Court in San Francisco, seeks to overturn the NMFS decision.

Despite the controversy surrounding labeling, the three major U.S. tuna processors—StarKist, Chicken of the Sea, and Bumble Bee—have said they will continue to use only tuna caught by methods other than encirclement. This decision does not seem to greatly affect the growth in the sales or volume of these three major processors, who share about 90 percent of the U.S. tuna market. StarKist Tuna, part of the H. J. Heinz Company, has stated in its fourth quarter fiscal 1999 report that seafood sales volume for the quarter increased by 6 percent.[1]

In the midst of the legal action and the continued debate, the NMFS will continue the second half of its scientific study. The finding of this study will be announced by December 31, 2002. At that point, the secretary of commerce will make yet another decision regarding the dolphin-safe label.

---

1. www.starkist.com/insidekt/corp/press/index.html, accessed December 1999.

QUESTIONS FOR DISCUSSION

1. Is the denial of market access an appropriate tool to enforce a country's environmental standards?

2. Did the U.S. denial of market access ultimately work?

3. What is your view on the quote, "Once again trade trumps science"? Is this case an example of that?

4. Is a zero-dolphin-death goal realistic?

Pepsi One

case 7

INTRODUCTION

On June 30, 1998, PepsiCo shocked the beverage industry with its introduction of a revolutionary new sugar-free cola with no aftertaste. Within one hour of FDA approval of acesulfame potassium (ace K), the main sweetening ingredient, the launch of Pepsi One was announced. Samples of the new drink were in the hands of reporters and bottlers within hours.

How was PepsiCo able to formulate a new core brand so quickly? The answer is that Pepsi is no longer an American company but has become a truly global organization. Pepsi has proven this by developing a new product to satisfy an overseas market segment. As the product was highly successful in foreign markets, PepsiCo brought it back to the U.S. market for a successful launch once ace K was approved.

PEPSICO CORPORATE HISTORY

EARLY GROWTH

In the 1890s the soda fountain was an integral part of the town drugstore. In New Bern, North Carolina, a pharmacist named Caleb Bradham decided to develop a new beverage that was both delicious and healthful. This beverage would aid digestion and boost energy by eliminating many of the chemicals and narcotics in popular fountain drinks. His new beverage was a huge success. He started producing the flavoring syrup in his basement and shipping it out to other drugstores in the region. By 1902 the formula was so successful that he decided to file incorporation papers to expand into Virginia, Maryland, Pennsylvania, and New York.

Now, some 100 years later, PepsiCo has developed into a global giant with sales in the range of $21 billion per year and a global sales force of 63,000 people. The current corporate entity of PepsiCo truly began in 1965 when Pepsi-Cola, under the leadership of Donald Kendall, and Frito-Lay, under the direction of Herman W. Lay, merged their companies to create a company with sales of $510 million. By 1970, PepsiCo had grown to annual sales of $1 billion and transferred the corporate headquarters to Purchase, New York.

Source: This case was prepared by Jason Blondé, Hemal Salot, Tanya Savio, and Florian Schmid of Temple University's Fox School of Business and Management under the supervision of Professor Masaaki Kotabe, October 1999. Reprinted by permission.

Table C7.1

PepsiCo acquisitions, divestitures, and international expansion

1898	Pepsi-Cola is formulated by Caleb Bernham
1964	Pepsi-Cola purchases Mountain Dew soft drink brand
1965	PepsiCo is founded by merger of Pepsi-Cola and Frito-Lay
1967	North American Van Lines (transportation company) purchased
1970	PepsiCo world headquarters moved to Purchase, New York; Wilson Sporting Goods is purchased
1972	Pepsi-Cola is sold in the USSR in exchange for Stolichnaya vodka
1974	Pepsi-Cola starts production in USSR
1977	PepsiCo acquires Pizza Hut restaurants (founded 1958)
1978	Taco Bell restaurants acquired (founded mid-1960s)
1981	PepsiCo reaches agreement for production in China; PepsiCo founds PepsiCo Food Systems (restaurant supplies)
1984	North American Van Lines is divested
1985	Wilson Sporting Goods is divested
1986	PepsiCo acquires Kentucky Fried Chicken restaurants (founded 1952); PepsiCo acquires 7-Up International (third-largest beverage brand); PepsiCo acquires Mug Root Beer brand
1987	PepsiCo headquarters relocated to Somers, New York
1988	PepsiCo establishes joint venture agreement in India; Hostess Frito-Lay partnership formed in Canadian snack food market
1989	PepsiCo acquires Walker Crisps and Smith Crisps in UK snack food market; PepsiCo acquires Smartfood ready-to-eat popcorn
1990	PepsiCo acquires controlling interest in Mexican cookie company, Gamesa
1991	PepsiCo acquires equity in leading Polish confectioner, Wedel SA
1992	PepsiCo purchases Carts of Colorado mobile merchandising equipment; PepsiCo purchases equity in California Pizza Kitchen restaurants; PepsiCo and General Mills merge European snack food operations
1993	PepsiCo acquires East Side Mario's Italian Restaurants; PepsiCo acquires D'Angelo Sandwich Shops
1994	PepsiCo becomes first soft drink producer in Vietnam; PepsiCo acquires bottler in India
1995	Cart of Colorado is divested
1997	Pizza Hut, Taco Bell, and Kentucky Fried Chicken restaurants are divested into Tricon Global Restaurants with PepsiCo shareholders receiving shares in the new company; other restaurant brands sold individually (California Pizza Kitchen, East Side Mario's, and D'Angelo Sandwich Shops); PepsiCo Food Systems is sold to AmeriServe; PepsiCo purchases Cracker Jack snack food from Borden Foods Corp.
1998	PepsiCo acquires Tropicana Juices from Seagram Company; PepsiCo acquires Smith's Snackfood Company in Australia; Wedel SA chocolate is divested

DIVERSITY AND FOCUS

Throughout the history of PepsiCo, there have been several purchases and sales of separate business entities (Table C7.1). In the late 1990s, PepsiCo experienced a period of rationalization and began to focus on the beverage and snack food markets. The most dramatic change during this period was the divestiture of the restaurant brands, Kentucky Fried Chicken, Taco Bell, and Pizza Hut, into the new Tricon Global Restaurants. Tricon was spun off to shareholders on the basis of 1 share in the new company for every 10 shares of PepsiCo held.

BRAND DEVELOPMENT

PepsiCo has concentrated on the development of major global brands. In 1997 they held nine different brands with over $1 billion in global sales (Lay's, Doritos, Ruffles, Cheetos, Pepsi, Diet Pepsi, Mountain Dew, 7-Up, and Mirinda). Table C7.2 shows the development of Pepsi slogans and brands.

Table C7.2

Brand and image development

Over the past 100+ years Pepsi has developed into one of the world's most recognizable brands. This brand growth has taken place in all of the core soft drink and snack food brands. The marketing slogans used by Pepsi have evolved in line with the product image.

Slogans and campaigns for Pepsi Cola

1963	Pepsi Generation advertising begins with slogan, "Taste that beats the others cold. Pepsi pours it on!"
1967	New theme and slogan, "Come Alive! You're in the Pepsi Generation."
1968	New package using bold red, white, and blue logo. New theme and slogan, "You've got a lot to live, Pepsi's got a lot to give."
1973	New theme focused on individualism with slogan, "Join the Pepsi people, feelin' free."
1976	Start of The Pepsi Challenge taste test campaign. New slogan, "Have a Pepsi day!"
1979	New campaign and slogan, "Catch that Pepsi Spirit!"
1980	New campaign and slogan, "Pepsi's got your taste for life!"
1984	New campaign with spokesman Michael Jackson. Advertising focuses on music marketing and slogan, "The Choice of a New Generation."
1990	New campaign with Ray Charles and new slogan, "The Right Ones."
1991	Eighth Pepsi logo introduced since 1898. Ray Charles campaign extended, "You Got The Right One Baby, Uh-Huh."
1992	New "Gotta Have It" campaign and membership card.
1993	Pepsi Max introduced in European markets.
1994	New slogan, "Be Young—Have Fun—Drink Pepsi."
1995	New slogan, "Nothing else is a Pepsi."
1996	New marketing campaign for "Pepsi Stuff" products.
1998	New three-dimensional logo, "The Globe." New blue ice logo backdrop. Introduction of Pepsi One in the United States.
1999	New slogan, "The Joy of Cola."

INTERNATIONAL OPERATIONS

PepsiCo's revenues are highly skewed toward the American marketplace, and international revenues account for only a small portion of total revenues and an even smaller portion of profits. During fiscal year 1997, PepsiCo reported a strong balance between their snack foods and beverage divisions. Each accounted for approximately $10.5 billion in revenue, although profits in the snack food division were significantly larger at $1.7 billion, as opposed to $1.1 billion for beverages.

In the beverage market, $8 billion was realized in North America, whereas international operations accounted for only $2.6 billion, with a net loss of $137 million. The snack food business was also skewed with $7 billion in North American revenue; however, PepsiCo achieved $3.5 billion in international revenue, for an international profit of $318 million.

THE HISTORY OF PEPSI ONE—PEPSI MAX

The soft drink market is one of the most active in terms of product development. This drive for innovation provides manufacturers with the tools to produce top-class beverages from milk and fruit juice combinations to great-tasting reduced-calorie carbonates.

Pepsi One, launched in the U.S. market in October 1998, is one of the latest and biggest of these innovations. The product is an innovation in the U.S. market, but was actually already launched in Europe in 1993 under the name Pepsi Max.

Carbonated soft drinks are not as popular in Europe as they are in other markets, especially in the United States. In terms of servings per capita, they rank only seventh, tied with bottled water (Table C7.3). With only 191 eight-ounce servings per capita, compared to 861 in the United States, European soft drink consumption is only one-eighth of what it is in the United States. It only accounts for 5.6 percent of the total beverage consumption, compared to almost 30 percent in the United States. Europeans prefer, in descending order, tap water (including "other"; see Table C7.2), milk, tea, coffee, and beer. But these facts do not mean that Europe, and especially Western Europe, is a small market. On the contrary, Western Europe consumes 26 percent of the world production of soft drinks (Table C7.4).

Table C7.3

1997 8-oz servings per capita			
	Canada	USA	Europe
Carbonated soft drinks	471	861	191
(% of total consumption)	(15.3%)	(29.5%)	(6.2%)
Coffee	402	315	248
Milk	380	301	271
Beer	274	357	221
Tea	246	112	252
Juices	240	139	115
Bottled water	90	184	191
Powdered drinks	72	78	N/A
Wine	27	30	89
Sports drinks	17	26	12
Spirits	16	21	24
All other/tap water	848	496	1470
Total	3083	2920	3084

Table C7.4

World consumption of soft drinks by region (1992–1996, in millions of liters)			
	1992	1996	% of total in 1996
Africa/Middle East	4,546.6	6,246.0	3.0
Australasia	2,284.3	2,801.8	1.4
Eastern Europe	5,650.7	11,794.2	5.7
Japan	8,488.1	10,456.0	5.1
North America	74,181.8	84,896.0	41.0
South America	16,630.9	24,514.0	11.9
South Asia	872.1	1,181.9	0.6
Southeast Asia	7,621.0	11,930.0	5.8
Western Europe	44,501.2	53,128.4	25.7
World total	**164,776.7**	**206,948.2**	**100**

International market share of diet soft drinks in 1993 at 4 percent paled in comparison to the U.S. market share of diet soft drinks, a whopping 27 percent. Rival Coke's international sales were three times that of Pepsi's in 1992, and its edge on diet sales in particular was even wider. In competing with Coke overseas, Pepsi has to deal with Coke's greater visibility and dominance in Europe.

Hoping to expand their share of the international soft drink market, Pepsi launched Pepsi Max. The idea grew out of foreign consumers' reluctance to try diet colas. Pepsi decided to find out what customers really wanted. In market research with overseas consumers, Pepsi discovered that consumers were hesitant to try colas that were labeled *diet* or *light*, as these terms were perceived to indicate that the products were meant for the obese or diabetics.

The name Pepsi Max was cleverly chosen to avoid any reference to the word *diet*. "Maximum Taste. No Sugar" was the line used to convince reluctant consumers. Interestingly enough, the name Pepsi Max was chosen from a list of 13 possible names, including Pepsi One.

Not only were overseas consumers turned off by the negative image associated with the word *diet*, they also did not like the taste of artificial sweetener–based diet colas. Consumers tested expressed dislike of the aftertaste. Because there are many ways to explain tastes and flavors, Pepsi set up panels from its research centers to define a common vocabulary to describe subtle variations in taste of colas. After extensively cross-checking their findings with consumers, Pepsi determined four different elements that defined "aftertaste." With this information, Pepsi was able to focus on finding a suitable blend of ingredients that would produce a muted aftertaste.

Pepsi spent three years developing a product that would not taste like typical diet cola. Pepsi Max contains the same base oils as Pepsi, but in the place of sugar, there is a mixture of aspartame and acesulfame K, a product that was not yet approved for consumption in the United States at the time. Pepsi Max is described as a no-sugar product with a full-bodied cola taste. According to Jesse Meyers, publisher of the *Beverage Digest* newsletter, it tastes more like Pepsi than Diet Pepsi.

In April 1993, Pepsi Max was launched in two test markets—the United Kingdom and Italy. These two countries were chosen because they represented opposite ends of the European diet cola consumption spectrum. In the United Kingdom in 1993, diet colas represented approximately 17 percent of the total carbonated soft drink market, and in Italy they represented only 3 percent of the market.

In September 1993, Pepsi Max was launched in Ireland because of research showing that more than two-thirds of regular cola drinkers are concerned about sugar intake. Pepsi Max was then introduced in France, the Netherlands, Ireland, and Australia in December 1993. In the beginning of 1994, Pepsi Max was introduced in Canada, where market research found that Canadians appreciate product innovation in soft drinks.

By the end of 1994, Pepsi Max was present in 20 markets, including Spain, Portugal, Sweden, Denmark, Norway, Greece, Japan, Thailand, New Zealand, and Uruguay and planned to enter 30 more markets by the end of 1995. By early 1994 Pepsi Max held 1.3 percent of the cola market in France, 3 percent in Australia, 3.2 percent in the Netherlands, 3.5 percent in Britain, and 4.8 percent in Ireland. In September 1995, PepsiCo stated that Pepsi Max would have over $500 million in sales and projected a growth rate of 70 percent for that year. The steady growth in the European market is shown in Table C7.5.

The target market was principally men between the ages of 16 and 29 with a fast-paced, exciting lifestyle. In terms of promotion, Pepsi concentrated on the suggested image for Pepsi Max that was discovered during the market research: masculine and adventurous. Two commercials were made with rock climbers and sky divers to promote the adventurous, risk-taking image. Other promotional

Table C7.5	Western Europe low–calorie carbonated consumption
Year	**Consumption (in thousands of liters)**
1990	2,345
1991	2,670
1992	2,935
1993	2,959
1994	3,142
1995	3,254
1996	3,256
1997	3,435

support included outdoor advertising, product sampling, point-of-sale displays, and consumer promotions. In 1994, $40 million was spent in promotional support. This represented one-third of Pepsi's international advertising budget. The "Live Life to the Max" theme was maintained through 1995.

An exceptionally extravagant promotion involved a competition for teenagers from all over Eastern and Western Europe. Those that were successful in a variety of promotions including finding lucky-number ring pulls and composing slogans were flown to Club Med in Ibiza for an all-expenses-paid weeklong holiday.

In Britain, promotion for Pepsi Max included commercials featuring teens accomplishing dangerous feats including skydiving from Big Ben, rollerblading off the Sphinx, and surfing down the dunes of the Sahara. Pepsi engaged a London club called the Ministry of Sound that promoted Pepsi Max at dance parties all around the country. Since its launch in England, Pepsi has increased its market share by 2 percentage points.

Another unusual but highly successful campaign took place in the United Kingdom. In order to gain the interest of the Generation X crowd, Pepsi mounted an aggressive "in your face" type of tasting campaign. Actors that emulated the risk-taking characters from the Pepsi Max commercials were hired to take Pepsi Max on a road show. This was an attempt to prove that Pepsi Max, with its "Live Life to the Max" slogan, was not simply an image-based product. In the process of product sampling, they found that when people tried the product, repeat purchasing was quite strong.

In terms of packaging, it was decided that traditional blue should be kept but jazzed up a bit. It seemed that consumers associated red and white with Coke, red and blue with cola in general, and that anything else was confusing.

THE HISTORY OF PEPSI ONE—THE LAUNCH

It is a formidable challenge to introduce a new soft drink into the already saturated U.S. soft drink market. In 1994, according to the *Market Share Reporter*, cola was the most popular flavor, with 65.9 percent of sales, followed by lemon-lime with 12.3 percent, pepper with 7.6 percent, root beer with 2.7 percent, and orange with 2.3 percent. All flavors are usually available in regular, caffeine-free, diet, and diet caffeine-free versions. The U.S. market includes nearly 450 different soft drinks.

Three major players occupy more than 90 percent of market share and dominate the U.S. market (see Table C7.6). In 1998, Coca-Cola Co. held 44.5 percent,

Table C7.6

All channel carbonated soft drink companies/brands

Companies	1998 share	1997 share	Share change	98 cases (millions)	97 cases (millions)	Volume % change	1997 rank
1. Coca-Cola Co.	44.5	43.9	+0.6	4399.5	4208.6	+4.5	1
2. Pepsi-Cola Co.	31.4	30.9	+0.5	3100.2	2965.7	+4.5	2
3. Dr. Pepper/Seven-Up	14.4	14.5	−0.1	1423.9	1392.5	+2.3	3
4. Cott Corp.	2.7	3.2	−0.5	270.0	305.0	−11.5	4
5. National Beverage	2.0	2.0	Flat	194.0	188.0	+3.2	5
6. Royal Crown	1.3	1.5	−0.2	126.1	148.4	−15.0	6
7. Monarch Co.	0.5	0.5	Flat	46.0	51.9	−11.4	7
8. Big Red	0.3	0.3	Flat	33.7	30.4	+10.9	8
9. Seagram's	0.3	0.3	Flat	28.0	26.5	+5.7	N/A
10. Private label/other	2.6	2.8	−0.2	258.6	273.0	−5.3	10
Industry totals	100.0	100.0		9880.0	9590.0	+3.0	

Brands	1998 share	1997 share	Share change	98 cases (millions)	97 cases (millions)	Volume % change	1997 rank
1. Coke Classic	20.6	20.6	Flat	2037.5	1978.2	+3.0	1
2. Pepsi-Cola	14.2	14.5	−0.3	1399.8	1391.5	+0.6	2
3. Diet Coke	8.6	8.5	+0.1	851.8	819.0	+4.0	3
4. Mountain Dew	6.7	6.3	+0.4	665.1	605.2	+9.9	4
5. Sprite	6.6	6.2	+0.4	651.8	598.0	+9.0	5
6. Dr. Pepper	6.1	5.9	+0.2	599.4	566.8	+5.8	6
7. Diet Pepsi	5.4	5.5	−0.1	529.7	524.5	+1.0	7
8. 7-Up	2.1	2.3	−0.2	210.9	216.7	−2.7	8
9. CF Diet Coke	1.8	1.8	Flat	179.7	172.8	+4.0	9
10. Minute Maid	1.2	1.0	+0.2	121.5	93.6	+29.8	N/A

Pepsi-Cola 31.4 percent, and Dr. Pepper/Seven-Up 14.4 percent of the market. However, in 15 major markets Pepsi and Coke are the dominant brands (see Table C7.7). In 1997 the retail sale of soft drinks totaled over $54 billion, and soft drinks accounted for more than 27 percent of America's beverage consumption. The amount spent on advertising these drinks is shown in Table C7.8.

Although the three companies mentioned above dominate the market, production of soft drinks is managed at a local level. Approximately 5,000 mostly independent bottlers bottle and sell the different beverages under exclusive licensing agreements. The bottlers provide the capital needed, and the big companies provide the concentrates and beverage bases to produce the final product, which consists mainly of carbonated water, sweeteners, and flavors. While nondiet soft drinks, which account for 75 percent of the total market are currently sweetened with high-fructose corn syrup, sugar, or a combination of both, diet soft drinks are mostly sweetened with aspartame. This intense sweetener provides less than one calorie in a 12-ounce can.

Although beverages with cola flavor still account for more than half of all carbonated soft drinks sold, its share is on the decline. The share of colas within total consumption of carbonated soft drinks has slightly but steadily declined from 63.5 percent in 1986 to 57.1 percent in 1997. The share of diet cola drinks

Table C7.7

Fifteen U.S. markets: Coca-Cola versus Pepsi

Market	Company	Cola	Diet Cola
Atlanta	Coke	Coke	Diet Coke
Boston	Coke	Coke	Diet Coke
Chicago	Coke	Pepsi	Diet Coke
Dallas/Ft. Worth	Coke	Coke	Diet Coke
Denver	Pepsi	Pepsi	Diet Pepsi
Detroit	Pepsi	Pepsi	Diet Pepsi
Los Angeles	Coke	Coke	Diet Coke
Miami/Ft. Lauderdale	Coke	Coke	Diet Coke
Minneapolis/St. Paul	Coke	Coke	Diet Coke
New York	Coke	Pepsi	Diet Coke
Philadelphia	Pepsi	Pepsi	Diet Pepsi
Phoenix/Tucson	Pepsi	Pepsi	Diet Coke
Providence	Coke	Coke	Diet Coke
San Francisco/Oakland	Coke	Coke	Diet Coke
Seattle/Tacoma	Coke	Coke	Diet Coke

Table C7.8

Soft drink ad spending rises slightly in 1997: U.S. tracked media spending ($ million)

	1997	1996	1995	1994
Coca-Cola Co.	277.1	327.6	215.0	237.2
Pepsi-Cola	197.8	169.3	177.5	148.3
Dr. Pepper/Seven-Up	129.4	128.7	108.2	N/A
Dr. Pepper	79.9	67.0	62.1	59.8
7-Up	38.7	33.2	23.1	27.0
Cadbury Bev	10.8	28.5	23.0	19.6
Triarc	26.4	4.5	6.4	8.5
Total	**630.7**	**630.1**	**507.1**	**500.4**

within carbonated soft drinks has increased continuously between 1977 and 1990 from 9.0 percent to 20.9 percent, but has been on the decline since then. In 1997 diet cola drinks accounted for only 18.0 percent of the market. After having expanded its share compared to regular colas, diet cola drinks have stagnated at around one-third of the total share of cola drinks (Table C7.9).

Today's consumers demand a much better tasting product in the low-calorie sector, which has led to the introduction of drinks based on multisweetener concepts and sugar-reduced mainstream products. As Pepsi-Cola North America is trying to reposition itself more as a marketing services firm and less as a manufacturing company, the company has transformed its American operations into

Table C7.9

		Cola shares of the market for carbonated soft drinks in the United States				
Year	Total	+/−	Regular	+/−	Diet	+/−
1977	61.0		51.7		9.3	
1986	63.5	+2.5	46.2	−5.7	17.3	+8.0
1987	63.3	−0.2	45.2	−1.0	18.1	+0.8
1988	63.0	−0.3	43.9	−1.3	19.1	+1.0
1989	61.3	−1.7	41.0	−2.9	20.3	+1.2
1990	61.8	+0.5	40.5	−0.5	21.3	+1.0
1991	60.4	−1.4	39.5	−1.0	20.9	−0.4
1992	59.0	−1.4	38.9	−0.6	20.1	−0.8
1993	58.6	−0.4	39.0	+0.1	19.6	−0.5
1994	58.3	−0.3	39.2	+0.2	19.1	−0.5
1995	58.1	−0.2	39.1	−0.1	19.0	−0.1
1996	58.2	+0.1	39.5	+0.4	18.7	−0.3
1997	57.1	−1.1	39.1	−0.4	18.0	−0.7

five sales and development markets. One of the newly created groups, the innovation and technology department, is responsible for maintaining an innovation pipeline that is filled with new products, packaging, and equipment.

The first challenge for this department—induced by the market research department that identified a market niche—was to develop the only soft drink left to brew: a diet cola that does not taste like one. On June 30, 1998, only one hour after the FDA had given approval for the new sweetener ace K, Pepsi announced the introduction of a new low-calorie drink using the new sweetener in combination with aspartame: Pepsi One.

The idea of Pepsi One was born almost 10 years earlier, but the U.S. government only approved the sweetener in 1998. This very quick move reflects a lesson Pepsi had learned in 1983 when the sweetener aspartame was approved. Coca-Cola reached a deal with NutraSweet to use the new sweetener in Diet Coke, which kept Pepsi out of the market for months and left it to Coca-Cola. In consumer marketing and especially in the highly competitive, oligopolistic market of carbonated soft drinks, being first really matters and is a determinant of market share and the success of new products.

The concept for the new product was to develop a low-calorie drink that tastes like a sugared soft drink but avoids the bitter aftertaste of diet drinks and the word *diet*. Pepsi One, as officials stress, is not a replacement for Diet Pepsi. The fundamental difference between the two drinks is the taste. "Diet Pepsi is light, crisp and refreshing . . . Pepsi One has a taste that's closer to regular brand Pepsi for people who are entering the category."

Market research and tests had been analyzed to determine the best positioning for Pepsi One. The new drink's target group are young men in their 20s and 30s who are scared away from diet drinks by the word *diet* and by the bitter aftertaste. The product also targets consumers who switched to bottled waters instead of diet drinks. Pepsi believes that the new product will reach a whole new audience. Initial cannibalization of Diet Pepsi is not considered to be severe, because "Diet Pepsi consumers love the taste of Diet Pepsi . . . and Pepsi One has a unique taste all to itself."

The new product was supported by a new and unique marketing strategy to capture the American market. At this point, the chairman of PepsiCo, Inc. stated, "This is a real-time business, and we're going to be a real-time company." Pepsi's launching strategy for Pepsi One, which started in October 1998, was to quickly attract consumers and make them try the new drink over and over again. Pepsi went for a national launch using all available channels, packages, and geographies. The only place where Pepsi One was not available initially was in fountains. But in March of 1999, five months after the launch, Pepsi One was also distributed through fountains. Industry analysts estimate that Pepsi will spend $100 million in the first year to promote the product, to boost sales in the low-calorie market, and to gain market share. Pepsi predicts that Pepsi One will attain sales of $1 billion in its first year.

In the initial phase of the launch, Pepsi shipped millions of free six-packs to the doorsteps of cola drinkers. Pizza Hut distributed free cans with every pizza delivery. 7-Eleven gave away free samples to buyers of sandwiches, and even greeters at 2,500 Wal-Mart stores were equipped with free samples. Because the drink targets young men, Pepsi created Pepsi One lounges in approximately 100 shopping malls. While waiting for their wives or girlfriends, men can watch sports and enjoy Pepsi One. Free samples were distributed at all targeted malls, and the turn-around to buy the drink was 60 percent the next day. The initial launch was very successful.

To support the national rollout of Pepsi One, Pepsi signed Academy Award winner Cuba Gooding, Jr., as spokesman. Cuba Gooding, Jr., starred in Pepsi One commercials featuring the slogan: "Only One has it all." The actor, who can be seen in adventurous and humorous settings, was signed to reinforce the message that Pepsi One is for everybody, not just dieters. The first spot, "Parachute," finds Gooding in an airplane with a group of sky divers (see Exhibit C7.1) and communicates the message that "You haven't tasted life until you've tasted the massive cola taste of Pepsi One!" The second spot, "Wired," plays in the boardroom of an Internet company where a young millionaire can't help but feel that something "big" is missing from his life, which of course turns out to be Pepsi One. The spots dominated airwaves during the 1998 World Series, the season premiere for the *X-Files* television show, the Oscars, and the 1999 Super Bowl. For commercials during the NCAA tournament ("March Madness") the spots were shot on college campuses to position Pepsi One as a drink for everybody—and especially for men in their 20s and 30s.

Marketing Pepsi One in addition to Diet Pepsi is not an easy task. Pepsi One is the first low-calorie drink that does not contain the word *diet*, and the word *Pepsi* seems to be secondary on the packaging. This is purposely done to avoid confusion with Diet Pepsi and to avoid the word *diet*. In consumer tests, Pepsi One reached very high scores. Nearly 70 percent of consumers who tried Pepsi One in an extensive home-use test stated that they would most likely purchase the product again.

According to Pepsi-Cola North America, Pepsi One will be treated as a core brand. This means that it will available everywhere Pepsi, Diet Pepsi, and Mountain Dew are available. Figure C7.1 shows where Pepsi core brands are sold. Supermarkets account for more than half of Pepsi's soft drink sales, with fountains following at 21 percent.

Exhibit C7.1

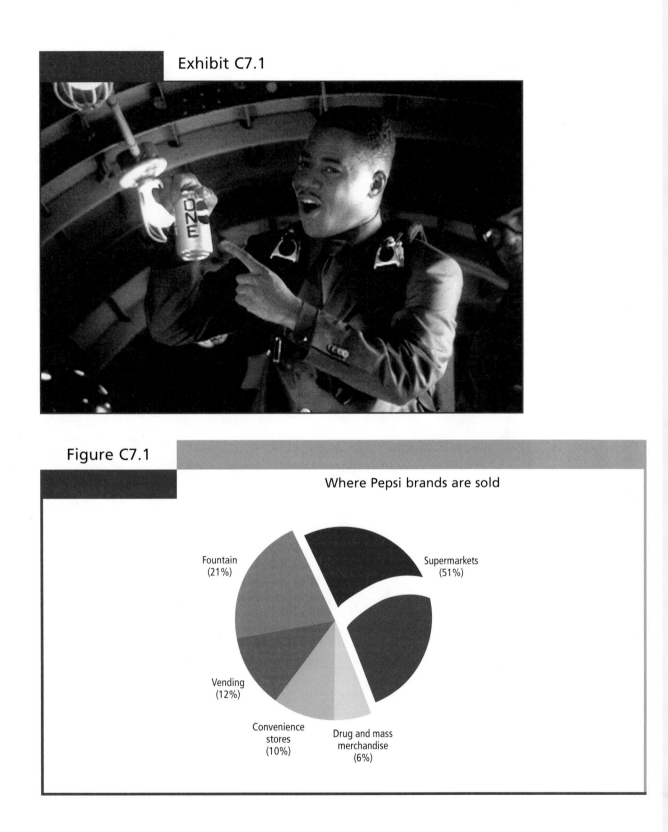

Figure C7.1

Where Pepsi brands are sold

Fountain (21%)

Supermarkets (51%)

Vending (12%)

Convenience stores (10%)

Drug and mass merchandise (6%)

QUESTIONS FOR DISCUSSION

1. Address the following issues regarding market positioning and segmentation.

   - What market positioning and segmentation strategy has PepsiCo chosen in this case?

   - How does this approach influence the marketing mix decisions for Pepsi One/Pepsi Max?

   - To what degree is the soft drink industry able to standardize products and marketing mix elements on a global basis?

2. "Pepsi core displays will include Pepsi, Mountain Dew, Diet Pepsi, and Pepsi One," says Philip Marineau, CEO Pepsi North America. Pepsi One will be treated as a Pepsi core brand and it will be sold everywhere the other core brands are available. Will Pepsi One take away market share from Diet Pepsi or will it generate more revenues and increase the market share for PepsiCo? Given the limited amount of fountains, shelf space, and vending machines, how can Pepsi effectively manage two products in the diet soft drink market?

3. "We'd be thrilled if consumers just call it 'One,'" says Steve Fund, director of marketing for Pepsi-Cola. What are the possible reasons why Pepsi wants to de-emphasize the corporate brand name *Pepsi* for this new product? How can Pepsi One still enhance the corporate brand image of Pepsi?

Spectrum Color Systems, Inc
r Systems, Inc.

Spectrum Color Systems, Inc.

case 8

The executive vice president of Spectrum Color Systems, Inc., Anthony Cordera, sighed as he hung up the phone. The conversation still raced through his mind as he surveyed the fall foliage outside his office window. Cordera went over every nuance of the telephone conversation he had just completed with Roberto Cortez, vice president of European operations at BASF International. BASF had been a good customer for Spectrum, but today Cortez spoke with disdain, accusing Spectrum of questionable practices in its dealings with BASF. Cordera hated to see such a profitable relationship sour, but he saw no solution. As he turned back toward his desk, he wondered whether Spectrum might soon face similar sentiment from other large multinational clients. At the same time, he wondered how to address this issue at the upcoming board meeting without alarming the company president and the board of directors.

HISTORY

Spectrum Color Systems is a medium-sized industrial firm with headquarters in the eastern United States. The firm was founded in 1952 when Daniel Clark, a government scientist working on techniques to measure aspects of color and appearance, was approached by Procter & Gamble (P&G).

Procter & Gamble recognized that customers held a perception of quality related to the color of its products. In order to offer consistency to its customers, and as part of its quality-control program, P&G sought a process to help standardize the color and appearance of the products it manufactured. Clark balked at the request to work for P&G building a machine that could quantify aspects of color, but, as he recognized widespread commercial applications of such a machine, Clark went into business for himself. Spectrum Color Systems started with the simple philosophy of providing solutions to customers' problems relating to measurement and control of color and appearance attributes. The first machines were developed under contract with P&G. As the quality-control movement developed throughout the industrialized world, the demand for Spectrum's products grew.

Spectrum Color Systems remains privately held; majority ownership and controlling voting rights remain in the Clark family. In 1990, Daniel Clark passed away. His son Paul is CEO and president; he runs domestic sales, finance, and human resources. Anthony Cordera joined Spectrum in 1985. As executive vice president, he is responsible for manufacturing, engineering, international sales, shipping, and receiving. He reports directly to Paul Clark.

Source: This case study was developed by Professor Michael R. Czinkota © and MBA candidate Marc. S. Gross. Reprinted by permission.

The Clark family retains approximately 55 percent of company stock, including all voting stock. The executive and associate staff participate in an employee stock ownership plan and together own the remaining 45 percent of shares.

PRODUCT LINE

Spectrum Color Systems manufactures an sells an extensive array of colorimeters and spectrophotometers. These machines quantify aspects of color and appearance. As Appendix A discusses, such measurements are important, but no easy task. A colorimeter is the most basic instrument, with some models starting at $2,000. Most large manufacturers choose spectrophotometers, which are more exacting in their measurement ability, providing better performance and more options. These are generally integrated systems that can cost as much as $150,000.

Spectrum offers both online products and lab products. Online products are designed for use on a production line, where products run under the instrument, which continuously monitors the product's appearance. These systems are manufactured in batch operations and customized to meet customer specifications. Typically, custom features are oriented to specific user applications and include hardware components such as moving optical scanners that measure lateral color variance as well as software components designed to meet the needs of specific industries. The first instruments built in the 1950s provided users with numerical values via a primitive screen and tape printer system with a 15- to 30-second lag between measurement and numerical output. Today, all of Spectrum's products are driven by user-friendly software that monitors color trends throughout a production run with real-time output. Lab products are used when a customer takes a sample from a production line and brings it to the instrument for measurement.

Spectrum instruments are used in a wide variety of industries. Large food product companies measure the color of their products and packaging to ensure consistency. Paint companies purchase instruments to match colors and lease the machinery to paint stores. Automobile companies use Spectrum products to ensure that the color of interior cloth material, plastic molding, and exterior paint match. Some companies have forced suppliers to provide color variance data sheets with all shipments. Spectrum recently supplied several instruments to a large bakery that produces buns for McDonald's. McDonald's had stipulated in its contract that buns be produced not only on time, but within certain color specifications. The bakery approached Spectrum to help meet these color standards.

A major manufacturer and supplier of denim uses Spectrum's "Color Probe" spectrophotometer in its dye house to measure and grade the color of every strand of denim it produces. Color determines the value of the denim; it has tremendous impact when millions of yards of denim are produced and the price fluctuates significantly depending on color.

THE COMPETITION

The color- and appearance-measurement market is considered a niche market with approximately $130 million to $140 million in annual sales worldwide. Spectrum has averaged $20 million annually in both retail and wholesale sales revenue over the last three years, placing it second in terms of market share. The industry became concentrated in 1990 when Color Value, a Swiss company with $5 million to $10 million in annual sales revenue, decided to dominate the color business. Color Value International, owned by a large Swiss brewery, purchased two competitors: Color Systems (CS), based in the United States and representing $35 million in annual sales, and International Color, based in the United Kingdom and representing $20 million in annual sales. Two smaller companies occupy the third and fourth market share positions; Speare accounts for approximately $12 million a year in sales and Scientific Color generates about $9 million a year in sales (see Figure C8.1).

Although Color Value International holds almost 50 percent of world market share, Cordera believes that Spectrum now has a unique window of opportunity. The confusion associated with integrating three companies and the loss of good-will caused by changing CS's company name, a well-established and respected

Figure C8.1

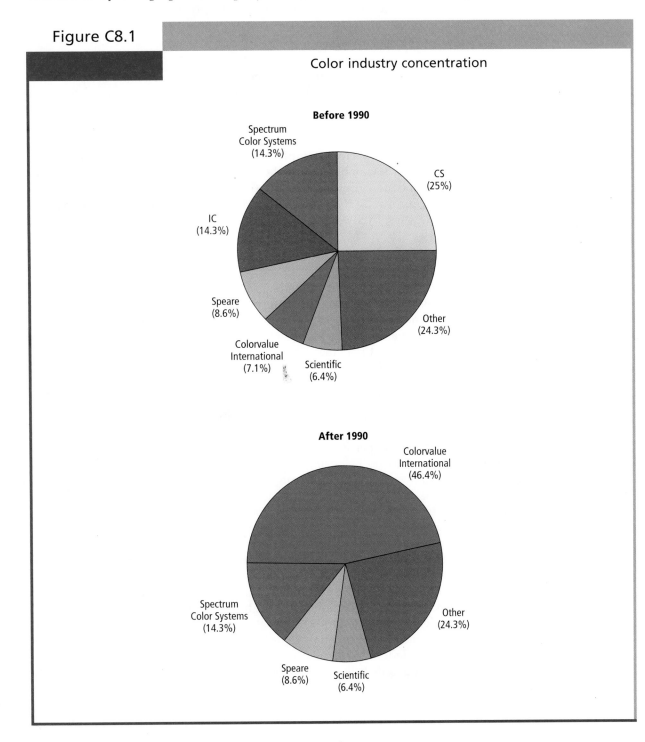

Color industry concentration

Before 1990

Spectrum Color Systems (14.3%)
CS (25%)
IC (14.3%)
Speare (8.6%)
Colorvalue International (7.1%)
Scientific (6.4%)
Other (24.3%)

After 1990

Colorvalue International (46.4%)
Spectrum Color Systems (14.3%)
Speare (8.6%)
Scientific (6.4%)
Other (24.3%)

brand, to Color Value International gave Spectrum a sales advantage. In addition, Spectrum entered the color matching and formulation market, one of Color value's most profitable product lines. To gain market share in the United States, Spectrum's management decided to become the low-cost vendor and offered its new machines and color-matching software at prices of about one-half of the competition. Whereas the typical color-matching spectrophotometer by Color Value International was priced at $50,000, Spectrum offered a simpler $25,000 machine. In order to compete, Color Value International was forced to drastically reduce its prices to meet those of Spectrum, thus cutting deeply into profits.

INTERNATIONAL EXPANSION

In the 1950s and 1960s, Spectrum's management spent most of its time building the instruments and getting them out the door to meet the demand rather than developing a strategy to expand the company domestically and internationally. Spectrum's expansion into international markets succeeded despite its lack of strategic planning.

In the early days, Spectrum simply responded to requests from large companies such as Procter & Gamble to provide instruments to overseas subsidiaries. As the Clarks became more comfortable with this process, they decided to begin selling actively in Europe. By 1984, international sales comprised about one-fourth of total corporate sales. By 1992, the share had grown to more than one-third.

SALES FORCE

Spectrum Color Systems used independent sales agents domestically from its inception until 1986, when it developed an internal sales force. Cordera, drawing on his experience in marketing, set up the domestic sales force to provide more direct control over the marketing and sales strategies. After touring a number of agent offices, Cordera began to calculate the real cost of such a sales relationship. Working closely with Bob Holland, Spectrum's chief financial officer, Cordera tried to quantify some of the intangible and hidden costs of the agent relationship. Spectrum spent significant resources lobbying for agents' time and attention to sales of Spectrum products and provided all the technical support, as few of the agents had technical expertise. Additionally, although Spectrum was responsible for billing customers and paid 15 percent of the sales price to the agent as commission, it had no access to lists of end users and decision makers within the client's organization. Spectrum is an application-oriented company; thus, access to decision makers and end users within client organizations provides valuable information for product development and sales of transferable applications to current and future clients. A detailed financial analysis compared the true cost of using sales agents to the anticipated cost of an internal sales force. The analysis indicated that Spectrum could increase sales, reduce cost, and increase its control by developing its own sales force.

Internationally, Spectrum still relied mainly on independent distributors for its sales. Spectrum sold instruments outright to distributors at wholesale price. Spectrum billed the distributors 30-day net terms. Spectrum provided its distributors sales brochures and manuals in English. Distributors then translated these brochures as needed.

In the early days, distributors were selected largely through happenstance. Distributors of other products would hear about Spectrum and write a letter to the Clarks expressing interest in the distribution of their instruments. The Clarks would invite the distributor to the United States to see the products and be trained in their operation and thus become a Spectrum distributor. Spectrum now has distributors all over the world, with extensive market penetration in Europe and the Far East. Although the company has encountered a steady international demand for its products, it continues to encounter problems with international distributors.

In 1984, Spectrum's sole French distributor, Gerard Bieux, abruptly closed his operation for medical reasons. Bieux had kept his sales operation close to his vest and thus maintained no customer lists or sales records. There was no one who could fill the void Bieux left, and Spectrum's management was forced to start over again, building up its French distribution.

Cordera spent a great deal of time locating another French distributor and developing a profitable relationship. The relationship served Spectrum well until 1990, when a major competitor purchased the distributor. Again Cordera was left without a French representative for Spectrum instruments.

Cordera realized that the distributor-selection process was critical to Spectrum's international expansion and decided to become more proactive in selecting distributors. He worked closely with Holland to establish selection criteria for distributors based on financial stability, formal training programs, and financial goals. Additionally, Spectrum insisted that all distributors have service technicians trained at its U.S. facility. The distributor was responsible for paying the airfare for the technician, and Spectrum supplied food, lodging, and training. This strategy was not pursued so much for financial reasons, but to force the distributor to make both a financial and emotional investment in selling Spectrum products.

With the domestic direct sales force up and running, Cordera decided that if he was going to put the effort into forging an international presence, Spectrum should move toward an international direct sales force. In 1991, Spectrum opened its first European sales office in Paris. It opened an office in Germany in 1992.

DEVELOPMENT OF AN INTERNATIONAL DIRECT SALES FORCE

In spite of the detailed planning, financial budgeting, and strategy analysis that preceded the opening of both European offices, each showed a net loss in its first year of operation. Cordera consulted with large accounting firms in both France and Germany to gain insight into European business law and to develop first-year budget projections. In addition, Spectrum management solicited information from its state Department of Economic Development on issues of taxation, international shipping, work permits, and Visa restrictions for U.S. nationals working abroad. Despite such effort, the combination of operating costs, which exceeded Spectrum's estimates, and slow sales associated with the European recession resulted in first-year losses in both France and Germany.

Cultural differences contributed to rising costs. Unlike the U.S. sales force, where the majority of sales representatives' compensation consists of commission, European sales representatives are traditionally paid high salaries and relatively low commissions. In addition, employees are paid an annual salary bonus equivalent to one month's salary regardless of performance. Terminated employees can receive up to one year of severance pay based on the longevity of their relationship and position with the company. Middle managers and above expect to be provided with company cars, which was particularly difficult for Spectrum management to swallow, as neither Cordera nor Clark was provided with a company car. Despite his uneasiness, Cordera agreed to provide these benefits because he felt it was important to attract high-quality employees for the new offices. All of these benefits were stipulated in the long-term employment contracts required in Europe.

Difficulties soon became apparent with Spectrum's sales representatives in Paris. In staffing the Paris office. Cordera, largely out of a desire to get someone out on the road in France, settled for an individual who, although the most qualified of the candidates, lacked the aggressiveness, sales orientation, and technical competence for the position. Cordera was disappointed by the sales representative's performance but found the process of terminating the employee a long and arduous one. Spectrum began working with an attorney in Paris, providing the employee with written documentation detailing the reasons for dissatisfaction, as well as sales goals that were to be met in order to retain the position. In the end, Spectrum was forced to negotiate an expensive severance package.

But now, the international activities seem to be back on track. Spectrum has two international offices abroad. The Paris office consists of the international sales director, one sales representative, one service technician, and two secretaries. From that office, Spectrum conducts marketing activities, sales, installation, and service for France. The German office employs two sales representatives, one secretary, and one service technician covering the German market.

To avoid future hiring difficulties, Cordera instituted a program that brings key individuals from European operations to its headquarters facility. The mission of this program is to integrate those individuals into Spectrum's corporate culture and create a team environment. On this point Cordera remarked, "The fax machine and telephone are great pieces of equipment, but nothing beats a face-to-face dinner or lunch where we can sit down and talk to each other."

COMMITMENT TO EUROPEAN CUSTOMERS

Spectrum management had historically marketed the same products throughout the world. Over time, Spectrum recognized that the European market and the U.S. market had different needs and preferences in both hardware and software. For example, Spectrum sales representatives frequently found their sales efforts focusing on the software that accompanies the instruments, because that is the part the customer sees, feels, and touches.

To achieve market success, Spectrum management felt it had to design products to meet the needs of European customers. There were two choices. The first was to translate existing software and then add the nuances the Europeans wanted. This proposition promised to be time consuming and very costly. The second option was to acquire a software company abroad.

In 1991, Cordera located a small software company in Switzerland that already had software written in German, French, Italian, and Spanish that was very applicable to the Spectrum system. Spectrum purchased the company for $275,000. Along with the company's assets and software copyrights, Spectrum also acquired the services of the company founder. This proved invaluable, as he speaks five languages and can adapt Spectrum's software products to meet the needs of the European market.

Spectrum Color Systems paid for its acquisition with the cash it had generated from operations. Spectrum management has historically taken a conservative view of financing. The focus is on cash management, trying to generate enough cash to finance any expansion. In fact, Spectrum would not have made the purchase unless it had the cash.

Spectrum does maintain a line of credit, but as yet it has not used loans to finance expansion. Occasionally, management borrows $500,000 on its credit line, invests in short-term CDs, and repays the loan early just to show activity on its account.

DECISION SITUATION

In all remaining international markets, Spectrum still uses distributors. Recently, this has resulted in significant problems. When BASF International in Germany purchased an instrument from Spectrum's German operation, it recommended that the BASF subsidiary in Spain buy the same instrument. When BASF received the invoice from Spectrum's Spanish distributor, the price was more than 50 percent higher than that paid in Germany. Cortez naturally felt that BASF was somehow being taken advantage of in Spain. However, there is little Spectrum can do about such disparities, because, pursuant to the distributor agreements, distributors purchase Spectrum products outright and determine the markup themselves. In addition, European Union antitrust regulations prevent Spectrum from setting a standardized price for its distributors.

This distributor arrangement is particularly advantageous in Italy and Spain. Given Spectrum's focus on cash management, the firm is leery about setting up direct operations in these countries. Cordera believes it is difficult to manage cash effectively in Italy and Spain, where vendors can wait six months to a year to receive payment from customers. There is an advantage to selling through distributors, because Spectrum can collect cash on the sale in 30 or 45 days and the distributor has to wait for payment.

FUTURE STRATEGIES

By 1993, both European sales offices had become profitable. The European Union allowed Spectrum to use its French and German operations as a base to expand into other countries without duplicating tasks. For example, the firm could place direct sales representatives throughout Europe with support provided by central office service technicians who would cross borders to perform installation and service. Yet Cordera still considered direct offices to be an expensive and somewhat risky proposition. His experience indicated that direct sales offices would not become self-sufficient for at least a year, and these types of financial losses caused friction with Spectrum's president and board of directors. Therefore, Cordera was not prepared for direct confrontation with distributors over markup. He dreaded the thought of being prematurely forced into opening other direct sales offices and repeating or even compounding the problems Spectrum had already endured.

In addition, recent changes in the exchange rates between the U.S. dollar and the euro had tightened margins on export sales and decreased available cash. This pinch threatened to delay Cordera's planned expansion in the Far East.

Currently, Spectrum sells through distributors in the Pacific Rim and China, but Cordera was in the process of negotiating a joint venture in China. Cordera thought that in order for Spectrum to continue its growth throughout the world and especially in the Pacific Rim, it should establish a joint operation. The cultural differences in the Pacific Rim seemed to great for Spectrum to overcome alone, so Cordera sought to marry Spectrum's technology and sales distribution to a company that has manufacturing capabilities similar to Spectrum's.

THE BASICS OF COLOR AND APPEARANCE

What words would you use to describe a school bus? Yellow or slightly reddish yellow or perhaps orange? You might add the word shiny or maybe even glossy. But could the person on the other end of a telephone be expected to make a gallon of this paint for touch-up based on these words? Most likely not.

To further complicate matters, is your color vision the same as the person making the paint? What about the lighting under which you made the initial judgment of color? Have you ever noticed how some colors appear quite different under the lamps used in your home or office compared to outdoors?

Appearance characteristics are difficult to communicate objectively. Certainly a sample of the product could be sent to another person, but what is "close enough" when deciding if a match exists?

THE LANGUAGE OF COLOR

Color is a three-dimensional characteristic of appearance consisting of a lightness attribute, often called "value," and two chromatic attributes, called "hue" and "chroma." Colors can be distinguished from one another by specifying these three visual attributes. Figure C8.2 shows a common arrangement of these three attributes often termed "color solid" or "color space."

HUE

Hue is often the first attribute of color that is mentioned. Consider the school bus. The most obvious thing is that it is a shade of yellow rather than blue or green. Hue is the attribute of color perception by which an object is judged to be red, yellow, green, blue, and so forth.

CHROMA

A color specification requires more than just a designation of hue. How concentrated is the yellow? That is, how much color does there appear to be? Words such as *depth*, *vividness*, *purity*, and *saturation* have been used to convey how different the color is from gray. *Chroma* is the more accepted term and is used to specify the position of the color between gray and the pure hue.

Figure C8.2

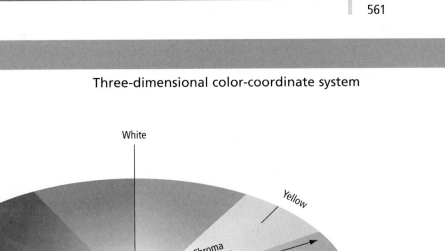

Three-dimensional color-coordinate system

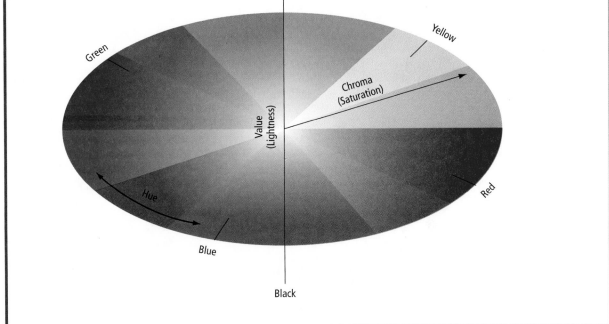

VALUE

A third dimension is necessary to complete our specification. This is a luminous or lightness attribute, which distinguishes "light" colors from "dark" colors. *Value* is the term commonly used to express this attribute and is shown as the vertical axis in Figure C8.2.

Unisys: The Repositioning

case 9

THE PROBLEM

In 1986, Unisys, after reorganization into three separate businesses, positioned itself as "The Information Management Company," a term that was very vague. Because of this, Unisys was faced with a dilemma on a global level. What do you do when many of your prospective customers are not even aware of who you are, let alone what you do?

In Europe, awareness of Unisys was low. When asked "What names come to mind when you think of companies that provide information technology?" respondents in France placed Unisys behind IBM, Microsoft, Compaq, and Hewlett-Packard. In some countries, Unisys placed behind Digital, Groupe Bull, and Olivetti. In Germany, Unisys was not thought of at all.

In most of Unisys' target market, awareness of the name was much lower than it should have been. The familiarity with what they did was also much lower than it should have been. Although some people had a reasonably warm feeling about Unisys, they still thought of it in terms of being simply a mainframe supplier.

Further research looked at people's familiarity with Unisys in the United Kingdom, France, Germany, and Italy compared with Unisys' major U.S. competitors. The picture was not a pretty one, with only 30 percent of respondents being "very familiar" or "somewhat familiar" with Unisys, compared with 90 percent for IBM, 78 percent for Hewlett-Packard, and 76 percent for Compaq. Worse still, this 30 percent had declined from 41 percent back in 1992, although it does represent a recovery from 27 percent in 1996. Therefore, this meant that Unisys' target market did not know the company very well and that they were in a worse position than they were five or six years prior.

HISTORY: THE FORMATION OF UNISYS

In 1986, two successful companies merged to form Unisys, the largest computer company after IBM. Each had approximately 60,000 employees and revenue of $7 billion. Billed as the merger of two complimentary companies, it was in reality a hostile leveraged buyout of Sperry by Burroughs at the end of the takeover craze in the 1980s.

Burroughs ran in a lean and mean manner, tight on staff that manufactured mainframe computers, work stations, and desktops (PCs). Employees started with the company when young and grew with it. Stock rose to $100 a share. Then

Source: This case was prepared by Rosalind Lewis, Joe McQuillan, Brian Sawyer, Barbara Yount, and Tim Silar of Temple University's Fox School of Business and Management under the supervision of Professor Masaaki Kotabe, January 1999. Reprinted by permission.

Michael Blumenthal, formerly the Secretary of the Treasury in the Carter administration, was invited to be CEO. He planned the Sperry buyout and moved his headquarters to the spacious campus of the acquired company in Blue Bell. Blumenthal spent freely and imported outside personnel at above-market salaries. Many came and went. Technology companies were bought and sold.

Sperry was formed from a portfolio of diverse, autonomous, decentralized companies (manufacturing mainframes to tractors). Electronics had brought in 88 percent of the revenue and 94 percent of operating profit. The year before the merger, five different companies were merged into one unified operating company. Sperry had been headquartered in New York and guided the Univac division at Blue Bell. At the merger Blumenthal insisted on a 50/50 job split of Burroughs and Sperry managers, so that some capable people were lost.

Here is a quote from Blumenthal's report in the 1986 Annual Report:

> We concluded that combining the resources, talent, and market positions of Sperry and Burroughs would materially enhance our credibility in the global marketplace for advanced systems. . . . In key markets, we would have the depth needed to deploy a genuine line-of-business strategy, tailoring our systems solutions to specialized customer needs. . . . The advent of Unisys proved to be a good "financial deal."

DEBT BURDEN AND ECONOMIC DOWNTURN

The name Unisys was the result of a companywide competition for a new name, with the tag line "Power of 2." However, the expensive merger caused the company to go exponentially down, not up. Company debt was high, reaching $4 billion when the economy and high-tech sales went sour. There was two of everything from payroll systems to order entry systems, and no money was available to integrate. Infrastructure was a mess. There was significant resizing in reponse to changes in the industry and a lack of revenue growth. Reductions were made by selling off various divisions.

UNISYS' LOWEST POINT

James Unruh became CEO in 1991. As an accountant and former CFO he cut, cut, and cut, but could not grow revenue. He reduced some debt slowly and in effect saved the company from bankruptcy. The stock fell to its lowest price at $2 1/8 per share. Analysts expected bankruptcy, international bankers had to be constantly placated; even former customers were refusing to buy, causing sales to suffer further. The company was trying to concentrate on four areas of marketing: finance, public sector, transportation, and communications. Unruh believed it made sense to diversify and get into services with the intent to build services and distribution worldwide. There was no strategy, and everything was tried in all directions by a shotgun approach, losing more money.

Personnel was reduced to 33,000 worldwide, and morale in the company deteriorated. This was one employee's dilemma:

> What are you to do, leave or stay? You've been with the company all your working life. You rose to top line manager overseas, then transferred to Corporate and International environments in Detroit. You were happy to work those 12–14 hour days. The work was exciting, challenging, always changing.
>
> Your future now is tied to this company. Yet your company stock and options are worthless. You need to hang on till you are 65 to be able to live reasonably for the next 25 years. In its cost cutting fervor, top management

has stopped employee health care for retirees. So you'd have to pay $1,100 a month in health care premiums till you're 65. You've been at the top of your salary range for some time so a younger person could be paid much less to do the job. You are threatened with a 25 percent pay cut next year—a hint to leave if there ever was one. The department you joined in Blue Bell was 30 strong; now there are three of you left. "Brown nosing" is a way of life for many in Unisys. Who you know is very important, but your mentors and friends have all retired or been laid off.

So, again, what should you do? Throw it in and have some peace of mind maybe? You hate going to work. No one smiles there any more. You have lost your creativity. You've lost 50 pounds. Suicide seems the only way out and you wouldn't be the first since the merger. The company has a stress help referral line inundated with employees seeking help. And you can always look around to see people in a worse state: Your colleague, for instance, whose husband is a chronic invalid and son has been in major car accidents, took several weeks off with stress. She came back to be told to clear her desk in one hour and not return.

You decide to stay on till thrown out and endure the daily hell. Surely it can't get any worse. . . . Mechanically, you do only what you have to do.

UNISYS REORGANIZATION

In 1996 Unisys was reorganized into three separate businesses:

Global Customer Services maintains and repairs computers and sells networking systems. However, this is a dying market, as computers now rarely need repair. **Computer Systems** manufactures and markets enterprise servers—a euphemism for mainframes, begun when PC networks were in the ascendancy and mainframes were thought to be finished. However, there is a resurgence, as they are seen to be needed for certain large environments. **Information Services** is perceived as the future and saving of the company, selling information solutions through consulting. Starting from scratch seven years ago, the company expected its first profits in 1999.

NEW CEO BRINGS CONFIDENCE

In 1998, after an extensive search, Larry Weinbach joined Unisys from Anderson Worldwide. Weinbach had an immediate impact on the perception of Unisys by the investment and banking communities and on employee morale. The stock shot up from $10 to $30 per share in twelve months. People began smiling again.

SWOT ANALYSIS

STRENGTHS

Unisys' own prepositioning research within its customer base, as well as research via interviews with current and former company executives, confirmed that the company enjoys a talented and determined workforce. Strong internal training programs and selective hiring practices have built a solid base of employees upon which the company can rely to recover from its prior weakness.

Unisys' server and mainframe products are reliable and of high quality. They have the reputation of being among the best in the industry, and Unisys' focus on the banking, airline, and government sectors has allowed the company to achieve leadership status in these large-dollar-purchase industries. Although much mainframe business has been supplanted by smaller, desktop-based systems, hardware sales still account for 60 percent of the company's revenue. In addition, profit margins are higher on hardware sales than on service sales.

As previously noted, the company suffered through years of weak leadership. However, Weinbach has infused the company with energy and focus. The 58-year-old joined Unisys in 1998 from Anderson Worldwide, where he grew revenue from $3 to $11 billion during his eight years as CEO. During his first year at Unisys, Weinbach refinanced and reduced debt, divested Unisys' PC business, visited all major customers and 11,000 of the 40,000 employees, and launched the global positioning campaign.

WEAKNESS

The company is highly leveraged, partially as a result of lingering debt from the Burroughs buyout of Sperry and partially as a result of more recent losses funded with additional debt. Interest expense on the relatively high debt diverts cash flow from growth and investment to debt service requirements. As seen in Table C9.1, revenue declined from a peak of $10 billion in 1990 to a low of $5.9 billion in 1994. During the same time frame, profits were minimal, and a $625-million loss in 1995 pushed the company to the brink of bankruptcy. Unisys experienced another large loss in 1997; however, the majority of that loss was attributable to writing off $1.1 billion of goodwill from the 1986 merger. Without the one-time charge, the company was profitable in 1997, and they netted over $300 million in 1998. Although it appears that the company's financial performance has "turned the corner," Unisys remains burdened by past financial difficulties.

A second major weakness stems from the recent low morale of the workforce as a result of poor financial performance, layoffs, and a declining stock price. Although it seems as though Weinbach's efforts have helped increase morale, many employees suffered through very difficult times, and it may be difficult for them to "buy into" the new Unisys.

OPPORTUNITIES

The convergence of three factors presents substantial opportunities for Unisys: (1) they enjoy a core of large, loyal global customers in the banking, airline, and government sectors; (2) these large customers are increasingly in need of information services; and (3) Unisys has begun to build positive momentum. These factors together present the opportunity to build upon existing hardware sales relationships by cross-selling information services to the existing customers. Fifty-six percent of Unisys' sales are international, and successful capitalization on newfound positive momentum could lead to the successful growth of information services on a global basis.

Table C9.1

Unisys revenue and profits, 1990–1998 (in millions of U.S. dollars)

	1990	1991	1992	1993	1994	1995	1996	1997	1998 (annualized)
Revenue	10,111	8,696	8,422	7,743	5,978	6,202	6,371	6,636	6,880
Profit	256	193	296	565	101	(625)	50	(854)	331

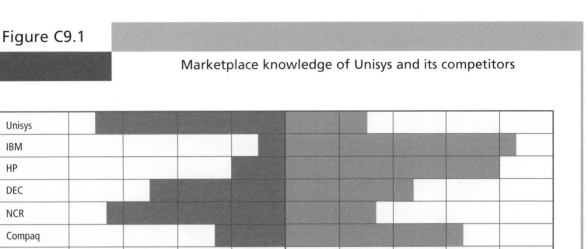

Figure C9.1

Marketplace knowledge of Unisys and its competitors

	80%	60%	40%	20%	20%	40%	60%	80%	100%
Unisys									
IBM									
HP									
DEC									
NCR									
Compaq									

Know only the name or don't know at all · *Very/Somewhat familiar*

THREATS

The computer hardware and services industry is very competitive, and no one company holds greater than a 10 percent market share. Primary competition comes from IBM, Hewlett-Packard, DEC, Digital, NCR, Compaq, and Anderson Worldwide.

The industrywide shift from mainframes nearly put Unisys out of business in the early 1990s, and computer technology continues to evolve at a rapid pace.

There is a lack of positive (or any) perception of Unisys in the marketplace. Unisys has been known as a stodgy, slow, "old" computer company, and competitors have bypassed Unisys in terms of positive recognition in the marketplace. Consultants to Unisys, Ronin Corporation, conducted a survey throughout Europe in 1997 asking medium- and large-sized companies, "When you think of companies that provide information technology and services, what names come to mind?" As seen in Figure C9.1, marketplace knowledge of Unisys lags behind that of primary competitors.

THE GOAL

When Weinbach joined Unisys, he immediately said that the Unisys brand was tarnished. That was putting it mildly. In fact, he loathed the positioning that Unisys was taking as "The Information Management Company." He did not understand what "information management" meant, and furthermore, he thought it was boring. He knew the reason behind this tarnished Unisys brand was that their marketplace execution and financial performance in recent years had been weak at best.

Weinbach knew, however, that any brand could be rebuilt. He was convinced that the Unisys brand could be strong again, and defining the right market position for the new Unisys would be key. Weinbach's number one goal, therefore, was to build a new Unisys brand.

The first thing Unisys had to do before they could begin accomplishing this goal was to make several assumptions about what a brand is:

- A brand is the totality of the thoughts, feelings, associations, and expectations a prospect or customer experiences when exposed to a company's name, its trademark, or its products.

- A brand is a company's reputation and, therefore, its promise of quality.

- Great brands are differentiated from competitors, and they deliver more relevant benefits to their target customers than their competitors.

- Great brands deliver on their promise—in everything they do, every time, and in every country in which they operate.

POSITIONING: THE PROCESS

Positioning a company is not an easy task. It is not a creative exercise like advertising. It must be developed from careful research about a brand. Several questions must be addressed, such as how the marketplace sees your company; how your customers see your company and what they value; and what you know about your own company. Unless positioning decisions are based on solid research, the results are likely to be wrong. Positioning should be a foundation for action to engineer, manage, and defend your brand. Positioning should really inform everything you do: how you communicate with customers; how you interact with customers; how you conduct the business; what you value and recognize in your employees; and what you communicate to the outside world.

This is a pretty tall order and not something that is easy to accomplish. Knowing this, Unisys was faced with several questions:

- Just what is the Unisys positioning and branding challenge?

- How can Unisys create interest and grab the attention of their target market by identifying the compelling capabilities that span their diverse businesses and deliver measurable value?

- How do they position Unisys to retain the position associated with their technology heritage, but shed the "stodgy, outdated mainframe company" image?

To launch a new positioning effort, Weinbach wanted to challenge a team to develop a new Unisys positioning based on a solid, global research with customers, employees, and outside audiences.

RESEARCH BY THE "GANG OF NINE"

Weinbach formed the team in November of 1997. It became known as "The Gang of Nine" and included representation from corporate advertising, corporate PR, corporate identity, Europe, Pacific America, Asia, Africa, information services, global customer services, computer systems, and federal. Weinbach functioned as team leader with direct involvement at all stages. The agency Bozell Worldwide was named to work with Unisys on this repositioning effort.

The first stage of this 10-month repositioning project was global research. Four types of research were conducted. First was *theme analysis*. Here, they interviewed 43 senior managers worldwide to look for patterns of consistency of what was felt about the company, both good and bad. The next type of research was *customer perception sampling*. Unisys conducted 20 interviews with major worldwide customers to find answers to such questions as:

- What do you like/dislike about Unisys?

- What do you think of when you hear the name Unisys?

The third type of research was a *Unisys Reputation Tracking Study*. Here, Unisys went out to global customers and noncustomers to test the recognition and association of Unisys with certain core attributes. The goal of this study was to find out how Unisys is perceived on those key attributes versus the competition by geography and product area. Finally, a *Fortune Corporate Equity Study* was conducted on Unisys. This is a national branding study done by a major business medium on the relative perceptions of top industry players. External focus groups were also part of the research process. This research was conducted with senior executives in New York, Chicago, London, Paris, Taipei, Tokyo, and São Paulo.

RESEARCH RESULTS

The results of the research were clear and consistent:

- What customers valued most was the Unisys people they worked with to solve their business problems.
- Customers described Unisys as having three important characteristics. They said Unisys people were (1) creative in devising solutions, (2) technically excellent in implementing them, and (3) tenacious in overcoming obstacles on the way.
- Customers applauded the "can-do" attitude.
- Customers said Unisys people were the kind that "rolled up their sleeves" and worked alongside them to help them become more competitive and successful.

Given all this information, there were four themes that Unisys thought were critical positions they could take: technical superiority, global, vertical expertise, and people positioning.

POSITIONING STATEMENT

Each positioning theme had a specific statement written that was tested in focus groups around the world (two cities in each the United States, Brazil, China, Japan, and Australia). The result was that the people positioning was the most attractive. All of this research led to formal internal and external statements based on people positioning:

> *Internal Positioning:* to large organizations that desire long-term partnerships to realize business value from the application and integration of information technology. . . . Unisys is thousands of highly skilled team players and alliance partners . . . who are willing to roll up their sleeves and work alongside you, creating and applying technology until your business problem is solved.
>
> *External Positioning:* Unisys is 40,000 creative, technically excellent, tenacious people willing to roll up their sleeves and work alongside you, creating and applying information technology to help you solve your business problems. In more than 100 countries around the world, leading financial services institutions, airlines, communications providers, commercial market leaders, and government agencies rely on Unisys to help them become more competitive and successful.

Now that Unisys had completed thorough global research and identified their positioning statement, it was up to their advertising agency and corporate advertising department to create a campaign that would communicate the new Unisys brand.

IMPLEMENTATION

CREATIVE DEVELOPMENT

The creative force behind the new advertising campaign is Unisys' longtime advertising agency, Bozell Worldwide. Weinbach told Bozell to create new advertising that would show the marketplace that Unisys was alive again, would push the envelope with a creative approach, and would make them smile. After several months of market research discussed in the earlier sections, the Bozell agency showed Weinbach a half-dozen proposals, including a way-out one that was tucked into the project, just in case.

Weinbach rejected all the proposals except the way-out one. He asked the agency to pursue the way-out proposal, which was based on a play on words. However, that campaign was ultimately rejected because it did not translate well globally.

Bozell went back to work and came up with the concept of the "thinkers." The tag line, "We eat, sleep and drink this stuff," was developed to stress the Unisys brand values of being "tenacious, technically excellent, and creative." The tag line has been translated into local colloquialisms, all relating the idea that Unisys goes the extra mile. There are different words used in each language, but all have to do with food, drink, and the personal side of life. The tag line has been translated into Portuguese, Spanish, German, French, Japanese, and Chinese. Many countries, like the Nordic countries, can use English, and other countries, like Italy, can use Spanish or French.

THE CAMPAIGN IS LAUNCHED

The $20-million computer monitor–head campaign was launched in September 1998, on Weinbach's one-year anniversary with the company, in the *Wall Street Journal* and the *Financial Times*. The advertisements featured Unisys people as "thinkers" solving customers' problems. The advertisements also featured customer examples such as Delta Airlines, the City of Rome, Amadeus, and others. In television and print advertisements, the general theme was computer monitor–head employees who cannot stop thinking about their clients' network problems—not even when they are skiing, dancing, or having coffee. In one particular television spot, two friends played golf, all perfectly normal, except one of them had a computer monitor for a head. As his friend waited patiently, the computer-headed Unisys employee pondered his shot, as well as a client's networking problem. The employee exclaimed, "I've got it." The monitor screen dissolved and the employee's head appeared. He putted, and the ball went into the hole. A voice-over said, "Solving problems this way isn't unusual for us. In fact, it's par for the course."

CREATIVE TESTING

The advertisements were tested to make sure that they cut through the clutter; that is, they were tested in the context of other corporate advertisements to see which ones were recalled after viewing them. The recall level amounted to about 84 percent in total. The recall percentages from around the world are among the highest that Bozell has ever seen. Examples of the levels of recall were 83 percent in São Paulo, 83 percent in London, 89 percent in Paris, 72 percent in Shanghai, and 100 percent in Tokyo!

MEDIA PLAN

Because Unisys is a global company, it is important that it has a global campaign, which is something that the company has not been able to afford in some time. The media plan consists of targeting business publications and trade journals; advertising on national television, cable television, and radio; and assuming sponsorships. Examples of some of the key media and regions that the advertisements appeared in are: *60 Minutes*, the *Wall Street Journal*, Monday and Sunday night NFL games, sponsorship of the *Cold War Series* on CNN (United States); *Financial Times*, the *Economist*, *Echos*, *Die Aktuelle*, *Handelsblatt* (Europe); *Exame*, ESPN, CNN, *Latin Finance*, *America Economia* (Latin America); and the *Herald Tribune*, *Yazhou Zhoukan*, the *World's Daily Newspaper* (Asia).

"LIVING THE BRAND"

At times, advertising claims behavior that is not institutionalized in corporate culture as behavior expected from employees. There arises a need to establish an infrastructure to motivate and support expected behavior. Such an internal infrastructure at unisys is known as "living the brand." This is a program developed to help the employees understand, articulate, and promote the new positioning.

Some of the basic tenets of the "living the brand" program as presented to employees are as follows:

- The Unisys brand going forward will be based in the company and the value that it delivers to its customers.
- Living the brand is Unisys' best strategy to make it strong—that means that each day Unisys applies its creativity, its technical excellence, and its tenacity in all it does.
- Living the brand means that Unisys focuses its energies on serving its customers, developing its employees, and building its reputation.
- Living the brand means that an inspired solution to a customer problem may well occur any time, any place . . . on the golf course, walking the dog, skiing down a mountain slope . . . and Unisys is happy it does.
- To use a popular phrase, "it's like we eat, sleep, and drink this stuff."

Other aspects of this program feature a CEO monthly newsletter and achievement awards that are redirected to recognize those people who exhibit "living the brand" behavior. Unisys University has been established to offer professional development programs. There is also a new compensation structure that is based on skills related to "living the brand"—those skills associated with being tenacious, technically excellent, and creative.

OUTCOME

There has been massive public relations coverage and overwhelming employee and customer support of Unisys' repositioning. There are no post-campaign results yet, as testing is presently in process. Weinbach feels that the advertisements take 20 years off Unisys' image, and that they are certainly not what would be expected from a company like Unisys.

CONCLUSION

Unisys typically spends about $30 million a year in advertising. In 1999, they held back $20 million of the budget to launch the campaign. They planned to significantly increase the advertising budget in the future, but would not say by how much. Unisys will have to spend more to get out their message because most people do not care as much about a corporation as they do about products that they use or with which they are familiar. However, Unisys can spend less than, for example, a carmaker that typically spends about $74 million a year to sustain each car brand, according to an advertising trade publication. Unisys can buy less-expensive media time targeting business people, rather than more-expensive time slots that would reach a larger audience.

Unisys has taken first steps toward revitalizing the company. They have a new energetic leader with good ideas who communicates and interacts with the employees. Employee morale is up, and market price of Unisys stock has risen. However, an advertising campaign is never really over. Unisys must advertise year after year with a consistent message: Get associated with Unisys, whose people worry about taking care of your business.

QUESTIONS FOR DISCUSSION

1. Does Unisys' advertising message translate well globally? English translations for the seven tag lines along with the appropriate countries are summarized below:

   It is life as we enjoy it.
   China, Japan, Korea, New Zealand, South Africa

   We live for this.
   Spain, Brazil, Austria, Belgium, Sweden, United Kingdom

   We are always switched on.
   Portugal

   It's completely natural to us.
   France, Germany, Hungary, Italy, the Netherlands

   We don't stop halfway.
   Denmark, Finland

   We live this stuff.
   Czech Republic

   We really care about it.
   Poland

2. Does Unisys have doubts or concerns about its steadfast repositioning based on their clients' perception?

3. Would the image of Unisys employees in the ad campaign have any effect on recruitment? Positive or negative? Why?

4. How will Unisys determine if the campaign is successful?

Water from Iceland

Water from Iceland

case 10

Stan Otis was in a contemplative mood. He had just hung up the phone after talking with Roger Morey, vice president of Citicorp. Morey had made him a job offer in the investment banking sector of the firm. The interviews had gone well, and Citicorp management was impressed with Stan's credentials from a major northeastern private university. "I think you can do well here, Stan. Let us know within a week whether you accept the job," Morey had said.

The three-month search had paid off well, Stan thought. However, an alternative plan complicated the decision to accept the position. Stan had returned several months before from an extended trip throughout Europe, a delayed graduation present from his parents. Among other places, he had visited Reykjavik, Iceland. Even though he could not communicate well, he found the island enchanting. What particularly fascinated him were the lack of industry and the purity of the natural landscape. In particular, he felt the water tasted extremely good. Returning home, he began to consider making this water available in the United States.

THE WATER MARKET IN THE UNITED STATES

In order to consider the possibilities of importing Icelandic water, Stan knew that he first had to learn more about the general water market in the United States. Fortunately, some former college friends were working in a market research firm. Owing Stan some favors, these friends furnished him with a consulting report on the water market.

THE CONSULTING REPORT

Bottled water has an 11 percent market share of total beverage consumption in the United States. The overall distribution of market share is shown in Figure C10.1.

Water is classified into two broad groups: surface water and groundwater. Surface water is typically found in a river or lake. Groundwater is trapped underneath the ground. Primary types of water available for human consumption in the United States are treated or processed water, mineral water, sparkling or effervescent water, spring well water, club soda, and tonic water.

Treated or processed water originates from a central reservoir supply or a well stream. This water usually flows as tap water and has been purified and fluoridated. Mineral water is springwater that contains a substantial amount of minerals, which may either be injected or occur naturally. Natural mineral water

Source: This case study was prepared by Professor Michael R. Czinkota © with assistance from George Garcia. Reprinted by permission.

Figure C10.1

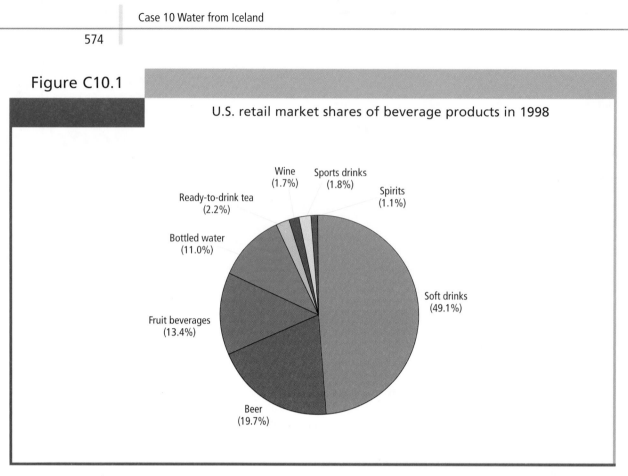

U.S. retail market shares of beverage products in 1998

- Wine (1.7%)
- Sports drinks (1.8%)
- Spirits (1.1%)
- Ready-to-drink tea (2.2%)
- Bottled water (11.0%)
- Fruit beverages (13.4%)
- Soft drinks (49.1%)
- Beer (19.7%)

Source: *Beverage World*, April 1999.

is obtained from a natural spring or underground aquifers. The composition of the water at its source is constant, and the source discharge and temperature remain stable. Mineral water is distinguished from other types of water by its constant level and relatively high proportions of mineral and trace elements at the point of emergence from the source. An artificial process does not modify the natural content of the water at the source.

Sparkling or effervescent water contains natural or artificial carbonation. Some mineral waters come to the surface naturally carbonated through underground gases, but lose their fizz on the surface with normal pressure. Many of these waters are injected with carbon dioxide later on. After treatment with carbon dioxide, such water contains the same amount of carbon dioxide that it had originally at emergence from the source.

Club soda is obtained by adding artificial carbonation to distilled or regular tap water. Mineral content in this water depends on the water supply used and the purification process the water has undergone. Tonic water is derived from the same process as club soda, but has bitters added to it.

Minerals are important to the taste and quality of water. The type and variety of minerals present in the water can make it a very healthy and enjoyable drink. The combination of minerals present in the water determines its relative degree of acidity. The level of acidity is measured by the pH factor. The pH scale runs from 0 to 14; the neutral point is 7. A higher rating indicates that the water contains more solids, such as magnesium and is said to be "hard." Conversely, water with a lower rating is classified as "soft." Most tap water is soft, whereas the majority of commercially sold waters tend to be hard.

WATER CONSUMPTION IN THE UNITED STATES

Tap water has generally been inexpensive, relatively pure, and plentiful in the United States. Traditionally, bottled water has been consumed in the United States by the wealthy. In the past decade, however, bottled water has begun to appeal to a wider market. The four main reasons for this change are:

1. An increasing awareness among consumers of the impurity of city water supplies (see Figure C10.2).
2. Increasing dissatisfaction with the taste, odor, and quality of tap water.
3. Rising affluence in society as well as lower prices for bottled water.
4. An increasing desire to maintain one's health and to avoid the excess consumption of caffeine, sugar, and other substances present in coffee and soft drinks.

Bottled water consumers are found chiefly in the states of California, Florida, Texas, New York, and Arkansas. These states combined represent 53.7 percent of nationwide bottled water sales for 1998, with California alone accounting for 26 percent of industry sales. Nationwide, bottled water is drunk by 1 out of every 13 households. The average national per capita consumption was estimated to be 13.3 gallons. For a comparison of per capita consumption of bottled water and other beverages see Table C10.1.

Before 1976, bottled water was considered primarily a gourmet specialty, a luxury item consumed by the rich. Today, there are over 750 brands of bottled water available on the U.S. market. The volume of bottled water sold rose from 255 million gallons in 1976 to 3.6 billion gallons in 1998. From 1988 to 1998, U.S consumption of bottled water increased by over 200 percent, taking market share from beverages such as coffee, tea, milk, juice, and alcoholic drinks (see Figure C10.3).

Figure C10.2

Gallup Poll Monthly, June 1998

How would you rate the job being done by the state and federal governments in protecting the safety of public drinking water?	Very good—20% Somewhat good—49% Somewhat poor—18% Very poor—11%
What kind of water do you normally drink at home, straight tap water, tap water that has been filtered, or bottled water?	Tap water—53% Filtered tap water—24% Bottled water—22%
Have you ever received a notice or heard a community alert concerning safety problems with your drinking water supply?	Yes—21% No—79%

Source: Gallup Monthly, June 1998.

Table C10.1

U.S. beverage consumption in 1998

	Retail receipts ($ billions)	Per capita consumption (gallons)
Soft drinks	53.7	54.6
Beer	53.3	21.9
Spirits	34.1	1.3
Fruit beverages	15.2	15.0
Wine	13.0	2.5
Bottled water	5.1	13.3
RTD tea	3.2	2.7
Sports drinks	2.2	2.2

Source: Beverage Marketing Corporation, "Bottled Water in the U.S.," 1999 Edition.

Figure C10.3

U.S. beverage consumption growth, 1988–1998

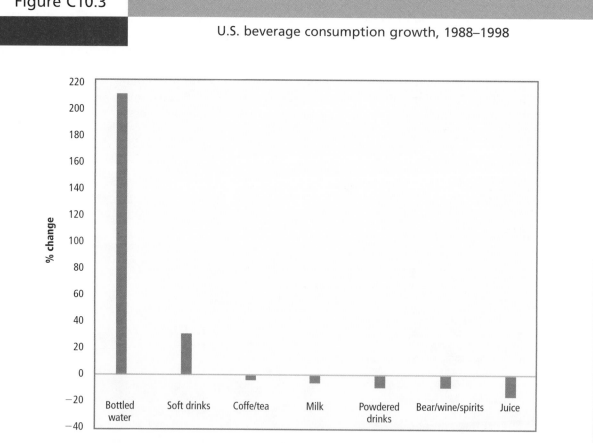

Source: Norland International.

In 1998 the water industry's receipts totaled just under $4 billion at the wholesale level and $5.1 billion at the retail level. Bottled water gallonage increased by almost 9 percent between 1997 and 1998. For more information on the sales of bottled water consumption in the United States, see Figure C10.4. Nonsparkling water accounts for around 91 percent of total bottled water gallonage and increased by 11.9 percent from 1997 to 1998. Sparkling water, on the other hand, decreased by 3.6 percent.

Figure C10.4

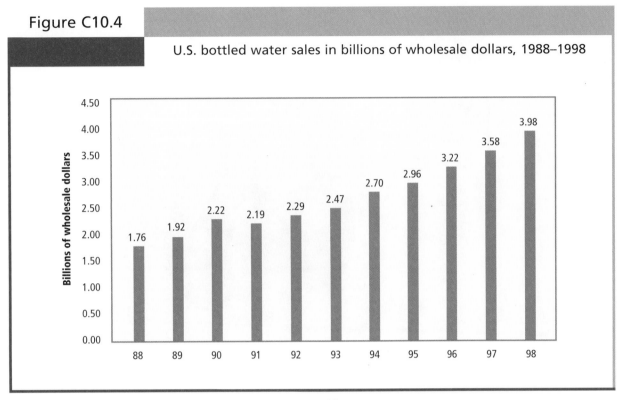

U.S. bottled water sales in billions of wholesale dollars, 1988–1998

Source: Beverage Marketing Corporation, "Bottled Water in the U.S.," 1999 Edition.

Table C10.2

Shares of imports in U.S. bottled water market

	% estimated wholesale dollars	% gallonage
1984	8.0	1.8
1985	11.7	2.8
1986	10.0	2.6
1987	11.0	2.7
1988	12.1	3.1
1989	11.9	3.1
1990	13.0	3.7
1991	11.2	3.5
1992	12.6	4.1
1993	15.0	4.1
1994	16.2	4.2
1995	14.4	3.6
1996	15.3	3.8
1997	17.9	4.6
1998	18.5	4.5

Source: International Bottled Water Association, www.bottledwater.org, accessed November 1999.

In 1998, imported water held a 4.5 percent share of the U.S. domestic market in terms of volume, but an 18.5 percent share in terms of wholesale dollars (see Table C10.2). The leading country importing water to the United States is France, home of Perrier, with a 61.2 percent share of total bottled water import volume. Canada, home of Naya Water, is second with 25.3 percent, and Italy is third with 7.2 percent of the imported gallonage (see Figure C10.5).

Figure C10.5

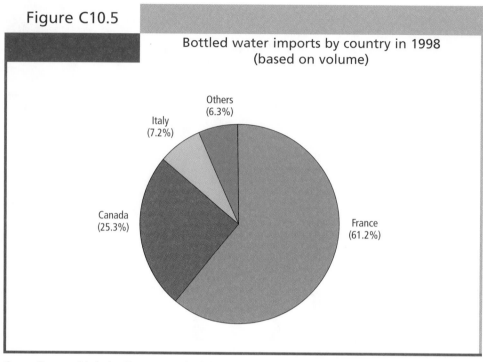

Bottled water imports by country in 1998 (based on volume)

Others (6.3%)
Italy (7.2%)
Canada (25.3%)
France (61.2%)

Source: Beverage Marketing Corporation, "Bottled Water in the U.S.," 1998 Edition.

Table C10.3

Top 10 bottled waters of 1998

Rank	Brand	Sales ($ millions)
1	Poland Spring (Perrier)	350.90
2	Arrowhead (Perrier)	283.20
3	Sparkletts (McKesson)	205.00
4	Evian (Danone International)	200.70
5	Aquafina (Pepsi-Cola)	165.00
6	Zephyrhills (Perrier)	134.40
7	Hinckley & Schmitts (Suntory)	128.60
8	Deer Park (Perrier)	123.60
9	Ozarka (Perrier)	122.80
10	Crystal Geyser (Suntory)	113.10

Source: *Beverage World*, April 1999.

Among domestic producers, Perrier Group of America is a strong leader with a 29.4 percent market share. The Perrier Group's three top-selling brands are Poland Spring, Arrowhead, and Zephyrhills. With the top two brands and five of the biggest eight, Perrier Group is approaching the ownership of one quarter of the market (see Table C10.3).

ADDITIONAL RESEARCH

SEGMENTS. Within the bottled water business there are two distinct industries and segments. The biggest by volume is the five-gallon, or returnable container, water business. Companies like Arrowhead, Sparkletts, and Hinckley & Schmitt are leaders in this field. Often associated with the office cooler, bottlers also use two-and-one-half-gallon as well as one-gallon containers for supermarket distribution. This type of bottled water is sold as an alternative to tap water. Premium bottled waters, such as Evian, Vittel, and Perrier, are sold as soft drink and alcohol alternatives. Packaging ranges from six ounces to two liters and from custom glass and polyethylene terephthalate (PET) plastic to aluminum cans. More and more bottled water producers have switched from glass to plastic because of the increased acceptance of this kind of packaging. PET bottles were a breakthrough in the bottled water industry. They protect nutritive properties without transfer of taste; they are recyclable and reused by a number of industries. These PET bottles come in different sizes and are the most widely displayed forms of bottled water on the market today.

The bottled water market is getting more competitive as major beverage companies such as Coca-Cola are introducing new brands of bottled water. Prices of bottled water continue to decrease. Image is also very important. That is why a lot of bottled water containers show pictures of mountains and springs to capture consumers' attention and to make them feel like they are drinking the purest water available.

BOTTLED WATER REGULATION IN THE UNITED STATES. The bottled water industry in the United States is regulated and controlled at three levels—by the federal government, state government, and trade association. The U.S. Food and Drug Administration (FDA), under the Federal Food, Drug and Cosmetic Act (FFDCA), regulates bottled water as a food product. This includes packaged water sold in small containers at retail outlets as well as large five-gallon containers distributed to the home and office market. Like all food products except meat and poultry (which are regulated by the U.S. Department of Agriculture), bottled water is subject to the FDA's extensive food safety and labeling requirements. In addition, all bottled water products imported from countries outside of the United States must not only meet the standards established by their own country but also comply with all of the U.S. regulations. Producers engaged in interstate commerce are subject to periodic, unannounced FDA inspections.

THE ICELANDIC SCENARIO

Iceland's economy is basically market oriented, with an extensive welfare system, low unemployment, and a remarkably even distribution of income. In terms of products exported, the economy depends heavily on the fishing industry, which provides 75 percent of export earnings and employs 12 percent of the workforce. The economy remains sensitive to declining fish stocks as well as to drops in world prices for its main exports: fish and fish products, aluminum, and ferrosilicon.

The government has the diversification of its export base as one of its key goals. It also plans to continue its policies of reducing the budget and current account deficits, limiting foreign borrowing, containing inflation, revising agricultural and fishing policies, and privatizing state-owned industries. The government remains opposed to EU membership, primarily because of Icelanders' concern about losing control over their fishing resources.

In recent years, economic growth has been high, inflation has been low, unemployment has declined, and living standards have risen. On these measures, Iceland is among the best performers in the OECD. Economic growth averaged over 3.4 percent per year from 1994 to 1997 and reached a respectable 3.9 percent in 1998. Unemployment fell from 5 percent of the labor force in 1995 to 4 percent in 1996 and remained even lower in 1998, at 3.8 percent. For comparison purposes, unemployment in 1998 averaged 11.1 percent in the European Union. Inflation, which has often been a problem in the economy, declined from 2.3 percent in 1996 to 1.8 percent in 1998.

The Ministry of Commerce, after consulting the Central Bank, has the ultimate responsibility in matters concerning import and export licensing. The Central Bank is responsible for the regulation of foreign exchange transactions and exchange controls, including capital controls. It is also responsible for ensuring that all foreign exchange due to residents is surrendered to authorized banks. All commercial exports require licenses. The shipping documents must be lodged with an authorized bank. Receipts exchanged for exports must be surrendered to the Central Bank.

In general, the business climate in Iceland is favorable to foreign investments. All investments by nonresidents in Iceland are subject to individual approval. The participation of nonresidents in Icelandic joint venture companies may not exceed 49 percent. However, the government has started abolishing restrictions in order to create a more favorable investment climate. One restriction being analyzed is the fact that non-resident-owned foreign capital entering in the form of exchange must be surrendered.

Iceland is a member of the European Economic Area (EEA), which opens up the possibility of a duty-free access to European Union member states for U.S. and Canadian firms. It is also part of the United Nations, the European Free Trade Association, and the World Trade Organization. Iceland enjoys normal trade relations (formerly most favored nation) status with the United Sates. Under this designation, mineral and carbonated water from Iceland is subject to a tariff of 0.33 cents per liter. Natural (still) water is tariff free.

QUESTIONS FOR DISCUSSION

1. Is there sufficient information to determine whether importing water from Iceland would be a profitable business in the United States market? If not, what additional information is needed to make a determination?

2. Is the market climate in the United States conducive to water imports in Iceland?

3. What are some possible reasons for the fluctuation in the market share held by imports over the past 10 years?

Company and Organization Index

Name Index

Subject Index

Photo Credits